03/08

The
Improving
State of the
World

WHY WE'RE LIVING LONGER, HEALTHIER, MORE

COMFORTABLE LIVES ON A CLEANER PLANET

The Improving State of the World

WHY WE'RE LIVING LONGER, HEALTHIER, MORE COMFORTABLE LIVES ON A CLEANER PLANET

INDUR M. GOKLANY

CATO INSTITUTE
WASHINGTON, D.C.

Copyright © 2007 by Cato Institute.
All rights reserved.

Library of Congress Cataloging-in-Publication Data

Goklany, Indur M.
    The improving state of the world: why we're living longer,
healthier, more comfortable lives on a cleaner planet/Indur M.
Goklany.
        p. cm.
    Includes bibliographical references and index.
    ISBN 1-930865-98-8 (paper)—ISBN 1-930865-99-6 (cloth)
        1. Economic development—Environmental aspects.   2. Quality
of life.   3. Technological innovations--Environmental
aspects.   4. Human ecology.   I. Title.

HD75.6.G64 2006
304.2—dc22

                                                                  2006051792

Cover design by Jon Meyers.

Printed in the United States of America.

CATO INSTITUTE
1000 Massachusetts Ave., N.W.
Washington, D.C. 20001
www.cato.org

Contents

v

Acknowledgments

I dedicate this book to Maya, Sam, and Karen. This book would have been impossible without their patience, support, and encouragement over the many years that this book was written and revised.

The first draft was penned in the summer of 2000 while I was the D&D Foundation Julian Simon Fellow at the Political Economy Research Center in Bozeman, Montana. Since then, the D&D Foundation renamed itself the Searle Freedom Trust, and the Political Economy Research Center is now the Property and Environment Research Center (PERC). I thank both institutions for their generous support.

I was also fortunate during my tenure in Bozeman to have the company and support of Terry Anderson, Rick Stroup, Jane Shaw, Roger Meiners, P. J. Hill, Dan Benjamin, Roger Sedjo, Don Leal, and the PERC family. I am also grateful to Juliette Shaw and Eric Noyes, as well as the Meiners' family, for their kindness and generosity in hosting me in Bozeman.

I am indebted to Kimberly Dennis and Chris DeMuth for their active support and sponsorship while I was a Visiting Fellow with the American Enterprise Institute (AEI) in 2002 and 2003. I am grateful to the Searle Freedom Trust's National Research Initiative housed within AEI for funding this stint, during which I wrote the second draft. That draft was also made possible with Ryan Stowers' invaluable assistance.

I thank the Cato Institute's David Boaz, Jerry Taylor, and, particularly, Ian Vasquez, director of Cato's Center for Global Liberty and Prosperity, without whose active interest I probably would not have finished the third draft in 2006. Ian also gave this book a thorough review, and he brought in Cato's excellent publication team and Ashley Young to smooth out the many rough edges in the draft. However, any remaining errors are my responsibility.

PART A

ECONOMIC DEVELOPMENT, TECHNOLOGICAL
CHANGE, AND THE HUMAN CONDITON

1. Introduction

A long suburb of red brick houses—some with patches of garden-ground, where coal-dust and factory smoke darkened the shrinking leaves, and coarse rank flowers, and where the struggling vegetation sickened and sank under the hot breath of kiln and furnace, making them by its presence seem yet more blighting and unwholesome than in the town itself, . . . they came by slow degrees upon a cheerless region, where not a blade of grass was seen to grow; where not a bud put forth its promise in the spring; where nothing green could live but on the surface of the stagnant pools, which here and there lay idly sweltering by the black road-side.

On every side, and as far as the eye could see into the heavy distance, tall chimneys, crowding on each other and presenting that endless repetition of the same dull, ugly form, which is the horror of oppressive dreams, poured out their plague of smoke, obscured the light, and made foul the melancholy air. . . . Then came more of the wrathful monsters . . . and still, before, behind, and to the right and left, was the same interminable perspective of brick towers, never ceasing in their black vomit, blasting all things living or inanimate, shutting out the face of day, and closing in on all these horrors with a dense dark cloud.

But night-time in this dreadful spot!—night, when the smoke was changed to fire; when every chimney spirted up its red flame; and places that had been dark vaults all day, now shone red-hot, with figures moving to and fro within their blazing jaws . . . night, when carts came rumbling by, filled with rude coffins (for contagious disease and death had been busy . . .) . . . night, when some called for bread, and some for drink to drown their cares . . . night, which unlike the night that Heaven sends on earth, brought with it not peace, nor quiet, nor signs of blessed sleep. . . .

— Charles Dickens (1840–41),
The Old Curiosity Shop, pp. 346–48[1]

Dickens's vision of the industrial town as Hell on earth was penned when modern economic growth was still young. With the advent of industrialization and urbanization that initially accompanied such economic growth, mankind's history—until then largely one of constant poverty, hunger, disease, and death, periodically punctuated by epidemics, floods, droughts, famines, war, and other natural and unnatural disasters—seemed destined to take a turn for the worse. But with hindsight, we now know that even as Dickens was chronicling the dark phase of economic development, the forces that would lift Britain from that Stygian gloom had already been set in motion.[2] Those forces gathered steam over the next few decades, and, today, more than a century and a half later, the average Briton has never been richer, better fed, healthier, or longer lived.

The British experience with modern economic growth has been repeated, to one degree or another, in other countries. It first spread to other parts of Western Europe and its mainly white colonies, for example, Australia, Canada, New Zealand, and the United States. It has since diffused broadly to other parts of the globe, albeit with varying degrees of success. And the average inhabitant of planet earth—such as the average Briton today—is also wealthier, freer from hunger and disease, and likely to be longer lived than ever before.[3] And although epidemics, floods, droughts, and other natural disasters still occur, their consequences, while still severe, are generally not as lethal as in times past,[4] except where poverty stalks the land because of war—civil or otherwise—and dysfunctional state policies.[5]

Modern economic growth is characterized by unparalleled technological change, which has transformed the world more in the past two centuries than all the other events put together since the beginning of agriculture 10 millennia ago. This technological change was accompanied by a prodigious increase in the use of inanimate energy, particularly fossil fuels and other renewable and nonrenewable natural resources. The associated industrialization and increases in agricultural productivity, urbanization, population, mobility, trade, and consumption of material goods have transformed the social, cultural, and physical landscapes of societies.

Together, economic growth and technological change have redefined the role of women and children, restructured the workplace, undermined age-old arrangements of caste and class, expanded the

4

middle class, and developed new institutions and organizations. In turn, societies aspiring to faster economic growth are restructuring themselves—freeing economies, bestowing property rights on private parties, giving individuals more latitude, and strengthening education—even as those very factors reinforce economic growth in empowering middle classes to create the basic conditions for democracy in societies that have never tasted it.

Economic development, however, is also changing humanity's relationship to the rest of nature. At first, industrialization and urbanization—in many countries, the first steps in modern economic growth—may have made people wealthier but, as Dickens so vividly depicted, not necessarily better, particularly for the masses. For many urban dwellers, crowding, unsanitary conditions, polluted air, and unsafe water may have led, at least initially, to a life that was nastier, more brutish, and, perhaps, even shorter than for their rural compatriots.[6] The countries that industrialized first were the first to experience those problems. But, by the same token, they were also the first to devise solutions to those problems, which now benefit those who came later to the path of economic growth. But even as old problems were solved, new ones cropped up. Today, with technology enabling us to detect one molecule of a pollutant among a billion other molecules, we feel beset by trace gases and debris of human origin in the atmosphere and the stratosphere, in the Arctic and the Antarctic, at the bottom of the ocean, and even at the top of Mt. Everest.

The twin forces of economic growth and technological change having, first, given us a degraded environment, now have provided, as antidotes, environmentalism, as well as a romanticized view of nature. Despite significant reductions in the past few decades in various forms of pollution, especially in wealthier countries, many Neo-Malthusians and environmentalists remain suspicious of these two forces.[7] They argue that economic growth and technology are among the driving forces behind environmental impacts and natural resource use, which—unless checked—will eventually degrade both human welfare and environmental quality.[8] All the progress to date may yet prove to be ephemeral. In this view, because of economic growth and technology, the world may yet come to resemble Dickens's "cheerless region, where not a blade of grass was seen to grow; where not a bud put forth its promise in the spring; where nothing green could live but on the surface of the stagnant pools. . . ."

Dickens's words—written long before DDT, dioxins, and radiation were discovered and humanity learned to loathe, if not fear, acid rain, ozone depletion, and carbon dioxide—echo throughout Rachel Carson's evocative first chapter of *Silent Spring*, which imagined a future in which synthetic pesticides and the effluents of civilization would lay waste a bucolic countryside so that neither bird nor bee nor beast would bestir itself in that blighted land.

Similar sentiments, although not always expressed with the same elegance, can be found in several works by Neo-Malthusians that have appeared since *Silent Spring*. Those works interweave concerns about population growth and food—Malthus's original concerns—with broader concerns about the environment and natural resources. Some contain quite remarkable proposals. Shortly after the first successful manned mission to the moon, Paul Ehrlich, a Stanford biologist, followed his best-selling book, *The Population Bomb*,[9] with a manifesto titled, *How to Be a Survivor: A Plan to Save Planet Earth* (coauthored with Richard Harriman). The book comes complete with a new constitution for the United Republics of America, which is provided as a "model for discussion."[10] The authors declare the following:

> Dramatic changes in the living arrangements on Spaceship Earth must commence immediately. The directions in which we must move are clear . . . [and] simple:
> 1. Population control must be achieved in both overdeveloped countries (ODCs) and underdeveloped countries (UDCs).
> 2. The ODCs must be de-developed.
> 3. The UDCs must be semi-developed.
> 4. The procedures must be set up for monitoring and regulating the world system in a continuous effort to maintain an optimum population-resource-environment situation.[11]
>
> Hopefully, [National Congresses on Optimum Population and the Environment] will provide some basis for deciding how far below the present level of 205 million people the population of the United States should be. Final decisions will, of course, depend in part on planetary planning. Strict limits will have to be placed on the resource consumption and pollution output of all nations. . . .[12]

Lester Brown—an agricultural scientist who later conceived *The State of the World* series, which, each year since 1984, has warned that the state of the world is bad and could get worse—echoed many of Ehrlich's ideas and lamented that "expanding economic activity is rendering our air unfit for breathing, water unfit for drinking, beaches unfit for bathing, and fish unfit for eating. Eco-catastrophes are occurring with increasing frequency."[13]

Those concerns captured the public imagination with the 1972 publication of the Club of Rome's *The Limits to Growth*,[14] whose general thesis was reiterated eight years later in the *Global 2000 Report to the President* (of the United States): "If present trends continue, the world in 2000 will be more crowded, more polluted, less stable ecologically, and more vulnerable to disruption than the world we live in now. Serious stresses involving population, resources, and environment are clearly visible ahead. Despite greater material output, the world's people will be poorer in many ways than they are today."[15] Others, even more pessimistic, argue that we are already living "beyond the limits" of the earth's carrying capacity.[16] Yet others have argued that technology is at least as culpable as population size and resource consumption for the sorry state of the planet.[17]

The pessimistic Neo-Malthusian world view did not go unchallenged. The dissenters—not all optimists—included the game theorist Herman Kahn who helped develop the doctrine of mutually assured destruction as a strategy to dissuade the Soviet Union from deploying thermonuclear weapons against the United States when he was at the RAND Corporation; Kahn's collaborator on *The Resourceful Earth*, the economist Julian L. Simon; Wilfred Beckerman, an economist at Oxford University; Ronald Bailey, currently a science correspondent for *Reason* magazine; Gregg Easterbrook, a senior editor of *The New Republic*; and, more recently, Bjørn Lomborg, a Danish statistician with previously impeccable environmental credentials who set out to discredit Simon with reams of empirical information but ended up writing *The Skeptical Environmentalist* instead.[18]

Both Easterbrook and Lomborg were viewed as apostates. For that, they were either praised or vilified in book reviews, depending on the reviewer's prior bent. Websites were established to attempt to debunk their books.[19] In one of the more bizarre episodes concerning science and faith since Galileo's conviction for heresy, a complaint was filed against Lomborg with a body having the Orwellian name of the Danish Committee on Scientific Dishonesty (DCSD). This committee ruled that Lomborg's book was scientifically dishonest and "clearly contrary to the standards of good scientific practice." It did not, however, find that Lomborg misled his readers deliberately. But then the Danish Ministry of Science, Technology, and Innovation rebuked the committee, noting that the DCSD verdict was not backed by documentation, "lacks any arguments" for the claims of dishonesty, and poor scientific practice. It also criticized the DCSD's treatment of Lomborg as unsatisfactory, deserving criticism, and "emotional," and it faulted the DCSD for not permitting Lomborg an opportunity to respond. The DCSD dropped its earlier finding, and Lomborg was cleared of scientific dishonesty.[20]

Despite the empirical data trotted out by the optimists to argue their case, the new millennium has brought forth a new crop of books from Neo-Malthusians essentially reaffirming their original message—that mankind was fast approaching the limits to growth and would face the Apocalypse, unless it changed its ways.[21] In the years since the publication of *Limits to Growth*, we are told that a new and more terrible specter has matured and joined the ranks of the four horsemen of the Apocalypse. The fifth horseman—climate change—was born out of the crucible of technology and perfected with fire. It feeds on economic and population growth, and where she rides, it is claimed, the other horsemen—hunger, pestilence, destruction of nature, and death—will surely follow.

She is the focus of much of the concerns of the Neo-Malthusians and will be among the horsemen addressed in this book.

The Environmental Impact of Growth and Technology

The general distrust of population growth, economic development, and technology exhibited by most Neo-Malthusians is captured by the identity, $I = PAT$ (IPAT), where I is a measure of environmental impact, P is the population, A stands for affluence—a surrogate for production or consumption per capita, often measured in terms of the gross domestic product per capita—and T, denoting technology, is a measure of the impact per unit of production or consumption.[22]

Technology, as used throughout this book, includes both hardware (e.g., scrubbers, catalytic convertors, and carbon adsorption systems) and software technologies (e.g., policies, management techniques, computer programs to track waste or model environmental quality, and emissions trading).[23] According to the IPAT identity, if all else remains the same, an increase in population, affluence, or technology would act as a multiplier for environmental impact, that is, it would increase that impact.[24] Based partly on this identity, Neo-Malthusians contend that the human enterprise as currently constituted is unsustainable in the long run, unless the population shrinks;[25] we diminish, if not reverse, economic development;[26] and apply the precautionary principle to new technologies, which, in their view, essentially embodies a presumption against further technological change unless the technology involved is proven absolutely safe and clean.[27]

Despite recognizing that technology could reduce some impacts, many Neo-Malthusians argue that, to quote Jared Diamond, a University of California at Los Angeles philosophy professor, it's a mistake to believe that "[t]echnology will solve our problems."[28] In fact, goes this argument, "All of our current problems are unintended negative consequences of our existing technology. The rapid advances in technology during the 20th century have been creating difficult new problems faster than they have been solving old problems. . . ."[29] Moreover, for most important activities, new technology would bring diminishing returns because as the best resources are used up (e.g., minerals, fossil fuels, and farm land), society would increasingly have to turn to marginal or less desirable resources to satisfy demand, which would increase energy use and pollution.[30]

This skepticism of economic growth and technological change is manifested, for instance, in the seeming disregard among many advocates of greenhouse gas (GHG) controls of the socioeconomic impact of costs associated with such control schemes.[31] It is also evident in calls to eschew genetically modified foods despite their promise to reduce agriculture's use of land, water, pesticides, and fertilizers, which could result in net benefits to the world's environment and biodiversity even as it increases the quantity and nutritional quality of food supplies for a rapidly growing world population that has yet to be free from hunger and malnutrition.[32] The precautionary principle has sometimes also been used to rationalize the refusal to countenance nuclear or hydroelectric power as substitutes for fossil fuel-generated electricity, despite assertions that there is no greater environmental problem facing the world

9

today than global warming.[33] It was also used in an attempt to justify a global ban on the insecticide DDT despite its obvious benefits in reducing malaria's toll—currently amounting to a million or more deaths annually out of about a half a billion cases worldwide, almost exclusively in poverty-stricken developing countries—until that position became untenable.[34] This last perversion of the precautionary principle was only possible because, in some minds, the principle gives license to cherry pick which public health or environmental risk one wants to focus on.[35] Thus, a global ban makes eminent sense only if one ignores the public health costs of not having access to DDT to reduce malaria (and other insect-borne diseases) in poverty-stricken areas. However, consideration of both public health and environmental impacts of DDT use (and nonuse) leads to a more nuanced policy on DDT, to whit, that its use is appropriate for public health purposes in areas where its use can reduce the burden of disease, but it is unnecessary in other areas.[36] Fortunately, this conclusion was also the one of the international community, and it is now accepted policy under the Stockholm Protocol on Persistent Organic Pollutants, although it did increase the transaction costs of developing countries using DDT even for public health purposes, which could be burdensome, if not counterproductive.

Others, including some Neo-Malthusians such as James Gustave Speth, for instance, while recognizing the role of technology in creating environmental problems, also view technology as part of their long-term solution. This duality is likewise evident in the ambivalence of U.S. environmental laws, which sometimes mandate a multiplicity of exotic and often untested technological standards, such as best available (control) technology, maximum achievable control technology, and lowest achievable emission rate technology, while, at the same time, raising barriers to the construction of new and usually cleaner sources and technologies. However, even some technological optimists continue to view economic growth as a multiplier of environmental impacts, rather than a critical contributor to their solution.[37]

The Environmental Transition Hypothesis

Yet another view, formalized as the environmental transition hypothesis, is that for any specific country, the forces of technological change and economic growth, acting in conjunction, can initially cause environmental degradation, but eventually an "environmental transition" takes place after which those forces become necessary for reversing that degradation.[38] This view, however, acknowledges that because economic growth and technological change are not inevitable, environmental cleanup is, likewise, not a foregone conclusion. So in this regard, the environmental transition hypothesis provides a reason to be hopeful, without necessarily being optimistic.

Basic assumptions underlying the environmental transition hypothesis are that society is always trying to improve its quality of life and that there is a mechanism for converting that desire into action. At relatively low levels of economic development, a society may justifiably conclude that its quality of life would be advanced through economic development, because such development provides the means for reducing poverty and the numerous problems that follow in its wake, for example, hunger, malnutrition, lack of access to safe water and sanitation, malaria, lack of education, and lack of public health services, to name just a few. Thus, in the early stages of development, a society would likely emphasize economic development over the environment. However, over time, as the society gets wealthier, it solves—or starts to solve—its most urgent public health problems. Even as other aspects of environmental quality deteriorate, it begins to realize that poor environmental quality detracts from its quality of life. Accordingly, it begins to give greater emphasis to environmental quality. Over time, society goes through a transition during which environmental deterioration, which had initially been growing, is first halted, and then reversed. Hence the term, the "environmental transition."

During this transition, economic growth and technology go from being causes of environmental problems to solutions for those very problems. However, it should also be kept in mind that, at all times—before, during, and after the environmental transition—the focus of society is to improve its quality of life. It just so happens that at low levels of economic development, quality of life is approximated by such development, while at higher levels of development, it's environmental quality that's a better surrogate.

Because it is each society's quality of life that drives environmental transitions, it should be expected that the timing of the transition and the level at which environmental deterioration peaks will necessarily vary with both the precise environmental indicator that is under consideration and the specific society being examined, if for no other reason than society—or, for that matter, individuals within that society—will weigh the various determinants of its quality of life differently.

The environmental transition hypothesis is superficially similar to the environmental Kuznets curve (EKC) hypothesis, which is based on an examination of data across countries or political jurisdictions to obtain a relationship between various environmental indicators and the level of economic development (or per capita income) of a country (or jurisdiction). According to the EKC hypothesis, initially at low levels of wealth, a country's (or jurisdiction's) environmental quality is generally poorer. However, in wealthier countries (or if a country becomes wealthier), its environment becomes cleaner. Therefore, a plot of environmental degradation against the level of economic development should result in an inverted U-shaped curve. Such inverted U-shaped curves are sometimes called "environmental Kuznets curves" after Simon Kuznets, the Nobel Prize-winning economist who first discovered such a shape when he plotted economic inequality as a function of per capita income (a measure of the level of economic development).[39] However, the EKC hypothesis tends to emphasize economic development as the explanatory variable at the expense of technological change as the source of eventual environmental cleanup,[40] while the environmental transition hypothesis emphasizes that both these forces (i.e., economic development and technological change) are coequal. The latter hypothesis also focuses on the fact that the two forces coevolve and reinforce each other in ultimately improving environmental quality.

This book is designed to determine whether modern economic growth has, as optimists claim, improved humanity's lot or whether well-being has deteriorated, as pessimists contend. To make this determination, I will, where feasible, apply the IPAT framework using empirical data over the past century—a period of unprecedented growth in population (P), affluence (A), and their product (PA) both in the United States and worldwide—to see whether the data support one or the other competing views outlined with respect to the relationship of technological change and economic growth to human and environmental well-being.

However, whether modern economic growth has performed admirably in raising the quality of life, past performance—as mutual fund ads tell us—is no guarantee of future results. Accordingly, to the extent that humanity is near or beyond the limits of growth, this book will outline approaches to extend those limits so that improvements in human well-being can be sustained despite increases in industrialization (in some countries), postindustrialization (in others), population, and consumption.

What This Book Covers

This book is divided into four parts. Part A, consisting of this introduction and the following three chapters, addresses trends in human well-being and the factors responsible for those trends. Chapter 2 examines whether, notwithstanding the attendant environmental problems, modern economic development has improved human well-being over the past century or so. To the extent that societies have, in fact, improved their well-being even as environmental quality first declined and then improved, such a progression would be consistent with the environmental transition hypothesis. Chapter 2 also examines how some of the most critical determinants of human well-being (e.g., access to food, safe water and sanitation, mortality, life expectancy, educational attainment, and level of economic development) vary across countries as functions of both economic development and time, a proxy for technological change. The chapter will give readers an idea as to whether, with regard to human well-being, advances in technology have created more difficult new problems faster than they have solved old ones, as Diamond has contended.

Chapter 3 addresses whether globalization has contributed to a widening of gaps between rich and poor nations in the critical determinants of well-being. But unlike most discussions on this topic, it does not limit its inquiry to the issue of whether the rich are getting richer and the poor poorer. Instead, recognizing that wealth is not an end in itself but the means to ensuring improvements in other, more important determinants of well-being (such as infant mortality, food supplies, education, child labor, and life expectancy). Chapter 3 also analyzes trends in the gaps for these determinants between the high-, middle-, and low-income countries, with special attention to those in sub-Saharan Africa. It then takes a brief detour to examine the trend in the gaps between black and white America with respect

13

to the three components of the human development index championed by the United Nations Development Program—namely, income, life expectancy, and education. Chapter 4 then discusses the reasons for the progress in human well-being, if any, over the past two centuries.

Part B, comprised of the next four chapters, examines the effects of economic development and technological change on environmental quality. Chapter 5 is devoted to providing a framework for examining and understanding factors driving long-term (decades-long) environmental trends, which are presented later in this book. It outlines the environmental transition hypothesis in greater detail, while the next chapter indicates how and in what respects that hypothesis differs from the EKC hypothesis. Chapter 5 also develops an approach for using the IPAT identity to estimate technological change from long-term trends in environmental indicators.

Chapter 6 examines long-term trends in various key environmental indicators, which serve as surrogates for man's impacts on land, air, and water. Among other things, the chapter examines trends in cropland, a surrogate for habitat loss; traditional air pollution emissions, as well as indoor and outdoor air quality; and deaths due to water-related diseases, an indicator of water pollution that is more relevant to well-being than measurements of chemical concentrations in the water. In addition, the chapter analyzes trends for various climate-sensitive indicators of human welfare and environmental quality, which, in the view of proponents of GHG controls and, arguably, in the popular imagination, might become worse with global warming. This examination verifies whether those trends, in fact, indicate increasing losses of human welfare in the past few decades, a period during which the earth has apparently warmed.[41] The specific indicators examined in the chapter include agricultural productivity, as well as deaths and property losses as a result of extreme weather events, such as hurricanes and floods.

Chapter 7 determines whether the long-term environmental trends presented in chapter 6 are consistent with one or the other view offered regarding the effects of economic development and technological change on the environment.

Chapter 8 draws upon the trend information developed in the previous two chapters to discuss various factors that affect the magnitude of environmental impacts. The chapter focuses on technological change, wealth, property rights, economic incentives, and the role of regulation. It also identifies factors that might affect the shape and timing of various environmental transitions from pollutant to pollutant and from country to country.

Part C examines whether and how human well-being and environmental quality can coexist in a more populated and richer world with the focus on a number of today's hotly debated environmental and natural resource issues. Chapter 9 specifically evaluates the promises and perils of bioengineered or genetically modified (GM) crops in terms of their ability to reconcile the competing goals of meeting the human demand for food, fiber, and timber while conserving habitat and biodiversity. Satisfying both those opposed goals is critical to advancing human and environmental well-being. Those human demands—despite being inadequately met, as witnessed by the millions who die from hunger and malnutrition each year—are the most important threats to terrestrial, freshwater, and marine biodiversity today. Those threats are likely to multiply as the population inevitably increases for the next few decades and, probably, becomes wealthier, whether Neo-Malthusians approve of those outcomes.

Chapter 9 also analyzes the public health and environmental benefits and costs of GM crops by using a framework consistent with the articulated rationale for the precautionary principle, namely, to identify and to implement policies that would most reduce risks to public health, the environment, or both. Accordingly, Chapter 9 compares the benefits and costs of both introducing GM crops on one hand and, on the other hand, persisting with "conventional" agriculture. It qualitatively evaluates the net consequences for (a) global public health, in terms of death and disease because of hunger and malnutrition, as well as over-consumption of food, and (b) the environment, in terms of habitat loss, soil erosion, and use of pesticides and fertilizers.

Chapter 10 addresses climate change. Notably, climate change will not create brand new problems as much as it might exacerbate existing ones, such as malaria, hunger, water stress, coastal flooding, loss of carbon sink capacity, and habitat loss. This allows us to estimate the contributions of climate change to those problems and to compare them against contributions from other sources, as well as to determine whether climate change is, in fact, as many have suggested, the most important public health and environmental problem facing the world through the foreseeable future.

Significantly, developing countries are most at risk of climate change because they lack the necessary economic, human, and social resources to obtain and to operate technologies to cope with its impacts. But the problems that climate change would exacerbate—particularly, malaria, hunger, water stress, and coastal flooding—are among the major hurdles that currently stand in their path to sustainable economic development. Accordingly, chapter 10 also develops a unified approach that would advance developing countries' sustainable development by reducing those hurdles while simultaneously increasing their capacity to adapt to climate change (both by reducing their vulnerability to those very hurdles and by advancing their ability to cope with any residual impacts of climate change). The chapter will show that this approach, which, for lack of a better name, I will call the "adaptive management approach to climate change," will also incidentally help reduce emissions of GHGs and advance the capacity of nations to mitigate greenhouse emissions, if and when that becomes essential.

Chapter 10 will also show that such an adaptive management approach will, over the short to medium term, advance human and environmental well-being faster, more efficiently, and much more surely than would attempts to just mitigate climate change through GHG emission reductions. This is due to the inertia of the climate system because of which it takes decades before any changes in emissions register as changes in temperatures or other climatic variables. However, because some mitigation may be inevitable in the longer run, the chapter also recommends pursuing existing no-regret actions—actions that should be undertaken on their own merits regardless of their effects on climate change per se, for example, reduction of subsidies to the energy and agricultural sectors that increase emissions as a byproduct—while expanding the range of no-regret options through research and development efforts to make additional emission reductions more cost-effective by developing new, or improving existing, technologies. At the same time, there should be an active program to monitor trends in impacts to avoid any surprises and to improve our knowledge and understanding of the science, economics, and policies related to climate change and its impacts. Combining the latter program with strategies that would advance adaptive capacity and mitigate GHG concentrations form the basis of an adaptive management approach toward climate change, under which the strategies could be modified and resources moved between them as knowledge in those areas accumulates and, one hopes, uncertainties are reduced.

Part D is a synthesis of the information presented in the previous chapters. Chapter 11 addresses the future sustainability of modern economic growth, with the focus on natural resource and environmental problems associated with land and water use (i.e., food and forests), air and water pollution, and potential global warming. It first develops priorities for those problems based on their public health impacts and, then, offers approaches to deal with those priorities. Finally, chapter 12 lays out the conclusions of this book, focusing on the roles of technological change, economic growth, and free trade in extending the limits to growth.

Although the United States is a major focus of this book, it also examines, where data allow, global trends for selected indicators of human well-being and environmental quality. This allows us to evaluate whether the U.S. experience is unique or if it fits a more general pattern. Because the United States is the country that probably has traveled the furthest on the path of modern economic growth, others—especially developing countries—might learn from its experience regarding which approaches may be more successful than others to ensure continuing improvement in human well-being, of which environmental quality is but one aspect.

2. The Improving State of Humanity

In the past two centuries, global population has increased more than seven-fold from about 900 million to about 6.5 billion today;[1] manufacturing industry by more than 75-fold;[2] carbon dioxide emissions from fossil fuel combustion by 600-fold;[3] and global economic product has increased more than 60-fold.[4]

In the following, I will address whether, and the extent to which, all this economic activity has improved humanity's lot. I will limit myself to the following handful of key indicators of human well-being:[5]

- *Hunger* has been synonymous with misery through the ages. It is no accident that famine was one of the four horsemen of the Apocalypse. Less than half a century ago, famine, natural or man-made, claimed more than 30 million Chinese in 1959–61.[6] Having sufficient quantities of food is, perhaps, the first step to a healthy society.[7] It also enables the average person to live a more fulfilling and productive life.[8] Hunger and undernourishment, moreover, retard education and the acquisition and development of human capital. Thus, inadequate food supplies could slow down both technological change and economic growth. I will use available food supplies per capita as a surrogate for hunger and malnourishment. I will supplement this with the prevalence of child malnutrition as measured by the percent of children whose weight is substantially below internationally accepted reference levels.[9]
- *Infant mortality* is another index for misery through the ages. Perhaps nothing has sown more sorrow and grief for womankind than the untimely death of children. For most of humankind's tenure on Earth, infant mortality has been one of nature's cruel mechanisms for keeping human populations in check.
- *Life expectancy* is undoubtedly the single most important indicator of human well-being. As we will see, longer life expectancy

is also generally accompanied by an increase in disability-free life years. Thus, both quantity and quality of life go hand-in-hand.

- *Economic development* is another key indicator as measured by the gross domestic product (GDP) per capita—itself a surrogate for per capita income (PCI)—not because it's an end in itself, but because it provides the means to many ends, such as higher crop yields, greater food supplies per capita, greater access to safe water and sanitation, improved public health services, and better education, which, in turn, help lower mortality rates and raise life expectancies.[10] Economic development, as we will see, accelerates the process of creating and diffusing new technologies, even as new technologies stimulate economic growth. Economic development is also critical for raising the material well-being of populations and for providing them with creature comforts.
- *Education*, in addition to being an end in itself, is essential for conserving and creating new human capital. It can, in the right setting, that is, with the appropriate set of institutions, accelerate the creation and, once created, the diffusion of technology.[11] Moreover, education (particularly of women) seems to be a key factor in spreading knowledge regarding basic hygiene, safe drinking water, sanitation, nutrition, and other public health practices that help reduce mortality and increase life expectancies.
- *Political rights and economic freedom* enable individuals to live life creatively and productively. Such rights and freedoms are critical to maintaining liberty and the pursuit of happiness, which are among the "unalienable Rights" of humankind.
- A composite *"human development index" (HDI)*, which combines three measures of well-being—life expectancy, the levels of education, and the levels of economic development—uses an approach similar to that employed in the annual Human Development Reports by the United Nations Development Programme (UNDP).[12]

As part of this examination, I will also address how factors contributing or related to the improvements in these indicators also vary with economic development, for example, access to safe water and sanitation, crop yields, and child labor.

In the following, I will use a country's GDP per capita as a measure of its wealth, which I will use interchangeably with PCI and income.

Hunger and Malnutrition

Concerns for the world's ability to feed its burgeoning population have been around at least since Malthus's *Essay on Population* 200 years ago. Several 20th century Neo-Malthusians confidently predicted apocalyptic famines in the latter part of that century in developing countries.[13] But today, although the world's population has never been larger, the average person has never been better fed.

Since 1950, the global population has increased by more than 150 percent,[14] and PCIs, as measured by global economic product per capita, by more than 190 percent.[15] Both those factors increase the demand for food. Yet the real price of food commodities has declined 75 percent.[16] Greater agricultural productivity and international trade have made this possible.[17] As a result, as indicated by table 2.1 and illustrated in figure 2.1, average daily food supplies per capita (FS/cap) increased 24 percent globally from 1961 to 2002.[18] The increase for developing countries, at 38 percent, was even larger.[19]

To put the increases in available food supplies into perspective, the scale in figure 2.1 for available food supply begins at 1,500 kcals/capita/day in recognition that the basal metabolic rate, which is the minimum energy needed by the body to perform basic activities at rest in a supine position, is in the general range of 1,300–1,700 kcals/day for adults with different physiological characteristics (i.e., age, sex, height, body weight).[20] Taking the age/sex structure and body weights of the adult populations of the different developing countries for 1990–92, and making allowances for the growth requirements of children, as well as for light activity, the Food and Agriculture Organization (FAO) estimates the minimum daily energy requirement to be between 1,720 and 1,960 calories per person per day for the different developing countries. Individuals with lower food intakes are undernourished because they do not eat enough to maintain health and body weight and to engage in light activity.[21] The result, as Robert W. Fogel, the Nobel Prize-winning economic historian, notes, is physical and mental impairment, characteristics that are evidenced in anthropometric surveys.[22] Add to this threshold an allowance for moderate activity, and the result is an estimate of the national average requirement, which for the different developing

21

Table 2.1
DAILY FOOD SUPPLIES (KCALS/CAPITA/DAY), C. 1800–2002

Areas	Pre- or Early-Industrial Phase [a,b]	1961	1975	1989	2002
United Kingdom/England	2,068 (1785–95)[c]	3,290	3,171	3,244	3,412
France	1,753 (1790)	3,194	3,247	3,563	3,654
Developed Countries	NA	1,928	3,147	3,308	3,314
Eastern Europe	NA	3,118	3,412	3,436	3,194
India	1,635 (1950–51)	2,072	1,942	2,417	2,459
China	2,115 (1947–48)[d]	1,641	2,090	2,642	2,951
Brazil	2,150 (1934–38)	2,516	2,494	2,766	3,066
Developing Countries	NA	1,930	2,144	2,519	2,666
Sub-Saharan Africa	NA	2,055	2,065	2,093	2,207
World	NA	2,254	2,422	2,710	2,804

a. Data are for the year(s) shown in parentheses. b. Many developing countries, for example, India and China, barely embarked upon industrialization until after World War II. c. For England. Calculated from Fogel (1995), p. 65, assuming the ratio of per capita consumption to calories per consuming unit would have been the same in England as it was in France. d. Based on data for 22 provinces.

NA = not available.

SOURCES: Joyce Burnette and Joel Mokyr, "The Standard of Living through the Ages," in The State of Humanity, ed. Julian L. Simon (Oxford, UK: Blackwell, 1995), pp. 135–48; Robert W. Fogel, "The Contribution of Improved Nutrition to the Decline of Mortality in Europe and America," in The State of Humanity, ed. Julian L. Simon (Cambridge, MA: Blackwell, 1995), pp. 61–71; Indur M. Goklany, "Meeting Global Food Needs: The Environmental Trade-Offs Between Increasing Land Conversion and Land Productivity," Technology 6 (1999): 107–30; World Resources Institute, EarthTrends database,

Figure 2.1
FOOD SUPPLIES VS. TIME, 1936–2002

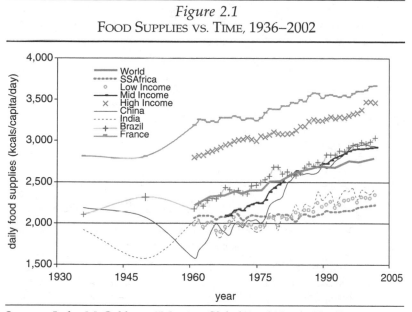

SOURCES: Indur M. Goklany, "Meeting Global Food Needs: The Environmental Trade-Offs Between Increasing Land Conversion and Land Productivity," *Technology* 6 (1999): 107–30; World Resources Institute, EarthTrends database, www.wri.org (accessed June 23, 2005).

countries ranges from 2,000 to 2,310 calories per person per day. All this assumes that food provisions will be equally divided among the entire population.[23]

The improvements for India since 1950–51 and China since 1961 are especially noteworthy. By 2002, China's food supplies had gone up 80 percent to 2,951 kcal/capita/day from a barely subsistence level of 1,636 kcals/capita/day in 1961,[24] while India's went up 50 percent to 2,459 from 1,635 kcals/capita/day in 1950–51.[25] Between 1969–71 and 2000–02 such increases in food supplies reduced chronic undernourishment in developing countries from 956 million to 815 million (or from 37 to 17 percent of their population) despite an 83 percent growth in their population.[26]

Notably, despite a doubling in China's population since 1960,[27] there has not been a repeat of the 1959–61 famine that claimed an estimated 30 million (or more) lives.[28] That is progress.

What are the factors responsible for such progress?

Figure 2.2
FOOD SUPPLIES PER CAPITA VS. INCOME, 1975–2002

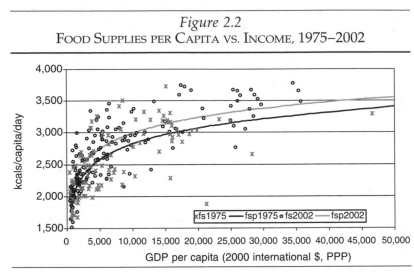

SOURCE: Based on data from World Resources Institute, EarthTrends database, www.wri.org (accessed June 23, 2005); World Bank, *World Development Indicators*, http://devdata.worldbank.org/dataonline (accessed July 12, 2005).

Figure 2.2 shows the raw cross-country data for 1975 and 2002 for average daily FS/cap plotted as a function of the country's wealth, as measured by GDP per capita in constant 2000 international (purchasing power parity [PPP]-adjusted) dollars.[29] It also shows the curves that "best fit" these raw data.[30] These curves indicate the following:

- Available food supplies per capita per day increase as countries become wealthier. These upward trends with respect to wealth for both 1975 and 2002 are statistically significant at the 99.9 percent confidence level. Moreover, FS/cap is equally sensitive to changes in income levels in both 1975 and 2002. In either year, going from an income of $100 to $1,000 would have increased FS/cap by 816 kcal/capita/day.
- The positive effect of wealth on available food supplies per capita per day is most pronounced at low levels of income. Because the dependence of FS/cap on income is logarithmic, the increase in FS/cap is the same whether income increases from $100 to $1,000 or from $1,000 to $10,000.
- The upward displacement of the entire FS/cap curve from 1975 to 2002 is also statistically significant (again, at the 99.9 percent

confidence level).[31] Because of this displacement, for any specified level of income, FS/cap was 166 kcal/capita/day higher
in 2002 than in 1975. This displacement can be ascribed to overall
technological change over this period because of the introduction of new, and the diffusion of existing, technologies that
increased agricultural production per capita. In general, the
flow of technology has been from the richer to poorer countries.

- Because of the combination of increasing incomes and technological change, according to the best-fit equation, the globally
averaged FS/cap rose 323 kcal (from 2,540 to 2,863 kcal/capita/
day) between 1975 and 2002. This change suggests that during
this period, while technology increased FS/cap by 166 kcal/
capita/day, the general increase in wealth was responsible for
another 157 kcal/capita/day (166 + 157 = 323). The average
improvement was somewhat greater for low-income countries,
for which it increased by 363 kcal/capita/day (from 2,027 to
2,390 kcal/capita/day) because they are situated on the steeper
part of the FS/cap versus income curve.

One reason for the improvement in FS/cap with income is that
average agricultural productivity increases with wealth, as indicated
in figure 2.3.[32] All else being equal, cereal yields increased by 117
kg/hectare for every $1,000 increase in income levels in either 1975
or 2003. This increase is because richer farmers and richer countries
can better afford new and more productive technologies.[33] Figure
2.3 also indicates that for any specific income level, cereal yields
improved by 526 kg/hectare between 1975 and 2002 because of
technological change. The increases in productivity with both wealth
and technological change are statistically significant at the 99 percent
confidence level. With both those factors acting in combination,
the increase in global food production outstripped the increase in
population growth and FS/cap increased, as indicated in figure 2.2.
This contributed to the 75 percent decline in global food prices (in
constant dollars) during the second half of the 20th century, which
increased access to food supplies for people at lower levels of income,
in particular. Reinforcing the increase in food supply was the fact
that wealthier populations could also afford more food whether
it was grown domestically or had to be imported, through trade,
from abroad.[34]

Figure 2.3
CEREAL YIELD VS. INCOME, 1975–2003

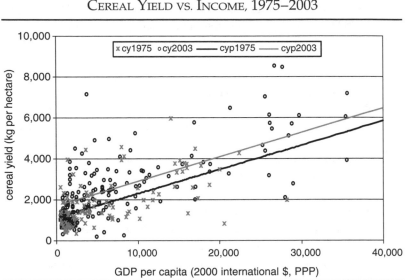

SOURCE: Based on data from World Bank, *World Development Indicators,* http://devdata.worldbank.org/dataonline (accessed July 12, 2005).

Because improvements in FS/cap translate into lower levels of malnutrition, malnutrition prevalence—measured as the percentage of children under five whose weight is substantially less than the normal for an international reference population—not surprisingly, also declines with economic growth and, possibly, time, as illustrated in figure 2.4.[35] According to this figure, if a country's average income had stayed constant at a dollar a day (in 2000 international dollars), a level that is sometimes considered to be approximately at "absolute poverty,"[36] then prevalence of malnutrition in its population would have dropped from 79.5 percent to 58.6 percent. If average income had doubled, malnutrition would have dropped further to 35.2 percent.

Like figure 2.2, figures 2.3 and 2.4 indicate that the most rapid improvements in cereal yields or malnutrition prevalence also occur at low levels of economic development. Thus, the poorer the society, the more important is economic development to its ability to keep hunger and malnutrition in check.

Figure 2.4
MALNUTRITION PREVALENCE VS. INCOME, 1987–2000

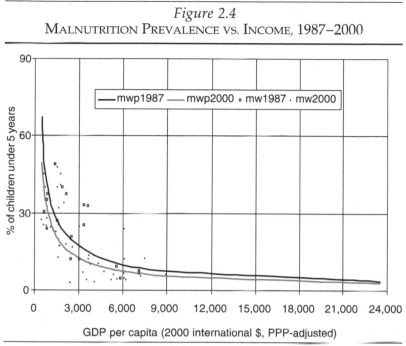

SOURCE: Based on data from World Bank, *World Development Indicators,*
http://devdata.worldbank.org/dataonline (accessed July 12, 2005).

Infant Mortality

Before industrialization, at least one out of every five children
died before reaching his or her first birthday; that is, infant morality,
measured as the number of children dying before the age of one,
typically exceeded 200 per 1,000 live births.[37] As indicated in table
2.2, the rate fell to 57 worldwide in 2003.[38] This level is approximately
the same one that more developed countries had reached in the mid
1950s.[39] In the United States, as late as 1900, infant mortality was
about 160; but by 2004 it had declined to 6.6.[40] In developing countries, the declines started later but may be occurring more rapidly
in many areas. For instance, between 1950–55 and 2003, India's infant
mortality fell from 190 to 63, and China's fell from 195 to 30.[41]

It is well known that infant mortality declines (i.e., improves)
with wealth.[42] Figure 2.5, based on World Bank data, shows infant
mortality declining (i.e., improving) with GDP per capita and the
entire curve being displaced downward with the passage of time

Table 2.2
INFANT MORTALITY (< 1 YEAR OF AGE PER 1,000 LIVE BIRTHS) FROM THE MIDDLE AGES TO A.D. 2003

Areas	Middle Ages	Pre- or Early-Industrial Phase[a,b]	1950–55	1970–75	1985–90	2003
Sweden		240 (1800)	19.7	10.2	6.0	2.8
France		182 (1830)	45.0	15.9	7.8	4.4
Developed Countries	> 200		59.1	21.4	12.7	7.1
Russia			97.5	27.7	23.7	16.0
China			195.0	61.1	50.0	33.0
India			190.0	132.0	94.5	63.0
Developing Countries			179.8	104.7	77.9	62.4
Sub-Saharan Africa			177.0	134.2	112.4	101.0
World	> 200		156.9	93.2	70.4	56.8

a. Data are for the year(s) shown in parentheses. b. Many developing countries, for example, India and China, had barely embarked upon industrialization until after World War II.

SOURCES: Brian R. Mitchell, *International Historical Statistics: Europe 1750–1988* (New York: Stockton Press, 1992); Kenneth Hill, "The Decline in Childhood Mortality," in *The State of Humanity*, ed. Julian L. Simon (Cambridge, MA: Blackwell, 1995), pp. 37–50; UN Population Division, *World Population Prospects: The 2004 Revision Population Database*, http://esa.un.org/unpp; World Bank, *World Development Indicators*, http://devdata.worldbank.org/dataonline (accessed July 12, 2005).

Figure 2.5
INFANT MORTALITY VS. INCOME, 1980–2003

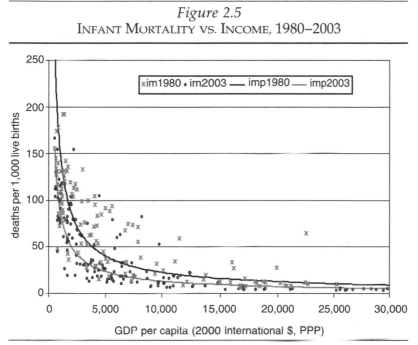

| xim1980 • im2003 —— imp1980 —— imp2003 |

GDP per capita (2000 International $, PPP)

SOURCE: Based on data from World Bank, *World Development Indicators,* http://devdata.worldbank.org/dataonline (accessed July 12, 2005).

from 1980 to 2003. This figure shows that infant mortality drops with greater affluence and with time.[43] According to this figure, if a hypothetical country doubled its GDP per capita from a dollar to two dollars a day, it would have decreased infant mortality from 355 deaths per 1,000 live births to 199 in 1980 and from 207 to 116 in 2003.

What accounts for the improvements in infant mortality with the level of economic development and with time?

First, as shown in figures 2.2 and 2.3, available food supplies and cereal yields increase with a country's level of economic development and with time (or technology). That increase reduces malnutrition in both mothers and children (see, for example, figure 2.4), which, in turn, improves their health and reduces their mortality rates. In addition, richer societies are better able to afford health care and, by and large, put more resources into health care as shown

Figure 2.6
HEALTH EXPENDITURES PER CAPITA VS. INCOME, 2002

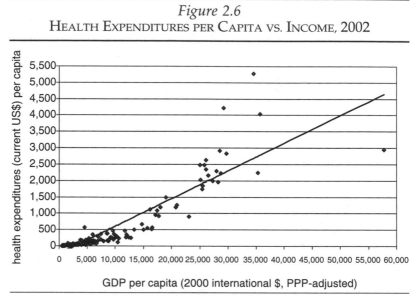

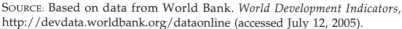

GDP per capita (2000 international $, PPP-adjusted)

SOURCE: Based on data from World Bank. *World Development Indicators,* http://devdata.worldbank.org/dataonline (accessed July 12, 2005).

by figure 2.6.[44] Moreover, figures 2.7 and 2.8 show that wealthier countries generally have greater access to safe water[45] and to sanitation,[46] and this ability has generally advanced with time and with the accretion of, and improvements in, technology. In addition, better health care, safer water, and increased sanitation reduce the amount of food supplies needed to maintain health, that is, the same amount of food supplies go further in ensuring good health,[47] at least until the point beyond which additional food supplies contribute mainly to obesity. Thus, all those factors reinforce each other in reducing infant mortality rates and generally improving public health.

One can get an idea of the significance of technological change from table 2.3, which compares infant mortality in the United States in 1913 (when it had a per capita income level of $5,301, in 1990 international dollars)[48] with data from 1998 for a sampling of the developing countries. In each case, developing countries in 1998 were much better-off in terms of infant mortality than the United States was in 1913 although their real income levels were substantially lower (by 31 to 77 percent).

Figure 2.7
ACCESS TO SAFE WATER VS. INCOME, 1990–2002

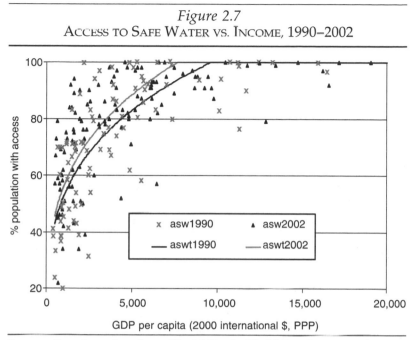

SOURCE: Based on data from World Bank, *World Development Indicators,* http://devdata.worldbank.org/dataonline (accessed July 12, 2005).

However, because income does not always increase monotonically with time, and poor countries frequently lack the resilience to cope with adversity, infant mortality does not always decline with the passage of time or, for that matter, increasing incomes. Thus, between 1990 and 2002–03, infant mortality increased in 26 countries (out of 186 countries that had data for both years, according to the World Bank's online database).[49] Twenty of those were in sub-Saharan Africa, and about half (or more) of those 20 had declining incomes during that period.

Life Expectancy

For much of human history, average life expectancy used to be 20–30 years.[50] By 1900, it had climbed to about 31 years (see figure 2.9).[51] By 2003 it had increased to 66.8 worldwide.[52] For the richest group of nations, the high-income countries of the Organisation for Economic Co-operation and Development (OECD), it was 78.5 years while for sub-Saharan Africa, which has some of the world's poorest

Figure 2.8
ACCESS TO SANITATION VS. INCOME, 1990–2002

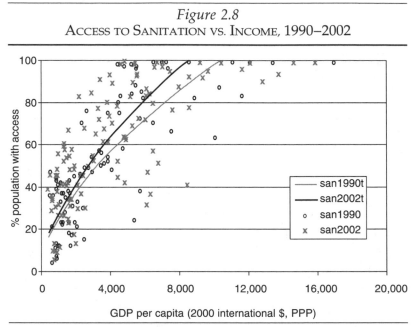

SOURCE: Based on data from World Bank, *World Development Indicators,* http://devdata.worldbank.org/dataonline (accessed July 12, 2005).

countries, life expectancy was 45.6 years.[53] However, as shown by recent, post-1980, trends for sub-Saharan Africa and Russia, whose experience mirrors other areas in the former Soviet Union, increases in life expectancies are neither monotonic nor inevitable.

Trends from the 1800s onward for the currently developed countries (CDCs) show that life expectancy fluctuated in the early part of the 19th century, followed by (small) declines in the middle two quarters of the 1800s before commencing, with a few notable exceptions and some minor fluctuations, a sustained improvement that continues to this day. In England and Wales, life expectancy, which had been 35.9 in 1801, declined from 40.8 in 1831 to 39.5 in 1851. After some fluctuations in the 40 to 40.2 range, it has been climbing more or less steadily since 1871.[54] The same broad pattern seems to fit the United States from the 1850s to the present, with improvements in life expectancy from 1880 onward.[55]

The fluctuations until the last quarter of the 19th century were due to a combination of factors. Urbanization, coupled with ignorance of

Table 2.3
TECHNOLOGICAL PROGRESS AND INFANT MORTALITY AND LIFE EXPECTANCY

Country	Year	Per Capita Income (1990 international $)	Infant Mortality (deaths per 1,000 live births)	Life Expectancy at Birth (years)
United States	1913	5,301	~100	52
United Kingdom	1913	5,150[a]	NA	~54[b]
Ghana	1998	1,244	57	59
India	1998	1,746	71	63
China	1998	3,117	31	70
Peru	1998	3,666	40	68

a. For England, Scotland, and Wales. b. For England and Wales.

SOURCES: Angus Maddison, *The World Economy: A Millenial Perspective* (Paris: Organisation for Economic Co-operation and Development, 2001), pp. 247, 264, 288, 323; World Bank, *World Development Indicators CD-ROM* (Washington, DC: World Bank, 2001); Roderick Floud and Bernard Harris, "Health, Height, and Welfare: Britain, 1700–1980," in *Health and Welfare During Industrialization*, ed. Richard H. Steckel and Roderick Floud (Chicago: University of Chicago Press, 1997), p. 116.

Figure 2.9
LIFE EXPECTANCY, 1820–2003

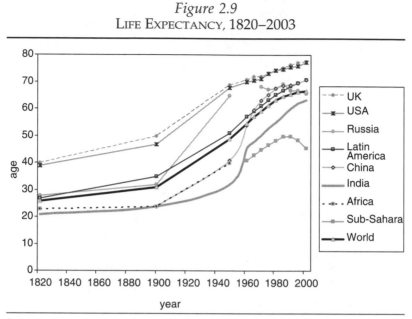

SOURCES: Angus Maddison, *The World Economy: A Millennium Perspective* (Paris: OECD, 2001); World Bank, *World Development Indicators,* http://devdata.worldbank.org/dataonline (accessed July 12, 2005).

the germ theory and rudiments of safe water and sanitation, facilitated the spread of infectious and parasitic diseases, such as cholera, smallpox, malaria, tuberculosis, and typhoid. This not only raised mortality rates directly, but it also increased a stricken individual's requirements for food and nutrition. Thus, even in years where it seemed that the harvest was adequate, mortality rates may have increased due to an effective increase in food requirements.[56]

Once solutions to those diseases were identified—in some cases ahead of an understanding of their causes[57]—the CDCs cleaned up their water supplies and instituted basic public health measures, such as water filtration, chlorination, sanitation, pasteurization, and vaccination, which rapidly dropped mortality rates in the latter part of the 19th and early part of the 20th centuries. In the first half of the 20th century, antibiotics, pesticides such as DDT, and a wider array of vaccines were added to this arsenal. Having essentially conquered the traditional infectious and parasitic diseases, CDCs have, over the past half century, turned their wealth and human capital to dealing with the so-called diseases of affluence—cancer, heart diseases, and strokes—and, since the 1980s, HIV/AIDS, a nontraditional infectious disease. They have, at the same time, trained their resources on more uncertain—and, in some cases, downright trivial—risks to public health, such as the effects of genetically modified crops, cloned pigs, electromagnetic forces, and even cell phones.

The diffusion of knowledge gained and technologies devised by the CDCs was also critical to a greater appreciation of the importance of safe water and sanitation services, particularly in developing countries. As a result, there has been general improvement in such access worldwide in the past few decades, as shown in figures 2.7 and 2.8 by the upward shift in those indicators with the passage of time. Such improvements, coupled with increases in food supplies per capita (figures 2.1 and 2.2); greater expenditures on, and availability of, basic public health services (figures 2.6 through 2.8); and the arrival and spread of antibiotics, vaccinations, and DDT combined to reduce mortality rates, particularly over the past half century (table 2.2). As a result, life expectancies increased worldwide—and not just in the richest nations (table 2.4).

The aggregate effect of all those factors is captured in figure 2.10, which is similar to curves previously presented by the World Bank and Harvard's Barry Bloom,[58] shows life expectancy increasing with per capita income for both 1977 and 2003.[59] In this figure, to better illustrate the dependence of life expectancy on income, the y-axis commences at 30 years, the approximate average life expectancy worldwide before the start of modern economic growth.

Figure 2.10 indicates that if a country's average income had been fixed, then between 1977 and 2003 its life expectancy would have increased by 4 years because of gains from technological change with the passage of time. It is consistent with the notion that over time the creation and diffusion of existing and new technologies (which includes knowledge) to improve public health and lower mortality will improve life expectancy for a given level of real income. A hypothetical doubling of GDP per capita from a dollar to two dollars a day would have increased life expectancy from 40.7 to 46.2 years in 1977 and from 44.6 to 50.2 years in 2003.

Figure 2.10 also suggests that, because of technological change, today's developing countries may have higher life expectancies than

Table 2.4
LIFE EXPECTANCY AT BIRTH (IN YEARS) FROM THE MIDDLE AGES TO A.D. 2000

Area	Middle Ages	Pre- or Early-Industrial Phase[a,b]	1900[d]	1950–55[f]	1975–80[f]	1985–90[f]	2003[g]
France	22 (1395–1505)[e]	~30 (1800)[e]	47.0	66.5	73.7	76	79.3
United Kingdom		35.9 (1799–1803)[c]	50.0	69.2	72.8	75	77.6
Developed Countries	20–30[e]			66.1	72.1	74.1	75.6[f]
Eastern Europe						70.3	67.9
India		24–25 (1901–11)[e]	24.0	38.7	53.3	57.2	63.4
China		24 (1900)[d]	24.0	40.8	65.3	67.1	70.8
Sub-Saharan Africa	20–30[e]			37.4	47.2	49.4	45.6
Developing Countries		26 (1820)[d]		40.9	56.8	60.4	63.4[f]
World	20–30[e]	31 (1900)[d]	31.0	46.5	59.7	62.9	66.8

a. Data are for the year(s) shown in parentheses. b. Many developing countries, for example, India and China, had barely embarked upon industrialization until after World War II. c. 1799–1803 data are for England and Wales only; from Wrigley and Schofield (1981). d. Maddison (2001). e. Preston (1995). f. WPP (2004), unless noted otherwise. g. World Bank (2005), unless noted otherwise.

SOURCES: Edward A. Wrigley and Roger Schofield, *The Population History of England, 1541–1871* (Cambridge, MA: Harvard University Press, 1981); Samuel H. Preston, "Human Mortality throughout History and Prehistory," in *The State of Humanity*, ed. Julian L. Simon (Oxford: Blackwell, 1998), pp. 30–36; Angus Maddison, *The World Economy: A Millennial Perspective* (Paris: OECD, 2001); UN Population Division, *World Population Prospects: The 2004 Revision Population Database*, http://esa.un.org/unpp; World Bank, *World Development Indicators*, http://devdata.worldbank.org/dataonline (accessed July 12, 2005).

Figure 2.10
LIFE EXPECTANCY VS. INCOME, 1977–2003

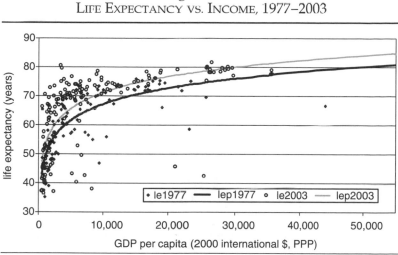

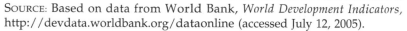

SOURCE: Based on data from World Bank, *World Development Indicators,*
http://devdata.worldbank.org/dataonline (accessed July 12, 2005).

did the developed countries at equivalent levels of income. This,
indeed, is the case for China and India, countries once synonymous
with poverty and wretchedness. In 1913, when the United States
had a GDP per capita of $5,301 (in 1990 international, PPP-adjusted
dollars),[60] its life expectancy at birth was 52.5 years.[61] In 1977, when
China and India had GDP per capita of a mere $895 and $937,
respectively (also in 1990 international dollars), they had life expectancies of approximately 65.4 and 52.9 years.[62] So far, this phenomenon also holds for sub-Saharan Africa. In 2003, its average life expectancy was 45.6 years, approximately the same as the United States
in 1890, while its GDP per capita was $1,613 (in 2000 international
dollars). In comparison, the U.S. GDP per capita stood at $3,392 (in
1990 international dollars).[63]

Figure 2.11 highlights trends in life expectancies from the years
1950–55 to 2003 for various income groups and other entities.[64] Consistent with figure 2.10, in any given year, life expectancy increases
with per capita income. Although life expectancy has on average
increased worldwide since the 1950s, more recently there have been
dramatic declines in many areas of sub-Saharan Africa, as well as less

Figure 2.11
LIFE EXPECTANCY, 1950–2003

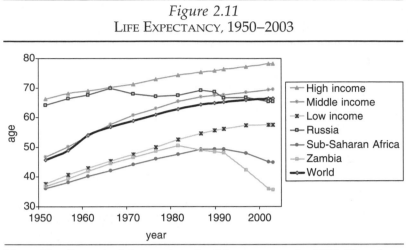

NOTE: The first set of data points for this curve are for 1950–55 and are plotted as 1952.5.

SOURCES: World Bank, *World Development Indicators,* http://devdata.worldbank. org/dataonline (accessed July 12, 2005); World Resources Institute, Earth-Trends, www.wri.org (accessed June 23, 2005).

pronounced declines in Russia, which is somewhat representative of the former Soviet Union.

Of the 176 entities for which the World Bank's online database had data, 39 had lower life expectancy in 2003 than in 1990. Of those, 25 were in sub-Saharan Africa, 9 were part of the former Soviet Union, 4 were from Latin America and the Caribbean, and 1 was North Korea.

Russia's life expectancy peaked in 1988 at 69.5 years.[65] By 1994, it had dropped by 5 years. In part, these ups and downs reflected economic deterioration concurrent with, and following, the fall of the communist government. Between 1989 and 1998, GDP per capita (in 1990 international dollars) declined 44 percent.[66]

The drop in income and the loss of subsidies for agricultural inputs and food consumption—both victims of a failed economic system—reduced cereal yields, as well as lowered food supplies per capita and nutritional levels. In addition, the decline in Russia's economic condition diminished public health services and contributed to alcoholism, which might have accounted for the large increase in accidental deaths, to homicides, and, possibly, to hypertension and to suicides.[67] All those factors combined to increase mortality and to reduce life expectancies. Life expectancies similarly declined in other countries in Eastern Europe and the former Soviet Union. However, since their lows, both life expectancies and GDP per capita have rebounded somewhat in both regions. The recovery is more or less complete in the former region, with both GDP per capita and life expectancies rivaling pre-1990 levels. But, based on 2003 data, recovery still lags in many countries that were part of the former Soviet Union, but here too there are signs of progress.[68] By 2003, life expectancy for Russia, for instance, had increased slightly, and erratically, to 65.7 years, while GDP per capita had increased by 41 percent since its nadir in 1998.

Life expectancies have dropped much more dramatically since the late 1980s in a number of sub-Saharan countries, because of a vicious cycle involving new and resurgent diseases, particularly malaria, HIV/AIDS, and tuberculosis, as well as a drop in economic output, all mediated by poor governance.[69] From 1990 to 2003, GDP per capita (in 2000 international dollars) declined by about 12 percent in sub-Saharan Africa (from $1,863 to $1,613) while average life expectancy dropped from 50.0 years to 45.6 years.[70] According to World Bank data available as of August 2005, no country for which data are readily available has life expectancy lower than Zambia.[71] At 36.5 years, it has fallen below its 1950–55 level.[72]

Twenty-five of the 40 countries that had lower life expectancies in 2003 compared to 1990 were in sub-Saharan Africa. Of those, 13 also experienced a decline in their economic fortunes, as measured by GDP per capita in international (PPP-adjusted) constant dollars. The remainder, despite some economic growth, were apparently unable to surmount the problems associated with death and disease.

In terms of life expectancy, inhabitants of developing countries, by and large, with some possible exceptions, are better off today than the United States, United Kingdom, and other CDCs were at the same stage of economic development, mainly because of the diffusion of technology from developed to developing nations. Thus, if today's developing countries learn from history and adapt the lessons and technologies developed by the CDCs to their own circumstances, it should be possible in the long run for the former to increase their life expectancies to the levels currently attained by the rich countries (that is, in the upper 70s), as well as to advance to those levels much more rapidly than did the CDCs historically.

We Are Living Longer, But Are We Healthier?

Not only are we living longer; but we are also healthier.[73] Disability in the older populations of such developed nations as Canada, France, and the United States has been declining.[74] In the United States, for instance, the disability rate dropped 1.3 percent per year between 1982 and 1994 for persons aged 65 and over.

Robert W. Fogel notes that age-specific prevalence rates of specific chronic diseases and disabilities were much higher in the century preceding World War II than they are today. White males aged 60–64 are two-and-a-half times more likely to be free of chronic diseases today than their counterparts of a century ago. During the course of the 20th century, the onset of chronic diseases has been significantly delayed—by 9 years for heart diseases, by about 11 years for respiratory diseases (despite higher smoking rates), and by nearly 8 years for cancers.[75] According to the World Health Organization (WHO), health-adjusted life expectancy (HALE) for the United States, China, and India, were 69.3, 64.1, and 53.5 years, respectively, in 2002.[76] This is substantially more than those countries' corresponding total life expectancies before industrialization (see table 2.4).

Figure 2.12 shows, somewhat predictably, that HALE increases along with income.[77]

Economic Development

Table 2.5 and figure 2.13, based on data from economic historian Angus Maddison and the Groningen Growth and Development Centre,[78] show the trends in economic development for the past two millennia for the world and for various regions of the world. Although these estimates are less than precise, they indicate that by today's standards, for much of this period, everyone was very poor. For the first millennium after Christ, there was virtually no growth in global per capita incomes, which were stuck around $400–$450 (in 1990 international dollars). This is less than what Chad's per capita income level was in 1998 ($471, also in 1990 international dollars).[79] Looked at another way, during the first millennium after Christ, the average person was living on slightly more than a dollar a day (which is usually the definition of abject poverty nowadays). For the following eight centuries, average global per capita income grew imperceptibly at 0.05 percent per year.[80] By 1800, it had

Figure 2.12
HEALTH ADJUSTED LIFE EXPECTANCY (HALE) VS. INCOME, 2002

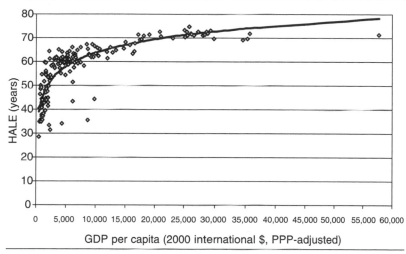

GDP per capita (2000 international $, PPP-adjusted)

SOURCES: Based on data from World Bank, *World Development Indicators,*
http://devdata.worldbank.org/dataonline (accessed July 12, 2005); World
Resources Institute, EarthTrends, www.wri.org (accessed June 23, 2005).

increased by about 50 percent to $650 (or less than two dollars a day).
However, in the past two centuries, because of modern economic
growth, which started with the industrialization of Great Britain
and spread first to Western Europe and its mainly white colonies
before infecting the rest of the world in the decades following World
War II, per capita income today has grown nine-fold to more than
$6,000 in 2001.

Figure 2.13 also shows that around 1800, Western Europe (initially
led by the United Kingdom) and the United States opened up gaps
in income levels between themselves and the rest of the world,
which, for the most part, have only widened since, although they
might have shrunk somewhat in the last two decades of the 20th
century (see chapter 3). So we have gone from an era when there
was broad parity in incomes between countries but all were desper-
ately poor by today's yardsticks to one where there is widespread
inequality but virtually everyone is far better off than their compatriots of a half a century ago. However, as indicated by tables 2.2 and
2.4, which show trends in infant mortality and life expectancy for

Table 2.5
GROSS DOMESTIC PRODUCT PER CAPITA (IN 1990 INTERNATIONAL $, PPP-ADJUSTED), A.D. 1–1998

Area	1	1000	1500	1700	1820	1913	1950	1989	1996	2001	2003[c]
Western Europe	450	400	771	998	1,204	3,458	4,579	15,856	17,097	19,256	
United States	400[a]	400[a]	400	527	1,257	5,301	9,561	23,059	25,066	27,948	28,797
USSR/former-USSR	400	400	499	610	688	1,488	2,841	7,098	3,854	4,626	5,267
Latin America	400	400	413[b]	441[b]	692	1,481	2,506	5,123	5,556	5,811	
China[d]	450	450	600	600	600	552	439	1,827	2,820	3,583	4,185
India	450	450	550	550	533	673	619	1,270	1,630	1,957	2,194
Japan	400	425	500	570	669	1,387	1,921	17,942	20,494	20,683	21,104
Africa	430	425	414	421	420	637	894	1,463	1,403	1,489	
World	445	436	566	615	667	1,525	2,111	5,140	5,517	6,049	

NOTES: a. Based on Maddison (1999): Angus Maddison, "Poor Until 1820," *Wall Street Journal*, The Millennium, January 11, 1999, p. R54. b. Based on the arithmetical average for Brazil and Mexico. c. Based on Groningen Growth and Developmental Centre, adjusted per Maddison. d. China's GDP for recent years has been revised upward to better account for its service sector. See James T. Areddy, "China Raises Growth Figures for Recent Years," *Wall Street Journal*, January 10, 2006, p. A12.

SOURCES: Angus Maddison, *The World Economy: Historical Statistics* (Paris: OECD, 2003), www.ggdc.net/~maddison (accessed July 30, 2005); Groningen Growth and Development Centre, Total Economy database, http://www.ggdc.net.

Figure 2.13
GLOBAL ECONOMIC DEVELOPMENT, A.D. 1–2003

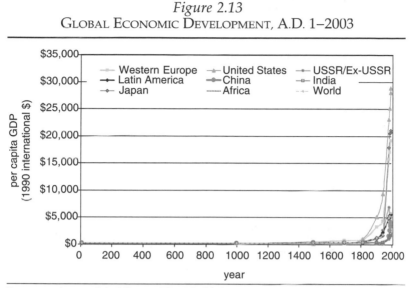

SOURCES: Angus Maddison, *The World Economy: Historical Statistics* (Paris: OECD, 2003), www.ggdc.net/~maddison (accessed July 30, 2005); Groningen Growth and Development Centre, Total Economy database, http://www.ggdc.net.

a variety of countries, it does not necessarily follow that gaps in other measures of human well-being are also widening. As we will see in greater detail in the following chapter, in terms of these other measures—food availability, prevalence of malnutrition, infant mortality, life expectancy, and child labor—which are much more directly relevant to the well-being of humanity, for the majority of the world's population, the gaps have diminished over the long term. However, for some indicators, particularly malnutrition and life expectancy, they have begun to expand once again between the rest of the world and sub-Saharan Africa and, to a lesser extent, the major portion of the former Soviet Union. Together, these regions comprise 17 percent of the human population.

Equally important, notwithstanding gaps in income, basic necessities of life, such as food, are much more easily available than they used to be even a few decades ago. For instance, between 1897–1902 and 2001–03, U.S. retail prices of flour, bacon, and potatoes relative to per capita income dropped by 92, 85, and 82 percent,[81] respectively. And, as noted, the real global price of food commodities has declined 75 percent since 1950. Thus, 100 real dollars today go further in providing food security than 100 real dollars in 1950 or, for that matter, in 1900.

Figure 2.13 (continued)
UPDATE: GLOBAL ECONOMIC DEVELOPMENT, A.D. 1950–2003

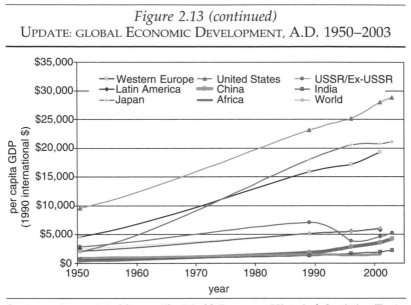

SOURCES: Angus Maddison, *The World Economy: Historical Statistics* (Paris: OECD, 2003), www.ggdc.net/~maddison (accessed July 30, 2005); Groningen Growth and Development Centre, Total Economy database, http://www.ggdc.net.

Moreover, not only is the average person's annual labor worth more (in real dollars), he or she is working less per year. Thus, from an economic perspective, the paradox is that despite the tremendous growth in population, human labor is more valuable and, therefore, scarcer. Average hours worked per person employed have declined since at least the 1800s, as shown in figure 2.14. Jesse Ausubel of Rockefeller University, one of the founders of the field of Industrial Ecology, and Arnulf Grübler, an authority on technological change in the energy sector at the International Institute for Applied Systems Analysis in Laxenburg, Austria, estimate that, for the average British worker, total life hours worked declined from 124,000 in 1856 to 69,000 in 1981.[82] This translates into a reduction in total life hours worked for the average British worker from 50 percent to 20 percent of "disposable life hours."[83]

Notably, Ausubel and Grübler didn't take into consideration the fact that because of improved and cheaper lighting since the middle of the 19th century (largely a result of electrification), the average

Figure 2.14
ANNUAL HOURS WORKED PER PERSON, 1870–1978

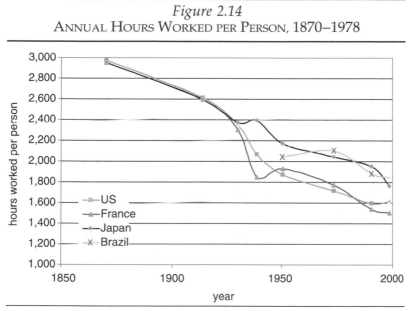

SOURCES: Angus Maddison, *Chinese Economic Performance in the Long Run* (Paris: OECD, 1998); Angus Maddison, *The World Economy: A Millennial Perspective* (Paris: OECD, 2001).

person now has more hours to pursue a wider array of activities to get whatever he or she may want of life. Therefore, arguably, the amount of disposable life hours estimated for the mid 1800s was overestimated relative to the amount available today, and improvements in the fraction of disposable life hours spent at work was, thus, underestimated.

Note that comparing so-called real GDP per capita for any two years separated by even as much as a generation apart can lead to a very misleading picture of the magnitude of changes. This is especially true during periods of rapid technological change. The goods and services that could be purchased in the year 1200, for instance, were probably not all that different from what could be purchased in 1100 or 1300. But if we compare 2000 with 1970, for instance, we can identify several goods and services (e.g., personal computers, cell phones, VCRs, and instant access to the Library of Congress's electronic catalogue), which simply were not available or, if so, they were at prices that exceeded the per capita GDP of

45

Figure 2.15
POST-SECONDARY SCHOOLING VS. INCOME, 1990–2002

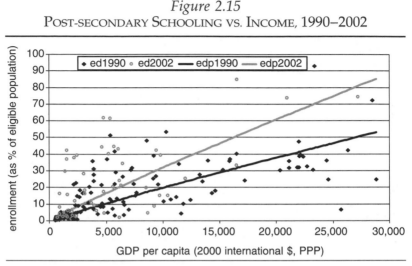

SOURCE: Based on data from World Bank, *World Development Indicators*, http://devdata.worldbank.org/dataonline (accessed July 12, 2006).

the richest nations (at that time). Clearly, you can buy a lot more with $1,000 (in *constant* dollars) today than you could in 1800 or, for that matter, 1900, and the improvements in the level of economic development shown in figure 2.13 are substantial underestimates.

Education

Literacy, an albeit imperfect surrogate for education, has also increased worldwide, as have other measures of educational attainment. Between 1970 and the early 2000s, global illiteracy rates dropped from 46 to 18 percent.[84]

Figure 2.15 shows what, by now, ought to be a familiar pattern, namely, human well-being—in this case measured by the percentage of the eligible population enrolled in tertiary education—growing with both time and affluence across countries.[85] The upward migration of the curve over time is consistent with the increasing realization (i.e., knowledge) about the benefits of education that, in turn, leads to a greater willingness in societies (and families) to incur the costs associated with longer periods of education. This greater willingness is then translated into action as countries (and families) become wealthier. Globally, the percentage of relevant population

The Improving State of Humanity

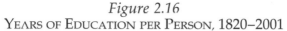

Figure 2.16
YEARS OF EDUCATION PER PERSON, 1820–2001

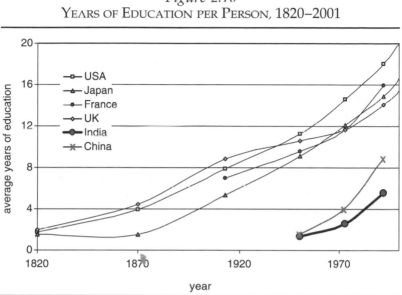

SOURCES: Angus Maddison, *Monitoring the World Economy, 1820–1992* (Paris: OECD, 1995); Angus Maddison, *Chinese Economic Performance in the Long Run* (Paris: OECD, 1998); Angus Maddison, *The World Economy: Historical Statistics* (Paris: OECD, 2003), http://ggdc.net/~maddison (accessed July 1, 2005).

enrolled in tertiary education increased from 6.8 percent in 1965 to 25.6 percent in 2001.[86] Figure 2.16 and table 2.6 also show long-term improvements in the levels of education for China, France, India, and the United States based on data from 1820 through the 20th century.[87]

Complementing the increases in literacy and education levels are declines in the portion of the population aged 10 to 14 years who are working (see figure 2.17). Worldwide child labor using this measure has been more than halved from 24.9 percent in 1960 to 10.5 percent in 2003.[88]

Figure 2.17 shows that for this indicator of human well-being as well, matters improve with the level of economic development and the passage of time,[89] suggesting that opponents of globalization and economic growth only hurt those they claim to champion.

Political Rights

In 1900, no country had universal adult suffrage, and only 12.4 percent of the world's population enjoyed even limited democracy.[90]

Table 2.6
EDUCATION (AVERAGE NUMBER OF YEARS PER PERSON AGED 15–64),
C. 1820–2001

Country	1820	1870	1913	1950	1973	1992	2001
France	—	—	6.99	9.58	11.69	15.96	—
United Kingdom	2.00	4.44	8.82	10.60	11.66	14.09	15.45
United States	1.75	3.92	7.86	11.27	14.58	18.04	20.21
Japan	1.50	1.50	5.36	9.11	12.09	14.87	16.61
India	—	—	—	1.35	2.60	5.55	—
China	—	—	—	1.60	4.09	8.93	—

SOURCES: Angus Maddison, *Monitoring the World Economy, 1820–1992* (Paris: OECD, 1995); Angus Maddison, *Chinese Economic Performance in the Long Run* (Paris: OECD, 1998); Angus Maddison, *The World Economy: Historical Statistics* (Paris: OECD, 2003).

Figure 2.17
CHILD LABOR VS. INCOME, 1975–2003

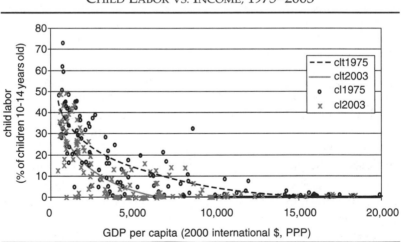

SOURCE: Based on data from World Bank, *World Development Indicators*, http://devdata.worldbank.org/dataonline (accessed July 12, 2005).

Today, 44.1 percent of the world's population is deemed free by Freedom House, while another 18.6 percent is considered partly free.[91] Multiparty electoral systems were introduced in 113 countries

Figure 2.18
GLOBAL ECONOMIC FREEDOM, 1980–2002

SOURCE: James Gwartney and Robert Lawson, *Economic Freedom of the World: 2004 Annual Report* (Vancouver, BC: Fraser Institute, 2004)

in the quarter century following 1974.[92] And there are even rumblings of democracy in the Middle East.

Economic Freedom

Economic freedom is also ascendant around the world. Economists James Gwartney and Robert Lawson have constructed an index of economic freedom that takes into consideration personal choice, protection of private property, and freedom to use and exchange property (so long as it does not violate the identical rights of others).[93] According to this index, economic freedom has been advancing globally at least since the mid 1970s.[94] Figure 2.18 shows this improvement from 1980 onward.[95] Moreover, economic freedom has increased in 102 of the 113 countries for which data were available for both 1990 and 2000.[96] Over the years, James Gwartney, Robert Lawson, and co-workers have shown the following:

Figure 2.19
AVERAGE INCOME VS. ECONOMIC FREEDOM INDEX, 2002

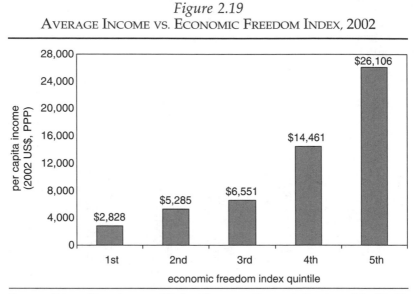

SOURCE: James Gwartney and Robert Lawson, *Economic Freedom of the World: 2004 Annual Report* (Vancouver, BC: Fraser Institute, 2004).

- The more economically free a country's population, the higher its economic growth during the 1990s and PPP-adjusted per capita income in the late 1990s (see figure 2.19).[97]
- Life expectancy—not surprising, given the previous discussion—is positively correlated with the index of economic freedom.
- Income inequality is not correlated with the index.[98]

Human Development Index

The HDI is an effort to construct a single index that captures various dimensions of human well-being and can be used to compare trends in well-being over time and across countries. The UNDP, which has popularized this approach, constructs an HDI based on life expectancy, education, and the log of GDP per capita. The logarithm is used to account for the fact that each additional dollar of income adds less to the quality of life than did the previous dollar; the logarithms of one, ten, hundred, and thousand, for instance, are zero, one, two, and three, respectively.

Figure 2.20
HUMAN DEVELOPMENT INDEX, UNITED STATES, 1870–2002

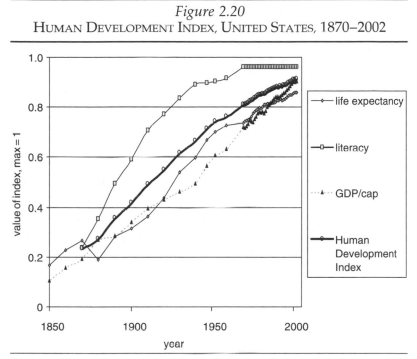

SOURCES: National Center for Health Statistics, *Health, United States, 2004 with Chartbook on Trends in the Health of Americans with Special Feature on Drugs* (Hyattsville, MD: Centers for Disease Control and Prevention, 2004), table 27; Michael R. Haines, "Estimated Life Tables for the United States, 1850–1900," National Bureau of Economic Research Historical Paper no. 59, Cambridge, MA, 1994; USBOC, *Historical Statistics of the United States, Colonial Times to 1970* (Washington, DC: GPO, 1975); Dora L. Costa and Richard H. Steckel, "Long-Term Trends, Health, Welfare, and Economic Growth in the United States," in *Health and Welfare during Industrialization*, ed. Richard H. Steckel and Roderick Floud (Chicago: University of Chicago Press, 1997), p. 72; USBOC, *Statistical Abstract of the United States 2004–2005* (Washington, DC: GPO, 2004); Angus Maddison, *The World Economy: Historical Statistics* (Paris: OECD, 2003), http://www.ggdc.net/~maddison (accessed July 1, 2005); Groningen Growth and Development Centre, Total Economy database, http://www.ggdc.net (accessed July 1, 2005).

Figure 2.20, based on certain assumptions, shows trends in the composite HDI and its individual components for the United States from 1870 to 2002 (see appendix B). It shows that, despite minor fluctuations in the components, there has been a general improvement in overall human well-being in the United States during the 20th century because of a continual improvement in each of its components (except for literacy, which reached "saturation" around 1970).[99]

Dora Costa and Richard Steckel have developed an HDI for the United States from 1800 to 1970, using heights rather than life expectancy as one of the three components of HDI.[100] Their analysis shows that heights declined in the third quarter of the 19th century, perhaps due to urbanization, which led to an increase in infectious diseases, and in the demand for food and nutrition for affected individuals. However, heights recovered in the last quarter due to the previously noted improvements in public health, and they have continued to improve since. These variations in height are generally consistent with Michael R. Haines's estimates for U.S. life expectancies from 1850 to 1900.[101]

In general, because the United Kingdom was the first to industrialize, public health developments there preceded developments in the United States, and the latter was a substantial beneficiary of the former's experience with regard to unsafe water, sanitation, soot, and smoke. In a joint analysis of human well-being for England and Wales from 1756 to 1981, the economic historian Sir Roderick Floud of London Metropolitan University and the social historian Bernard Harris of Southampton University also show some drops in human well-being in the middle decades of the 19th century due to lowered life expectancies because of urbanization.[102] However, those declines were turned around sooner than in the United States, and HDI in England and Wales has been increasing more or less steadily since 1850. Those results are broadly consistent with Sandberg and Steckel's analysis of HDI for Sweden from 1820 to 1965,[103] and Twarog's analysis for Germany from 1851 to 1950.[104]

According to the UNDP's *Human Development Report 2004*, HDI has been going up for most countries.[105] Specifically, it shows the following:

- All but three of the 102 countries for which data are available showed improvement in HDI between 1975 and 2002. The exceptions—the Democratic Republic of Congo, Zambia, and Zimbabwe—were all in sub-Saharan Africa. Each had increased its HDI between 1975 and 1985 (due to longer life expectancy and higher literacy rates despite a decline in GDP per capita).[106] However, those gains have been more than erased since then because of continuing economic declines in affluence, lower life expectancy due to HIV/AIDS and the resurgence of malaria, and the conflict in the Democratic Republic of Congo (which Zimbabwe chose to involve itself in and which created refugee problems in neighboring countries, including Zambia).[107] Intermittent droughts and their effects, exacerbated by poor governance, also contributed to declines in Zambia and, to a greater extent, in Zimbabwe.

- Twenty of the 138 countries with available data showed a decline in HDI between 1990 and 2002. The majority of those countries (13) were in sub-Saharan Africa. For this set of countries too, the declines could be attributed to HIV/AIDS, resurgent malaria, and, in some areas, declining affluence, as well as the direct or indirect effects of conflict within—or in nearby—countries.

- Of the 20 countries that had lower HDIs in 2002 than in 1990 (based on UNDP data), five were in the former Soviet Union; none were in Eastern Europe. Following the collapse of the communist regimes in Eastern Europe and the former Soviet Union, the drop in affluence in those areas accompanied by the deterioration in health status (as measured by life expectancy) led to a decline in their HDIs. However, by the mid to late 1990s, the economic situation in those countries had bottomed out. As a result, despite drops in the early 1990s, a number of those countries had higher HDIs in 2002 than in 1990.

- The remaining two countries with HDIs known to be lower in 2002 than 1990 were the Bahamas and Belize. Their declines, which were relatively minor, had nevertheless been reversed by the mid to late 1990s.

In summary, the data indicate that human well-being has improved and continues to improve for the majority of the world's population. During the past 15 to 20 years, however, well-being has been reduced in many sub-Saharan countries, and it continues to deteriorate. However, while matters had also regressed in Eastern European and the former Soviet Union nations, they now seem to be rebounding. These broad regional trends can be grasped when one considers that between the mid 1970s and the early 2000s

- Affluence broadly advanced around the world for most income and regional groups with some exceptions—major oil exporting countries,[108] sub-Saharan Africa, the former Soviet Union, and a handful of Latin American countries (e.g., Argentina, Bolivia, Honduras, Nicaragua, and Peru). A common thread for Argentina, Bolivia, and Peru was that they all suffered from internal conflicts or failed economic policies.
- Life expectancy also increased generally around the world except in sub-Saharan Africa and some areas in the former Soviet Union.

The critical factor underlying declines in HDI is the lethal combination of deteriorating wealth exacerbated by serious public health problems (e.g., deadly new diseases, such as HIV/AIDS, or resurgent diseases, such as malaria and tuberculosis), and vice versa. This problem is most painfully illustrated by the experience of sub-Saharan countries.

When AIDS first appeared, it resulted in almost certain death. Developed countries, particularly the United States, launched a massive assault on the disease. United States deaths due to HIV/AIDS dropped from a high of approximately 52,000 in 1995 to 19,000 in 1998.[109] Since then, fatalities have leveled off at around 18,000 per year. In 1996, HIV/AIDS was the eighth leading cause of death in the United States; by 1998, it had dropped off the worst-15 list. But similar improvement is unlikely to occur soon in sub-Saharan countries because they cannot afford the cost of treatment unless it's subsidized by the governments, charities, or industry from the richer nations.

Notably, the UNDP's HDI suffers from a measure of arbitrariness. It could be improved by incorporating within it metrics for the levels of hunger (and malnourishment) and infant mortality, because they are measures for misery in their own right whose contributions to (negative) welfare are not fully captured by either life expectancy or wealth, as well as metrics for economic and political freedom.

Had the metrics for hunger and infant mortality been included in the HDI, that might well have shown a larger increase in HDI since 1975 than what was seen by the UNDP. As previously noted, the increase in food supplies per capita during the past half-century is a major reason for the worldwide improvement in health status during that period.

In summary, the data indicate that human well-being has improved and continues to improve for the vast majority of the world's population. However, despite the past improvements, there is room for additional improvement. But such improvements are contingent on the creation of and access to additional resources—financial, human, and technological—which is more likely if a society's institutions and policies favor economic growth and technological change. Moreover, over the past 10 to 15 years, certain aspects of well-being have declined in some countries in sub-Saharan Africa, Eastern Europe, and the former Soviet Union. Although there are several proximate causes for those reductions, as will be discussed in greater detail in the next chapter, one of the critical underlying factors for this deterioration can be traced to lack of sufficient wealth.

3. Has Globalization Widened the Gaps in Human Well-Being?[1]

Despite the absolute improvements in human well-being (in general) and per capita income (in particular) that have accompanied globalization, much of the debate over globalization and its merits has revolved around the issue of income inequality and whether in the past few decades globalization has made the rich richer and the poor poorer.[2] For example, Laura D'Andrea Tyson, the former national economic adviser, in an article written jointly with two other alumni of the Clinton administration—W. Bowman Cutter, now managing director of Warburg Pincus, and Joan E. Spero, now president of the Doris Duke Foundation—claimed that "as globalization has intensified, the gap between per capita incomes in rich and poor countries has widened."[3] Another not atypical observation is the following from the 1999 *Human Development Report* by the United Nations Development Programme (UNDP).

> Nearly 30 years ago the Pearson Commission began its report with the recognition that "the widening gap between the developed and developing countries has become the central problem of our time." But over the past three decades the income gaps between the richest fifth and the poorest fifth have more than doubled. . . . Narrowing the gaps between rich and poor . . . should become explicit global goals—to be rigorously monitored by [the United Nations Economic and Social Council] and the Bretton Woods institutions."[4]

And, indeed, there are wide disparities between the developing and the developed world. But it wasn't always so. Table 2.5 and figure 2.13 indicate that, for much of the past two millennia, there was broad equality between regions. Everyone was, by today's standards, very poor. For the first millennium after Christ, per capita incomes were stuck around $400–$450 (in 1990 international dollars, adjusted for purchasing power parity [PPP]). That is, virtually everyone was on, or below, the threshold of "absolute poverty," defined as subsisting on less than one dollar per day or $365 per year.[5] As another yardstick, consider that per capita income levels in 2001 for Afghanistan, Rwanda, and Zaire were $453, $871, and $202, respectively.[6] By 1500, a relatively modest gap had opened up between Western Europe and the other parts of the world (table 2.5). The former's average income level in 1500 was 40 percent greater than the world average. These gaps grew gradually until the start of industrialization in Great Britain around 1800, after which the gap between Western Europe and its predominantly European colonies exploded. Today, incomes in Western Europe are three times the world average. Similarly, incomes in Africa, estimated to be at par with the United States five centuries ago, are now one-twentieth as large (table 2.5).[7] In addition, today's average American has an annual income in excess of $30,000 (in 1990 international dollars) even as, according to the World Bank, in 2001, 1.1 billion people, mostly in the developing world, lived in "absolute poverty" and 2.7 billion lived on less than two dollars per day.[8]

The UNDP's *Human Development Report 2002*, citing work done by Milanovic using 1993 data, goes on to state that the world's richest 1 percent of people have an income equal to that of the poorest 56 percent and that the income of the richest 25 million Americans equals that of almost 2 billion of the world's poorest people.[9]

It is such disparities that drive claims similar to the ones contained in the earlier quote—that the world is getting more unequal, that the rich are getting richer while the poor are getting poorer, and that globalization is responsible for the widening gaps. Those claims have become a rallying cry for critics of globalization.[10]

But the UNDP's own report acknowledges that, in recent decades, trends in inequality between country groups have been ambiguous.[11] Specifically, it notes that between 1975 and 2000, relative to per capita income levels in the Organisation for Economic Co-operation and Development (OECD) countries, sub-Saharan Africa's level (in PPP terms) dropped further behind, from one-sixth to one-fourteenth (of the income in OECD countries); income levels in Eastern Europe and former Soviet Union countries also fell behind; Latin America and the Carribean levels fell from one-half to one-third; and Arab states' levels dropped from one-fifth to one-fourth.

Figure 3.1
GLOBAL POVERTY, 1820–1992

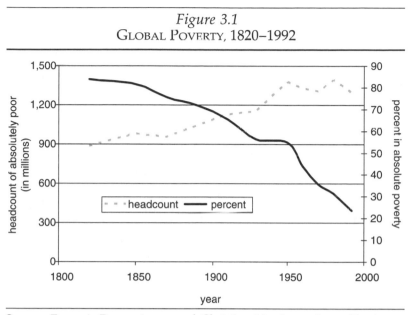

SOURCE: François Bourguignon and Christian Morrisson, *Inequality Among World Citizens: 1820–1992* (Paris: Départment et Laboratoire d'Economic Théorique et Applequéc, Ecole Normale Superieure, 2001).

However, South and East Asia, the most populous areas of the world, experienced remarkable progress because of their rapid and substantial economic growth in the past decades. And China's income, which had grown very rapidly during that period, went from one-twenty-first to one-sixth of the OECD level, while India's income, which had grown more modestly until the 1990s at least, also increased from one-fourteenth to one-tenth.

Similarly, the UNDP reports that trends in inequality between *people* (as opposed to *nations*) since 1970 is also ambiguous. Various measures of inequality showed small and not significant trends.[12]

However, a number of recent studies have disputed the claim that poverty has been growing or income inequalities have been widening in recent decades. David Dollar and Aart Kraay, economists at the World Bank, argue that "the best evidence available shows the exact opposite to be true . . . [and that] . . . the current wave of globalization, which started around 1980, has actually promoted economic equality and reduced poverty."[13] Figure 3.1, based on data

Figure 3.2
GLOBAL POVERTY, 1980–2001

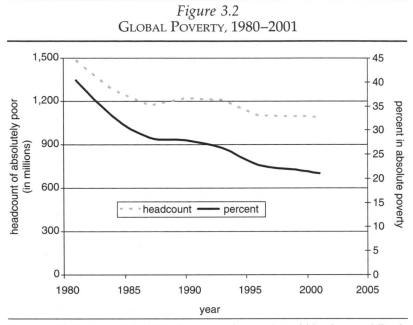

SOURCE: World Bank, *World Development Indicators*, http://devdata.worldbank. org/dataonline (accessed July 12, 2005).

from François Bourguignon and Christian Morrisson, shows that indeed, in terms of the headcount (i.e., raw numbers), the size of the population in absolute poverty—defined as income less than one dollar a day in 1985 international (PPP-adjusted) dollars—increased until around 1950 after which it dropped, only to rebound in the 1970s. However, in the 1980s, the headcount saw a drop.[14] As a result, despite the fact that the global population in 1992 was more than five times its 1820 level, the poverty headcount increased by only a third. Consequently, the proportion of the global population in absolute poverty, which has been dropping since the 1820s, declined from 84 percent in 1820 to 24 percent in 1992.

Since that time, there have been further drops in absolute poverty, as indicated by figure 3.2. Specifically, this figure shows that the economic boom and globalization of the 1990s is associated with a decline in global poverty in terms of absolute numbers, as well as the percentage of the global population.[15] According to the World Bank, the poverty headcount dropped from 1,218 million to 1,089 million (or from 27.9 percent to 21.1 percent of the global population) between 1990 and 2001. The majority of those declines were in China and, to a lesser extent, India, indicating—as if proof were needed—that economic growth is the route to lower poverty!

The poverty levels shown in figures 3.1 and 3.2 are based on consumption per capita. Growth economist Xavier Sala-i-Martin, using *income* data that covered 90 percent of the world's population,[16] estimated that poverty rates declined substantially between the 1970s and 1998. Between 1976 and 1998, a period during which global population increased 42 percent,[17] the number of people subsisting on an income of one dollar a day declined from 16.1 percent to 6.7 percent of the population or by 235 million, while those living on an income of two dollars a day declined from 39.1 percent to 18.6 percent or by 450 million.[18] Consistent with the World Bank's analyses, he finds that the bulk of the decline took place in Asia. Latin America reduced poverty overall, but most of the gains occurred during the 1970s with little or no gains after that. However, the number of people living in poverty in Africa increased by 175 million people (from 22 percent to 44 percent of the population) according to the one-dollar definition and by 227 million (from 53 percent to 64 percent) according to the two-dollar definition.

Sala-i-Martin's basic result is confirmed by the Indian economist, Surjit Bhalla, who also looked at inequality within the global population rather than inequality between countries. He estimated that globally, inequality increased during the 1960s and early 1970s after which it shrank—slowly at first, but with increasing rapidity through the 1980s and 1990s.[19] Using the so-called *Gini coefficient* as a measure of inequality, he estimated that inequality increased from 66.4 in 1960 to 69.3 in 1973, and it then declined to 68.5 in 1980 and 65.1 in 2000, which is the lowest level since 1910.[20] The majority of this drop was due to economic growth and rising incomes in China and, to a lesser extent, India.[21]

Xavier Sala-i-Martin, using each of nine separate indices of income inequality, also showed that global income inequality during the 1980s and 1990s was reduced substantially. Thus, broad claims of increasing poverty and rising income inequality are not substantiated by data from recent decades whether one uses income or consumption data.

Nevertheless, the controversy about the direction of the trends in income gaps misses the larger point. The central issue with respect to globalization is neither income inequality nor whether the issue is getting larger. Rather it is whether globalization advances human well-being and, if inequalities in well-being have, indeed, expanded, whether that is because the rich have advanced at the *expense* of the poor.

In fact, as critics of globalization frequently note, human well-being is not synonymous with income[22] nor—to echo a catchy anti-globalization slogan—can you eat GDP.[23] To conflate the two is to confuse ends with means. Although per capita income (or its surrogate, GDP per capita) is probably the best indicator of material well-being, its greater importance stems from the fact that either it helps provide societies (and individuals) the means to improve other, more important measures of human well-being (e.g., freedom from hunger, level of health, mortality rates, child labor, educational levels, access to safe water and sanitation, and life expectancy)[24] or it is associated with other desirable indicators (e.g., adherence to the rule of law; government transparency; economic freedom; and, to some extent, political freedom).[25] In fact, as we saw in the last chapter, although cross country data indicate that these other indicators generally improve as per capita income rises, their relationships are not linear. The improvements are usually rapid at low levels of economic development, but slow down or, in some cases, halt altogether as they reach their practical or theoretical limits, for example, 100 percent for literacy and access to safe water and 0 percent for child labor (measured as the percentage of children aged 10–14 years in the labor force). Therefore, per capita income would not, by itself, be a good measure of human well-being. This premise, in fact, is a fundamental one behind the UNDP's human development index (HDI). Thus, any determination of whether globalization has benefited humanity in general, or favors the rich at the expense of the poor, should be based primarily on an examination of how and why gaps between rich and poor countries in these more relevant measures of human well-being have evolved as globalization has advanced.

The following examines trends in the gaps between countries grouped by various income levels for various indicators of human well-being. Specifically, it examines such trends for hunger and malnutrition, infant mortality, life expectancy, child labor, and the HDI.

Hunger and Malnourishment

As was indicated in table 2.1, hunger and malnourishment used to be chronic conditions the world over, at least until a couple of centuries ago. But by the 1950s and 1960s, despite the privations of the Second World War and the Great Depression, it seemed that the problem, if any, would be restricted to developing countries. Several Neo-Malthusians, such as Paul Ehrlich[26] and William and Paul Paddock,[27] confidently predicted apocalyptic famines in the latter part of the 20th century in the developing world. But remarkably, despite an unprecedented increase in the demand for food fueled by equally unprecedented population and economic growth, its average inhabitant has never been better fed and less prone to hunger and undernourishment.

Since 1961, developing countries' available food supply has, on average, gone from inadequate to above adequate. But those averages mask the fact that hunger still persists today since, unlike the children of Lake Woebegone, food availability for many people, unfortunately, is below average. Nevertheless, as we saw in chapter 2, although developing countries' population grew by 83 percent between 1969–71 and 2000–02, the numbers of undernourished people declined by 15 percent while the proportion of the undernourished was more than halved.[28] Thus, gaps between developing and developed countries in hunger and malnourishment have, in the aggregate, declined in both absolute and relative terms. But the trends for sub-Saharan Africa tell a somewhat more complex tale. Between 1969–71 and 2000–02, the share of population that was undernourished declined from 36 percent to 33 percent, but the absolute numbers increased substantially from 125 million to 204 million.[29]

As indicated by figures 2.2 through 2.4, economic development has played a big role in reducing the level of hunger and malnutrition. Those figures show, by and large, that the richer the country, the higher its available food supplies and lower the level of malnutrition. Therefore, to the extent globalization contributes to economic growth, it too has helped reduce hunger and malnutrition.

Globalization has helped in other ways as well. First, the green revolution, which is a major proximate cause for the increase in food production in developing countries, is itself the product of the globalization of knowledge regarding agronomics and agricultural technology. Also, because it is always possible to have local food shortages in the midst of a worldwide glut, the importance of trade—a key factor in globalization—should not be underestimated. Specifically, trade helps augment food supplies. In fact, between 2000 and 2002, international trade allowed developing countries to enhance their grain supplies by 11.6 percent.[30] The corresponding figure for sub-Saharan Africa was 23.5 percent.

Moreover, the inputs needed to power the green revolution, for example, seeds, fertilizers, and pesticides, are often obtained through trade, both internal and external. Without such direct food imports and trade in inputs, food prices in developing countries would no doubt be higher and more of their people would be priced out of the market. In essence, globalization, through trade and economic growth, has enhanced food security. And, in doing so, it has reduced the severe health burdens that accompany hunger and undernourishment.[31]

To summarize, the developing countries where hunger and malnutrition were reduced the most are those that also experienced the most economic development.

Infant Mortality

Before industrialization, infant mortality generally exceeded 200 per 1,000 live births.[32] Starting in the 19th century, infant mortality started to drop in several of the currently developed countries because of advances in agriculture, nutrition, medicine, and public health. As indicated in table 2.2, by the early 1950s, there was a large gap between developed and developing countries as infant mortality dropped to 59 in the former and 180 in the latter.[33] By 2003, further medical advances reduced infant mortality in developed countries to 7, but because existing health care technology (including knowledge) diffused even faster from developed to developing countries, it had declined to 62 in the latter.[34] Thus, during the past half century the gap between developed and developing countries has been halved.

The drop in infant mortality has been broad and deep. Since at least 1960, infant mortality has dropped more or less continuously for each of the country groups shown in figure 3.3.[35] Note that in this figure sub-Saharan Africa is a subset of the low-income country group. It also illustrates that in any given year, consistent with figure

Figure 3.3
GAP IN INFANT MORTALITY, 1960–2002
(relative to high-income OECD countries)

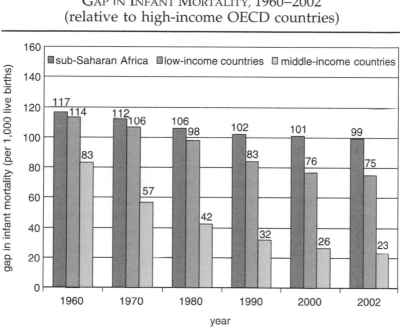

SOURCE: World Bank, *World Development Indicators,* http://devdata.worldbank.org/dataonline (accessed July 12, 2005).

2.5, higher per capita income is generally associated with lower infant mortality. Between 1960 and 2003, the gaps in this indicator between high-income OECD countries and the other income groups shrank rather than increased. These gaps closed the fastest for medium-income countries and the slowest for sub-Saharan Africa. But for the influence of globalization and economic growth, this would have been counterintuitive since, all else being equal, one would expect that the larger the initial gap, the faster it ought to shrink because the closer infant mortality is to zero, the harder it should be to reduce it further.

Consistent with the lowering of the infant mortality curve with the passage of time (illustrated in figure 2.5) and the rapid technological diffusion from developed to developing countries in the past few decades, we saw in table 2.3 that many developing countries have much lower infant mortality rates today than the currently developed countries did at equivalent levels of economic development. In 1913, when the United States had a per capita income of $5,301 (in 1990 international dollars), its infant mortality was about 100. By contrast, in 2003, China's and India's infant mortality, for example, were 33 and 63, respectively, despite having per capita incomes of $4,437 and $2,159—16 to 59 percent lower![36]

Thus, just as for hunger and malnutrition, the areas where infant mortality has improved the least are those with insufficient economic development or, for whatever reason, have been unable to fully capitalize on existing knowledge and technology. Once again, globalization seems to be part of the solution rather than the problem.

Life Expectancy

Historically, the decline in infant mortality was a major factor in the improvement in life expectancy. Not surprisingly, therefore, there are certain parallels between the progress in these two indicators, especially in the earlier years.

Because the public health and medical advances that have contributed to both declines in infant mortality and increases in life expectancy in the past two centuries were discovered, developed, and adopted first by the developed countries, a substantial gap opened up in average life expectancy between developed and developing countries. By the early 1950s, the gap stood at 25.0 years in favor of the former (see table 2.4).[37] But by 2003, with the diffusion and transfer of those technologies (including knowledge) to developing countries, this gap had closed to 12.2 years.

A closer look at trends for different country groupings, however, reveals a more complex situation. Figure 3.4 compares life expectancies between high-income OECD, middle-income, and low-income countries and sub-Saharan Africa (which is also included in the low-income group). Between 1960 and 2003, average life expectancy improved steadily for high-income OECD, middle-income, and low-income countries. This pattern also held for sub-Saharan Africa until 1990, but since then its average life expectancy has dropped.

With respect to gaps in life expectancy, the gap between high-income OECD and middle-income countries, which had shrunk from 15.0 years in 1962 to 8.2 years by 1990, increased slightly to 8.8 years by 2003, mainly because the latter group includes many Eastern

Figure 3.4
GAP IN LIFE EXPECTANCY, 1962–2003
(relative to high-income OECD countries)

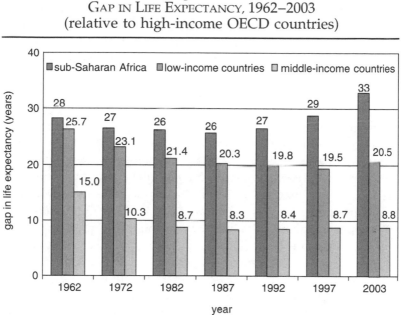

SOURCE: World Bank, *World Development Indicators*, http://devdata.worldbank. org/dataonline (accessed July 12, 2005).

Europe and former Soviet Union nations whose life expectancies regressed as their economies contracted during that period.[38]

The gap between high-income OECD and low-income countries also declined for most of the post-World War II period. Between 1950–55 and 1997 life expectancy dropped from 28.0 to 19.5 years, but by 2003 it had increased to 20.5 years because while life expectancy in the former continued to increase because of medical advances, it dropped slightly in the latter.[39] This drop was particularly severe in sub-Saharan Africa, where life expectancy declined by 4.4 years from 1990 to 2003 due to the HIV/AIDS epidemic and—in some cases, even more important—the resurgence of malaria,[40] aggravated by civil unrest and cross-border conflicts in several areas. Consequently, the gap between rich and poor expanded in the 1990s, reversing the direction of the trend from previous decades. But it didn't expand because the rich increased their life expectancy at the expense of the poor; rather it was because, when faced with new diseases (such as

AIDS) or new forms of ancient ones (such as drug-resistant tuberculosis), the poor lacked the economic and human resources not only to develop effective treatments but also to import and to adapt treatments invented and developed in the rich countries. Notably, both economic and human resources are more likely to be augmented with globalization than without it.

Sub-Saharan Africa's experience with AIDS is in stark contrast with that of the richer nations. When this disease first appeared, it was tantamount to a death sentence for rich as well as poor. But the rich countries of the world, particularly the United States, drew upon their wealth, human capital, and entrepreneurial skills to develop several technologies to contain this disease and to reduce its toll. As a consequence, United States deaths because of HIV/AIDS dropped from a high of approximately 52,000 in 1995 to around 18,000 per year currently, and it is no longer featured among the top 15 killers in the United States.[41] But sub-Saharan countries cannot afford the cost of treatment and are short on the human capital necessary to manage this disease unless their efforts are underwritten by the governments, charities, or industries from richer nations. And, indeed, that is exactly what the worldwide effort to contain HIV/AIDS hopes to mobilize. This is as clear of an illustration as any that the greater the economic resources, the greater the likelihood not only of creating new technologies but also, equally important, of actually putting those technologies to use.

But it might be argued that the rapid spread of AIDS and other diseases was, in fact, one of the unintended consequences of globalization. Without the transportation network that enables goods and people to move great distances, AIDS, for instance, might have been an isolated phenomenon rather than a pandemic. And indeed that much is true. But the same network also helped reduce public health problems in numerous ways. It helped reduce hunger and malnourishment by moving agricultural inputs and outputs between farms and markets. This help was critical to increasing global food supplies in the past half century, which, as noted, was one of the first steps to improved public health. Second, the transportation network is crucial to the worldwide diffusion of medical and public health technologies through, for instance, the distribution of medicines, vaccines, medical equipment, insecticides for vector control, and equipment for water treatment plants. But globalization is more than

Figure 3.5
GAP IN CHILD LABOR, 1962–2003
(relative to high-income OECD countries)

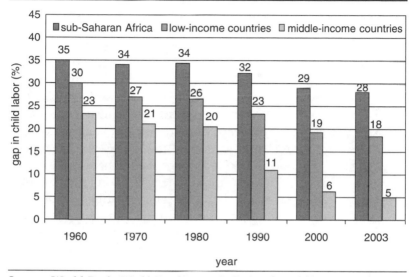

SOURCE: World Bank, *World Development Indicators,* http://devdata.worldbank. org/dataonline (accessed July 12, 2005).

the movement of goods; it also involves the movement of people and the diffusion of their ideas, knowledge, and expertise. These, too, were enabled by the transportation network as doctors, nurses, agronomists, engineers, and scientists—and those aspiring to those professions—moved back and forth between the developing and developed worlds. Despite the AIDS epidemic, average life expectancy in sub-Saharan countries of 45.6 years still exceeds the 20–30 years that was typical before globalization.

Child Labor

Figure 3.5 shows that the proportion of children in the workforce has also been declining steadily for each of the income groups, and the richer the group, the lower that percentage. Gaps in child labor between sub-Saharan Africa, the low- and middle-income countries, and the high-income OECD countries have been shrinking at least since 1960. For this indicator also, the gap between high-income

Figure 3.6
HUMAN DEVELOPMENT INDEX (HDI), 1975–2002
(different country groups)

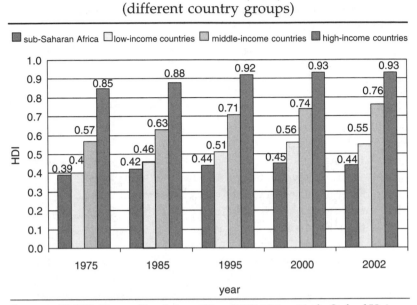

■ sub-Saharan Africa □ low-income countries ▨ middle-income countries ■ high-income countries

SOURCES: UNDP, *Human Development Report 2004* (New York: Oxford University Press, 2004); World Resources Institute, EarthTrends, www.wri.org (accessed June 23, 2005).

OECD and middle-income countries has diminished the most, and the least for the gap between the former and sub-Saharan Africa.[42]

Human Development Index

Figure 3.6, based on the UNDP's *Human Development Report 2004*, shows that since 1975—the first year that report provides data—the *population-weighted* HDI has improved for the so-called high-, middle-, and low-development tiers of countries, as well as for sub-Saharan Africa (much of which is also included in the low-development tier). This is because of the broad improvements in life expectancy, literacy, and economic growth that have combined to increase the HDI for most countries and country groups since 1975. However, for reasons discussed previously, HDI has been more or less stuck for sub-Saharan Africa since around 1990, and since 2000, it has declined slightly. This also helped to slow improve-ments for the low-income countries during the 1990s; since 2000, the HDI for this group of countries has also seen a slight decline.

Notably, according to the UNDP's *Human Development Report 2001*, Zambia had the unique, but dubious, distinction of having a lower HDI in 1999 than in 1975 because both GDP per capita and life expectancy declined over this period. (Curiously, in terms of aid as a fraction of GDP, at 22.8 percent, Zambia is also among the world's largest recipients of foreign aid.[43] Its downward spiral can hardly be attributed to rich countries having enriched themselves at the expense of the poor.) Despite the broad improvement for the various groups of countries, we saw in the previous chapter that at least 20 countries' HDIs have deteriorated since 1990. Thirteen of those were in sub-Saharan Africa, and five were part of the former Soviet Union. Many of those countries saw concurrent declines in per capita income and average life expectancies. However, the countries of the former Soviet Union seem to be reversing their economic fortunes, and their HDIs have seen a rebound since the late 1990s.

All else being equal, one would have expected that HDI improve-ments would generally be largest for the lowest tier and least for the highest tier of countries because the latter are closer to the top of the HDI scale and because with each improvement in HDI, it becomes harder to improve it further (just as each additional dollar adds less to the quality of life than the previous dollar). But, in fact, as figure 3.6 shows, between 1975 and 2002, the middle-tier countries saw the most progress, followed, in order, by the progress for low-tier, high-tier, and sub-Saharan countries. As a result, the HDI gap between the high- and medium-tier countries diminished the most. The gap between high- and low-tier countries also declined slightly but, for the reasons discussed earlier, it expanded between the high-tier and sub-Saharan countries.

Summarizing International Trends in Gaps in Human Well-Being

In summary, human well-being has improved and continues to improve for the vast majority of the world's population. Because of a combination of economic growth and technological change, compared to a half century ago, today's average person lives longer and is less hungry. They are also healthier, more educated, and more likely to have children in a schoolroom than in the workplace. During that period, indicators of well-being have improved for every country group, although life expectancies have declined in many sub-Saharan and Eastern Europe and former Soviet Union countries since the late 1980s because of HIV/AIDS, malaria, or problems related to their economic deterioration.

For every indicator examined, regardless of whether the rich are richer and the poor are poorer, gaps in human well-being between the rich countries and other income groups have, for the most part, shrunk over the past four decades. However, comparing rich countries and sub-Saharan Africa, although the gap in infant mortality between the two has continued to close, the gap in life expectancy has once again expanded in the past decade or so (but not enough to erase the large reductions made previously). Despite this, in the aggregate, the corresponding gap in HDI has decreased.

In other words, although income inequalities may or may not have been exacerbated, in the aspects of human well-being that are truly critical—life expectancy, infant mortality, hunger, literacy, and child labor—the world is far more equal today than it was a half century ago, in large part because of globalization.

Surprisingly, the UNDP, which takes such great pains to note that human well-being is more important than economic development and in recognition of which it has tried to institutionalize the HDI, is—as the quote at the beginning of this chapter reveals—among the organizations most guilty of focusing inordinately on the income gap.

Trends in the Black-White Divide in the United States

What about gaps in inequality in the United States: have they increased? This question is a difficult one to answer *with respect to incomes* because of the tremendous mobility in and out of the various income brackets in the United States. Stephen Moore and Julian L. Simon, quoting a study by the Alexis de Tocqueville Institute, note that between 1975 and 1991 families in the lowest fifth (quantile) of income levels were five times as likely to have moved up to the top quantile than to have stayed at the bottom quantile.[44] At the same time, 37.5 percent of the families in the top quantile experienced downward mobility out of that bracket. Thus, to determine whether income inequality has expanded one needs to examine data on family

Figure 3.7
U.S. BLACK-WHITE DIVIDE FOR THE COMPONENTS OF HDI, 1940s–2003

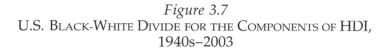

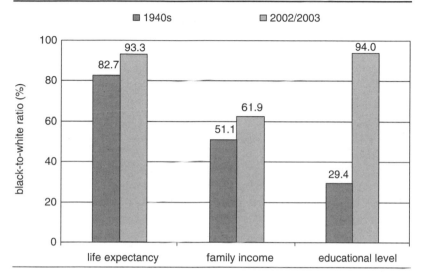

SOURCE: USBOC *Historical Statistics of the United States: Colonial Times to 1970* (Washington, DC: GPO, 1975), pp. 14, 55, 297, 380; USBOC, *Current Population Survey, 2003 and 2004 Annual Social and Economic Supplements,* www.census.gov/hhes/www/img/incpov03/fig07.jpg (accessed August 7, 2005); USBOC, *Statistical Abstract of the United States 2004–2005* (Washington, DC: GPO, 2004); Donna L. Hoyert, Hsiang-Ching Kung, and Betty L. Smith, "Deaths: Preliminary Data for 2003," *National Vital Statistics Reports 53*, no. 15 (Hyattsville, MD: National Center for Health Statistics, 2005).

incomes averaged over several years. Instead, I will use an indirect method to investigate whether inequalities might have increased. Specifically, I will examine whether gaps in key indicators of human well-being between a historically disadvantaged group—black Americans—and the majority group—white Americans—have shrunk or expanded over the long term. Figure 3.7 shows the approximate trends in the gaps between black and white Americans for median income, life expectancy at birth, and educational attainment (as measured by the fraction of the population aged 25 years or more with at least a high school degree), which are three indicators that are similar to the components of HDI. The figure indicates the following:

- The median family income levels for blacks as a percentage of what it was for whites was 51.1 percent in 1947; by 2003, the median household income for blacks had increased to 61.9 percent of the level for whites.[45] However, it had been higher in 2000—68.8 percent—when the economy was more robust.[46]
- Life expectancy at birth for blacks was 82.7 percent of that for whites in 1940, and it is estimated to be 93.3 percent in 2003.[47]
- Educational attainment for blacks was 29.4 percent of that for whites in 1940. By 2003, that had grown to 94.0 percent.[48]

Clearly, although gaps persist between blacks and whites in the components of HDI (which, arguably, is a composite measure of human well-being), these gaps have closed in the latter half of the 20th century. This also suggests—but does not prove—that gaps between rich and poor might have also shrunk.

Are Rural Residents Better Off?

In the currently developed countries, which were the first to embark upon modern economic growth, the welfare of urban dwellers historically used to lag behind their rural compatriots.[49] Robert W. Fogel notes that U.S. cities with populations in excess of 50,000 had twice the death rates of rural areas in the 1830s.[50] This was because overcrowding, as well as a lack of knowledge of basic hygiene and the germ theory coupled with the lack of safe water and sanitation, made the urban population more susceptible to infectious diseases such as cholera, typhoid, and tuberculosis.

The stereotype of the suffering urban resident compared to the healthier country cousin is reinforced in the mind of anyone who visits the overcrowded and polluted urban areas of the developing world. But, in fact, in most developing countries, the country cousin is worse off. As the UNDP notes, when the HDI and a related index, the human poverty index, are disaggregated along the urban-rural divide, there is more progress and less deprivation in urban areas.[51] For instance, in Swaziland, the rural HDI was 35 percent below the urban level. Reasons for this include reduced access to safe water, sanitation, and public health services; lower rates of literacy; and

Figure 3.8
RURAL VS. URBAN DIVIDE, ACCESS TO SAFE WATER AND
SANITATION, 2000

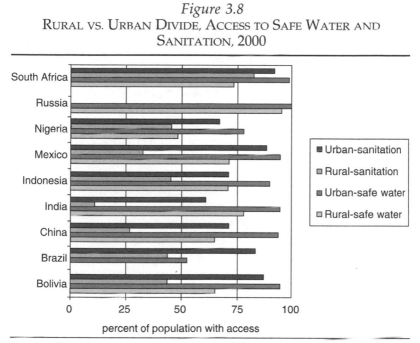

SOURCE: World Resources Institute, EarthTrends, www.wri.org (accessed June 23, 2005).

higher rates of malnourishment. Figure 3.8 shows, for 2000, the urban-rural divide for access to safe water and the divide between the total population and rural areas for access to sanitation for some of today's populous developing nations (namely Brazil, China, India, Indonesia, Mexico, Nigeria, and South Africa). In each of these cases, rural residents have reduced access. In 1994, in developing countries as a whole, access to safe water for rural populations was 72 percent compared to 80 percent for urban populations; similarly, the corresponding figures for access to sanitation are 18 percent and 63 percent, respectively.[52]

Is Inequality Always for the Worse?

Conventional wisdom decries income inequality, but there may be situations where some inequality would benefit humanity. Consider, for instance, that because most of the easy improvements in public health have been largely captured (except where globalization has lagged), the search and implementation of cures and treatments for today's unconquered diseases (e.g., strokes, heart diseases, and cancers) could progressively become more expensive. Richer societies are in a better position to invest in the research and development of new or improved technologies in general, as well as for detecting, treating, or eliminating those diseases, in particular. AIDS is a case in point. Moreover, new technologies often cost more initially. The rich, therefore, are usually the first customers for any new or innovative technology. As the rich purchase this technology, the supplier can increase production and its price drops because of economies of scale and learning-by-doing, if nothing else. Such declines allow the less wealthy to also afford that technology, which then paves the way for further price drops and induces people of more modest means to enter the market. Thus, arguably, wealth inequality spurs the invention, innovation, and diffusion of new technologies. This pattern has been repeated time and again for goods and services (such as telephones, VCRs, personal computers, and even vacations to exotic places) and for health technologies (such as antibiotics; organ transplants; CAT scans; and, now, AIDS treatments) where innovations started expensive but ended up cheaper. Therefore, some inequality in wealth probably benefits humanity. Presumably, for a given set of supply-and-demand characteristics for a particular technology, there is an optimal level of inequality that would maximize the rate of adoption of that technology, as well as the rate at which that technology improves human well-being. In other words, even if one were to ignore trends in inequalities in other, more significant indicators of human well-being, income inequality is a poor lens for viewing the merits of globalization.

Without restricting himself only to income inequality, Amartya Sen claims that inequality is the central issue with respect to globalization and that a "crucial question concerns the sharing of the potential gains from globalization, between rich and poor countries, and between different groups within countries."[53]

If one accepts Sen's contention regarding the centrality of inequality, the previous data indicate that whether income inequalities have been exacerbated, in terms of the truly critical measures of well-being—hunger, infant mortality, life expectancy, and child labor—the world is much more equal now than it was a few decades ago.

But in the past dozen years the life expectancy gap between the richest and some of the poorest has expanded. Therefore, it might be argued that, with respect to this most significant of all indicators at least, globalization might yet fail to address Sen's "crucial question." But it is no more reasonable to expect that globalization would lead to equal gains among countries than, say, a course in economics would lead to equal gains in knowledge among its students. Sen, for instance, benefited much more from his education than his erstwhile classmates, not because someone else gained less but perhaps because of better preparation, harder work, or, dare I say it, greater natural ability. Just as unequal sharing of benefits or outcomes does not indict education, unequal progress in human well-being does not damn globalization.

In fact, figures 3.3 through 3.6 suggest that where gaps in well-being have expanded, it is not because of too much globalization, but too little. The rich are not better off because they have taken something away from the poor, rather the poor are better off because they have benefited from the technologies developed by the rich, and their situation would have been further improved had they been better prepared to capture the benefits of globalization. In fact, if the rich can be faulted at all, it is that by protecting favored economic sectors through subsidies and import barriers—activities that have not necessarily improved their own economic welfare—they have retarded the pace of globalization and made it harder for many developing countries to capture its benefits.

4. The Cycle of Progress: Factors Propelling Humanity's Progress

In chapter 2 we saw that human well-being has improved more in the past two centuries, that is, since the start of industrialization, than it did in all the rest of humankind's tenure on earth.

Figure 4.1, which draws on several figures (and analyses) presented in chapter 2, illustrates one of the major findings from that chapter—namely, improvements in the most critical indicators of human welfare are associated with advances in the level of economic

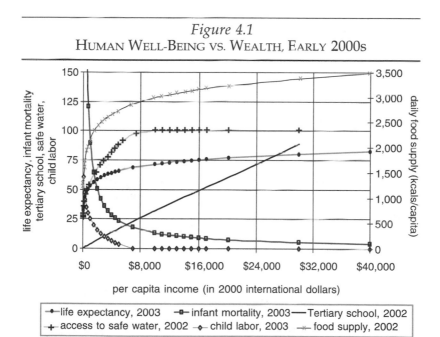

Figure 4.1
HUMAN WELL-BEING VS. WEALTH, EARLY 2000s

per capita income (in 2000 international dollars)

— life expectancy, 2003 — infant mortality, 2003 — Tertiary school, 2002
+ access to safe water, 2002 — child labor, 2003 — food supply, 2002

SOURCES: World Resources Institute, EarthTrends, www.wri.org (accessed June 23, 2005); World Bank, *World Development Indicators,* http://devdata.worldbank.org/dataonline (accessed July 12, 2005).

development (or wealth, as measured by the gross domestic product [GDP] per capita). Although figure 4.1 limits itself to availability of food, infant mortality, schooling, children in the labor force, access to safe water, and life expectancy, similar curves could also have been drawn for crop yield, prevalence of malnutrition, access to sanitation, and other indicators of well-being addressed in chapter 2.

Table 4.1, which is also based on the analyses in chapter 2, indicates the effects of technological change on each of the critical indicators shown in figure 4.1. It shows that even if the level of economic development for a country had historically been frozen at a constant level (in purchasing power parity [PPP]-adjusted international dollars), the various indicators of human well-being would have advanced with the passage of time, which is a surrogate for technological change (over that period). Specifically, it shows the improvements in the indicators if a country's average per capita income (a surrogate for wealth) had been frozen at $1 a day, $2 a day, $1,000 per year, and $10,000 per year (in 2000 international dollars). It also shows the changes that would have occurred had a country's average income tracked either the average for low-income countries or the world average. Thus, if a country's income had stayed constant at $2 a day (for instance), then because of technological change alone, average daily food supplies would have gone up by 167 kilocalories per day between 1975 and 2002, while between 1980 and 2003 infant mortality would have declined by 83 points (from 199 to 116 deaths per 1,000 live births), life expectancy would have increased 4 years, and so forth.

Notably, for each of the six indicators shown in figure 4.1 and table 4.1, the improvements, whether because of economic development or technological change, are most rapid at the lowest levels of wealth. Thus, in 2003, going from an annual per capita income of $365 to $1,000 would have improved the infant mortality rate by 117 points (from 207 to 90 deaths per 1,000 live births) but going further to $10,000 would have resulted in a smaller additional improvement (of 77 points). Table 4.1 also confirms what should be obvious from the previous figures—increases in wealth are much more critical for poorer countries than equivalent increases for richer ones because the former live closer to the margin. In other words, the poorer the country, the more crucial are wealth and the ability to obtain (and use) technology for the well-being of its population.[1]

Table 4.1

IMPROVEMENT IN HUMAN WELL-BEING WITH TIME (OR TECHNOLOGICAL CHANGE) AND ECONOMIC GROWTH

Income (2000 international $)	Daily food supplies per capita[a] (kcal)		Infant mortality (per 1,000 live births)		Life expectancy (years)		Tertiary student enrollment (percent)		Access to safe water (percent)		Child labor (percent)	
	1975	2002	1980	2003	1975	2003	1975	2002	1990	2002	1975	2003
$1 a day	1,652	1,818	355	207	40.7	44.6	0.9	1.5	39.1	41.7	49.3	39.0
$2 a day	1,897	2,064	199	116	46.2	50.2	1.7	2.8	47.7	50.9	39.9	29.6
$1,000 per year	2,009	2,175	154	90	48.7	52.7	2.3	3.8	52.2	55.7	35.6	25.3
$10,000 per year	2,825	2,991	23	13	67.2	71.2	19.8	31.9	100.0	100.0	4.3	0.0
Average for low-income countries[b]	2,027	2,390	147	52	49.2	58.0	2.4	6.6	53.0	66.3	34.9	16.4
World average[b]	2,540	2,863	44	17	60.8	68.5	9.4	22.8	80.3	97.4	15.2	0.0

a. Based on data from World Resources Institute's EarthTrends database online at www.wri.org (accessed June 23, 2005), except as noted. b. Based on data from World Bank's *World Development Indicators*.

SOURCES: Based on calculations using data from World Bank, *World Development Indicators*, http://devdata.worldbank.org/dataonline (accessed July 12, 2005), except where noted.

And, in fact, because of the combination of technological change and general increases in income, the progress in these indicators over the past few decades has been pretty remarkable, as shown in table 4.1. If a country's average income kept pace with the average for low-income countries, for example, between 1975 and 2003, its life expectancy would have increased by 8.8 years, infant mortality would have dropped by 95 points, and the rate of child labor would have dropped by more than 50 percent, while between 1990 and 2002 access to safe water would have increased from 53.0 percent to 66.3 percent of the population.

There are several possible explanations for the association between the various human well-being indicators and the level of economic development or technology. First, economic development (or technology) indeed improves those indicators. Second, the causation might be in the reverse direction. Perhaps it is advances in human well-being that stimulate economic development (or technology), rather than vice versa. Or perhaps there is a measure of truth to both explanations, that is, the various aspects of human well-being and wealth (or technology) reinforce each other in a set of interlinked cycles. Or perhaps human welfare, wealth, and technology are all propelled by a common set of forces.

In the following, I will examine various mechanisms that might be consistent with one or another of those explanations for the correlation between economic development, technological change, and the various indicators of well-being, with the focus on the six indicators plotted in figure 4.1 and table 4.1.

How Wealth Advances Human Well-Being

Greater wealth can advance human welfare in a myriad of direct and indirect ways. First, it means increased resources for advancing literacy and education, which itself is one of the more important indicators of well-being. Hence, the proportion of the population enrolled in post-secondary educational institutions increases with wealth. Second, greater wealth also reduces the incentives for parents to put children to work to supplement family income. Those two factors act together to help reduce child labor rates.

Moreover, increased education helps provide populations with the knowledge and information necessary to live a healthier life through wider understanding of the importance of better food and

Figure 4.2
HEALTH EXPENDITURES PER CAPITA VS. INCOME, 2002

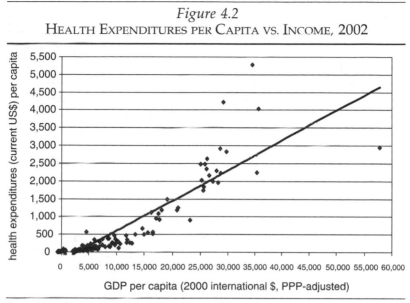

SOURCE: Based on data from World Bank, *World Development Indicators*, http://devdata.worldbank.org/dataonline (accessed July 12, 2005).

nutritional habits, proper hygiene, safe water, immunization and pasteurization, and other things. It also enables populations to better and more easily assimilate and keep track of new information relevant to these matters as such knowledge is created and becomes available. Equally important, wealthier societies, not surprisingly, can better afford welfare-enhancing technologies.[2] For instance, they spend proportionately more on health care than poorer ones. That, combined with the fact that their GDPs per capita are higher translates into significantly more spending on health care per capita by or on their behalf (see figure 4.2). Thus, they have better access to improved health technologies. Such technologies include not only "old" technologies (such as water treatment to produce safe water, sanitation, basic hygiene, vaccinations, antibiotics, and pasteurization, which are still underutilized in the poorer countries, precisely because they are too poor to afford them),[3] but also newer science-based technologies (such as AIDS and oral rehydration therapies, organ transplants, mammograms, and other diagnostic tests, some of which are quite expensive at present).

Health can also be advanced indirectly through technologies that increase food availability. Wealthier countries can better afford yield-enhancing agricultural technologies, such as special seeds; inputs, such as fertilizers for nutrient-poor soils or lime for acidic soils; and methods to reduce pre- and post-harvest and end-use losses to pests, as well as to reduce spoilage and wastage on and off the farm.[4] Although many of those technologies are pretty mundane and far from "high-tech," not everyone can afford their costs. For instance, while farmers in richer countries have sometimes overused fertilizers, especially in the past, the problem in poorer countries is that their farmers are unable to afford sufficient fertilizers to realize the productive potential of their land. This problem, as well as the inability to afford other yield-enhancing technologies, are the reasons figure 2.3 shows that the richer the country, the higher its crop yield. Higher crop yields translate into more food. And if, despite that, supply can't meet demand and additional food is needed, then if one is wealthy, one can buy what one cannot produce locally. Trade facilitates that by moving agricultural crops and products voluntarily from surplus to deficit areas. Global trade has, in fact, globalized food security.[5] Trade allows not only richer states, such as Hong Kong, Japan, Saudi Arabia, and Singapore, but also developing countries in sub-Saharan Africa to make up their food shortfalls. In 1998–2000, net cereal imports by countries of sub-Saharan Africa were equivalent to 20.4 percent of their production. Thus, United States wheat goes to China, while produce from Chile, for instance, comes to the United States. Moreover, the transportation systems and associated infrastructure that trade depends on—hardware such as ships, refrigerated trucks, roads, and rails, as well as software such as mechanisms and techniques to transfer money, hedge risks, and so forth—are themselves products of technology, capital, and human resources. Not surprisingly, richer countries have more food supplies per capita, as shown in figure 4.1. Greater wealth also makes it more likely that a society will establish and sustain food programs for those on the lower rungs of the economic ladder. Therefore, although "you can't eat GDP," if GDP is larger you are less likely to go hungry or be undernourished (except by choice).

But more food not only means fewer hungry stomachs, it also means healthier people who then are less likely to succumb to infectious and parasitic diseases.[6] Historically, reductions in hunger and undernourishment have been among the first practical steps nations have taken to improve public health, to reduce infant mortality, and to increase life expectancy.[7] Analysis by the Food and Agriculture Organization (FAO) indicates that malnutrition can increase the child mortality rate from common childhood diseases.[8] Compared to children who have adequate nourishment, FAO's analysis shows that the risk of death is 2.5 times higher for children with mild malnutrition, 4.6 times higher for children suffering from moderate malnutrition, and 8.4 times higher for the severely malnourished.[9] Moreover, wealthier societies are more able to target capital and human resources on public health measures and technologies in order to increase the availability of sanitation, water supplies, immunization, and antibiotics, which further reduces infant mortality and increases life expectancies.[10]

Thus, as figure 4.1 illustrates, greater wealth—through a multiplicity of sometimes overlapping pathways—leads to greater education; to lower rates of child labor; to higher food production; to greater access to food supplies and safe water; and, eventually, to better health, to lower mortality, and to higher life expectancies.[11]

How Well-Being Advances Economic Development

Earlier, we saw that wealthier is more educated, less hungry, and healthier.[12] But the converse is also true: more educated, less hungry, and healthier is generally also wealthier. Less hungry and healthier people are more energetic, less prone to absenteeism, and, therefore, more productive in whatever economic activity they undertake.[13] Robert W. Fogel, the Nobel Prize-winning economist, estimates that the levels of food supplies in 18th-century France were such that the bottom 10 percent of the labor force did not have sufficient food to generate the energy needed for regular work, and the next 10 percent had enough energy for about half an hour of heavy work (or less than 3 hours of light work).[14] Economic historian Richard A. Easterlin, notes that, on the basis of a United Nations study, when malaria was eradicated in Mymensingh (now in Bangladesh), crop yields increased 15 percent because farmers could spend more time and effort on cultivation. In other areas, elimination of seasonal malaria enabled farmers to plant a second crop.[15] Similarly, according to the World Bank, the near-eradication of malaria in Sri Lanka between 1947 and 1977 is estimated to have raised its national income by 9 percent.[16]

Moreover, healthier people can also devote more time and energy to their own education and the development of their human capital. Good health is particularly important during children's formative years. Similarly, improved food supplies and nutrition by themselves might help increase a population's educability, which is one of the premises behind school meals programs.[17] A healthier and longer-lived population is also more likely to invest time and effort for its members' educational and intellectual development.[18] Thus, a healthier population is likely to more fully develop its human capital, which, then, aids in the creation and diffusion of technology. The benefits to individuals, families, and societies of investing in higher education, post-doctoral research fellowships, and medical residencies increases significantly if individual beneficiaries live to 70 rather than a mere 30 to 35, as was the case, for instance, before the advent of modern economic growth. Thus, it is not surprising that levels of education have gone up as life expectancy has advanced or that more and more aspiring doctors and researchers today spend what literally used to be a lifetime to acquire the skills and expertise necessary to pursue careers in medicine, research, and institutes of higher learning. And once having acquired this expertise, those researchers are poised to contribute to technological innovation and diffusion in their chosen fields and to guide yet others along the same path. Thus human capital breeds additional human capital.[19] Hence, better health helps raise human capital, which aids the creation and diffusion of technology, further advancing health and accelerating economic growth.

In addition, several measures undertaken to improve public health provided a bonus in helping economic productivity increase in other ways. For instance, draining swamps not only reduced malaria but also added to the agricultural land base.[20] The World Bank reported that the international Onchocersiasis Control Program, an admixture of drug therapy and insecticide-spraying, is freeing up 25 million hectares (100 million acres) of land for cultivation and settlement, while having protected 30 million people (including 9 million children) born since the program's inception in 1974 from river blindness.[21] Notably, a joint study by the Harvard University Center for International Development and the London School of Hygiene and

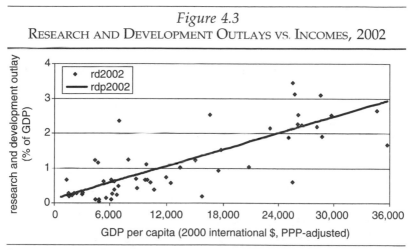

Figure 4.3
RESEARCH AND DEVELOPMENT OUTLAYS VS. INCOMES, 2002

SOURCE: Based on data from World Bank, *World Development Indicators*, http://devdata.worldbank.org/dataonline (accessed July 12, 2005).

Tropical Medicine states that if malaria had been eradicated in 1965, Africa's GDP would have been 32 percent higher today.[22]

The Cycle of Progress

We saw in the previous sections how greater wealth through greater education and less hunger leads to better health, and, in turn, better health leads to greater wealth. Yet another cycle consists of food production, food access, education, and human capital, all of which also help turn the health-wealth cycle. Both cycles are embedded in a more general cycle of progress in which pervasive technological change, broad economic growth, and globalized trade reinforce each other in advancing human well-being.[23] In this cycle, technological change, in general, reinforces economic growth.[24] In turn, richer countries have more resources to research and to develop new and improved technologies. Predictably, as shown in figure 4.3, analysis of cross-country data shows that expenditures on research and development rise with per capita GDP.[25] Also, wealthier countries have better-educated populations, which increases human capital and is generally conducive to greater technological innovation and diffusion in a society.[26] Moreover, anecdotal evidence based on an informal survey of fellow immigrants suggests the major reason many of the best and brightest from poorer countries end up in the universities and research establishments of the richer nations is that they perceive that the latter not only provide a higher quality of education, but also offer greater job opportunities for employing their human capital to the fullest extent. It is, therefore, hardly surprising that in 1993, for instance, 10 of the richest (and most well-educated) countries accounted for 84 percent of global research and development and controlled more than 80 percent of the patents in the United States and in developing countries.[27]

Advances in human capital have helped not only devise new technologies but also to adapt and refine them for a variety of uses, which were not always contemplated by their original inventors. Consider, for example, broadly used ("general") technologies that were originally invented and developed for other reasons but have found uses in numerous other economic sectors. Such technologies, which are well nigh becoming ubiquitous, include electricity, integrated circuits, microprocessors, lasers, global positioning systems, plastics, the internal combustion engine, the personal computer, word processing, and spreadsheets. They can, and do, improve productivity in virtually every sector of human activity. Consider, for instance, the food and agricultural sector. Microprocessors, lasers, personal computers, and global positioning systems can be used in precision agriculture to optimize the timing and quantities of fertilizers, water, and pesticides. This increases agricultural productivity per unit of land, water, and pesticide used, which, in addition to producing more crops, also reduces agriculture's environmental impact.[28] Similarly, plastics, by packaging and preserving food, have reduced wastage and spoilage, essentially stretching food supplies from a ton of agricultural produce and increasing the overall productivity of the agricultural sector. Moreover, trucks, trains, and planes—powered mainly by the internal combustion engine or other fossil fuel-dependent prime movers—are indispensable for moving critical inputs such as seeds, fertilizers, and pesticides from markets to farms, as well as the produce from farms to markets. Thus, we see that global agriculture productivity has been boosted—and hunger diminished—by a multiplicity of inventions that were never designed with either of those outcomes in mind.

Similarly, broad advances in physics and engineering, for instance, have led to new or improved medical technologies. Examples include electricity without which virtually no present day hospital or operating room could function, nor could other ubiquitous technologies such as x-rays, nuclear magnetic resonance, lasers, refrigeration, and personal computers. In the future, biotechnology and its products, unless shackled by technophobia, could have a similar widespread impact cutting across a variety of economic sectors—food, agriculture, forestry, medicine, and even manufacturing of products that have analogs in the biological sphere.

Trade is an integral part of the cycle of progress. Freer trade—in tangible goods, intellectual property, and intangible ideas—directly stimulates economic growth,[29] helps disseminate new technologies, and creates pressures to invent and innovate.[30] We saw earlier how trade has globalized food security. It also enables countries that lack sufficient financial or natural resources (e.g., energy and minerals) to import them from countries where it is relatively more abundant. It also allows a country that either lacks sufficient human capital or might have focused its human resources on certain economic sectors to obtain products and designs developed in another country and other economic sectors. For instance, competition from foreign car makers accelerated the introduction of several automobile safety and emission control systems to the United States, improving both environmental and human well-being.[31] Similarly, through trade, the rest of the world will eventually benefit from the United States's investment in AIDS cures. In that case, therapies invented and developed in the United States are available to be used in other countries without having to be re-invented. In other instances, trade allows technologies invented in one country to be developed and improved, if not perfected, in another. For example, the transistor was invented in the United States but its commercial potential was first realized by the Japanese, and the whole world gained.

Competitive trade also helps contain the costs of basic infrastructure, including water supply, sanitation, and power generation (although the full benefits are often squandered because of corrupt, inefficient, and opaque bureaucracies and governments). A vivid example of the importance of trade in improving human well-being comes from Iraq whose inability, because of trade sanctions, to fully operate and to maintain its water, sanitation, and electrical systems or to obtain sufficient food for its population contributed to a deterioration of public health and lowered life expectancies since the Gulf War. The need to alleviate those problems was the basis for various

United Nations Security Council resolutions to extend what became its scandal-ridden "Oil-for-Food" program.[32]

Thus the individual components of the cycle of progress—higher yields, increased food supplies, lower mortalities, and higher life expectancies—are strengthened by the general forces of economic growth, technological change, and trade, which, in turn, reinforce each other. Box 4.1 provides a schematic depiction of the cycle of progress and a brief description of the numerous paths linking the elements of the cycle.

To summarize, the progress in human well-being in the past two centuries was sustained, if not put into motion, by a cycle consisting of the mutually reinforcing, coevolving forces of economic growth, technological change, and free trade.

Factors Propelling the Cycle

In the description of the cycle of progress, the various components—higher food supplies, reduced malnutrition, better health, greater wealth—build on each other. But it is just as easy to visualize the cycle being kicked into reverse (e.g., by wars or poor policies) with both health and wealth going in the wrong direction as seems to be the case currently in many parts of sub-Saharan Africa, East Europe, and the former Soviet Union.

So what propels this cycle forward? Why did some countries get on the cycle before others? How do countries that have yet to get on the cycle, do so? Why do some societies cycle forward faster than others? Why have others barely begun to move economically and socially? Why have yet others slipped back in terms of various indicators of well-being? Can their situation be turned around?

Several excellent treatises and monographs provide insights into the second of those questions,[33] that is, why did modern economic growth begin in Europe or its colonies populated by its descendants? The question itself is not only significant historically, its study also provides valuable lessons for those who are not yet on the cycle, or whose seat on it is still wobbly.

Lessons from history, coupled with the real world "experiments" with various social and economic systems during the 20th century, and economic analyses of recent differences in the indication of human well-being give us clues as to what may or may not work to propel the cycle of progress forward. Geography, geology, and

Box 4.1

Interlinkages in the Cycle of Progress

The figure in this box is a depiction of the cycle of progress, indicating the various links and the paths connecting those links.

Because this is a cycle, it has no definitive beginning or end. Here I will arbitrarily begin its description with economic growth (which leads to wealth) on the right-hand side.

Wealth harnesses human capital to create new or improved technologies (paths A and B). It also makes those new or improved, as well as existing-but-underemployed, technologies affordable (path C), which, among other things, enhances crop yields (path D). Crop yields help increase available food supplies (path E), boosting health (path F), as well as reducing mortality and increasing life expectancy. Better health then leads to greater wealth (path G).

If a nation cannot grow sufficient food, it can use wealth to trade (path H) in order to augment food supplies (path I).

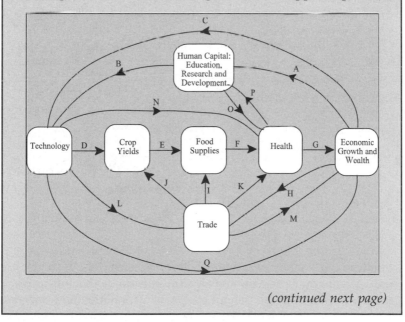

(continued next page)

(continued)

Trade (in ideas as well as products) can also help improve a country's crop yield through obtaining technologies or inputs produced elsewhere (path J). Similarly, trade can be used to help improve a country's health status (path K).

This trade is facilitated by technology (path L), which enables rapid movement of large quantities of inputs and outputs from one location to another. Also, trade, by allowing specialization and economies of scale where they are useful, accelerates economic growth (path M).

Technology also improves health independent of food supplies and trade (path N), as does education, particularly of women (path O). In turn, better health enables fuller development of human capital (path P; see text), which, among other things, helps countries to develop, absorb, and diffuse new technologies (path B), which further enhances economic growth (path Q).

Thus, technological change and economic growth (supplemented by trade) are mutually reinforcing, coevolving mechanisms that drive the cycle of progress.

One may well ask which—technological change or economic growth—came first. This, in fact, is the chicken-and-egg question. Although the answer is historically important and intrinsically interesting, it is not all that relevant to today's world. We know that regardless of which may have come first, today we need both chicken and egg to have a sustainable population of chickens (although technology might change that in the future).

The interconnection shown in the diagram provides one explanation for the associations seen between per capita income and the levels of tertiary education, crop yields, available food supplies, infant mortality, and life expectancies, as well as the progress in those measures over time.

climate may have played a role in helping Western European nations be the first to take off economically, but technology—and historical lessons of the successes and failures of economies and societies around the world—is making those factors increasingly irrelevant.

Industrial ecologist and Director of Rockefeller University's Program for the Human Environment Jesse Ausubel's perceptive question, "Does climate still matter?" is equally valid for geography and geology, especially given that human capital is becoming increasingly more important than natural or other forms of capital.[34] In fact, Robert W. Fogel estimates that two-thirds of all capital in the United States is human capital.[35] Moreover, the location-specific factors of geography, geology, and climate, author Jared Diamond's arguments notwithstanding, may never have been as important as the fact that Western nations *happened* upon the web of institutions that undergird economic growth and technological change.[36] Those institutions include economic and legal systems providing for free market economies; fair, equitable, and transparent rules to govern markets and to enforce contracts; secure and enforceable property rights to both tangible and intellectual products; and institutions for accumulating and converting knowledge into useful and beneficial products. Equally important was that Western nations also adopted attitudes that, by allowing those who venture their labor, intellectual capital, and financial resources to profit from the risks they incur, encouraged competition not only in the commercial sphere but also in the scientific, intellectual, and, not least, the political spheres.[37] Notably, those institutions and attributes are also the foundations of civil societies and democratic systems.

It is important to recognize that the cycle of progress evolved and was not the result of a conscious design. It fell into place as a result of self-organization. And the principle behind this self-organization was the desire on the part of every individual, family, and other social and economic unit to improve their well-being, and a political and economic system was necessary that would let them pursue that goal or was too weak to prevent them from doing so. This entire process took place in the context of Western societies' attitudes toward change, risk and reward, commerce, education, knowledge, and science and technology.[38]

Today, most countries know about the cycle of technological and economic progress. The most important question for those that are not on it is how to get on it, and for those who are on it, how to move faster forward.

First, what does not work? As the examples of the erstwhile Communist societies show us, a command-and-control economy is not sustainable in the long run if for no reason other than that command-and-control is not compatible with the institution of property rights, which is key to each individual pursuing his or her own well-being. A second reason is that the ability to command and control an economy itself requires a big government (or bureaucracy), and big bureaucracies never make small mistakes—and there will be occasional mistakes, despite the best of intentions. A market system in which a lot of smaller entities make decisions—some good, some bad—in essence is a mechanism for society to hedge its bets. Also, big bureaucracies require high taxes. High taxes are an invitation to corruption. It used to be that the front-line collectors themselves were prone to corruption (hence, the reference to the "cheating tax collector" in the Bible). Nowadays, where you have orderly government, favoritism by legislators in the form of special legislation and subsidies to special interests has replaced old-fashioned corruption. More important, high taxation itself cuts down the rate of economic growth.

A detailed analysis by James Gwartney and others of the relationship between annual economic growth rates and government expenditure from 1960–96 found that as the size of government (measured as government spending as a percentage of GDP) increased, the annual growth rate declined.[39] When countries had government spending at less than 25 percent of GDP, annual growth rates were 6.6 percent; when government spending was more than 60 percent of GDP, the annual growth rate dropped to 1.6 percent. Essentially, they found that a 10 percent increase in government expenditure (as a share of GDP) translated into a 1 percent drop in annual economic growth rate. These results are broadly consistent with those of other leading researchers.[40]

In an examination of a broader set of countries (60) from 1980 to 1995, James Gwartney and others also found that security of property rights (based on risk of expropriation, risk of contract violation, and presence of rule of law) was strongly correlated with the rate of economic growth.[41] The level of educational attainment is also correlated with an increased growth rate. Finally, the rate of economic growth in the 1980–95 period was negatively correlated with the growth of government expenditure from 1985–90. These results are also similar to those of other leading researchers.[42]

Other studies have shown that openness to trade (measured as exports and imports relative to GDP) is good for growth,[43] as well as that inflation is bad, at least at high rates.[44] Harvard University economist Robert Barro also indicates that at low levels of political rights, democracy can increase economic growth rates but reduce them at higher levels, perhaps because of the impulse to redistribute from the few to the many (which, generally, would lead to an increase in the size of government).[45]

World Bank economists David Dollar and Aart Kraay also found that increased rule of law (or protection of property rights) and fiscal discipline (defined as low government consumption) raise overall incomes without increasing income inequality. Dollar and Kraay did not find any relationship between formal democratic institutions or public spending on health care to have any systematic effect on the incomes of the poor. However, they did find that high rates of inflation do more harm to the poor.

Many of the factors to which economic growth seems to be sensitive have been combined into the *Economic Freedom of the World* index.[46] The index is a composite of 37 factors designed to characterize the extent to which individuals can pursue their economic interests with minimal interference and dictation from the state.[47] These factors measure economic freedom on a 0 to 10 scale in five broad areas: size of government; the legal system, rule of law, and security of property; soundness of money; freedom to trade with foreigners; and regulation of credit, labor, and businesses.

As was noted previously, James Gwartney and others have shown that the economic freedom index is correlated to levels of economic development (see figure 2.19) and to economic growth.[48] Not surprisingly, it also is associated with higher life expectancies.[49]

Future Dependence of Well-Being on Economic Development

With the passage of time, the level of economic development needed to reach a specific level of human well-being keeps dropping. This is the natural consequence of a dynamic in which new technologies are brought online and existing technologies are perfected and adopted more widely, thus allowing old problems to be solved more effectively and efficiently. Because of this dynamic, so long as new problems do not arise, one should expect that at some time in the future the level of economic development may become less of a factor in improving well-being. This would certainly seem to be the case for those indicators that have a natural limit. For example, literacy and access to safe water and sanitation cannot exceed 100 percent, and the share of children in the labor force (that is, child labor) cannot go below 0 percent. For such indicators, if the technology-driven dynamic is coupled with economic growth, it is not too far fetched to conceive of a time when access to safe water, sanitation, literacy, and absence of child labor become, for practical purposes, almost universal. A corollary of this is that future cross-country analyses may show that levels of such indicators are not as sensitive to the level of economic development as current analyses indicate.

The situation could be somewhat different with regard to life expectancy. First, in the last quarter century or so we have seen a brand new, life shortening disease—AIDS—take hold in the human population. As already discussed, it took significant commitments of human and fiscal resources—both products of society's wealth—to devise methods to treat this disease. Because of the high cost of treatment, we currently have a situation where the disease is spreading but the poorer countries cannot afford these treatments. Until the cost of treatment is reduced or more effective methods and approaches adopted to prevent its spread, we will continue to have a situation in which life expectancy is significantly dependent on the level of economic development. It's also conceivable that if the AIDS situation is addressed successfully in the poor (and rich) countries, humanity may in the future fall victim to other new diseases or new forms of old diseases (e.g., drug-resistant tuberculosis), which would also put a premium on wealth as a factor in determining longevity. Moreover, it seems that even if there is a "natural" limit to a human being's life span, with enough human and fiscal resources these limits can be raised, albeit slowly. Therefore, one should expect that wealthier populations will have higher life expectancies into the foreseeable future.

With respect to infant mortality, the situation will probably be in between what one would expect for indicators such as access to safe water and life expectancy. There is indeed a limit to the infant mortality rate—it's zero. In fact, it already is in the 4 to 5 range for several of the richest countries. Although these levels have been dropping steadily—it dropped from 5.7 in 1995 to 4.2 per 1,000 in 2003 for the countries of the European Monetary Union[50]—it is probably getting as close to zero as is practically possible.[51] However, there is always the risk of new or renewed diseases that might lead to its increase. But if that does not happen, we should see the continuation of the current pattern of the dependence of the infant mortality rate on wealth, namely, a sharp plunge in the rate at low levels of wealth with a flattening out at higher levels (see table 4.1 and figure 2.5). In the future one might see a deeper plunge in infant mortality, and the flattening out to occur, at lower levels of wealth.

Is Nonrenewable Resource Use Unsustainable?

It may be argued that the improvements in human well-being have been obtained through massive and unsustainable depredation of the earth's nonrenewable resources and degradation of its environment. While deferring the latter issue to subsequent sections, in the following I will address the issue of nonrenewable resources. This discussion is brief because it has been addressed comprehensively in Julian L. Simon's *The State of Humanity*, as well as elsewhere, and the general finding is that we are not likely to run out of critical energy and mineral resources any time soon, if at all.[52]

The contention that we are depleting "nonrenewable" resources stems from a static view of what a "resource" is. For example, while every atom of copper is a potential resource for humanity, it is not a usable resource unless it is accessible at an affordable price. But what is accessible and affordable depends on technology, which, as we have already seen, is constantly advancing. Economic geologists classify the amount of resources that can be extracted profitably at current prices as current, proven, or economic reserves. However, at any time, there will be resources that can be extracted using current technology, but which could not then be sold profitably. Such resources are classified as potential reserves, and they are a function of current prices and technology.

Consider, for instance, that technology limited us to bore a hole no deeper than a thousand feet. All the copper beyond that, even if it comprised 99 percent of the earth's total resource endowment of copper, would be inaccessible. Therefore, the price of copper (assuming free markets and good information) would not consider the 99 percent that would be inaccessible. But if technology advances so that we can access copper beyond that thousand feet and be able to sell that additional amount at a profit, its price would drop in recognition of the expansion of the resource base. In fact, it is not necessary for a technology to actually be functioning for markets to factor it into prices. The likelihood that a technology may increase economic reserves itself would be considered in the pricing. The greater the likelihood, the lower prices would drop in anticipation. Thus, prices are always changing in response to short- and long-term prospects for accessing and using a commodity.

In a free market system, the fact that prices are attached to commodities means that suppliers are in a constant quest to increase supplies so that they can sell more while at the same time reducing prices so that they are not undersold. Meanwhile, direct and indirect users of the commodities are on their own quest to reduce consumption so that they can reduce their costs.

The higher the price of a resource, the greater the response from both suppliers and consumers. This response can take the form of greater penetration of improved-but-less-used technologies, as well as research, development, and adoption of brand new technologies. For suppliers, this leads to technological change in the search for more efficient methods to locate, extract, and refine the resource. For consumers, higher prices stimulate technological change in the reuse, recycling, and conservation of that resource. Thus, today with global steel demand at record heights (around a billion tonnes annually), more than a third of the steel produced each year comes from recycled scrap, which is a \$100 billion per year business.[53] High prices also intensify the search for substitutes for that resource. And sometimes those substitutes can drive out the "original" resource. To paraphrase Bjørn Lomborg, the stone age didn't end because we ran out of stones, the iron age because we ran out of iron, or the bronze age because we ran out of bronze.[54]

As a result of this dynamic, technology increases the amount of resources that can be used or there is increased substitution, which would stabilize if not reduce prices. Alternatively, if these efforts fail to reduce prices, its usage would drop and efforts to find substitutes would increase until they are, in fact, found. Consider whale blubber. Once it was the preferred fuel used to light households. It became scarce, prices went up, and substitutes were found. Today, although there might be a niche for whale blubber somewhere, it no longer has an international market as a lighting fuel. So although reportedly you can get a pound of whale blubber for half-a-penny in Norway (down from 15 cents per pound in 1999), its current price is irrelevant.[55]

Figure 4.4
PRICE OF VARIOUS METALS RELATIVE TO WAGES, 1800–2005

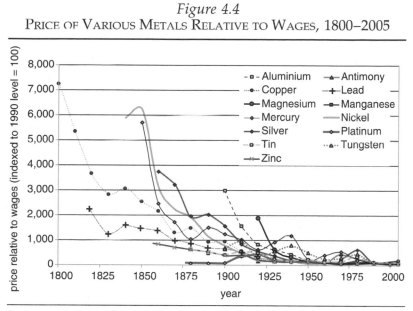

SOURCES: Stephen Moore, "The Coming Age of Abundance," in *True State of the Planet*, ed. Ronald Bailey (New York: Free Press, 1995), pp. 109–39; U.S. Geological Survey (USGS), *Metal Prices in the United States through 1998* (Reston, VA: USGS, 2004), http://minerals.usgs.gov/minerals/pubs/metal_prices (accessed March 19, 2006); USGS, *Mineral Commodity Summaries*, http://minerals.usgs.gov/minerals/pubs/mes/ (accessed March 19, 2006); USGS, *Minerals Yearbook 2004*, http://minerals.usgs.gov/minerals/pubs/commodity/tungsten/index.html (accessed March 19, 2006); Bureau of Labor Statistics, *Establishment Data: Historical Hours and Earnings.*

Thus, it is hardly surprising that despite short-term fluctuations, the long-term price trend of virtually every commodity that is used today has been downward over the past two centuries not only in terms of "real," inflation-adjusted dollars but also more importantly in terms of the amount of effort an average individual has to expend to obtain or to purchase a given mass of that commodity.[56] As one illustration of this general phenomenon, figure 4.4 shows that, despite a recent upturn in prices probably because of increased demand in Asia, there has been a long-term decline in the price of 13 metals relative to wages.[57] On that basis, in 2005, the price of copper was an 1/80th of its 1800 level, aluminum dropped to a 1/40th of its 1900 price, silver declined to a 1/40th of its 1860 level, and tin to a 1/7th of its price in 1880. These long-term declines in prices indicate that those commodities are not getting any scarcer. In fact, the only metal that had a price-relative-to-wages higher in 2005 than in 1900 was platinum: in 2005, it was 35 percent more expensive that it was in 1900, but its price had peaked around 1920, at a level three and one-half times higher than today's.

Given that commodity prices have, by and large, dropped, it is interesting to ponder on the etymology of the phrase "searching for a needle in a haystack." Before the industrial revolution when metals were scarcer than they are today and needles, therefore, more costly, it might have made sense to search a haystack for a lost needle. But today that would be a sheer waste of time and energy.

Finally, in recent years there have been a spate of books and articles trumpeting the imminent end of oil.[58] As Jerry Taylor of the Cato Institute notes, "Fortunately, the debate over the likelihood of declining production is in a sense irrelevant."[59] Perhaps the end of oil will come about sometime in the future but whenever it comes, it will only be a footnote to history, just as the end of blubber is today. The end of oil does not mean an end to energy production. Even today we have a number of technologies waiting in the wings ranging from "clean coal" to nuclear as a substitute for fossil fuels to different forms of renewables that could generate electricity for ultimate use in the home, workplace, and even in transportation. And when the price is right, they will step in, either because oil becomes more expensive as it becomes scarcer or technological innovation reduces the price of substitutes.

THE EFFECTS OF ECONOMIC DEVELOPMENT AND TECHNOLOGICAL CHANGE ON THE ENVIRONMENT

5. Competing Views Regarding Affluence, Technology, and the Environment

The remarkable improvement in the human condition over the past two centuries documented in the previous chapters was driven by economic growth; technological change; and trade in ideas, services, and goods, which helped meet the burgeoning demands of a vastly greater population. But the drive to meet these human demands for food, clothing, shelter, energy, and material goods— among other things—have led to an expansion of humankind's dominion over earth. In many locations, land and water appropriated for human use have displaced much of the rest of nature; air and water pollution threaten both humans and the rest of nature; and some claim that human influences on global biogeochemical cycles could lead to potentially disastrous climatic change.

Although the past few decades have seen substantial environmental cleanup, particularly in the richer countries, there is a deep skepticism, if not outright suspicion, of economic growth and technological change in many quarters.[1] Those claims, right or wrong, have substantial credibility within the body politic. Such skepticism is displayed, for instance, in the dismay among many environmental groups regarding the vast quantities of energy used to power the human enterprise, as well as in their reaction to the use of genetically engineered foods, even in instances where there could be net public health or environmental benefits, such as the use of pest-resistant crops to increase crop productivity and to decrease use of synthetic pesticides.[2] It is also evident in the ambivalence of the United States environmental and public health statutes, which erect numerous hurdles to the development and dissemination of new technologies even as they require the use of best available technologies.[3] United States Clean Air laws, for instance, have often mandated new, untested technologies for automobiles even as they have raised barriers to the siting of new stationary sources and technologies, which then might displace older, less-efficient plants.[4]

Many Neo-Malthusians and environmentalists claim that economic growth and technology are among the driving forces behind environmental degradation and natural resource use. They argue that the progress, if any, in human welfare is illusory and unsustainable, and sooner or later, environmental degradation will reverse all that progress.[5]

The IPAT identity on environmental impact introduced in chapter 1 has often been used to justify such skepticism. Clearly, an unquestioning application of the IPAT identity leads to the conclusion that A (affluence) and T (technology) act as multipliers for environmental impact, if all else remains equal. While noting that the IPAT identity is a simplified representation, its formulators have nevertheless used it to support sweeping and bold, though somewhat differing, conclusions. Barry Commoner contends that technology, specifically that adopted widely since World War II, is the source of environmental degradation.[6] Paul and Anne Ehrlich, however, conclude that the primary causes are population and affluence, particularly "overconsumption" in the United States, and they have to be curbed.[7] Despite recognizing that "benign" technologies could reduce impacts, they argue that for most important activities, new technology would bring diminishing returns because as the best resources are used up (e.g., minerals, fossil fuels, and farm land), society would increasingly have to turn to marginal or less desirable resources to satisfy demand, which would increase energy use and pollution.[8]

There are alternate views of the role of technological change and economic growth regarding human and environmental well-being. Jesse Ausubel and other systems-oriented industrial ecologists believe that additional technological change has to be part of the solution to reduce the environmental impact of the processes designed to meet human needs.[9] However, even these ardent advocates of technology view economic growth as a multiplier of impacts, rather than a contributor to the solution.[10]

Another view, formalized as the environmental transition hypothesis, is that, for any specific country, the forces of technological change and economic growth may initially be the causes of environmental impacts, but eventually they can combine to effect an "environmental transition"—after which they become a necessary part of the solution to environmental problems.[11]

Figure 5.1
THE ENVIRONMENTAL TRANSITION

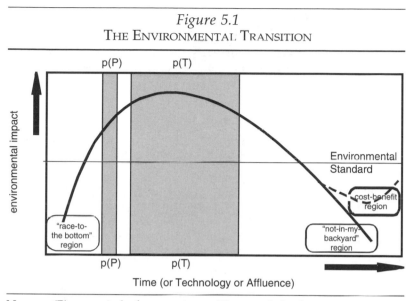

NOTES: p(P) = period of perception; p(T) = period of transition; "not-in-my-backyard" region (environmental impact enters this region if benefits far exceed costs to beneficiaries); cost-benefit region (where benefits and costs have to be more carefully balanced).

SOURCE: Indur M. Goklany, *Clearing the Air: The Real Story of the War on Air Pollution* (Washington, DC: Cato Institute, 1999), p. 96.

Environmental Transition Hypothesis

The environmental transition hypothesis, depicted in figure 5.1, aims to provide a general framework for explaining the influence of technological change and economic growth on various indicators of environmental impact and natural resource use. In this figure, the environmental impact on a single country as measured by a particular indicator (e.g., indoor and outdoor air quality for sulfur dioxide [SO_2] and particulate matter, availability of safe water and sanitation, and PCB and DDT residues in human tissue) is represented on the y-axis. The x-axis represents time.

Under the environmental transition hypothesis, environmental impact first goes up, then it goes through an "environmental transition" after which the environmental impact declines, at least to a point.[12] Until that point, the trajectory for environmental impact is shaped like an inverted U. The precise height, width, and timing of

105

an environmental transition curve varies with the specific indicator. For some indicators (e.g., lack of access to sanitation or safe water), the transitions currently occur early in a country's developmental history, sometimes even before the period for which time-series data are available. In such cases, the curve representing the historical trend will be downward sloping; it will look like the post-transition curve in figure 5.1. For other indicators, for a variety of reasons to be clarified later, an environmental transition may not be evident in the historical trend, that is, the country may still be on the upward slope of the transition curve.

Notably, cross-country data for some pollutants also result in inverted U-shaped curves when environmental impact is plotted against *affluence*. Such curves have been called "environmental Kuznets curves" after the Nobel Prize-winning economist Simon Kuznets who first discovered such a shape in a plot for economic inequality as a function of per capita income.[13] Despite the apparent resemblance between the environmental transition and the environmental Kuznets curve (EKC), the two are not identical. In the former, the x-axis represents time (a proxy for both affluence and technological development), while in the latter it only represents affluence. Thus, the EKC hypothesis, which suggests that environmental degradation increases with affluence at low levels of affluence but declines with affluence at higher levels, misses half the story regarding the factors that determine environmental degradation. For this, and other reasons outlined in the following section, a set of single-country inverted U-shaped environmental transition curves does not necessarily result in a similarly shaped cross-country EKC.

An explanation offered for an environmental transition is that society is on a continual quest to improve its quality of life, which is determined by numerous social, economic, and environmental factors. The weight given to each determinant is constantly changing with society's precise circumstances and perceptions. In the early stages of economic and technological development, which go hand-in-hand, society places a higher priority on increasing affluence than on other determinants, even if that means tolerating some environmental deterioration, because increasing wealth provides the means for obtaining basic needs and amenities (e.g., food, shelter, water, and electricity) and reducing the most significant risks to public health and safety (e.g., malnutrition, infectious and parasitic diseases, and child mortality). Also, in those early stages, society may, in fact, be unaware of the risk posed by a deterioration in the specific environmental impact, measured by the particular indicator in question. However, as society becomes wealthier; tackles these problems; and, possibly, gains more knowledge about the social, health, and economic consequences of the environmental impact in question, reducing the environmental impact due to the specific indicator automatically rises higher on its priority list (even if the impact does not worsen). But because the first increments of economic activity further increase environmental impact, it becomes an even more important determinant of the overall quality of life. Accordingly, lowering the specific impact becomes even more urgent. This stage is represented in figure 5.1 as the period of perception or p(P). (I deliberately use that term, because in matters determining the strength of actions undertaken to improve quality of life, perception often trumps reality.)

Before p(P), one should not expect conscious actions to reduce the environmental impact, although reductions may occur because of long-term improvements in technology as both manufacturers and consumers strive to reduce costs and to improve efficiencies associated with their use of energy and other natural resources, as well as other reasons.[14] For example, for SO_2 in the United States, the start of p(P) dates to the early 1950s after the October 1948 Donora air quality episode, which resulted in 18 excess deaths in a population of 14,000, and the notorious five-day London episode in December 1952 that reportedly killed as many as 4,000 people in a population of 8.5 million.[15] Both episodes resulted from atmospheric inversions in which a cold air mass near the ground is trapped by a warm layer above it. Such an inversion prevents pollutants at ground level that are trapped along with the cold air from being dispersed, which allows their concentrations to build up. Usually such an inversion is a relatively brief affair, but it lasted for four days during the Donora episode and five days during the London episode. The fog during the latter episode was so thick that people reportedly couldn't see their own feet at times.[16] The resulting publicity about these events woke the population in the United States (and Europe) to the dangers of extreme air pollution.[17] However, indoor SO_2 levels had begun to improve at least by the 1940s, and perhaps much earlier, because households started moving away from burning coal and wood inside homes and commercial establishments in

Figure 5.2
RESEARCH AND DEVELOPMENT OUTLAYS VS. INCOMES, 2002

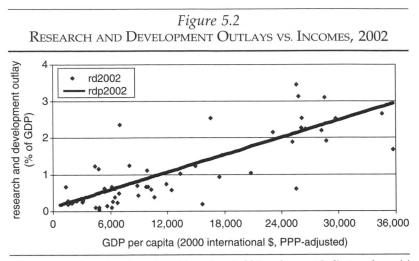

SOURCE: Based on data from World Bank, *World Development Indicators*, http://devdata.worldbank.org/dataonline (accessed July 12, 2005).

the 1910s and 1920s once they became wealthier and technologies (in the form of cleaner fuels, such as oil and natural gas) became more readily available. Regardless of precisely why reductions might have first been undertaken, from p(P) onward, a democratic society, because it has the political means to do so, will translate its desire for a cleaner environment into laws, either because clean up is not voluntary or rapid enough or because of sheer symbolism. The wealthier such a society, the more affordable—and more demanding—its laws.

At the same time, with increasing affluence and the secular march of technology, society is able to improve its environmental quality better and more cheaply. Affluence makes the purchase and use of new or existing-but-unused cleaner technologies more affordable, especially if their up-front costs are higher, as is often the case. Greater affluence also means more resources will be available for research and development (R&D) targeted on cleaner technologies. Moreover, a richer country is better able to fund broad-based R&D. In fact, by comparison with poorer countries, richer countries spend disproportionately more of their gross domestic product (GDP) on R&D in general. Figure 5.2 shows that across countries, R&D expenditures in 2002 as a *percentage* of GDP generally increased linearly with per capita income.[18] Spending on R&D is beneficial even if it is not targeted to specific problems, because the course of scientific and technological progress is unpredictable and advances in one field often spread to and stimulate innovations in others.

In addition, affluence provides the funds for developing and nurturing the human capital that a technologically advanced society needs to sustain itself, that is, a more or less universal educational system that ultimately feeds the entire web of universities, laboratories, banks, corporations, entrepreneurs, and even lawyers that participate in the process of invention, innovation, and diffusion of technologies. Participation at the post-secondary education level increases with wealth. In turn, such education helps the cycle of progress move faster. Thus, with affluence and technological change reinforcing each other, the environmental impact undergoes, first, a period of transition and, then, a decline.[19]

Other factors might reinforce environmental transitions for traditional (industry-related) pollutants. Historically, economic development has involved technology-mediated transformations from, first, an agrarian to an industrial society and, then, an industrial to a post-industrial knowledge- and information-based society. Emissions of industrial pollutants per capita or per GDP (both leading, rather than true, indicators of environmental impacts)[20] increase with the first transformation but decline with the second. Hence, temporal trends for these leading indicators should also look like stylized inverted U-shaped curves. Second, as the industrial sector waxes and wanes so does its political power. In 1900, the United States mining and manufacturing sectors, traditionally associated with pollution, employed 40.2 percent of nonfarm labor.[21] After declining during the Depression, the employment in those sectors rebounded into the 40 percent or more range during World War II before dropping to 28.2 percent in 1970 and 17.0 percent in 1997.[22] A decline in a sector's economic and demographic power only makes stiffer environmental laws more likely for that sector, particularly in a democracy. Currently, we see this principle in operation for the U.S. industrial, ranching, mining, lumbering, and agricultural sectors.[23]

Once past the environmental transition, and if (and when) the impact drops below the environmental standard, environmental impact could then move in one of several different directions. If the (perceived) benefits of control substantially exceed (perceived) social and economic costs, or if the costs are shifted to others while benefits are retained, the impact will be driven down farther (as indicated by the solid post-transition curve in figure 5.1). In effect, the trajectory enters a "not-in-my-backyard" phase. However, if the impact enters a region where costs approximate benefits, which may occur if technological progress has been unable to substantially reduce costs or costs cannot be shifted to someone else, then the precise trajectory will depend on a more careful balancing of the perceived costs and benefits. Such a region is denoted in figure 5.1 as the "cost-benefit" region. In a democracy such balancing is often done by legislators or agencies authorized by them. Almost inevitably, such balancing is qualitative and imprecise.

The dashed line in figure 5.1 depicts a case where further control is no longer perceived to enhance the quality of life, that is, the additional costs of further control once again exceed additional benefits, and the environmental impact swings upward. That may occur, for example, if, as is not unusual, the costs of additional cleanup increase exponentially while benefits diminish; society decides that for the particular environment impact, the environment is clean enough and scarce resources should now be spent on other unmet needs; and limits of clean technologies have been reached and no cleaner substitutes are available.

Several points need to be emphasized with respect to the environmental transition hypothesis. First, because economic growth and technological change are not inevitable, environmental cleanup and environmental transitions are, likewise, not a foregone conclusion. Second, a basic assumption implicit in this hypothesis is that society is always trying to improve its quality of life and that the quality of life does not always track with environmental quality. Third, the hypothesis also assumes that a mechanism exists to convert the desire for a better quality of life into action. Clearly, the stronger that mechanism, the greater the likelihood that we should see a transition. A corollary is that transitions are more likely to occur in democracies.

It is also worth noting that an environmental transition (see figure 5.1) resembles a demographic transition in that the latter also exhibits an initial increase in the population growth rate (due to a decline in the mortality rate), which is followed by a decrease in that growth rate (due to a decline in the birth rate).[24] The environmental transition curve can also be adapted to apply to broad indicators of human welfare. Because reductions in indicators such as infant, maternal, or age-adjusted mortality, for instance, are more critical to human well-being than improved environmental quality, one ought to expect that societies would take measures to reduce mortality rates before indicators of environmental quality, unless the latter are known to be proximate causes of the former. Indeed, now that we know environmental improvements such as greater access to safe water, sanitation, and better air quality help reduce mortality rates, today's developing countries are instituting such improvements relatively early in their process of economic development (compared to the currently developed countries). Thus, not surprisingly, we see mortality rates declining—and life expectancies improving—at relatively early stages of a country's economic development.

Differences between the Environmental Transition and the Environmental Kuznets Curves

The environmental transition hypothesis (ETH) depicted in figure 5.1 suggests that, in general, a plot of environmental impact (EI) against time follows an inverted U shaped path except, possibly, at very high levels of affluence where it may swing up under some circumstances. (If the upswing were to continue, the plot would resemble the letter N.) But despite the similarity in the pre-upswing region between a depiction of the ETH and an EKC, there are fundamental differences between the two hypotheses as the latter has usually been derived or proposed.

First, the ETH applies to individual groups (usually countries), while the existence (or nonexistence) of EKCs is usually postulated based on statistical analyses of data sets spanning several groups (also, usually countries). Second, as already noted, the ETH incorporates consideration of both technological change and economic development as determinants of environmental quality, whereas the EKC hypothesis focuses on economic development as the critical explanatory variable. The latter, therefore, misses an important factor that determines environmental quality. Under the ETH, the independent variable is time, which over the past two centuries at least, has in most areas, by and large, served as a surrogate for both affluence and technological change. However, the EKC is usually based on a plot of EI against affluence. If technology were propagated instantly from country to country, then using a data set drawn from a narrow time period would exclude technological change as a confounding variable in the derivation of an EKC. But technology is not propagated instantaneously, and analytical techniques have to be used to filter out the effects of technological change (as well as other confounding variables). However, separating out the effects of technological change and economic growth is easier said than done because economic growth and technological change coevolve.

It is easy to see how a set of single-country environmental transitions followed by upswings (as indicated by the curve ending in the cost-benefit region in figure 5.1) may lead to a similar N-shaped cross-country EI versus affluence curve. However, I will show that cross-country EI versus affluence curves need not be inverted U-shaped even if the single-country EI curves are.

In order to make this point I will start from a set of single-country EI versus affluence curves and use them to construct a cross-country EI versus affluence curve. This approach is fundamentally different from the approach of other researchers who have started with cross-country curves and tried to use those to develop shapes for or to derive conclusions or policies about the evolution of EI for single countries.[25]

For a given pollutant, one should expect that the shape of an environmental transition will vary from country to country depending on its particular circumstances. For any given pollutant and indicator employed to characterize that pollutant's environmental impact, environmental transitions for some countries may be narrower, some may have steeper ascents, and others may have faster declines. The precise timing of a single-country environmental transition and the magnitude of EI at which that occurs will depend on numerous interdependent factors in addition to the level of economic development and availability and affordability of technology. These factors include the distribution and quantities of its natural resource endowments; population density; climate; geography; level of knowledge (or perhaps more importantly, perceptions) about the pollutant in question; cultural and religious attitudes toward the environment, as well as the numerous other determinants of the aggregate quality of life; political and economic structures; and the precise nature and magnitude of its unmet social and economic needs.

112

Because no two countries are identical in all those respects, we should not, in general, expect their peaks for environmental impact to be of the same magnitude or occur at the same time or level of affluence. A divergence in just one of the several factors noted could result in differences in the timing and the levels of affluence or EI at which their environmental transitions may occur. For example, if it is possible for two countries to be identical in every respect except that one's economic take-off occurs later, then the lagging country's environmental transition is more likely to occur at a lower level of affluence because it has the opportunity to benefit from technologies invented by the leading country (assuming trade in ideas and a willingness to learn on the part of the lagging country). For the same reason, the time between economic take-off and the peak in the environmental impact plot is more likely to be shorter for the lagging country.

Consider two countries, A and B. For the sake of simplicity, I will assume that both countries are past their respective periods of perception. If country A is well endowed in coal, while country B imports fossil fuels, then it should not be surprising if the former's economy is more dependent on coal and invests less on energy efficiency. (Compare, for example, the United States against Japan.) As a result, country A is more likely to have higher SO_2 emissions per capita and per GDP, and its environmental transition for ambient SO_2 air quality is likely to occur at a higher level of EI and when it is more affluent than country B.

A similar result could be obtained if both countries are identical in every respect except that the latter has a higher population density. That would result in greater SO_2-related impacts on the population of country B, which, since all else is deemed equal, ought to result in higher benefit-to-cost ratio for any given level or method of SO_2 control. In turn, that should generally lead to country B instituting earlier and a more drastic level of control. (Countries with greater population densities are also more likely to justify mass transit and, hence, to have less intensive automobile usage, which can be a major source of other fossil fuel-related emissions.)

Next, assume that country A, which is better endowed with coal and fossil fuels, launched on its economic growth path earlier. This could occur for a variety of reasons. Through an accident of history or conscious design it may have developed the appropriate institutions for stimulating economic growth and technological change

Figure 5.3
EXAMPLES OF SINGLE-COUNTRY ENVIRONMENTAL TRANSITIONS

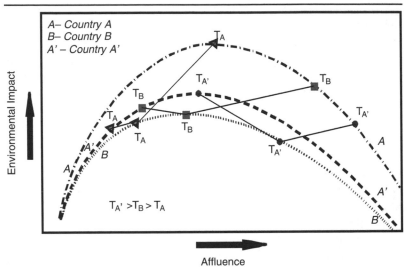

SOURCE: Indur M. Goklany, *Clearing the Air: The Real Story of the War on Air Pollution* (Washington, DC: Cato Institute, 1999).

sooner, or it may have gained leverage from its natural resource endowments earlier. Thus, as illustrated in figure 5.3, country A could be past its environmental transition (which it reaches at time T_A) by the time country B reaches its point of transition at time T_B (with $T_B > T_A$).[26] At times beyond T_B, the environmental impact for country A could, nevertheless, be above that for country B even after both have gone past their individual environmental transitions despite country B being less affluent. This is illustrated in figure 5.3 in which both A and B have inverted U-shaped curves for EI versus affluence. This situation clearly is at odds with the general notion of an inverted U-shape postulated by the EKC hypothesis (namely, that at high affluence levels, the more affluent country will also have a lower level of EI).

Now let us consider a third country, A', which is identical to A, except that its economic take-off occurred after A and B. Country A' would peak at a lower EI level than country A at time $T_{A'}$ (with $T_{A'} > T_B > T_A$). But conceivably, this peak could be higher than that for B, although A' was the last to take off economically and could avail itself of the technological changes devised by both the leaders (see figure 5.3).

Figure 5.3 indicates the levels of EI and affluence for each country at times T_A, T_B, and $T_{A'}$. We can construct cross-country EI versus affluence plots by connecting the three points on the three country plots corresponding to each of those times. The three resulting cross-country plots do not look like inverted U's for any of those times. If anything, they look like upside-down EKCs.

Thus, it does not necessarily follow that an EKC will emerge from cross-country data even if each country has an environmental transition shaped like a Kuznets curve.

The second point illustrated by figure 5.3 is that, given the numerous factors that govern the evolution of EI for any country, there is no reason why, left to their own devices, the "turning point" or peak EI for a particular pollutant should occur at the same level of affluence (or time) for all countries. (Of course, if each country is not left to its own devices, then the timing and possibly the peak EIs may be interrelated—for instance, if they band together in an international agreement with similar obligations for each party.) Nor is there any reason, given the numerous factors that could determine the evolution of EI for any country, why the turning point in an EKC should be universally applicable to individual countries (in the absence of collective action or, perhaps, even then).[27] In fact, it is not clear what, if anything, is represented by the various inflection points in a cross-country EI versus affluence curve, although with time the peak corresponding to the environmental transition is likely to move down and to the left because of technological change and increased awareness (or perception) of the problems due to environmental impact.

The earlier example is based on a very limited number of hypothetical countries. If we construct a cross-country curve from a much larger set of single-country curves covering the spectrum with respect to the numerous factors that could affect the shape, height, and timing of environmental transitions, then, based on the ETH, we should expect to see countries that have very low and very high affluence levels to have generally low levels of EI, and those countries with medium levels of affluence to have generally higher levels of EI. Hence, it is possible to obtain, in a very general sense, a stylized inverted U-shaped cross-country curve from a set of single-country

ET curves with, possibly, some peaks and troughs here and there, particularly toward the extremes of affluence because the precise shape in these regions is necessarily determined by the few countries at those extreme reaches. As figure 5.3 shows, these details can lead to some mighty peculiar shapes.

In summary, an inverted U-shaped curve for EI against per capita income derived from a cross-country analysis would be consistent with the (single-country) ETH. However, if the cross-country analysis fails to result in an inverted U-shaped curve, that does not disprove the ETH.

Deciding between the Competing Views

In the following two chapters I will examine long-term trends in various key environmental indicators in order to establish whether they are consistent with one or the other view offered earlier regarding the effect of economic growth and technological change on the environment. To do so, I will use the IPAT identity to determine how well changes in impacts track with changes in population, affluence, and T, the technology factor.[28]

6. Long-Term Environmental Trends

Chapter 2 showed that over the past two centuries there has been a more or less steady improvement in the average person's quality of life and material well-being. In this chapter, I will examine, where data are available, trends in various environmental indicators of the impacts of humankind on land, air, and water that accompanied these improvements in human well-being. Specifically, I will focus on trends in cropland, traditional air pollution emissions and air quality, and deaths due to water-related diseases—critical indicators for habitat loss and air and water pollution, respectively. In addition, I will examine trends for various metrics of human welfare that in the view of some greenhouse gas control advocates and, arguably, in the popular imagination, might be sensitive to global warming to verify whether these trends, in fact, indicate increasing losses of human welfare. The climate-sensitive metrics examined here include changes in agricultural productivity, deaths, and property losses due to extreme weather events, such as hurricanes and floods.

My focus is primarily on the United States, but I will also examine, where data allow, global trends to evaluate whether the U.S. experience is unique or if it fits a more general pattern. Because the United States is, arguably, the country that has traveled the farthest on the path of economic growth and has been a pioneer in many environmental matters, others—especially developing countries—might learn from its experience as to which approaches may be more successful than others to ensure continuing improvement in human well-being, of which environmental quality is one aspect.

Cropland

Conversion of land to human use is the major cause of loss and fragmentation of natural habitat, as well as the consequent reduction in biodiversity and carbon sinks.[1] According to the World Conservation Union, habitat loss and degradation, to which agriculture is the single largest contributor, affect 86 percent of threatened birds, 86

Figure 6.1
TECHNOLOGICAL CHANGE IN U.S. AGRICULTURE, 1910–2004

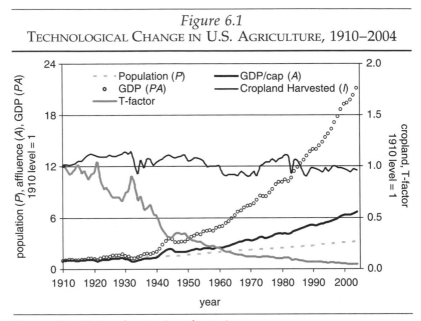

SOURCE: See Notes, chapter 6, endnote 4.

percent of threatened mammals, and 88 percent of threatened amphibians that it assessed.[2] Much of this conversion has been to cropland.[3] Hence, cropland is a particularly important indicator for the cumulative impact of humankind's activities not only on land itself but also on the rest of nature. Moreover, the fear that there is insufficient cropland to meet the needs of expanding populations for food and fiber has historically been a major factor in the debate over population, resources, and the environment. It was, for instance, Malthus's original concern regarding the limits to growth.

U.S. Trends

Figure 6.1 shows U.S. trends from 1910 to 2004 in the amount of cropland harvested (*I*), population (*P*), and affluence (*A*) as measured by gross domestic product (GDP) per capita, and the GDP, that is, *PA*.[4]

Indexed so that the 1910 level equals 1, in 2004, the amount of cropland (I_f), population (P_f), affluence (A_f), and GDP ($P_f A_f$) were 0.96, 3.18, 6.63, and 21.07, respectively (see table 6.1). In other words, although the population increased 218 percent, affluence by 563

Table 6.1
LONG-TERM CHANGES IN CROPLAND (I), POPULATION (P), AFFLUENCE (A), TECHNOLOGY (T) AND GDP (PA)

Indicator	Area	Period	Population (P_f)[a]	Affluence (A_f)[a]	GDP (P_fA_f)[a]	Impacts (I_f)[a]	Technological Factor (T_f)[a,b]	Technological Change $(\Delta T,$ in $\%)$[c]
Area harvested	United States	1910–2004	3.18	6.63	21.07	0.96	0.046	−95.4
Cropland	World	1961–2001	2.00	2.13	4.26	1.13	0.265	−73.5
Cropland	World	1700–2001	10.06	9.84	98.97	5.82	0.059	−94.1
Cropland	World	1950–2001	2.44	2.86	6.99	1.32	0.189	−81.1

a. Values at the end of the period relative to values at the beginning of the period. b. Calculated as $I_f/(P_fA_f)$, as given in the previous two columns. c. Calculated using equation 5-6 (see last note in chapter 5); the negative sign indicates a decline in impact due to technological change.

SOURCES: Angus Maddison, *The World Economy: Historical Statistics* (Paris: OECD, 2003), www.ggdc.net/~maddison (accessed July 30, 2005); Colin McEvedy and Richard Jones, *Atlas of World Population History* (New York: Penguin, 1978); USBCC, *Historical Statistics of the United States, Colonial Times to 1970* (Washington, DC: GPO, 1975), and various issues; FAO, *FAOSTAT 2005*, http://apps.fao.org; USDA, "USDA Data on Major Land Uses," www.ers.usda.gov/data/Major LandUses/spreadsheets/c1910_00.xls (accessed December 20, 2005); USDA, "Agricultural Statistics 2005," pp. IX–17.

percent, and GDP by 2,000 percent, the amount of cropland harvested stayed more or less constant during the past century. (It actually declined by 4 percent during this period, as shown in figure 6.1.)

However, if the prognostication that the T-factor (or technology-factor, defined as the impact per unit of GDP) ought to increase (i.e., the impact should worsen) progressively with time is correct, I_f should be greater than P_f if not $P_f A_f$.[5] Instead, T_f, calculated as $I_f/P_f A_f$, rather than going up, declined substantially during this period (table 6.1). Using the IPAT formulation, the T-factor declined to 0.05. That is, technological change since 1910 reduced the impacts of agriculture from what it otherwise would have been by a factor of 20 (= 1/0.05), as measured by the amount of cropland that would have been harvested. (This calculation does not consider whether the proportion of land accounting for net exports may have changed since 1910.)[6] Thus, technology, far from making matters worse, in fact reduced impacts substantially, and it enabled U.S. agriculture to feed a much larger domestic population, feed it better, and still have a surplus for export or aid.

Without the U.S. surplus, global food supplies would have been reduced. Unless those reductions were made up, global food prices would have increased, which would have priced many poorer individuals and households out of the food market. In turn, that would have led to greater hunger and undernourishment. However, efforts to make up any shortfall that would be created due to any loss in the U.S. surplus would have resulted in cultivation of marginal lands, which would have increased environmental degradation.[7]

Assuming that the demand for and consumption of food is determined only by population size, then absent technological change since 1910, the United States would have needed to harvest at least 1,007 million acres to provide the same quantity of crops as were produced in 2004 as opposed to the approximately 305 million acres that were actually harvested that year.[8] The additional 702 million acres that would have gone under the plow exceeds the entire area of the United States east of the Mississippi.

Moreover, using the 1997 Natural Resources Inventory,[9] I estimate total U.S. potential cropland at 628 million acres.[10] To gain yet another perspective on the magnitude of habitat saved from conversion to cropland by agricultural technological change since 1910, consider that the total amount of specially protected land and habitat reserved in the United States (i.e., national parks, wildlife refuges, and wilderness areas) totaled 217 million acres in 1999.

In other words, had there been no technological change since 1910, it is improbable that the United States could have produced as much food as it does today even if it had sacrificed much of its habitat, forests, and biodiversity in the bargain. It would, for instance, have made *in situ* conservation virtually impossible except in areas that had virtually no agricultural potential. Thus, ironically, although productivity-enhancing agricultural technologies are responsible for numerous environmental problems (such as excess nitrogen, phosphorus, and pesticides in rivers and other water bodies), nothing else has saved more habitat and forests than these very same technologies.[11]

Remarkably, these actions resulted not from any specific government mandate to explicitly reduce habitat conversion but from indirect factors including the following: (a) economic and legal institutions that allowed both farmers and would-be innovators to profit from any risks taken to improve their productivity, (b) public and private investments in research and development of new and improved technologies, (c) the extension system that was critical to the spread and adoption of new technology, and (d) farmers who are better educated and trained in the agricultural sciences. In fact, to the extent government involvement consists of direct subsidies or tinkering with markets, it may well have increased cropland harvested.[12] Indeed, past government subsidies may well have increased the amount of cultivated land, as well as contributed to the historical overuse of pesticides and fertilizers. For instance, Roger E. Meiners and Andrew P. Morris note that for a period in the 1950s the U.S. Department of Agriculture began giving dieldrin away free for the eradication of fire ants, after some farmers and states resisted its use because of its poisonous effects on livestock and, possibly, human health.[13]

Global Trends

The relative reduction in cropland with respect to population, affluence, or their product and the resulting environmental benefit is not merely a U.S. phenomenon. It is also a global phenomenon, as shown in figure 6.2.[14]

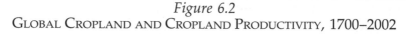

Figure 6.2
GLOBAL CROPLAND AND CROPLAND PRODUCTIVITY, 1700–2002

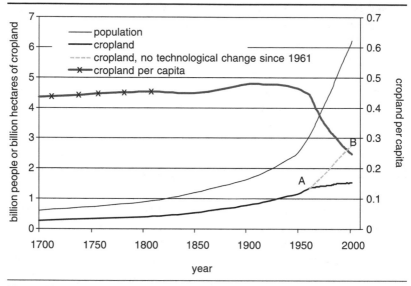

NOTE: AB = cropland needed if no technological change since 1961.

SOURCES: Indur M. Goklany, "Strategies to Enhance Adaptability: Technological Change, Economic Growth, and Free Trade," *Climate Change* 30 (1995): 427–44; Indur M. Goklany, "Meeting Global Food Needs: The Environmental Trade-Offs Between Increasing Land Conversion and Land Productivity," *Technology* 6 (1999): 107–30; FAO, *FAOSTAT 2005*, http://apps.fao.org (accessed July 12, 2005).

Table 6.1 shows that relative to their 1950 levels, although population (P_f), affluence (A_f), and GDP ($P_f A_f$) increased 2.44-fold, 2.86-fold, and 6.99-fold, respectively, global cropland in 2001 increased 1.32-fold because the T-factor (T_f) improved to about 0.19.[15] Thus, using the IPAT formulation, the global environmental impact of agriculture between 1950 and 2001 (in terms of cropland usage) would have been more than five times higher had it not been for the technological change that occurred since 1950. A good deal of the credit, of course, goes to the Green Revolution in developing countries, particularly Asia and Latin America.[16] Notably, the foregoing calculation underestimates the improvement in technology because it does not account for the increase in the average daily intake of calories and protein. Between 1961 and 2001, they increased 24 percent and 21 percent, respectively.[17]

Perhaps even more important is that those improvements occurred despite a 44 percent decline in cropland per capita between 1961 and 2002 (see figure 6.2).

Assuming that there were no improvements between 1950 and 2002 in the food and protein intake levels in the average global inhabitant's diet and that technology (i.e., average productivity) was frozen at 1950 levels, then at least another 3.33 billion acres would have been needed to feed the world's population in 2002, an area greater than Brazil, India, and South Africa combined.[18] That would have increased global cropland requirements to *at least* 7.14 billion acres. By contrast, actual cropland is currently estimated at 3.81 billion acres.[19] The earlier calculation underestimates cropland requirements because the majority of the best and most productive lands are probably already under cultivation.

Potential global cropland (excluding China) has been estimated at 8.25 billion acres, of which about 2.1 billion acres may be forested and 0.56 billion acres were in protected status as of the mid 1990s.[20] Therefore, the requirement for 7.05 billion acres of cropland could have been met in theory, but only at a heavy cost in terms of land conversion and loss of forests and other habitat, as well as a substantial increase in global threats to biological diversity.

To further place in context the magnitude of habitat saved from conversion since 1950, consider that in 2004 only 3.72 billion acres worldwide were reserved in fully and partially protected areas.[21] Clearly, technological change has been crucial to conserving habitat and biodiversity globally.

A longer-term view shows that between 1700 and 2002, the global cropland increased by 481 percent while population and affluence increased by 918 percent and 890 percent, respectively (figure 6.2). As a result, cropland per capita, which is estimated to have been 0.43 hectare in 1700, has dropped to 0.25 hectare today, its lowest level ever; it peaked in the early 20th century at 0.48 hectare per capita.

Some Neo-Malthusian observers have bemoaned such drops in cropland per capita, claiming they presage an impending shortage of cropland.[22] But this decline has not been accompanied by declines in available food supplies per capita. Instead, per capita food supplies for many regions have actually increased. India and China are cases in point. As shown in chapter 2, available food supplies per capita in those two countries—once prime candidates for Malthusian famines—have never been higher in recorded history. Therefore, the current decline in cropland per capita is correctly viewed as a victory for both humankind and the rest of nature: humans now meet their needs with less land—the very essence of natural resource conservation.

The magnitude of this achievement can perhaps be gauged by estimating what food supplies might have been in 2002 if cropland and population levels had grown to their 2002 levels but agricultural productivity had been frozen at 1961 levels. Table 6.2, which displays the results of such a calculation for China, India, the developing world, and the world, shows that had it not been for increased productivity (and technological change), people worldwide would have been at below-starvation diets, well below levels needed to maintain essential bodily functions.

One important factor in reducing malnourishment worldwide was the relatively large increase in agricultural productivity in richer countries. During the past few decades their food production has outstripped the increase in demand. Much of the resulting crop surpluses are transferred voluntarily—through either trade or aid—to developing countries. Such trade (or aid) keeps global food prices down and reduces the level of hunger and undernourishment worldwide.

The effect of affluence on agricultural productivity was discussed in chapter 2 and is also evident in figure 6.3, which shows that cereal yields increase significantly with wealth, as measured by per capita GDP.[23] This is because richer nations can afford to acquire, operate, and maintain more productive technologies, such as adequate fertilizers and methods to reduce crop losses to pests and weeds. Such crop losses are estimated to reduce net crop production by 42 percent worldwide.[24] This has helped countries located outside of the tropics, most of whom are developed countries, add forest cover in recent decades. According to the Food and Agriculture Organization's *Global Forest Resource Assessment 2000*, those countries added 29 million hectares (about 72 million acres) to their forests from 1990 to 2000.[25] However, that assessment estimated that forest cover in tropical and subtropical countries declined by 123 million hectares because the growth in agricultural productivity was outstripped by

Table 6.2
CHANGES IN POPULATION, CROPLAND AREA, AND FOOD SUPPLIES PER CAPITA, 1961–2002

Area	Changes from 1961 to 2002 (%)			Food Supplies/Capita/Day (kcal/capita/day) in 2002	
	Population	Cropland	Food supplies per capita	Actual (with technology change)	Estimated (without technology change)
World	102	13	24	2,804	1,387
Developing countries	133	31	38	2,666	1,142
China	94	46	80	2,951	1,524
India	132	6	19	2,459	1,060

SOURCES: Updated from Indur M. Goklany, "Agricultural Technology and the Precautionary Principle," in *Environmental Policy and Agriculture: Conflicts, Prospects, and Implications*, ed. Roger E. Meiners and Bruce Yandle (Lanham, MD: Rowman and Littlefield, 2003), using data from FAO, *FAOSTAT 2005*, http://apps.fao.org, and World Resource Institute, EarthTrends database, www.wri.org (accessed June 23, 2005).

Figure 6.3
CEREAL YIELD VS. INCOME, 1975–2003

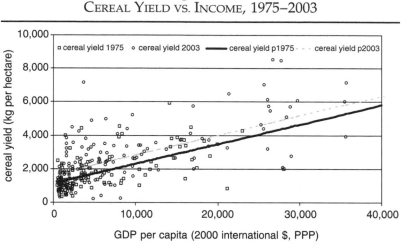

SOURCE: Based on data from World Bank, *World Development Indicators,* http://devdata.worldbank.org/dataonline (accessed July 12, 2005).

increases in food demand due to higher population growth rates, and, outside of some nations in sub-Saharan Africa, greater wealth.

Figure 6.3 also shows that the cereal yield curve has shifted upward with time because of new—and increased use of existing, but previously underused—technologies. However, not every country has sufficient land or land that is sufficiently productive. But what a country cannot produce, it can purchase through trade if it is wealthy enough to do so. Not surprisingly, therefore, figure 6.4 shows that daily food supplies per capita across countries also increase significantly with wealth as well as time. The rise in the curve from 1975 to 2002 in figure 6.4 indicates that, over time, technological change has made it possible for poorer populations to have access to more food. In fact, between 1961 and 2004, global cereal yields increased by about 150 percent between 1,353 kilograms per hectare (kg/ha) to 3,330 kg/ha,[26] which helps explains why, despite increases in global food supplies per capita and population, cropland per capita actually declined and habitat conversion was limited.

Thus, in the absence of technological change and economic growth, developing nations would have had lower food supplies, and their populations would have suffered from greater hunger and

Figure 6.4
FOOD SUPPLIES PER CAPITA VS. INCOME, 1975–2002

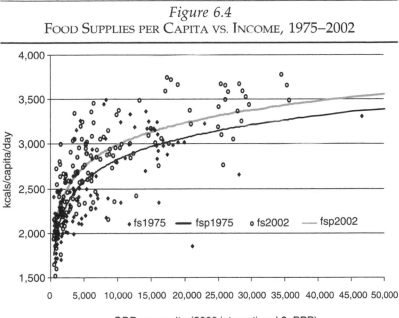

GDP per capita (2000 international $, PPP)

SOURCES: Based on data from World Resources Institute, EarthTrends, www.wri.org (accessed June 23, 2005); World Bank, *World Development Indicators*, http://devdata.worldbank.org/dataonline (accessed July 12, 2005).

undernourishment, poorer health, higher mortality rates, and lower life expectancies. In other words, affluence and technological change have, so far, helped stave off Malthusian corrections, such as famine and disease.[27] As recently as 1959–61, an estimated 30 million (or more) perished in China's last famine.[28] Nothing comparable has occurred there since then, despite a doubling of the population.[29] Moreover, cereal yields would have been lower and deforestation would have been higher.

However, although cropland is probably the single most important indicator of agriculture's impact on the environment, it does not capture the full range of those impacts, such as pesticide residues in tissues of human beings, avian species, and aquatic species; excess nitrates and phosphorus; and reductions in dissolved oxygen levels in water.

Nevertheless, the experience of developed countries indicates that with technology and wealth, these problems might be surmountable if a long-term effort is undertaken to reverse them. Trends for various pollution indicators related to agricultural sources in the United States and Europe show recent reductions in their rates of growth, if not outright improvements.[30]

Since the 1960s and 1970s, partly because of pressure from environmental laws, concentrations of many organochlorine pesticides, such as DDT, toxaphene, dieldrin, and chlordane, have declined in human adipose tissues and fresh water fish, and concentrations in some avian species have dropped substantially. For example, total DDT, chlordane, and dieldrin in whole fish in the United States dropped exponentially from the late 1960s and early 1970s through the 1990s, with a half-life of 7 years for DDT, 11–13 years for chlordane, and 30 years for dieldrin.[31] Between 1974 and 1996, levels of various pesticide metabolites and residues (DDE [a derivative of DDT], dieldrin, mirex, and HCB) in herring gull eggs from each of the five Great Lakes of North America declined by more than 80 percent.[32] Consistent with those findings, between 1980–88, DDT in fall-run coho salmon declined 40 percent and 60 percent in Lakes Erie and Michigan, respectively.[33] Between 1966 and 1985, levels of DDE in waterfowl dropped from 0.70 to 0.09 parts per million (ppm)[34] in the Atlantic flyway, from 0.65 to 0.05 ppm in the Pacific flyway, and from 0.15 and 0.25 ppm to below detection levels in the Mississippi and Central flyways.[35] Partly because of such reductions, some species that were once endangered in the United States by those chemicals, such as bald eagles and peregrine falcons, are now rebounding and have been dropped from the endangered species list.[36]

Such improvements are not limited to the United States. They also extend to the other richer nations. For example, between the 1960s and 1990s, studies on various aquatic and avian species in the Baltic show that total DDT (including its metabolites) declined 8–12 percent per year for herring and cod and 11 percent per year for guillemot eggs.[37]

All those improvements have also reduced pesticide residues entering the human food chain. Monitoring of pesticide residues on various food commodities in the United States indicates that between 1973 and 1986, 3 percent of the samples tested violated pesticide residue standards while between 1987 and 1998 that level had dropped to 1 percent.[38]

Perhaps most important, DDT and related compounds have declined in human adipose tissue and breast milk. DDT in human adipose tissue dropped by 80 percent between 1970 and 1983.[39] Similarly, concentrations of *o,p'*- and *p,p'*-DDT—two different forms of DDT—declined from 1.066 mg/kg of human adipose tissue to 0.066 mg/kg in Canadian citizens.[40] DDT concentrations in similar tissue also dropped by an order of magnitude in the Netherlands. Also, based on a review of about a hundred studies, Daniel Smith, who is with the Environmental Health Investigations Branch, California Department of Health Services, concludes that DDT levels in human breast milk declined 11–21 percent per year in the United States and Canada since 1975, and it declined 9–13 percent per year in Western Europe. Notably, Smith's analysis suggests that DDT levels in human breast milk have also declined substantially since the early to mid 1970s in parts of Asia, Middle East, Latin America, and Eastern Europe, although data for these regions are more sparse.[41]

Water quality in the richer countries has also improved for other agriculture-related pollutants. From 1975–76 to 1996–97, violation rates in the United States for water quality standards for dissolved oxygen[42] declined from 5.5 percent to 1.5 percent of all rivers and streams in which measurements were taken.[43] But for fecal coliform (FC), they rebounded to 31.5 percent in 1994–95 after having declined from 34 percent in 1975–76 to 20.5 percent in 1990–91.[44] However, because water-borne disease rates have dropped over the long term and are currently at relatively low levels (see section in this chapter), the significance of this trend (or lack of it) for public health is unclear.

There has been a general improvement in other water quality indicators that are potentially sensitive to agricultural inputs and practices. Nitrogen fertilizer usage in the United States in 1996–98 was 8 percent above the 1978–80 level, which is a marked improvement over the previous 18-year period during which it increased 195 percent despite increases in population and GDP of 18 percent and 56 percent, respectively.[45] In the 1980s, the number of water monitoring stations with "extreme" concentrations of nitrates (in excess of 3 mg/L) dropped about 25 percent.[46] Moreover, large investments in sewage treatment plants and limitations on phosphate content of detergents in the 1960s and 1970s supplemented by point source controls and an 18 percent drop in phosphorus fertilizer usage since 1978–80 have led to widespread reductions in phosphorus loadings of water bodies.[47] As a result, between 1975–76 and 1996–97, violation rates for water quality standards for total phosphorus declined from 5.0 percent to 1.5 percent.[48]

Because of those efforts and large investments in point sources by and large during the past few decades, there has been substantial improvement in the condition of rivers in the developed world. Dissolved oxygen levels have slowly but steadily improved. The number of species in the sediment of the Rhine, one of Western Europe's major rivers, increased from 27 in 1971 to 97 in 1997.

Thus, we see that recent improvements in the T-factor, even for those agricultural impacts, have outstripped the increases in overall economic growth. Similar improvements are occurring in many Organisation for Economic Co-operation and Development (OECD) nations.[49]

Traditional Air Pollution

The impacts of poor air quality were major factors in galvanizing public support for environmental cleanup not only in the United States but also around the world. Because long-term national data are unavailable for "primary" indicators of those impacts, for example, mortality (i.e., death) rates, incidence of sickness (i.e., morbidity) or visibility, or even "secondary" indicators such as concentrations of air pollutants inhaled by a representative sample of the public, I will examine trends in air quality impacts using a variety of surrogate air quality indicators.

U.S. Trends

This section presents U.S. trends in the traditional air pollutants, namely, particulate matter (PM), sulfur dioxide (SO_2), nitrogen oxide (NO_x), carbon monoxide (CO), and ozone (O_3) or its precursor volatile organic compounds (VOC), using three sets of indicators.[50] The first set, national emissions, were obtained from emissions trends reports from the Environmental Protection Agency (EPA). The reports provide data from 1900 onward for SO_2, NO_x, and VOC and from 1940 for PM and CO. The second set, based on measurements of outdoor air quality, were developed by stringing together national-level averages for each pollutant using data in EPA (or predecessor agencies') reports on air quality trends, Council on Environmental Quality's annual reports (*Environmental Quality*), and the *Statistical Abstracts of the United States*. These publications usually provide data for a few years at a time. By combining several of these series, it is possible to construct a longer series, going back to 1957 for total suspended particulates (TSP) in the ambient air and 1962 for SO$_2$. But for the other pollutants, the data are of more recent origin. The third set, "indoor" air quality, was derived from 1940 through 2002 using, as a crude proxy, residential combustion emissions per occupied household.[51]

In order to better appreciate factors behind the ups and downs in long-term trends in U.S. air quality, it is useful to identify two milestones for each of the pollutants. The first milestone is the "time of federalization" [t(F)], which indicates when the federal government asserted its authority to control the air pollutant under consideration. In theory, at least, one might expect a greater degree of control following t(F). For CO and VOC, both motor vehicle-related pollutants, t(F) dates to 1967, the year when federal requirements for automobile exhausts first went into effect. For the other traditional pollutants, t(F) dates to 1971 because the federal Clean Air Act of 1970, which essentially put the federal government in charge of air pollution control in the United States, was enacted on the very last day of 1970.[52]

The second milestone is—in the parlance of the environmental transition hypothesis—the "period of perception" [p(P)]. This period is the one during which the general public and policymakers begin to recognize or perceive that a substance in the air is a pollutant that needs to be controlled because of its adverse effects, real or otherwise, on the public's health and welfare. Before p(P), one should not expect governmental or voluntary private measures to specifically control that substance. Thus, one ought not to be surprised if air quality indicators worsen before p(P). However, as will be shown shortly, improvements might well occur before then because of either purely economic factors or chance.

At least as early as the beginning of this century, smoke and dust, both composed of PM, were synonymous with air pollution. Hence, p(P) for PM probably dates to 1900 or even earlier.[53] But for the other "traditional" air pollutants, the notion that they could also be detrimental to human health and welfare was accepted much later. SO$_2$ was not generally considered to be an air pollutant in need of control until after the fatal 1948 Donora, Pennsylvania, episode, which was associated with 18 deaths in a population of 14,000, and the December 1952 London episode, which was associated with 4,000 deaths. Thus, p(P) for SO$_2$ can be fixed at around 1950.

The story with regard to CO is more complex. CO was perceived to be a problem indoors because of the publicized cases of CO poisoning that would occur periodically.[54] However, it was only after automobiles became more prevalent that it was recognized to be a problem outdoors.

With respect to O_3, VOCs, and NO_x, it was not until the mid 1950s that Californians recognized that Los Angeles' legendary smog problem was due to O_3 (and other oxidants) formed by the reaction of VOC and NO_x emissions as they were "cooked" in the presence of sunlight. Until the late 1960s and early 1970s most air pollution authorities outside California, however, believed that photochemical smog problems were limited to California because of its unique mix of geography, climate, and high automobile emissions. In fact, they were convinced otherwise only after wider air pollution monitoring (instituted pursuant to the Clean Air Act of 1970) measured violations of the national primary (i.e., public health-related) ambient air quality standards for oxidants. Thus, p(P) for O_3, VOC, and NO_x dates to the 1950s for California but the 1960s (or later) elsewhere.

Trends in Emissions

Between 1900 and 2003, U.S emissions of SO_2, VOC, and NO_x peaked several times and are now generally declining (figure 6.5a).[55] At the end of that period, they stood at 1.60, 1.89, and 7.94 times, respectively, their 1900 levels, while population (P_f), affluence (A_f) and GDP (P_fA_f) were at 3.82, 8.26, and 31.58, respectively (figure 6.5b and table 6.3). In 2003, levels of CO were at 1.14 of their 1940 levels,[56] while P_f, A_f, and P_fA_f were at 2.20, 4.53, and 9.98, respectively. In 2002, PM less than 10 micrometers (PM-10) were 0.29 times their 1940 value[57] compared to 2.18, 4.46, and 9.72 for P_f, A_f, and P_fA_f, respectively. In all cases over these time periods, the improvements in technology (T) outstripped any increases in GDP (i.e., PA) or, with the exception of NO_x, its individual components, population, and affluence (table 6.3).

Notably, in 2000—one of the worst years for wildfires—both PM-10 and CO levels were at their highest levels since 1988, another banner year for wildfires. But for such fires, emission reductions for those two pollutants would have been significantly higher. In 2000, more than 16 percent of the national CO emissions were because of wildfires.

The swings in emissions for the various pollutants can be better understood when one considers the various factors that might determine the technologies employed in the processes and activities that

132

Figure 6.5a
SO₂, NOₓ, AND VOC EMISSIONS, 1900–2003

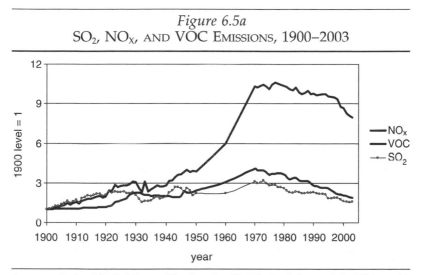

SOURCES: Indur M. Goklany, *Clearing the Air: The Real Story of the War on Air Pollution* (Washington, DC: Cato Institute, 1999); EPA, *National Air Pollutant Emission Trends, 1900–1998* (Research Triangle Park, NC: Office of Air Quality Planning and Standards, 2000); EPA, *1970–2002 Average Annual Emissions, All Criteria Pollutants*, www.epa.gov/ttn/chief/trends/ (accessed August 13, 2005); David Brzezinksi and Harvey Michaels, EPA, personal communications, Ann Arbor, MI, August 2005; USBOC, *Statistical Abstract of the United States 2006* (Washington, DC: GPO, 2006); USBOC, *Historical Statistics of the United States, Colonial Times to 1970* (Washington, DC: GPO, 1975); Bureau of Economic Affairs, *National Income and Products Accounts,* table 1.1.6, www.bea.gov/bea/dn/nipaweb/SelectTable.asp?Popular = Y (accessed August 13, 2005).

produce emissions. Those factors include times of federalization and periods of perception because these milestones could, at least in theory, affect emission trends. Also, it is useful to examine emissions per gross national product and emissions per capita because in a society where economy and population are expanding, these measures serve as *leading* environmental indicators. Until a sustained decline in those leading indicators occurs, there will be no eventual downturn in emissions, though air quality may well improve. Accordingly, an examination of whether—and when—these leading indicators peaked, indicates the year by which "cleanup" efforts had commenced (at the latest).[58] Especially significant are trends in national emissions per GDP (E/GDP), which, as noted in chapter 5,

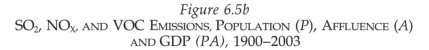

Figure 6.5b
SO₂, NOₓ, AND VOC EMISSIONS, POPULATION (*P*), AFFLUENCE (*A*)
AND GDP *(PA)*, 1900–2003

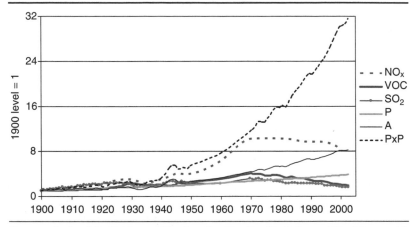

SOURCE: Indur M. Goklany, *Clearing the Air: The Real Story of the War on Air Pollution* (Washington, DC: Cato Institute, 1999); EPA, *National Air Pollutant Emission Trends, 1900–1998* (Research Triangle Park, NC: Office of Air Quality Planning and Standards, 2000); EPA, *1970–2002 Average Annual Emissions, All Criteria Pollutants,* www.epa.gov/ttn/chief/trends/ (accessed August 13, 2005); David Brzezinksi and Harvey Michaels, EPA, personal communications, Ann Arbor, MI, August 2005; USBOC, *Statistical Abstract of the United States 2006* (Washington, DC: GPO, 2006); USBOC, *Historical Statistics of the United States, Colonial Times to 1970* (Washington, DC: GPO, 1975); Bureau of Economic Affairs, *National Income and Products Accounts,* table 1.1.6, www.bea.gov/bea/dn/nipaweb/SelectTable.asp?Popular = Y (accessed August 13, 2005).

is an aggregate measure of the net effect of technology on all of society's emissions-producing activities. E/GDP for PM-10 and SO₂, for instance, may increase if coal replaces natural gas, or it may decrease if old processes are replaced by new, more efficient technologies because of either economic factors or regulatory requirements. Alternatively, E/GDP may change with the evolution of the economy, for example, from an agricultural to an industrial to a post-industrial service and information economy.

Figure 6.6 shows emissions, emissions per GDP, and emissions per capita from 1900 to 2003, as well as the t(F) and p(P) for SO₂. This figure shows that emissions per GDP peaked in the 1920s for

Table 6.3

LONG-TERM CHANGES IN THE UNITED STATES FOR IMPACTS (I) OF VARIOUS AIR POLLUTION INDICATORS, POPULATION (P), AFFLUENCE (A), TECHNOLOGY (T) AND GDP (PA)

Indicator	Period	Population $(P_f)^a$	Affluence $(A_f)^a$	GDP $(P_f A_f)^a$	Impacts $(I_f)^a$	Technological Factor $(T_f)^{ab}$	Technological Change $(\Delta T$, in $\%)^c$
		Outdoor Air Pollution (annual emissions)					
SO$_2$	1900–2003	3.82	8.26	31.58	1.60	0.051	−94.9
VOC	1900–2003	3.82	8.26	31.58	1.89	0.060	−94.0
NO$_x$	1900–2003	3.82	8.26	31.58	7.94	0.251	−74.9
PM-10	1940–2002	2.18	4.46	9.72	0.29	0.030	−97.0
CO	1940–2003	2.20	4.53	9.98	1.14	0.114	−88.6
Lead	1970–2000	1.38	1.88	2.60	0.02	0.007	−99.3
		Indoor Air Pollution in the Home (emissions/occupied home)					
SO$_2$	1940–2002	2.18	4.46	9.72	0.02	0.002	−99.8
VOC	1940–2002	2.18	4.46	9.72	0.14	0.014	−98.6
NO$_x$	1940–2002	2.18	4.46	9.72	0.39	0.040	−96.0
PM-10	1940–2002	2.18	4.46	9.72	0.05	0.005	−99.5
CO	1940–2002	2.18	4.46	9.72	0.05	0.005	−99.5

a. Values at the end of the period relative to values at the beginning of the period. b. Calculated as $I_f/(P_f A_f)$, as given in the previous two columns. c. Calculated using equation 5-6 (see last note in chapter 5); the negative sign indicates a decline in impact due to technological change.

SOURCES: See text.

Figure 6.6
SO₂ EMISSIONS, EMISSIONS/GDP, AND EMISSIONS/CAPITA, 1900–2003

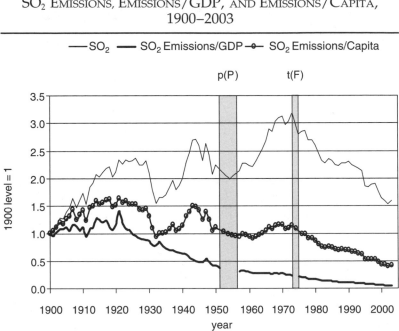

SOURCES: Indur M. Goklany, *Clearing the Air: The Real Story of the War on Air Pollution* (Washington, DC: Cato Institute, 1999); EPA, *National Air Pollutant Emission Trends, 1900–1998* (Research Triangle Park, NC: Office of Air Quality Planning and Standards, 2000); EPA, *1970–2002 Average Annual Emissions, All Criteria Pollutants,* www.epa.gov/ttn/chief/trends/ (accessed August 13, 2005); David Brzezinksi and Harvey Michaels, EPA, personal communications, Ann Arbor, MI, August 2005; USBOC, *Statistical Abstract of the United States 2006* (Washington, DC: GPO, 2006); USBOC, *Historical Statistics of the United States, Colonial Times to 1970* (Washington, DC: GPO, 1975); Bureau of Economic Affairs, *National Income and Products Accounts,* table 1.1.6, www.bea.gov/bea/dn/nipaweb/SelectTable.asp?Popular = Y (accessed August 13, 2005).

SO₂ and have been declining steadily since then. That is, "cleanup" apparently commenced decades before federalization. A similar pattern is also evident for the other traditional pollutants. Emissions per GDP peaked in the 1930s for both VOC and NOₓ and in the 1940s (or earlier) for PM-10 and CO. Notably, except for PM-10, for each pollutant E/GDP commenced declining substantially before the corresponding p(P), which indicates that market-driven techno-logical change was key to these preregulatory reductions.

Steady declines in E/GDP following their peaks eventually reduced total emissions, but not until after the periods of perception had been completed. Emissions peaked in 1950 for PM-10, 1970 or earlier for VOC and CO, and 1973 for SO_2 (see figure 6.5a).[59] NO_x emissions peaked in the late 1970s.

Trends in Outdoor Air Quality

Outdoor (ambient) concentrations are much better indicators of the public health impacts of air pollutants than emissions. In recognition of this, public health-related standards are almost invariably specified in terms of the ambient concentration at any point on the ground, although, given the relatively small amount of time any individual spends outdoors at any one fixed spot, it is very difficult to relate such measured outdoor levels to public health impacts.

Composite nationwide air quality data from the EPA and its predecessor agencies show that ambient air quality for each of the traditional air pollutants (i.e., PM, which is also an indicator for soot and smoke, SO_2, O_3, CO, NO_x, and lead) has been improving for almost as long as such data are available. Figure 6.7 illustrates this for SO_2 from 1962 to 2000; SO_2 peaked in 1963.[60] Similarly, nationwide data for PM show it declining continually from 1957, the first year for which such data were available; CO data from the 1960s onward indicate it has been improving since 1970, if not earlier; and O_3 and NO_x data from 1974 onward show they had peaked by the late 1970s.

For the pollutants of greatest concern before federalization—O_3 and VOC in California and SO_2 and PM everywhere—the improvements in outdoor air quality began before federalization, and they have continued since. The improvements were especially pronounced in urban areas, which traditionally have had the worst pollution problems. Particulate levels, which had been in decline at least since the 1940s, fell an additional 15 percent just between 1957 and 1970 (based on data from 60 cities). SO_2 declined 40 percent between 1962 and 1969 (based on data from 21 cities) (see figure 6.7).

Consider trends in Pittsburgh, Pennsylvania, once synonymous with smoke around the world. Dustfall in Pittsburgh, measured at 58 tonnes per square km per month in 1923–24, had fallen by an order of magnitude by the mid 1970s. Total suspended particulate

Figure 6.7
SO₂, AIR QUALITY, 1962–2000
(mean annual average)

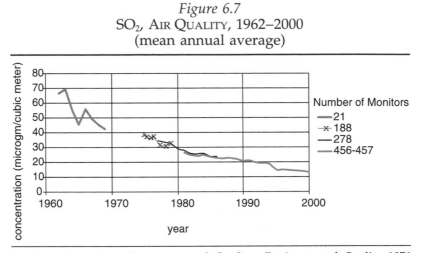

SOURCES: Council on Environmental Quality, *Environmental Quality 1971* (Washington, DC: CEQ, 1971); USBOC, *Statistical Abstract of the United States 1981* (Washington, DC: GPO, 1981); EPA, *National Air Quality and Emissions Report, 1996* (Research Triangle Park, NC: Office of Air Quality Planning and Standards, 1998); *National Air Quality and Emissions Report, 2003: Special Studies Edition,* table A-11, www.epa.gov/air/airtrends/aqtrnds03/ (accessed August 15, 2005).

(TSP) levels (annual arithmetic averages) declined 60 percent between 1959 and 1971 from 275 micrograms per cubic meter ($\mu g/m^3$) to 110 $\mu g/m^3$. By 1993, the highest annual reading in Allegheny County, where Pittsburgh is located, had dropped to 56 $\mu g/m^3$. Since that time, TSP has been replaced by PM-10 and PM-2.5 as a measure of particulate matter in the atmosphere, but the downward trend continues. The highest (weighted) annual mean for PM-10 in the Pittsburgh metropolitan area dropped by 7.5 percent between 1993 and 1999.[61]

Similarly, New York City was the site of several killer air pollution episodes in the 1950s and even the 1960s. Daily TSP levels in New York, which were as high as 1,000 $\mu g/m^3$ during one November 1953 episode, declined to 280 $\mu g/m^3$ in 1972 and below 207 $\mu g/m^3$ in 1993— an overall reduction of about 80 percent. In addition, between 1993 and 1999, peak levels for the weighted annual means in the metropolitan area for PM-10 dropped by 6.2 percent. Concurrently, daily SO₂ levels in New York declined from an estimated 2,200 $\mu g/m^3$ during the 1953 episode to 392 $\mu g/m^3$ in 1972 and below 120 $\mu g/m^3$ in 2000—an overall reduction of 95 percent.[62] Between 1963 and 1972, after peaking in 1964, peak annual SO_2 levels dropped from about 570 $\mu g/m^3$ in 1964 to about 81 $\mu g/m^3$ in 1972 mainly because of fuel switching and sulfur-in-fuel requirements. In 2000, they were below 34 $\mu g/m^3$.[63]

Also, photochemical smog—a problem first and foremost in the Los Angeles area—had been improving there since the mid 1950s. However, because p(P) for smog arrived later elsewhere, nationwide "composite" ozone and oxidant air quality levels peaked in the mid to late 1970s. With respect to the other traditional pollutants, ambient levels have been dropping since the mid to late 1960s for CO and the late 1970s for NO_x.[64]

Because of all these improvements in outdoor air quality, United States air quality, by and large, is better now than it has been in several decades.

Trends in Indoor Air Quality

Seventy percent of the average person's time is spent indoors at home (89 percent for the average homemaker).[65] Therefore, all else being equal, indoor air pollution levels in the home ought to be even better indicators for the public health impacts of air pollution than outdoor air quality. However, since long-term measurements of indoor air pollution levels are unavailable, I have constructed a surrogate indoor air quality indicator from 1940–2002 using EPA's estimates of residential emissions and the U.S. Bureau of the Census data on the number of occupied households.[66]

Based on this indicator, between 1940 and 2002, indoor air levels declined (i.e., air quality improved) 95 percent for PM-10 and CO, 98 percent for SO_2, 61 percent for NO_x, and 86 percent for VOC, as illustrated in figure 6.8.[67] T_f—the technology-factor—for these indoor air pollutants improved by more than two orders of magnitude for SO_2, VOC and PM-10; more than one order of magnitude for VOC; and 96 percent for NO_x (table 6.3).

Interestingly, for all indoor air pollutants, except NO_x, more than 90 percent of the indoor improvements between 1940 and 2000 occurred before 1970, that is, before the passage of the Clean Air Act of 1970. Thus, the major reductions in the public health impact of air pollution preceded the imposition of federal regulations of stationary sources.[68]

Figure 6.8
INDOOR AIR QUALITY, 1940–2002

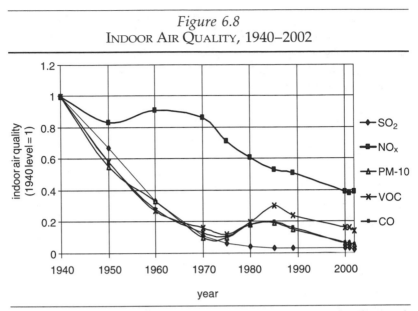

SOURCES: EPA, *National Air Pollutant Emission Trends, 1900–1998* (Research Triangle Park, NC: Office of Air Quality Planning and Standards, 2000); EPA, *1970–2002 Average Annual Emissions, All Criteria Pollutants*, www.epa.gov/ttn/chief/trends/ (accessed August 13, 2005); USBOC, *Statistical Abstract of the United States 1995* (Washington, DC: GPO, 1981), 733; USBOC, *Housing Vacancies and Homeownership*, www.census.gov/hhes/www/housing/hvs/historical/histtab7.html (accessed August 14, 2005).

However, for NO_x, only 23 percent of the reduction preceded federalization. The relatively smaller effect on NO_x was because switching from wood and coal to oil and gas, one of the primary reasons for improvements in PM and SO_2 air quality, has a more modest improvement on NO_x. Moreover, many methods to burn fuel efficiently result in higher temperatures during combustion, which increases NO_x formation.[69] The relatively small increases in indoor levels of PM-10, VOC, and CO were due to an increase in wood burning in response to the 1973 and 1979 oil crises. However, by 1982, usage of wood in households started declining once again.[70] That, combined with technological improvements, helped recommence the long-term declines in indoor levels of those pollutants.

Figure 6.9
U.S. ENERGY USE, 1800–2004

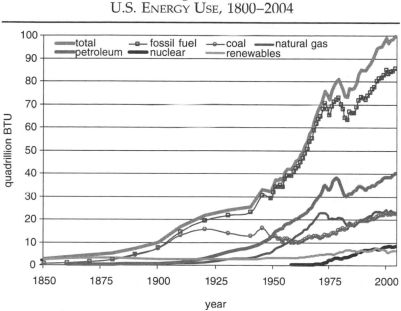

year

SOURCES: USBOC, *Historical Statistics of the United States, Colonial Times to 1970* (Washington, DC: GPO, 1975); U.S. Department of Energy, *Annual Energy Review 2004* (Washington, DC: Energy Information Administration, 2004).

Energy Use and Other Factors Affecting U.S. Air Pollution Trends

The data presented earlier suggest that technological change is generally a far more important determinant of air pollution than either affluence or population. This technological change was driven by various social, economic, and technological developments that gathered steam during the first three decades of this century and then took off in earnest after World War II. These developments ensured that much of the pre-1970 cleanup was voluntary.

Energy consumption, which had been growing steadily during the third quarter of the 19th century, picked up significantly with industrialization during its last quarter, and it accelerated even further in the first two decades of the 20th century (figure 6.9). Much of this growth was due to increased coal combustion in industry, in electrical power generation, and for heating and cooking in an increasingly populous and urbanized society. This era was when smoke and soot were equated to prosperity.[71]

Between 1880 and 1900, total energy use almost doubled from 5.0 quadrillion BTUs (British thermal units) (or Quads [Q]) to 9.6 Q; consumption of coal, which displaced wood as the most-used fuel, more than tripled from 2.0 Q to 6.8 Q. Consequently, coal's contribution to total energy consumption increased from 41 percent to 71 percent. Between 1900 and 1920, both total energy and coal consumption increased about 125 percent to 21.4 Q and 15.5 Q, respectively.[72]

Fortunately, even as coal use was growing, cleaner energy sources were gaining a foothold. Starting around the turn of the century, cleaner energy sources, such as natural gas, oil, and electricity, became increasingly available. And with increasing prosperity, these cleaner energy sources began to displace coal and wood as the fuel of choice, initially in households and commercial establishments. Today, they are favored even by industry. Urbanization, although responsible for many environmental woes, accelerated the process of substitution because higher population densities reduce access to wood and ensure that distribution systems for natural gas and electricity are more cost-effective and economical. Natural gas usage, which had been only 0.2 Q in 1900 and 0.9 Q in 1920, had climbed to 6.0 Q in 1950; in 2004, it stood at 23.0 Q (or 23.1 percent of total energy consumption).[73]

Moreover, soot and smoke, although they might still have signified prosperity, were also recognized by engineers and consumers to be symptoms of incomplete combustion and fuel wastage. New technologies entered the marketplace that not only increased the efficiency of all types of combustion equipment but also reduced soot and smoke. These technologies included more efficient and cleaner furnaces and boilers for homes, businesses, industries, and power plants, as well as diesel locomotives to replace coal-fired ones. Most important, increasing affluence made it possible for individual households and businesses to voluntarily purchase these new technologies because they valued their evident cleanliness and convenience, as well as the possibility of lower fuel bills. Steam locomotives, a notoriously dirty mode of transportation, began to be replaced by diesel locomotives. Thus, except for a rebound associated with World War II, bituminous coal consumption in railways dropped more or less steadily from 120 million tonnes (MT) in

1920 to less than 0.001 MT in 1970.[74] In homes and commercial establishments, coal consumption declined from 117 MT in 1949 to 11.7 MT in 1972 and 4.3 MT in 2004.[75]

The 20th century also saw the ascendancy of the automobile in the United States. In 1900, there was about one motor vehicle for every 10,000 Americans.[76] This number had grown to 3,240 by 1950 and 8,247 by 2001.[77] Greater prosperity not only increased automobile ownership, but also its usage, which pushed petroleum usage from 0.2 Q in 1900 to 13.3 Q in 1950 and 40.1 Q in 2001 (or 40.2 percent of total energy consumption).[78]

Because of all those factors, although total energy use continued to climb, in the 1920s coal usage began a long-term decline that was interrupted, temporarily, by the war effort. In 1950, petroleum consumption surpassed coal, and in 1958, natural gas usage overtook coal. After hitting a minimum in 1959, coal usage began to grow once again to meet the demand for electrical power, but it still lags behind gas and oil usage.

In contrast to the situation during the early phases of industrialization and the early part of the 20th century, the post-1959 growth in coal use was concentrated in rural areas, which, coupled with air pollution controls, softened its air pollution impact on public health. Coal usage hit a minimum in 1959 at 9.5 Q. Although by 2004 it had climbed to 22.4 Q, at 22.5 percent of total energy consumption, coal is no longer the dominant energy source it used to be in the first decades of the 20th century.

Increased usage of oil and diesel also facilitated sulfur-in-fuel regulations. It is easier to desulfurize these fuels and to enforce these regulations because authorities need only focus on a few fuel distributors, and even fewer refiners, rather than millions of consumers. Moreover, desulfurization of natural gas is self-enforcing because it is necessary for marketing; any significant sulfur in the gas corrodes the distribution system and home appliances and creates obnoxious odors.[79]

Because the first improvements came from PM, CO, and SO_2 emission reductions from low-level combustion sources in urban areas, their public health-related benefits were disproportionately high. First, many of these reductions were in the home, which translated into substantial reductions in population exposure to air pollutants both inside (where most people spend most of their time) and around

143

neighborhoods. Second, urban areas have higher population densities. Third, lower-level emissions cause higher concentrations outdoors at ground level.

Much of the resulting gains for public health due to improved outdoor air quality could have been lost because of increased electrical generation and industrial activity. Electrical generation, for instance, increased from 6 billion kilowatt-hours (BkWh) in 1902 to 1,535 BkWh in 1970 and 3,957 BkWh in 2004.[80] Once again technological change came to the rescue. Power plants became more efficient, burning less coal per unit of electricity generated. The energy needed to produce 1 kwh of electricity in fossil fuel-power plants dropped from 121,000 BTU in 1899 to 58,900 BTU in 1913. It dropped even more to 23,400 BTU in 1929 to 10,500 BTU in the mid 1950s. In 1997, the heat rate was 10,300 BTU.[81] Technology enabled these plants to be located farther from consumers and closer to coal mines, reducing population exposure. The plants installed tall stacks, a practice once encouraged by federal agencies but now officially frowned upon in the United States,[82] to reduce ground-level concentrations in their immediate vicinity. Also, control technology improved dramatically for all types of processes. For example, for PM, cyclones (which were 60 percent to 75 percent efficient) were replaced, first, by "high efficiency" multicyclones (85 percent to 95 percent efficient), then by electrostatic precipitators (initially, 90 percent to 97 percent efficient) and, finally, in the 1970s, by baghouses (99 percent or more efficient).[83] Finally, a greater share of electricity is now produced in clean nuclear power plants. That share went from zero in 1955 to 1.4 percent in 1970 and 19.9 percent in 2004.[84]

Those technological improvements were supplemented by the establishment of air pollution control programs at the municipal, county, and state levels, as shown in figure 6.10. However, given that most accounts of the pre-1970 state and local regulations claim that they were badly written and poorly enforced, it is not clear how much credit for these improvements before 1970 can be laid to regulatory intervention. No doubt it is due some credit, but perhaps even more critical was that households, businesses, and industries recognized that they would not only reduce costs (by conserving energy and materials) but also improve the air within their premises, with the added bonus that they would be viewed as good neighbors.

Initially, air pollution control focused on stationary sources. Motor vehicles were first controlled in California only after Los Angeles'

Figure 6.10
GROWTH IN AIR PROGRAMS, 1880–1980

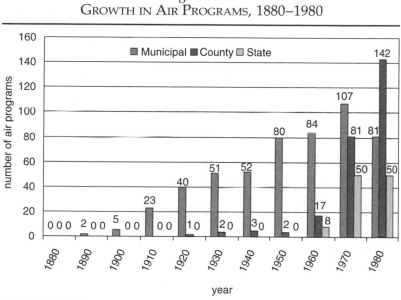

SOURCE: Authur C. Stern, "History of Air Pollution Regulation in the United States," *Journal of the Air Pollution Control Association* 32 (1982): 44–61.

smog problems refused to be solved despite substantial control of industrial and other fixed sources. Following that standard, and threats by other states to promulgate their own standards for vehicles, the federal government established its primacy in regulating tailpipe emissions in the remaining 49 states, beginning with 1968 model year vehicles. Automobile manufacturers welcomed this outcome because they would rather adhere to one more set of standards rather than 49. Moreover, they might have harbored hopes of capturing the regulating agency.[85]

Despite these advances, the general perception was that progress was too little, too late. The Clean Air Act of 1970 was born out of the attempts of President Richard Nixon and Senator Edmond Muskie—both contenders for the 1972 presidential sweepstakes—to outbid each other for the favors of an increasingly environmentally oriented citizenry. Under this act, the federal government asserted responsibility for stationary sources and established the current air pollution control framework, which has survived, with embellish-ments, to the present day. This regulatory structure, with its uncom-promising stance that economics has little, if any, role to play in setting ambient standards or attainment deadlines, could be imposed in a democratic society only if the general public perceived itself to be sufficiently affluent so that cost was of little or no concern or that its cost of compliance—whatever it might be—would be worth it, given that other, more urgent problems (such as infectious and parasitic diseases, safe water, and sanitation) were under suffi-cient control.[86]

The 1970s oil shocks and associated energy price increases further reduced emissions per capita and per unit of GDP, as did the increased reliance on nuclear power. Nuclear power, which pro-vided less than 0.4 percent of total energy use in 1970, had grown to 8.3 percent by 2004.[87]

Many of the previously mentioned factors improved the overall efficiency of the U.S. energy system. As indicated in table 6.4, carbon dioxide (CO_2) emissions due to fossil fuel combustion per unit of GDP were reduced; in 2002, they were below their 1900 level. In 2002, the T-factors for CO_2 emissions were 0.34 and 0.41 relative to 1900 and 1950, respectively. However, despite technological change, CO_2 emissions from these sources were 8.8 times their 1900 levels.[88]

Trends in Other Developed Countries

Examination of long-term air quality and emission trends in other developed nations show that their trends are similar in many respects to those in the United States: SO_2, PM, and CO levels have generally peaked. Figure 6.11 shows that for 15 European and North American nations where composite "national" SO_2 ambient data are available from 1980 onward, concentrations seem to have peaked and are converging.[89]

Data from 1990 to 2002 for 30 member states of the OECD, which includes most of the world's richest countries,[90] indicates that SO_2 emissions for 25 of them had peaked before 1990 or sometime between 1990 and 2002.[91] Four—Australia, Iceland, Mexico, and Tur-key—showed emissions increasing during this period. One, New Zealand, hit a maximum in 1996, but showed no obvious downward trend in the following years.

Table 6.4
LONG-TERM CHANGES IN CARBON EMISSIONS FROM COMBUSTION AND INDUSTRIAL SOURCES

Indicator	Area	Period	Population (P_f)[a]	Affluence (A_f)[a]	GDP (P_fA_f)[a]	Emissions (E_f)[a]	Technology Factor (T_f)[a,b]	Technological Change $(\Delta T,$ in %$)$[a]
CO_2	United States	1900–2002	3.77	6.90[d]	25.97	8.80	0.339	−66.1
CO_2	United States	1950–2002	1.89	2.95[d]	5.57	2.30	0.412	−58.8
CO_2	World	1900–2001	3.93	4.79	18.84	13.06	0.693	−30.7
CO_2	World	1950–2001	2.44	2.86	6.99	4.28	0.613	−38.7

a. Values at the end of the period relative to values at the beginning of the period. b. Calculated as $E_f/(P_fA_f)$, as given in the previous two columns. c. Calculated using equation 5–6 (see last note in chapter 5); the negative sign indicates a decline in impact due to technological change. d. Based on work by Maddison and the Groningen Growth and Development Centre, rather than data from USBOC's *Historical Statistics* and Bureau of Economic Analysis' "National Income and Product Accounts."

SOURCES: Gregg Marland, Thomas A. Boden, and Robert J. Andes, "Global, Regional, and National CO_2 Emissions," in *Trends: Compendium of Data on Global Change* (Oak Ridge, TN: Carbon Dioxide Information Analysis Center, Oak Ridge National Laboratory and U.S. Department of Energy, 2005); Angus Maddison, *The World Economy Historical Statistics* (Paris: OECD, 2003), www.ggdc.net/~maddison (accessed July 30, 2005); Groningen Growth and Development Centre, Total Economy database, http://www.ggdc.net.

Figure 6.11
AMBIENT SO₂ CONCENTRATIONS, 1980–1997,
VARIOUS OECD COUNTRIES

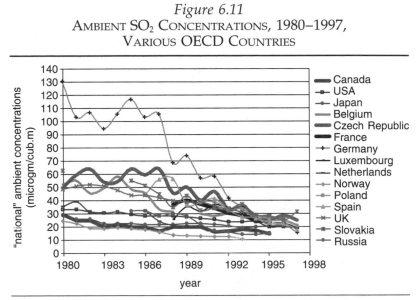

SOURCES: OECD, *OECD Environmental Data Compendium 1997* (Paris: OECD, 1997); OECD, *OECD Environmental Data Compendium 1999* (Paris: OECD, 1999).

Complementing these data, the European Environment Agency's 2005 environmental report indicates that SO_2 emissions in the European Union (EU) peaked in the 1970s and have declined two-thirds since 1980 through a combination of fuel switching, efficiency improvements, and add-on controls.[92] Also contributing to these reductions were the shutdown of inefficient industries in East Germany and other former communist nations caused by their transition to a more market-based economy, which by its very nature is much more sensitive to the cost of energy (or any other input) than a command-and-control economy. Emissions in Austria, Denmark, Germany, and the United Kingdom dropped by more than 90 percent. Overall, SO_2 emissions in the EU-15[93] dropped by about 59 percent between 1990 and 2002.[94] For CO, all but 2 of the 30 OECD countries (New Zealand and Finland) had clear downturns during the 1990 to 2002 period.[95]

For NO_x, 22 of the 30 OECD countries had their maxima before or during this period. The remainder—Australia, Greece, Ireland, Mexico, New Zealand, Portugal, Spain, and Turkey—had higher emissions at the end of the record than in 1990, with no clear downward trend in recent years.[96] Between 1990 and 2002, NO_x emissions declined by a quarter in the EU-15, and they declined between 24 percent and 50 percent or more in the Czech Republic, Hungary, Latvia, Lithuania, Poland, and Slovakia.[97]

For VOC, emissions of all OECD countries, except New Zealand, had peaked before the end of the data record (2002 for most countries).[98]

As a combination of such reductions

- Emissions of the precursors of acidic deposition (which include SO_2, NO_x, and ammonia) were reduced by 43 percent in the EU-15 and 58 percent in the EU-10.[99]
- Precursors of ground-level ozone (VOCs and NO_x) declined by a third between 1990 and 2002 for the EU-15 and 40 percent for the EU-10.[100]
- Thirteen of the EU-15 reduced primary and secondary fine particles between 1990 and 2002.[101] The exceptions, Greece and Portugal, saw their emissions increase by 0.3 percent and 6.0 percent, respectively.[102] As a group, the EU-15 reduced these emissions by 39 percent, with reductions in the 55–60 percent range from Germany and the United Kingdom.[103]

Just as in the United States, for the most part, air quality in the richer countries of the world has improved quite substantially.

Trends in Developing Countries

Air quality in developing countries is substantially worse than it is in developed countries. As any visitor to Beijing; Mexico City; New Delhi; and Cairo, Egypt, knows, those cities are among the most polluted in the world. Nevertheless, developing countries seem to be learning from the history of developed countries. They have embarked on cleaning their air at much earlier stages of their economic development. In 1975, when unleaded gasoline was first introduced in the United States, its GDP per capita was $19,414 (in 1995 dollars using market exchange rates), while India and China, which instituted some controls for lead in gasoline by 1997, had GDP per capita in 1997 below $1,000.[104]

In 1990, leaded gasoline comprised about 57 percent of the total worldwide gasoline market.[105] However, by 2000, the market for leaded gasoline had shrunk to less than 20 percent and, by mid 2002, to less than 10 percent.[106] Most of that market was then located in Africa, East Europe, and the former Soviet Union. Since then, progress has continued. In January 2006, South Africa phased out leaded gasoline, the last country in sub-Saharan Africa to do so.[107] It is, however, still sold in several Pacific islands and 27 countries, mainly in the Middle East and Central Asia. Such reductions led to rapid improvements in air quality for lead in some of the world's most populated areas. In New Delhi, for instance, lead levels in 1999 at traffic intersections were 79 percent lower than in 1995, when unleaded gasoline was first introduced.[108] In addition, between 1998 and 1999, lead content of suspended PM in industrial areas fell by 45 percent; in residential areas the decline was 52 percent. Moreover, the introduction of compressed natural gas and four-stroke engines for motorized cycles helped CO levels drop by 22 percent.[109] And in Mexico City, ambient lead levels dropped more than 90 percent between 1986 and 2003.[110]

Ambient levels of PM in some of the other most polluted spots in the developing world have dropped dramatically. In China, the average annual suspended PM (SPM) reading for more than 50 cities declined about 40 percent between 1987 and 1995, from almost 500 to about 300 micrograms per cubic meter. Progress has continued since. Chinese environmental scientists Jiming Hao and Litao Wang indicate that between 1990 and 2002, despite an increase in China's energy consumption of approximately 50 percent, average TSP concentrations in its cities declined by 25 percent.[111] However, in Beijing itself, average TSP concentrations increased by about 25 percent; but PM-10, which has greater impact on public health, dropped by about 10 percent.[112] In Mexico City, the percentage of readings exceeding ambient standards for PM-10 declined from about 40 percent to 18 percent between 1989 and 1997. And PM-10 measurements in the industrial region of Cubatao in São Paulo state—Brazil's dominant industrial region—declined from 180 to about 70 micrograms per cubic meter (a 60 percent drop). Notably, these are among the fastest growing industrial regions of the world.[113] Also, in Santiago, Chile, ambient fine PM concentrations (i.e., PM that is less than 2.5 micrometers in diameter and, therefore, liable to have a higher impact on public health) decreased 52 percent in the 12-year period from 1989 to 2001.[114] Similarly, average SO_2 concentrations in China's cities declined by more than 44 percent between 1990 and 2002 despite a

30 percent increase in national emissions.[115] Average concentrations in Beijing dropped by more than 30 percent over the same period.[116] And between 1986 and 2003, ambient SO_2 and CO levels dropped by 84 percent and 50 percent, respectively, in Mexico City, while O_3 declined by 36 percent after having peaked in 1991.[117]

Despite those improvements, further improvements are needed. Lead emissions, for example, seem to be increasing from developing countries as a whole (at least into the early 1990s), although global lead emissions have declined from 400,000 tonnes in the 1970s to 100,000 tonnes, mainly because of controls in the developed countries.[118]

However much outdoor air needs to be improved in many of the faster growing developing countries, their major air pollution problems are indoors. Half of the world's population continues to use solid fuels, such as coal, dung, and wood. This includes 75 percent of India, China, and other South Asian countries, as well as 50–75 percent of Africa and Latin America.[119] The *Global Burden of Disease 2000 (Version 2)* from the World Health Organization (WHO) study estimates that in 2000 air pollution was responsible for 2.4 million premature deaths (or 4.3 percent of all deaths), two-thirds of which were attributed to indoor pollution from PM in developing countries from cooking and heating with coal, dung, and wood and the remainder to outdoor air pollution.[120]

However, on the basis of disability-adjusted life years (DALYs), a measure that purports to account for the quality of life for the period during which a risk (such as air pollution) may shorten a life, the impact of air pollution, particularly outdoor air pollution, is somewhat smaller.[121] Therefore, indoor air pollution accounts for 2.7 percent of lost DALYs worldwide, and outdoor air accounts for 0.5 percent.

Economic growth, by giving the inhabitants of developing countries the means to switch from solid fuels to cleaner, but no-longer-exotic, technologies such as natural gas, oil, or even electricity, would help reduce the disease burden in these countries significantly, essentially allowing today's developing countries to follow the same path so successfully taken by the rich nations in reducing population exposure to air pollutants.

Mortality Due to Various Water-Related Diseases

Globally, two of the most serious environmental problems are inadequate sanitation and insufficient availability of safe water for drinking, washing food, and personal hygiene.[122] About 1.1. billion people (18 percent of the world's population) lack access to safe water, and 2.4 billion (or 40 percent) have inadequate sanitation.[123] The majority of these people live in Asia and Africa, mainly in rural areas.[124] Because sanitation coverage in rural areas is less than half that in urban settings, 2 billion of the 2.4 billion lacking adequate sanitation live in rural areas, of which 1.3 billion are in China and India.[125]

The WHO's *Global Burden of Disease 2000 (Version 2)* study attributes 1.7 million deaths in 2000 (or 3.1 percent of the total deaths worldwide) to unsafe water, inadequate sanitation, and poor hygiene. These deaths account for 3.7 percent of the lost DALYs globally.[126] Notably, this study probably understates the mortality and lost DALYs due to these factors because, based on "models with considerable uncertainty" and an opaque methodology (as noted in the next section, "Climate-Sensitive Indicators"), it assigns some of the mortality because of diarrhea to climate change (by which it apparently means human-induced climate change).[127] Another water-related disease, malaria—a natural rather than man-made environmental problem—claimed 1.1 million lives (or 2.0 percent of the global total), which, in turn, accounted for 2.9 percent of the lost DALYs. Thus, the mortality and morbidity rates for these diseases are among the most significant indicators not only of a nation's environmental quality but also its quality of life.

There has been, in the past few decades, enormous progress in addressing these issues. Access to safe water in low-income countries is estimated to have increased from 19.6 percent in 1975 to 69.3 percent in 1993.[128] By 2002, 76 percent of the population of low-income countries had access to improved water sources.[129] And in 2000, 82 percent of the world's population (or 4.9 billion people) had access to some form of improved water supplies, which is up from 79 percent (or 4.1 billion) in 1990.[130] During the same period, the proportion of the world's population with access to sewage disposal facilities increased from 55 percent (or 2.9 billion people) to 60 percent (or 3.6 billion). In other words, between 1990 and 2000, each year 70–80 million additional people were provided with some access to safer water and sanitation. Figures 6.13 and 6.14 suggest that the number of people lacking access to safe water and sanitation could be reduced much faster if economic growth accelerates.

U.S. Trends

During the 19th century, water-related diseases were rampant in the United States. Cumulatively, the death rate in 1900 due to typhoid and paratyphoid, various gastrointestinal diseases (gastritis, duodenitis, enteritis, and colitis), and all forms of dysentery was 1,860 per million. To put this in context, the annual crude death rate due to all causes was 8,650 per million in 1997,[131] and society today seems willing to pay millions of dollars to eliminate cancer risks (not deaths) of the order of one in a million.[132] Today, as a result of one of the greatest environmental triumphs in the United States, deaths due to these water-related diseases are regarded almost as anachronisms.

Following the introduction of slow sand-filtration units in the United States in Poughkeepsie and Hudson, New York, in the 1870s, several towns and cities in Massachusetts built water supply systems. As the number of water supply systems increased, typhoid and paratyphoid death rates in Massachusetts declined from about 1,337 per million in 1865 to about 221 in 1900.[133] In 1908, chlorination was introduced to the United States. Mortality due to typhoid and paratyphoid dropped from 313 per million in 1900 to 76 in 1920, and 11 in 1940. By 1960, it was virtually eliminated (figure 6.12).[134] According to the Centers for Disease Control and Prevention's WONDER database, there were no deaths attributed to typhoid and paratyphoid in 1997.[135]

Similarly, the death rate due to various gastrointestinal diseases declined from 1,427 per million in 1900 to 6 in 1970 corresponding to a 235-fold improvement in technology (see table 6.5). For all forms of dysentery, the death rate declined from 120 per million in 1900 to 3.3 in 1957 and 1.7 in 1998,[136] equivalent to a 65-fold improvement in technology.

By the time the federal Clean Water and Safe Drinking Water Acts were passed in 1972 and 1974, the major battle regarding U.S. public health and water quality had been largely fought and won. At least since 1920, only a small fraction of cases of the earlier diseases have been due to ingestion of contaminated water.[137] There were no deaths attributed to drinking water systems in the United States in 1997–98, and only two deaths in 1999–2000 (equivalent to a death rate of less than 0.005 per million), while a total of nine deaths were attributed to recreational water use during that four year period (equivalent

153

Table 6.5
LONG-TERM CHANGES IN DEATH RATES DUE TO WATER-RELATED DISEASES, POPULATION (P), AND TECHNOLOGY (T)

Indicator	Area	Period	Population (P_f)[a]	Technology Factor (T_f)[ab]	Technological Change (ΔT, in %)[d]
Typhoid and paratyphoid	Massachusetts	1865–1900	2.09[c]	0.165	–83.5
	United States	1900–1997	3.58	0.000	–100
GI diseases[d]	United States	1900–1970	2.68	0.004	–99.6
Dysentery	United States	1900–1998	3.62	0.014	–98.6

a. Values at the end of the period relative to values at the beginning of the period. b. Calculated as I_f/P_f, which is equivalent to the change in death rate. c. Assumes exponential population growth rate between 1860 and 1870. d. GI = other gastrointestinal diseases, including gastritis, duodenitis, enteritis, and colitis. e. Calculated using equation 5-6 (see last note in chapter 5); the negative sign indicates a decline in impact due to technological change.

SOURCES: USBOC, *Historical Statistics of the United States, Colonial Times to 1970* (Washington, DC: Government Printing Office, 1975) and various issues; Centers for Disease Control and Prevention (CDC), WONDER Compressed Mortality Data Base, http://wonder.cdc.gov/mortSQL.shtml (accessed January 14, 2003).

Figure 6.12
DEATH RATES FOR VARIOUS WATER-RELATED DISEASES, UNITED STATES, 1900–70

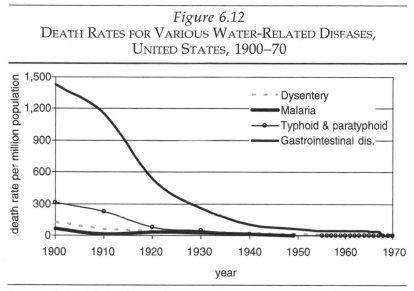

SOURCE: Indur M. Goklany, "Factors Affecting Environmental Impacts: The Effects of Technology on Long-Term Trends in Cropland, Air Pollution, and Water-Related Diseases," *Ambio* 25 (1996): 497–503.

to a death rate of less than 0.01 per million).[138] Recent outbreaks such as the *E. coli* episode in Walkerton, Ontario, Canada, which killed about six people perhaps because of inadequate chlorination,[139] serve as a warning against complacency and relaxing vigilance in treating and disinfecting water supplies.[140]

Global Trends

The trends in death and sickness rates from water-related diseases are not unique to the United States. Figures 6.13 and 6.14, based on analyses of cross-country data, show that fractions of population with access to safe water and sanitation services—major determinants of the improving trends in water-related diseases—increase with both GDP per capita and the passage of time.[141] These significant upward displacements of the curves with the passage of time is most likely because of the diffusion of technology that includes, in particular, the spread of knowledge about safe drinking water and sanitary practices. Historically, this diffusion has been from developed to developing countries.

Figure 6.13
ACCESS TO SAFE WATER VS. INCOME, 1990–2002

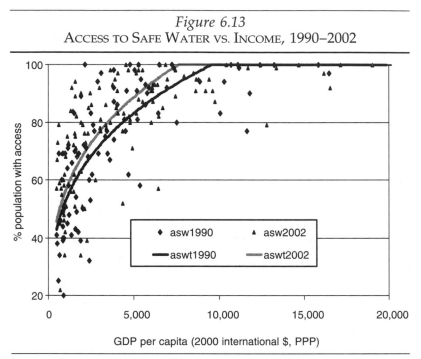

GDP per capita (2000 international $, PPP)

SOURCE: Based on data from World Bank, *World Development Indicators,* http://devdata.worldbank.org/dataonline (accessed July 12, 2005).

Climate-Sensitive Indicators

Table 6.4 indicates that global carbon emissions from fossil fuel and industrial emissions have grown more than four-fold since 1950.[142] Between 1950 and 2004, this was accompanied by an 18 percent increase in atmospheric CO_2 concentrations[143] and, according to one set of surface data, a global temperature increase of about 0.66°C.[144]

Although some have disputed the magnitude of the temperature trend,[145] many policymakers and scientists have noted that such temperature increases would be consistent with the observed increases in greenhouse gas concentrations in the atmosphere during the past two centuries. Some have also speculated that various recent extreme weather events (such as hurricanes, floods, heat waves, or even cold spells) might be linked to global warming.[146] Concerns regarding global warming also extend to the possibility that it may

Figure 6.14
ACCESS TO SANITATION VS. INCOME, 1990–2002

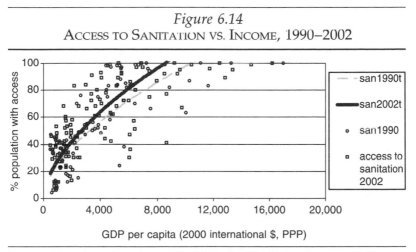

GDP per capita (2000 international $, PPP)

SOURCE: Based on data from World Bank, *World Development Indicators*, http://devdata.worldbank.org/dataonline (accessed July 12, 2005).

increase incidences of infectious and parasitic diseases, decrease agricultural productivity and forest cover, and raise sea levels.

These possibilities have prompted some scientists and, more important, policymakers to claim that climate change is—to use President Bill Clinton's words—"the overriding environmental challenge facing the globe today."[147] This claim is in no small way responsible for the emphasis policymakers place on implementing the Kyoto Protocol, which would reduce greenhouse gas emissions from the developed countries.[148]

However, changes in emissions, temperature, or other meteorological variables are very poor indicators of the impacts of human-induced global warming on either human well-being or environmental quality. The amount of temperature change is not (directly) proportional to the amount of greenhouse gas emissions, nor is temperature change proportional to the magnitude of impacts on public health or the environment. Accordingly, instead of focusing on meteorological variables that are relatively poor surrogates for the impacts of any warming, I will, in the following, examine long-term empirical trends for various climate-sensitive measures of socioeconomic or environmental well-being to check whether the trends are consistent with the putative effects of global warming and whether they have worsened human well-being and environmental quality.

The climate-sensitive indicators that I will examine include rates of damages due to or impacts on various types of extreme weather events, crop productivity, forest cover, ranges of wildlife and vegetation, death rates due to vector-borne diseases, and sea level rise. Such analyses might also instruct us as to the factors that determine adaptation and vulnerability to climate-related challenges. Arguably, examination of such trends is more fruitful than an examination of trends in meteorological variables and then speculating what that might imply for rates of death or disease, agricultural productivity, forest cover, and so forth.

Agriculture and Food Security

As discussed at the beginning of this chapter, although the amount of cropland per capita has never been lower, the average person has never been better fed. This is only possible because global productivity in the food and agricultural sector is at an all time high. This outcome is in contrast to the contention that warming may reduce global agricultural productivity through a combination of factors including more frequent floods, droughts and loss of soil moisture, and pest and disease outbreaks[149]—especially given Mann and coworkers' centuries-long reconstructions of temperature trends, which suggest that the earth today is the warmest it has been in the last several hundred years,[150] and others' analysis indicating an increasing trend in the global combined areas of severe drought and severe moisture surplus since the 1970s.[151]

So how can one explain the historical increases in agricultural productivity and improved food security at a time when the climate is purportedly getting worse?

One possible explanation for this divergence is that, perhaps, the net effects of global warming at current CO_2 and temperature levels are not particularly detrimental to global agricultural productivity or, more important, global food security. In fact, there is substantial evidence that so far CO_2-enhanced warming may be contributing to increased agricultural productivity:

- Neville Nicholls estimated that 30–50 percent of the post-1950 increases in corn yields in Australia may be because of higher minimum temperatures.[152]
- An analysis of the effect of variations in temperature, precipitation, and solar radiation on county corn and soybean yields in

the United States for 1982–98 indicated that 25 percent of corn and 32 percent of soybean yield trends can be explained by temperature, while precipitation and solar radiation trends did not show significant relationships with crop yields.[153]

• Comparing agricultural yields in Argentina between the period 1950–70 with 1971–99, Graciela Magrin and coworkers estimate that yields for corn, wheat, and sunflower increased by 110 percent, 56 percent, and 102 percent, respectively, because of higher precipitation, higher minimum temperatures in spring and summer, and higher minimum temperatures during the rest of the year. They also estimate that climate change contributed significantly to these increases—38 percent of the increased yield in soybean, 18 percent in corn, 13 percent in wheat, and 12 percent in sunflower.[154]

Part of these increases could also be because of a lengthening of growing seasons. In the far northern latitudes—north of 45°N—the active growing season seems to have lengthened by 12 ± 4 days in the 1980s because of warming, human-induced or otherwise, and plant growth has apparently accelerated.[155] Analysis of data from 41 stations in Germany from 1951 to 2000 indicates that the dates of the last spring frost advanced by an average of 2.4 days per decade on average while autumn frosts were delayed up to 2.5 days per decade.[156] Similar trends in the climatological growing season were also reported in other European countries. The frost-free period increased by 5.0 days per decade in Austria and Switzerland (1951–99, 18 stations) and 3.4 days per decade in Estonia (1951–2000, two stations).[157] These results are consistent with findings that, worldwide, spring events have advanced by 2.3 days per decade.[158] Another global study detected an advance of 5.1 days per decade in spring blooming.[159]

In addition, numerous controlled field experiments show that increasing atmospheric CO_2 concentrations increase crop yields. The 1995 impact assessment by the Intergovernmental Panel on Climate Change (IPCC) suggests that yields of C3 crops (i.e., the majority of crops) may increase an average of 30 percent due to a doubling of CO_2.[160] Sylvan H. Wittwer, the eminent agronomist, estimates that the increase in CO_2 concentrations during the past two centuries may have increased production by as much as 14 percent.[161] Between

1961 and 2004, global cereal yields increased 146 percent,[162] while CO_2 concentrations increased less than 19 percent,[163] and annual global temperature increased 0.44°C.[164] Thus, CO_2-enhanced warming is unlikely to explain more than a small portion of the increase in global agricultural productivity.

A second explanation for the increase in global agricultural productivity and global food security is that it is due to technological progress driven by the mutually reinforcing, coevolving forces of economic growth, technological change, and trade, which have overwhelmed the impacts of global warming that might otherwise, one might argue, have been negative.[165] But the most plausible explanation is that both CO_2-enhanced global warming and technological progress have contributed to reduced human vulnerability to hunger and malnourishment, with technological progress being the major contributor.

Forest Cover and Biodiversity

Through the ages, human demand for land for agriculture and—to a much lesser extent—settlements and infrastructure, has been the major reason for the loss of forest cover and diversion of habitat away from the rest of nature.[166] Such deforestation and habitat conversion, in turn, is the greatest threat to global biodiversity. Between 1990 and 2000, global population increased 15.3 percent.[167] To meet the additional food demand, net agricultural land increased by about 1.3 percent or 95 million hectares (Mha) (including a 20 Mha increase in cropland), and, according to the latest (2005) Global Forest Resource Assessment (GFRA), net forest cover decreased by about 89 Mha.[168] This loss in forest cover, which occurred mainly in tropical and subtropical areas, would have been substantially greater but for offsetting increases in forest cover in developed countries.[169]

Notably, according to the previous (2000) GFRA, the net loss of forest cover from 1990 to 2000 was 27 percent less than the estimated 130 Mha lost between 1980 and 1990.[170]

There is no evidence that anthropogenic global warming has contributed to the loss of forest cover, significantly or otherwise. In fact, for forests as for agriculture, CO_2-enhanced warming and fertilization due to higher CO_2 concentrations in the atmosphere—aided by longer growing seasons in the higher latitudes and increased nitrogen deposition from agricultural activities and fossil fuel combustion—may have increased forest productivity, thereby stimulating timber growth and forest mass.[171] An analysis of satellite-based data on vegetation cover indicates that the earth's net primary productivity increased by 6 percent from 1982 to 1999.[172] The Amazon rain forests accounted for 42 percent of that increase, mainly because of decreasing cloud cover, which increased solar radiation. According to another estimate, a one-day extension in the growing season could increase the net primary production in deciduous forests by an average of 1.6 percent, with greater increases in colder areas (1.9 percent for Burlington, Vermont) and smaller increases in warmer areas (1.4 percent for Charleston, South Carolina).[173] Supporting these notions are analyses that indicate that carbon sinks in ecosystems in the northern latitudes strengthened markedly in the 1990s.[174]

The trends in developing and developed countries (taken as groups) confirm the importance of economic growth and technological progress in limiting deforestation.[175] Forest cover continues to decline in developing countries largely because their increases in agricultural and forest productivity lag behind the demands of their growing populations for food and other products. Meanwhile, developed countries are being reforested because—despite diversion of land for urbanization and infrastructure projects—productivity in the agricultural and forestry sectors is growing faster than the increase in the demand for food and timber. Without science-based and market-driven increases in food and agricultural productivity between 1990 and 2000 alone, at least an additional 831 Mha of agricultural land (including 265 Mha of cropland) would have been needed to compensate for the lost productivity, global deforestation would have been greater, and biodiversity would have been in greater peril, especially in the developing world.[176]

Table 6.6 shows the effect of increased agricultural productivity between 1961 and 2002 in stemming habitat conversion to cropland in a number of areas. In each case, the amount of land potentially saved from being plowed is substantial relative to the amounts set aside in fully or partially protected areas as of 2004.[177] In India, for instance, 273 Mha were saved from conversion during that period because of increased productivity. By contrast, it only has 16 Mha set aside in fully or partially protected areas. For China, the corresponding numbers were 212 Mha saved versus 110 Mha actually set aside; for the developing world as a group, 1,315 Mha saved and 994 Mha reserved, while on a global basis 1,894 Mha were saved

Table 6.6
HABITAT SAVED BY AGRICULTURAL TECHNOLOGY, 1961–2002

| Area | Cropland (Mha) | | | Habitat Saved from Conversion by 2002 (Mha) | Partly or Wholly Protected Area in 2004 (Mha) |
	1961 Actual	2002 Actual with Technology Change	2002 Estimated with No Technology Change		
China	105	154	366	212	110
India	161	170	443	273	16
Developing world	687	899	2,214	1,315	994
World	1,366	1,541	3,435	1,894	1,506

SOURCES: Updated from Indur M. Goklany, "Agricultural Technology and the Precautionary Principle," in *Environmental Policy and Agriculture: Conflicts, Prospects, and Implications*, ed. Roger E. Meiners and Bruce Yandle (Lanham, MD: Rowman and Littlefield, 2003), using data from FAO, *FAOSTAT 2005*, http://apps.fao.org, and World Resource Institute, EarthTrends database, www.wri.org (accessed June 23, 2005).

compared to 1,506 Mha set aside. In each case, the amount of land reserved for conservation is exceeded by the amount saved through productivity-enhancing technological change. Ironically, individual farmers, through base motives such as maximizing profits by increasing productivity to meet food demand, inadvertently did more for conservation than all the other actions taken explicitly to advance conservation. In fact, it's likely that the former enabled the latter because it is inconceivable that populations—particularly populations such as China and India's, which were on the verge of starvation in the third quarter of the last century—would have forgone food production in lieu of nature conservation.[178]

Vegetation and Wildlife

Higher CO_2 concentrations, longer growing seasons in the northern latitudes, and accompanying changes in climatic variables that have occurred over the past several decades should have modified the distribution and abundance of vegetation and wildlife species. And indeed scientists have seen many changes in the vegetation and wildlife that are consistent with these trends. Gian-Reto Walther and her colleges, for instance, note, that they saw "earlier breeding or first singing of birds, earlier arrival of migrant birds, earlier appearance of butterflies, earlier choruses and spawning in amphibians, earlier shooting and flowering of plants."[179] This change has been accompanied by the later arrival of autumn and autumn colors in some places. Based on meta-analyses of trends with respect to 99 species of birds, butterflies, and alpine herbs, Camille Parmesan and Gary Yohe found significant range shifts averaging 6.1 km per decade toward the poles.[180] They also found a significant mean advancement of spring events by 2.3 days per decade based on data for 172 species of shrubs, herbs, trees, birds, butterflies, and amphibians.[181]

The Finnish branch of the World Wildlife Fund notes, for example, the following:

> Thanks to the warming trend, the growing season has grown. . . . At the same time the spring migration of birds, including finches, larks, wagtails, and swifts, has begun an average of ten days earlier than before.
>
> The warmer temperatures have brought new, more southerly species of butterflies to Finland. Many existing types of butterflies have extended their habitats further north.[182]

163

Similarly, some birds in the United Kingdom have become more abundant, possibly due to milder winters. These birds include the blackcap, nuthatch, great spotted woodpecker, various herons, the song thrush, little ringed plovers, woodlarks, and Dartford warblers (the latter three being scarce breeders). Notably, the number of new bird species breeding in Britain has increased steadily in the past three decades, with a net gain of 10 species. However, climate change might have contributed to the redistribution of waders from the warmer west to the colder east. It has also been suggested that the climate change might have contributed to the decline in seabirds along the North Sea, but this link has not been established.[183]

The ranges of 15 butterfly species in the United Kingdom have expanded substantially since the 1970s, "almost certainly" because of warming (human-induced or not).[184] They also appear earlier in the year and some have spawned an extra generation during the summer. In addition, some moths, crickets, and dragonflies have migrated into the United Kingdom.[185] The ranges of dragonflies and damselflies in the United Kingdom have expanded northward faster than they have shrunk at their southern margins, suggesting that "their southern range margins are less constrained by climate than by other factors."[186]

In Antarctica, Adélie penguins, which require access to winter pack ice, are declining around Faraday, whereas chinstrap penguins, which usually require open water, are increasing.[187]

Recently, J. Alan Pounds and others have hypothesized that the presumed extinction of two-thirds of the harlequin frog species in the American tropics caused by a deadly fungus was, in fact, mediated by global warming.[188] Under this hypothesis, global warming contributes to greater evaporation and, therefore, greater cloud formation, which reduces daytime temperatures but increases night temperatures, resulting in conditions that favor the fungus. It is currently premature to determine whether this hypothesis will stand the test of time; however, Pat Michaels has noted that the area in question seems not to have become cloudier during the periods the extinctions were presumed to have occurred.[189]

With respect to vegetation, a study of the earliest flowering dates of 385 wildflower species in the United Kingdom shows that, on average, they bloomed more than 4.5 days earlier in the 1990s compared to their 1954–90 average, with 16 percent blooming significantly earlier while 3 percent bloomed significantly later; one plant bloomed fully 55 days earlier.[190] Similarly, the ranges of flowering plants and mosses seem to have expanded in the parts of Antarctica that have warmed.[191] Soil invertebrates have also advanced with changes in vegetation.[192] A study of plant biodiversity in the Netherlands during the 20th century indicates that, in recent decades, the number of thermophilic (warm-loving) species increased, coinciding with observed warming, but there was no decline in cold-loving species.[193] About half of the increase in thermophilic species could be explained by warming due to urbanization.

So obviously there have been changes in vegetation and wildlife. But whether these changes constitute a net benefit or loss is unclear not only because the "final" distribution and abundance of biological resources are uncertain but also because there are no universally accepted criteria for establishing whether the change has resulted in a net loss or benefit to either humanity or the rest of nature. Proponents of greenhouse gas controls, however, implicitly assume that any change is inherently detrimental, more as an article of faith rather than as the product of a rational inquiry.

Undoubtedly, warming, whether due to man's activities or nature's machinations, will have a profound impact on the distribution and abundance of species. It might favor some species over others. It has been suggested that climate change might be the coup de grâce for some already-threatened species, but might it not just as well increase the likelihood of survival of other threatened species? Another concern is that climate change might disrupt the synchronous arrival of a species and its food source, and the former might be unable to adapt to such a change.[194] However, because the ranges of birds and butterflies change over time, one may infer that they are capable of at least some adaptation. In addition, new research provides greater direct evidence that some species may be more adaptable than previously thought. Dutch researchers have shown that the blue tit adapts its egg-laying date to coincide with the timing of when its natural food source was most abundant the previous year. This suggests that some birds, at least, can learn from experience and, therefore, adapt.[195] Perhaps equally remarkable about this anecdote is that about half of the blue tits never survive from one year to the next, which means that they are least likely to apply the lessons learned from their experiences.[196] Despite that handicap, they apparently have learned how and when to modulate their egg-laying.

165

Mortality and Mortality Rates Due to Extreme Weather Events

U.S. Trends. Among the problems in developing aggregate long-term trends for U.S. deaths and death rates due to extreme weather events is that the length of the record varies according to the type of event. The *Annual Summaries* published by the National Oceanic and Atmospheric Administration (NOAA) provides time series data on fatalities due to tornadoes and lightning, respectively, from 1916 and 1959 onward.[197] Each year's summary also gives that year's death toll due to various other weather-related phenomena, such as hurricanes, floods, extreme cold, extreme heat, drought, mudslides, winter storms, and avalanches, but it does not provide any time series data for these other categories.

A second problem is that the data for several categories of events from these summaries are at variance with data from other sources. Specifically, there are discrepancies between mortality data from the *Annual Summaries* and (a) the Hydrologic Information Center (HIC) estimates for floods,[198] (b) the National Hurricane Center (NHC) data for hurricanes,[199] and (c) the Centers for Disease Control and Prevention WONDER database for extreme cold and extreme heat.[200] Thus, based on conversations with personnel from the various agencies,[201] in order to develop long-term trends, I use HIC data for floods (commencing in 1903) and NHC data for hurricanes (commencing in 1900) because those agencies are primarily responsible for tracking information related to these categories of events within NOAA. The WONDER database was used for fatalities *directly* attributable to extreme heat and cold, because it is based on actual death certificate records. As of this writing, these data are readily available only from 1979 to 2002.[202]

Notably, the WONDER database attributes many more deaths to excessive heat and cold than do the *Annual Summaries*. For 2001 and 2002, for example, WONDER has 300 and 350 deaths due to extreme heat, while the latter lists 166 and 167, respectively. The discrepancies are even greater for extreme cold. According to WONDER, there were 646 deaths due to extreme cold in 2002, while the *Annual Summaries* has 11; similarly, for 2001, the corresponding numbers are 599 and 4.

Despite the much higher numbers of fatalities according to the WONDER database, it does not capture excess deaths indirectly

Table 6.7
U.S. DEATHS DUE TO WEATHER-RELATED EVENTS, 1979–2002

	Cumulative deaths 1979–2002	Deaths per year	Percent of annual deaths
Lightning	1,512	63	0.003
Tornado	1,321	55	0.002
Flood	2,395	100	0.004
Hurricane	460	19	0.001
Extreme cold	16,313	680	0.028
Extreme heat	8,589	358	0.015
Other (e.g., drought, mudslides, winter storms, and avalanches		< 75	0.003
Sum	**30,590**	**1,350**	**0.056**
Total deaths (in 2002)		**2,448,000**	**100**

SOURCE: See text.

caused by extreme heat or extreme cold (i.e., deaths above a background level in the absence of the extreme event, adjusted for the period of the year). Deaths due to all causes (e.g., strokes or heart disease) on average go up more due to extreme heat than due to extreme cold events.[203] This is true even if one considers that the death rate drops below the background level after the extreme event has ended, and such drops (like the increases) are more pronounced for extreme heat events. But there are many more deaths during the winter months than in the summer months. A proper evaluation of the net effect of any warming on mortality ought to consider these factors—as well as possible changes in background death rates—within a framework that considers adaptation and uses "years of life lost" and DALYs lost.[204] However, there might be some cancellation of mortality effects due to climate change with an increase in deaths from extreme heat offset by a reduction due to extreme cold,[205] although such effects might be dampened if temperature variability declines.

Table 6.7 shows that from 1979 to 2002, there were 1,350 annual deaths directly attributable to weather-related natural disasters in the United States.[206] By contrast, there were about 2.45 million annual deaths due to all causes in 2002.[207] Thus, cumulative mortality directly attributable to extreme weather events is generally less than 0.06 percent of all deaths. And if one assumes that the deadly hurricane season of 2005 becomes an annual fixture with fatalities to match (about 1,500),[208] annual mortality due to all weather events is nevertheless unlikely to exceed 3,000 (or 0.12 percent of mortality due to all causes). By comparison, each year more than 45,000 people die from motor vehicle accidents, 3,400 die from accidental drowning or accidental fires, and 3,200 die from smoke inhalation.[209] Thus, despite the copious amount of press garnered by such extreme weather events, their contribution to overall mortality is relatively tiny.

Table 6.7 also shows that half of the weather-related deaths in the United States during the 1979–2002 period were caused by extreme cold. Extreme heat, floods, lightning, tornados, and hurricanes contributed 27, 7, 5, 4, and 1 percent, respectively, to the average annual cumulative death toll from weather-related events.

Figure 6.15 shows that from 1979 to 2002 the trends in cumulative deaths and death rates for hurricanes, floods, tornados, lightning, and extreme heat and cold are downward, despite any warming that may have occurred. This result is not unexpected because the trends are dominated by fatalities due to extreme heat and cold, and earlier studies have shown no upward trends in U.S. deaths or death rates due to extreme temperatures, despite the aging of the population, which, if all else is equal, ought to have increased risks of death due to either type of event.[210]

Examination of longer-time series due to various categories of extreme weather events generally confirms the earlier findings. Specifically, notwithstanding the 2005 hurricane season, average annual fatalities due to lightning, tornados, floods, and North Atlantic hurricanes and cyclones hitting the U.S. mainland through the last century have declined substantially in the past several decades:

- Deaths due to lightning have declined more or less steadily since the beginning of the fatality record in 1959. The 10-year moving average (MA) for annual deaths was at its peak at 118 at the end of the first period (in 1968). (Note that I will refer to that period as the "10-year MA in 1968.") For instance, in 2004, for the period ending in 2004, it was 58 percent lower with 49 deaths per year.[211]

Figure 6.15
U.S. Deaths and Death Rates from Tornados, Floods, Lightning, Hurricanes, and Extreme Temperatures, 1979–2002

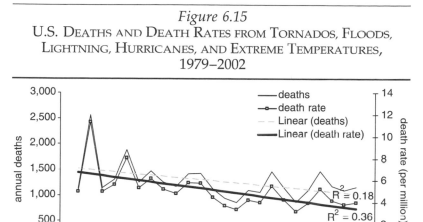

Sources: E. S. Blake, P. J. Herbert, J. D. Jarrell, M. Mayfield, and C. W. Landsea, "The Deadliest, Costliest, and Most Intense United States Hurricanes of This Century (and Other Frequently Requested Hurricane Facts)," *NOAA Technical Memorandum NWS TPC-1* (Miami, FL: National Weather Service, 2005; National Hurricane Center, *2005 Atlantic Hurricane Season*, www.nhc.noaa.gov/2005atlan.shtml (accessed April 10, 2006); Stuart Hinson, National Climatic Data Center, personal communications, August 22, 2005); Hydrologic Information Center, *Flood Fatalities*, www.nws.noaa.gov/oh/hic/flood_stats/recent_individual_deaths.shtml (accessed October 15, 2005); National Weather Service, *2003 Annual Summaries*, www.nws.noaa.gov/om/severe_weather/sum03.pdf (accessed October 15, 2005); National Weather Service, *Summary of U.S. Natural Hazard Statistics*, www.nws.noaa.gov/om/severe_weather/sum04.pdf (accessed October 15, 2005); Centers for Disease Control and Prevention, *WONDER Database*, http://wonder.cdc.gov (accessed October 15, 2005); USBOC, *Statistical Abstract of the United States 2004–2005* (Washington, DC: GPO, 2004); *National and State Population Estimates: Annual Population Estimates 2000 to 2004*, www.census.gov/popest/states/NST-ann-est.html (accessed on August 14, 2005).

- For tornados, the 10-year MA for annual deaths peaked in 1933 at 319. By 2004, it had dropped by 82 percent to 57.[212]
- With respect to floods, although researchers have generally agreed that precipitation has increased in the past few decades (for the United States), there is controversy over whether the

intensity of heavy and extreme precipitation events has increased for the United States since the early decades of the 20th century.[213] Regardless of whether frequency and intensity of flooding may have increased or decreased, what is more pertinent is that fatalities from floods have declined. The 10-year MA for annual deaths from floods, which peaked in 1978 at 198, had declined by 56 percent to 88 by 2004.[214]

- The hurricane record commences in 1900, the year of the great Galveston hurricane, which may have killed as many as 10,000–12,000 people. (I use 8,000, per NHC's estimate.) At the end of the first period, 1909, the 10-year MA was 873 deaths per year. By the end of 2004, it was down to 30 deaths per year, a drop of 97 percent.[215] Based on the previous assumption of 1,500 hurricane fatalities in 2005, by the end of the year the 10-year MA had rebounded to 177 deaths per year—nevertheless, a decline of 80 percent from its peak. While a portion of the pre-1990s declines in deaths from hurricanes may be due to a reduction in the number and wind speeds of violent Atlantic hurricanes since the 1940s,[216] some credit is perhaps also due to technology-based adaptation.[217]
- Based on the record from 1959 to 2004, the 10-year MA for cumulative fatalities for lightning, tornadoes, floods, and hurricanes peaked at the end of 1974 at 451. By the end of 2004, it had dropped by 50 percent.

The declines in death rates (measured as deaths per million population) are even more dramatic (see figure 6.16). For the 10-year period ending in 2004, the 10-year MA for death rates for lightning, tornados, floods, and hurricanes had dropped by 72, 93, 76, and 99 percent, respectively, from their earlier peaks.[218] And despite the rebound in the death rate for hurricanes at the end of 2005, the overall decline for hurricanes from its earlier peak was a still-impressive 95 percent.

The cumulative death rate for lightning, tornados, floods, and hurricanes peaked in 1974. It had declined by 64 percent at the end of 2004, then rebounded so that at the end of 2005 it was 42 percent below its peak.

The bulk of the long-term decreases in deaths and death rates for extreme events is most likely caused by increased wealth and new

Figure 6.16
U.S. DEATH RATES DUE TO TORNADOS, FLOODS, LIGHTNING, AND HURRICANES, 1900–2005
(deaths per million population, 10-year moving average)

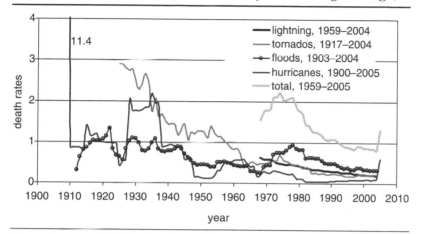

NOTE: Assumes 1,500 deaths due to hurricanes in 2005.

SOURCES: E. S. Blake, P. J. Herbert, J. D. Jarrell, M. Mayfield, and C. W. Landsea, "The Deadliest, Costliest, and Most Intense United States Hurricanes of This Century (and Other Frequently Requested Hurricane Facts)," *NOAA Technical Memorandum NWS TPC-1* (Miami, FL: National Weather Service, 2005); National Hurricane Center, *2005 Atlantic Hurricane Season*, www.nhc.noaa.gov/2005atlan.shtml (accessed April 10, 2006); Stuart Hinson, National Climatic Data Center, personal communications, August 22, 2005; Hydrologic Information Center, *Flood Fatalities*, www.nws.noaa.gov/oh/hic/flood_stats/recent_individual_deaths.shtml (accessed October 15, 2005); Indur M. Goklany, "Potential Consequences of Increasing Atmospheric CO_2 Concentration Compared to Other Environmental Problems," *Technology* 7S (2000): 189–213; National Weather Service, *2003 Annual Summaries*, www.nws.noaa.gov/om/severe_weather/sum03.pdf (accessed October 15, 2005); National Weather Service, *Summary of U.S. Natural Hazard Statistics*, www.nws.noaa.gov/om/severe_weather/sum04.pdf (accessed October 15, 2005); USBOC, *Historical National Population Estimates, 1900 to 1999*, www.census.gov/popest/archives/pre-1980/ (accessed August 14, 2005); USBOC, *Statistical Abstract of the United States 2006* (Washington, DC: GPO, 2006).

technologies (which include greater human and social capital). These advances have enabled people to benefit from adaptation measures, such as more reliable forecasts, early warning systems, elaborate evacuation plans, more robust construction of houses and infrastructure, an extensive transportation network, and the constant drumbeat of television and radio weathermen once a storm registers on the radar screens.[219] But for such technologies, the 2005 hurricane season in the United States would have been even more deadly.

Finally, in hindsight—particularly in light of the damage caused by levee breaks subsequent to Hurricane Katrina's passage through New Orleans and the tardy response to that event—it seems obvious that many of the fatalities that occurred during the 2005 hurricane season were avoidable. Some, for instance, Jürgen Trittin, Germany's erstwhile environment minister, suggested that Hurricane Katrina was nature's payback for a recalcitrant United States that refused to go along with the Kyoto Protocol, implying that catastrophe could have been avoided had the United States adhered to the protocol.[220] Many hurricanologists and other scientists who study natural disasters, however, ascribe the 2005 hurricane season's ferocity to the return of an extremely active phase in a natural cycle.[221] But even if climate change contributed to its fury, neither the protocol nor any other emission reduction scheme for greenhouse gas would have reduced its destructiveness significantly because whatever reductions might have been instituted would have been too little and too late, if for no reason other than the inertia of the climate system, which precludes either climate change or efforts to reverse it from taking effect rapidly. However, casualties could have been reduced much more effectively (and surely) through better adaptation, that is, smarter hazard management. This topic is one that I will return to in subsequent chapters.

Global Trends. Global trends in deaths and death rates from extreme weather events are broadly consistent with the experience in the United States outlined earlier. Figure 6.17, based on data from the Emergency Disaster Database (EM-DAT), the international disaster database maintained by the Office of Foreign Disaster Aid and Center for Research on the Epidemiology of Disasters at the Université Catholique de Louvain in Brussels, Belgium,[222] shows cumulative global trends in these critical measures between 1900 and 2004 for droughts, extreme temperatures (both extreme heat and extreme cold), floods, landslides, waves and surges, wild fires, and wind storms of different types (e.g., hurricanes, cyclones, tornados, and typhoons).[223] It indicates that both deaths and death rates

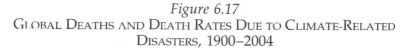

Figure 6.17
GLOBAL DEATHS AND DEATH RATES DUE TO CLIMATE-RELATED DISASTERS, 1900–2004

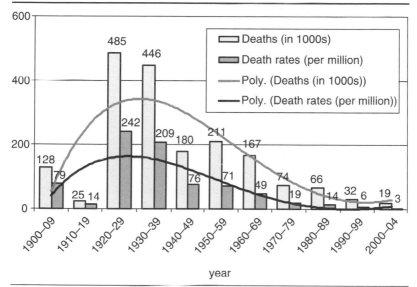

year

SOURCES: EM-DAT, *The OFDA/CRED International Disaster Database,* Université Catholique de Louvain, Brussels, Belgium, www.em-dat.net (accessed September 6, 2005); Colin McEvedy and Richard Jones, *Atlas of World Population History* (New York: Penguin, 1978); World Resources Institute, Earth-Trends, www.wri.org (accessed June 23, 2005).

have trended downward since the 1920s. Specifically, comparing the 1920s to the 2000–04 period, the annual number of deaths has declined from 485,200 to 19,400, a 96 percent decline, while the death rate per million has declined from 241.8 to 3.1, a decline of 98.7 percent.

Notably, these figures include 45,755 deaths attributed to the European heat wave of 2003, the lessons of which parallel that of Hurricane Katrina, namely, casualties are more easily and effectively reduced by bringing adaptive technologies to bear through expenditures of human and social capital rather than through greenhouse gas emission reductions. Perhaps, if the countries of the EU had spent a fraction of the amount and effort they devoted to the Kyoto Protocol on gearing up for adaptation they might have saved several thousand of their compatriots from an untimely death. The important thing is that such adaptation would have been effective whether or not climate change played a role in the intensity and duration of the heat wave.[224] However, reducing climate change would only have had a positive effect if it contributed significantly to the heat wave and if measures had been instituted decades ago.

Table 6.8 compares the average number of annual fatalities worldwide from extreme weather-related events against other causes of death. In 2002, according to the WHO, a total of 57.0 million people died worldwide from all causes, including 2.8 million from HIV/AIDS, 1.8 million from diarrheal diseases, 1.3 million from malaria, and 129,000 from other tropical diseases.[225] In other words, notwithstanding the headlines garnished by extreme weather-related events, they contribute only about 0.03 percent of global deaths.

Finally, a recent review paper in *Nature* claims that global warming may have been responsible for about 166,000 deaths worldwide in 2000.[226] The majority of these deaths, according to this study, were ascribed to malnutrition (77,000), diarrhea (47,000), and malaria (27,000).

This estimate, which is the centerpiece of the review article, is taken from an analysis put out under the auspices of the WHO.[227] However, its authors acknowledge the following:

> "Climate change occurs against a background of substantial natural climate variability, and its health effects are confounded by simultaneous changes in many other influences on population health. . . . Empirical observation of the health consequences of long-term climate change, followed by formulation, testing and then modification of hypotheses would therefore require long time-series (probably several decades) of careful monitoring. *While this process may accord with the canons of empirical science, it would not provide the timely information needed to inform current policy decisions on [greenhouse gas] emission abatement*, so as to offset possible health consequences in the future."[228] [Emphasis added.]

In other words, science was sacrificed in pursuit of a predetermined policy objective.[229] But, absent serendipity, one cannot base sound policy on poor science. Sound science, at best, is a necessary, but not sufficient, condition for sound policy.

If one nevertheless accepts these problematic estimates at face value, global warming currently accounts for about 0.3 percent of all global deaths. Clearly, there are other more significant public health matters today that deserve to be addressed before climate change.

Table 6.8
GLOBAL DEATHS PER YEAR DUE TO VARIOUS CAUSES, EARLY 2000s

Cause of Death	No. of Deaths	Percent of Total Deaths
Communicable Diseases	*18,324,000*	*32.13*
Tuberculosis	1,566,000	2.75
HIV/AIDS	2,777,000	4.87
Diarrhoeal diseases	1,798,000	3.15
Malaria	1,272,000	2.23
Other tropical diseases	129,000	0.23
Other infectious and parasitic diseases	3,362000	5.90
Subtotal—Infectious and parasitic diseases	10,904,000	19.12
Respiratory infections	3,963,000	6.95
Nutritional deficiencies	485,000	0.85
Maternal and perinatal conditions	2,972,000	5.21
Noncommunicable Conditions	*33,537,000*	*58.81*
Malignant neoplasms	7,121,000	12.49
Cardiovascular diseases	16,733,000	29.34
Respiratory diseases	3,702,000	6.49
Other noncommunicable conditions	5,981,000	10.49
Injuries	*5,168,000*	*9.06*
Road traffic accidents	1,192,000	2.09
Violence	559,000	0.98
War	172,000	0.30
Extreme weather events	**19,400**	**0.03**
All other injuries	3,225,600	5.66

NOTE: All data are for 2002, except for deaths due to extreme weather events, which are based on the annual average from 2000–04.

SOURCES: World Health Organization, *World Health Report 2004* (Geneva: WHO, 2004); EM-DAT, Emergency Disaster database, Office of Foreign Disaster Aid and Center for Research on the Epidemiology of Disasters at the Université Catholique de Louvain, Brussels, Belgium, www.em-dat.net/disasters/statisti.htm (accessed September 6, 2005).

Property Losses Due to Floods and Hurricanes

One might expect that while a wealthier society may take extra effort to limit loss of life, it may be less concerned about property losses. A wealthier society is also likely to have more property at risk.

One could also argue that as people have grown richer, insurance becomes more affordable. Moreover, over time, private insurance has become more widely available, and governments seem to be more willing to come in with disaster aid every time there is an adverse weather event. Hence, not only has the property at risk increased, the willingness to take risks is further enhanced. In addition, as time marches on and populations increase, one ought to expect that more property would be built in flood plains and other more risky locations. For all these reasons, it should be no surprise if property losses caused by floods and hurricanes increase with time regardless of whether the frequency and intensity of floods in the United States might have increased due to climatic change.

In a recent paper on property damage from floods in the United States from 1934 to 1999/2000, Downton, Miller, and Pielke Jr. show that total losses and per capita losses have increased significantly since 1934, but losses per unit of wealth have declined slightly (but not significantly).[230] This is consistent with Goklany's finding that between 1903 and 1997 although total property losses due to U.S. floods increased in terms of real dollars, there was no significant upward trend between 1926 and 1997 if those losses are measured as a percentage of the nation's wealth measured as fixed tangible reproducible assets (excluding land values).[231]

Similarly, with respect to hurricanes, Goklany found an upward trend in property losses in terms of real dollars between 1900 and 1997. However, when losses were measured in terms of percent of wealth, there was no trend between 1926 and 1997. This is generally consistent with Pielke Jr. and Landsea's analysis of property losses due to hurricanes between 1925 and 1995, which showed no increasing in trends once increases in assets-at-risk had been considered.[232]

Figure 6.18 shows trends from 1929 to 2004 for property losses from hurricanes in terms of the personal income in the 19 Gulf of Mexico and Atlantic states that have received at least one direct hit from a hurricane between 1850 and 2004.[233] In effect, this figure uses the change in a state's personal income as a proxy for the change in its wealth.[234] This was done to allow for growth in assets at risk over time.[235] This figure reaffirms the earlier finding, that is, there has been no significant trend in property losses measured in terms of weighted assets at risk, at least through 2004.

An analysis of economic losses per unit of GDP for natural disasters in Australia between 1967 and 1999 also showed no clear trend

Figure 6.18
PROPERTY LOSSES DUE TO HURRICANES, UNITED STATES, 1929–2004

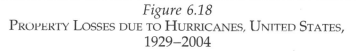

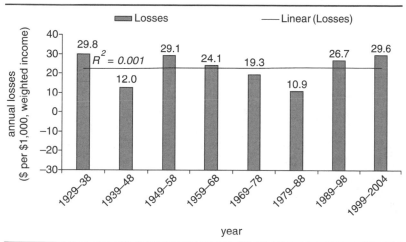

year

SOURCES: E. S. Blake, P. J. Herbert, J. D. Jarrell, M. Mayfield, and C. W. Landsea, "The Deadliest, Costliest, and Most Intense United States Hurricanes of This Century (and Other Frequently Requested Hurricane Facts," *NOAA Technical Memorandum NWS TPC-1* (Miami, FL: National Weather Service, 2005); Bureau of Economic Affairs, *National Economic Accounts, Section 1—Fixed Assets and Consumer Durable Goods*, www.bea.gov/bea/dn/FA2004/SelectTable.asp (accessed on August 22, 2005); USBOC, *Historical National Population Estimates, 1900 to 1999*, www.census.gov/popest/archives/pre-1980/ (accessed August 14, 2005); USBOC, *Statistical Abstract of the United States 2006* (Washington, DC: GPO, 2006).

in any direction. The bulk of these losses (87 percent) were because of extreme climate-related events, such as floods, severe storms, cyclones, and bushfires.[236] Within these categories, trends for absolute losses were flat, upward, and downward for floods, severe storms, and cyclones, respectively.

According to the IPCC's 2001 assessment based on information from reinsurance companies, however, the annual economic costs of catastrophic weather events has grown 10.3-fold (from about $4 billion in the 1950s to $40 billion from the 1950s to the 1990s).[237] However, it is not clear whether or what part of the increases are because of more severe weather; increases in the property at risk as the population becomes larger and wealthier; migration of people into riskier and more vulnerable locations as population increases and the less vulnerable locations are occupied; and inappropriate state policies and the availability of insurance, which allows individuals to bear less than their full burden of risk, better reporting, and wider coverage in recent years.

Infectious and Parasitic Diseases and Other Health Impacts

Malaria alone accounts for 75 percent of the cumulative DALYs lost from the 10 vector-borne diseases that the IPCC's 2001 report identifies as being potentially sensitive to climate change.[238] Thus, with respect to the impacts of climate change, malaria serves as a good proxy for the entire suite of climate-sensitive infectious diseases.

Despite major advances in public health, infectious and parasitic diseases are still among the major causes of higher mortalities and lower life expectancies in developing countries (see chapter 2). Malaria was estimated to have killed between 1.5 and 2.7 million people in 1996 and 1.3 million in 2002.[239] Some fear that because of global warming vectors such as the anopheles mosquito—the carrier of malaria—could become more widespread and the malaria parasite might be able to survive better.[240] Accordingly, the potential spread of malaria and vector-borne diseases in a warmer world has been raised as one of the major concerns regarding anthropogenic climate change.

However, others have argued that global warming would not necessarily expand the range of all vectors, nor need it otherwise increase the incidence of malaria.[241] Today, as is evident from the previous chapters and figures 6.12 through 6.14, the prevalence of these diseases has less to do with their potential ranges than with the public health measures taken to deal with the vectors and the diseases they spread. Malaria, cholera, and other diarrheal and parasitic diseases used to be prevalent around the world during the past century, including in the United States and Western Europe.[242] For instance, mainly because of cholera, yellow fever, typhoid, and various diarrheal and gastrointestinal diseases, the mean crude death rate (CDR) in New Orleans for a 30-year period between 1830 and 1859 was 60,000 per million.[243] By comparison, in 2000, it was 24,160 per million for Malawi—the nation with the world's highest CDR—

and 8,770 for the United States.[244] In 1900, the cumulative death rate in the United States for typhoid, paratyphoid, various gastrointestinal diseases, and all forms of dysentery was 1,860 per million population.[245] But, today, because of a host of public health measures, those diseases barely show up in current statistics—accounting for a death rate of less than 5 per million.[246]

Advances and investments in, and greater availability of, food, nutrition, and medical and public health technology helped reduce infectious and parasitic diseases worldwide—particularly among the young in developing countries. As a result, crude global death rates dropped from 20 per 1,000 population in 1950–55 to 9 in 2000–05, helping push global life expectancy at birth from 46.6 to 65.4 years during that period.[247] Those improvements would have been unlikely, if not impossible, without the transfer of knowledge and technologies generated in the richer nations, as well as the wealth generated by economic growth, which made those technologies more affordable.[248]

It has been suggested that climate change may be a factor in the recent resurgences in vector-borne diseases.[249] Resurgences include malaria in Henan Province, China; malaria and dengue in the Americas; and cholera in Peru and Rwanda. Studies, however, fail to show any clear link between changes in temperature and precipitation with increases in malaria.[250] However, increases in drug resistance; increased urbanization, which can lead to unsanitary conditions and facilitates the spread of infectious diseases; premature discontinuation of control measures, such as indoor spraying and use of impregnated mosquito nets; and faltering mosquito control and public health measures (e.g., reduction in DDT usage and chlorination) aggravated by poor nutrition seem to be more likely causes.[251] Interestingly enough, in many developing countries, malaria has retreated, advanced, and, in some places, retreated once again as levels of in-home malaria spraying have been increased, decreased, and, occasionally, increased again.[252]

This is amply illustrated by the history of malaria control in South Africa. DDT spraying in that area started in 1946.[253] By 1974, *Anopheles funestes*, the mosquito species associated with year-round prevalence of malaria in that region, had been eradicated (see figure 6.19).[254] In the 1991/92 malaria season, the number of malaria cases was around 600 in the Province of KwaZulu-Natal (KZN).[255] However, in 1996,

Figure 6.19
MALARIA CASES AND DEATHS - SOUTH AFRICA, 1971–JULY 2005

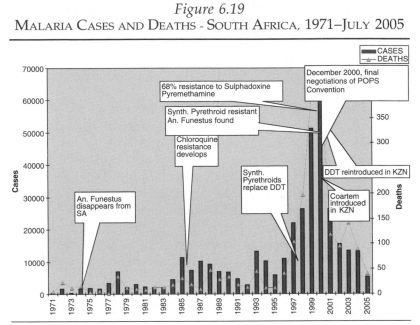

SOURCE: R. Tren, "IRS & DDT in Africa—Past and Present Successes," *54th Annual Meeting, American Society of Tropical Medicine and Hygiene (ASTMH),* Washington, DC, December 11–15, 2005.

DDT was replaced by synthetic pyrethroids. In 1999, members of *Anopheles funestes* were found in houses in KZN that had been sprayed. In 1999/2000, there were more than 40,000 cases in KZN. In 2000, DDT was brought back. By 2002, the number of cases had dropped to 3,500.

Craig and coworkers used 30 years of data from KZN to examine the variation in malaria case numbers due to climatic and nonclimatic factors. They found that cases were significantly associated with mean maximum daily temperatures from January to October of the preceding season and total rainfall during the current summer months of November–March, but they found no evidence of association between case totals and climate.[256] Because of the intensity of malaria control operations in KZN, climate appears to drive the interannual variation of malaria incidence, but not its overall level. Thus, although climate is a major limiting factor in the spatial and temporal distribution of malaria, many nonclimatic factors may alter

180

or override the effect of climate.[257] These nonclimatic factors include, primarily, drug resistance and HIV prevalence and, secondarily, cross-border people movements, agricultural activities, emergence of insecticide resistance, and the use—or perhaps more important, nonuse—of DDT for indoor residual spraying.[258]

South Africa's experience with DDT perfectly illustrates the perils of implementing the precautionary principle without applying a framework that would allow the risks of employing a technology to be compared against the risk of forgoing that technology, as well as of giving greater weight to hypothetical or uncertain problems than to known or more certain problems.[259]

To summarize, climate-sensitive diseases nowadays are problems only where the necessary public health measures are unaffordable or inadequate because societies lack sufficient economic, human, and social resources to cope with and address these problems or, as the experience with DDT and malaria amply illustrate, societies have—for whatever reason—eschewed available technologies.

Accelerated Sea Level Rise

A major concern related to global warming is that it could accelerate the rate at which the sea level has been rising for millennia due to the natural retreat from the ice ages. It is useful to examine trends in sea level rise although it is, unlike the indicators explored earlier, a physical measure rather than an indicator of socioeconomic impact. Such an examination would give us another clue as to whether human-induced warming might be having a significant impact.

The IPCC's 2001 estimate during the past century, based mainly on tide gauge observations, is 1–2 mm/year.[260] However, a 2006 paper by Church and White, also using tide gauge data, estimates that the global mean sea level rose by 1.7 ± 0.3 mm/year from 1870 to 2004, with a significant annual acceleration of 0.013 ± 0.006 mm/year. They estimate that if this acceleration remained constant, then, between 1990 and 2100, sea level would rise from 280 to 340 mm (or between 11.0 and 13.4 inches).[261]

However, estimates from Cazenave and Nerem, based on satellite (TOPEX/Poseidon) altimetry from 1993 to 2003 give an estimate of 2.8 ± 0.4 mm/year. Accounting for an average change in the altitude of land mass of 0.3 mm/year because of post-glacial rebound gives an overall sea level rise of 3.1 mm/year, which would be significantly larger than the rate of increase estimated by the IPCC for the 20th century.[262]

However, these data also show that there is substantial regional variation in sea level change. Some regions exhibit trends that are about 10 times the global mean. The highest rise is in the western Pacific and eastern Indian Oceans although sea level has been dropping in the eastern Pacific and western Indian Oceans, for example. They note that this high regional variability, "has led to questions about whether the rate of 20th century sea level rise, based on poorly distributed historical tide gauges, is really representative of the true global mean. Such a possibility has been the object of an active debate, and the discussion is far from being closed."[263]

In a more recent paper, Lombard and coworkers note that the year-to-year variability in the thermosteric component is dominated by the signatures of El Niño Southern Oscillation and decadal oscillations, such as the Pacific Decadal Oscillation and, to a lesser extent, the North Atlantic Oscillation.[264] Consequently, the global mean thermosteric sea level trends computed over 10-year windows exhibit an oscillatory pattern with a period of about 20 years. Accordingly, they conclude that "deriving trends from intervals shorter than the longest oscillatory time scale cannot be used for extrapolating backward or forward in time."

Suffice it to say, so far any accelerated sea level rise because of human-made warming is unlikely to have caused anything other than a minor impact on human or natural systems compared to other environmental stressors, such as development of coastlines, conversion of lands for aquaculture, drainage for other human land uses, sediment diversion due to dam construction up-river, construction of seawalls, and subsidence owing to water, oil, and gas extraction.[265]

The issue of sea level rise is deceptively simple, particularly for the lay person. What could be more obvious than the fact that higher temperatures would melt snow and ice in glaciers and the polar regions and would expand the volume of the ocean thereby raising sea levels worldwide? However, the noted regional variabilities, as well as an examination of the causes of the ups and downs of sea level during the past half-century in the Mediterranean Sea, for instance, indicate the issue of sea level rise is quite a bit more complex than that.[266] Further complicating matters are recent findings based on measurements from the European Remote Sensing Satellites (ERSS) that while the ice sheets in the Antarctic Peninsula and West Antarctica are thinning, the East Antarctica, a much larger region, has apparently been thickening from 1992 (the first year satellite data became available) to 2003. As a result, the total volume of ice in Antarctica has increased, and the net contribution of the Antarctic ice sheet to sea level rise is slightly negative (− 0.02 mm/year).[267] Measurements from the ERSS also show that although the ice margins of Greenland are shrinking, its interior is growing due to higher snowfall, such that on the whole the volume of the Greenland ice sheet is increasing.[268] However, it should be kept in mind that in the context of climate change, 11 years worth of data are not sufficient to establish a long-term trend, a fact frequently forgotten by journalists and sometimes even scientists.

Notably, since the previous words were written, a couple of new papers addressing the polar ice sheets have garnished a substantial amount of press. One paper, based on 34 months of data, found that Antarctic ice sheets are losing 152 cubic kilometers (km³) of ice per year, which would raise sea levels by 0.4 mm/year or 1.6 inches a century.[269] The other paper, based on a 9-year-long record and a combination of empirical data and model results, estimated that the Greenland ice sheet is losing 224 km³/year, which is clearly at odds with the estimate provided earlier, but which was based on a slightly longer record. In any case, according to this paper, it will take another 5,400 years to melt the remaining 1,200,000 km³ in that ice sheet, which might raise sea level by 23 feet (7 meters) or 0.05 inches/year,[270] which is a pretty modest amount.

Summary

For some climate-sensitive sectors and indicators (e.g., agricultural productivity and food security, deaths and death rates due to extreme events, overall death rates, life expectancies, and biomass in the northern forests) matters have improved despite any climate change that may have occurred. For others (e.g., global deforestation, loss of biodiversity, and sea level rise), where matters continue to worsen, the effect of any human-made climate change so far has, at worst, been relatively minor.

The WHO's *World Health Report 2002*, based on the results of its *Global Burden of Disease 2000 (Version 2)* study, attributes 154,000 deaths in 2000 (or 0.3 percent of the global total) to human-induced climate change, which translates into 0.4 percent of the lost DALYs globally.[271] These estimates were apparently derived by attributing to climate change 2.4 percent of global deaths due to diarrhea, 6 percent of deaths due to malaria in some middle-income countries, and 7 percent of deaths due to dengue, as well as an unspecified percentage of deaths due to malnutrition and flooding.

Although the methods by which these percentages were obtained is not transparent, they seem to be based on precursors to methods used for developing the estimate of 166,000 deaths provided in the previously mentioned 2005 review article in *Nature*,[272] which, as has been noted, is suspect. The 154,000 estimate is apparently based on climate modeling using three climate change scenarios.[273] It too acknowledges that "current estimates of the potential health impacts of climate change are based on models with considerable uncertainty."[274]

The problem is not only that climate models are uncertain at the global level, but also that the uncertainty of their outputs escalates as one goes to the finer geographical scales at which most impact analyses necessarily have to be undertaken. (The issue of the credibility of existing models to estimate the impacts of climate change is addressed in greater detail in chapter 10.) Moreover, the meager information made available on both the *World Health Report 2002* and *Global Burden of Disease 2000* websites provides no details on the methodologies used to translate changes in climatic variables into health impacts; hence, one cannot judge the credibility of the exercise.

But there are, nevertheless, grounds for skepticism. Although temperature and precipitation can affect the incidence of malaria, for example, it is less clear whether the combination of the changes in temperature and precipitation will increase its incidence. More important, as was discussed earlier, the overall incidence is more sensitive to the public health measures taken (or not taken) rather than climate change. The materials on the Internet do not elaborate whether or how the analysis filtered out the effect of confounding variables such as wealth, education, access to public health and medical facilities, the prevalence of AIDS, smoking, indoor air pollution, unsafe water, and nutrition. Moreover, if warming is indeed causing additional deaths, the signal that it is doing so in the aggregate seems to be nonexistent at the *global* level or, if it is, it is swamped by other factors. Despite any warming that may have occurred, fewer people are dying from non-HIV infectious diseases; deaths and death rates due to extreme weather events have declined; global food production has increased, and between 1969–71 and 1998–2000 the number of people suffering from hunger and undernourishment worldwide has declined from 37 percent to 17 percent of the population of the developing countries.[275] But, in the past couple of decades, we have indeed seen backsliding on hunger and malaria in sub-Saharan Africa; however, this is due not to climate change but to a deterioration in economic development, public health services, and institutional and policy failures.

Nevertheless, even if one accepts the *World Health Report 2002* estimate that climate change is responsible for 0.15 million deaths per year, that same report attributes 6.2 million deaths to childhood and maternal undernutrition; another 16.9 million deaths to other diet-related risk factors (e.g., blood pressure, cholesterol, obesity, and low fruit and vegetable intake); 1.7 million deaths due to unsafe water and inadequate sanitation and hygiene; 1.6 million deaths due to indoor air pollution from indoor heating and cooking with wood, coal, and biofuels; and 1.1 million deaths due to malaria. Not surprisingly, therefore, with climate change contributing 0.28 percent of mortality and 0.38 percent of lost DALYs globally, data from the *World Health Report 2002* ranks it at 16th or 15th out of 19 global health risk factors related to food, nutrition, and environmental and occupational exposure, depending on whether the rankings are based on mortality or lost DALYs.

These risks account for a total of 54 percent of all mortality and about 38 percent of lost DALYs globally.[276]

In summary, based on the current level of impacts, climate change today does not rank among the top global public health or environmental priorities. However, if the world becomes wealthier and more technologically advanced, one should expect greenhouse gases to continue to build up in the atmosphere, exacerbating climate change even as other existing problems are diminished. Thus, climate change should rise on the list of priorities.

Chapter 10 will address whether climate change is likely to advance sufficiently on this list to warrant being labeled the most important or urgent environmental problem facing the globe, as many have claimed.

7. Are Long-Term Trends Consistent with Environmental Transitions?

In the previous chapter I examined long-term trends in various indicators to gauge the diverse impacts of man's activities on the environment. Those environmental trends indicate, among other things, that despite increasing affluence and material well-being, which increased demands for food, land, water, and other natural resources, in many instances environmental indicators have actually improved during the past few decades. The trends presented in chapter 6 also indicate that although in the developing countries environmental impacts might be higher and, often, increasing, they are lower in the richer countries and generally decreasing. In addition, tables 6.1 through 6.4 show that over the long term, technology eventually has actually reduced impacts per capita or per gross domestic product (GDP). Hence, long-term trends do not support prognostications that affluence and technology will necessarily increase environmental impacts (as suggested by simplistic interpretations of the IPAT identity). In fact, these trends might be consistent with the notion of an environmental transition, introduced in chapter 5.

However, before addressing whether the trends presented in chapter 6 are indeed consistent with the environmental transition hypothesis, it is critical to recognize that environmental transitions are not inevitable. For such transitions to occur, economic growth and technological change should increase with time, as should the quality of life for the general population. Moreover, implicit to the environmental transition hypothesis is the existence of a relatively effective functioning mechanism for translating a populace's desires for a better quality of life into private or public actions.

Those four conditions are generally valid for the United States and the other rich nations of the world during the periods for which historical trends in environmental indicators were examined in chapter 6. Figure 2.13 shows that economic development has advanced steadily in these countries for the past two centuries. More specifically, tables 6.1 through 6.4 show that economic development increased during the periods for which environmental trends were examined in chapter 6. Those tables also indicate concurrent advances in technology in the United States and worldwide with respect to the specific indicators that were examined. The improvement in the state of humanity documented in chapter 2 confirms that the third condition (i.e., the quality of life should also improve) is also satisfied for the United States and other rich nations. This improvement is also reflected in the fact that during the past century or more the human development index (HDI), one measure for the quality of human life, has advanced for the wealthy countries (see chapter 2). Finally, because these countries are democracies, the electoral system ensures the existence of a mechanism—however imperfect—for translating society's desire for a better quality of life into actions.

Note, however, that advances in the quality of life (or HDI) do not necessarily mean that the reverse is true, that is, societies have functioning mechanisms for converting desires into actions. Secular improvements in technology might by themselves improve quality of life (or reduce environmental impacts, for that matter) without any conscious action on society's part. For instance, as noted previously, indoor air pollution and emissions per GDP for many substances, such as sulfur dioxide (SO_2), volatile organic compounds (VOC), and nitrogen oxide (NO_x), began to be reduced decades before they were generally perceived as being detrimental to public health or the environment (i.e., before individuals, the general population, or policymakers had good reasons to try to reduce the impacts of these substances).[1] In the absence of such perceptions, such improvements can be attributed to secular advances in technology driven by market forces. With respect to coal usage, for instance, these market forces were powered by the urge to reduce costs by conserving energy, the desire for convenience, or the appeal of a cleaner domicile or commercial establishment.

Nor does a declining quality of life or HDI imply that society does not desire an improved quality of life or lacks mechanisms to convert desires into actions. Poor policies, despite the best of intentions, might conceivably reduce HDI or its components. However, considering the spectacular advances in technology during the past century or more and that technology keeps improving, the policies have to be exceedingly poor to bring about declines in HDI. Yet, this is not impossible, as evidenced by the deterioration in HDI during the late 1980s and 1990s in most of the former Communist countries and in sub-Saharan Africa (see chapters 2 and 3).

Another reason quality of life might decline could be the introduction of a brand new or more virulent disease that may overwhelm a society's human and capital resources or technological ability to devise, pursue, and implement solutions. We saw previously that the advance of a new disease, HIV/AIDS, and the return of more lethal versions of old diseases, such as drug-resistant tuberculosis, indeed rolled back life expectancy (and HDI) in many parts of sub-Saharan Africa, but not in the United States (and other wealthy countries). The difference, of course, is that wealth enables the mobilization of economic and human resources to more easily and quickly devise, and implement, solutions to such problems.

Although most countries outside of the wealthiest nations now have adopted some of the trappings of democracy, their democratic tradition, if it exists at all, is not very deep. Yet, despite the lack of a robust mechanism to translate the population's desires into actions, many of their HDIs have indeed improved during the past several decades (see chapter 2). Two reasons might account for this improvement. First, knowledge about good hygiene, sanitation, safe drinking water, food, and nutrition has continued to expand and diffuse from the richer to the poorer nations. At the same time, technologies to address them are relatively cheap and widely available worldwide. Third, except in the rarest of instances, even undemocratic regimes strive to improve the lot of their citizenry, if for no reason other than because it reduces the possibility of unrest and provides the rulers with a patina of legitimacy. However, this has its limits because the quality of life of the general population takes second place behind the well-being of the rulers (or ruling groups)—or their ideologies. Thus, despite an increase in technological ability and broad technological advances worldwide, the quality of life declined in the latter decades of the 20th century for the average Iraqi and North Korean, though not necessarily for their ruling elites.

Given all these considerations, one ought not to be surprised if the environmental trends presented in chapter 6 for the richer nations at least—and, possibly, the globe—exhibit stylized environmental transitions as depicted in figure 4.1. But do they?

Cropland

For the United States, figure 6.1 shows that cropland harvested—a measure of man's impact on the land—followed a stylized path consistent with the environmental transition hypothesis. It peaked earlier in the 1930s, and it is now at a level slightly below its 1910 level.

Globally, cropland per capita—a leading environmental indicator—peaked around 1930 (figure 6.2). As a result, cropland growth has slowed significantly in recent decades. Between 1961 and 2002, cropland increased by less than 13 percent although population increased by more than 120 percent. In fact, figure 6.2 indicates that cropland seems to be reaching a plateau, although whether this presages an actual decline, in consonance with expectations under the environmental transition hypothesis, will depend largely on whether society allows farmers worldwide to continue bringing—and adopting—newer and more productive technologies online, as they have been doing since at least the 1950s.

Significantly, the decline in cropland per capita has been accompanied by a significant increase in food production per capita because of an enormous surge in the productivity of the food and agricultural sector (figures 6.2 and 6.3). Accordingly, food prices have declined and the world is better fed (figures 2.1 and 6.4), less hungry, and less susceptible to disease today than ever before.

In addition, the increases in productivity across the food and agricultural sector have allowed the richest countries to add to their forest cover. That is, those countries have apparently gone past their environmental transition for habitat loss. However, developing countries, as a group, continue to lose forest cover because the increase in their demand for food exceeds their growth in productivity of their food and agricultural sector. Thus, historical trends over the past century or more suggest that collectively the world might be approaching a transition for cropland, which, ultimately, might help halt further global losses of habitats (including forests), particularly if population growth continues to slow. But we are not there yet. And we won't get there unless we are willing to adopt new and more productive technologies that, moreover, require fewer external inputs, some of which, as we will see in chapter 9, are already available for adoption.

Traditional Air Pollution

In chapter 6, I examined long-term trends in three sets of national air pollution indicators for the United States, namely, emissions, indoor air quality, and outdoor (ambient) air quality. Table 7.1 summarizes for each combination of indicator and pollutant, various milestones and features based on the history of the control of that pollutant.[2] Specifically, this table indicates the period of perception [p(P)] and the time of federalization [t(F)] for each *pollutant*.[3] It also shows for each *indicator*, the period of transition [p(T)], which is the period subsequent to or contemporaneous with p(P) during which the indicator went through its dominant peak. Table 7.1 also shows the periods of transition for emissions per gross national product (GNP) although, as noted previously, this is a leading, rather than a true, air pollution indicator because it is not directly related to socioeconomic or environmental impacts of that pollutant but could signal the future trend in its emissions.

An examination of table 7.1 in conjunction with figure 6.5 shows that despite several ups and downs in U.S. emissions of SO_2, VOC, and NO_x during the 20th century, there has been only one pronounced peak for each of these pollutants once it entered into its p(P), although subsidiary peaks are also possible. This is also illustrated more clearly in figure 6.6 for SO_2. This observation is also, by and large, valid for emissions for VOC, NO_x, and carbon monoxide (CO).[4] With respect to particulate matter (PM), emissions data from 1940 to 1997 also show one peak, but since p(P) precedes 1940 for PM, it is not clear whether there might have been additional peaks before 1940 but after p(P).[5] Thus, to the extent we have information, the emissions data for the traditional air pollutants in the United States are consistent with *stylized* environmental transition curves (see figure 5.1).

Figure 6.8 and table 7.1 show that trends for indoor air pollution in the United States exhibit relatively well-defined environmental transitions. These transitions occurred because of a combination of fuel shifts away from coal and wood to cleaner fuels such as oil and natural gas, which produced less smoke and ash (and dirt generally) and improvements in combustion efficiency, against a background of increasing number of households (and larger houses). These transitions apparently occurred in the 1940s, if not earlier. Note, however, that NO_x has a subsidiary peak around 1960, which is not evident

Table 7.1

MILESTONES AND TRANSITIONS FOR VARIOUS POLLUTANTS AND INDICATORS

Substance	Period or Year When Substance Was		Worst Year(s) or Period of Transition (Nationally, Unless Noted Otherwise)			
	Recognized or perceived as a pollutant [p(P)]	First federally regulated [t(F)]	Indoor air quality	Outdoor air quality	Emissions	E/GNP[a]
PM	<1900	1971[e]	<1940	<1957	1950[c]	1940s or earlier
SO₂	approximately 1950	1971[e]	<1940[f]	early to mid 1960s	1973	1920s
CO	approximately late 1950s[d]	1967[e]	<1940	mid 1960s, but not after 1970	1960s	1940s or earlier
VOC/O₃	CA 1950s elsewhere—1960s or later	1971[b, g]	NE	CA mid 1950s	NE	NE
		1967[e]	<1940[f]	elsewhere— mid to late 1970s	1960s	1930s

(continued on next page)

Are Long-Term Trends Consistent with Environmental Transitions?

Table 7.1

MILESTONES AND TRANSITIONS FOR VARIOUS POLLUTANTS AND INDICATORS (*continued*)

Substance	Period or Year When Substance Was Recognized or perceived as a pollutant [p(P)]	First federally regulated [t(F)]	Worst Year(s) or Period of Transition (Nationally, Unless Noted Otherwise)			
			Indoor air quality	Outdoor air quality	Emissions	E/GNP[a]
NO_x	CA 1950s, elsewhere—1960s or later	1971[b]	<1940, secondary peak around 1960[f]	1978–79	1977–78	1930s

a. The peak in this leading indicator shows the latest time by which "cleanup" had begun either through deliberate actions or by happenstance (see text). b. The Clean Air Amendment of 1970 was signed on the last day of 1970, but most federal regulations went into effect later. c. For CO: long known to be deadly indoors, but its status as an outdoor air pollutant was recognized much later. d. For PM-10. e. Model Year 1968 for automobiles. f. Not generally recognized by the public or policymakers as needing remediation indoors. g. Because federal vehicle emissions were borrowed from, and went into effect after, California's, federalization did not have any effect until after the 1970 amendment was signed. NE = not estimated.

NOTE: This table summarizes data provided in chapter 6 on U.S. air trends of traditional air pollutants.

SOURCE: Updated from Indur M. Goklany, *Clearing the Air: The Real Story of the War on Air Pollution* (Washington, DC: Cato Institute, 1999).

in the record for the other pollutants in figure 6.8 because its emissions were not reduced as dramatically by the shifts toward oil and gas as were emissions of PM less than 10 micrometers (PM-10), VOC, CO, and SO_2.

The transitions for SO_2, VOC, and NO_x occurred as much by serendipity as by conscious effort because these transitions preceded their periods of perception (see table 7.1). By the time these three substances were perceived by the general public as potential sources of health problems, they had been reduced substantially indoors as a side effect of all the voluntary (market-driven) measures taken to reduce smoke, ash, dust, and CO inside the home and to save household fuel costs. Therefore, although these improvements could be ascribed to secular improvements in technology, it would, arguably, be inappropriate to portray reductions in indoor air quality for SO_2, VOC, and NO_x as consequences of "true" *environmental* transitions.

Table 7.1 and figure 6.7 show that long-term trends in ambient SO_2 air quality for the United States are consistent with the environmental transition hypothesis. National composites for ambient air quality for the other traditional air pollutants also follow a similar pattern.[6]

The air pollution trends furnished in chapter 6 for the other rich countries are also generally consistent with the environmental transition hypothesis. This is clearly the case for traditional air pollutants (i.e., PM, SO_2, and CO) that have been perceived for sufficiently long periods to be inimical to a better quality of life because they contribute to major public health problems and environmental degradation.

Significantly, an earlier analysis using 1990/91 data had not seen much improvement in either VOC or NO_x emissions for many of the richer countries (except for the United States).[7] However, the analysis in chapter 6 uses data for 1990–2002 for a group of 30 Organisation for Economic Co-operation and Development (OECD) countries, and it shows that for most of these countries, trends for VOC and NO_x also seem to fit a stylized inverted U-shaped pattern. For VOC, 25 of those countries seem to have gone past their peak emission levels, while four more (Norway, South Korea, Spain, and Turkey) might also be on the downward (post-transition) part of the environmental transition curve. New Zealand is the sole country for which VOC levels might be increasing; however, given its geography and climate, it's not readily apparent how critical that might be for the formation of ground-level ozone, the secondary pollutant that necessitates VOC control in other areas of the world.[8] Significantly, air quality monitoring from 1992 to 2002 did not measure any exceedances of ozone guideline values in New Zealand.[9] Regarding NO_x, 22 of the 30 countries seem to have moved beyond their transitions, but six others (Australia, New Zealand, Mexico, Portugal, Spain, and Turkey) and, possibly, Ireland, had yet to go through a clear transition. Notably, the last five countries arrived relatively late to prosperity levels rivaling those of other OECD countries. These trends are also consistent with the notion that for many of these countries the periods of perception for VOC and NO_x were late in coming and that, just as for the United States, transitions for NO_x might have been further delayed because of the relatively high costs of NO_x control (compared to economic and human resources that those countries could mobilize), especially when one simultaneously attempts to reduce CO and VOC emissions. Despite those problems, by the mid 1990s the richer countries were at or beyond the environmental transitions for VOC and NO_x.

Water-Related Deaths

Regarding deaths due to water-related diseases, the data presented here for the United States show only a declining trend from 1900 onward. This is because by that time, the United States had passed its transition for these diseases. Figures 6.13 and 6.14, which show broad improvements in access to safe water and sanitation with time, suggest that for these indicators much of the rest of the world is today to the right side (i.e., the downward side) of their respective environmental transition curves. Equally important, the per capita income level at which a country reaches full access to safe water and sanitation services has dropped over time.

Global Warming

Global carbon emissions from fossil fuel and industrial sources have continued to grow through the last two centuries. By 2002, they had grown to 13 times their 1900 level (see table 6.4 and figure 7.1). However, the carbon intensity of the global economy as measured by global carbon emissions per global economic product (GEP)[10]—a measure of technological change and a *leading* indicator for total emissions rather than an indicator of the socioeconomic or

Figure 7.1
GLOBAL AND U.S. FOSSIL FUEL AND INDUSTRIAL CARBON
EMISSIONS, 1820–2002

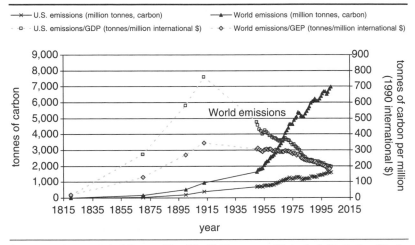

SOURCES: Angus Maddison, *The World Economy: Historical Statistics* (Paris: OECD, 2003), www.ggdc.net/~maddison/Historical_Statistics/horizontal-file.xls (accessed July 1, 2005); GGDC,*Total Economy Database*, www.ggdc.net (accessed July 1, 2005); Gregg Marland, T. J. Boden, and R. J. Andres, *National CO₂ Emissions from Fossil-Fuel Burning, Cement Manufacture, and Gas Flaring: 1751–2002* (Oak Ridge, TN: Carbon Dioxide Information Analysis Center, Oak Ridge National Laboratory, 2005), http://cdiac.esd.ornl.gov/ftp/trends/emissions/usa.dat (accessed December 21, 2005).

environmental impact of climate change—peaked around the time of World War I. Since then, the carbon intensity, however, has been declining more or less continually. These declines are the result of market forces that, first, led to the decarbonization of the global energy system at a rate of 0.3 percent per year since 1850.[11] Second, consumers, large and small, invested in conservation and more efficient technologies to maximize profits (or, in the case of individuals and households, money in their pockets and bank balances) by, among other things, reducing their energy costs. These declines in carbon emissions per GDP only accelerated after the 1973 oil shock. As a result, the rate of technological change, measured by the annual decline in emissions per GEP, which had been improving at the rate of 0.3 percent per year between 1913 and 1973, accelerated to 1.6

percent per year after the oil shock. Impressive as this seems, the growth in GEP between 1973 and 2001 was, at 3.1 percent per year, even more impressive.[12] Thus, emissions continued to grow 1.5 percent per year. Then, after the price of oil retreated in the 1980s and 1990s, technological change, measured by the rate of decline of emissions per GDP, moderated.

Another leading "indicator," industrial carbon dioxide (CO_2) emissions per capita, has essentially remained more or less stuck around 1.10 to 1.20 tonnes of carbon per capita per year since 1970, although it seems to have touched a maximum at 1.23 tonnes per capita in 1979.[13] The lack of improvement in per capita emissions is because improvements in technology (i.e., efficiency) have been offset by the increase in per capita energy use around the world, which, moreover, is magnified by the rapid industrialization and "automobilization" of China and India, in particular. And because population growth, despite decelerating since the late 1960s, continued to be positive, total carbon emissions continued to grow.[14]

Although declining emissions per GDP and per capita might presage eventual downturns in emissions, that is, environmental transitions, such transitions have not yet come to pass for either the United States or global CO_2 emissions. And, in fact, one should not expect such transitions to have occurred yet.

First, although some environmentalists and scientists claimed in the 1980s (or even before) that CO_2 could be a major environmental problem, for the majority of the global public and, certainly, policymakers, the period of perception for CO_2 emissions or global warming did not commence until the late 1980s or even the spring of 1996, when the second assessment report of the Intergovernmental Panel on Climate Change (IPCC) was released.[15] That report spawned the 1997 Kyoto Protocol, although several scientists, including a number of climatologists, continued to question the immediate need for CO_2 controls.[16] Perhaps, more important, policymakers in some key countries remain skeptical as evidenced, for instance, by the United States and Australia's rejection, and Russia's very tardy acceptance, of the protocol. As a result, the protocol only went into effect in 2005.

To compound matters, despite various claims from politicians, journalists, newspapers, and even some scientists,[17] there has never been any showing that global warming is today, or will be over the next few decades, as important as the numerous other social, economic, and environmental problems facing humanity and the globe. Those other problems include, as will be shown in chapters 10 and 11, indoor air pollution due to burning of solid fuels inside the home or sulfates outdoors, loss of habitat and forests to agricultural needs, malaria, and water-related deaths and diseases due to insufficient access to sanitation and safe water. The few studies that have compared the magnitude of potential problems caused by global warming against those caused by other existing environmental and public health problems indicate that, by and large, the latter outweigh those problems caused by global warming, at least for the foreseeable future, that is, 50 to 100 years from now.[18]

Second, even if p(P) for CO_2 had ended with the IPCC's second assessment report in 1996, it would be premature to expect a downturn in CO_2 emissions by 2005. After all, it only took a decade for the Kyoto Protocol to enter into effect, and it will take an additional four to five decades to replace the global energy system, which is the major source of human-made CO_2. Such a turnover has also been retarded by the inability of proponents of control to show that accelerated turnover of the energy infrastructure is worth the benefits, by the added costs associated with non-fossil fuel energy alternatives, and by the lack of enthusiasm for various commercially demonstrated noncombustion alternatives to fossil fuels (such as nuclear or hydro) even among the most vociferous institutional supporters of greenhouse gas controls. In addition, the relationship between CO_2 emissions and human or environmental well-being is far from linear.

More relevant to trends in human and environmental well-being than either CO_2 emissions or emissions per GDP are trends in climate-sensitive indicators of human well-being or environmental quality, many of which were examined in chapter 6. Those trends seem to have been more sensitive to technological change (and human adaptability) than to human-induced or natural climatic change. For some climate-sensitive indicators, matters have improved during the 20th century (e.g., global agricultural productivity and deaths caused by extreme climatic events both in the United States and globally). Other climate-sensitive indicators (e.g., sea level rise, U.S. property losses because of floods and hurricanes, and death rates because of extreme heat or cold events) do not show significant changes in impacts or level of risk, which are outside the range of natural climatic variability. Yet others (e.g., deforestation) have been more sensitive to the level of economic development and the ability to harness technology than to human-induced climate change. Although one might argue that the evidence regarding these indicators suggests that they are near or past their environmental transitions, it could also be posited that climate change is only now warming up, and it is premature to declare a victory (or a draw) now. This issue is addressed in greater detail in chapter 10.

Lessons from U.S. Air Pollution Trends

The U.S. experience with air quality outlined in chapter 6 is summarized in table 7.1. This table provides several clues as to the factors affecting the timing, width, and duration of various environmental transitions.

Table 7.1 suggests that people and society dealt with air pollution almost as if driven by a relentless logic. Initially, the indicators of air pollution worsened as people and communities strove to improve their quality of life through jobs and economic growth. As the population became more prosperous and new technologies became available, the problems perceived to be the worst, and the easiest to address, were dealt with first. Families (and individuals) cleaned up their personal environment, that is, inside their households, of the most obvious problem—smoke and, to some extent, CO—before anything else. The measures to reduce such air pollution indoors also improved the outside air in their neighborhood. By happenstance, they also reduced indoor concentrations of other coal-related pollutants, namely, VOC and SO_2, although they were not generally deemed by the general public or policymakers to be particularly harmful at that time.

Next, attention turned to outdoor air. Once again, the first target was smoke because it was also the most obvious. New technologies and prosperity helped move the fuel mix from coal and wood toward oil and gas and generally increased fuel efficiencies across all economic sectors. As a result, soon after World War II, if not earlier, most urban areas had gone through their environmental transitions for smoke.

With greater prosperity, the public's health improved and mortality dropped, in large part because of cleaner water, better hygiene, improved nutrition, antibiotics, vaccines, and other new medicines (see, for example, figure 6.12). Crude death rates, which were running at 17.2 per thousand in 1900, had dropped about 45 percent by 1950. Thus, in the years following World War II, when deadly air pollution episodes occurred on both sides of the Atlantic, it was easier to detect "excess" deaths above the norm. At the same time, advances in epidemiological methods and measuring techniques for various substances (adapted from studies of occupational safety) made it possible to ascribe the excess deaths to PM, SO_2, or both. Thus, transitions for ambient PM and SO_2 air quality came next, followed by the transitions for CO and ozone (O_3) air quality. That the transition for NO_x air quality came last is fitting for a pollutant that was never ranked very high in terms of adverse effects at the levels it occurred in the outdoor air and that was also the most expensive to control.

Notably, by the time the U.S. federal government took over air pollution control in 1970, matters had begun to improve for the pollutants of greatest concern to the public. For most of the nation these pollutants were those associated with excess mortality during the air pollution episodes of the 1940s, 1950s, and 1960s (i.e., total suspended particulates and SO_2). In California, however, the pollutant of greatest concern arguably was O_3 or oxidants. But for this case too, ambient air quality has been improving since the mid 1950s, long before federalization of air pollution control in California.

Curiously, table 7.1 also shows that it is possible to improve air quality even while emissions may be increasing. For SO_2 and probably CO, both primary pollutants, the transitions for outdoor air quality occurred before those for aggregate national emissions. The data on PM are unclear on which came first—the transition for air quality or for emissions—because the emissions data are for PM-10, while the national air quality data for PM-10 are only available from 1988 onward. (Note that based on national composites, ambient air quality for PM measured as TSP had peaked by the late 1950s.) However, with respect to O_3, a secondary pollutant, the transition for national emissions preceded that for air quality.[19]

The order in which the periods of transition occurred for the various pollutants suggests that for a particular society the environmental transition for a pollutant is determined by the general level of affluence, the state of the technology, the effects of the pollutant relative to other societal risks, the likelihood that an individual's action will result in a noticeable and quick improvement, and the affordability of measures to reduce those effects, as well as the strength of the relationship between the precise indicator used to characterize the pollutant's effects and the nature and magnitude of the impacts of that pollutant. But most of these factors are not independent of each other. As noted, affluence and technology are interdependent. Moreover, knowledge of a pollutant's effects on society is itself a product of technology (such as improved technology to measure, model, or estimate pollutants and their effects). In addition, affordability of control and mitigation measures is a function of both affluence and technology. Thus, environmental transitions for a particular society, in the final analysis, ought to be determined by affluence and technology.

Because the timing of a transition depends not only on the specific pollutant but also on the particular indicator chosen to represent the pollutant's impacts as well as the relative social, economic, and environmental costs and benefits of controls, it is possible for a society, group, or individual to be simultaneously to the left of the environmental transition for one pollutant but to the right of it for another. Hence, it is quite rational to oppose, say, CO_2 controls on one hand, while supporting stricter controls on CO on the other hand. Nor would it be unusual to support VOC controls at refineries but oppose mandatory inspection and maintenance of one's own vehicle. However, there is a line beyond which such rationalizations mutate into hypocrisies, such as bemoaning the environmental effects of sports utility vehicles while driving one or decrying the build-up of greenhouse gases while opposing windmills that obscure one's scenery or environmentally sound drilling for low-carbon natural gas or no-carbon nuclear power plants.[20]

Determinants of Environmental Transitions

In light of the earlier discussion and examination of empirical data from the United States and other rich nations, it is possible to list several factors that might affect the shape, height, and timing of single-country environmental transitions.

Fundamentally, an environmental transition comes about because neither economic growth nor environmental quality is identical to a society's aggregate quality of life at all times. At an early stage of economic development, greater economic development is a better indicator of an improvement in the quality of life, while at later stages environmental quality is a better surrogate, at least until the environment is deemed to be sufficiently clean.

Because society's quest for a better quality of life is a cornerstone of the environmental transition hypothesis, that hypothesis implicitly assumes that society's desire to improve its collective quality of life is converted into actions. As noted, such a conversion is more likely to occur in democratic societies where popularly elected legislators—in their eagerness to prove that they are responsive to the public's desires—will tend to enshrine those desires into laws and regulations.[21] Because symbolism, for better or worse, is important in electoral politics, these rules and regulations are likely to be promulgated even if cleanup is likely to be voluntary and virtually self-fulfilling due to market forces. Arguably, such was the case in the United States for the worst air pollutants, as well for access to safe water.[22] Nevertheless, federal legislators enacted the Clean Air Act of 1970, the Clean Water Act of 1972, and the Safe Drinking Water Act of 1974, allowing them to take enormous credit for battles that, for practical purposes, had already been won or were in the process of being won (see, e.g., figures 6.7, 6.8, and 6.13).

Thus, rules and regulations are probably an inescapable part of an environmental transition in a democratic society. However, even if more stringent regulation might be among the proximate causes for bringing about an environmental transition, such regulation does not arise—nor is its success achieved—in a vacuum. Eventual success, in fact, is a consequence of having not only the desire but also the means to improve quality of life.

Affluence and technological progress are the means whereby our desires and needs, including those for a clean environment, are converted into reality. The wealthier the nation, the more it can afford to research, develop, and install the technologies necessary for a cleaner environment. Figure 4.3, which shows that expenditures in research and development increase with the level of economic development, hints at this.

Moreover, it is insufficient to merely install technologies. They should be installed and operated properly, which requires adequate human and social capital. And as we saw in earlier chapters, the level of such capital, for which the level of educational attainment serves as a surrogate, increases with wealth (see figures 2.15 and 2.16). In other words, it is easier for wealthier societies to mobilize the economic and human resources needed to solve its problems. Perhaps nothing better illustrates this than the example of HIV/AIDS. It is no accident that the technologies, practices, and systems to cope with this disease, for which humanity had no previous defenses, were all developed in the affluent west and in a remarkably short time. Only after those methods are developed, is it possible to spread them around the world, no matter how imperfectly, through trade and aid.

In addition, as societies have become more affluent, their economies have generally followed a common path going, first, from an agricultural to an industrial economy and, then, to a knowledge- and service-based economy. Because of such an evolution, trends for emissions per GNP also go through a peak, which, in turn, accentuates an environmental transition for emissions. Affluence— or the desire for greater affluence—also helps establish conditions that moderate population growth rates, and, predictably, the richer nations have lower population growth rates.[23]

As the progression in the transitions for the various pollutant-indicator combinations for traditional air pollutants suggest, the existence and timing of p(P) can be critical. Consider, also, the apparently anomalous case of CO_2. Several analysts have noted that cross-country plots of several CO_2 emission indicators versus affluence do not follow inverted U-shaped paths or, if they do, the turning points are at such high levels of affluence that many developing countries will, they claim, never reach that point.[24] However, such a conclusion is premature, if not flawed, and CO_2 is not necessarily an anomaly with respect to the environmental transition hypothesis:

- As noted previously, it is somewhat unrealistic to expect CO_2 emissions to go through a transition because, at most, only a decade or so has passed since its p(P) ended, and energy systems—the major sources of CO_2 emissions—need decades rather than years to be turned over. Thus, conclusions based on current trends could be misleading because they are, arguably, drawn from the upward-sloping region of the environmental transition curve.
- The CO_2 analysis assumes no further technological change or technology transfer that would, in time, cause transitions to

occur at lower levels of affluence. If emissions per GDP continue to decline, as table 6.4 shows that it indeed has over the past few decades, the transition for CO_2 emissions would eventually occur at lower levels of affluence. The long-term trends summarized in tables 6.1 to 6.4 indicate that, over the long haul, technological change can reduce environmental impacts by as much as one or more orders of magnitude. Thus, ignoring technological changes will inevitably lead to serious errors in long-term projections of the magnitude and impacts of emissions.[25] In addition, as the previously discussed examples of lead emissions and access to safe water and sanitation indicate, developing nations seem to be learning from the experiences of today's developed countries. Hence, all else being equal, one should expect their transitions to occur later in time but at earlier levels in their economic development, and CO_2 emissions should be no exception.

- Given the numerous variables that affect the timing, height, and width of an environmental transition, it is perilous to extrapolate from the experience of one or a small set of countries to determine when and at what levels environmental transitions may occur in others. Using cross-country CO_2 analyses to predict the evolution and timing of single-country environmental transitions is, as suggested by figure 5.3 and the accompanying text, an inherently risky exercise. For such analyses to succeed, the data will have to be filtered using many more variables than have generally been tried. These variables include those to reflect the responsiveness of government to its population's perceptions of the quality of life; natural resource endowments; population densities; current level of economic development; structure of the economy; the type and magnitude of unmet needs, as well as the costs of meeting them; attitudes of peoples and ruling elites toward the environment; geography; and climate.

As table 7.1 indicates, the choice of environmental indicator is also important. Not all indicators are created equal. Some are better measures of the environmental and public health impacts of a substance than others. Even when one considers a specific pollutant, the transitions are determined by the relationship between the particular indicator used and its impact on public health or the environment.

In a democracy, all else being equal, public health impacts will generally be addressed before other environmental impacts. It is probably no accident that reductions in deaths because of water-related diseases preceded reductions in air pollution or that emissions of CO_2 have not yet been reduced (although CO_2 emissions per GNP—a leading indicator—has gone past its transition for the United States and the world). Moreover, as the historical progression of transition periods from indoor to outdoor air quality shown in table 7.1 suggests, the more closely an indicator reflects impacts, the sooner it is likely to be addressed. In addition, the progressions in table 7.1 are also consistent with the notion that the cheaper it is to address an indicator, the more likely that it will be addressed before others, which is a good reason to support not only research and development into new or improved technologies but also innovative approaches to increase the cost-effectiveness of controls in general.

8. Factors Affecting Environmental Trends

Technological Change

Table 8.1 consolidates much of the information regarding changes in population (*P*), affluence (*A*), gross domestic product (GDP) (*PA*), the environmental impact (*I*), the technology factor (*T*), and technological change (Δ*T*), which were gleaned from the examination of trends in environmental indicators undertaken in chapter 6. In this table, which is based largely on tables 6.1 through 6.4, the entries in each row for *P*, *A*, *PA*, *I*, and *T* are their values at the end of the period over which the trends were examined expressed as multiples of their values at the beginning of the period. That is, the entries are normalized to unity at the beginning of the period. Thus, the first row of data (for the amount of cropland harvested in the United States) indicates that relative to its 1910 level, population (*P*) stood at 3.18 in 2004, affluence (*A*) at 6.63, and GDP (*PA*) at 21.07.[1] Despite these increases, the environmental impact of U.S. agriculture, measured by the amount of cropland harvested, declined slightly so that at the end of this period it stood at 0.96 times its 1910 level. The *T*-factor, which is the change in the ratio of impact to GDP (calculated using equation 5-5 in the last note of chapter 5) tells us that in 2004 the amount of cropland harvested per GDP was 0.046 times what it was in 1910. Hence, the total amount of technological change (Δ*T*) during the intervening period—the percent change in impact per unit of GDP—is −95.4 percent (in the second to last column). The *minus* sign indicates that the environmental impact per GDP *declined*, that is, matters *improved*, by 95.4 percent during this period. Finally, the last column expresses the amount of technological change over this period in terms of an annual rate. Assuming an exponential change between 1910 and 2004, this rate of technological change is estimated to be −3.2 percent per year

For most rows, the *T*-factor and technological change (Δ*T*) in table 8.1 are calculated using equations 5-5 and 5-6 in the last note of

Table 8.1
CHANGES IN POPULATION, AFFLUENCE AND TECHNOLOGY FOR VARIOUS

Indicator	Area	Period	Population (P)	Affluence (A = GDP/P)	PA = GDP	Impact (I)	Technology factor (T)	Total ΔT in %	ΔT, in %/year
				Land (area)					
Cropland Harvested	United States	1910–2004	3.18	6.63	21.07	0.96	0.046	−95.4	−3.2
Cropland	World	1950–2001	2.44	2.86	6.99	1.32	0.189	−81.1	−3.2
			Air (national annual emissions)						
SO_2	United States	1900–2003	3.82	8.26	31.58	1.6	0.051	−94.9	−2.8
VOC	United States	1900–2003	3.82	8.26	31.58	1.89	0.060	−94.0	−2.7
NO_x	United States	1900–2003	3.82	8.26	31.58	7.94	0.251	−74.9	−1.3
PM-10	United States	1940–2002	2.18	4.46	9.72	0.29	0.030	−97.0	−5.5
CO	United States	1940–2003	2.20	4.53	9.98	1.14	0.114	−88.6	−3.4
Lead	United States	1970–2000	1.38	1.88	2.60	0.02	0.007	−99.3	−15.2

Air (indoor air pollution; residential emissions per occupied household)

SO_2	United States	1940–2002	2.18	4.46	9.72	0.02	0.002	−99.8	−9.5
VOC	United States	1940–2002	2.18	4.46	9.72	0.14	0.014	−98.6	−6.7
O_x	United States	1940–2002	2.18	4.46	9.72	0.39	0.040	−96.0	−5.1
PM-10	United States	1940–2002	2.18	4.46	9.72	0.05	0.005	−99.5	−8.2
CO	United States	1940–2002	2.18	4.46	9.72	0.05	0.005	−99.5	−8.2

Water (deaths due to water-related diseases)[a]

Typhoid and paratyphoid	United States	1900–97	3.52	NA	NA	0	0	−100.0	
Gastrointestinal diseases	United States	1900–70	2.68			0	0.002	−99.8	−8.5
Dysentery	United States	1900–97	3.52			0.02	0.004	−99.6	−5.5

(continued on next page)

Table 8.1
CHANGES IN POPULATION, AFFLUENCE AND TECHNOLOGY FOR VARIOUS (continued)

Indicator	Area	Period	Population (P)	Affluence (A=GDP/P)	PA= GDP	Impact (I)	Technology factor (T)	Technological change	
								Total ΔT in %	ΔT, in %/year
Global Warming—Carbon Dioxide Emissions from Combustion and Industrial									
CO_2	United States	1900–2002	3.77	6.90	25.97	8.80	0.339	−66.1	−1.1
CO_2	United States	1950–2002	1.89	2.95	5.57	2.30	0.412	−59.4	−1.7
CO_2	United States	1900–2001	3.93	4.79	18.84	13.06	0.693	−30.7	−0.4
CO_2	World	1950–2001	2.44	2.86	6.99	4.20	0.600	−40.0	−1.0
Global Warming—Extreme Weather Events (deaths, based on 10-year averages for the United States and decadal averages for the world)[a]									
Deaths from hurricanes	United States	1900/09–1996/2005	3.41			0.18	0.053	−94.7	−3.0
Deaths from floods	United States	1903/12–1995/2004	2.71			2.75	1.016	1.6	0.02
Deaths from tornados	United States	1917/26–1995/2004	2.56			0.18	0.070	−93.0	−3.4

Deaths from lightning	United States	1959/68–1995/2004	1.48	0.42	0.281	−71.9	−2.7
Deaths due to climate-related disasters	World	1900/09–1995/2004	3.57	0.15	0.042	−95.8	−3.3

a. Death associated with these indicators are expected to increase with population but not with affluence (except through its effect on technology, which is captured in the T-factor). Therefore, the values of A and PA are not relevant in these cases, and ΔT = percent reduction in death rates over this period. NA = not appropriate.

211

chapter 5. However, for trends in deaths caused by water-related diseases and extreme weather events, technological change is calculated using P rather than $P \times A$, on the basis that—all else being equal—deaths would increase with population but not with affluence. This underestimates the technological change with respect to water-related diseases because one ought to expect that, all else being equal, population density by itself might contribute to the environmental burdens that contribute to such diseases.[2]

Table 8.1 also shows that with the exception of deaths from floods, in each case, technological change, by itself, has improved matters (because it is always associated with a negative sign, indicating that it has reduced impacts). This table shows, for example, that per unit of GDP, technological change has reduced the global environmental impact of agriculture, as measured by cropland, by 81 percent between 1950 and 2001; indoor PM-10 (particulate matter less than 10 micrometers) levels in the United States by 99.5 percent between 1940 and 2002; and carbon dioxide (CO_2) emissions by 59.4 percent in the United States between 1950 and 2002, and 40.0 percent for the world between 1950 and 2001. With respect to water-related diseases, technological change reduced U.S. death rates by 100 percent for typhoid and paratyphoid from 1900 to 1997, 99.8 percent for gastrointestinal diseases from 1900 to 1970, and 99.6 percent for dysentery from 1900 to 1997. Death rates because of extreme weather events declined in the United States by at least 71.9 percent to 94.7 percent (for lightning, tornados, and hurricanes) for the periods analyzed, but it increased by 1.6 percent for floods (from 1903/12 to 1995/2004). At the global level, death rates declined by 95.8 percent from all extreme weather–related events (including droughts, floods, wind storms, wave surges, and extreme temperatures) between the first decade of the 20th and 21st centuries.

Note, however, that, as with all trends, these results can be quite sensitive to the starting and ending year used for compiling the data. This is particularly true for trends related to episodic events, for example, extreme weather events such as hurricanes and floods. The flood record, for instance, starts in 1903, and the first 10 years of that record (1903–12) apparently coincides with a relatively quiescent period in the nation's flood history. In fact, if the record had started in any other year in that decade except 1903, I would have obtained an improvement in the *T*-factor for flood fatalities because 1903–12 had the lowest death rate for any 10-year period since.

Just as the flood record starts with a whimper, the hurricane record starts with a bang. The first year for which data are available is 1900, the year of the great Galveston hurricane. Accordingly, as figure 6.16 shows, the beginning of that record is literally off the chart. Without the 1900 data point, the reductions in the *T*-factor for hurricanes would have been much less impressive. If the data series had commenced in any other year, the *T*-factor for hurricane fatalities would have been less impressive. And if it had started in the 1980s, one would have seen an upward trend in the data.

Regardless of the vagaries of the starting and ending years for the various data series, long-term environmental trends have not conformed to the notion that, sooner or later, technology will necessarily increase environmental impacts. This notion is based on the argument advanced by Ehrlich and coworkers that with the passage of time we will increasingly have to rely on resources that are harder to access.[3] Therefore, the energy used to extract, refine, and distribute any resource ought to increase, which, in turn, should increase environmental impacts. And, in fact, where the historical record goes back far enough, such as, for air pollution emissions, the trends indicate that impacts initially increased. In the beginning, the standard interpretation of the IPAT identity would seem to be qualitatively valid, that is, *P*, *A*, and *T* seem to combine to increase impacts. But once the indicator enters the transition region, this interpretation begins to fail. Then after the transition, despite substantial increases in population and affluence, the environmental impact begins to decline because technology no longer acts as a multiplier but as a divisor for the environmental impact. As table 8.1 shows, the long-run decline in impact can often be of an order of magnitude or more. Thus, notwithstanding plausible arguments that technological change would increase environmental impacts in the long run, historical data suggest that, in fact, technological change *ultimately* reduces impacts, provided technology is not rejected.

Figures 6.13 and 6.14 not only show that access to safe water and to sanitation has increased with economic development, but also show that time (a surrogate for technological change) can bring about improvements in environmental quality.

Wealth

Clearly, technological change is one key to continued improvement in environmental and human well-being.

At least two ingredients are necessary to bring about technological change. First, better technology must be brought into existence. Figure 5.2 shows that with greater wealth, expenditures on research and development increase. Therefore, the likelihood of developing new or improved technology should rise with wealth. Moreover, levels of education also increase with wealth, which helps maintain and enhance human capital. This, in turn, not only further enhances the possibility of devising better technologies but it also propagates knowledge about the existence and operation of existing and new technologies, which is a key element for the diffusion of technology.

But there is more to technological change than creating technology or being aware of its existence. Although poor countries (and their farmers) are cognizant of technologies that would improve agricultural productivity, they are unable to capitalize on that information, despite that many such technologies, for example, fertilizers and crop protection measures, are quite mundane. Thus, their agricultural yields are substantially lower (see figure 6.3) as are their food supplies (figure 6.4). As a result, hunger and malnourishment are higher, and pressures for deforestation are greater. Similarly, notwithstanding that nowadays authorities in even the poorest countries know how to extend access to safe water and sanitation to 100 percent of the population, they lack the wherewithal to do so. Consequently, 1.1 billion people worldwide still lack access to safe water and 2.4 billion to adequate sanitation, virtually all in the poorer countries.

The missing ingredient, of course, is wealth, without which not only is it harder to invent, develop, perfect, and use new technologies, but even old technologies are often unaffordable. Greater wealth increases the likelihood of acquiring, operating, and maintaining new as well as existing technologies. That is, wealth not only helps create technology and conditions favorable for its diffusion but wealth also ensures that technology is, in fact, used to make technological change a reality. It is hardly surprising that in previous chapters, we saw repeatedly that virtually every indicator of human well-being or environmental impact sooner or later improves with wealth. Hence, wealth increases cereal yields, which helps reduce rates of deforestation. It boosts the ability to install air pollution controls and to substitute cleaner fuels for dirty ones. Wealth also increases access to safe water and sanitation, which then reduces mortality due to water-related diseases.

And just as wealth helps create technology and accelerates its adoption, so does technological change create wealth. As we saw in chapter 4, economic growth and technological progress reinforce each other in a cycle of progress, that is, they coevolve.[4] Thus, economic growth and new technology, acting in tandem, were key to moving the richer countries toward and, in many cases, beyond their environmental transitions, which have led to long-term environmental improvements in recent decades.

Does the Environment Worsen at Very High Levels of Affluence?

The fact that cross-country and single-country data for a variety of environmental indicators seem to fit stylized patterns consistent with the environmental Kuznets curve and environmental transition hypotheses suggests that as a country gets richer, then through some agency or the other, it will ultimately get cleaner, at least until—as shown in figure 5.1—it is clean enough. One of the major arguments advanced against this proposition is that some analyses indicate that a cross-country plot of ambient sulfur dioxide (SO_2) concentrations versus affluence shows concentrations first going through a transition and then swinging up once again at relatively high levels of affluence (i.e., the cross-country curve may be somewhat N-shaped).[5] This observation has been generalized to argue that richer is not necessarily cleaner.

Before examining the empirical basis for this contention, it is critical to recognize that an upswing at very high levels of affluence should be a concern only if that also diminishes the overall quality of life. But once a sufficient level of cleanup as measured by the specific environmental indicator has been achieved, there is no reason to presume *a priori* that further improvements in environmental quality (as measured by that indicator) would necessarily also result in a net improvement in the quality of life. As illustrated in figure 5.1, once sufficiently past the transition, the environmental impact as measured by the indicator might well go up once again because the cost of additional control is likely to rise while benefits are likely to decline. Thus, sooner or later, marginal costs will exceed marginal benefits, and overall quality of life will no longer be improved by further reducing that indicator.

An upswing is also possible if society has other unmet needs that it may want to address despite a less-than-total victory over the specific environmental problem characterized by the indicator in question. For example, it may make more sense today for the United States to spend additional resources on expanding health insurance, broadening cancer screening, or even reducing fine PM than on continuing to reduce ground-level ozone concentrations.

Now let us turn to the question of whether empirical data show any upswings in environmental impacts at high levels of affluence. I showed in chapter 5 that it was possible to construct an N-shaped cross-country curve from a hypothetical set of inverted U-shaped single-country environmental transition curves. Thus, the existence of an N-shaped cross-country curve does not necessarily disprove the notion that as a country gets richer, it might ultimately become cleaner.

More to the point, despite the theoretical possibility of an upswing, the trends presented in chapter 6 do not provide any empirical support for a sustained upswing following any transition. In particular, with respect to ambient air quality for SO_2—the source of the original concern that at very high levels of affluence there might be an upswing in environmental impacts—figure 6.11, which is based on "national" composite ambient SO_2 concentrations for 15 of the world's richest countries from 1980 to the mid to late 1990s, shows that the single-country curves seem to be converging. Each of these countries is currently on the downhill side of the environmental transition, and none of them, so far, has had a sustained upswing.[6] The likely reason for this is that none of these countries has been on a downward slope long enough.

Moreover, given that the height, width, and timing of an environmental transition depends on the specific country, the pollutant in question, and the particular indicator used to characterize the pollutant's impact, one should expect that the ambient SO_2 air quality for a country would be influenced, but not determined solely, by its level of affluence. Indeed, a regression analysis of national SO_2 concentrations against PPP (purchasing power parity)-adjusted GDP per capita for the richest set of countries using a single year (in this case, 1993) showed no correlation between environmental impact and affluence.[7] However, there is, as should be expected, a much stronger correlation between national SO_2 concentrations and a country's dependence on solid fuels, as measured by the fraction of total fuel consumption due to solid fuel consumption ($R^2 = 0.62$, and the slope is significant at the 0.01 level).

Finally, among the key findings of a set of recent Environmental Protection Agency (EPA) reports titled *America's Children and the Environment*, are that national trends for various pollutants in the air, water, and food to which children's health is supposed to be most sensitive have all improved in the 1990s.[8] In other words, it too finds no evidence for any upswing in its key measures of environmental quality. Among its key findings are the following:

- The percentage of days with unhealthy air quality dropped from 3 percent in 1990 to less than 1 percent in 1999.[9]
- The percentage of homes with children under 7 years of age in which someone smokes regularly declined from 29 percent in 1994 to 19 percent in 1999.[10]
- Between 1993 and 1998, the percentage of children living in areas served by public water systems in which a drinking water standard for chemicals, radiation, or microbial standards was exceeded decreased from 20 percent to 8 percent.[11]
- Between 1993 and 1998, the percentage of children living in areas served by public water systems in which nitrate or nitrites standards were exceeded declined by about 20 percent.[12]
- Detectable pesticide residues in fruits, vegetables, grains, dairy, and processed foods declined from 62 percent in 1994 to 55 percent in 1998.[13]
- Median lead concentrations in the blood of children under 5 years of age declined 85 percent between 1976–80 and 1999–2000.[14]

Clearly, despite the theoretical possibility of upswings, there apparently are, as yet, no sustained upswings in these data.

The absence of upswings in the cases examined here suggest that, so far, the limits of technology have not yet been reached, the beneficiaries of additional controls feel the costs are justified by the benefits, or the beneficiaries have managed to shift control costs to other parties while retaining the benefits (i.e., we are in "not in my backyard" territory). So apparently, one or more of those conditions continue to hold for now.

Wealth and the Population Growth Rate

Greater wealth also affects environmental quality through its direct and indirect effect on total fertility rate (TFR). Factors that are conducive to economic growth are also consistent with reductions in TFR. At the same time, economic growth helps create conditions that tend to lower TFRs. For example, consider education. As shown in figure 2.15, the amount of education is associated with the level of economic development. Simultaneously, education boosts human capital, which indirectly contributes to economic growth and technological change.

Second, education, particularly of women, helps propagate good habits of diet, nutrition, sanitation, and safe drinking water. This improves health and reduces mortality, in general, and infant and maternal mortality, in particular. This step is the first one in families starting to realize that they do not need to maximize birth as a method of hedging for a more secure future, as well as to consider what size family would be "optimal." At the same time, improved health leads to greater wealth (or economic growth).

Educated women, compared to those not as well educated, also have higher human capital, and, like all capital, its owners would want to maximize their return on capital. Because these women have a higher probability of being employed—and if employed—more likely to have higher wages—the time taken for childbirth and raising children could result in substantial economic losses to these women (and their families).

Fourth, economic growth also helps generate the funds for non-family-based social security systems, which would reduce the reliance of the aged on their offspring.

In addition, in a low technology world, children used to be economic assets from relatively young ages. But in today's society, children are more likely to be an economic drain for the first several years. Historically, children used to help out on the farm. But technological change (which requires both technology and wealth) has reduced the need for additional farm hands in many parts of the world. A similar dynamic could occur with respect to child labor in urban areas, which today is confined to the developing world. Figure 2.17 shows that the percentage of children between 10 and 14 years of age employed as child labor has declined with both economic growth and time (i.e., technology). Moreover, families

Figure 8.1
TOTAL FERTILITY RATE VS. WEALTH, 1977–2003

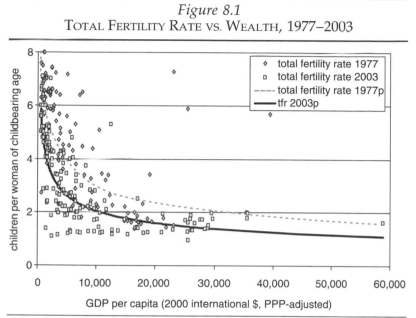

SOURCE: Based on data from World Bank, *World Development Indicators,* http://devdata.worldbank.org/dataonline (accessed July 12, 2005).

recognize that a good education is the key to future economic success for their offspring. Thus, they are willing to forego the quantity of their children for the quality of their education.

Finally, it seems evident that many couples prefer to postpone having children in favor of current consumption, possibly fueled, among other things, by images of the consumer society so ubiquitous on the world's televisions and movie screens.

Because of all these reasons, it is not surprising that TFR—a measure of how many children a woman might have during her lifetime—is associated with poverty and has dropped progressively with time. Figure 8.1 shows that, in fact, TFRs generally dropped from 1977 to 2003 across the spectrum of countries, as well as with the level of economic development. Both these drops are statistically significant at the 99.9 percent confidence level.[15] Therefore, if per capita income for a typical country had been held constant at $2 a day (in PPP-adjusted 2000 international dollars), then TFR would have declined from 7.8 in 1977 to 5.2 in 2003 if all else was held constant. If a country had the average global per capita income level of $4,958 in 1977 and $7,162 in 2003, its TFR would have declined by 41 percent from 3.9 to 2.3. For the average high-income country, TFR would have gone from 2.6 in 1977 to a below-replacement level of 1.5 in 2003.[16] (The replacement level is about 2.1.)

Thus, sooner or later, the richer the nation the lower its population growth rate, which might lead to a cleaner environment.

Summary

Because of the numerous determinants of environmental transition, which can vary from country to country, it does not follow that richer countries are necessarily always cleaner than poorer countries. However, as a country gets richer, ultimately it is also likely to become cleaner, at least until it is "clean enough." But once a country gets clean enough, it does not follow that its quality of life will necessarily be improved by cleaning up further, particularly if its citizens have to bear a larger social and economic burden for additional cleanup that provides diminishing environmental benefits.

The Role of Property Rights, Markets, and Other Economic Incentives

Comparing Trends in Agricultural Use of Land and Water[17]

Land and water are probably the two most critical natural resource inputs for agriculture. Predictably, no other human activity uses more land and water than agriculture. Worldwide, agriculture accounts for 38 percent of land use, 66 percent of freshwater withdrawals, and 85 percent of freshwater consumption.[18] Not surprisingly, agriculture can have a critical impact on terrestrial and freshwater habitats, ecosystems, and biological diversity.[19]

Earlier we saw that enormous amounts of habitat were saved from conversion to cropland because of the increased productivity of land in agriculture. This forestalled further increases in threats to terrestrial habitats and biodiversity. And although increased water diversions for agriculture might increase agricultural land productivity, such diversions can be as serious a problem for many aquatic species as land conversion is for terrestrial species.[20] In fact, although global information on this topic is poor, one report suggests that more than 20 percent of freshwater species might be threatened, endangered, or extinct.[21] The *2004 IUCN Red List of Threatened Species* cites a regional case study in Eastern Africa, which estimated that 27 percent of freshwater species assessed were listed as threatened.[22]

One of the most interesting conundrums in natural resource use is why the spectacular decades-long increases in agricultural productivity per unit of land in the United States and worldwide (chapter 6; table 8.1) have not been matched by comparable increases in productivity per unit of water.

In the United States, as in the rest of the world, agriculture is the predominant user of water. In the United States, it accounts for one-third of the surface water withdrawals and two-thirds of groundwater withdrawals.[23] More significantly, it is responsible for 85 percent of consumptive water use.[24] Between 1910 and 2004, during which the United States population increased by 205 percent, the amount of cropland harvested declined 3 percent while total water withdrawn for irrigation increased by 251 percent (figure 8.2).[25] During the same period, corn and wheat yields increased by 391 percent and 208 percent, respectively.[26] Figure 8.2 also shows that the amount of irrigated land increased by 374 percent from 1910 to 2004.

The contrast in U.S. trends in cropland per capita, irrigation water use, and irrigated land is illustrated in figure 8.3. As noted previously, per capita indicators (such as per GDP indicators) are leading indicators in societies where population (or GDP) is growing. That is, one cannot, for such societies, expect to see a downturn in aggregate indicators unless they are preceded by or, at the latest, concurrent with downturns in their corresponding per capita (or per GDP) indicators. And, in fact, comparing figures 8.2 and 8.3, we see that cropland per capita has been declining at least since 1910, while aggregate cropland has remained more or less stable with, perhaps, a minor peak around 1930. With respect to irrigation water, both aggregate and per capita levels have been declining since around 1980. Notably, between 1910 and 2000, cropland per capita declined by 68 percent while irrigation water use per capita and irrigated land per capita increased 15 percent and 55 percent, respectively.

Figures 8.2 and 8.3 show that between 1910 and 1950, U.S. irrigation water use grew more rapidly than irrigated land, but this trend was reversed in the 1950s. Currently, irrigated land seems to be increasing at a faster rate than irrigated water use.

Figure 8.2
U.S. CROPLAND AND IRRIGATION WATER USE, 1910–2004

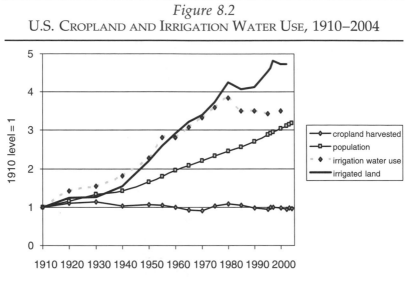

SOURCES: USBOC, *Historical Statistics of the United States, Colonial Times to 1970* (Washington, DC: GPO, 1975); USBOC, *Historical National Population Estimates, 1900 to 1999*, www.census.gov/popest/archives/pre-1980/ (accessed August 14, 2005); USBOC, *Statistical Abstract of the United States 2006* (Washington, DC: GPO, 2006); U.S. Department of Agriculture, *Agricultural Statistics 2001*, www.nass.usda.gov/Publications/Ag_Statistics/ index.asp, p. ix–17 (accessed December 20, 2005); U.S. Department of Agriculture, *Agricultural Statistics 2005*, www.nass.usda.gov/Publications/Ag_ Statistics/index.asp, p. ix–17 (accessed December 20, 2005); N. Gollehon, W. Quinby, and M. Aillery, "Agricultural Resources and Indicators: Water Use and Pricing in Agriculture," in *Agricultural Resources and Environmental Indicators 2003*, ed. R. Heimlich, www.ers.usda.gov/publications/arei/ ah722/ (accessed August 19, 2005); U.S. Department of Agriculture, *Data on Major Land Uses*, www.ers.usda.gov/data/MajorLandUses/spreadsheets/ c1910_00.xls (accessed December 20, 2005); Wayne B. Solley, Robert R. Pierce, and Howard A. Perlman, *Estimated Use of Water in the United States in 1995*, USGS Circular 1200 (Denver, CO: U.S. Geological Survey, 1998); Susan S. Hutson, Nancy L. Barber, Joan F. Kenny, Kristin S. Linsey, Deborah S. Lumia, and Molly A. Maupin, *Estimated Use of Water in the United States in 2000*, USGS Circular 1268 (Denver, CO: U.S. Geological Survey, 2005) (released March 2004, revised April 2004, May 2004, February 2005), http:// pubs.usgs.gov/circ/2004/circ1268/ (accessed December 20, 2005).

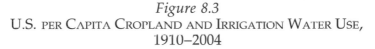

Figure 8.3
U.S. PER CAPITA CROPLAND AND IRRIGATION WATER USE, 1910–2004

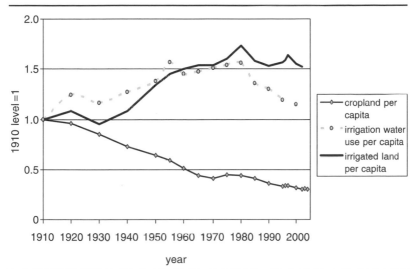

SOURCES: USBOC, *Historical Statistics of the United States, Colonial Times to 1970* (Washington, DC: GPO, 1975); USBOC, *Historical National Population Estimates, 1900 to 1999*, www.census.gov/popest/archives/pre-1980/ (accessed August 14, 2005); USBOC, *Statistical Abstract of the United States 2006* (Washington, DC: GPO, 2006); U.S. Department of Agriculture, *Agricultural Statistics 2001*, www.nass.usda.gov/Publications/Ag_Statistics/ index.asp, p. ix–17 (accessed December 20, 2005); U.S. Department of Agriculture, *Agricultural Statistics 2005*, www.nass.usda.gov/Publications/Ag_ Statistics/index.asp, p. ix–17 (accessed December 20, 2005); N. Gollehon, W. Quinby, and M. Aillery, "Agricultural Resources and Indicators: Water Use and Pricing in Agriculture," in *Agricultural Resources and Environmental Indicators 2003*, ed. R. Heimlich, www.ers.usda.gov/publications/arei/ ah722/ (accessed August 19, 2005); U.S. Department of Agriculture, *Data on Major Land Uses*, www.ers.usda.gov/data/MajorLandUses/spreadsheets/ c1910_00.xls (accessed December 20, 2005); Wayne B. Solley, Robert R. Pierce, and Howard A. Perlman, *Estimated Use of Water in the United States in 1995*, USGS Circular 1200 (Denver, CO: U.S. Geological Survey, 1998); Susan S. Hutson, Nancy L. Barber, Joan F. Kenny, Kristin S. Linsey, Deborah S. Lumia, and Molly A. Maupin, *Estimated Use of Water in the United States in 2000*, USGS Circular 1268 (Denver, CO: U.S. Geological Survey, 2005) (released March 2004, revised April 2004, May 2004, February 2005), http:// pubs.usgs.gov/circ/2004/circ1268/ (accessed December 20, 2005).

Figure 8.4
GLOBAL CROPLAND AND IRRIGATION WATER USE, 1900–2000

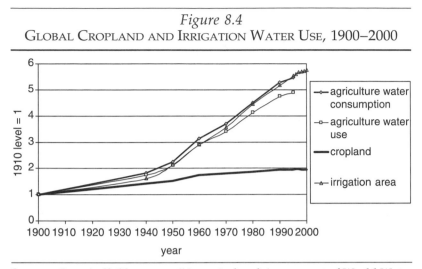

SOURCES: Igor A. Shiklomanov, "Appraisal and Assessment of World Water Resources," *Water International* 25, no. 1 (2000), 11–32; Indur M. Goklany, "Potential Consequences of Increasing Atmospheric CO_2 Concentration Compared to Other Environmental Problems," *Technology* 7S (2000): 189–213; Colin McEvedy and Richard Jones, *Atlas of World Population History* (New York: Penguin, 1978); FAO, *FAOSTAT 2001*, http://apps.fao.org (accessed October 3, 2001).

Figure 8.4, which shows global trends in aggregate land and water use and consumption by agriculture between 1900 and 2000, suggests that they too are on paths similar to that of the United States, except they are not as far along.[27] This figure also shows that although cropland seems to be leveling off, agricultural water use and consumption, as well as irrigated land area, continue to increase, albeit less rapidly than previously. Moreover, relative to population growth, water use and consumption have increased much more than cropland. Between 1900 and 1995, population increased 249 percent, cropland increased 95 percent, and agricultural water use increased 388 percent. Agricultural water consumption and irrigated land area increased even faster—by 446 percent and 453 percent, respectively. Not surprisingly, the amount of irrigated land tracks relatively closely with agricultural water consumption because the two sets of data are related and come from the same source.[28]

Figure 8.5 provides the same information, but on a per capita basis, that is, using leading indicators. This shows that global cropland per

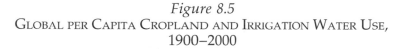

Figure 8.5
GLOBAL PER CAPITA CROPLAND AND IRRIGATION WATER USE,
1900–2000

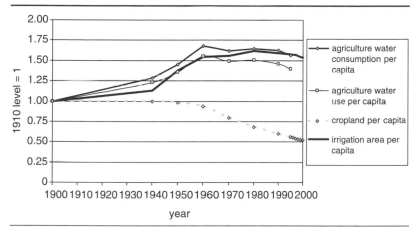

SOURCES: Igor A. Shiklomanov, "Appraisal and Assessment of World Water Resources," *Water International* 25, no. 1 (2000), 11–32; Indur M. Goklany, "Potential Consequences of Increasing Atmospheric CO₂ Concentration Compared to Other Environmental Problems," *Technology* 7S (2000): 189–213; Colin McEvedy and Richard Jones, *Atlas of World Population History* (New York: Penguin, 1978); FAO, *FAOSTAT 2001*, http://apps.fao.org (accessed October 3, 2001).

capita has been declining since around the 1930s. Between 1900 and 1995, it dropped by 44 percent. However, per capita agricultural water use and consumption both peaked around 1960. Although they have declined since then, per capita withdrawals and per capita water consumption due to agriculture, as well as per capita irrigated land, were higher in 1995 than in 1900 (by 40 percent, 56 percent, and 58 percent, respectively).

Just as for the United States, figures 8.4 and 8.5 show that global agricultural water withdrawals and consumption grew more rapidly than irrigated land in the first four decades of the 20th century, but this trend has since been reversed. Since 1980, irrigated land has increased at a faster rate than either agricultural water withdrawals or consumption. Between 1980 and 1995, irrigated land area increased 25 percent while water withdrawals and consumption increased by 19 percent and 21 percent, respectively.

So what accounts for the large differences in the trends for agricultural water and land use in both the United States and worldwide? Why has agricultural water use increased much more rapidly than it has for land use? Why did increases in the efficiency of cropland use precede those of agricultural water use?

U.S. Situation. Figures 8.2 and 8.3 show that for the United States, aggregate and per capita irrigation water use have both gone beyond their environmental transitions (or peaks). Aggregate cropland is close to—and, perhaps, also past—the transition while cropland per capita is clearly past its environmental transition. These figures also indicate that although aggregate cropland has stayed more or less static for the 20th century, the increase in the productivity of agricultural land use substantially exceeds the increase in water use productivity.

One possible reason the decline in cropland per capita commenced earlier than agricultural water use per capita might be that land, in contrast to water, has often been privately owned. Although there are several reasons this has traditionally been the case (e.g., water supplies are uncertain and variable, not all its uses are rival, and water use can result in externalities),[29] private property rights to land provides its owner with powerful incentives to maximize long-term productivity per unit of land[30] (more on this in the next few paragraphs). These incentives are less compelling where, as is the case for water, private property rights are either absent or unclear.

Notably, had U.S. agricultural technology and its penetration been frozen at 1910 levels (i.e., had cropland per capita stayed at 1910 levels), then in 2004 the United States would have needed to harvest 1,007 million acres rather than the 305 million acres that were actually harvested that year.

This calculation is based on three relatively optimistic assumptions. First, sufficient new cropland would be available, but this is unlikely because the total amount of potential cropland in the United States is estimated to be only 647 million acres.[31] Second, the additional cropland would be just as productive as existing cropland. Third, the productivity of existing cropland would be maintained without any new technologies. Clearly the increase in land productivity averted a potential catastrophe for biodiversity in the United States. One can obtain another perspective on the amount of land saved from conversion when one considers that the total amount of land and habitat under special protection in the United States was 217 million acres in 1999. This land includes national parks, national wildlife refuges, and national wilderness areas.

By contrast, water use per capita increased between 1910 and 1995, possibly because water use is more dependent on political muscle and machinations than on economics. Once access to water has been secured, in the absence of the ability to sell excess water or transfer it to other users for a compensation, the incentive to increase the productivity of water used in agricultural activities is limited. However, even where de facto water "rights" are not fully transferrable, there is an incentive to optimize water use within the constraints that exist. One method of doing this is to improve irrigation efficiency, which, in turn, would allow more land to be irrigated. Let's examine the U.S. experience more closely.

In the early part of this century, farmers and the agricultural sector had their way with water. However, throughout the 20th century, the demographic and economic power of the agricultural sector declined, while that of urban, suburban, and environmental interests—interests with broad overlap in membership—increased. Agriculture's share of national income dropped from 18.9 percent for 1899–1903 to 7.2 percent for 1948–53 and 3.1 percent in 1970.[32] In 1899, agriculture accounted for 36.9 percent of the population engaged in production; by 1948–53 that had declined to 10.6 percent before dropping to 4.3 percent in 1970.[33] Concurrently, the percentage of the population in rural areas declined from 60 percent in 1900 to 41 percent in 1950 and 26 percent in 1970.[34] Also by 1970, the demand for water and the costs of tapping new sources of water had gone up for all sectors. Thus, the politics and economics came together to enable the urban-suburban-environmental groups to often challenge agriculture's claims to water. While all these challenges might not have been fully successful, by the 1980s they did serve to reduce the amount of water diverted as well as irrigation water use per capita.[35] One of the adjustments made to cope with the difficulty of obtaining additional water for agriculture is to increase irrigation efficiency and expand the amount of land under irrigation. This would help account for the decline in the amount of irrigation water applied per acre of land from about 2.5 acre-feet in 1980 to 2.1 acre-feet in 1995 and explain the rapid increase in irrigated land during this period even as irrigation water use declined.[36]

Global Situation. Figure 8.4 shows that while aggregate cropland seems to have leveled off, that is, arrived at an environmental transition, aggregate water use and consumption, as well as irrigated land use, continue to increase, albeit less rapidly than before. Moreover, except for cropland, they have all increased faster than population.

On a per capita basis, however, cropland and irrigation water use and consumption have all gone past their environmental transitions. But these levels have not yet dropped off as much as the levels for the United States.

Despite the pressures agriculture has brought to bear on global biological resources, similar to the situation in the United States, those pressures could have been much worse had global agricultural productivity, and therefore yields, been frozen at, say, 1961 levels. This is equivalent to freezing technology—and its penetration—at 1961 levels. In that case, agricultural land area would have had to more than double its actual 1998 level of 12.2 billion acres to at least 26.3 billion to produce as much food as was actually produced in 1998.[37] Thus, agricultural land area would have had to increase from its current 38 percent to 82 percent of global land area.[38] Cropland would also have had to more than double, from 3.7 to 7.9 billion acres. In effect, an additional area the size of South America minus Chile would have to be plowed under. Thus, increased land productivity forestalled further increases in threats to terrestrial habitats and biodiversity.

However, these improvements were not matched by similar increases in efficiencies of irrigation water use. Not surprisingly, some analysts now believe that the major resource constraint for satisfying future global demand for food is likely to be water rather than—as Malthus and others had traditionally thought—land.[39]

A similar rationale, as was suggested for the United States, also helps explain the global lag in the increase in water use efficiency relative to the increase in cropland efficiency, namely, in most areas of the world, farmers have some property rights to their land but often not to water; nor is water usually treated as an economic commodity in other ways. In fact, the tremendous increase in irrigation in the United States and worldwide over the past few centuries could be viewed,[40] at least in part, as the substitution of often-subsidized water for land, supporting free market environmentalist Terry Anderson's lament that when water is cheaper than dirt, it will be treated that way.[41]

Property rights include long-term tenure to land, the right to trade, and the right to profit from selling products and improving productivity.[42] Farmers would not invest—a euphemism for risk taking—their time, money, and effort to increase productivity and efficiency without such rights, which include their right to profit from such investments. Property rights also provide an incentive for the farmer to engage in long-term sustainable practices.

A good example of the beneficial effects of property rights comes from China's experience in improving agricultural productivity in the early 1980s and its subsequent slowdown in improving yields.[43] In the early 1980s, Chinese farmers were given an albeit imperfect measure of property rights to a portion of their produce. The rate at which agriculture productivity increased annually soared, only to decline again because once it became clear that long-term tenure was not yet forthcoming, farmers held back further investments in "their" plots.

Not surprisingly, economists James Gwartney, Robert Larson, and Dextel Samida find cereal yields increasing across countries with their degree of economic freedom,[44] which Seth Norton has argued,[45] serves as an aggregate measure for the deference given by a country to property rights because it includes components for the security given to property rights under law as well as components that would diminish those rights indirectly through inflation or through limitations on the freedom to trade or exchange. Norton also finds that rates of deforestation decline with increased property rights. These two sets of results—increased yields and lowered deforestation—are consistent with the notion that higher agricultural productivity leads to greater land conservation.[46]

However, the failure to develop and to assign property rights to water only encourages waste and reduces incentives to adopt existing—or develop new—conservation, reuse, or recycling technologies. To make matters worse, on the basis that water is crucial to human beings, most societies subsidize its use, particularly in agriculture.[47] But, perversely, such subsidies further reduce the incentive for conservation. Predictably, water conservation technologies remain underutilized and underresearched. Yet another perverse consequence of these subsidies is that in many urban areas in the developing world, the poor pay more for water than do the middle and upper classes who are connected to subsidized municipal water systems.[48] Ironically, many in these subsidized groups are happy enough to pay larger sums for Coca-Cola or Pepsi even when they are not needed to quench their thirst.

If institutions and policies are modified to price water and private entities are assigned transferrable property rights to water (which would encourage markets and trading in water), then it might be possible to replicate for water the almost universal historical experience with land, which shows the latter's use being made progressively more efficient. The success of such policies has been demonstrated in cultures and milieus as diverse as Chile, India, Indonesia, Jordan, Pakistan, and the United States.[49] For example, in Chile, water trading increased efficiency of water use by 22–26 percent between 1976 and 1992, effectively expanding irrigated area by that much.[50] The experience in India and Pakistan shows that gains in efficiency can be obtained even where markets are based on informal and imperfect property rights.[51]

Marine versus Land Resources

Yet another natural resource conundrum is that although the oceans cover 71 percent of the earth's surface area, aquatic species provide only 1 percent of humankind's caloric intake and 4.5 percent of protein consumed by humankind.[52] By weight, 67 percent of fisheries production comes from marine capture fisheries, between 6 percent and 7 percent from inland capture fisheries, and 26 percent from aquaculture.[53] Despite its relatively meager contribution to the overall food supplies, 47–50 percent of the marine fisheries are fully exploited and 15–18 percent are overexploited.[54] The problem here is that in the absence of well-defined property rights, technology has been harnessed to harvest, but not to stock, ocean fisheries.[55] Hence, marine resources are being depleted even as land resources are becoming more productive.[56]

It stands to reason that if entrepreneurs' property rights to any increases in stocks that they had brought about were recognized and protected, then people would make the investments to enhance stocks. And, in fact, aquaculture's share of global fish production doubled from 13 percent to 26 percent between 1990 and 1999,[57] stimulated perhaps because entrepreneurs investing in aquaculture have greater confidence in capturing the profits from their investments.

The absence of property rights for ocean fisheries helps resolve yet another conundrum, namely, why do oceans contribute so little to humankind's food needs while the land contributes so much, despite that its surface area is larger by 130 percent?

Secular Trends in Technological Change and Economic Growth

The environmental benefits of property rights are also evident in the case of air pollution. As noted, the initial major improvements in air quality came in the first few decades of the 20th century when some households and businesses switched from coal and wood burning stoves and fireplaces to oil and gas, while others adopted more efficient combustion equipment and practices. By and large, homeowners and businesses undertook these measures willingly because they were cleaning up their own private property, and they were confident that their investments would result in direct benefits—reduced smoke, dust, and grit—to themselves, their families, and, in the case of businesses, their employees and customers. No less important was the fact that the use of newer, more efficient technology reduced their fuel costs. Thus, by virtue of the institution of property rights, they had an economic as well as an environmental incentive for cleaning up.

The ability of property owners to capture the economic benefits associated with greater efficiency also provided much of the impetus behind the secular improvements in technology that helped reduce emissions per GDP for SO_2, volatile organic compounds (VOC), and nitrogen oxide (NO_x) long before these substances were generally recognized to be environmental problems or, for that matter, before the federal government got involved in air pollution control.[58] SO_2 was not perceived to be a public health problem until after the Donora, Pennsylvania, episode in 1948 and the London episode of December 1952, yet SO_2 emissions per GDP have been in decline since the early 1920s. Similarly, VOC and NO_x emissions per gross national product (GNP) have been dropping nationwide since the 1930s, decades before these substances were either implicated in the 1950s as being responsible for the formation of photochemical smog or recognized (in the late 1960s and early 1970s) to be nationwide air quality problems.[59] Likewise, CO_2 emissions per GDP have been declining at the rate of 1.3 percent per year for the past century and a half,[60] long before global warming hit the public consciousness in the late 1980s.

Economics was also the fillip for much of the decline in energy use per GNP and per capita in the decade or more following the oil shocks of the 1970s. Those declines translated into lower energy use and contributed to reduced emissions per GNP, especially for SO_2, VOC, and NO_x.

The institution of property rights also indirectly helps improve environmental quality because it stimulates generalized technological change and economic growth.[61] Property rights (and its hand-maidens, markets) in general are among the key institutions that have propelled the developed nations ahead of developing nations and the former Communist nations, which flirted with economic systems that eschewed or drastically limited property rights for individuals. Property rights help explain, in large part, why East Germany and North Korea fell behind West Germany and South Korea economically despite similar endowments in human capital. And although there were differences in natural capital, it's not obvious where the advantage lay. In any case, natural capital, as the cases of Hong Kong, Singapore, and Switzerland suggest, is less critical and, in any case, insufficient to explain the large gaps between the two Koreas and, before reunification, the two Germanys. Moreover, property rights embedded in legally protected patents and copyrights provide a critical stimulus to invention, innovation, and diffusion of new and improved technologies, which, in turn, stimulates further economic growth.

As noted, Gwartney, Lawson, and Samida find that countries with greater economic freedom also have higher growth rates.[62] And, consistent with this and the environmental transition hypothesis, Norton finds that life expectancy and access to sanitation and safe water increase with this (and other measures) of property rights, while the rate of deforestation declines.[63]

National Regulation and Government Intervention

One of the enduring myths about the environment is that before federal takeover of environmental regulations, air, water, and other pollutants were increasing, and, in the absence of such a takeover, matters would necessarily have continued to deteriorate. But as the cases of the Clean Air Act of 1970, Clean Water Act of 1972, and Safe Drinking Water Act of 1974 show, much of the improvements in the United States for the air and water quality indicators examined in chapter 6 preceded the enactment of stringent national environmental laws. That, however, did not deter federal legislators from enacting those statutes and from taking enormous credit for battles that, for practical purposes, had already been won or were in the process of being won (see, for example, figures 6.7 and 6.12).

Table 7.1 showed that, with the notable exception of NO$_x$, improvements in indoor and outdoor air quality preceded federalization. In fact, NO$_x$ is the exception that proves this rule, because it was never deemed to be an important enough source of health or environmental impacts to be vigorously addressed (at least well into the 1990s).

Moreover, as I have shown elsewhere, for the air pollutants of greatest concern, the federalization of stationary air pollution control under the Clean Air Act of 1970 seems not to have accelerated cleanup significantly.[64] Although federalization may have further improved air quality, the nation has paid substantially more than it needed to for getting the same level of cleanup or, alternately, reductions in risks to health, mainly because of the federal government's embrace of one-size-fits-all command-and-control regulations. Notably, in theory, federalization does not inevitably have to lead to command-and-control or one-size-fits-all approaches nor does command-and-control have to lead to uniform requirements. But if they don't, it undercuts a good portion of the rationale for federal regulatory control. If one size-is-not-to-fit-all or if command-and-control is abandoned, why does the federal government have to be in the business of regulation in the first place? Why not let each jurisdiction do its own calculus of optimizing how much control it prefers, while letting the federal government do research and collect and distribute information?

With respect to water quality, as figure 6.12 shows, by the time stringent federal regulations were enacted under the Clean Water Act of 1972 and the Safe Drinking Water Act of 1974, death and disease because of water-related diseases had virtually been eliminated. Nevertheless, the federal government did play an important role in funding the construction of water and sanitary facilities before the passage of those acts.[65] Moreover, there have been significant improvements in water quality since federalization, especially in terms of improvements in fishability and swimmability of streams and reductions of residual public health impacts, as well as non–public health–related environmental impacts.[66] Also, as we saw earlier, federal laws governing pesticide use also helped improve water quality in the nation.

Although national intervention can lead to environmental benefits, it has, in the long term, also contributed to environmental degradation. Without federal subsidies, the amount of land and water diverted to agriculture would have been significantly lower than what it is today (see also figure 8.2);[67] loss of wetlands would have been lower;[68] and, at least in some cases, pesticide use would have been diminished.[69]

Finally, although stringent national regulations might be the proximate cause of environmental improvements since the 1970s, according to the environmental transition hypothesis, the very stringency is itself a product of wealth and technology. First, as a country becomes more wealthy, the shares of employment and national income due to the knowledge and service sectors increase at the expense of agriculture, mining, manufacturing, and other polluting sectors. This makes it possible for democratic societies to enact stringent environmental laws affecting those sectors. Second, the richer a society the more control it can afford and the less concerned would it be about the associated costs. Third, a richer society is also likely to have addressed its primary public health risk factors (e.g., hunger and lack of access to basic public health services, safe water, and sanitation) first and would then be more inclined to address secondary or even tertiary risks (such as outdoor air quality), which, with the march of time, would inevitably loom larger.[70]

PART C

RECONCILING HUMAN WELL-BEING WITH
ENVIRONMENTAL QUALITY

9. The Promise and Peril of Bioengineered Crops

Despite the evidence presented in the previous chapters that technological progress enables human needs to be met while limiting environmental damage, many environmental groups remain skeptical about such progress. This is evident in the angst over bioengineered or genetically modified (GM) crops. Probiotechnology advocates argue that it is essential for reducing hunger and malnutrition in the developing world, as well as the environmental impacts of agriculture worldwide. Environmental groups, citing uncertainty about its impact on public health and the environment, have invoked the precautionary principle in calling for a ban on GM crops.[1]

A popular formulation of the precautionary principle—and the one that I will use in this chapter—is contained in a declaration on that principle that was developed at a conference of environmentalists and like-minded academics at the Wingspread Conference Center, Racine, Wisconsin, in January 1998. According to the Wingspread Declaration:

> When an activity raises threats of harm to human health or the environment, precautionary measures should be taken even if some cause and effect relationships are not established scientifically.[2]

This principle captures much of the skepticism many environmentalists feel about technology. Although some scholars claim that the precautionary principle derives from the German articulation of *vorsorgeprinzip*[3] from the 1970s—translated as the "precaution" or "foresight" principle—it is essentially a verbose rendering of every mother's admonition that it is "better to be safe than sorry."[4] In the 1980s, various versions of the precautionary principle started to appear in international environmental declarations and agreements. By the 1992 United Nations Conference on Environment and Development in Rio de Janeiro, the precautionary principle was well-nigh ubiquitous: it was incorporated not only in principle 15 of the Rio Declaration, but in article 3.3 of the United Nations Framework Convention on Climate Change, as well as in the preamble to the Convention on Biological Diversity.[5] In January 2000, out of those declarations and agreement eventually emerged the Cartagena Protocol on Biosafety to the Convention on Biological Diversity. It repeatedly endorses the precautionary principle as a basis for decisionmaking and risk assessment with respect to the transboundary transfer (and associated handling and use) of GM organisms that may have adverse effects on the conservation and sustainable use of biological diversity.[6] As Frances Smith has noted, the Cartagena Protocol is seen as a major victory for the precautionary principle and its advocates.[7]

In keeping with its origins in technological skepticism, the mantra of the precautionary principle has also been increasingly invoked to justify, among other things, international regulation and control, if not outright bans, of various technologies, which—despite providing substantial benefits to humanity and, in some cases, to certain aspects of the environment—could adversely affect some facet of the environment or public health.[8] Among the technologies against which the precautionary principle has been invoked are DDT, a pesticide that has had spectacular success in reducing one of nature's dread diseases—malaria—worldwide, but that also has been associated with declines in the population of various avian species, such as the bald eagle and the peregrine falcon; fossil fuel combustion, on which much of the world's current prosperity and human well-being is based but which could contribute to global warming; and GM crops, which promise reductions in global hunger and malnutrition and a less chemical-dependant agriculture but which have also raised the specter of "frankenfoods."[9]

In addition to the precautionary principle itself, the justifications for those policies all share something else: a common flaw. The flaw is that each of those justifications takes credit for the public health and environmental risks that might be reduced by implementing the policy, but they ignore those public health and environmental risks that the policy itself might generate or prolong. As a result, there is a risk that the policy cures could be worse for humanity and the environment than the underlying diseases they seek to redress.[10] This one-sided application of the precautionary principle can be attributed to the fact that the principle itself provides no guidance on its application in situations where an action (such as a ban on GM crops) could simultaneously lead to uncertain benefits and uncertain harms.

To rectify this state of affairs, I first present a "framework" for applying the precautionary principles to policies in which outcomes might be ambiguous because their benefits might be offset in whole or in part by their harms. Next, I briefly survey the public health and environmental benefits and costs of GM crops. Then, I apply the framework to the broad range of consequences of a ban on GM crops to determine whether an unbiased and comprehensive application of the precautionary principles would justify such a ban. Next, I examine whether a ban would be consistent with, or further the stated aims and objectives of, the Convention on Biological Diversity. Finally, I will analyze whether GM crops (as a class) could or should be banned under the Cartagena Biosafety Protocol.

A Framework for Applying the Precautionary Principle under Competing Uncertainties

Few actions are either an unmitigated disaster or an unadulterated benefit, and certainty in both science and the real world is the exception rather than the rule. How, then, do we formulate precautionary policies in situations where an action could simultaneously lead to uncertain benefits and uncertain harms (or costs) to public health and the environment? Before applying the precautionary principle it is necessary to formulate criteria on how to rank various threats based on their characteristics and the degree of certainty attached to them. Consequently, I offer a set of criteria to construct a precautionary "framework."

The first of these criteria is the *human mortality criterion*, that is, the threat of death to any human being—no matter how lowly that human—outweighs similar threats to members of other species— no matter how magnificent that species. Moreover, in general, other nonmortal threats to human health should take precedence over threats to the environment, although there might be exceptions based on the nature, severity, and extent of the threat. I will call this the *human morbidity criterion*. Those two criteria can be combined into the *public health criterion*.

However, in instances where an action under consideration results in both potential benefits and potential harms to public health, additional criteria have to be brought into play. These additional criteria are also valid for cases where the action under consideration could result in positive as well as negative environmental impacts unrelated to public health. I propose five such criteria:

- *The immediacy criterion.* All else being equal, more immediate threats should be given priority over threats that could occur later. Support for this criterion can be found in the fact that people tend to partially discount the value of human lives that might be lost in the more distant future.[11] Although some may question whether such discounting may be ethical, it may be justified on the grounds that if death does not come immediately, with greater knowledge and technology, methods may be found in the future to deal with conditions that would otherwise be fatal, which, in turn, may postpone death even longer. For instance, between 1995 and 1999, estimated U.S. deaths because of AIDS dropped by more than two-thirds even though estimated cases increased by almost half.[12] Thus, if an HIV-positive person in the United States did not succumb to AIDS in 1995, because of the advances in medicine there was a greater likelihood in 1998 that he or she would live out a "normal" life span. Thus, it would be reasonable to give greater weight to premature deaths that occur sooner. This is related to, but distinct from, the adaptation criterion noted later.
- *The uncertainty criterion.* Threats of harm that are more certain (have higher probabilities of occurrence) should take precedence over those that are less certain if otherwise their consequences would be equivalent.
- *The expectation value criterion.* For threats that are equally certain, precedence should be given to those that have a higher expectation value. An action resulting in fewer expected deaths is preferred over one that would result in a larger number of expected deaths (assuming that the "quality of lives saved" is equivalent). Similarly, if an action poses a greater risk to biodiversity than inaction, the latter ought to be favored.
- *The adaptation criterion.* If technologies are available to cope with, or adapt to, the adverse consequences of an impact, then that

240

impact can be discounted to the extent that the threat can be nullified.

- *The irreversibility criterion.* Greater priority should be given to outcomes that are irreversible, or likely to be more persistent.

Ideally, each criterion should be applied, one at a time, to the various sets of public health and environmental consequences of the action under review (and weighted against, for each category, the consequences of persisting with the *status quo*, or whatever the other options might be). Such an approach could work relatively easily if the factors critical to each criterion were kept constant, except the ones related to the criterion under evaluation. But because the various factors are rarely equal, the net effects (on each of the sets of consequences) usually have to be evaluated by applying several of the criteria simultaneously. Then, if the results are equivocal with respect to the different sets of consequences, one should apply the human mortality and morbidity criteria. Thus, if the action, for example, might directly or indirectly increase net human mortality but improve the environment by, for instance, increasing the recreational potential of a water body, then the action ought to be rejected. Of course, there will be instances where no cut-and-dried answer will emerge readily (e.g., if an action might reduce cases of a nonlethal human disease while at the same time potentially killing a large number of animals). In such cases, in addition to considering factors such as the nature, severity, and curability of the disease; the cost of the disease or treatment; and the numbers of human and other species affected (factors subsumed in the previously specified criteria, namely, the adaptation, irreversibility, and expectation value criteria), decisionmaking should also consider factors such as the abundance of the species, whether the species is threatened or endangered, and so forth.

In the following, I will outline the potential benefits and costs to public health and the environment due to research, development, and commercialization of GM crops before applying the relevant criteria to determine whether a GM crop ban would be appropriate under the precautionary principle.

Potential Environmental Benefits of Bioengineered Crops

Agriculture and forestry, in that order, are the human activities that have the greatest effect on the world's biological diversity (see chapter 6). Today, agriculture worldwide accounts for 38 percent of land use, 66 percent of freshwater withdrawals, and 85 percent of water consumption.[13] It is responsible for most of the habitat conversion and fragmentation that threaten the world's forests, biodiversity, and terrestrial carbon stores and sinks. Between 1980 and 2005, there was a net loss of approximately 250 million hectares (Mha) of forest cover, despite significant expansion of forest cover in nontropical (mainly developed) countries because of increases in agricultural productivity that outstripped the demand for staple crops.[14] Moreover, current agricultural practices not only are responsible for most of the diversions of freshwater from the rest of nature, but also what they haven't withdrawn has often been polluted. Agriculture is among the prime contributor to environmental and water quality problems—oxygen depletion, pesticide and fertilizer runoff, and soil erosion—which are the major threats to aquatic and avian species. Their effects are evident not only inland but are also often felt in estuaries, oceans, and even in the atmosphere far from where the actual agricultural activities might have been undertaken.

Demand for agricultural and forest products is almost certainly going to increase substantially. The world's population is projected to grow from about 6.5 billion in 2005 to, perhaps, between 7.7 and 10.6 billion in 2050 under the low and high assumptions of population growth, an increase of 19–65 percent.[15] Under the United Nations (UN) Population Division's medium-growth scenario, the 2050 population is estimated at 9.1 billion (40 percent higher than today). The average person is also likely to be richer, which ought to increase agricultural demand per capita.[16] Accordingly, as will be shown in greater detail in chapter 10, the predominant environmental and natural resource challenge facing the globe for the remainder of the 21st century is probably the problem of meeting the human demand for food, nutrition, fiber, timber, and other natural resource products while conserving biodiversity.[17]

The question is whether biotechnology can help, hinder, or reconcile these often opposing goals. Although most of the following discussion focuses on agriculture, with particular emphasis on developing countries, much of it is equally valid for other human activities that use land and water, such as forestry, and also in developed countries.

Figure 9.1
THE TRADE-OFF BETWEEN HABITAT LOSS AND INCREASED AGRICULTURAL YIELDS, 2000–50

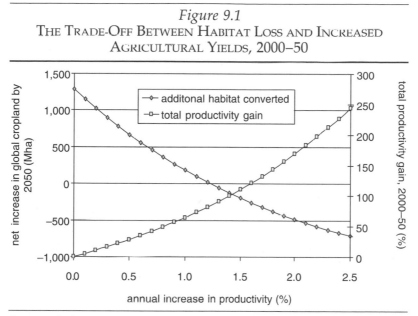

SOURCES: Indur M. Goklany, "Potential Consequences of Increasing Atmospheric CO_2 Concentration Compared to Other Environmental Problems," *Technology* 7S (2000): 189–213; FAO, *FAOSTAT 2006*, http://apps.fao.org (accessed January 8, 2006).

Decrease in Land and Water Diverted to Human Uses

Figure 9.1 shows, as a function of the annual increase in productivity in the food and agricultural sector per unit of land, how much additional land would need to be converted to cropland between 2000 and 2050 in order to meet the food demand of a larger and richer global population.[18] This figure assumes that the global population would grow from the 2000 level of 6.1 billion to 9.1 billion in 2050, per the UN's 2004 "medium variant" estimate.[19] It also assumes that global cereal production per capita, a surrogate for crop production per capita, will grow at the same rate between 2000 and 2050 as it did between 1961–63 and 1999–2001. And in the absence of any further technological improvements, all cropland will, on average, be as productive in 2050 as existing cropland was in 2000 (an optimistic assumption because soil degradation, nutrient depletion, and tighter water supplies are occupational hazards of farming).

Nevertheless, if the average productivity in 2050 stays at its 2000 level, then the entire increase in production (84 percent under the earlier assumptions of growth in population and food demand) would have to come from an expansion in global cropland. This expansion would translate into additional habitat loss of at least 1,287 Mha (see figure 9.1) beyond the 1,531 Mha devoted to cropland in 2000.[20] Much of that expansion would necessarily have to come at the expense of forested areas. It would lead to massive habitat loss and fragmentation, and it would put severe pressure on the world's remaining biodiversity, as well as on *in situ* conservation.

However, a productivity increase of 1 percent per year, equivalent to a cumulative 64 percent increase from 2000 to 2050, would reduce the net amount of new cropland required to meet future demand to 182 Mha. Such an increase in productivity is theoretically possible without resorting to biotechnology, provided sufficient investments are made in human capital, research and development, extension services, infrastructure expansion (to bring new lands, where needed, into production and integrate them with the rest of the world's agriculture system), inputs such as fertilizers and pesticides, and the acquisition and operation of technologies to limit or to mitigate the environmental impacts of agriculture.[21]

A 1.0 percent per year increase in the net productivity of the food and agricultural sector (per unit area) is within the bounds of historical experience given that it increased 2.2 percent per year between 1961–63 and 1999–2001.[22] In fact, there are numerous existing but underused opportunities to enhance productivity in an environmentally sound manner—underused, largely because of insufficient wealth (one reason why cereal yields are usually lower in poorer nations; see figure 2.3).[23] Merely increasing the average cereal yields in developing and transition nations to the level attained in 1999–2001 by the Netherlands (the country that had the highest average yield, that is, the yield ceiling) would increase global production by 95 percent, while increasing the average global cereal yield (3.09 tonnes per hectare [T/ha] in 1999–2001) to the yield ceiling (7.55 T/ha) would increase global cereal production by 144 percent.[24] To put those levels into perspective, one estimate of the theoretical maximum yield is 13.4 T/ha or 333 percent greater than the average global cereal yield in 1999–2001.[25]

Specifically, conventional (i.e., nonbioengineering) methods could be used to increase net productivity in the food and agricultural sector from farm to mouth by (a) further limiting preharvest crop losses to pests and diseases, which currently reduce global yields by an estimated 42 percent;[26] (b) increasing fertilizer use; (c) liming acidic soils; (d) adapting high-yielding varieties to specific locations around the world, although many scientists believe that opportunities to further increase yields through conventional breeding techniques are almost tapped out;[27] and (e) by reducing post-harvest and end-use losses,[28] which are estimated at about 47 percent worldwide.[29] Moreover, precision farming could help reduce chemical and water use without lowering yields, which would reduce many of the adverse effects of modern agriculture.

Productivity improvements are likely to come much more rapidly and more surely if biotechnology is used, particularly now that DNAs of *Arabidopsis thaliana* (a plant related to the mustard family and frequently used as a simplified biological model for crops consumed by humans) and rice have been decoded and with DNA sequencing of other crops (e.g., corn and soy) in the works. Biotechnology would more easily and quickly reduce current gaps between average yields and yield ceilings and between yield ceilings and the theoretical maximum yield, as well as push up the theoretical maximum yield. This begs the question as to whether environmental costs of such productivity increases will also increase and whether the latter are sustainable in the long run. This issue will be discussed in greater detail in subsequent sections.

If through biotechnology the annual rate at which productivity can be increased sustainably goes up from 1.0 percent to 1.5 percent per year, then cropland could actually be reduced by 193 Mha rather than increased by 182 Mha (relative to 2000 levels), while, at the same time, meeting the increased food demand of a larger and richer population. This corresponds to a net increase in productivity of 28 percent in 2050 because of biotechnology alone. And if it would help increase productivity to 2 percent per year, then by 2050 at least 484 Mha of current cropland could either be returned to the rest of nature or made available for other human uses (e.g., carbon sequestration, forest cover, or conservation areas). This would correspond to a net improvement in productivity because of biotechnology alone of 64 percent in the first half of the 21st century (figure 9.1).

Several biotechnological crops, currently in various stages between research and commercialization, could increase yields and, more important, put more food on the table per unit of land and water diverted to agriculture. A partial list of such crops, which could be particularly useful in developing nations, are described next.

Cereals That Are Tolerant of Poor Climatic and Soil Conditions. Soil and climatic conditions are frequently less than optimal for specific agricultural crops. Farmers virtually everywhere have had to cope with insufficient water or drought at one time or another; 43 percent of tropical soils are acidic;[30] 30 percent of the world's arable land is too alkaline; and salinity—to which more cropland is lost annually than is gained through forest clearance—has rendered one-third of the world's irrigated land unsuitable for growing crops.[31] Several efforts are underway to engineer crops that would better cope with such adverse conditions. These crops include cereals that would be tolerant to aluminum (which is associated with acidic soils), drought, high salinity levels, submergence, chilling and freezing, and low iron levels (associated with alkaline soils).[32] The ability to grow crops in the presence of such abiotic stresses is critical for developing countries, and it would only increase in urgency with population growth, particularly if global warming increases the need to rely on marginal soil and climatic conditions to achieve food security.

The mechanisms by which crops succumb to primary stresses (e.g., drought, salinity, cold, and heat and chemical pollution) are often interconnected.[33] Osmosis is the process whereby a plant absorbs water from its surroundings and moves the water into its root cells. This process continues until water pressure inside the cell builds up and reaches an equilibrium with the water outside. Once there is sufficient water inside the plant cell, osmosis stops. The same process transfers water from cell to cell within the plant. The pressure from water inside plant cells gives shape to the cells and allows plants to stand up. The water is also needed to transport nutrients and wastes in and out of the plant and to help provide the energy needed for photosynthesis. However, if the soil lacks sufficient water or if it contains high levels of salt, instead of accumulating water in the plant cells, the cells will be dehydrated as the water is transported outside. The resulting "osmotic stress" can affect the structure and function of the different cell components, damage the plant's cells, and shut down photosynthesis.

Freezing a plant also effectively dehydrates the cell. Because they share a common mode of action, it is possible to develop crops that simultaneously tolerate drought, salinity, and freezing. Developing tolerance to abiotic stress, however, is complicated because, among other things, responses to these stresses are controlled by multiple genes, which increases the difficulty of developing stress tolerant crops. Consequently, such plants are still in the development stage.

In one approach to developing salt tolerant plants, Eduardo Blumwald, then at the University of Toronto, and coworkers first identified a gene in *Arabidopsis thaliana* that produces a "transport protein" that is capable of moving salt from the root system into compartments (called vacuoles) in leaf cells where the salt can no longer disrupt the plant's biochemical activity.[34] Blumwald and Zhang engineered this gene into tomato plants and showed that the plants remove salt from the soil, sequestering it in leaves without affecting the fruit.[35] They also showed that their GM tomato plant could grow even if it was irrigated with water containing 200 millimoles (mM) of sodium chloride (common salt). For reference, this is 50–100 times saltier than normal and about 40 percent as salty as seawater.[36, 37] In 2003, for his work, Blumwald received the Alexander von Humboldt Award for contributions to agriculture.

More recently, Blumwald and coworkers have developed a transgenic cotton using the same *Arabidopsis* gene. This cotton generated greater fiber yield and higher quality fibers when irrigated in greenhouses with water containing 200 mM of sodium chloride.[38] The transgenic plants also had higher nitrogen assimilation rates compared to wild-type cotton plants under saline conditions.

A second approach to conferring salt tolerance would be to protect cells from the damage caused by osmotic stress. Substances that prevent such damage—called "osmoprotectants"—include various amino acids, amines, sugars, and sugar alcohols.[39] In an application of this approach, an international team of plant scientists from the United States and South Korea engineered indica rice varieties to increase the production of trehalose, a sugar molecule, when the plant is under stress. (Trehalose, one molecule of which is formed from two molecules of glucose, also helps stabilize biological structures under abiotic stress in bacteria, fungi, and invertebrates). These transgenic plants showed higher tolerance to salt, drought, and low temperatures compared to nonengineered plants. In one experiment, the photosynthetic yield of nontransgenic plants decreased by two-thirds, whereas that of the two best-performing transgenic lines only decreased by about one-third (both compared to the unstressed controls). Moreover, under unstressed conditions, photosynthetic rates in the transgenic plants were 5–15 percent higher than in the nontransgenic controls. These results demonstrate that it should be possible to enhance rice productivity while also increasing the tolerance to common stresses.[40]

A recent paper in the *Proceedings of the National Academy of Sciences* identified a gene that confers tolerance to salt, drought, freeze, and oxidative stress in a fungus that survives in the extreme environment of the Dead Sea despite it being 10 times saltier than the world's oceans. Transferring this gene (or a gene with a similar effect) into crops could help enhance their productivity under similar extreme conditions.[41] That this could be more than just a pipe dream is suggested by experiments in which it was shown that there is very little penalty in the yield of salt-tolerant transgenic tobacco under unstressed conditions and that these plants suffered only a 5 percent loss in total productivity when grown in a medium containing 200 mM of sodium chloride.[42]

Another source of stress is low availability of iron in the soil, a condition that is common in moderate to high alkaline soils characteristic of arid and semiarid areas, which according to one estimate occupy 30 percent of the world's arable land.[43] Because of the high alkalinity, iron in the soil is not soluble and cannot be used by plants. But iron is needed to catalyze the formation of chlorophyll. Thus, iron-deficient plants suffer from chlorosis (i.e., yellowing of the leaves) and low plant growth.

Japanese scientists have developed a transgenic rice that incorporated two barley genes designed to increase, in the event of iron deficiency, the amount of compounds released into the soil that help solubilize iron and transport it back into the plant. The yield of the transgenic rice was four times that of the nontransgenic variety, and it contained more iron.[44] If such a rice—a staple to at least half the world's population—is successfully commercialized, it could not only increase the quantity of grain but also its nutritional quality because an iron-deficient diet leads to anemia, one of the major causes of perinatal and maternal mortality.[45]

Rice Varieties That Combine the Best Traits of the African and Asian Varieties. These rices, which are called NERICA—for NEw RIce for

AfriCA—combine the former's ability to shade out weeds when young with the high-yield capacity of the Asian variety.[46] In addition, the GM variety is highly resistant to drought, pests, and diseases. This resistance could be particularly useful for Africa because its increases in rice yields have so far lagged behind the rest of the world's. This lag is one reason why malnourishment in sub-Saharan Africa has increased in the past several decades, in contrast to improved trends elsewhere. In Guinea, NERICAs increased the yield ceiling by 50 percent. But in field conditions, yields increased by 25–250 percent with little to modest inputs (compared to traditional varieties).[47] Typically, weed removal also accounts for 30–40 percent of the labor used to grow a crop. Thus, the ability of NERICA to reduce weed growth boosts yields while reducing labor on the farm, which is an important consideration in Africa where a significant proportion of the working population has been lost to or weakened by AIDS, malaria, and other diseases.

Rice with the Property of Being Able to Close Stomata More Readily.[48] Stomata are microscopic pores on the underside of leaves that allow carbon dioxide (CO_2) and water vapor to enter and exit the leaves. Closing stomata reduces the amount of water vapor leaving the plant, in effect increasing its water use efficiency. It also increases net photosynthetic efficiency. This ability ought to increase water use efficiency and net photosynthetic efficiency. Both aspects will be useful under dry conditions—conditions that, moreover, may get more prevalent in some areas under global warming.

Rice with the Alternative C4 Pathway for Photosynthesis.[49] About 95 percent of plants, including most conventional crops (e.g., rice and wheat), fix atmospheric CO_2 into the plant as sugars through the C3 pathway of photosynthesis—so-called because the initial step in this pathway involves the formation of a compound containing 3 carbons. This step occurs through a chemical reaction catalyzed by RuBisCO—an enzyme critical to all photosynthesis. But RuBisCO also catalyzes the breakdown of sugars through respiration in the presence of light (i.e., photorespiration), which releases CO_2. Thus, C3 photosynthesis is inherently inefficient in daylight, as well as in environments with high oxygen and low CO_2. Photorespiration reduces net carbon fixed by C3 plants by up to 40 percent. As a result, current CO_2 levels in the atmosphere, which are low by

249

evolutionary standards, frequently limit photosynthesis.[50] The C3 pathway is also inefficient when it is hot and dry.

Some tropical species (e.g., maize and sugarcane), however, have evolved to employ the C4 pathway of photosynthesis, which involves the formation of a compound containing 4 carbons (hence the name) and reduces photorespiration. C4 plants exhibit several desirable agronomic traits particularly under hot and dry conditions: high rate of photosynthesis in current atmospheric conditions (i.e., fast growth) and high efficiency in water and mineral use. Unfortunately, there are no closely related C3 and C4 crops that can be used to transfer the C4 traits to C3 crops by traditional breeding approaches. But by introducing the photosynthesis genes of maize into rice through bioengineering, researchers have demonstrated that the new rice strains could boost photosynthesis and grain yield by up to 35 percent.[51] Small-scale field trials in China and South America have reportedly increased yield up to 90 percent, although it is unclear whether the improvement is because of the presence of the C4 pathway or perhaps greater tolerance in the engineered plant to the area's saline soils or more intense ultraviolet light.[52] In the real world, especially under poor soil conditions, the reason for the increase, however, may not be that important. Moreover, because the C4 pathway is more efficient at higher temperatures and drier conditions, this trait could be especially useful if there is significant global warming. In addition, efforts are underway to try to reengineer RuBisCO by using RuBisCO from red algae, which is a far more efficient catalyst for photosynthesis than that found in crops.[53]

Maize, Millet, Rice, and Sorghum with Resistance to Striga, *a Parasitic Weed.* Striga can reduce yields by 20–80 percent.[54] This weed, which infests an estimated 20–40 Mha in sub-Saharan Africa, attaches itself to the roots of the growing crop and sucks away the crop's water and nutrients, diverting them for its own growth. The International Center for Corn and Wheat Improvements and Israel's Weizmann Institute of Science have developed a unique system for *Striga* control in maize. It combines a seed coating containing a low dose of an herbicide (imazapyr) for killing *Striga* with an imazapyr-resistant (IR) maize. Small quantities (30–45 grams) of the herbicide are delivered when the weed attaches to the maize root thereby preventing *Striga* from affecting the crop. In addition, imazapyr can diffuse into the soil killing ungerminated *Striga* seeds. Field trials in Africa indicate that IR-maize yields can increase between 38 percent and 82 percent.[55]

Recent work on arbuscular mycorrhiza (AM)—an extremely common symbiotic complex composed of fungi (called AM fungi) and plant roots in which the fungi extracts nutrients from the soil and delivers it to the roots in exchange for carbohydrates produced within the plant—suggests possible mechanisms whereby *Striga* infects its hosts. These studies indicate that before the formation of AM, the plant root exudes a chemical that increases production of filaments (called hyphae) by the AM fungi, which then increases the likelihood of the latter attaching itself to a plant root. Notably, this same chemical stimulates seed germination by *Striga*, and its production is increased if phosphate availability in the soil is low. This condition is precisely the one in which *Striga* thrives. Better understanding of the mechanisms by which this chemical is produced and regulated might provide new avenues for controlling *Striga*.[56]

Cereals with the Ability to Fix Nitrogen[57] and to Enhance Uptakes of Phosphorus and Nitrogen.[58] Efforts toward this goal were advanced with the genetic sequencing of *Sinorhizobium meliloti*, a bacterium that, in a symbiotic relationship with the alfalfa root system, fixes nitrogen for the alfalfa. In exchange, the alfalfa provides the bacterium with sugars and other nutrients.[59] Such symbiosis is responsible for a substantial proportion of the approximately 100 million tons of nitrogen fixed annually in terrestrial ecosystems.

Other approaches for enhancing nutrient uptake could be developed based on the recent discovery of a previously unknown mechanism for transferring nitrogen from the soil into the plant, which is mediated by AM fungi.[60]

Rice, Maize, Cotton, Potato, Sweet Potato, Papaya, Zucchini, and Cucumber with Resistance to Insects, Nematodes, Bacteria, Viruses, and Fungi.[61] Crops resistant to viruses, weeds, insects, and other pests, such as the *Striga*-resistant maize, rice, and sorghum, ought to reduce pesticides and their residues in the environment. Other examples include crops that contain genes from the *Bacillus thuringiensis* (Bt), a soil bacterium, which has been used as an insecticide (as a spray) in conventional agriculture for almost half a century. Such crops include Bt corn, Bt cotton, Bt potato, and Bt rice, which are discussed in greater detail in subsequent subsections.

The potential of such crops was probably first made evident with the experience of papaya in Hawaii. Between 1995 and 1998, production of papaya, a fruit rich with vitamin A and Hawaii's second most important crop, dropped 50 percent because of the papaya ringspot virus (PRV). In 1998, however, the commercialization of bioengineered varieties of papaya resistant to the virus enabled production levels to rebound and exceed their pre-1998 levels.[62] For this signal achievement, Dennis Gonsalves and the team of scientists who developed the PRV-resistant varieties, received the 2002 Alexander von Humboldt Award for Agriculture. As of 2005, GM papaya had reached the field trial stage in Australia, Brazil, China, Cuba, and Mexico.[63] However, in Thailand, commercialization is stymied because of a government ban on field trials of GM plants, which has placed these plants into a regulatory limbo, despite demonstrations by some papaya farmers asking for progress on field trials.[64] Scientists in other tropical areas where papaya is popular (e.g., Africa, Bangladesh, Jamaica, and Venezuela) are also trying to develop disease-resistance varieties for their locales.[65]

Cassava with Resistance to the Cassava Mosaic Virus (CMV).[66] CMV can reduce yields of cassava, a staple in much of Africa, by 20–95 percent. Efforts are underway to develop a CMV-resistant variety of cassava, which includes a gene with an enzyme (replicase) that can disrupt the life cycles of several other viruses. Also, because cassava naturally contains substances that can be converted to cyanide, cassava has to be adequately prepared to detoxify it prior to consumption. Work is proceeding on producing a GM cassava that would be less toxic.[67]

Despite success in laboratories, field tests in African nations have been held up because of government inaction caused by suspicion and controversies over biotechnology.[68]

Spoilage-Prone Fruits Bioengineered for Delayed Ripening. Such fruits would have longer shelf life and reduce post-harvest losses. In fact, the first commercialized GM plant was the FlavrSavr tomato, a tomato engineered to delay rotting. But it was a commercial bust in the United States. Despite that failure, several efforts are underway to increase the shelf life of fruits. Such work is being undertaken not only in the United States, where scientists are working on, among other things, melons, strawberries, and raspberries,[69] but also in many developing countries. For instance, in Mexico, field studies are being undertaken on melon, papaya, chili pepper, and pineapple.[70] Scientists in the Philippines are working on mangos, papaya, and tomatoes.[71] Slow-ripening tomatoes are near commercialization in China, while papaya is in the experimental phase.[72] In India, the focus is on bananas and tomatoes.[73]

Crops Bioengineered to Reduce the Likelihood of Their Seed Pods Shattering. Shattering seed pods reduce yields of crops such as wheat, rice, and canola. It is estimated that this change could increase canola yields, for instance, by 25 percent to 100 percent.[74]

Maize and Soybeans with High-Lysine Content, Maize with High-Oil and Energy Content, and Forage Crops (Such as Alfalfa) with Lower-Lignin Content. Such crops ought to improve livestock feed and to reduce the overall demand for land needed for livestock.[75] In late 2005, Rennesen LLC, a joint venture of Cargill and Monsanto, announced it was preparing to market the first genetically engineered animal feed, a high-lysine corn.[76] Lysine is an amino acid that improves the efficiency of protein utilization in animal feeding. According to one estimate, displacing soy-based feed with high-lysine corn can reduce the amount of arable land needed to produce an equivalent amount of protein in the feed by three-fourths, while also reducing nitrogen excreted from livestock.[77]

Crops That Will Be Better Able to Cope with Earlier Springs and Summer Droughts. Among the concerns about global warming is that spring will arrive earlier and soil moisture may be diminished in summer. If that occurs, to increase yields, the crop should flower earlier and its growth completed before the advent of the hot or dry period. Scientists at the John Innes Centre in the United Kingdom have identified the gene in barley that controls the timing of flowering and could help in developing crops that are better adapted to global warming.[78]

If the methods and genes used to bioengineer those crops can be successfully adapted and transferred to other crops or even trees, it would help reduce future land and water needed to feed, clothe, and shelter humanity, as well as free up those resources for the rest of nature.

Reductions in Nutrients, Pesticides, Silt, and Carbon in the Environment

By increasing the amount of food produced per unit of land and water, GM crops would significantly reduce the environmental impacts associated with agricultural activities. Increasing crop yields would translate into substantial environmental benefits, whether that was the original intent. Higher yields reduce habitat loss and the potential for soil erosion. In turn, less erosion translates into better water quality for streams, rivers, estuaries, and other water bodies, as well as lower impacts on species using those water bodies. It also reduces loss of carbon sinks and stores into the atmosphere. And to the extent that usage of agricultural chemicals is determined by the area under cultivation, reductions in cropland would also reduce pollution from fertilizer and pesticides. Equally important, many of the mentioned GM crops would maintain, if not enhance, yields without increasing inputs such as water, fertilizers, and pesticides. In some instances, they may enable the displacement of more toxic pesticides with ones that are less toxic or persistent.[79]

In fact, the experience since GM crops were commercialized in 1996 in the United States (and elsewhere) confirms that they indeed provide environmental benefits. In 2004, U.S. farmers planted biotech crops on 118 million acres, an increase of 11 percent over the previous year. Compared to conventional crops, biotech varieties increased food production by 6.6 billion pounds while pesticide use declined by 62 million pounds (measured by weight of active ingredients). The combination of reduced input costs and higher production increased net returns to farmers by $2.3 billion.[80] No wonder such crops are increasingly accepted by farmers. GM crops are now cultivated on more than 35 percent of cultivated land in the United States.[81]

Use of Bt cotton—planted on 7.1 million acres (or 51 percent of cotton area in the United States, up from 42 percent in 2001)—reduced pesticide use by 1.76 million pounds, increased yields by 587 million pounds (or 82 pounds per acre), and netted farmers $297 million (or $42 per acre).[82] The Agricultural Research Service of the U.S. Department of Agriculture (USDA) completed a four-year study in a 7,000 square mile watershed in the Mississippi Delta. It compared insecticide runoff from Bt cotton and conventional cotton sites and found that the former had lower levels of pyrethroid insecticides.[83] Comparing the period before the introduction of Bt cotton

(1993–95) to the year 2000, pesticides that are most toxic to birds and fish decreased by two-thirds, while those most toxic to humans decreased by one-third.[84] Notably, this dramatic reduction coincided with substantial increases in average bird counts in cotton growing areas in the South. The North American Bird Breeding Survey from the U.S. Geological Service shows that bird counts increased from the five years before the introduction of Bt cotton (1991–95) to the five years after (1996–2000). The counts are positively correlated with the Bt cotton adoption rates, the reduction in insecticide use, and the relative presence of the species in cotton fields.[85] These increases, on average, range from 10 percent for Texas to 37 percent for Mississippi.

Moreover, reductions in pesticide use translate into lower environmental impacts and energy use from the manufacture and distribution of pesticides, as well as fuel and water savings on the farm.[86]

Developing countries can also reduce pesticide usage by using pest resistant crops. Conventional cotton cultivation is one of the most pesticide-intensive agricultural activities worldwide. In India, the world's third-largest cotton producer, in the late 1990s cotton occupied only 5 percent of its land but accounted for about 50 percent of its pesticide use.[87] In 1998, the devastation caused by pests reportedly contributed to 500 suicides among Indian cotton farmers whose crops had failed. Some Indian farmers—aware of reports that yields might increase from 14 percent to 38 percent despite suspension of any spraying,[88] desperate for more reliable technologies, and fearful of their livelihoods—planted Bt cotton illegally on about 10,000 acres, even before *it* had been officially approved by government authorities. The Indian government threatened to confiscate and burn the resulting bumper crop, but it eventually relented.[89] In March 2002, the Indian government finally approved, for the first time, the commercialization of a bioengineered crop—Bt cotton.[90] That first year, 29,415 ha were planted with Bt cotton.[91] By 2005, that amount had increased to 1,300,000 ha (or 14 percent of India's cotton acreage).[92] A 2003 nationwide survey indicated that Bt cotton growers in India increased average yields by about 29 percent because of effective control of bollworms, reduced chemical spraying by 60 percent, and increased net profit by 78 percent compared to non-Bt farmers.[93] Thus, cultivation of Bt cotton in India is good for the farmer, the environment, and the consumer (because increased production reduces the price of cotton).

Elsewhere, other countries' experience with commercialized Bt cotton has been less contentious, but also positive.[94] For instance, in 1999, China's Bt cotton farmers reduced pesticide use by an average of 49.9 kg per ha (or 80.5 percent) per season while increasing yields by 5.8 percent.[95] Another study indicated that because of Bt cotton, China's pesticide usage in 2001 was 25 percent lower than its mid 1990s level.[96] And during the 1999/2000 season in South Africa, farmers who adopted Bt cotton had 60 percent higher yields and 38 percent lower pesticide consumption compared to nonadopters.[97]

Similarly, with respect to Bt corn in the United States, which was planted on 25.1 million acres (or 32 percent of the country's corn area) in 2004, pesticide use dropped by 4.8 million pounds and production increased by 5.9 billion pounds (or 237 pounds per acre).[98] As a result, farmers' net income increased by an estimated $210 million ($8.36 an acre). However, in years when insect pressure is low, farmers may, in hindsight, lose money. For example, they lost $35 million because of Bt corn in 1999 because of low prevalence of insects that year.[99] However, insecticide usage was reduced by 1 million acre-treatments and production was up 66 million bushels.[100] Therefore, until one can reliably forecast insect pressure months in advance, planting Bt corn serves as an insurance policy from the point of view of the farmer's bottom line. From the perspective of the environment, it provides greater assurance of lower pesticide use.

A two year preproduction field trial on two kinds of Bt rice in China also indicates that such rice could provide substantial economic and public health benefits to farmers. A recent paper in *Science* indicates that, compared to conventional varieties, Bt rice increased yields by 6–9 percent and reduced pesticide use by 80 percent.[101] Recent reports that Iran has commercialized a Bt rice indicate that yields increased by 10 percent.[102] Equally important, in the Chinese study none of the households of the farmers who adopted Bt rice reported any adverse health effects from pesticide use in either year of the study. Of those who cultivated both, Bt and conventional rice, none reported adverse effects while the farmer was working on the GM rice, but between 8 percent and 11 percent reported such effects while working the conventional rice field. Of those using only conventional varieties, between 3 percent and 8 percent of households reported ill effects.[103]

The experience in the United States with commercial varieties of bioengineered herbicide tolerant (HT) crops is also positive. Those crops are designed to tolerate various herbicides, so that those herbicides can be used to kill weeds competing with the crop for space, sunlight, water, and other nutrients, but not the crop itself. The point of HT crops is not to eliminate herbicide use, but to reduce the amount, toxicity, and persistence of pesticides employed.

Moreover, it is important to remember that because the major reason for tilling the soil is to reduce pressure from weeds, HT crops facilitate no-till cultivation. By stemming soil erosion, no-till cultivation protects future agricultural productivity, reduces the transport of particles containing fertilizers and pesticides into aquatic systems and into the atmosphere, and reduces the loss of carbon stored in the soil into the atmosphere.

Consider the case of soybean in the United States, which competes with more than 30 kinds of weeds that, left unchecked, can reduce yields by 50–90 percent.[104] Thus, even before the development of HT soybean, farmers relied heavily on herbicides. However, an HT soybean ("Roundup Ready" soybean), which is engineered to be tolerant to a broad spectrum herbicide, glyphosate, helps farmers rid their fields of weeds more effectively using lower amounts of less toxic and less persistent pesticides. Because of farmers' successful experience with HT crops, they are among the most common applications of biotechnology today. In 2004, for instance, Roundup Ready soybean was planted on 64 million acres or 85 percent of the U.S. soybean acreage, up from 69 percent in 2001.[105]

It is estimated that, in 2004, the use of HT soybean reduced pesticide usage by more than 22 million pounds (in terms of active ingredients) while increasing farmers' net income by more than $1.4 billion. Other HT crops—canola, corn, and cotton—reduced pesticide use by an additional 33 million pounds (and increased farmers' incomes by more than $410 million).[106]

Wider use of HT soybean has helped boost the amount of soy acreage that is no-till from 16 million acres in 1995 to 26 million acres in 2004.[107] According to a survey done by the American Soybean Association, because of the increased popularity of Roundup Ready soybean, 73 percent of the soy farmers were leaving more crop residue on the soil, and soy acreage that was "reduced till" acres increased by one-fourth between 1996 and 2001.[108] Cumulatively, such practices are estimated to save hundreds of millions of tons of topsoil from being eroded as well as hundreds of millions of gallons of fuel because farmers have to run equipment over the field fewer times.

Conservation tillage, over the long term, also increases the number and diversity of surface and subsurface arthropods, including many beneficial predatory species.[109] For instance, the density of carabid beetles was 50 times greater in no-till soils than in conventionally treated soils, while the density of earthworms was more than 3.5 times greater. These worms not only serve as a good food source for birds, but some of them—nightcrawlers, in particular—create vertical burrows, which improves the ability of water to percolate into the ground and reduces the potential of flooding.[110]

Other potential environmental benefits that have not yet been realized because the affected crops have yet to be commercialized include the following:

- Reduced usage of nitrogen and phosphorus for agriculture. For example, nitrogen-fixing rice and rice and maize bioengineered with the ability to increase uptakes of phosphorus and nitrogen from the soil would reduce nutrient load in the environment. In Europe and the United States, an estimated 18 percent of the nitrogen and 30 percent of the phosphorus in fertilizers are incorporated into crops, between 10 percent and 80 percent of the nitrogen and 15 percent of the phosphorus end up in aquatic ecosystems, and much of the remainder accumulates in the soil, to be later eroded into aquatic systems.[111] Nitrogen-fixing crops would reduce reliance on fertilizers and, thereby, reduce ground and surface water pollution, risks of chemical spills, and atmospheric emissions of nitrous oxide (N_2O), which is a greenhouse gas that, pound for pound over a 100-year period, is about 300 times more potent a greenhouse gas than is CO_2.[112]

- Reduced phosphorus in animal waste and in runoff into streams, lakes, and other water bodies, mitigating one of the major sources of excess nutrients in the environment. It would also reduce the need for inorganic phosphorus supplements in feed.[113] Phosphorus is one of the essential nutrients for animal growth. About two-thirds of the phosphorous in corn and soy feed for animals is bound up as phytic acid and cannot be absorbed by animals. Any unabsorbed phosphorous passes into the environment in animals' manure and through the manure into the environment. One way to make this phosphorous available for nutritional use (and reduce nutrient loading in the environment) is to introduce the enzyme phytase into the animals' diet. This introduction can also be facilitated through the use of bioengineered corn and soybean, which are low in phytic acid and/or contains phytase. In an interesting variation of the latter approach, scientists have developed a transgenic pig that contains phytase in its saliva and excretes 75 percent less phosphorus.[114]

Other Environmental Benefits of Bioengineered Plants and Trees

Crops can also be engineered to directly cleanup environmental problems. For instance, GM plants can be used for bioremediation by developing crops that selectively absorb various metals and metal complexes containing aluminum, copper, cadmium, nickel, zinc, and arsenic from contaminated soils.[115] Such plants could, for instance, detoxify methyl mercury in soils, thereby removing it from the food chain. GM plants might also be used to detect and remove groundwater pollutants such as tetrachloroethene (PCE) and trichloroethene (TCE) or explosives such as pentaerythritol tetranitrate (PETN) and trinitrotoluene (TNT).[116]

Researchers have also genetically modified aspen trees to produce 50 percent less lignin and 15 percent more cellulose. Lignin, a component of all wood, must be chemically separated from cellulose to make the pulp used in paper production. The GM tree has half the normal lignin cellulose ratio of about 1 to 2. Overall, 15 percent more pulp may be produced from the same amount of wood. Moreover, the GM trees are 25–30 percent taller. Thus, the requirements of land, chemicals, and energy used to make a given quantity of paper ought to be reduced substantially and result in significantly lower environmental impacts at every stage—from tree farming to paper production.[117]

Other potential applications of biotechnology that could reduce environmental impacts include production of biodegradable plastics using oilseed rape and colored cotton (which could reduce reliance on synthetic dyes).[118]

Potential Public Health Benefits of Bioengineered Crops

Having sufficient quantities of food, as we saw in previous chapters, is often the first step to a healthy society. The increase in food supplies per capita during the past half-century not only reduced the absolute and relative level of hunger and malnutrition worldwide, it also helped lower global infant mortality rates from 157 to 57 per 1,000 live births between 1950–55 and 2003, increase life expectancies from 46.5 years to 66.8 years, and enable the average person to live a more fulfilling and productive life.[119]

Despite the unprecedented progress during the past century, billions of people still suffer from undernourishment, malnutrition, and other ailments due, in whole or part, to insufficient food or poor nutrition. Globally, about 852 million people are currently undernourished, that is, cannot meet their basic needs for energy and protein.[120] Underweight children are at greater risk of death due to diarrhea, malaria, measles, pneumonia, and other infectious diseases. Reducing these numbers over the next half-century despite projections that population will increase by 1.2–4.1 billion (or 18–63 percent)[121] while simultaneously reducing pressures on biodiversity will require increasing the quantity of food produced per unit of land and water. As discussed earlier, GM crops could help in this struggle.

But increasing food quantity is not enough. Improving the nutritional quality of food is just as important. The diets of more than half the world's population are deficient in iron, vitamin A, zinc, or other micronutrients. Such deficiencies compounded by underweight can cause disease, if not death.[122] About 2 billion people do not have enough iron in their diet, making them susceptible to anemia (see table 9.1).[123] According to one estimate, in Asia about 60 percent of all pregnant women and 40 percent of school children are iron deficient.[124] As a result, iron deficiency is a major contributor to perinatal and maternal mortality. Between 100 million and 140 million children suffer from vitamin A deficiency, which can cause clinical xerophthalmia—a condition of the eye, caused primarily by a lack of vitamin A, that causes thickening and drying of the conjunctiva and cornea and could lead to blindness.[125] As a result, between 250,000 and 500,000 children become blind each year from vitamin A deficiency.[126] Vitamin A deficiency also compromises the immune system. Zinc deficiency, which affects about one-third of the world's population, has also been implicated in lower respiratory tract infections, malaria, and diarrheal diseases.[127] Through the cumulative effect of these deficiencies, malnutrition was responsible for 6.2 million deaths each year including 5.6 million children below

Table 9.1

PUBLIC HEALTH PROBLEMS THAT COULD BE ALLEVIATED USING GM,
RATHER THAN CONVENTIONAL, CROPS

Problem	Current extent (year)	Likelihood of GM crops reducing problem
Undernourishment	852 million people (2000–02) (Source: SOFIA 2004)	very high
Malnutrition	5.6 million deaths per year in children < 5 years (Source: Bryce et al. 2005)	very high
Stunting	182 million people (2000) (Source: de Onis et al. 2000)	high
Iron-deficiency anemia	~ 2,000 million people (Source: WHO 2003)	high
Vitamin A deficiency	100–140 million children suffer from deficiency each year; 0.25–0.5 million children blinded per year, and half die each year; 0.6 million women die each year from childbirth-related causes (Source: WHO 2003)	high

(continue on next page)

Table 9.1

PUBLIC HEALTH PROBLEMS THAT COULD BE ALLEVIATED USING GM,
RATHER THAN CONVENTIONAL, CROPS *(continued)*

Problem	Current extent (year)	Likelihood of GM crops reducing problem
Ischemic and cerebrovascular diseases	2.3 million deaths per year in HIC (2001) 10.3 million deaths per year in MIC and LIC (2001) (includes those due to smoking) (Source: WHO 2002, Annex Table 2)	moderate
Cancers	2.0 million deaths per year in HIC (2001) 5.1 million deaths per year in MIC and LIC (2001) (includes those due to smoking) (Source: WHO 2002, Annex Table 2)	moderate

NOTE: HIC = high-income countries; LIC = low-income countries; MIC = mid-income countries.

SOURCES: FAO, *The State of World Fisheries and Aquaculture* (SOFIA) 2004, http://www.fao.org/sof/sofia/index_en.htm (accessed) February 10, 2006; Jennifer Bryce, Cynthia Boschi-Pinto, Kenji Shibuya, and Robert E. Black, "WHO Estimates of the Causes of Death in Children," *Lancet* 365 (March 26, 2005): 1147–52; WHO, *Micronutrient Deficiencies: Battling Iron Deficiency Anemia,* 2003, www.who.int/nut/vad.htm (accessed January 16, 2006); WHO, *The World Health Report 2002* (Geneva: WHO, 2002).

the age of five (see tables 9.1 and 9.2).[128] It also contributes to stunting in 182 million children.[129] Malnutrition in early childhood also seems to lead to long-term developmental deficits and impaired intelligence, if not severe retardation.[130]

In addition, poor nutritional habits and overconsumption of food can lead to so-called diseases of affluence such as high blood pressure, high cholesterol levels, obesity, and nutritional imbalances, which contribute to strokes, heart diseases, type 2 diabetes, and, perhaps, various forms of cancer.[131] In 2001, an estimated 16.6 million deaths resulted from cerebrovascular and ischemic heart diseases alone, of which 20 percent were in the highest-income countries.[132]

The *World Health Report 2002* attributes 41.3 percent of the global death toll of 55.78 million in 2000 directly or indirectly to food and nutrition. That number includes 3.75 million deaths caused by insufficient food supplies, equivalent to 6.7 percent of total deaths (see table 9.2). However, its toll in terms of disability-adjusted life years (DALYs) lost worldwide is somewhat higher at 9.5 percent. This report also attributes 2.41 million (or 4.3 percent) of total deaths, accounting for 6.2 percent of total DALYs lost, to insufficient intake or absorption of three micronutrients, namely, iron, vitamin A, and zinc. In addition, another 14.15 million (or 25.4 percent) of deaths are attributed to other diet-related conditions—high blood pressure, high cholesterol, overweight—which contribute to strokes, heart disease, and various cancers and are frequently, although not exclusively, the result of poor dietary habits. However, despite the high death toll, these other diet-related conditions account for only 9.5 percent of DALYs lost, mainly because they strike people who are relatively older.[133] Finally, 2.73 million (or 4.9 percent) of total deaths and 1.8 percent of total DALYs lost are attributed to low fruit and vegetable intake, which too seems to be a factor in strokes, heart disease, and various cancers.

Not surprisingly, the vast majority of deaths because of insufficient food and micronutrients occur in developing countries, with Africa accounting for 47 percent and Southeast Asia for another 34 percent of those deaths.

Bioengineered crops can help reduce the toll of death and diseases due to each of the conditions noted in table 9.2. They would help ensure that adequate quantities of food are available and reduce micronutrient deficiencies. Not least, they could create alternatives

Table 9.2
MORTALITY AND BURDEN OF DISEASE DUE TO DIET-RELATED
CONDITIONS, 2000

	Mortality		DALYs Lost	
Attributed cause	Number (in thousands)	% of all deaths worldwide	DALYs lost (in thousands)	% of total DALYs lost
Childhood and Maternal Undernutrition				
Underweight	3,748	6.7	137,801	9.5
Iron deficiency	841	1.5	35,057	2.4
Vitamin A deficiency	778	1.4	26,638	1.8
Zinc deficiency	789	1.4	28,034	1.9
Subtotal	*6,157*	*11.0*	*227,530*	*15.7*
Other Diet-related Risks				
Blood pressure	7,141	12.8	64,270	4.4
Cholesterol	4,415	7.9	40,437	2.8
Overweight	2,591	4.6	33,415	2.3
Low fruit and vegetable intake	2,726	4.9	26,662	1.8
Subtotal	*16,873*	*30.2*	*164,784*	*11.3*
Deaths due to all diet-related factors—Total	*23,030*	*41.3*	*392,314*	*27.0*
Deaths due to all causes	**55,775**	**100.0**	**1,453,617**	**100.0**

SOURCE: WHO, *World Health Report 2002* (Geneva: WHO, 2002), Statistical Annexes 11 and 12, also available at www.who.int/whr/2002/annex/en/ (accessed January 16, 2006).

to foods that contribute to high blood pressure, high cholesterol, obesity, and various cancers and would be just as tasty as, if not tastier than, existing foods.

A relatively efficient method of reducing micronutrient deficiencies would be to introduce the micronutrients into dietary staples such as rice, which provides half the daily calories for Asia, home to 60 percent of the world's population.[134] In line with this approach, Swiss scientists working at Syngenta developed "golden rice," which is rich in beta-carotene, a precursor to vitamin A, and crossed it with another bioengineered strain rich in iron and cysteine (which allows iron to be absorbed in the digestive tract). Such rice would help reduce deaths and diseases in the developing world related to vitamin A deficiency and iron deficiency. Iron-fortified rice— whether golden or not—would also reduce the need for meat, which is one of the primary sources for dietary iron. As a result, overall demand for livestock feed, as well as the land, water, and other inputs necessary to produce that feed, might be reduced.[135] More recently, British scientists working for Syngenta announced the development of golden rice 2, which increased the amount of beta-carotene in golden rice by 23-fold.[136] Syngenta is providing the rice free to research centers across Asia, which will begin field trials provided their governments can shake their inertia and permit testing.

Similarly, Indian scientists are working on a protein-rich potato— the "protato." Such a potato, which is part of everyone's diet in India, would be one more arrow in the battle against chronic malnutrition that India's masses suffer from. Thinking even more broadly, scientists at the International Rice Research Institute have conceived a project to grow the "dream rice," which would be bioengineered to contain iron, beta-carotene, and lysine, all essential micronutrients. Although commercialization of the crop will take several years to ensure that it would be safe for human consumption, such a rice could help improve health dramatically in the developing world and reduce death and disease (see table 9.2).[137]

Scientists are also working on using edible foods such as bananas and other fruits as vehicles to deliver vaccines against the Norwalk virus, E. coli, hepatitis B, and cholera.[138] Edible vaccines can be created by introducing genes from a virus or bacterium into the plant, which then create proteins that trigger immune reactions in people ingesting the plants. Scientists in Australia have developed a transgenic tobacco plant in which the leaves contain a protein from the measles virus that produced the measles antigens in mice that fed on them.[139] Other examples include a potato containing a vaccine for hepatitis B. Such advances could eventually lead to low cost, efficient immunization of whole populations against common diseases with broader coverage than likely with conventional needle delivery.

Bioengineered crops can also help battle the diseases of affluence. In 2001, ischemic heart disease, hypertension, and cancer diseases accounted for 4.3 million or 54 percent of the total deaths in the highest-income countries and 15.4 million or 32 percent of deaths in the rest of the world.[140] Several GM crops can help reduce this toll. For instance, genetically enhanced soybeans that are lower in saturated fats are already in the market. Scientists at the Max Planck Institute for Molecular Plant Physiology have developed a transgenic potato, which, compared to the wild type plant, increased tuber yields up to 60 percent, doubled or quadrupled concentrations of certain beneficial amino acids, and increased starch concentration by 60 percent,[141] which ought to reduce the amount of oil absorbed during processing of foods such as French fries or potato chips. The International Food Information Council also notes that biotechnology could also make soybean, canola, and other oils and their products, such as margarines and shortenings, more healthful.[142] Bioengineering could also produce peanuts with improved protein balance; tomatoes with increased antioxidant content; fruits and vegetables fortified with or containing higher levels of vitamins such as C and E; and higher-protein rice, using genes transferred from pea plants.

Moreover, levels of mycotoxins, which increase with insect damage in crops, are lower on Bt corn. Some mycotoxins such as fumonisin, can be fatal to horses and pigs, and they may be human carcinogens.[143] Morton also argues that GM Bt food crops are safer than conventional crops sprayed with Bt because the sprays contain several toxins that could affect both insects and mammals, while the GM variety contains a single toxin known to be harmful to insects but not to mammals.[144] In fact, a doubling of the incidence of neural tube defects—embryonic defects of the brain and spinal cord resulting from failure of the neural tube to close, which can cause, among other problems, *Spina bifida*—in women along the Mexico-Texas border in 1990–91 has been attributed to fumonisin from contaminated corn used to make tortillas.[145] Thus, Bt corn, whether used as food for humans or feed for livestock, may be safer and healthier than conventional corn.

Transgenic crops can reduce health risks to human beings in other ways as well. Edible vaccines (in transgenic feeds) could also be developed to protect livestock from viral and bacterial diseases. This could reduce the use of antibiotics in feeds and the likelihood of generating any antibiotic resistant organisms that could strike human beings.[146] GM plants may also be able to save life and limb, if they can be successfully engineered to biodegrade explosives around land mines and abandoned munitions sites.[147] Finally, to the extent pest-resistant GM plants can, as noted previously, reduce the amount, toxicity, or persistence of pesticides used in agriculture (by themselves or as parts of integrated pest management systems), they would reduce accidental poisonings and other untoward health effects on farm workers. For instance, there apparently have been instances of food poisoning and human infections from Bt sprays but none (so far) from Bt crops.[148]

Potential Environmental Costs of Bioengineered Crops

The major environmental concerns regarding GM crops are those related to crops that are designed to be resistant to pests or tolerant of herbicides. One potential risk is that adjacent crops grown in the vicinity of herbicide-tolerant plants may acquire tolerance to those herbicides. In Canada, oilseed rape plants (also known as canola) have apparently acquired tolerances to three herbicides—two from different GM crops and the third from a conventional variety.[149] This indicates that herbicide-tolerant crops—whether developed through conventional or transgenic techniques—have to be managed appropriately and/or molecular techniques have to be employed to reduce the likelihood of gene escape (discussed later).

Another risk is that target pests will become resistant to toxins produced by pest-resistant GM crops, such as Bt corn or Bt cotton. In fact, such resistance has evolved through the use of conventional Bt sprays in a number of insects in laboratory studies—in the cabbage looper under greenhouse conditions and the diamondback moth under field conditions.[150] On the basis that, under conventional spraying, target pests are exposed to Bt toxins only for brief periods, whereas currently available Bt crops produce toxins throughout the growing season, which could increase the chances of developing Bt-resistant pests, it has been argued that such resistance is more likely with Bt plants.[151] In fact, some laboratory studies suggest that target pests may evolve resistance more rapidly than had previously been thought possible.[152]

In response to such concerns, existing strategies to deter pest resistance to conventional pesticides have been adapted for use with pest-resistant GM crops. Such strategies include ensuring that plants deliver high doses of Bt, while simultaneously maintaining refuges for non-Bt crops to ensure pest populations remain susceptible to Bt. In fact, the Environmental Protection Agency (EPA) has established the requirement that Bt corn farmers plant 20 percent of their land in non-Bt corn, as refuges. For Bt corn grown in cotton areas, farmers must plant at least 50 percent non-Bt corn.[153] The EPA also requires expanded monitoring to detect any potential resistance. Other strategies to delay development of pesticide resistance include rotating crops,[154] developing crops with more than one toxin gene acting on separate molecular targets,[155] and inserting the bioengineered gene into the chloroplast because that ought to express Bt toxin at higher levels.[156] Notably, farmers have an economic stake in implementing such adaptive strategies so that their crop losses to pests are kept in check in the long, and the short, term.

Field monitoring studies from Arizona and Mississippi in the United States, as well as Australia and China, indicate that these strategies have been more effective in retarding the evolution of resistant pests than had been feared. Contrary to prognostications, pink bollworm, a major cotton pest, for instance, did not increase its resistance to Bt toxin produced by genetically modified Bt cotton.[157] A recent study by Bruce Tabashnik, an entomologist at the University of Arizona, and coworkers, published in the *Proceedings of the National Academy of Sciences* indicated that bioassay results showed no net increase from 1997 to 2004 in pink bollworm resistance to Bt toxin in Arizona.[158] They note that the lack of "field-evolved" resistance in the pink bollworm, despite extensive use of Bt cotton and rapid evolution of resistance in the laboratory, may be caused by the presence of refuges of non-Bt cotton, recessive inheritance of resistance, incomplete resistance, and fitness costs associated with resistance.

Equally important, a 10-year study in 15 regions across Arizona showed that Bt cotton suppressed pink bollworm, independent of effects of weather and demographic variation among regions.[159] Pink bollworm population density declined only in regions where Bt cotton was abundant. Such long-term suppression, which has not been observed with insecticide sprays, suggests that transgenic crops open new avenues for pest control that might lead to long-term regional pest suppression and reductions in the need for insecticide sprays.

Another source of risk is that Bt from pest-resistant plants could harm, if not kill, nontarget species. This could happen if, for instance, Bt-laden pollen were to drift away from the field or if the toxin were to leak through the roots and was consumed by nontarget organisms susceptible to the Bt toxin.[160] Losey and others in a laboratory study indicated a 44 percent mortality rate for monarch butterfly larvae fed on milkweed dusted with Bt corn pollen compared to zero for the control case (which used milkweed dusted with ordinary pollen).[161] In a more sophisticated study, Jesse and Obrycki showed a 20 percent mortality rate to monarch butterfly larvae fed in the laboratory with leaves exposed to pollen in or near a field of Bt plants.[162] However a subsequent set of papers in the *Proceedings of the National Academy of Sciences*, which suggest that the risk to monarchs is negligible under field conditions, essentially laid to rest this particular set of concerns.[163]

Yet others have argued that the major threat to monarchs is the habitat loss in their wintering grounds in Mexico,[164] which is a result of pressure from a growing population in need of land. Vagaries of the winter itself can also lead to high monarch mortality. A freeze in January 2002 was estimated to have killed as many as 250 million monarchs or 80 percent of its Mexican population.[165] Bt could also enter the food chain through root leakage or if predators prey on target pests.[166] For instance, studies have shown that green lacewing larvae, a beneficial insect, that ate maize borers fed with Bt maize were more likely to die,[167] but whether—and the extent to which—these studies represent real world conditions is also debatable,[168] particularly given the long history of Bt spraying on crops and other studies that showed beneficial insects essentially unharmed by such spraying, particularly under field conditions.[169]

Earlier, the EPA had concluded that "the weight of evidence" indicates "no hazard to wildlife from the continued registration of Bt crops," and Bt corn is unlikely to cause widespread harm to monarchs.[170] The EPA also concluded that continued cultivation of Bt corn is unlikely to "cause harmful widespread effects to monarch butterflies at this time." It also noted that the only endangered species of concern are in the Lepidoptera and Coleoptera group (i.e., butterflies, moths, and beetles), but the majority of these species have very restricted habitat range and do not feed in, or close to, the Bt crop planting areas. These basic conclusions were reaffirmed in the EPA's decision to reregister various Bt corns and cottons until 2008 and 2006, respectively.[171]

Perhaps more important, the inadvertent effects of Bt crops because of pollen dispersal or root leakage could be reduced by more than four orders of magnitude by bioengineering genes into the chloroplast rather than into nuclear DNA.[172]

There is also a concern that bioengineered genes from herbicide- or pest-tolerant crops might escape into wild relatives leading to "genetic pollution" and creating "superweeds."[173] This would have an adverse economic impact on farmers. It would reduce crop yields and detract from the very justification for using such GM crops.[174] Clearly, the farmer has a substantial incentive for preventing weeds from acquiring herbicide tolerance and, if that fails, to keep such weeds in check.

Gene escape is possible if sexually compatible wild relatives are found near fields planted with GM crops, as is the case in the United States for sorghum, oats, rice, canola, sugar beets, carrots, alfalfa, sunflowers, and radish.[175] In a paper published in *Nature* in 2001, David Quist and Ignacio Chapela claimed to have detected gene flow from GM corn to "traditional" corn landraces in Oaxaca, Mexico.[176] But their methodology has been challenged as flawed and prone to forming artifacts.[177] *Nature* later retracted their paper.[178] Regardless of this, using similar procedures, the Mexican government confirmed the presence of transgenes in Mexican maize.[179]

Recently, however, a joint research team from Mexico and the United States, including two of the Mexicans who had also previously confirmed the presence of the transgenes, analyzed DNA from a sample of more than 150,000 seeds from 870 plants in 125 fields and 18 localities in the state of Oaxaca during 2003 and 2004, including areas that were in the area covered in the Quist and Chapela study, after subjecting the seeds to polymerase chain reaction to magnify traces of genes that might have been introduced through bioengineering.[180] They failed to find any detectable traces of these genes. The results of their paper in the *Proceedings of the National Academy of Sciences* suggests that either these genes were never there in the first place, or if they had been, they are now greatly diminished, if not extinct, at least in the area sampled. Based on this recent study, Peter Raven, the eminent biologist, concludes "that the introduction of the transgenes currently in use for maize poses no danger to maize near its center of origin, to the Mexicans, or generally."[181]

Regardless of whether such gene flow might have occurred in the first place—no one doubts its possibility[182]—the ecological significance of such an event is unclear,[183] particularly if it had once occurred but has now, presumably, been suppressed naturally. To quote Raven, "It is unlikely that the presence of transgenes could reduce the genetic diversity of the landraces in which they might occur."[184]

In any case, as noted, there are methods to limit and discourage, if not preclude, such gene flow if it is deemed to be important enough. As the Royal Society pointed out in its assessment of this issue, centuries of conventional breeding have rendered a number of important crops, such as maize and wheat, "ecologically incompetent" in many areas.[185] It also noted that despite the use of conventionally bred herbicide-tolerant plants, there has been no upsurge in problems due to herbicide-tolerant weeds.[186] Although these theoretical arguments by themselves do not guarantee safety,[187] they seem confirmed by a 10-year-long British study of four different herbicide-tolerant or pest-resistant GM crops (oilseed rape, corn, sugar beet, and potato) and their conventional counterparts grown in 12 different habitats.[188] This study indicated that within four years, all plots of rape, corn, and beet had died out naturally. Only one plot of potatoes survived the 10th year, but that was a non-GM variety. In other words, GM plants were no more invasive or persistent in the wild than their conventional counterparts.[189] Moreover, had any herbicide-tolerant or pest-resistant weeds begun to spread, available crop management techniques (such as another herbicide) could have been used to control them.

The fact that the most common GM crops, namely, soybeans or corn, have no wild U.S. relatives, also offers some measure of additional protection (for the United States).[190]

The 10-year British study also provides reassurance with respect to another potential environmental concern, namely, that herbicide-tolerant or pest-resistant "superweeds" could invade natural ecosystems. It confirms that such GM plants do not have a competitive advantage in a natural system unless that system is treated with the herbicide in question. But if it were so treated, would it still qualify as a natural system? Moreover, if it had to be treated, another herbicide to which the superweed is not resistant could be used.

However, if the area is not treated with the herbicide in question, what difference does it make to the ecosystem whether the weed is tolerant? And what is the significance of "genetic pollution" with respect to ecosystem function and biodiversity? Would gene escape affect ecosystem function negatively? Does gene escape diminish or expand biodiversity?

To bring this issue into focus, consider the case of human beings: if an Indian from Calcutta comes to Washington, D.C., and has an offspring with a native-born American, would that not, as the term has been used, be considered genetic pollution? (Not very long ago, xenophobes labeled that miscegenation.) Does that diminish, or expand, biological diversity? Is such genetic pollution acceptable for human beings, but not for other species? But if the answer varies with the species, it raises questions about the validity of the notion that gene escape can be equated to pollution—genetic, or otherwise.[191]

Also, genes may escape from GM crops to non-GM crops of the same species. If this were to occur, it would be unpopular with organic farmers, who are afraid it might "adulterate" their produce, as well as producers and farmers of GM seeds, who are not eager to have someone else profit from their investments. The 10-year British study noted previously is consistent with the Royal Society's prognosis that because more crops (including corn, sorghum, sugar beet, and sunflower) are now grown from hybrid seeds, that provides a measure of built-in security against such gene transfers.[192] Moreover, the chances of such gene escape can be further reduced by maintaining a buffer between the two crops.

Of course, gene escape could be limited with greater certainty if the GM plant were engineered to be sterile or prevented from germinating using, for instance, "terminator technology." As discussed earlier, among the other molecular approaches to reduce the probability of gene flow would be to insert the gene into the chloroplast, which would reduce, if not prevent, their spread through pollen or fruit, or through root leakage.[193]

Finally, there is a concern that in the quest to expand yields, GM plants will work too well in eliminating pests and weeds, leading to a further simplification of agricultural ecosystems and further decreasing biodiversity. This concern, in conjunction with the other noted environmental concerns, needs to be weighed against the cumulative biodiversity and other environmental benefits of reduced conversion of habitat to cropland and decreased use of chemical inputs.

Adverse Public Health Consequences

Perhaps the single most important fact about the safety of GM crops is that 300 million Americans and tens of millions of visitors to the United States have been eating GM crops since 1996 with no ill effects that anyone can point to. Therefore, the health effects, if any, are too subtle to be noticed. This suggests that if one is truly concerned about improving public health, there are probably far more efficient and effective methods of achieving that than banning GM-bioengineered crops even if one discounts all the potential health benefits outlined previously. Curiously enough, life expectancy in the 5 years preceding 1996 (i.e., 1990–95) increased 0.4 years from 75.4 to 75.8, but between 1996 and 2000 (a shorter period of time), it advanced by twice as much (from 76.1 years to 76.9 years).[194]

A major health concern regarding bioengineered crops is that the new genes inserted into GM plants could be incorporated into a consumer's genetic makeup. However, because there is no evidence that any genes have ever been transferred to human beings through food or drink despite the fact that plant and animal DNA has always been a part of the daily human diet, the Royal Society concluded twice in four years that the risk to human health, if any, is negligible.[195] A recent study assessing the survivability of transgenic DNA in the human gastrointestinal tract following ingestion of GM soybean concluded that the transgene neither survived passage through the gut nor had gene transfer occurred during the feeding experiment on subjects who had intact tracts.[196] However, the researchers observed the transgenes in the intestinal microflora of subjects whose intestinal tract had been diverted to colostomy bags, although levels of the transgene were the same before and after feeding, raising the mystery as to how that could be.[197] It is also worth pondering whether consuming, for instance, beans that have been genetically modified with genes from a pig would pose a greater risk to public health than consuming a dish of non-GM pork and beans.

Another concern is that genes transferred from foods to which many people are allergic could trigger allergies in unsuspecting consumers of such GM crops. Between 1 percent and 3 percent of

273

the adults and 5 percent and 8 percent of the children in the United States suffer from food allergies, and each year, food allergies cause 135 fatalities and 2,500 emergency room visits.[198] This concern regarding allergic reactions to GM foods can be traced to precommercialization tests conducted by Pioneer Hi-Bred, which showed that a soybean that had been bioengineered to boost its nutritional quality using a gene from the Brazil nut was, in fact, allergenic.

More recently, after years of effort, the development of a GM pest-resistant pea was abandoned in late 2005 after a standard "multiple immune challenge" procedure designed to test for allergenicity showed it caused or contributed to allergic lung damage in mice. The original gene, which expressed a protein that kills the pea weevil, had been transferred from a bean. The protein, which does not cause any allergic reactions when extracted from the bean, however, underwent subtle changes in its structures that may have been responsible for the allergic reaction from the GM product.[199]

Opponents of GM foods have used these examples as arguments against bioengineered crops. But, if anything, they show that GM foods can be tested before commercialization for their allergenic potential and that the current process has safeguards that work. First, several databases of known allergens can be used to help identify problematic GM products before they are developed.[200] Following that, it is necessary to undertake a case-by-case evaluation of the GM plant's risks (and associated rewards), as has often been noted.[201]

In fact, because bioengineering allows more precise manipulation of genes than does conventional plant breeding, it could be used to render allergenic crops nonallergenic,[202] and efforts are underway attempting that for peanuts, wheat, and other crops to which people are most frequently allergic.[203] In fact, scientists at the USDA and Pioneer Hi-Bred, the same company that did *not* commercialize the soybean containing the Brazil nut gene, have developed a soybean that lacks the ability to make a protein that causes much of the allergic reactions some human beings have to the soybean.[204]

Yet another potential negative effect on public health is that antibiotic resistant "marker" genes that are used to identify whether a gene has been successfully incorporated into a plant could, through consumption of the antibiotic gene by humans, accelerate the trend toward antibiotic-resistant diseases. However, by comparison with the threat posed by the use of antibiotics in feed for livestock and their overuse as human medicines, the increased risk because of such markers is slight.[205] Moreover, alternative markers are being devised for many crops, with more in the offing.[206] Progress is also being made in eliminating the marker genes after they have served their function of identifying transgenic plants.[207]

Applying the Precautionary Principle

The earlier discussion indicates that there are risks associated with either the use or the nonuse of GM crops. Here I will apply the criteria outlined in the framework presented earlier in the chapter for evaluating actions that could result in uncertain costs and uncertain benefits. Ideally, each criterion should be applied, one at a time, to the human mortality, the nonmortality public health, and the non-public health-related environmental consequences of GM crop use (or nonuse). However, because there are variations in the severities, certainties, and magnitudes associated with the various competing costs and benefits regarding each of these sets of consequences, one may have to apply several criteria simultaneously.

Public Health Consequences

Population could increase 50 percent between 2005 and 2050 (from 6.1 billion to 9.1 billion, according to the UN's best estimate). Hence, one ought to expect that undernourishment, malnutrition, and their consequences on death and disease would also increase by 50 percent worldwide, if global food supply increases by a like amount and all else remains equal. But the problem is not just the quantity of food, but also its quality. As tables 9.1 and 9.2 indicate, unless food production outstrips population growth significantly during the next half century—and its nutritional quality improves—billions in the developing world may suffer annually from undernourishment, hundreds of millions may be stunted, and millions may die from malnutrition. Given the sheer magnitude of people at risk of hunger and malnutrition, as well as the degree of certainty attached to their public health consequences, limiting GM crops will, by slowing the rate at which the quantity and quality of food is enhanced, almost certainly increase death and disease, particularly among the world's poor.

GM crops could also reduce or postpone deaths because of diseases of affluence. Although the probability that might occur is lower than that of reducing deaths due to hunger and malnutrition, the expected number of deaths postponed could run into the millions. A 5 percent decrease, for instance, in the 19.7 million annual deaths nowadays due to cancer, and ischemic and cerebrovascular diseases translates into almost a million lives saved each year (see table 9.1). And these numbers could increase in the future as populations increase and become older.

By contrast, the negative public health consequences of ingesting GM foods are speculative (e.g., the effects due to ingesting transgenes), relatively minor in magnitude (e.g., a potential increase in antibiotic resistance), or both (e.g., increased incidence of allergic reactions). Moreover, it is possible to contain, if not eliminate, the effects of even those impacts. As noted previously, not only is it possible to reduce the likelihood of allergic reactions from GM foods through vigilance and premarket testing, it is possible to more easily and rapidly develop GM foods that are less allergenic than their conventional counterparts. With respect to the risk of increasing antibiotic resistance, progress has been made on devising a variety of solutions. Novartis (now part of Syngenta), for instance, developed a sugar-based alternative to antibiotic-resistant marker genes, which has been used to develop about a dozen GM crops, including maize, wheat, rice, sugar beet, oilseed rape, cotton, and sunflowers.[208] With additional research, it ought to be possible to devise alternative marker genes for other crops or to develop practical methods to remove or repress antibiotic-resistant marker genes.[209]

Thus, based on the *uncertainty, expectation value,* and *adaptation criteria* applied either singly or in conjunction, the use of GM crops must be favored over their nonuse. Hence, the precautionary principle *requires* that we continue to research, develop, and commercialize (with appropriate safeguards, of course) those GM crops that would increase food production and generally improve nutrition and health, especially in the developing world.

Some have argued that many developed countries are "awash in surplus food."[210] Thus, goes this argument, developed countries have no need to boost food production. However, this argument ignores the fact that reducing those surpluses would be almost as harmful to public health in developing countries as curtailing the latter's food production. At present, net cereal imports of the developing countries exceed 10 percent of their production.[211] Without trade (and aid), which moves the surplus production in developed countries voluntarily to developing countries suffering from food deficits, food supplies in developing countries would be lower; food prices would be steeper; undernourishment and malnutrition would be higher; and associated health problems, such as illness and premature mortality, would be greater. And, as already noted, developing countries' food deficits are only expected to increase in the future because of high population growth rates and, possibly, be further worsened by global warming. Therefore, developed countries' food surpluses will at least be as critical for future food security in developing countries as it is today.[212]

Also, the earlier argument against GM crops implicitly assumes that such crops will provide little or no public health benefits to the inhabitants of developed countries. But, as noted, GM crops are also being engineered to improve nutrition in order to combat diseases of affluence afflicting populations in developed, as well as developing, nations. These diseases, which are major causes of premature death globally, killed about 4.3 million in 2001 in the developed countries (table 9.1). Even a small reduction in these numbers because of GM crops would translate into relatively large declines in their death tolls. Moreover, the health benefits of "golden rice" or food vaccines, for instance, do not have to be confined to developing countries; also, developed countries could avail themselves of its benefits. Thus, even for developed countries, the potential public health benefits of GM crops far outweigh in magnitude and certainty the speculative health consequences of ingesting GM foods.

Another argument against using GM foods to increase food production is that there is no shortage of food in the world today, that the problem of hunger and malnutrition is rooted in poor distribution and unequal access to food because of poverty. Therefore, it is unnecessary to increase food production; ergo, there is no compelling need for biotechnology.[213] Significantly, this argument tacitly acknowledges that GM crops would boost production (and productivity). Although this part of the argument is valid, it still has several flaws. First, unequal access is a perennial problem that continues to persist despite the successes of conventional agriculture. The case for bioengineered crops is not that it is the one and only solution for solving hunger and malnutrition. It should be sufficient that GM crops can contribute to the solution, and they are among the most efficient solutions for that problem. Second, and more important, increasing food production and improving access are closely related. The best method of improving access is to reduce food prices, something that is facilitated by overproduction. In fact, the world's experience since the 1950s attests to this strategy. As noted earlier, despite a much larger and wealthier global population, the price of food has dropped by 75 percent, and fewer people suffer from hunger today (see chapter 2).

Notably, conventional agriculture has been relatively successful in improving global access to food. This is obvious from the fact that hunger and malnourishment have declined substantially in the past few decades despite a substantial increase in population (see chapter 2). The principal reasons for these improvements are production increases, which outstripped population growth and brought food prices down worldwide; economic growth, which made food more affordable to all and sundry, particularly in developing countries; investments in infrastructure, which enable rapid and efficient distribution of agricultural products; and greater democratization, which increases the political accountability of rulers to those ruled.[214] Although GM crops (in comparison with conventional crops) are unlikely to directly increase democratization or increase economic growth, they can indirectly boost the latter. Moreover, as the anti-GM crop argument (that "there is sufficient food") seems to recognize, GM crops could increase productivity more rapidly and by larger amounts, which would further increase food availability and reduce costs to consumers. In addition, one of the problems contributing to poor distribution is spoilage of crops before they are consumed. As noted, various GM crops could increase shelf life and reduce spoilage and wastage. Thus, although GM crops cannot guarantee equal access, they can improve access for the poorer segments of society more rapidly than can conventional crops.

Second, if the argument that there is sufficient food is truly a compelling one against GM crops, then it should be equally valid for increases in production using conventional technologies. If that's indeed the case, perhaps developing countries, such as India and Bangladesh, should forego increasing agricultural productivity altogether and focus only on improving access and distribution. For obvious reasons, no one makes this argument.

Third, this argument completely overlooks the fact that GM crops can improve the nutritional quality, and not merely the quantity, of food, which, as table 9.2 shows, can contribute substantially to reductions in human mortality and morbidity.

Environmental Consequences

A figure similar to figure 9.1 could be developed for any level of food demand whether it is, say, half that of today (perhaps because of a perfect, cost- or transaction-free distribution system and a magical equalization of income) or whether it is four times that (possibly due to runaway population growth). And regardless of the level of demand, limiting GM crops would lower crop and forest yields per unit of land and water used. To compensate for the lower yields, more land and water would have to be pressed into humankind's service, leaving that much less for the rest of nature.[215]

Reductions in the amount of land and water available for the rest of nature would be further aggravated because the price of land and water, relative to other goods, would necessarily rise, as would the opportunity costs for these resources. This means that the socio-economic costs of setting aside land or water for conservation and preservation of nature would increase, further inhibiting *in situ* conservation of species and biodiversity, which is one of the major goals of the Convention on Biological Diversity beyond one of merely conserving biodiversity itself (see next section).[216]

Moreover, if bioengineering succeeds in improving the protein and micronutrient content of vegetables, fruits, and grains, it might persuade many more people to adopt and, more important, to persevere with vegetarian diets, thereby reducing the additional demand of meat-eating places on land and water. In addition, giving up GM crops will, more likely than not, further increase pressures on biodiversity due to excess nutrients, pesticides, and soil erosion. Finally, reduced conversion of habitat and forest to cropland and timberland coupled with reduced soil erosion due to increased no-till cultivation would further limit deterioration of water quality and losses of carbon reservoirs and sinks.

Arrayed against these benefits to ecosystems, biodiversity, and carbon stores and sinks are the environmental costs of limiting pest-resistant and herbicide-tolerant GM crops *minus* the environmental costs of conventional farming practices. These costs include a potential decrease in the diversity of the flora and fauna associated with or in the immediate vicinity of GM crops if they are more effective

279

in reducing nontarget pests and weeds than conventional farming practices, as well as the possible consequences of gene escape to weeds and non-GM crops.

Between 1999 and 2005, in an effort to shed light on this issue with respect to herbicide-tolerant GM plants, the British government undertook extensive farm-scale evaluations (FSEs) of the effects of cultivating genetically modified herbicide-tolerant (GMHT) spring beet, spring and winter canola, and maize on farmland wildlife.[217] The FSEs found that in comparison to their conventional counterparts, although GMHT canola resulted in about the same number of seeds (a food source for a variety of wildlife), it produced more grass weeds (and seeds) and fewer broadleaf weeds (and seeds). Consequently, there were fewer butterflies and bees in the fields and field margins of GMHT winter canola but springtails—tiny wingless insects that feed on decaying organic matter and serve as prey for larger insects (e.g., spiders and centipedes)—were more abundant. The results for spring canola and beet were generally similar, except that the GMHT variety also produced fewer weeds. GMHT maize, however, resulted in more weeds, seeds, butterflies, bees, and springtails.

The studies, somewhat predictably, found that differences in the distribution and abundance of wildlife species in farms and farm margins were the result of the type and timing of herbicides that were used to control weeds, rather than because the crops were genetically modified. Thus, the results would probably have been the same had the herbicide-tolerant variety been developed through conventional breeding, instead of being bioengineered.

Equally important, although these studies provided a bumper crop of scientific and technical information on the effects of varying the timing and quantities of weed killers, they fell short of a full-scale assessment of the biodiversity effects of using and managing GMHT crops versus conventional varieties.

The environmental rationale for GMHT crops—and other GM crops—is based on the trade-off between one set of environmental risks for another, that is, the environmental justification, if any, for GMHT crops hinges on risk-risk analysis.[218] On one side of this risk equation is the possibility that the use of GMHT crops would indeed lead to more efficient weed control with predictably negative effects, in the short run, on species dependent on those weeds. And the

FSEs, in fact, evaluated only this side of the equation. But they left unexamined the other side of the equation, namely the possibility that with judicious use and management of GMHT crops, the overall benefits for biodiversity could be positive.

These countervailing benefits, as discussed earlier in this chapter, include facilitating conservation tillage and its numerous environmental and economic benefits, including protection of future agricultural productivity, better water quality, reduction in the transport of fertilizers and pesticides into aquatic systems and into the air, and lower loss of soil carbon into the atmosphere. Second, more efficient weed control ought to enhance yields, which means less land needs to be cultivated to maintain a given level of production. That, in turn, should help relieve the single largest threat to biodiversity because it would reduce the total amount of land under cultivation, while further reducing land subject to erosion. But this argument was not evaluated because FSEs "were not intended to compare the performance of the crops but rather the effects on biodiversity of management of the crops, data on yields were not necessary and were not collected routinely."[219] So much for comparing the ecological consequences of using GMHT crops against those of conventional crops!

There are, nevertheless, reasons to believe that yields might be higher for GMHT beet[220] and canola[221] although not necessarily for GMHT corn.[222]

Third, judicious selection of the herbicide to which GMHT crops would be tolerant could enable reductions in the amount, toxicity, and persistence of pesticides, as seems to have occurred in the United States. But these benefits cannot be evaluated in small-scale studies that look at individual farms and farm margins. They require analysis at a wider scale. Thus, inadvertently, the FSEs resulted in a biased treatment of the underlying issue.

Given that the potential positive aspects of GMHT crops were not even evaluated, it is surprising that GMHT crops did not fare worse in the FSEs in comparison with more conventional crops. In fact, the FSEs only confirmed what we always knew or suspected, namely, that weed killers kill weeds, that delayed application of weed killers might result in larger weeds before they are killed, and that killing weeds disadvantages weed-feeding invertebrates but might favor species that feed on decaying matter.

Hence, with respect to the net environmental consequences of the use or nonuse of GM crops, one must conclude, based on the *uncertainty* and *expectation value criteria*, that the precautionary principle requires the cultivation of GM crops. On net, GM crops should conserve the planet's habitat, biodiversity, and carbon stores and sinks, provided due caution is exercised, particularly with respect to herbicide-tolerant and pest-resistant GM crops.

It may be argued that although gene escape to "natural" ecosystems might be a low-probability event, it may cause irreversible harm to the environment; thus, under the *irreversibility criterion*, GM crops ought to be banned. However, increased habitat clearance and land conversion resulting from such a ban may be at least as irreversible, particularly if it leads to species extinctions.

It is worth noting that the precautionary principle supports using terminator-type technology and other molecular techniques that would minimize the possibility of gene transfer to weeds and non-GM plants without diminishing any of the public health or environmental benefits of GM crops.[223] Notably, some of the same groups that profess environmental concerns about genetic pollution subjected terminator technology to unbridled criticism because, it is claimed, farmers in the Third World need to propagate these plants without having to continually buy new seeds from evil multinationals.[224] Obviously, in these groups' policy calculus, the potential environmental costs of GM crops are outweighed by the presumed negative economic consequences to farmers due to their inability to propagate GM crops from sterile seeds, as well as these groups' antipathy toward multinationals' profits. Yet, at the same time, they oppose the use of Bt cotton, for instance, despite the fact that farmers in developing countries are clamoring for it because it increases their profits, exposes them to fewer public health risks, and generally reduces the labor needed to produce cotton.

It is debatable whether putting antipathy to profits ahead of public health or the environment is any more commendable than putting profits ahead of them. It certainly does not advance either human or environmental well-being.

Global Economic Consequences of GM Crops

Many so-called environmental groups also claim that GM crops will enrich multinational seed producers while impoverishing Third

World farmers. One study of the global impact of GM crops, however, estimates that in 2004 alone, such crops were grown by 8.25 million farmers, 90 percent of them in resource-poor developing countries; increased farmers' incomes by $4.8 billion (or between 3.1 percent and 4.2 percent); and reduced pesticide use by at least 6 percent (measured in terms of active ingredients).[225] This report was criticized by anti-GM groups more because it was funded by industry groups and, of course, its results, rather than because of its methodology or data that it relied on.

Nevertheless, real world experience indicates that there is at least a grain of truth in that estimate—perhaps it's a GM grain and, therefore, inherently biased? Unless farmers were relatively confident that GM crops would increase their profits, adoption rates would have been low. And if its promise was not borne out, each subsequent year fewer farmers would plant them, and GM crops would have been, as an entire class, pulled from the market, as indeed was the first GM crop, the FlavrSavr tomato. But acreage under GM crops continues to grow year after year. GM crops first became commercially available in 1996, yet by 2005 they were planted on 222 million acres, or 6 percent of the world's cropland. (To put this into context, consider that for the United States the combined contribution of biomass, solar, and wind—energy sources that have been around since the dawn of time—stayed more or less constant at 4.5 percent since 1996.[226])

Despite losing the battle on GM crops in farmers' fields, anti-GM groups continue to hinder the development of such crops by trying to erect and raise regulatory barriers despite the lack of any credible evidence that they are any worse than conventional crops. In fact, there is every reason to believe that with common-sense precautions and due consideration of the consequences not only of cultivating GM crops but also of foregoing them, they are likely to be better for both people and the planet.

Would a Ban on GM Crops Further the Convention on Biological Diversity's Goals?

The earlier analysis indicates that banning GM crops would more likely than not magnify threats to biodiversity and *in situ* conservation. But the preamble to the Convention on Biological Diversity (CBD) states that "it is vital to anticipate, prevent and attack the causes of significant reduction or loss of biological diversity at source," and that "the fundamental requirement for the conservation of biological diversity is the in-situ conservation of ecosystems and natural habitats and the maintenance and recovery of viable populations of species in their natural surroundings."[227] Article 1 of the CBD also identifies as the first of its various objectives, "the conservation of biological diversity." Thus, a ban on GM crops would be directly counter to the convention's *raison d'etre*.

Banning GM crops would also contradict the letter of the CBD. Article 8(d), which addresses *in situ* conservation, requires that "[each contracting party shall, as far as possible and as appropriate] . . . [p]romote the protection of ecosystems, natural habitats and the maintenance of viable populations of species in natural surroundings."[228] Moreover, a GM ban would also make it harder to satisfy the requirements of article 8(a), which requires contracting parties to "[e]stablish a system of protected areas or areas where special measures need to be taken to conserve biological diversity" because,[229] as noted earlier, there would be less land and water available for *in situ* conservation and what would be available would be socially and economically costlier to obtain and maintain.[230]

Would a Ban on GM Crops Advance the Cartagena Biosafety Protocol's Goals?

Both the objective and scope of the Cartagena Biosafety Protocol (articles 1 and 4, respectively) are specifically limited to GM organisms "that may have adverse effects on the conservation and sustainable use of biological diversity, taking also into account risks to human health."[231] But we have seen that *in the aggregate*, by contrast with conventional crops, GM crops are not only unlikely to have adverse impacts on the environment, conservation, sustainable use, and human health but also, as the previous discussion indicates, GM crops might result in net benefits. Thus, it can be argued that the case for a general ban on GM crops under the protocol is, at best, weak. And it looks even weaker when one considers the sources of the protocol's authorities.

As noted in its preamble and article 1, the protocol derives its authority regarding the regulation of the transfer, handling, and use of GM organisms largely from principle 15 of the Rio Declaration[232] and articles 8(g), 17, 19(3), and 19(4) of the CBD. Let's examine whether a general ban on GM crops would be supported under each of these sources of authority:

- Principle 15 of the Rio Declaration is a statement of the precautionary principle. But in the previous section we saw the precautionary principle does not support a broad ban of GM crops.
- Article 8(g) of the CBD requires that contracting parties shall "[e]stablish or maintain means to regulate, manage or control the risks associated with the use and release of living modified organisms resulting from biotechnology, which are likely to have adverse environmental impacts that could affect the conservation and sustainable use of biological diversity, taking also into account the risks to human health." This language parallels that in articles 1 and 4 of the protocol, and the same rationale applies to why it would be inappropriate to use such language to ban GM crops, namely, GM crops in the aggregate are likely to have a positive rather than an adverse impact on conservation and sustainable use of biodiversity or on human health.
- Article 17 of the CBD only addresses the facilitation of exchange of information, so it cannot be used to justify a general ban on GM crops either.
- The same rationale applies to why article 19(3) of the CBD also cannot be used to justify a ban on GM crops. This article requires that "[t]he Parties shall consider the need for and modalities of a protocol setting out appropriate procedures, including, in particular, advance informed agreement, in the field of the safe transfer, handling and use of any living modified organism resulting from biotechnology that may have an adverse effect on the conservation and sustainable use of biological diversity."
- Article 19(4) of the CBD only operates through article 19(3).[233] But because article 19(3) cannot justify a ban on GM crops, neither can article 19(4).

A counterargument could be made that the appropriate test to determine whether GM crops as a class should be subject to the protocol's requirements would be to evaluate whether it may have *any*—and not just *aggregate*—adverse impact on the environment, conservation, sustainable use, and human health. However, as the *any* in article 19(3) of the CBD indicates, the CBD's negotiators seem to have been cognizant of that word's significance. Notably, *any* appears 43 times in the protocol (and 66 times in the convention).

More important, had the CBD explicitly said *any adverse impact*, and had that then been used to impose a blanket ban on GM crops, then that would have been counterproductive—and inconsistent with the goals of the convention and the protocol.

Conclusion

The precautionary principle has often been invoked to justify a prohibition on GM crops.[234] However, this justification is based on a selective application of the principle to a limited set of consequences of such a policy. Specifically, the justification takes credit for the potential public health and environmental benefits of a ban on GM crops but ignores any discredit for foregoing or delaying the worldwide benefits to public health and the environment that such a ban would probably cause.

By comparison with conventional crops, GM crops would, in fact, increase the quantity and nutritional quality of food supplies. Therefore, such crops would improve public health by reducing mortality and morbidity rates worldwide. In addition, cultivation of GM, rather than conventional, crops would, by increasing productivity, reduce the amount of land and water that would otherwise have to be diverted to humankind's needs. GM crops could also reduce the environmental damage from soil erosion and the use of synthetic fertilizers and pesticides. Thus, GM crops would be more protective of habitat, biological diversity, water quality, and carbon stores and sinks than would conventional agriculture.

Hence, a ban on GM crops—whether accomplished directly through the invocation of the precautionary principle or indirectly through application(s) of the Biosafety Protocol—is likely to aggravate threats to biodiversity and further increase the already considerable hurdles facing *in situ* conservation. Therefore, a ban would be counterproductive and contravene the spirit and letter of the Convention on Biological Diversity. The precautionary principle properly applied, with a more comprehensive consideration of the public health and environmental consequences of a ban—argues instead for a sustained effort to research, develop, and commercialize GM crops, provided reasonable caution is exercised during testing and commercialization of the crops.

In this context, a "reasonable" precaution is one in which public health benefits are not negated by the harm incurred due to reductions (or delays) in enhancing the quantity or quality of food. The public health costs of any reductions (or delays), which would make food more costly and reduce broader access to higher quality food at least for a period, would be disproportionately borne by the poorest and most vulnerable segments of society. Also, the environmental gains flowing from a "reasonable" precaution should more than offset the environmental gains that would otherwise be obtained.

10. Climate Change and Sustainable Development

Perhaps no environmental issue arouses greater passion than climate change (which I will use interchangeably with global warming).[1] In 2001, for example, the Organisation for Economic Co-operation and Development (OECD) Ministerial Council declared that "climate change is the most urgent global environmental challenge, requiring strong leadership and action by OECD Members. . . ."[2] In 2004, British Prime Minister Anthony Blair and French President Jacques Chirac jointly proclaimed that "climate change is the world's greatest environmental challenge."[3] Sir David King, chief scientific adviser to the British government, in a much quoted paper in *Science*, claimed that it was "more serious even than the threat of terrorism,"[4] while Lord Robert May, then president of the Royal Society, asserted that its consequences "invite comparison with 'weapons of mass destruction.' "[5]

Such sentiments have fueled calls for urgently instituting policies to reduce anthropogenic emissions of greenhouse gases that would go beyond "no regret" actions—that is, actions that should be undertaken on their own merits unrelated to any presumed benefits related to global warming.[6] But considering the multiplicity of unmet challenges facing the globe today—1.1 billion people living in absolute poverty, 850 million people suffering from chronic hunger, 500 million cases of malaria each year, 1.1 billion people lacking access to safe water, and continuing deforestation, to name just a few—and that insufficient resources are devoted to these challenges, these claims merit closer examination.

We saw in previous chapters that despite any warming that might have occurred during the past century, the average person's welfare as measured by the most important climate-sensitive measures of human well-being has improved. Global agricultural productivity is up, food prices are down, hunger and malnutrition have dropped worldwide, public health has improved, mortality rates are down, and life expectancies are up. However, despite worldwide advances since the middle of the past century, human well-being has regressed in recent decades in sub-Saharan Africa and parts of Eastern Europe and the former Soviet Union. But as discussed in chapter 3, these relapses are the result of declines in economic development, public health services, and the institutions that underpin them, caused by poor policy choices (such as forsaking the appropriate use of DDT), participation in armed conflicts, poor governance, and the emergence of AIDS coupled with initial denial of its existence.

Ironically, some credit for increasing agricultural and forest productivity, which has helped limit habitat conversion, is probably due to higher carbon dioxide (CO_2) concentrations compounded in temperate areas by higher winter and springtime temperatures, which have substantially lengthened the growing season in the northern latitudes (see chapter 6). Most of the improvements in climate-sensitive indicators of human well-being, however, are because of technological progress, driven by market- and science-based economic growth, secular technological change, and trade. Such progress has overwhelmed whatever impacts—positive or negative—climate change may have had to date.[7]

Notably, the *current* consequences of anthropogenic climate change are dwarfed by numerous other environmental and public health problems facing humanity today. Even if one accepts the dubious estimates of present-day health consequences of climate change presented in the *World Health Report 2002*, that same report shows that climate change contributes less than 0.4 percent to the global burden of disease (see chapter 6). Climate change, in fact, ranks 15th or 16th in importance out of 19 global health risk factors related to food, nutrition, and environmental and occupational exposure, depending on whether the ranking is based on mortality or lost disability-adjusted life years (DALYs).[8] Cumulatively, these 19 risk factors account for 54 percent of all mortality and 38 percent of lost DALYs globally.

The contribution of climate change to the global burden of disease is dwarfed by that of hunger and malnutrition; indoor air pollution; lack of access to safe drinking water, water for hygiene, and sanitation; and malaria.[9] And with regard to the natural world, current problems include diversion of habitat (including forests, wetlands, and ecosystems) and freshwater to human uses, as well as overexploitation of marine biological resources. These activities constitute the greatest threats to global terrestrial, freshwater, and marine bio-diversity, outweighing any impacts of climate change to date.

Thus, based on effects manifested to date, climate change is today outranked by other problems. But what about tomorrow and the day after? How robust are claims that global warming is—or is likely to be—the most important public health and environmental issue facing the globe in the foreseeable future? This chapter will examine that issue, along with related issues.

Specifically, it will address the following issues: Is global warming likely to be the most important public health and environmental issue facing the globe this century, or is it merely one more straw on the camel's back? If it's the latter, should we focus on climate change or on other burdens (or straws) that might more easily or effectively reduce the load on the camel's back? Because the burden of climate change is likely to become heavier with time if nothing is done to curb it, can we delay responding to climate change? If so, for how long? Over the foreseeable future, are these damages of climate change likely to be reduced most effectively and efficiently through mitigation (i.e., reductions in global warming), reactive adaptation to its impacts, or proactive measures to reduce vulnerability to climate change? What is the appropriate balance of resources that should be allocated in the short, medium, and long term to these strategies? How should that balance evolve with time?

Moreover, because human and economic resources are limited and there are several other global priorities begging to be solved, would humanity and the environment be better served if we addressed these other priorities ahead of climate change? Or can we address both simultaneously? How can we do that most effectively? Can we deal with other critical present-day problems, such as malaria and hunger, without compromising our ability to address future problems caused by further climate change, and vice versa? What is the appropriate balance of human and economic resources that should be expended on present-day problems such as poverty and longer-term problems such as climate change? How should this balance evolve over time so that we can maximize human and environmental well-being? Do we have to sacrifice the well-being of present generations for that of future generations, or vice versa?

This chapter will address those issues based on the premise that the primary objective of climate change policy—as it should be for other policies as well—is to advance human and environmental well-being, rather than to merely reduce either climate change or its impacts. This allows one to address climate change without losing sight of all the other problems facing the globe. Resources allocated toward dealing with climate change should be commensurate with its importance, as measured by its contribution to human and environmental problems. If it is indeed the most important problem facing the globe, it should receive, over time, the largest share of resources allocated to solving the suite of problems under examination.

But even if a problem is the most significant in the long run and must inevitably be addressed, it does not follow that policy measures must be taken right now to address that problem. Additional factors have to be considered in determining the urgency of the issue. For example, we know that for the human race to survive it is vital that its individual members propagate sooner or later. Despite this knowledge, it is neither necessary nor desirable to commence efforts to propagate at birth. It makes perfect sense for individuals to delay propagation until they are sufficiently mature—physically, mentally, and psychologically—to deal with the task at hand. And so it might be with efforts to curb climate change. The timing of implementing mitigation measures should, among other things, consider whether and when society will have access to sufficiently mature technologies—and the economic and human resources—needed for implementation, as well as whether there are other critical problems that might demand more immediate attention. This is important because unless one can get through the short and medium term in relatively decent shape, there may be little point in dealing with problems that might arise in the long term, much as it doesn't serve any purpose to buy a ticket from London to Paris if one can't get to London in the first place.

Biodiversity is a case in point. Currently, biodiversity is under threat because of the human appetite for land, water, and marine resources. If we can't address these successfully over the next few decades, it probably won't matter much what the future impacts of climate change might be on biodiversity. Thus, in the near term at least, urgency and importance are generally separable issues. The issue, therefore, is what is the appropriate mix of short-, medium-, and long-term policies so that human and environmental well-being is optimized.

A corollary to the previous is that the (secondary) objective of climate-change policies is to reduce net damages (i.e., net negative impacts) to society and the environment from climate-sensitive hazards (which includes capitalizing on any positive impacts of climate change), rather than reduce climate change per se. This consideration is often overlooked in the public debate on climate change, much of which centers on reducing climate change (and costs associated with that) rather than reducing climate-sensitive risks efficiently and effectively. We will see in subsequent sections that policies that would reduce climate change the most would not necessarily be the most effective policies to advance human and environmental well-being or, for that matter, the most effective method of reducing risks from climate-sensitive hazards.

That reasoning will be based on an analysis of the *global* impacts of climate change on various climate-sensitive threats or hazards that have frequently been invoked to justify greenhouse gas emission controls. These hazards include infectious and parasitic diseases (e.g., malaria), hunger, water stress, coastal flooding, and various threats to biodiversity. Notably, those climate-sensitive hazards are among the existing hurdles that many developing countries have to surmount in their quest toward sustainable economic development. Therefore reducing these hazards, in addition to helping developing countries cope with climate change, would also help advance sustainable economic development in these countries.

Because climate change mainly exacerbates these existing risks, it is possible to compare the contribution of climate change to these risks relative to the contribution of non-climate-change-related factors. Such a comparison allows us to determine whether climate change is likely to be—as has sometimes been claimed—the most important public health and environmental problem facing the world for the foreseeable future. It also allows us to analyze the relative costs, benefits, and effectiveness of different strategies that would reduce the combined risks due to climate change and non-climate-change-related factors.

The specific strategies examined here are (a) reductions in emissions or concentrations of greenhouse gases (or "mitigation") and (b) advances in the ability of society to deal with the impacts of climate change through proactive measures to reduce the vulnerability of society to climate-sensitive hazards that might be exacerbated by climate change and reactive measures to cope with any remaining or unavoidable impacts of climate change.

We will also see that policies that advance sustainable economic development will increase the capacity to adapt to or mitigate climate change and would, over the next several decades, reduce damages from climate-sensitive hazards more effectively and efficiently than would efforts focused on reducing greenhouse gas emissions. The analysis undertaken here is based on an evaluation of the results of assessments sponsored by the British government of the global impacts of climate change through 2085–2100, which use various scenarios developed by the Intergovernmental Panel on Climate Change (IPCC).

This chapter offers an "adaptive management approach" to dealing with climate change that would combine the earlier two strategies with a program to monitor trends to forestall any nasty surprises and to improve our knowledge and understanding of the science, economics, and policies related to climate change and its impacts. The latter will allow the strategies to be modified and resources moved between them as knowledge in these areas accumulates, uncertainties are reduced, and we gain a better understanding of the impacts.

How Robust Are Global Warming Impact Estimates?

For any rational discussion about global warming and what can or should be done about it, we first need to understand what its impacts are likely to be, their magnitudes, and how rapidly they might be visited on the globe. Accordingly, we must necessarily rely on projections of the impacts of climate change. Estimates of future global and regional impacts of human-induced climate change (or global warming) are, however, inherently uncertain. This is because projections of future impacts are based on a series of model calculations with each succeeding model using as its inputs increasingly uncertain outputs of the previous model.[10]

First, future emissions of greenhouse gases (GHGs) have to be estimated using uncertain projections of future population, economic conditions, energy usage, land use, land cover, and the rate of technological change in every sector that contributes to emissions and influences the options available for energy and land use. Table 8.1 shows that ignoring technological change could, over a few decades, lead to substantial overestimates of emissions and impacts, sometimes by orders of magnitude. Moreover, many of the factors that determine GHG emissions are themselves sensitive to climatic conditions. For example, land use, land cover, and energy use depend on climate and atmospheric concentrations (and vice versa), although the overall level of economic development is probably a more important determinant of energy use and, possibly, land use and land cover, than are climatic conditions.

Next, these emissions have to be converted into each GHG's atmospheric concentration. Ideally this means modeling the transport and fate of each GHG. For carbon emissions that entails modeling the carbon cycle (i.e., the exchange of carbon between the land, ocean, and atmosphere), for nitrogen emissions the nitrogen cycle, for chlorofluorocarbons the entire cycle involved in the generation and destruction of ozone, and so forth for each gas. In addition, it means modeling the interactions between these various cycles. Because this is a formidable set of tasks, often short cuts are taken, such as assuming a constant rate of growth in the accumulation of GHGs in the atmosphere.

For example, Knutson and Tuleya estimated that the maximum surface wind speed associated with hurricanes would increase by 6 percent over the next 80 years because of global warming, assuming that CO_2 concentrations would increase by 1 percent per year during that period, following an assumption used in some of the IPCC's earlier scenarios.[11] Although this reduces the computational burden in developing a numerical result, it lacks any support from empirical trends. The Mauna Loa CO_2 record shows an average year-to-year increase of about 0.46 percent from 1977 to 2004, with no significant (up or down) trend in that figure, with a maximum annual increase of about 0.79 percent (from 1997 to 1998).[12] With respect to methane, the GHG that is next in importance—for reasons that are not well understood but which could be caused by the closing of the stomata (i.e., the pores on the underside of the leaves that enable gases and water vapor to be exchanged between the leaves and the atmosphere) because of higher CO_2 concentrations[13]—the growth in atmospheric concentrations has slowed down substantially during the past several years after having grown exponentially for much of the 19th and 20th centuries. Measurements from Alert (in North West Territories, Canada), the South Pole, and Mauna Loa indicate that between 1992 and 2001 they grew at an average rate of between 0.15 percent and 0.26 percent per year.[14] Thus, the assumed 1 percent annual increase seems to be a significant overestimate for increases in GHG concentrations.

Third, the atmospheric concentrations projected in the previous step have to be used to determine future "radiation forcing." Here too there are uncertainties regarding the amount of longwave and shortwave radiation that GHGs can absorb and emit as the concentrations of these gases continue to increase (as the saturation of various absorption and emission bands changes).[15] These estimates of radiation forcing over time then need to be fed into climate models to estimate changes in climatic variables (such as changes in seasonal temperatures and precipitation, seasonal highs and lows, and changes in diurnal variability).

Nowadays the more sophisticated climate models consist of atmospheric general circulation models (GCMs) coupled to oceanic GCMs (or coupled to atmospheric-ocean GCMs) to project climatic changes. However, despite some progress, there are several model-related issues that have yet to be satisfactorily resolved. These issues include whether the models adequately or realistically characterize and treat clouds;[16] land use, land cover, and associated biological processes;[17] black carbon and other anthropogenic and natural aerosols in the atmosphere;[18] solar variability; and topography. Moreover, in addition to being able to accurately model the direct effect of these climate-forcing agents, the models should be able to account for their indirect effects and interactions.[19] Given all these uncertainties and unresolved complexities, it is unclear how much credence can be placed on GCM estimates of climatic variables that would affect human and natural systems at scales that are appropriate and relevant to estimating climatic effects on natural and human systems.

For example, Professor Roger A. Pielke Sr. and coworkers at the University of Colorado, using a coupled regional atmospheric and vegetation model, showed that (a) changes in vegetation have a larger effect on temperature and precipitation than does the change in radiative forcing due to a doubling of CO_2 and (b) a doubling of CO_2 has a greater impact on seasonal temperature and precipitation through its biological effects than through its radiative effects.[20] This suggests not only that climate-change models that exclude land use and land cover changes could be prone to large errors but that land use and land cover could be at least as important a determinant of local, regional, and possibly global climate than increases in CO_2 concentrations.[21]

Such shortcomings are particularly significant at the regional or smaller geographical scales because these are the scales at which most impacts have to be estimated. This is because geographical features are themselves important determinants of the climate. Moreover, the distribution and abundance of natural resources such as water, soil, vegetation, and other biological resources—the basis of most climate-sensitive natural and human systems—are themselves spatially heterogeneous. And so is precipitation, which for vegetation, agriculture, and forestry is just as, if not more, critical than temperature. But regardless of how much confidence one may have in the ability of climate models to estimate globally averaged climatic changes, the finer the geographic scale, the more uncertain the results. In fact, it is not uncommon for GCMs to disagree with each other regarding whether precipitation at any particular location will increase or decrease. But, if the models are not robust and cannot reliably project precipitation (and its temporal and spatial distribution), then how much reliance can be placed on any projections regarding plant growth and all else that depends on plant life such as agriculture, forestry, water resources, the abundance and distribution of species, and so forth?

Other anomalies and unresolved issues include the inability of current GCMs to explain why, on the whole, Antarctica has apparently cooled at least since 1971 despite warming in the Antarctic Peninsula;[22] why, despite globally averaged warming in the past two decades, the extent of Antarctic ice cover and sea ice has expanded in recent years (at least from the late 1970s to the early 2000s) and its average temperature has dropped;[23] and why evaporation seems to have decreased in both the northern and the southern hemispheres despite projections of a stronger hydrological cycle because of global warming.[24]

Fifth, these uncertain location-specific climatic changes serve as inputs to simplified and often inadequate models, which project location-specific biophysical changes (e.g., biological productivity of ecosystems, crop or timber yields, or the ability of mosquitos to transmit malaria).

Next, depending on the human or natural system under consideration, the outputs of these biophysical models may have to be fed into additional models to translate biophysical changes into social and economic impacts. For example, estimates of crop yields serve as inputs for models of the global agricultural system in order to project the overall impact on food availability in different parts of the world (through trade and commerce) and, through that, on food security and hunger.

But the biophysical changes are themselves affected by the level of economic development and technological change in the relevant sectors. For example, crop yield—a biophysical measure—is sensitive to both economic development and levels of technology. Thus, the coupling between biophysical and socioeconomic models should run both ways.

To further complicate matters, socioeconomic consequences are themselves dependent on the levels of economic development, access to technologies, and the capacity to implement those technologies. For instance, figures 2.2 and 2.4 show that available food supplies per capita and malnutrition—both food security-related socioeconomic measures that are affected by crop yield—are also dependent on the level of economic development and technology. Thus, the models should allow for the fact that socioeconomic impacts will themselves be modified by socioeconomic responses.

For both biophysical and socioeconomic impacts, the greater the impact, the greater the response. The effects of a reduction in crop yield in an area in this day and age, for example, is likely to be substantially diminished through a variety of "autonomous" or "automatic" responses (or adaptations) at the local, regional, or global levels.[25] At the local level, the farmer may, for instance, adapt his or her agronomic practices to reduce if not compensate for any revenues lost due to a drop in yield by modifying the timing of sowing or harvesting the crop or by shifting to crops or crop varieties that would be expected to perform better under the climatic and soil conditions projected on the farm. At the regional level, among other things, researchers may improve crops so they are better adapted to expected climatic conditions (given existing soil conditions), or governments may improve or extend infrastructure to move agricultural inputs and outputs to and from farms more efficiently. And at all levels—local, regional, and global—trade, commerce, and, in extreme cases, aid will tend to move agricultural inputs and outputs from surplus to deficit areas as a matter of course.

All such actions will serve to moderate any negative socioeconomic consequences of climate change-induced declines in yield while capitalizing on any potential gains.

Moreover, as we have seen in the previous chapters, individual and societal responses to reduce adverse impacts while capitalizing on positive elements are not restricted to socioeconomic impacts. They also extend to environmental impacts.

Therefore, modeling the future impacts of climate change on climate-sensitive systems or indicators that are or can be affected by human actions (e.g., agriculture, food security, forests, land use, land cover, habitat loss, and biodiversity) should include consideration of society's capacity to adapt to the consequences of climate change, whether they are positive or negative. Such "adaptive capacity" (or adaptability) is a key determinant of impacts (or damages) due to climate change because the greater that capacity, the greater society's ability to forestall or to reduce impacts through a combination of (a) anticipatory measures to reduce society's vulnerability to climate change and (b) reactive measures to cope with or adapt to any residual impacts.

In addition, the models should allow for society's adaptive capacity to increase with both the level of economic development and the secular advances in technology. However, as we will see in greater detail later, among the shortcomings of most present-day impacts studies is that although they use emission scenarios that assume relatively rapid economic growth (and technological change) in the future, their impact estimates frequently do not fully consider increases in society's adaptive capacity that should occur because of the same increases in economic and technological development.[26] Consequently, such impact assessments tend to systematically overestimate the net damages (or negative impacts) of climate change.

There also ought to be additional dynamic feedback loops between several of the individual models in the entire chain of models going from emissions to impacts estimates. For instance, the climate affects photosynthesis and respiration on the earth's surface, which, in turn, will affect global CO_2 emissions. But to ease calculations, these feedback loops are generally ignored or replaced by static inputs or "boundary" conditions.

Because impacts assessments lie at the very end of this chain of models, estimates of the impacts of global warming at any particular location or time are, in most instances, even more uncertain than estimates of the globally averaged temperature or precipitation. Net global impacts—because they are an aggregation of the various location-specific impacts—are also uncertain, although there may be some cancellation of errors. Nonetheless, the uncertainties are large enough that one cannot be confident either of the magnitude or, in many cases, even the direction of impacts (i.e., whether the net impacts are positive or negative). This is true not only for any specific geographic location but also globally, because global impacts are nothing but an aggregation of local impacts.

The Degree of Global Warming by the Late 21st Century

Based on climate models, the IPCC's Third Assessment Report (TAR)—*Climate Change 2001: The Scientific Basis*—states that global temperature could increase by 1.4°C–5.8°C between 1990 and 2100.[27] However, the TAR provides no central or most likely estimate of climate change. Moreover, given the uncertainties associated with such models, an alternate and, arguably, more robust approach to determining future levels of climate change would be to extrapolate recent trends into the future. In fact, the TAR notes, "On timescales of a few decades, the current observed rate of warming . . . suggests that anthropogenic warming is likely to lie in the range of 0.1 to 0.2°C per decade over the next few decades."[28]

Thus, if one accepts recent trend data from *surface* temperature measurements as valid, then, according to the TAR itself, the likely change in globally averaged temperature (GAT) could be of the order of 0.1°C–0.2°C per decade, which is essentially the same result as obtained by James Hansen and Makiko Sato based on an examination of trends in the growth of GHG emissions.[29] More recently, Hansen has suggested that under a business-as-usual scenario (i.e., 2 percent per year growth in fossil fuel CO_2 emissions), GAT would rise 2°C–3°C by 2100.[30]

Several skeptics challenged the surface temperature record because of the poor correspondence between temperature trends, as measured by satellite, radiosonde, and surface instruments,[31] and between trends in sea surface and air temperatures.[32] These discrepancies have not yet been fully resolved. These alternative data sets suggest that recent global warming is less than reported by the IPCC.[33] No less important, the satellite data are more representative of the globe than are the sets of surface stations used to determine temperature trends. [34] If one relies on the satellite data, then the measured rate of global warming is of the order of 0.13°C per decade (or 1.3°C per century).[35]

There are also ongoing debates as to whether the surface instrumental record continues to be contaminated by the urban heat island effect[36] and other effects due to changes in land use and land cover[37] in the vicinity of instruments.

Some skeptics have also noted that the warming to date is substantially less than ought to have occurred if the IPCC's high-end estimates for the climate's sensitivity to GHG concentrations were accurate. To explain this discrepancy, it has been suggested that some of the warming that ought to have occurred had been offset by cooling due to sulfates.[38] Moreover, goes this explanation, because developing countries are likely to impose more stringent sulfur dioxide (SO_2) controls in the future to reduce acidic deposition and sulfate formation—a reasonable assumption in light of the environmental transition hypothesis—the sulfate cooling effect would be reduced, boosting future global warming.[39] The counter to this argument is that if the amount of cooling attributed to sulfates was indeed accurate, then perhaps the southern hemisphere should have warmed more than the northern hemisphere because SO_2 has been emitted predominantly in the northern hemisphere (by both developed and developing countries). But, in fact, we see more warming in the northern hemisphere.

However, Stanford scientist Mark Jacobson notes that past sulfate cooling should have been offset by greater heat absorption by dark soot formed during combustion of fossil fuels and forest fires worldwide, which would not only absorb heat when the dark matter is suspended in the atmosphere (where it can affect cloud formation) but also when it is deposited on the snow, ice, and other ground cover.[40]

Is Global Warming This Century's Most Important Environmental Issue?

Despite the unresolved issues and uncertainties associated with models used to project global warming and its impacts, I will employ the results of various model studies to ascertain whether climate change is likely to be the most important environmental problem facing the globe for the foreseeable future. Specifically, I will, for the most part, adopt as valid projections made by the so-called Fast Track Assessment (FTA) of the global impacts of climate change.

The FTA was sponsored by the U.K. government's Department of Environment, Forests, and Rural Affairs (DEFRA). The results of the latest FTA were reported in a special issue of the peer-reviewed journal, *Global Environmental Change: Part A*, published in 2004.[41] Where necessary, I will also draw upon results from a previous global impact assessment that was also sponsored by DEFRA and undertaken by the same groups that were involved in this version of the FTA. Many of the results of that previous assessment, published in the peer-reviewed literature between 1999 and 2002,[42] were incorporated into the IPCC's TAR.

In recognition of the shamefully politicized nature of the debate about surrounding climate change and to defuse questions some readers may have, I should note that the authors of these sets of DEFRA-sponsored assessments are in good standing with the IPCC. Most—perhaps all—have been active participants in the writing of the IPCC's Third and Fourth Assessment Reports. They include the current chairman of the IPCC's Work Group II, which is charged with compiling the impacts, vulnerability, and adaptation volume of the forthcoming Fourth Assessment Report, as well as several lead authors, authors, and coauthors of that report.

These impacts assessments have been remarkably influential, especially in the United Kingdom, a leader in the international debate over climate change. In fact, the earlier set of impacts assessments provided the basis for the statement by Sir David King that "as a consequence of continued warming, millions more people around the world may in future be exposed to the risk of hunger, drought, flooding, and debilitating diseases such as malaria."[43]

In order to gauge the importance of climate change in affecting human well-being at the global level, I too will focus on the four climate-sensitive hazards to human health and safety invoked by Sir David and emphasized by the FTA, namely, malaria, hunger, water shortage, and coastal flooding. With respect to environmental impacts, I will, like the FTA, also focus on habitat loss and terrestrial carbon sink capacity.

Notably, the authors of the DEFRA-sponsored studies do not consider socioeconomic scenarios to be credible beyond the 2080s.[44]

Accordingly, I will assume that 2085 is at the limit of the foreseeable future although that seems wildly optimistic about our ability to foretell the future.

Like the FTA, this chapter does not consider low-probability but potentially high-consequence outcomes, such as the collapse of the Western Antarctic Ice Sheet or the Greenland Ice Sheet, either of which it is feared could raise the global sea levels by several meters over a few centuries, or the shut down of the thermohaline circulation in the North Atlantic, which ironically might, some claim, cool parts of Europe,[45] because such outcomes are deemed unlikely to occur during this century.[46] Moreover, many of these verge on the speculative at this time (see box 10.1).

Scenarios of SRES Employed by the Fast Track Assessment

The FTA used four scenarios that were developed in the IPCC's *Special Report on Emission Scenarios* (SRES) to project future climate change and its global impacts in 2085.[47]

Table 10.1 summarizes the dominant characteristics of the "storylines" associated with each scenario, as well as corresponding estimates in 2085 of atmospheric CO_2 concentrations and climate change. The latter is represented by the increase in the globally averaged temperature between 1990 and 2085, as estimated by the U.K. Meteorological Office's HadCM3 model.[48] The columns in this, and most subsequent, tables in this section are arranged by scenario from left to right in the order of decreasing CO_2 concentrations (and global temperature changes). As indicated, the globally averaged temperature increases between 1990 and 2100 are projected to range from 4.0°C to 2.1°C. Notably, the A1FI world is not only the warmest, it is also the richest of the four alternate worlds analyzed in the assessment. In addition to having the highest level of economic growth, under its SRES storyline it is assigned the most fossil fuel intensive economy (hence the "FI" within "A1FI"), low population growth, rapid technological change, and relatively low regard for the environment. The next warmest world, the A2 world, is the poorest and the most populous. It is also assigned globally uneven levels of technological change. Of the four alternate future worlds, the B1 world is the coolest. According to its storyline, it represents a moderately rich world reliant on highly efficient energy technologies, low population growth (equivalent to the A1FI world), and

Box 10.1
Daemon ex Machina

We are probably all familiar with *Deus ex machina*—the God from the machine—that descends on the stage, sets everything right before the play descends into tragedy, and ensures a happy ending. To many, global warming is precisely the reverse of *Deus ex machina*. It is, in fact, a *daemon ex machina*, which will inevitably turn everything into disaster unless we act now—or within 20 years. Among the most frequently mentioned disasters that this demon might unleash are abrupt climate change through the shutdown of the thermohaline circulation or melting of the polar ice sheets beyond the "tipping point." How likely are either of these disasters in the foreseeable future?

Thermohaline circulation

One of the popular myths about climate is that the major reason winters of Western Europe are mild relative to those of eastern North America is because of the thermohaline circulation (THC), so-called because it is driven by differences in the density of seawater because of changes in temperature and salinity (salts are *halides* in Latin). The thermohaline circulation, sometimes called the "Great Ocean Conveyor Belt" or "Meridional (i.e., north-south) Overturning Circulation," conveys heat from the lower latitudes in warm surface waters toward the poles. The Gulf Stream (and its tentacle, the North Atlantic Drift), which is part of this circulation, moves heat from the tropics to the northeast Atlantic Ocean. This heat is picked up by the mid-latitude westerlies over the Atlantic, which warm Western Europe. Thus, as the surface water moves north, it cools. Some of it also forms sea ice, which increases the salinity of the remaining water. Both cooling and sea ice formation, therefore, increase the density of the water, which then sinks toward the ocean depths becoming part of the North Atlantic Deep Water. This deep water travels south across the Atlantic between the new and old worlds toward the Antarctic and

(continued next page)

(continued)

then northward into the Indian Ocean or northeast around Australia to the northern Pacific Ocean, where mixing with warmer waters it rises and generates a warm, countercurrent close to the ocean's surface. The countercurrent from the Pacific travels south and west through the Indonesian archipelago where it joins the countercurrent established in the Indian Ocean. It then goes around the Cape of Good Hope into the Atlantic, where it becomes, once again, part of the Gulf Stream.

One of the doomsday scenarios about global warming is that it could inject extra freshwater in the North Atlantic through melting of the Greenland Ice Sheet or the permafrost or through increased runoff, which could then disrupt the sinking of the water into the North Atlantic Deep and halt the conveyor belt, sending Europe, if not the world, into a deep freeze. The latter scenario was the inspiration for the movie, *The Day After Tomorrow*. However, these fears seem to be overblown.[49] First, most of the winter warming of Western Europe seems to be caused by atmospheric circulation and seasonal release of heat stored in the ocean rather than heat transported by the ocean circulation.[50] Second, although recent data from 1957 to 2004 indicate that the conveyor belt may have slowed by 30 percent, this is "uncomfortably close" to the uncertainties in the observations.[51] In addition, Richard Kerr reports in *Science* magazine that "changing sea surface temperatures suggest that the conveyor has speeded up a bit since the 1970s."[52] Third, Gregory and others compared the response of the THC to a quadrupling of CO_2 concentrations over 140 years using 11 different models.[53] All the models indicated a gradual decline in the strength of the THCs by between 10 percent and 50 percent. However, none showed a rapid or complete collapse. None of the models shows a cooling anywhere that would more than offset any resulting warming.

(continued next page)

(continued)

Collapse of the Greenland and Antarctic Ice Sheets

It has been suggested that the collapse of the Greenland Ice Sheet could raise global sea levels by 7 meters over a millennium, while that of the West Antarctic and East Antarctic Ice Sheets could raise sea levels by another 7 meters and 84 meters, respectively.[54] Such rises in sea level, if they happen at all, would occur over the time scale of millennia or longer.

So what do data tell us is happening with respect to these ice sheets?

Recent findings (see chapter 6 and references therein) based on measurements from 1992 to 2003 using the European Remote Sensing Satellites indicate the following:

- Ice sheets in the Antarctic Peninsula and West Antarctica are thinning but the East Antarctica, a much larger region, has been thickening. As a result, the total volume of ice in Antarctica has increased, and the net contribution of the Antarctic ice sheets is to *lower* sea level ever so slightly (by 0.02 millimeters [mm] per year).
- The Greenland Ice Sheet is acquiring mass. Despite shrinking at the margins, its interior is growing due to higher snowfall.

Two recent papers, however, apparently contradict those results derived from an 11-year satellite record. One paper, based on 34 months of data, found that Antarctic Ice Sheets are losing 152 cubic kilometers (km^3) of ice each year, which would raise sea levels by 0.4 mm per year (or 1.6 inches a century). The other paper, based on a 9-year record and a combination of empirical data and model results, estimates that the Greenland Ice Sheet is losing 224 km^3 per year. At that rate, it will take 5,400 years to melt the remaining 1,200,000 km^3 in that particular ice sheet, which might raise sea levels by 7 meters (equivalent to a sea level rise of 5 inches per century).

(continued next page)

> *(continued)*
>
> Notably, none of these studies suggests that a catastrophic melting of the ice sheets is in the offing soon. But the contradictory results of the different studies suggest that it would be imprudent to base long-term policies on short-term data. Neither a 34-month period nor an 11-year period is sufficiently long to have captured the extent to which melting may be driven by natural or anthropogenic factors. Also it should be emphasized that it's not evident that a 14-meter rise over a millennium or more, while no doubt tragic for some populations, necessarily constitutes a catastrophe for humankind. In other words, a geologic catastrophe does not necessarily a socioeconomic catastrophe make, particularly if the situation is monitored carefully and measures are taken to avoid loss of life and property, such as retrenchment in due course of time of populations away from vulnerable coastlines. A millennium—or half that—ought to be sufficient to prepare for such an event.

the greatest regard for the environment. Finally, the B2 world lies between the A2 and B1 worlds in terms of economic growth, population growth, and concern for the environment.

Although the A2 world is the poorest of the four alternate worlds, it would nevertheless be substantially richer than the world of today. In 2100, under this scenario, the average per capita income for developing countries is projected to increase to $11,000 (in 1990 U.S. dollars, at market exchange rates) from $886 in 1990. Thus, even if there is no additional innovation or technological change for the rest of this century—an unlikely prospect—even under A2, the poorest of the four alternate future worlds, the adaptive capacity of the average developing nation at the end of the 21st century should be substantially higher than what it is today, if for no reason other than that a wealthier developing world should be better able to obtain, operate, and maintain technologies that are relatively commonplace in the developed world today but are underused in developing countries. They could, for example, improve their infrastructure,

Table 10.1

CHARACTERISTICS AND ASSUMPTIONS FOR THE VARIOUS SCENARIOS USED IN THE FAST TRACK ASSESSMENT

	Scenario			
	A1FI	A2	B2	B1
Population in 2085 (billions)	7.9	14.2	10.2	7.9
GDP growth factor, 1990–2100	525–550	243	235	328
GDP/Capita in 2100 (in 1990 US$)				
Industrialized countries	$107,300	$46,200	$54,400	$72,800
Developing countries	$66,500	$11,000	$18,000	$40,200
Technological change	Rapid	Slow	Medium	Medium
Energy use	Very high	High	Medium	Low
Energy technologies	Fossil intensive	Regionally diverse	"Dynamics as usual"	High efficiency
Land use change	Low-medium	Medium-high	Medium	High
CO_2 concentration in 2085	810	709	561	527
Global temperature change (°C) in 2085	4.0	3.3	2.4	2.1

SOURCES: Nigel W. Arnell, M. J. L. Livermore, R. S. Kovats, P. E. Levy, et al., "Climate and Socio-economic Scenarios for Global-Scale Climate Change Impacts Assessments: Characterizing the SRES Storylines," *Global Environmental Change, Part A* 14 (2004): tables 1, 6, 7; Nigel W. Arnell, "Climate Change and Global Water Resources: SRES Emissions and Socio-economic Scenarios," *Global Environmental Change, Part A* 14 (2004): 31–52.

install early warning systems, invest in drip irrigation or other irrigation systems, and better afford fertilizers and pesticides, which are among the reasons their crop yields are currently lower than the developed world's.[55]

In addition, as we saw in earlier chapters, there is a secular (time-dependent) component to technological change, because technology accretes with time, and for any given level of economic development. For instance, food availability per capita and crop yield increased with the passage of time (see, for example, figures 2.2 and 2.3).

Thus, the assumptions made in some impacts assessments that adaptive capacity would not improve with economic growth or with time are not only inconsistent with the assumptions used to drive emission estimates (and, therefore, climate change) under the various scenarios of the SRES, they are unrealistic, given real world experience of the past few centuries.

Contribution of Climate Change to Climate-Sensitive Hazards to Human Well-being through the Foreseeable Future

This section examines the FTA's results regarding the contribution of climate change over the foreseeable future to the total global population at risk (PAR) for malaria, hunger, water shortage, and coastal flooding. These climate-sensitive hazards to public health and safety, as has been noted, have often been cited as justification for controlling climate change.[56]

Hunger. Table 10.2 shows the FTA's estimates of the global PAR for hunger in 2085 both with and without climate change for each scenario, assuming that direct CO_2 effects will indeed be realized (i.e., higher CO_2 concentrations will enhance crop yields and increase the water use efficiency of plants).[57] In this table, PAR in the absence of climate change is denoted by P_0, and the increase in PAR because of climate change by ΔPAR. The total PAR (TPAR) with climate change is, therefore, the sum of P_0 and ΔPAR.

The FTA's analysis for hunger, which was undertaken by an international group of scientists headed by Martin Parry, the current chairman of the IPCC Work Group II, allows for some secular (time-dependent) increases in agricultural productivity, increases in crop yield with economic growth due to greater application of fertilizer and irrigation in richer countries, decreases in hunger due to economic growth, and adaptive responses at the farm level to deal with

Table 10.2
GLOBAL POPULATION AT RISK (PAR) IN 2085 FOR HUNGER WITH AND WITHOUT FURTHER CLIMATE CHANGE (MILLIONS)

	Baseline 1990	A1FI 2085	A2 2085	B2 2085	B1 2085
P_0 (no climate change)	798–872	105	767	233	90
ΔPAR (because of climate change only)		28	−28 to −9	−11 to +5	10
TPAR *with climate change*	798–872	133	739–758	222–238	100

NOTE: This table is based on results that assume direct CO_2 effects will be realized.

SOURCE: Martin L. Parry, Cynthia Rosenzweig, Ana Iglesias, Matthew Livermore, et al., "Effects of Climate Change on Global Food Production under SRES Emissions and Socio-economic Scenarios," *Global Environmental Change, Part A* 14 (2004): 53–67.

climate change.[58] However, Parry and others acknowledge that these adaptive responses are based on currently available technologies, not on technologies that would be available in the future or any technologies developed to specifically cope with or take advantage of any impacts of climate change.[59] But the potential for future technologies to deal with climate change is large especially if, as we saw in the previous chapter, one considers bioengineered crops. Moreover, each of the future worlds is projected to be substantially wealthier and, therefore, ought to have a much greater capacity to develop and employ new technologies. Consequently, the FTA underestimates the adaptive capacity of future worlds, which results in overestimates of ΔPAR and TPAR for each scenario.

These overestimates in TPAR for hunger are likely to be most pronounced for the A1FI world because, as shown in table 10.1, that scenario has the highest levels of economic and technological development, which empirical data indicate should increase agricultural yields, increase available food supplies per capita, and reduce hunger and malnutrition (see figures 2.2 through 2.4).[60]

Table 10.2 indicates that through 2085, the ΔPAR for hunger due to climate change under each scenario is smaller than the contribution of other non-climate change-related factors. That is, climate change is not as important as the other factors contributing to hunger, at least through the foreseeable future. Moreover, under each scenario, TPAR is projected to be lower in 2085 than it was in 1990. The FTA also indicates that, as expected, most of the population at risk of hunger will be in developing countries whether climate changes.

Table 10.2 also shows that eliminating climate change would, at best, reduce TPAR by 21 percent (under the A1FI scenario). At worst, it might *increase* the total population at risk (under the A2 and, possibly, B2 scenarios). TPAR, moreover, is not largest under the warmest scenario (A1FI). Therefore, given the uncertain nature of the projections of climate change and its impacts, reducing GHG emissions may well increase the total global population at risk of hunger. Precautionary principle, where art thou?

Notably, the results following from table 10.2 (and subsequent tables) are unaffected whether impacts are measured in terms of absolute numbers or as a proportion of total population.[61]

However, if the direct effects of CO_2 on crop growth are ignored, then the analysis by Parry and others shows that climate change would exacerbate TPAR under each scenario (including the A2 and B2 scenarios), although ΔPAR would still be less than P_0 for all but the A1FI scenario.[62] However, such outcomes are unlikely. First, the probability that direct CO_2 effects would be zero or negative for the major crops in the world is very low, if not nonexistent.[63] Second, as noted, the FTA most likely overestimates the declines in agricultural yield as well as TPAR for hunger because it underestimates the adaptive capacities of the substantially wealthier and more technologically advanced future societies depicted by the scenarios used by SRES.

Table 10.2 also illustrates a point that is critical for developing climate change policies, namely, when comparing outcomes under various scenarios, it is not sufficient to examine only the impacts of climate change (i.e., ΔPAR). One should also include in the analysis the impacts of non-climate change-related factors. Otherwise, based merely only on a superficial examination of ΔPAR, one would be forced to conclude, erroneously, that with respect to hunger, A2 is the best of the four scenarios and A1FI the worst. But, in fact, based on TPAR, A2 would be the worst and B1 the best. Thus, any policy that would minimize the consequences of climate change to the exclusion of other societal objectives would not, in general, be the most effective method of advancing human well-being, except through serendipity.

Finally, the magnitudes of ΔPAR shown in table 10.2 are disproportionately large compared to changes in yield due to climate change. This is because small declines in yield lead to large increases in food prices, which, then, prices a disproportionately large share of the population out of the food market, putting them at greater risk of hunger.[64] For example, the 21 percent increase in PAR in 2085 because of climate change under the A1FI scenario is the result of a 2 percent drop in the yield over a 95 year period (from 1990 to 2085). This suggests that a modest, but sustained increase in agricultural research and development for the next several decades, could more than compensate for any declines in agricultural productivity due to climate change.

Water Stress. Table 10.3, constructed from Nigel Arnell's contribution to the FTA, shows the global PAR for water shortage in 2085 both with and without climate change for each scenario.[65] In this

Table 10.3
GLOBAL POPULATION AT RISK (PAR) IN 2085 FOR WATER SHORTAGE, WITH AND WITHOUT CLIMATE CHANGE (MILLIONS)

	Baseline 1990	A1FI 2085	A2 2085	B2 2085	B1 2085
P_0 (no climate change)	1,368	2,859	8,066	4,530	2,859
ΔPAR because of climate change		−1,192	−2,100 to 0	−937 to 104	−634
TPAR with climate change	1,368	1,667	5,966–8,066	3,593–4,634	2,225

NOTE: PAR is measured as the number of people inhabiting countries where available water supplies are less than 1,000 m³ per person per year.

SOURCE: Nigel W. Arnell, "Climate Change and Global Water Resources: SRES Emissions and Socio-economic Scenarios," *Global Environmental Change, Part A* 14 (2004): 31–52.

313

table, a population is deemed to be under water stress if its available water supplies fall below 1,000 m^3 per capita per year.

By contrast to the FTA's analysis for hunger, which makes an effort to include autonomous adaptatation, the water stress estimates exclude *any* autonomous or proactive adaptations that might be undertaken, albeit at some cost, to alleviate future water shortages. Because these estimates do not include any adjustments for adaptive capacity as a function of economic progress or secular (i.e., time-dependent) technological development, both P_0 and TPAR are over-estimated for each scenario. The PAR for the A1FI scenario is likely to be overestimated the most because it is the richest of the four worlds and, therefore, should have the greatest adaptive capacity. Nevertheless, TPAR for water shortage in 2085 is smallest for precisely this scenario, although it is also the warmest.

Even more remarkable, table 10.3 shows that climate change by itself might, in fact, *reduce* the TPAR for water shortage. In other words, eliminating climate change might, in fact, *increase* the total population at risk for water shortage under all scenarios except, possibly, the B2 scenario. This result also illustrates one of the critical shortcomings of emission reduction strategies, namely, they indiscriminately eliminate the positive as well as the negative impacts of climate change. By contrast, adaptation strategies will allow societies to selectively capture the benefits of climate change while reducing, if not eliminating, its damages (or costs).

Moreover, just as for hunger, climate change is not as important as the other factors contributing to water shortage, at least through the foreseeable future. Table 10.3 also reaffirms that if the objective is to improve human well-being with respect to water shortage as opposed to reducing climate change (or its damages) as ends in themselves, one should attempt to minimize TPAR rather than ΔPAR (all else being equal).

Finally, note that for each scenario, P_0 is higher in 2085 than in 1990, and that P_0 in 2085 exceeds ΔPAR. This increase is because of the population increase projected in the intervening 95 years.

Malaria. As noted in chapter 6, malaria accounts for 75 percent of the burden of disease currently attributed to climate-sensitive diseases. Unfortunately, the FTA's analysis for malaria, undertaken by van Lieshout and others only provides numerical estimates for changes in global PAR due to climate change (i.e., ΔPAR) under the various scenarios, but not for PARs in the absence of climate change or for TPARs with climate change. Despite efforts, I was unable to obtain from van Lieshout and others the results for PAR with and without climate change.

Yet another problem with the van Lieshout and others paper was that although it attempted to include adaptive capacity as it was in 1990, it did not account for changes in adaptive capacity over time, that is, with advances in economic and technological development, as ought to occur between 1990 and 2085 (see table 10.1). Thus, their analysis sheds no light on the relative importance of climate change as a risk factor for malaria in 2085.

However, the results of the older (pre-SRES) set of impact assessments that were also sponsored by DEFRA allow us to estimate the contribution of climate change to the total population at risk for malaria in 2085.[66] That analysis used a "business-as-usual" scenario without any additional GHG controls that was developed for the 1995 IPCC impact assessment. The U.K. Meteorological Office's HadCM2 model projected that under that scenario, the globally averaged temperature would increase by 3.2°C between 1990 and 2085.[67]

That study's results for malaria indicate that the global population at risk of malaria transmission in P_0 would double from 4,410 million in 1990 to 8,820 million in 2085, while ΔPAR in 2085 would be between 256 million and 323 million. In other words, climate change would contribute about 3.2 percent of the TPAR for malaria in 2085.[68]

Note that these PARs for malaria transmission are substantially larger than the numbers of people who would actually contract or die from that disease in any given year. By comparison with the PAR of 4,410 million in 1990, the number of people who actually contracted malaria each year in the 1990s was an order of magnitude lower (300–500 million), while the number who died (about 1 million) was smaller by more than three orders of magnitude.[69] One reason for these differences is that the actual prevalence of malaria does not coincide with either its historical or its potential range based on the presence of the malaria transmitting vectors or the malaria parasite. This, in fact, reaffirms the importance of incorporating adaptive capacity—and changes in adaptive capacity due to economic growth and technological change—into impact assessments.

The current range of malaria is dictated less by climate than by human adaptability. Despite any global warming that might have taken place during the past century (or more), malaria has been virtually eradicated in richer countries although it was once prevalent there (e.g., the United States and Italy). This is because, in general, a wealthier society has better nutrition, better general health, and greater access to public health measures and technologies targeted at controlling diseases in general and malaria in particular (see chapter 4). In other words, today's wealthier and more technologically advanced societies have greater adaptive capacity, which is manifested in the current geographic distribution of malaria prevalence around the globe.

In fact, analysis by Richard Tol and Hadi Dowlatabadi suggests that malaria is functionally eliminated in a society in which annual per capita income reaches $3,100.[70] But table 10.1 indicates that under the poorest (A2) scenario, the average gross domestic product (GDP) per capita for developing countries is projected to be $11,000. Hence, few, if any, countries ought to be below the $3,100 threshold in 2085. Moreover, given the rapid expansion in our knowledge of diseases and development of the institutions devoted to health and medical research, one can be relatively confident that the $3,100 threshold will almost certainly drop in the next several decades as public health measures and technologies continue to improve and to become more cost-effective. Therefore, unless we squander our human and financial resources pursuing secondary or tertiary priorities, or unless we refuse to develop or adopt malaria-reducing technologies, the importance of climate in determining the ranges of malaria (and other climate-sensitive infectious and parasitic diseases) ought to diminish further. However, there is no guarantee against society shortchanging first order priorities in favor of lower order problems or, for that matter, declining to employ readily available technologies that could address first order priorities. In fact, malaria is a perfect example of such a failure, where in order to reduce the environmental impacts of DDT even its responsible use was eschewed in many parts of the world, allowing that disease to rebound.[71] But as we saw in chapter 6, fortunately this irrational and counterproductive response is currently being reversed, despite lukewarm support, if not warnings, from some officials from the malaria-free developed world.[72]

Coastal Flooding. Table 10.4, based on Robert Nicholls' study, shows the FTA's estimates of the global PAR for coastal flooding in

Table 10.4
GLOBAL POPULATION AT RISK (PAR) IN 2085 FOR COASTAL
FLOODING, WITH AND WITHOUT CLIMATE CHANGE (MILLIONS)

	Baseline 1990	A1FI 2085	A2 2085	B2 2085	B1 2085
PAR (no sea level rise)	10	1–3	30–74	5–35	2–5
PAR (because of sea level rise alone)		10–42	50–277	27–66	3–34
TPAR	*10*	*11–45*	*80–351*	*32–101*	*5–39*

SOURCE: Robert J. Nicholls, "Coastal Flooding and Wetland Loss in the 21st Century: Changes under SRES Climate and Socio-economic Scenarios," *Global Environmental Change, Part A* 14 (2003): 69–86.

2085 both with and without climate change for each scenario.[73] In this table, PAR is measured in terms of the average number of people projected to experience flooding each year by storm surge. These estimates assume that the coastal population grows twice as fast as the general population (or, if populations are projected to drop, it drops at half the pace of the general population), an "evolving" protection with a 30-year lag time. The low and high end of the ranges for PAR for each entry in the table assume low and high subsidence, repectively, because of non-climate change-related human causes.

Nicholls' coastal flooding study makes a creditable effort to incorporate improvements in adaptive capacity due to increasing wealth. Nonetheless, some of its assumptions are questionable. For instance, Nicholls allows societies to implement measures to reduce the risk of coastal flooding in response to 1990 surge conditions, but they ignore subsequent sea level rise.[74] But one would expect that no matter when any measures are implemented, they would consider the latest available data on surge conditions at the time the measures are initiated. That is, if the measure is initiated in, say, 2050, the measure's design would at least consider sea level—and sea level trends—as of 2050, rather than levels reflecting 1990 conditions. Nicholls also allows for a constant lag time between initiating protection and sea level rise. But one should expect that if sea level continues to rise, this lag between upgrading protection standards and higher GDP per capita will be reduced over time, and that the richer a society the faster this reduction. In fact, if the trend in sea level rise proves to be robust, it is conceivable that protective measures may be taken in advance (i.e., lag times may even become negative).

In addition, Nicholls does not allow for any slow down in the preferential migration of the population to the coasts, as is not unlikely if coastal flooding indeed becomes a greater problem. But if the preferential migrations continue unabated, it would not be implausible to expect a country's expenditures on coastal protection to increase as its coastal population increases relative to its total population. A plausible adjustment that could be made would be to increase such expenditures on a per capita GDP basis as the fraction of its population in coastal areas rises. Such an outcome would be consistent with democratic governance.

Nicholls also suggests that subsidence is more likely under the A1FI and A2 worlds than the B1 and B2 worlds.[75] Although this assumption conforms with the SRES's narratives regarding the priority given in each scenario to environmental issues, it contradicts real world experience, which indicates that once richer countries are convinced of a problem, whether it is environment or health related, they generally respond quicker to remedy the problem, spend more, and have greater environmental protection than poorer ones, especially at the high levels of development that, as indicated in table 10.1, are projected to exist virtually everywhere later this century under all the IPCC scenarios. Hence, one should expect that the richest (A1FI) world would spend more and be better protected from subsidence than would the B1 or B2 worlds. Even if greater concern for the environment translates into a higher fraction of GDP spent on the environment then, despite spending a smaller fraction under A1FI, total spending on, and the amount of, coastal protection could be higher under that scenario than, say, the B1/B2 scenarios, given the wide gaps in GDP per capita between these scenarios.

Putting aside these qualms and shortcomings, table 10.4 shows that, in the absence of climate change, the PAR for coastal flooding in 2085 under the A1FI and B1 worlds would be lower than what it was in 1990, but it would be higher under the A2 world. It may or may not be higher under the B2 world. With climate change, the PARs would increase under each scenario with A2 having the highest

TPAR by far, followed, in order, by B2, and perhaps A1FI and B1. Notably, the difference in TPAR between A1FI and B1 scenarios is not very large, despite the several assumptions noted earlier that tend to overestimate TPAR for A1FI more than for B1 (because they downplay the relationship between wealth and adaptive capacity).

Table 10.4 shows that, in contrast to the other climate-sensitive hazards discussed previously, the contribution of climate change to TPAR for coastal flooding would substantially exceed that of non-climate change-related factors. Eliminating climate change could reduce TPAR by as much as 93 percent in 2085 (under the A1FI scenario).

Summary. With respect to the various hazards to human health and safety, the contribution of climate change in general is relatively small compared to contributions of other non-climate change-related factors, with the notable exception of coastal flooding. But in terms of the human impacts at the global level (as measured by the number of annual fatalities or the burden of disease), hunger and malaria outrank coastal flooding. According to the *World Health Report 2002*, malaria was responsible for 1.12 million deaths in 2001. It attributes an additional 3.24 million deaths to underweight.[76] By contrast, weather-related floods, waves, surges, and wind storms caused less than 8,000 fatalities per year from 2000 to 2004,[77] or 0.2 percent of deaths because of malaria and underweight. Therefore, even if one assumes that climate change were to increase the relative share of the burden of disease for coastal flooding 100-fold, its toll would not rival that of either malaria or hunger, unless, of course, we solve those problems first—a topic that is addressed later in this chapter.

Contribution of Climate Change to Environmental Threats through the Foreseeable Future

This section examines the contribution of climate change over the foreseeable future to changes in various positive and negative indicators of environmental well-being. Following the lead of the FTA, we will examine the following indicators: the net biome productivity for the globe (which measures the terrestrial biosphere's net carbon sink capacity),[78] the area of cropland (a crude measure of the amount of habitat converted to human use and is perhaps

319

the single largest threat to global terrestrial biodiversity), and the global loss of coastal wetlands relative to its 1990 level.

Table 10.5 shows that net biome productivity (and terrestrial carbon sink capacity) is projected to increase under climate change, at least through the 21st century, mainly because of increased productivity of plant life in a higher CO_2 world and, to a lesser extent, a reversal of deforestation under the high CO_2 scenarios (i.e., A1FI and A2).[79]

After the middle of this century, however, higher temperatures begin to offset these productivity increases. Nevertheless, according to the FTA, net biome productivity through 2100 is higher under climate change than without it.[80] Second, the area of cropland is projected to be least under the A1FI, the warmest scenario, which should (all else being equal) lead to the lowest habitat loss. This is, in fact, a factor in the increase in the net biome productivity during the 21st century. Third, although sea level rise is projected to add substantially to the loss of coastal wetlands, total losses will be dominated by non-climate change-related factors through at least the 21st century.

Is Climate Change the Most Important Environmental Problem for the Foreseeable Future?

We saw in the foregoing that climate change does not manufacture new problems as much as it mostly exacerbates existing ones, such as malaria, hunger, coastal flooding, water shortage, and various threats to biodiversity. This enabled us to compare the relative contribution of climate change to these problems over the foreseeable future. This comparison, based on the global impacts of climate change with regard to each of these hazards, indicates that climate change is, in general, unlikely to be the most important determinant of the level of human and environmental well-being, at least through the foreseeable future. Coastal flooding is the exception to this rule. However, its contributions to global mortality and burden of disease should continue to be relatively minor compared to malaria and hunger, unless those problems are solved before then. Until then, climate change is unlikely to be the most important public health or environmental challenge facing the globe in the 21st century.

The fact that climate change exacerbates existing problems rather than creates new ones indicates that the magnitude of the total

Table 10.5
ECOLOGICAL INDICATORS UNDER DIFFERENT SCENARIOS, 2085–2100

	Units	Baseline 1990	A1FI	A2	B2	B1
Global temperature increase (ΔT), 1990–2085	°C	0	4.0	3.3	2.4	2.1
Global population (in 2085)	billions	5.3	7.9	14.2	10.2	7.9
GDP per capita, global average (in 2085 in 1990 US dollars)	$/capita	$3,800	$52,600	$13,000	$20,000	$36,600
CO_2 concentration (in 2100)	parts per million	353	970	856	621	549
Net biome productivity with climate change (in 2100)	Pg C/yr	0.7	5.8	5.9	3.1	2.4
Area of cropland with climate change (in 2100)	% of global land area	11.6	5.0	NA	13.7	7.8
Global losses of coastal wetlands in 2085						
Losses because of sea level rise alone	% of current area	NA	5–20	3–14	3–15	4–16
Losses because of other causes	% of current area	NA	32–62	32–62	11–32	11–32
Combined losses	% of current area	NA	35–70	35–68	14–42	14–42

NOTE: NA = not available in the original sources.

SOURCES: N. W. Arnell, M. J. L. Livermore, S. Kovats, P. E. Levy. et al., "Climate and Socio-economic Scenarios for Global-Scale Climate Change Impacts Assessments: Characterizing the SRES Storylines," *Global Environmental Change, Part A* 14 (2004): 3–20; Robert Nicholls, "Coastal Flooding and Wetland Loss in the 21st Century: Changes under SRES Climate and Socio-economic Scenarios," *Global Environmental Change, Part A* 14 (2003): 60–86; P. E. Levy, et al., "Modeling the Impact of Future Changes in Climate, CO_2 Concentrations and Land Use on Natural Ecosystems and the Terrestrial Carbon Sink," *Global Environmental Change, Part A* 14 (2004): 21–30.

problem (i.e., TPAR) will generally exceed the contribution of climate change to that problem (i.e., ΔPAR). As a result, policy strategies that would reduce the total problem have a larger target of opportunity than strategies that would merely reduce the climate change–related portion of the problem. Such policies, therefore, are more likely to enhance human well-being than policies that would only reduce climate change or just its impacts.

For example, a strategy to generally reduce society's vulnerability to malaria through, say, the development of a malaria vaccine would potentially be able to reduce the risk to the entire 9,143 million population at risk for malaria in 2085, while a policy to eliminate climate change would at most reduce risks to 323 million people (i.e., ΔPAR).[81] Therefore, the former strategy has a greater potential to advance human well-being with regard to malaria than any mitigation policy, regardless of how deep the mitigation.[82]

In subsequent sections, we will examine if this potential can indeed be realized in practice, that is, whether strategies that would target the total problem could, in fact, improve human and environmental well-being more effectively and efficiently than would mitigation. This will help us identify and devise integrated strategies to concurrently advance adaptation, mitigation, and well-being.

Is a Richer-but-Warmer World Better than Poorer-but-Cooler Worlds?

A key premise implicit in calls to take actions *now* that would go beyond "no regret" policies[83] in reducing GHG emissions is that before too long a warmer world will necessarily be worse for the globe than cooler worlds. Results from the FTA presented in the previous section allows us to test this premise for the period spanning 2085–2100 with respect to the four alternate worlds that the FTA analyzed. Accordingly, this section will address the issue of whether human and environmental well-being will inevitably be lower in a richer-but-warmer (e.g., A1FI) world than in poorer-but-cooler (e.g., A2, B1, and B2) worlds. It will also provide an estimate as to how much time we can wait, if at all, to institute mitigation measures that would go beyond no-regrets.

Table 10.6 ranks the four scenarios used by SRES for each indicator of human and environmental well-being examined in the foregoing, as well as for GDP per capita.[84] The latter, as we saw in chapters 2

Table 10.6
RANKING OF SCENARIOS PER EACH INDICATOR OF WELL-BEING,
2085–2100, ASSUMING CLIMATE CHANGE

Indicator	A1FI	A2	B2	B1
Indicators of Human Well-Being				
GDP per capita	1	4	3	2
Hunger (PAR in 2085)	2	4	3	1
Water stress (PAR in 2085)	1	4	3	2
Coastal flooding (PAR in 2085)	2	4	3	1
Indicators of Environmental Quality				
Terrestrial carbon sink strength (in 2100)	1.5	1.5	3	4
Cropland area (in 2100)	1	NA	3	2
Coastal wetland area (in 2085)	3.5	3.5	1.5	1.5

NA = not available.

SOURCES: Tables 10.1 through 10.5.

through 4, is itself a surrogate for numerous other indicators of human well-being, as implicitly acknowledged by its inclusion in the human development index by the United Nations Development Programme (UNDP) (see figure 10.1).

The rankings for each indicator in table 10.6 are based on the FTA's projection of the total impact in the 2085–2100 period, that is, the combined impact of climate change and non-climate change-related factors shown in tables 10.2 through 10.5. In the ranking scheme, "1" indicates the highest level of well-being, with respect to the specific indicator, while "4" indicates the lowest. If two scenarios have approximately the same level of well-being, then they would split their ranking. For example, scenarios A1FI and A2 share top ranking for carbon sink strength per table 10.5. Accordingly, their joint ranking is indicated as 1.5.

Table 10.6 assumes that the relative ranking of the scenarios with respect to GDP per capita (a surrogate for per capita wealth or income) will be maintained despite any climate change. This is likely because the gaps in GDP per capita from one scenario to the next are quite large (see tables 10.1 and 10.5) and the impacts of climate change are relatively small through 2085–2100. Moreover, the other

Figure 10.1
HUMAN WELL-BEING VS. WEALTH, EARLY 2000S

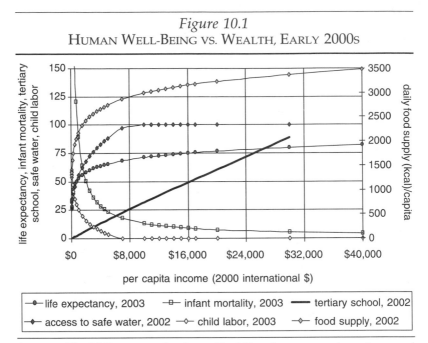

SOURCES: World Resources Institute, EarthTrends, www.wri.org (accessed June 23, 2005); World Bank, *World Development Indicators,* http://devdata. worldbank.org/dataonline (accessed July 12, 2005).

entries in table 10.6 suggest that the percent drop in the GDP per capita because of climate change will be largest for the A2 world and least for the A1FI world (because these scenarios are likely to result in the smallest and largest amount of climate change impacts on human well-being, respectively). Hence, if there is any re-ordering of the rankings for GDP per capita, it would probably be due to B2 and B1 trading places (because B1 is wealthier and, therefore, likely to have greater adaptive capacity; see table 10.1).

Of all the indicators of human well-being noted in table 10.6, GDP per capita—or, perhaps, the logarithm of the GDP per capita per the UNDP's human development index (see chapter 2)—should be given greatest weight because it's a surrogate for numerous, and more appropriate, human well-being indicators. GDP per capita can serve as a proxy for a wide variety of indicators of human well-being, including infant mortality rates, life expectancy, access to safe water and sanitation, educational status, and reduction in child labor,

Figure 10.2
TOTAL FERTILITY RATE VS. WEALTH, 1977–2003

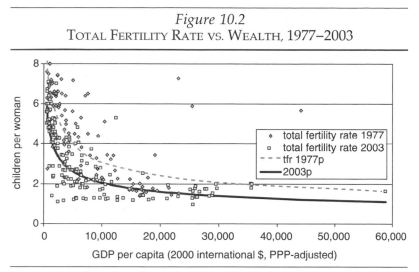

SOURCE: Based on data from World Bank, *World Development Indicators*, http://devdata.worldbank.org/dataonline (accessed July 12, 2005).

that contribute to human capital (see figure 10.1). Moreover, as noted earlier, impacts analyses have a general tendency to underestimate, if not ignore, changes in adaptive capacity because of increases in both economic development and technological progress (or time), which, in turn, overestimates the negative impacts of climate change. Because the A1FI world probably has the greatest adaptive capacity, negative impacts are likely to have been overestimated the most for that scenario for both human and environmental well-being. Accordingly, table 10.6 suggests that human well-being in 2085 would, in the aggregate, be highest for the A1FI scenario and lowest for A2.

Applying the same logic and considerations, it would seem that human well-being should be somewhat better under B1 than B2. Notably, these aggregate rankings stay the same whether climate changes, or whether the rankings are based on PAR in terms of absolute numbers or the proportion of global population.[85]

With respect to environmental well-being, based on the strength of the terrestrial carbon sink and cropland area, environmental quality should be superior under the A1FI scenario than under either the B1 or B2 scenarios through 2100, but these rankings could apparently be reversed for coastal wetlands, at least through 2085—"apparently," because, as noted previously, that could be an artifact of the assumption that subsidence would be lower under the B1 and B2 scenarios than the A1FI scenario despite the latter's greater adaptive capacity.

From the perspective of human well-being, the richest-but-warmest world characterized by the A1FI scenario would probably be superior to the poorer-but-cooler worlds at least through 2085, particularly if one considers the numerous ways GDP per capita advances human well-being. Human well-being would likely be the lowest for the poorest (A2) world. With respect to environmental well-being, matters may be best in the A1FI world for some critical environmental indicators through 2100, but not necessarily for others.

Because the warmest world, which is also the richest, is superior to the other worlds through the foreseeable future, it is unnecessary to launch an urgent program to reduce climate change *at this time*. If there is any urgency at all, it should be to increase the level of economic development and their technological prowess, particularly in developing countries. If one assumes that it takes 50 years to replace the energy infrastructure, then we have at least until 2035 (2085–50) before embarking on a GHG reduction program that goes beyond "no-regrets." In the interim, we use this time wisely by building up society's adaptive and mitigative capacities, even as we ensure no-regret actions are instituted.

Benefits and Costs of Mitigation and Focused Adaptation

In the foregoing we examined the impacts of climate change under various scenarios of the future assuming that there would be no reductions in GHGs beyond application of business-as-usual controls. In this section, we will compare the relative costs and benefits through the foreseeable future of various mitigation schemes against those associated with strategies that would focus on reducing society's vulnerability to each climate-sensitive hazard that might be exacerbated by climate change. For lack of an accepted term, I will call this alternate strategy "focused adaptation" to distinguish it from "broad development," which will be discussed later in this chapter.

Focused adaptation consists of measures focused on coping with and reducing vulnerability to malaria, hunger, coastal flooding, water stress, loss of habitat, and so forth. Such measures would include, for instance, developing a malaria vaccine, developing drought resistant crops to increase yields that might otherwise decline, using drip irrigation to cope with water shortage, building structures better able to withstand flooding, or reducing habitat loss to help conserve biodiversity. In theory, combinations of such measures should be capable of reducing the vulnerability of the TPAR for each climate-sensitive hazard regardless of whether individuals were placed at risk because of climate change or non-climate-change-related factors. TPAR, as we know, would usually exceed the additional population at risk because of climate change (ΔPAR) alone. For instance, we saw earlier that a successful malaria vaccine could reduce vulnerability of the TPAR for malaria (estimated at up to 9,143 million in 2085), while halting climate change would reduce that population at risk by 323 million.

Comparing Mitigation and Focused Adaptation

Table 10.7 provides (a) estimates of changes in globally averaged temperature from 1990 to 2085; (b) reductions in climate change damages in 2085 for malaria, hunger, water shortage, and coastal flooding; and (c) a notion of the annual costs associated with mitigation under four mitigation scenarios, namely, the Kyoto Protocol, stabilization of GHG concentrations at 750 parts per million (ppm) in 2250, stabilization at 550 ppm in 2150, and "no climate change."[86] In this table, damage reductions are expressed in terms of the percent reduction in TPAR from levels that would otherwise occur if emissions are not mitigated at all. This table is derived from the results of the earlier DEFRA-sponsored global impact assessments that were published in the peer-reviewed literature in the 1999–2002 time frame.

For the IPCC scenario used in these assessments, the U.K. Meteorological Office's HadCM2 model projects the global temperature change between 1990 and 2085, assuming no mitigation, to be 3.2°C.[87] The global temperature change due to the Kyoto Protocol is based on the optimistic assumption that by 2085 the protocol would reduce climate change by 7 percent, which would then reduce the impacts of climate change on malaria, hunger, and water shortage by a like amount, as well as the impacts of coastal flooding by thrice that.[88]

Table 10.7

PERCENT REDUCTION IN THE TOTAL GLOBAL POPULATION AT RISK (TPAR) IN 2085 UNDER VARIOUS MITIGATION SCENARIOS, AND ASSOCIATED COSTS

Climate-sensitive hazard	Because of the Kyoto Protocol	Reduction in TPAR[a] in 2085		
		Assuming stabilization at 750 ppm	Assuming stabilization at 550 ppm	Assuming no climate change
Malaria	0.2%	1.3%	0.4%	3.2%
Hunger	1.5%	16.6%	9.7%	21.1%
Water shortage[b]	−4.1%–0.8%			−58.6%–11.8%
Coastal flooding	18.1%	62.8%	80.1%	86.2%
ΔT (globally averaged), 1990–2085	3.0°C	1.8°C	1.4°C	0°C
Annual costs (in 2003 U.S. dollars)	~ $165 billion in 2010	> $165 billion	>> $165 billion	>>> $165 billion

a. TPAR = (PAR without climate change) + (PAR because of climate change). A negative sign indicates that emission reductions will *increase* TPAR. Reductions in water shortage are estimated as the net change in the global population under greater water stress using Arnell's 1999 data. Arnell did not provide any estimates for the stabilization scenarios. However, Nigel Arnell and others provided estimates for the stabilization scenarios but only for the population experiencing greater stress, ignoring the population for which climate change might relieve water stress.

SOURCES: Indur M. Goklany, "A Climate Policy for the Short to Medium Term: Stabilization or Adaptation?" *Energy and Environment* 16 (2005): 667–80; Nigel W. Arnell, M. G. R. Cannell, M. Hulme, R. S. Kovats, et al., "The Consequences of CO₂ Stabilization for the Impacts of Climate Change," *Climate Change* 53 (2002): 43–46; Martin L. Parry, Nigel Arnell, A. McMichael, Robert Nicholls, et al., "Viewpoint, Millions at Risk Defining Critical Climate Change Threats and Targets," *Global Environmental Change, Part A* 11 (2001): 181–83; Nigel W. Arnell, "Climate Change and Global Water Resources," *Global Environmental Change, Part A* 9 (1999): S31–S49.

Table 10.7 indicates that global temperatures will increase from 1990 to 2085 by 3.0°C under the Kyoto Protocol, and 1.8°C and 1.4°C under the 750 ppm and 550 ppm stabilization scenarios, respectively. Of course, there will be no temperature increase under the "no climate change" scenario.

Malaria. Table 10.7 shows that freezing climate change at its 1990 level—a virtual impossibility—would at best reduce the TPAR for malaria in 2085 by 3.2 percent. Reductions under either stabilization scenario would be even smaller, despite potentially costing trillions of dollars. Reductions under the Kyoto Protocol would, at 0.2 percent, be relatively trivial despite costing anywhere between 0.1 percent and 2.0 percent of the GDP of the countries subject to the protocol, according to the IPCC's Third Assessment Report. Assuming that the protocol's cost is at the lower end of this range, say 0.5 percent, then, in 2010, it would nevertheless cost about $165 billion (in 2003 dollars), which is the estimate used in table 10.7.[89] But, according to the United Nations Millennium Project (UNMP), malaria's current global death toll of about a million per year can be reduced by 75 percent at an additional cost of $3 billion per year through measures designed to reduce present-day vulnerabilities to malaria, that is, through focused adaptation measures.[90] Even if this cost has to be doubled by 2085 to keep pace with the projected increase in the global population at risk in the absence of climate change, the benefit-cost ratio for focused adaptation solely with respect to malaria would still be much greater than that of the Kyoto Protocol or, for that matter, any mitigation scheme listed on table 10.7.

Although this benefit-cost comparison does not account for the other nonmalaria-related benefits associated with reducing climate change, for example, reducing hunger, coastal flooding, and greater threats to biodiversity, neither does it account for the substantial cobenefits associated with reducing malaria more widely (see next paragraph). In any case, we will revisit the benefit-cost estimates in the following sections, taking into account the broader set of benefits that would pertain to mitigation.

Current vulnerabilities to malaria can be reduced through a mixture of measures targeted specifically at malaria as well as measures that would generally enhance the capacity to respond to public health problems and deliver public health services more effectively and efficiently. Malaria-specific measures include indoor residual (home) spraying with insecticides, insecticide-treated bednets, improved case management, more comprehensive antenatal care, and development of safe, effective, and cheap vaccines and therapies.[91]

These vulnerability-reducing strategies would enhance the adaptive capacity of societies currently plagued by malaria in a variety of ways. First, measures—technologies, practices, and institutions—developed to reduce vulnerability to malaria today, will also help reduce malaria tomorrow, whether the disease is due to climate change or non-climate change-related factors. That is, they would reduce risks to 100 percent of the TPAR today and in 2085 (estimated at 4 billion and 9 billion per year, respectively), while, as noted, mitigation would at most address only 3.2 percent of the problem in 2085 and even less than that for the billions at risk annually between now and then.

Perhaps even more important, reducing malaria in developing countries today would enhance their adaptive capacity to deal with a wider variety of problems than just malaria. It would improve public health in general, which would, as noted in chapter 4, ensure fuller development of their human capital and help advance economic development that would then enhance their resiliency and reduce their vulnerability to any adversity, whether it is caused by climate change or another agent.[92] Thus, it would help address, fundamentally, why countries where malaria is prevalent are mired in poverty and are more vulnerable to adversity in general and climate change in particular. In other words, it would reduce one of the major hurdles to their sustainable economic development and help move the cycle of progress in the right direction, thereby advancing many facets of sustainable development. However, mitigation, as table 10.7 shows, would only have a marginal impact on advancing sustainable development.

Curiously enough, table 10.7 indicates that stabilization at 750 ppm reduces the TPAR for malaria in 2085 by a greater amount than stabilization at 550 ppm—a reduction of 1.3 percent versus a reduction of 0.4 percent. This also suggests that for a period of time at least, deeper mitigation may increase climate change damages somewhat.

Hunger and food production. Just as for malaria, stabilization at 750 ppm reduces the TPAR for hunger in 2085 by a greater amount than stabilization at 550 ppm (see table 10.7). Table 10.7 also indicates that the maximum reduction that can be achieved through mitigation in 2085 in the TPAR for hunger is 21 percent, which is quite similar to the results from the newer FTA summarized earlier. This amount, seemingly large, is in fact the result of a small (1.9 percent) climate change-related drop in future global food production between 1990 and 2085. In other words, unmitigated warming would reduce the annual growth in food productivity from 0.84 percent per year to 0.82 percent per year. But in the 1990s, the world spent about $33 billion annually on agricultural research and development, including $12 billion in developing countries. Therefore, an increase in research and development investments, say $5 billion per year, which is relatively modest compared to the costs associated with the Kyoto Protocol, should help increase agricultural productivity sufficiently to more than compensate for the 0.02 percent annual shortfall caused by unmitigated warming, particularly if the additional investment is targeted toward solving developing countries' current agricultural problems that might be further exacerbated by warming.[93]

These problems include growing crops in poor climatic or soil conditions (e.g., low soil moisture in some areas, too much water in others, or soils with high salinity, alkalinity, or acidity). Because of warming, such conditions could become more prevalent, agriculture might have to expand into areas with poorer soils, or both. Thus, actions focused on increasing agricultural productivity under current marginal conditions would alleviate hunger in the future whether or not climate changes.

Similarly, because both CO_2 and temperatures will increase willy-nilly, crop varieties should be developed to take advantage of such conditions as, and when, they come to pass. Substantial progress can be and, in fact, is being made on these strategies (see chapter 9). Notably, in the initial stages at least, progress on these strategies does not depend on improving our skill in location-specific details of climate change impacts analyses.[94] These focused adaptation measures should be complemented by development of higher yield, lower impact crop varieties and agronomic practices so that more food is produced and used by consumers per unit of land or water devoted to food production.[95] Such measures would include reducing losses on the farm before and after harvesting, in processing, at the supermarket, in the home, during storage, and in transit between each of these stages. Many technologies to effect these measures already exist but are underused in developing countries because they lack the resources to afford them. Examples of existing-but-underused technologies include fertilizers, pesticides, precision agriculture, refrigerators, and even plastic containers and bags for storage. Insufficient penetration of these technologies is one reason why yields and available food supplies per capita are lower in poorer countries.

By 2085, focused adaptation measures, such as those mentioned earlier, would help reduce not only the 80 million increase in PAR for hunger due to uncontrolled warming but also the 300 million at risk because of nonwarming-related factors.[96] Equally important, focused adaptation would help reduce PAR for hunger in the near term (estimated at 521 million in 1990), whereas mitigation, no matter how drastic, will have virtually no effect on this population at risk because of the inertia of the climate system.

Similar to the case of malaria, focused adaptation directed toward reducing vulnerability to hunger would also boost adaptive capacity and advance sustainable development by improving public health and enhancing human capital and economic growth, which would then reduce developing countries' vulnerability to any adversity, whether caused by warming or another agent.

Other benefits associated with this strategy include the following:

- Reduced demand for additional agricultural land (because of increased availability of usable food per unit of land under cultivation), which would limit habitat conversion and reduce habitat fragmentation and loss of migratory corridors. In turn, that would help species adapt more "naturally" through migration and dispersion, as well as conserve carbon stores and sinks, thereby aiding mitigation.[97] As suggested by figure 9.1, increased agricultural productivity has great potential for reducing habitat loss, conserving carbon stores and stocks, and reducing the costs of setting land aside for *in situ* conservation.
- Reduced demand for water, which would generally reduce pressure on water resources (see next section) and help overcome what some have argued could be the major future constraint to meeting global food needs (i.e, insufficient water). That would also reduce pressure on global freshwater biodiversity.[98]

Water shortage. Table 10.7 indicates that warming might, in fact, increase the net population at risk of water stress. This result would be consistent with the results of the FTA noted previously. In other words, mitigation might make matters worse. It also reinforces one of the shortcomings of mitigation, namely, mitigation is indiscriminate in its effect—it reduces all impacts, whether they are positive or negative. This unfortunate outcome also holds for other hazards for which warming results in a mixture of positive outcomes at some locations but negative outcomes at others. This is also the case for hunger and malaria. By contrast, adaptation allows communities to capture the benefits while reducing, if not avoiding, the down sides.

Measures that would help societies cope with present and future water shortages regardless of cause include institutional reforms to ensure that water is treated as an economic commodity, allowing water pricing and transferable property rights to water. Such institutional reforms should stimulate greater adoption of existing-but-underused conservation technologies, as well as lead to more resources from the private sector for innovation and research and development that would reduce the demand for water by all sectors (e.g., by developing new or improved crops and techniques to increase agricultural water use efficiency). These resources should be supplemented by additional public sector resources.

Improvements in water conservation following such reforms are likely to be most pronounced within the agricultural sector because that sector is responsible for 85 percent of global water consumption.[99] Notably, an 18 percent reduction in agricultural water consumption would, on average, double the amount of water available for all other water uses, namely household, industry, and in-stream uses (e.g., conservation of aquatic species and recreation).

Cobenefits of focused adaptation designed to reduce present-day vulnerabilities to water stress include an increase in the amount of food produced per liter of water and a reduction in water diversions, which would help relieve pressures on freshwater biodiversity now and in the future.

Coastal flooding. If there is any hazard for which emission reductions ought to be more cost-effective than adaptation, it is coastal flooding. Table 10.7 indicates that by 2085, unmitigated warming, estimated by the study underlying this table to raise global sea level by 0.41 meter,[100] would contribute 86 percent of the TPAR. By 2085, stabilization at 550 ppm would reduce TPAR by as much as 80 percent at a cost of trillions of dollars, while the Kyoto Protocol would reduce TPAR by 18 percent. But, the global cost for protecting against a 0.5 meter rise in 2100 has been estimated at about $1 billion annually[101] or less than 0.005 percent of global economic product.[102] Thus, emission reductions would not only cost more but could also provide less protection in 2085 than an adaptive approach that would protect against flooding.

Comparing Mitigation with Focused Adaptation

The best one can do through mitigation is to halt climate change at its 1990 level. Table 10.7 shows that would, by 2085, reduce the TPAR for malaria and hunger by 3.2 percent and 21.1 percent, respectively. It would also reduce TPAR for coastal flooding by 86.2 percent, based on a sea level rise of 0.41 meter between 1990 and 2085. However, there is no guarantee that mitigation will not increase the net population at risk for water stress. Although the cost of freezing climate at its 1990 level has never been estimated, it would be astronomical compared to the cost of the Kyoto Protocol, which is estimated at $165 billion in 2010.

However, measures implemented today and focused on reducing current vulnerabilities to these climite-sensitive hazards would, throught 2085, provide greater aggregate benefits than halting climate change, but at less than a tenth of the cost of the Kyoto Protocol:

- At an additional cost of $3 billion per year, malaria's current global death toll of about 1 million per year can be reduced by 75 percent. These expenditures may have to be doubled by 2085 to keep pace with the projected increase in the global population at risk in the absence of climate change.
- An additional $5 billion annual investment in agricultural research and development should raise productivity sufficiently to not only erase any climate change-caused deficit in agricultural production in 2085 but also reduce the PAR in the absence of climate change. If such technologies are brought to fruition, that would also help conserve water, as well as habitat and migratory corridors, thereby reducing the pressure on both water resources and biodiversity.

- An annual investment of $1 billion per year is sufficient to protect coastal areas against a 0.5 meter sea level rise in 2100.

Not only does focused adaptation provide a greater target of opportunity than mitigation—because it would act on both the climate change and the non-climate change-related components of TPAR while mitigation would only affect the climate change-related component—the economics favor it as well.

There are other advantages associated with focused adaptation. First, it will not only reduce present-day climate-sensitive problems, it will also help reduce these problems in the future, whether they are caused by climate change or other factors. This is because the technologies, practices, systems, and human and social capital devised to cope with these problems today will aid societies coping with these problems in the future.

Second, it can be implemented without detailed knowledge of the impacts of climate change. In other words, it can be proactive with respect to climate change. Cases in point are the development of malaria vaccines, drought-resistant crops, transferrable property rights for water resources, or early warning systems for climate-sensitive events ranging from storms to potential epidemics of various kinds.

Third, focused adaptation will start to provide a steady stream of benefits in the very near term while, because of the inertia of the climate system, the benefits of mitigation will not be significant until decades have elapsed. This would be fine except that there are plenty of unsolved problems that afflict current generations that could use the economic and human resources that might otherwise be diverted toward mitigation.

Fourth, mitigation would indiscriminately reduce all impacts of climate change, whether they are positive or negative. But adaptation can capture the positive aspects of climate change, while reducing its negatives.

Fifth, while the impacts of global warming are uncertain, there is no doubt that malaria, hunger, water shortages, and coastal flooding are real and urgent problems here and now. Thus, focused adaptation is far more likely to deliver benefits than is mitigation, as well as to deliver those benefits sooner rather than later.

Not least, ancillary benefits of adaptation focused on reducing vulnerability to malaria and hunger include better health, increased economic growth, and greater human capital, which should advance human well-being and the capacity to address a much wider variety of problems, in addition to climate change. These benefits, in fact, are among the goals and purposes of sustainable development, as explicitly articulated in the Millennium Development Goals (MDGs).

Several measures to reduce hunger and water shortage would also provide benefits by enhancing agricultural productivity per unit of land and water. In turn, that would reduce human demand for agricultural land and water, which currently is the greatest threat to both terrestrial and freshwater biodiversity and is likely to remain so through the foreseeable future. It would also aid mitigation by limiting land under cultivation thereby reducing losses of carbon stores and sinks and the socioeconomic costs of reserving land for conservation or carbon sequestration. These benefits would, moreover, advance sustainable development in their own right.

Finally, the conclusion that focused adaptation is for the foreseeable future superior in terms of both global benefits and global costs is robust to the choice of discount rates, including a zero discount rate. This is because the benefits of focused adaptation will generally follow relatively soon after its costs are incurred. The climate system's inertia, however, ensures that costs of emission reductions will have to be borne for decades before any benefits are accrued.

Advancing Sustainable Development and Adaptive and Mitigative Capacities

One of the most persuasive justifications offered for instituting measures to mitigate GHG emissions is that "developing countries will suffer the most damage [from climate change], and their poor will be at an even greater disadvantage"[103] because they are the least able to adapt.[104] Because some climate change seems inevitable, if for no reason other than that even the world's richest nations lack the mitigative capacity to reduce their GHG emissions to 1990 levels, let alone to preindustrial levels, it is critical, therefore, to enhance adaptive capacity, particularly for developing countries.

In the previous section, we examined the relative costs and benefits of increasing adaptive capacity through focused adaptation, that is, by reducing vulnerabilities to urgent climate-sensitive risks—for example, hunger, malaria, water shortage, coastal flooding, and loss of habitat—that today are among the significant hurdles to sustainable development and would, moreover, be exacerbated by climate change. The low adaptive capacity of the developing world stems from a deeper set of problems, namely, they often lack the economic development and social and human capital to develop and to use the technological options to address the numerous problems that beset them. This compromises their ability to cope not only with climate change but many, if not most, other forms of adversity. As a result, as we saw in chapters 2 and 3, by virtually every objective indicator of well-being, developing countries lag behind developed countries whether the indicator itself is climate sensitive. Hence, an alternative strategy to increasing adaptive capacity would be to broadly advance economic development and social and human capital, as well as the ability to expand technological options and the ability to harness them. But this, of course, is the point of sustainable development. Moreover, because the determinants of adaptive and mitigative capacity are largely the same, enhancing the former should also boost the latter.

Thus, broad pursuit of development (i.e., "broad development") would simultaneously advance the capacity to adapt to or mitigate climate change. One part of this strategy would be to reduce the climate-sensitive hurdles to sustainable development (e.g., hunger and malaria), which would essentially subsume focused adaptation.

A strategy for pursuing broad development would be to meet the MDGs, which were devised to explicitly advance sustainable development in developing countries. The goals' benefits—halving global poverty, hunger, lack of access to safe water and sanitation; reducing child and maternal mortality by two-thirds or more; achieving universal primary education; and reversing growth in malaria, HIV/AIDS, and other major diseases—would generally exceed the benefits flowing from focused adaptation or even the deepest mitigation that were enumerated in the previous section (see table 10.7). Yet, the UNMP pegs the additional annual cost to the richest countries of attaining the MDGs by 2015 at about 0.5 percent of their GDP or $143 billion (in 2003 U.S. dollars) in 2010.[105] That is approximately the same cost as that of the barely effective Kyoto Protocol and less than the cost of stabilization at either 750 ppm or 550 ppm.

Table 10.8 compares the costs and benefits of the three different strategies to reducing the damages associated with climate change

Table 10.8

COMPARING BENEFITS AND COSTS ASSOCIATED WITH MITIGATION,
FOCUSED ADAPTATION, AND BROAD DEVELOPMENT
(as exemplified by the Millennium Development Goals)

Risk factor	Is risk factor sensitive to climate change?	Reduction in TPAR[a]			
		Because of Kyoto Protocol (in 2085)	Because of a halt in climate change (in 2085)	Focused adaptation (in 2085)	Because of MDGs (in 2015)
Malaria[b, c]	Yes	0.2%	3%	75%[f]	75%[f, h]
Hunger[b, c]	Yes	2.0%	21%	> 21%[d]	50%
Water shortage	Yes	−4 to +1%	−59 to +12%	Moderate +	Not addressed explicitly
Coastal flooding[c]	Yes	18%	86%	> 86%[g]	> 86%[g]
Poverty[b, c]	Indirectly	Unknown sign, but small	Unknown sign	+ +[b, e]	50%
Child mortality rate[b, c]	Indirectly	Small +	+[e]	+ +[b, e]	67%

Maternal mortality rate[b,c]	Indirectly	Small +	+[e]	++[b,e]	75%
Lack of access to safe water[c]	No	No effect	No effect	No effect	50%
Lack of access to sanitation[c]	No	No effect	No effect	No effect	50%
Lack of primary education[b,c]	No	Minor +	Small +[e]	+[b,e]	100%
AIDS, TB[b,c]	No	No effect	Zero to small +[e]	+[b,e]	++
Annual costs		~ **$165 billion in 2010**	**>>> cost of Kyoto Protocol**	~**$10–20 billion per year**	~**$145 billion in 2010**

(continued on next page)

Table 10.8
COMPARING BENEFITS AND COSTS ASSOCIATED WITH MITIGATION, FOCUSED ADAPTATION, AND BROAD DEVELOPMENT
(as exemplified by the Millennium Development Goals) (*continued*)

NOTES: a. + denotes a positive reduction in the magnitude of the problem or in population at risk, while + + denotes a larger positive reduction; − sign denotes matters are made worse. b. Reductions in malaria or hunger should directly or indirectly reduce risks associated with each other, poverty, child and maternal mortality rates, educability, AIDS, and tuberculosis. c. Risks associated with these categories should decline with economic development. d. Assumes $5 billion extra per year for agricultural research and development. e. Indirect improvements because hunger or malaria would be reduced. f. Assumes $6 billion per year would reduce malaria by three-fourths. g. Assumes $3 billion per year spent on coastal protection, which is three times the estimate for protection against a 0.5 meter sea level rise per IPCC (1996). h. The 75 percent reduction exceeds the formally adopted MDG, but it is the target established by the UNMP task force (UNMP 2005a).

SOURCES: Updated from Indur M. Goklany, "A Climate Policy for the Short to Medium Term: Stabilization or Adaptation?" *Energy and Environment* 16 (2005): 667–80; World Bank, "The Cost of Attaining the Millennium Development Goals," 2002, www.worldbank.org/html/extdr/mdgassessment.pdf (accessed December 10, 2002), UN Millennium Project, *Investing in Development: A Practical Plan to Achieve the Millennium Development Goals* (New York: Earthscan and UN Millennium Project, 2005); UN Millennium Project, *Coming to Grips with Malaria in the New Millennium*, Task Force on HIV/AIDS, Malaria, TB, and Access to Essential Medicines, Working Group on Malaria (London: Earthscan and Millennium Project, 2005); IPCC, *Climate Change 2001: Synthesis Report* (New York: Cambridge University Press, 2001); World Bank, *World Development Indicators*, http://devdata.worldbank.org/dataonline (accessed July 12, 2005).

through the foreseeable future, namely, mitigation, focused adaptation, and broad development. In this table, mitigation is represented by two scenarios—the Kyoto Protocol and a complete halt to climate change beyond 1990—focused adaptation is represented by the combination of measures outlined in the previous section; and broad development is represented by the MDGs. For focused adaptation, I have arbitrarily tripled the cost estimate provided in the previous section for protecting coastal areas through 2085 against a sea level rise of 0.5 meter. The table assumes that such protection would reduce TPAR for coastal flooding by at least as much as would halting climate change. This level of protection (and associated cost) has also been grafted on to the MDG column because those goals do not explicitly address coastal flooding.

Table 10.8 indicates that, over the next several decades, either focused adaptation or broad development would deliver greater benefits than could be obtained through a halt in further climate change but at a cost less than that of the Kyoto Protocol, let alone any stabilization scheme (see table 10.7).

Pursuing broad development would directly or indirectly advance human well-being in its many facets, while broadly increasing adaptive capacity to cope with adversity in general and climate change in particular. These benefits would be obtained sooner, at lesser cost, and, because of the uncertainties related to climate change and—more important—its impacts, far more certainly than through mitigation alone. In addition, increased adaptive capacity would either raise the level at which GHGs would need to be stabilized to forestall warming from becoming "dangerous," allow mitigation to be postponed, or both. If in the interim, resources are expended to improve the cost-effectiveness of mitigation options, costs (measured as a fraction of GDP lost, for instance) associated with any eventual stabilization might be further reduced even if cuts have to be deeper to compensate for the delay in implementing emission reductions. This would, of course, be supplemented by advances in mitigative capacity that should automatically follow as a result of attaining higher levels of development through adherence to the MDGs.

A benefit of pursuing broad development is that, based on empirical evidence, higher levels of economic development should generally reduce birth rates, thereby mitigating all manner of population-related environmental and natural resource problems. Lower population growth would mitigate GHG emissions across the board. It would also reduce the threats to biodiversity resulting from the human demand for food, freshwater, and marine resources, as well as reduce population exposure to climate-sensitive risks. In fact, the population increase between 1990 and 2085 is the major reason that, in 2085, increases in the populations at risk in the absence of climate change for hunger, malaria, and water shortage are projected to exceed the additional PAR due to climate change. It would, moreover, reduce the demand for adaptation.

An argument advanced for mitigation is that otherwise climate change would hinder sustainable development and lock developing nations into poverty.[106] However, through 2085, the impacts of unmitigated warming are, as shown, generally smaller than the "baseline" problems that would exist in the absence of warming—and where that isn't the case, as we found for coastal flooding, it is more cost-effective to reduce the magnitude of the total problem through adaptation than through mitigation. Thus, even if mitigation is inevitable, in the longer term (i.e., beyond 2085) the bigger problem through the foreseeable future is not that climate change will perpetuate poverty and hinder sustainable development, but that the lack of sustainable economic development will impede developing countries' ability to cope with all manners of adversity, including climate change.[107]

Finally, either the focused adaptation or the broad development strategies would be consistent with the United Nations Framework Convention on Climate Change's objectives outlined in article 2, namely, "to allow ecosystems to adapt naturally to climate change, to ensure that food production is not threatened, and to enable economic development to proceed in a sustainable manner." First, either strategy would reduce emissions. Second, by limiting habitat loss, the strategies would also limit loss of wildlife corridors and fragmentation of habitat. And if anything can aid "ecosystems to adapt more naturally to climate change," it would be limiting habitat fragmentation and conserving migration corridors. That would help species migrate and disperse with less need for human intervention. Third, either strategy would reduce threats to food production. Moreover, by increasing the productivity of the agricultural sector and reducing hunger and malaria, either strategy would help the cycle of progress move forward, thereby contributing to sustainable economic development, particularly in developing nations where employment is usually heavily dependent on the agricultural sector. Of course, the broad development strategy, almost by definition, should deliver higher levels of development and greater adaptive and mitigative capacities.

Additional Issues Relevant to Adaptation and Mitigation

Until the early 2000s, most of the focus on climate change policies was on mitigation, especially in developed countries.[108] However, since then there has been an increase in interest in adaptation. This interest has been fueled by a greater acknowledgment that some climate change is inevitable—whether because of natural or human-made causes—and the realization that although the Kyoto Protocol is insufficient to significantly lower the rate or magnitude of climate change, more drastic mitigation is not necessarily coming soon in light of the current experience with the reductions required under the protocol. There is also wider appreciation of the inverse relationship between adaptation and mitigation. Greater adaptability could raise the threshold at which GHG concentrations could be deemed to have become "dangerous," thereby reducing the urgency and depth of emission reductions, at least in the short to medium term. Postponing drastic cuts in emissions could, in turn, buy additional time to research and develop more (cost-)effective methods of limiting climate change and, if the rate of technological change could be accelerated, net costs of mitigation might be reduced even if the emission limitations are eventually more stringent. Accordingly, development of socially, economically, and environmentally optimal strategies to combat climate change must necessarily consider these trade-offs and combine elements of adaptation and mitigation.[109] However, integration of mitigation and adaptation strategies continues to be hindered by several misconceptions about adaptation and mitigation, which fuel the tendency to view adaptation as a very junior partner in climate change policy.[110] This section addresses some of these misconceptions.

The first misconception is that adaptation is of little use in reducing threats to biodiversity and natural systems. However, as we have seen, there are numerous opportunities under focused adaptation to increase the productivity of land and water used to produce food, which ought to reduce pressures on terrestrial and freshwater biodiversity while also reducing hunger and advancing sustainable development. Figure 9.1 illustrates the potential of increased productivity in helping reduce habitat loss.

The second misconception is that mitigation anywhere accrues to everyone's benefit.[111] Mitigation indeed reduces impacts in all sectors and regions but unless the amount of warming is excessive, the impacts of climate change are not necessarily negative in all areas. Thus, mitigation would increase risks in some areas while reducing them in others, at least in the short to medium term before warming becomes excessive. In fact, the IPCC's Third Assessment Report suggests that below 1°C–2°C[112] the global impact of unmitigated climate change could be positive while, based on a survey of the impacts literature, Joel Smith and Sam Hitz found that marginal adverse impacts increase in almost all sectors beyond a globally averaged temperature increase of 3°C–4°C, but not necessarily below that range.[113] Thus, in the next few decades there could be losers and winners because of mitigation. And even if everyone wins, the magnitude of the prize will vary from population to population (as will the costs of mitigation). Therefore, not everyone will receive benefits commensurate with their costs expended on mitigation. However, it is more likely that with adaptation, the winners from climate change can capitalize on their gains, while losers can reduce their losses. Thus, adaptation should generally leave everyone better off relative to the post-climate change situation, but not necessarily relative to the pre-climate change situation (unless there are maladjustments).

Third, although some acknowledge that adaptation can be proactive if it is based on projected impacts, it is generally deemed to be reactive.[114] This, however, is based on a narrow view of adaptation in that it assumes an impact-first-response-later model for adaptation. Several measures identified in this chapter to advance adaptability or to broadly reduce vulnerability to existing climate-sensitive problems that might be heightened by climate change have the virtue that they transcend this model. They are anticipatory in nature, and what's more, neither their design nor their effectiveness depends on the location-specific details of any impact assessment or projection of climate change. Examples of such measures include developing malaria vaccines, developing model plants to adapt to drought or salinity, instituting property rights for water to make its use more efficient, and building the necessary expertise and capacity to deal with adverse circumstances as they arise. Such measures, which are proactive by nature, would prepare societies to better cope with adversity by expanding the tools, expertise, and capacity available for autonomous action by individuals and governmental and non-governmental organizations.[115]

The fourth misconception is that mitigation is a necessary insurance policy. Table 10.8 shows that in the short to medium term, mitigation would, as an insurance policy, carry a hefty premium if it goes beyond "no-regret" actions. However, enhancing adaptive capacity through either focused adaptation or broad development will, by addressing urgent and larger existing problems, pay handsome dividends whether or not climate changes. Thus, either adaptive strategy provides a better climate insurance policy than mitigation. A mitigation-based insurance policy would pay off only if human-induced climate change is a fact. And if climate changes, either focused adaptation or broad development will help reduce attendant risks much more contemporaneously with incurred costs than is possible through mitigation.[116]

Some have also invoked the precautionary principle as an argument for immediately going beyond no-regret actions to mitigate GHG emissions. Table 10.8, however, indicates that in the short to medium term the precautionary principle would be better-served by addressing today those urgent climate-related hurdles to sustainable development that could be heightened by future climate change, especially if reducing these hurdles leads to some near-term mitigation; advances mitigative and adaptive capacities; and is complemented by efforts (a) to implement no-regret mitigation actions and (b) to expand and improve the cost-effectiveness of mitigation options (through greater investments in science and technology) so that in the future, mitigation, if and when it becomes necessary, is more affordable and effective.[117]

Sixth, it has been argued that not expending resources on mitigation now would be unfair to future generations because they would otherwise be left with a bigger mess and a larger clean-up bill. But the major share of the benefits of mitigation are likely to occur in the longer term. It might, therefore, be more equitable, especially to present generations, to expend resources on adaptive strategies now and to defer purely mitigative actions for a few years until they can better pay for themselves, especially since future generations are likely to be wealthier, have greater access to technology and human capital, and should, therefore, be able to solve many of their problems with relatively greater ease.[118] According to the IPCC scenarios, the average GDP per capita for developing countries could rise 12- to 75-fold between 1990 and 2085, and other indicators of adaptive capacity should also rise correspondingly (see table 10.1).

Table 10.8 shows that resources expended in the short to medium term on mitigation that goes beyond no-regrets could be put to better use in reducing current risks and vulnerabilities.[119] Focused and broad development would provide benefits in both the short and the long term because the technologies, processes, and systems developed to adapt to climate-sensitive risks today will be the basis for future, more effective adaptations.

Thus, future generations would also benefit from resources spent today on adaptive strategies, particularly if these resources go toward enhancing adaptive capacity. Although we do have an obligation to future generations, that obligation is discharged if we are diligent in expanding technological options and amassing the economic, social, and human capital that they can draw on to address the problems of their day.

Seventh, it is claimed that adaptation is "unfair" because those doing the adapting are "not always responsible for causing climate change"[120] and that responsible parties should compensate those who are not. However, before assigning responsibility, one has to first determine who is "responsible" and for what. On that score, although it is possible to assign GHG emissions to nations based on where the act of burning a ton of coal, for instance, physically occurs, we should be cognizant that GHG emissions are the effluvia of civilization and all its activities. It is not only energy consumption that contributes to it, but land clearance, crop production, animal husbandry, trade, tourism, and so forth. Moreover, because of the globalized economy, which sustains today's civilization, economic activity in one country helps provide livelihoods and incomes for many inhabitants of other countries, and vice versa. In fact, a substantial portion of economic growth in developing countries is attributable to trade,[121] remittances, tourism, and direct investment from developed countries. Without such economic activities, U.S. emissions, for example, might be lower, but so would jobs and incomes elsewhere (e.g., in Bangladesh, India, Jamaica, or the Philippines).

Thus, the improvements in human well-being that have occurred in many developing countries (particularly since World War II) are partly due to the GHG-fueled economic growth in developed countries.[122]

GHG-fueled economic growth also enabled today's rich societies to invest in research and development that helped, for instance, raise crop yields worldwide, develop new and more effective medicines (e.g., for HIV/AIDS), provide aid in times of famine or other natural disasters, provide funding for reducing tuberculosis and malaria, and create and support the Internet and other items now considered by some to be global public goods.[123] Also, absent such economic growth, the sum of human capital worldwide would have been much less. Consider, for instance, the millions of non-Americans who have been cycled through universities in the United States who, then, have gone back to help in their native countries' economic and technological development. Thus, all countries indulge in or benefit from activities that lead to climate change. Hence, before determining responsibility or compensation, one should try to estimate whether direct and indirect costs of climate change will, in fact, exceed direct and indirect benefits of the activities that fuel climate change.

It might be argued that if the actions of A produce both benefits and harms to B, A should compensate B for the harms, but A cannot subtract the benefits in escaping responsibility (because, after all, B did not solicit A to undertake the actions in question). This would be disingenuous because benefits are nothing but negative harms, and they should, therefore, necessarily be subtracted in estimating net harm to B. Also, if B insists on not subtracting benefits from the compensation package, B loses his moral claim for any compensation because one can't insist on compensation on one hand and be a free rider on the other hand.

Some might also argue that one should not take indirect effects of GHG-producing activities into consideration: only direct effects should be considered. But the notion of assigning responsibility (or demanding compensation) for climate change is itself based on indirect (and inadvertent) outcomes. After all, developed countries did not emit GHG emissions with the express intent to harm anyone. There has to be symmetry in these matters.

Let's assume for the sake of argument that one can indeed estimate the fraction of global warming caused by the United States (for instance). The next step is to estimate the net harm that has been caused to, say, Bangladesh (ignoring for now issues such as whether today's generation should be liable for damages incurred by previous generations). To make such estimates, it is not sufficient just to know the direct impacts of climate change on Bangladesh, but indirect consequences of all GHG-producing activities must also be known. This involves developing answers to questions such as the following: Had there been no GHG-producing activities in developed countries, what would have been Bangladesh's level of human well-being? What would be its life expectancy (which is currently 62 years and was about 35 years in 1945) had there been no GHG-emissions in the interim? What about its hunger and malnutrition rates? How many Bangladeshis were saved in the 1960s and 1970s because of food aid from the developed countries? How much of the past increase in Bangladesh's agricultural productivity is because of higher CO_2 levels or indirectly due to efforts that were possible because developed countries were wealthy enough to support and stimulate them? If future agricultural productivity declines because of climate change, how do you subtract out past benefits from future harms? These questions are just a small sample of issues that have to be addressed before assigning responsibility to various actors for climate change.

Finally, even if one could assign responsibility for climate change, it does not follow that it would be more fair if developed nations were to expend resources on ambitious mitigation measures now based partly on the premise that doing such would reduce future climate change risks for developing nations, when the same resources would, in the short to medium term, provide greater and faster benefits to precisely those nations by reducing existing—and generally larger—climate-sensitive risks and vulnerabilities (see table 10.8).

A Climate Change Policy for the Near and Medium Term

In the near to medium term, because of the inertia of the climate system, the benefits of mitigation are relatively small compared to its costs (see tables 10.7 and 10.8). Increasing adaptive capacity, however, would improve human and environmental well-being relatively rapidly while also reducing current and future damages from climate change. Moreover, during the next few decades, the impacts of climate change on well-being are for most indicators relatively small compared to the impacts of non-climate change-related factors. Therefore, greater improvements in well-being are possible during this period through advances in adaptive capacity, either through broad advances in sustainable development or focused adaptation.

In the long term, however, the adverse impacts of climate change should grow while the impact of non-climate change-related factors may diminish. Therefore, sooner or later mitigation may be inevitable. The issue, consequently, isn't whether adaptation or mitigation should be the sole approach to dealing with climate change. Clearly, both are necessary.

The issue, in fact, is one of the magnitude and relative balance of resources expended on these strategies, as well as how that balance might shift over time to ensure that well-being is optimized. Regardless of when mitigation becomes necessary, "no-regret" actions should be taken without further ado. Such actions include, as a general rule, removal of subsidies that contribute to GHG emissions (e.g., subsidies that lead to greater use of energy, fertilizer, and land) and elimination of unnecessary barriers to the use of existing or new technologies that would advance adaptation or mitigation. And, as the case of DDT, genetically modified crops, and nuclear power indicate, such barriers indeed exist, and they make the task of responding to climate change harder.

Through 2085, climate change is projected neither to be the most important environmental problem facing the globe nor to significantly diminish human or environmental well-being. Therefore, if it takes 50 years to replace the energy infrastructure, that means we have at least until 2035 (= 2085–50) before selecting hard and fast targets for any emission reduction program that goes beyond "no-regrets."

With aggressive efforts to increase adaptive capacity, it should be possible to buy even more time. Increasing adaptive capacity, whether through pursuit of broad development (e.g., MDGs) or through focused adaptation, could raise the level at which GHG concentrations might become "dangerous." Alternatively, it might allow mitigation to be postponed. In either case, the net present value cost of mitigation would be reduced. In the interim, we should strive to make mitigation more cost-effective so that, if or when mitigation becomes necessary, net costs would be lower even if emission reductions have to be more drastic.

Accordingly, in the near to medium term, we should pursue a strategy designed to broadly advance sustainable development. Second, we should take focused adaptation measures now to reduce vulnerability to today's urgent climate-sensitive risks—hunger, malaria, water shortages, coastal flooding, extreme events, and pressures on biodiversity—that could be exacerbated by warming. Together, these efforts would improve human and environmental well-being and enhance adaptive capacity of developing countries, which, it ought to be remembered, are most vulnerable to climate change. This can be accomplished more broadly by striving to augment economic resources, human capital, and the propensity for technological change. Focused adaptation and sustainable development would also advance sequestration and enhance mitigative capacity. Third, we should ensure that "no-regret" mitigation measures are implemented while constantly expanding the universe of such measures through research and development designed to improve their cost-effectiveness. Fourth, we should continue to advance knowledge of climate change science, economics, and responses to better evaluate and to determine trade-offs and synergies between adaptation and mitigation. Finally, we should continue to monitor trends to provide advance warning—and to rearrange priorities, if necessary—should the adverse impacts of warming occur faster or threaten to be more severe or more likely than is currently projected. Together, these policies constitute an adaptive management approach to addressing climate change.

Such a climate policy would solve some of the most critical problems facing the world today and tomorrow while preparing it to address the uncertain problems of the day after tomorrow, of which climate change is but one among many.

PART D

SUSTAINING THE HUMAN ENTERPRISE

11. The Future Sustainability of Human Populations

Despite uncertainties in projections of future populations, the world's population will almost certainly grow over the next few decades. The population growth rate is quite sensitive to assumptions regarding fertility rate of women in their childbearing years and mortality rate. Historically, all else being equal, a higher fertility rate is associated with a higher mortality rate.

According to the latest analysis by the United Nations (UN), global population would increase from 6.5 billion in 2005 to between 7.7 and 10.7 billion in 2050, with its medium-growth scenario (or "medium-variant") projection at 9.1 billion.[1] Earlier, based on slightly different assumptions regarding fertility and mortality rates worldwide, which had placed the medium variant slightly lower at 8.9 billion in 2050, the UN had projected that global population levels could be between 5.1 and 16.2 billion in 2100 (with the medium variant at 9.5 billion) and from 3.2 to 24.8 billion in 2150 (with the medium variant at 9.7 billion).[2] Clearly, population projections are uncertain, but the medium-growth scenario remains the best guess.

But which of the population scenarios is more likely to transpire?

Population growth will peak earlier and at lower levels under low mortality-low fertility assumptions. As discussed in chapters 2 and 8, low infant mortality and low fertility are both consistent with greater affluence and technological change (see figures 2.5 and 8.1).

Most people, except possibly Neo-Malthusians skeptical of economic growth, hope—if not expect—that the future population, although larger, will also be richer, because wealth is generally associated with, among other things, improved human welfare as measured by life expectancy, lower mortality, less malnourishment, greater education, and so forth.[3] However, as Neo-Malthusians fear, greater wealth is also likely to increase the per capita demand for food, water, energy, and material goods. But if that is indeed the case, will there be sufficient food and natural resources to meet humanity's future demands? And will the scale of activities undertaken to meet those demands be environmentally sustainable?

With respect to the scarcity issue, some, and not only Cornucopians, argue that the long-term declines in real worldwide prices of food, energy, and minerals (due to technological progress) that we have seen during the past two centuries—which, moreover, occurred during a period of unprecedented increases in demand—belie the notion of impending shortages.[4] More to the point, several recent analyses indicate that there is enough land, energy, and minerals provided technological change continues.[5] However, there is at least one natural resource—water—for which maintaining adequate supplies could be problematic.[6] But perhaps the most critical issue is whether the global economic enterprise necessary to meet the needs and wants of a larger and richer population is sustainable given the cumulative effects of various environmental problems (e.g., air and water pollution, habitat loss, human appropriation of land and water, and climate change).

The following briefly addresses global prospects with respect to the most critical resource and environmental problems for the foreseeable future. In the previous chapter, we looked at the impacts of climate change in the 2085–2100 time frame, because those estimates were readily available and for the sake of argument rather than because those impact estimates were necessarily credible. However, as the various estimates of future population indicate, the further out we go, the greater the uncertainties, and the more the results are driven by the underlying assumptions. Similar problems also arise with respect to projections of economic activity. Thus, I will assume, somewhat optimistically, that 2050 (or so) is as far as we can foresee into the future.

However, before discussing specific natural resource and environmental problems, it is useful to first establish priorities so we know which problems should be tackled before others.

Priorities in the Short to Medium Term

Table 11.1 provides a global ranking of 14 health risk factors associated with the use and management of natural resources and the environment based on estimates of lost disability-adjusted life years (DALYs) attributed to these factors in the *World Health Report 2002* (WHR 2002).[7] These risk factors, which in 2000 accounted for

Table 11.1

PRIORITY RANKING OF FOOD, NUTRITION, AND ENVIRONMENTAL RISK FACTORS BASED ON
LOST DALYs FOR 2000

Risk factors	Ranking	Attributable mortality in thousands	(%)	DALYs Lost in thousands	(%)
Underweight (insufficient food)	1	3,748	6.7	137,801	9.48
Blood pressure (unhealthy foods)	2	7,141	12.8	64,270	4.42
Unsafe water, sanitation, and hygiene	3	1,730	3.1	54,158	3.73
Malaria (see note, below)		1,121	2.0	42,080	2.89
Cholesterol (unhealthy foods)	4	4,415	7.9	40,437	2.78
Indoor smoke from solid fuels	5	1,619	2.9	38,539	2.65
Iron deficiency (malnutrition)	6	841	1.5	35,057	2.41
Overweight (unhealthy or too much food)	7	2,591	4.6	33,415	2.30
Zinc deficiency (malnutrition)	8	789	1.4	28,034	1.93
Low fruit and vegetable intake	9	2,726	4.9	26,662	1.83
Vitamin A deficiency (malnutrition)	10	778	1.4	26,638	1.83
Lead exposure (environmental)	11	234	0.4	12,926	0.89

(continued on next page)

355

Table 11.1

PRIORITY RANKING OF FOOD, NUTRITION, AND ENVIRONMENTAL RISK FACTORS BASED ON
LOST DALYS FOR 2000 *(continued)*

Risk factors	Ranking	Attributable mortality		DALYs Lost	
		in thousands	(%)	in thousands	(%)
Urban air pollution (environmental)	12	799	1.4	7,865	0.54
Climate change (environmental)	13	154	0.3	5,517	0.38
Subtotal (see note below)		27,566	49.42	511,319	35.18
Total in 2000 from all causes		55,776		1,453,617	

NOTE: Except for malaria, the deaths (and lost DALYs) for the various risk factors listed in the table are calculated by reassigning deaths (and lost DALYs) from immediate causes of death to the listed risk factors. Under this approach, deaths and lost DALYs due to malaria were redistributed into the totals for climate change and for underweight, zinc, and Vitamin A deficiencies. Because of that, the subtotal does not include the numbers for malaria. By itself, malaria would have been ranked at least fourth.

SOURCE: WHO, *World Health Report 2002* (Geneva: WHO, 2002), Annexes 2, 3, 11, 12, 14–16.

about 50 percent of mortality and 35 percent of the lost DALYs world-wide, include those associated with food, nutrition, water, air pollution, and other environmental factors.

The table also includes the estimates for deaths and lost DALYs attributed to human-induced climate change in the WHR 2002 report although, as noted in chapter 6, these figures are suspect. The major problem with these numbers is that a significant portion of the mortality and lost DALYs due to real and well-established causes (such as malaria, dengue, diarrhea, flooding, and malnutrition) have apparently been reassigned to climate change on the unsubstantiated hypothesis that there were, in 2000, excess deaths and disease from malaria, dengue, malnutrition, and so forth in which the underlying cause was, in fact, climate change. Although it might be scientifically justified for reassigning a portion of deaths and disease due to diarrhea to unsafe water and poor sanitation, for instance, the reassignments to climate change require a scientific leap of faith. There is no showing that climate change, in general, or human-induced climate change, in particular, has, in fact, caused excess death or disease from malaria, dengue, flooding, or malnourishment. One consequence of this unsubstantiated approach is that malaria, for instance, does not appear on WHR 2002's tables for mortality and lost DALYs "attributable" to various risk factors. This could lead some readers to mistakenly conclude that climate change, for instance, deserves higher priority than risks (such as malaria) that are not listed in the table. This could, as discussed in the previous chapter, lead to serious misallocation of resources. Nevertheless, despite the shortcomings of the WHR 2002 approach, it provides some useful information. So as not to lose sight of malaria or its importance relative to other risk factors, table 11.1 also contains entries for malaria.

Of the 14 food, nutrition, and environmental risk factors listed in table 11.1, hunger (underweight) should be accorded the highest priority, followed by blood pressure; unsafe water, sanitation, and hygiene; malaria; and cholesterol, to round out the top five. The bottom five, in terms of priority, should be low intake of fruits and vegetables, vitamin A deficiency, lead exposure, urban air pollution, and, at the very bottom, climate change.

Table 11.2 presents the same information aggregated into five groups of risk factors. In order of priority, these risk groups are

Table 11.2
PRIORITY RANKING BY FOOD, NUTRITION, AND ENVIRONMENTAL RISK GROUPS BASED ON LOST DALYS FOR 2000

	Mortality		DALYs Lost	
	in 1,000	(%)	in 1,000	(%)
Childhood and Maternal Undernutrition				
Underweight	3,748	6.72	137,801	9.48
Micronutrient deficiencies (iron, zinc, and Vitamin A)	2,408	4.32	89,729	6.17
Subtotal	**6,156**	**11.04**	**227,530**	**15.65**
Other Diet-Related Risks				
Diseases of affluence (blood pressure, cholesterol, and obesity)	14,147	25.36	138,122	9.5
Low fruit and vegetable intake	2,726	4.89	26,662	1.83
Subtotal	**16,873**	**30.25**	**164,784**	**11.33**
Poverty-Driven Environmental Risks				
Unsafe water, sanitation, and hygiene	1,730	3.10	54,158	3.73
Malaria (see note, below)	1,121	2.01	42,080	2.89
Indoor smoke from solid fuels	1,619	2.90	38,539	2.65
Subtotal	**3,349**	**6.00**	**92,697**	**6.38**
Other Environmental Risks				
Urban air pollution and lead exposure	1,033	1.85	20,791	1.43
Climate Change	**154**	**0.28**	**5,517**	**0.38**
Sum of the Above	**27,565**	**49.42**	**511,319**	**35.17**
Total from All Causes	*55,775*	*100*	*1,453,617*	*100*

NOTE: Except for malaria, the deaths (and lost DALYs) for the various risk factors listed in the table are calculated by reassigning deaths (and lost DALYs) from immediate causes of death to the listed risk factors. Under this approach, deaths and lost DALYs due to malaria were redistributed into the totals for climate change and for underweight, zinc, and Vitamin A deficiencies. Because of that, the sums do not include the numbers for malaria. By itself, malaria would have been ranked at least fourth or fifth (see table 11.1).

SOURCE: WHO, *World Health Report 2002* (Geneva: WHO, 2002), Annexes 2, 3, 11, 12, 14–16.

childhood and maternal undernutrition (i.e., insufficient food and micronutrient deficiencies); other diet-related risks (i.e., diseases of affluence—blood pressure, cholesterol, obesity risks—and low fruit and vegetable intake); poverty-related environmental risks (i.e., unsafe water, sanitation, and hygiene; malaria; and indoor air pollution); other environmental risks (i.e., lead exposure and urban air pollution); and, finally, climate change.

Tables 11.1 and 11.2 indicate that worldwide, the highest priority among *natural resource and environmental issues* should be to boost the quantity and quality of food available to consumers at large. Following that, in order of priority, are access to safe water and sanitation, malaria, indoor air pollution, urban air quality, and, finally, climate change, if the WHR 2002's estimates are to be believed.

The priority list not only helps to identify the areas that scarce fiscal and human resources should be focused on, but it can also help deal with trade-offs involving the various risk factors. For example, actions or policies that would increase the quantity and quality of food should be favored, in general, as a rebuttable presumption, even if that might create additional environmental problems with respect to climate change, for instance. Exceptions should, of course, be made if aggregate climate change-related risks can be reduced more cost-effectively than can food-related risks. But, as we saw in the previous chapter, that is unlikely to be the case through the foreseeable future.

Achieving Food and Nutrition Security while Conserving Biodiversity

Agriculture on Land

The major source of tension in meeting both the needs of human beings and those of the rest of nature is in resolving the competing demands for land to ensure that human beings have adequate quantity (and quality) of food while simultaneously conserving biodiversity.

The amount of cropland is one of the most critical indicators for habitat loss and the threat to biological diversity. At the same time, cropland is essential for agricultural production. However, figure 8.4 shows that despite unprecedented population growth in the 20th century, the increase in global cropland has almost come to a halt during the past few decades. This suggests that the globe may be on the verge of an environmental transition for this particular environmental indicator. A closer examination indicates differences in trends between various groups of countries, depending on their economic and demographic circumstances. The richest countries (i.e., the countries that belong to the Organisation for Economic Co-operation and Development), which also have relatively low population growth rates, have stabilized their cropland area. Between 1980 and 2003, it declined slightly (about 3.5 percent) from 462 million hectares (Mha) to 446 Mha.[8] Cropland in developing countries, however, increased by 17.7 percent from 768 Mha to 904 Mha over the same period. Cropland has also declined in the former Soviet Union and Eastern Europe, from 280 Mha to 251 Mha (or 10.5 percent), perhaps because subsidies for overuse were reduced during a period when demand dropped because of deteriorating economic circumstances. Although reductions in subsidies should be encouraged because they are detrimental both economically and environmentally,[9] needless to say, having the economy go in reverse is not a recommended strategy for ensuring that cropland goes past its environmental transition. That, as we have seen, can be severely detrimental to public health and human well-being and can tear the social fabric apart.

To increase the likelihood of effecting an environmental transition for land conversion while also increasing food production, humanity has to be able to take advantage of existing-but-underused technologies and to stimulate the development of new technologies. As chapter 9 shows, biotechnology is critical to ensuring that humanity meets the demand for food, fiber, and timber while reducing its demand on land (and water) and, at the same time, to containing the myriad other impacts associated with both ancient and modern agriculture, namely, soil erosion, water diversions, release of excess nutrients and pesticides into the environment, and emissions of various greenhouse gases into the atmosphere.

However, success depends on more than the mere existence of technology or, equally important, the willingness to use that technology. It will also depend, in large part, on the ability of developing nations to afford and operate the necessary technologies. In other words, success will depend on economic and human resources.

It is estimated that developing countries will need substantial agriculture-related investments.[10] The Food and Agriculture Organization (FAO) suggests that developed countries should contribute substantially to such investments.[11] But, realistically, most of these amounts will have to come through internal economic growth, probably supplemented by private capital flows from overseas. Accordingly, developing countries ought to provide a more hospitable climate for investments from abroad, which should include the relaxation of controls over capital flows. In particular, they need to convince investors that they will respect property rights and will allow profits to be repatriated.

There is yet another reason why trade in goods, capital, and intellectual properties will be even more important for attaining future food security in the developing world than it is today. Even if agriculture in developing countries can obtain investments of the magnitude noted earlier, their food and crop imports are expected to increase by 2050 because their rapid growth in demand is expected to outpace increases in productivity in the food and agricultural sectors. Climate change could further increase their food deficits.[12] But to finance food imports, developing countries will need to increase exports from, and increase economic growth in, nonagricultural sectors.[13]

Finally, just as increasing agricultural productivity would reduce the future amount of land conversion and habitat loss to cropland, so would increasing the productivity of forestry reduce the amount of forests harvested for timber and other products. And for forestry too, there are numerous existing and potential opportunities to increase efficiency.[14] Notably, 35 percent of the world's roundwood production comes from the 5 percent of global forests that are in plantations.[15] This lends credence to the contention that one method of conserving natural forests, and their biodiversity, might be to practice more intensive forestry on a small share of global forests.[16]

Agricultural Water Withdrawals and Consumption

The second source of tension in reconciling the food and nutrition needs of human beings and the rest of nature is agriculture's water demand. Unlike agricultural land use worldwide, agricultural water withdrawals and consumption continue to grow. In fact, many analysts have suggested that water, rather than land, could be the major constraint on future food production, which,[17] of course, would be bad news for both human beings and the rest of nature. However, because water is becoming oversubscribed and the economic and social costs of increasing its use have increased, the rates of growth of agricultural water withdrawals and consumption have slowed down substantially. As a result, withdrawals and consumption have declined on a per capita basis (see figures 8.4 and 8.5). This suggests that agricultural water use and consumption could, like cropland, also peak and go past their environmental transitions provided that appropriate policies are put in place.

One major reason for the continuing growth in agricultural water use is that water is generally not treated as an economic commodity. Remedying that requires policies to develop and assign property rights to water, to allow water to be priced, to remove barriers to water trading, and to eliminate subsidies to favored political groups.[18] Such policies would increase incentives for developing and using "hardware" and "software" options for recycling, reusing, and conserving scarce water supplies. Also, biotechnology and precision agriculture would help reduce water use in agriculture. Finally, if there is a real scarcity, prices would adjust accordingly, allowing desalination of ocean water, for instance, to become an economic proposition. Several new desalination technologies are now on the horizon. The cost of one such technology, reverse osmosis—a process in which water molecules under pressure pass through a semipermeable membrane while salt molecules do not—dropped by over an order of magnitude in the past quarter-century.[19] Current costs are estimated to be around $1.50 per 1,000 gallons for desalinating brackish water and $2.50–$3.00 per 1,000 gallons for seawater.[20] However, the energy (and, therefore, environmental) costs of desalination are quite substantial. Currently, although some form of desalination occurs in more than 120 countries, desalination is most prevalent in a number of oil producing countries that have easy access to fossil fuels combined with an acute need for fresh water. New technologies using solar, wave, or tidal power may eventually supplant fossil fuels as the preferred energy source in desalination plants, which would reduce their environmental impacts.[21]

Because, globally, agriculture is responsible for 66 percent of water withdrawals and 85 percent of water consumption, small increases in the efficiency of agricultural water use would free up water not only for other human uses (e.g., hygiene, drinking, and industrial uses) but also for the rest of nature. That is, it would help reduce current and future water stress and provide the world a necessary cushion in the event climate changes for whatever reason.

Marine Fisheries and Aquaculture

Increasing the productivity of terrestrial agriculture would also enhance the productivity and sustainability of fisheries whether they are located inland, on the coasts, or even further offshore in the oceans. Thus, increases in agricultural productivity could also benefit fisheries indirectly by reducing the erosion of soil and the usage of pesticides and fertilizers, much of which runs off into streams, rivers, and, finally, the oceans.

Agricultural biotechnology, in particular, could be especially beneficial for fisheries because, as we saw in chapter 9, bioengineered crops would help reduce the following:

- Soil erosion, through a general increase in agricultural productivity, as well as by facilitating no-till agriculture through the use of GM crops or herbicide-tolerant crops, such as Roundup Ready.
- Release of nutrients, by increasing the ability of plants to use phosphorus and nitrogen from the soil.
- Agricultural water use, through the development of drought-tolerant crops or crops with lower water demand.
- Phosphorus in animal waste, which would diminish its runoff into streams, lakes, and other water bodies. It would also reduce the need for inorganic phosphorus supplements in feed.
- Usage of synthetic pesticides and their release into the environment, including the oceans.

Just as terrestrial agriculture can affect the productivity of aquatic ecosystems, whether these are in fresh, brackish, or salt waters, so does the productivity of aquatic ecosystems affect agriculture on land. In fact, if more of humankind's food needs could be met from aquatic ecosystems, that would reduce pressure on the land.

Remarkably, although land comprises only 29 percent of the earth's surface area, it provides 99.0 percent of humankind's energy needs (i.e., caloric intake) and 95.5 percent of protein supplies (including 84.6 percent of animal protein).[22] Not only are aquatic ecosystems contributing a disproportionately small share of humanity's food needs, but also there is some concern that it might decline in the future. Specifically, although 24 percent of marine capture fisheries are underexploited or moderately exploited, 52 percent are fully exploited, 16 percent are overexploited, while 7 percent are depleted and 1 percent are recovering from depletion.[23] In other words, if there is an environmental transition curve for marine fisheries, we are currently on the wrong side (i.e., on the upward slope).

Why is the contribution of aquatic ecosystems to human food intake so low, and why might it diminish further? One reason is that, by and large, human beings have treated the ocean's bounty as our hunter-gatherer forebears treated the land's.[24] This hunter-gatherer mentality creates havoc, particularly when modern technology is pressed into service for harvesting, but not for increasing the population of the harvested species.[25] The demise or near-demise of species such as the beaver, American buffalo, and various whale species are cases in point. In fact, only after deliberate and more intensive management of the land (i.e., agriculture) started to replace hunting and gathering was it possible for the earth's human-carrying capacity to go from a few million to hundreds of million.[26] Today, the earth, mainly through intensive land-based agriculture, supports more than 6.5 billion people.

In order to allow humankind to coexist with the rest of nature, the realm of conscious and more intensive management may have to be expanded to at least a portion of its waters. On this score, it is encouraging to note the rapid increase in aquaculture worldwide. Although the net output of capture fisheries has been fluctuating since the early 1990s in the 90–95 million tonnes range, aquaculture's output has been climbing steadily since at least 1970. Between 1990 and 2003, aquaculture's share of the world's fish product has more than doubled from 13 percent to 32 percent.[27] This contrast might be partly explained by the fact that some degree of property rights exist for the latter but not the former because it is easier to establish, maintain, and enforce such rights on land than in water. This might also contribute to the fact that 60 percent of the world's aquaculture is in inland, rather than in marine, areas.[28] In fact, in inland areas, aquaculture provides 2.8 times as much fish as do capture fisheries.[29]

Another factor is that aquaculture is necessitated by the increasing pressures on agricultural demand for land and water resources. In fact, growth in aquaculture is led by some of the world's most populous and crowded nations providing some justification for the Boserupian hypothesis that increased pressure on natural resources due to population growth is an incentive for technological change. In 2002, China was responsible for 69.8 percent of the world's aquaculture production; another 12.7 percent came from Bangladesh, India, Indonesia, Thailand, and Vietnam.[30]

Further increases in aquaculture will depend on developing new or improved technologies to enhance productivity and on the ability to obtain additional inputs, including capital and human resources. All these can be facilitated by assigning property rights to fishery resources.[31] Assigning such property rights will also provide greater legal standing—and leverage—to the owners of those resources to insist on land management and use practices that might otherwise degrade marine productivity.

Rosamond Naylor and others note that farming some fish species ought to relieve pressures on ocean fisheries while farming others might increase them.[32] First, farmed fish have to be fed. This means that some of the oceans' and rivers' natural bounty has to be diverted to farmed species. The higher the farmed fish feeds on the food chain and the greater their feed requirements from other aquatic species, the greater the likelihood that farmed fish might displace wild varieties. Second, the extent and nature of marine and coastal habitat modification undertaken to prepare for aquaculture will affect the productivity of wild species. For example, in Southeast Asia, often mangrove forests have been cleared prior to shrimp farming. Not only does this affect species dependent on those forests, but such habitat clearance adds to sediment transported to adjacent coral reefs. Moreover, farms for fish, like their terrestrial counterparts, generate waste that can pollute the water and affect other species.[33] Thus, if current practices do not change, capture fisheries' share of the global food supply might decline, and only a portion of that decline might be restored by the increase in aquaculture. In addition, there is the concern that farmed fish might escape and interbreed with the wild stock and spread pathogens, thereby increasing pressure on an already dwindling wild population.[34]

However, James Tidwell and Geoff Allen note that eschewing aquaculture would only put greater pressure on wild stocks.[35] They suggest that it is more efficient to produce fish protein through aquaculture than through harvesting wild stock, and this efficiency should improve further because the economic incentives for fish farmers to reduce feed costs should stimulate efforts to replace relatively expensive fishmeal with lower cost plant-based feed formulations. According to their analysis, the ecological threat of aquaculture is lower than the alternative of continuing to supply the fish protein from wild capture. Moreover, one should not overlook the benefits for human beings of consuming fish protein in lieu of other forms of protein.

The analysis of Naylor and others is deficient in another, very significant respect. It ignores that there is a trade-off such that increasing fish production in the water might decrease meat production on land because the former might substitute for the latter. In such a circumstance, additional reliance on aquaculture should be offset by lower pressures on wildlands.

Moreover, the relatively low productivity of the oceans not only increases pressures on land to meet the demands humanity has for food, but it also limits the ocean's potential to serve as a greenhouse sink. Some research indicates that phytoplankton production in the oceans could be boosted through iron fertilization.[36] The type of phytoplankton that is stimulated by these iron amendments depends on the silicon content of the waters. If the waters are not silicon-limited, then diatoms—phytoplankton enclosed in silica shells—will be formed, which then can sink, thereby helping remove carbon from the ocean surface to the deep sea. If the waters are silicon-limited, however, non-siliceous phytoplankton species will be formed, which would be less efficient in sequestering carbon into the ocean, although presumably this could be remedied by adding silicic acid to the waters.[37] Another experiment in the open ocean indicated that 1 atom of iron may be able to sequester between 10,000 and 100,000 atoms of carbon.[38]

These experiments suggest that ocean fertilization by an appropriate mix of nutrients could not only enhance carbon sequestration in the oceans, but in theory, it could also increase the ability of oceans to support a more abundant fish population and to help meet global food demand. Other studies indicate, however, that iron fertilization might, by increasing phytoplankton, stimulate production of organic chemicals produced by these organisms (e.g., isoprene), which could lead to the formation of ozone at ground levels, and of methyl bromide, which could reduce stratospheric ozone.[39] This sets up an interesting exercise in risk-risk analysis: Would this increase the ultraviolet radiation incident at the earth's surface, or would it be a decrease? What would be the best course of action given the combined effects of changes in ultraviolet and the rate and magnitude of global warming in the context of the human demand for food and land to produce that food? Clearly, this is something that needs additional research.

In summary, to relieve the pressure on the land, the productivity of oceans and the intensity of its use might have to increase. Perhaps if humanity spends more time in the water, fewer footprints will be left on the land.[40] But, of course, even that would have some environmental impacts.

Air and Water Pollution

Based on experience to date, which is consistent with the environmental transition hypothesis, local- and regional-scale problems of air and water pollution (including access to better sanitation and safe water) will probably be of diminishing importance for countries that will be in their post-industrial phase. In those countries that are developing today, such pollution may or may not be lower depending on how far along they are in their individual environmental transitions for the various pollutants.[41] The wealthier they become, the more likely that they will reverse their air and water pollution problems, particularly if other easier-to-solve risks, such as malaria and hunger (where they are prevalent), are addressed and technological change continues to lower pollution control costs and to increase the efficiency of energy, land, water, and other natural resource use. In general, one should expect that, in a rational world, developing countries would learn from the experience of today's rich countries and improve upon the path taken by the latter on their way to advancing their well-being. Accordingly, it ought to be expected that, all else being equal, the developing countries would do the following:

- Focus initially on public health-related pollution problems before addressing other pollution impacts.
- Adapt control technologies and management approaches developed by the richer countries to their specific circumstances.

- Commence addressing their pollution problems at lower levels of economic development compared to the experience of the currently developed countries unless, of course, new information shows that the latter had overemphasized the benefits or underestimated the costs of meeting some control targets.
- Encourage advances in technology, so that, all else being equal, their environmental transitions would occur at lower levels of income, and peak at lower levels of environmental impact, compared to the countries that developed earlier.

And, in fact, historical experience confirms these expectations. For example, we saw in chapter 6 that today's developing countries were attacking their lead-in-gasoline problems at much earlier levels of economic development. Similarly, figures 6.13 and 6.14 show that with the passage of time access to safe water and sanitation has increased for any given level of economic development.

With respect to air and water pollution, as indicated by table 11.2, the first order of business for developing countries should be to continue to improve basic hygiene and access to safe water and sanitation because these three factors are still the major causes of easily preventable deaths and diseases in the developing countries. According to the World Health Organization (WHO), despite past improvements, each year about 1.8 million people, mostly children in the developing world, die annually from diarrhea.[42] The next environmental priority should be to reduce indoor air pollution from the burning of coal, wood, and dung in households, which is estimated to kill about 1.6 million annually, mostly in the developing world.[43] U.S. experience suggests that most households will suspend using solid fuels indoors more or less voluntarily as the population grows more affluent and cleaner substitutes become available.[44] Other options are to use more efficient heaters and cookers. Energy and environmental policies should be structured so as not to hinder the movement to cleaner fuels.

As historical experience has shown, economic growth will also hasten these improvements, as well as improvements in outdoor air quality, which should be the next priority.

Other public health problems could be addressed by siting (to the extent practicable without resorting to a command-and-control economy) pollution sources in less populated areas (which would help bring jobs to some rural areas and help reduce population pressures on some of the largest urban areas), using emissions trading (or bubble) strategies as opposed to stack-by-stack or pipe-by-pipe regulations, possibly taxing pollutants rather than income, and more fully using sink characteristics of the atmosphere and waters.

Adaptive Management of the Climate Change Problem

Some scientists and laymen alike have claimed that global warming is among the most important environmental challenge facing the globe. Based partly on this premise, they have invoked the precautionary principle to justify a policy of aggressively controlling greenhouse gas emissions beyond what would be achieved through the normal process of technological change and reductions in subsidies. However, as we saw in chapter 10, projections of the impacts of climate change indicate that, for the next several decades, climate change is unlikely to rival other environmental and public health and safety problems in either magnitude or urgency unless these other problems are reduced substantially.

Therefore, it would be more precautionary to focus on these larger problems facing the globe, which also happen to be more urgent today.

Nevertheless, climate change could arguably be the proverbial last straw, particularly for natural ecosystems and biodiversity. But given the magnitude of the impacts of climate change compared to other environmental problems, it may be futile to intercept that last straw if, as seems more likely, the cumulative load proves to be unsustainable well before that last straw drops. More important, it is possible to address climate change-related issues effectively while at the same time one deals with other, higher priority issues listed in table 11.2, such as hunger, malnutrition, other diet-related diseases, unsafe water, poor sanitation, malaria, and indoor and outdoor pollution. In addition, as table 10.8 shows, these larger and more urgent problems can be solved more economically than can reducing climate change (which is tantamount to reducing the size of the last straw).

Beyond focusing only on the last straw, there are other strategies that would also reduce the camel's burden. First, one could reduce the cumulative burden by removing or reducing some of the other straws weighing on the camel's back. Second, the camel's back could be strengthened, so that it can bear a heavier burden. Third, the total burden could be shared among several camels.

The first strategy—equivalent to the focused adaptation strategy outlined in the previous chapter—calls for measures to solve current problems that are urgent and may be exacerbated by climate change by reducing vulnerability to those problems. Hunger, malaria, water shortage, and extreme weather events all fall into this category. For instance, additional research into the causes, prevention, and treatment of malaria and other climate-sensitive diseases will help the world cope with current as well as future climate change-related problems. Some of these measures are also capable of addressing multiple problems, while also contributing to reductions in greenhouse gas emissions. Increasing agricultural and forest productivity with respect to land would, in addition to reducing hunger and helping meet human needs for fiber and timber, also limit—if not reverse—habitat loss and fragmentation, as well as reduce soil erosion. These reductions would, in turn, reduce threats to biological diversity, conserve carbon sources and sinks, and improve water quality in freshwater and marine systems. Similarly, creating institutions to allow water to be managed as an economic resource would likewise reduce pressure on water resources.

The second strategy—strengthening the camel's back—would address the root causes as to why the camel's back may not be strong enough to bear a heavy load, namely, lack of sufficient economic resources, human and social capital, and technological prowess. This calls for strengthening the institutions that support the forces that undergird economic growth, development of human capital, and the propensity for technological change. This is equivalent to the broad development strategy outlined in chapter 10, which would advance sustainable development. Strengthening these institutions would help perpetuate, if not set in motion, the virtuous cycle of progress that reduces society's vulnerability to adversity in general whether it is hunger, malnutrition, lack of access to safe water, malaria, or to climate change. It is also integral to moving society through its environmental transitions. Specifically, economic growth provides the means for creating, affording, and implementing cleaner, more productive technologies. In turn, technological change reinforces economic growth. Moreover, economic growth creates conditions conducive to a long-term reduction in population growth rates, which, in turn, will help limit greenhouse gas emissions.

The third strategy—sharing the burden—consists of unsubsidized trade. Because it facilitates movement of food from surplus to deficit areas, it is critical to global food security. Such trade also discourages exploitation of marginal land resources, helps disseminate new technologies, and boosts economic growth, which, in turn, reinforces the first two strategies.[45] Trade also advances economic growth and aids in the diffusion of technology.

Completing these three approaches is a strategy that would implement no-regret measures today to reduce greenhouse gas emissions, while striving to expand the universe of such no-regret options in the future through research and development to improve the cost-effectiveness of measures that would reduce greenhouse gas concentrations. Currently available no-regret actions include reducing, if not eliminating, inappropriate subsidies for energy and land use that would otherwise increase greenhouse gas emissions. They also include measures such as those outlined earlier that would address current urgent problems, while providing benefits in terms of mitigation, for example, increasing the efficiency of agricultural land use or agricultural nitrogen use. The latter, for example, would not only reduce water pollution but also contain nitrous oxide emissions, a potent greenhouse gas.

The strategies should be supplemented by a program to monitor trends with respect to climate change and, more important, its impacts. Such a program would help rearrange priorities between and within the various strategies, as necessary. It could, for instance, help direct resources toward interventions designed to manage a specific climate-sensitive disease in one area, improve yields for a particular crop in another, or provide more intensive efforts to reduce climate change to avoid widespread dangerous impacts. In combination, these strategies provide a framework for adaptive management of the climate change problem.

These strategies, used in tandem, would solve current problems, provide immediate and substantial benefits to humanity, limit greenhouse gas emissions, and reduce vulnerability and increase adaptability to climate and other environmental changes. Moreover, these strategies would provide benefits regardless of how rapidly climate change occurs, or whether it is due to natural, rather than human-made, emissions of greenhouse gases. They would also advance society's mitigative capacity, not only by specifically advancing the state of mitigation technology, but also by generally advancing access to economic resources and human and social capital, which are necessary to obtain and operate mitigation technologies if and when that becomes necessary, as well as for accelerating innovation in general.

In addition, some climate change is inevitable, even if one could wave a magic wand and freeze greenhouse gas concentrations at today's levels immediately. Therefore, like it or not, humanity will have to adapt. In fact, the issue is not whether we will adapt but, rather, how well—or how poorly—we will adapt. And the strategies outlined would help humanity adapt well.

Equally important, by increasing adaptability, the strategies outlined would also raise the level at which atmospheric greenhouse gas concentrations may become, to use the terminology of the Framework Convention on Climate Change, "dangerous." This would give humanity and the rest of nature more breathing room and reduce the eventual costs of controlling greenhouse gas emissions.[46] In fact, there can be no optimal approach to addressing climate change that does not explicitly incorporate the strategies outlined here.

12. Extending the Limits: The Role of Economic Development, Technological Change, and Free Trade

> "[Malthus'] worry has not been dispelled; demographers continue to speculate about the rapid increase of people as hygiene and medication recklessly prolong life."
>
> — Jacques Barzun, *From Dawn to Decadence*,
> (New York: Harper Collins, 2000) p. 525.

But for the advances in hygiene and medicine that the distinguished sociologist Barzun deplores, he would probably have been dead long before those words, written when he was 93 years old, appeared in print.

Despite "recklessly" increasing its numbers during the past millennium, humanity has never been better fed, healthier, or longer lived. The state of humanity has never been better.

Since Malthus wrote his *Essay on Population* two centuries ago, the average person's life span has more than doubled. He is better educated and wealthier. She is freer to choose her rulers and express her views. He is more likely to live under the rule of law and is less fearful of being arbitrarily deprived of life, limb, freedom, property, wealth, and other basic human rights. Her professional, social, and physical mobility, while still limited in many places, is less likely to be circumscribed by caste, class, location, or other accidents of birth. Not only is work less physically demanding, he works fewer hours, earns more, and—not least—has more leisure time at his disposal.

These advances in the state of humanity were accompanied by global industrialization and tremendous increases in material and energy consumption. Remarkably, the progress in human well-being occurred despite the catastrophes that Neo-Malthusians, enamored with the IPAT identity (see chapter 1), have often warned would befall humanity if population, affluence, and consumption of materials, chemicals, energy, and other natural resources continued to increase.

The proximate causes for the improvements in the human condition—and for the failure of the Neo-Malthusian specters from materializing—are the forces of technological change and economic growth, supplemented by trade in products, ideas, and technologies associated with those forces. In fact, these overall improvements in human well-being contradict the view advanced by Jared Diamond, for example, that new technology creates more problems than it solves because it replaces old problems with new, more difficult problems.[1] A more accurate characterization of new technology is that it generally replaces imperfect existing technologies with improved, but still-less-than-perfect technologies.

Virtually every indicator of human welfare also improves with wealth, as do the environmental indicators that we know to have the greatest bearing on public health. People in richer countries have higher access to food supplies, lower levels of undernourishment, greater access to safe water and sanitation, lower infant and maternal mortality rates, and higher life expectancies. They also have higher levels of education and lower levels of child labor.

In the countries that were among the first to develop, such as England and the United States, human well-being arguably worsened initially because of urbanization. And for a long period of time, well-being in their urban areas indeed lagged that in rural areas. But once food supplies per capita began to improve and the importance of basic hygiene, safe water, sanitation, and the germ theory were recognized, the broad indicators of human well-being commenced a long-term improvement that continues to this day.

In the United States, this upward march has been in progress at least since the 1880s. Occasionally, this march might have faltered. For example, U.S. life expectancy declined from 1915 to 1918 and from 1933 to 1938.[2] But these short-lived downturns cannot be attributed to economic growth or to increases in fuel, minerals, and chemical use and any associated pollution, because all these "factors" rose before, during, and after those periods.

During the 20th century, the U.S. population grew 3.7-fold and gross domestic product (GDP) per capita grew 8.1-fold; consumption

Figure 12.1
GROWTH IN CO$_2$ EMISSIONS AND METAL CONSUMPTION, POPULATION, AFFLUENCE (GDP/CAPITA), AND LIFE EXPECTANCY, UNITED STATES, 1900–2000

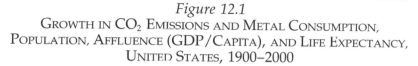

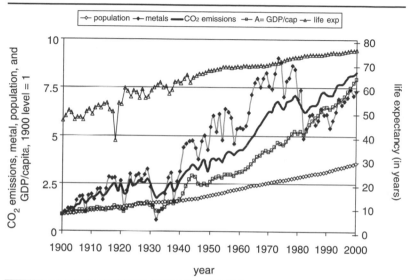

year

SOURCES: Grecia Matos, *Total U.S. Material Consumption, 1900–2000* (Washington, DC: USGS, 2005); USBOC, *Historical Statistics of the United States, Colonial Times to 1970* (Washington, DC: GPO, 1975); USBOC, *Historical National Population Estimates, 1900 to 1999*, www.census.gov/popest/archives/pre-1980 (accessed August 14, 2005); USBOC, *Statistical Abstract of the United States 2006* (Washington, DC: GPO, 2006); Bureau of Economic Affairs, *National Income and Products Accounts*, table 1.1.6, www.bea.gov/bea/dn/nipawcb/SelectTable.asp?Popular = Y (accessed August 13, 2005); Gregg Marland, T. J. Boden, and R. J. Andres, *National CO$_2$ Emissions from Fossil-Fuel Burning, Cement Manufacture, and Gas Flaring: 1751–2002* (Oak Ridge, TN: Carbon Dioxide Information Analysis Center, Oak Ridge National Laboratory, 2005), http://cdiac.esd.ornl.gov/ftp/trends/emissions/usa.dat (accessed December 21, 2005); National Center for Health Statistics, *Health, United States, 2004 with Chartbook on Trends in the Health of Americans with Special Feature on Drugs* (Hyattsville, MD: Centers for Disease Control and Prevention, 2004), table 27.

grew 3.4-fold for forestry products, 3.3-fold for coal, 10.3-fold for energy, 7.5-fold for metals, 26.5-fold for all materials, and 101.0-fold for nonfuel organic chemicals; and CO$_2$ emissions increased 8.5-fold (see figures 12.1 and 12.2).[3] Despite these increases in population,

Figure 12.2
CONSUMPTION OF ORGANIC CHEMICALS AND TOTAL MATERIALS,
CO_2 EMISSIONS AND LIFE EXPECTANCY, UNITED STATES,
1900–2000

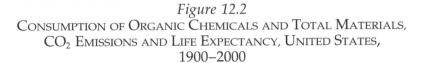
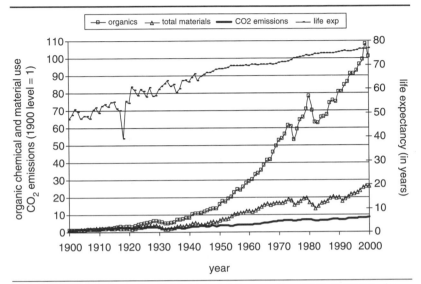

year

SOURCES: Grecia Matos, *Total U.S. Material Consumption, 1900–2000* (Washington, DC: USGS, 2005); USBOC, *Historical Statistics of the United States, Colonial Times to 1970* (Washington, DC: GPO, 1975); USBOC, *Historical National Population Estimates, 1900 to 1999*, www.census.gov/popest/archives/pre-1980 (accessed August 14, 2005); USBOC, *Statistical Abstract of the United States 2006* (Washington, DC: GPO, 2006); Bureau of Economic Affairs, *National Income and Products Accounts*, table 1.1.6, www.bea.gov/bea/dn/nipaweb/ SelectTable.asp?Popular = Y (accessed August 13, 2005); Gregg Marland, T. J. Boden, and R. J. Andres, *National CO_2 Emissions from Fossil-Fuel Burning, Cement Manufacture, and Gas Flaring: 1751–2002* (Oak Ridge, TN: Carbon Dioxide Information Analysis Center, Oak Ridge National Laboratory, 2005), http://cdiac.esd.ornl.gov/ftp/trends/emissions/usa.dat (accessed December 21, 2005); National Center for Health Statistics, *Health, United States, 2004 with Chartbook on Trends in the Health of Americans with Special Feature on Drugs* (Hyattsville, MD: Centers for Disease Control and Prevention, 2004), table 27.

affluence, consumption of virtually every resource, and unprecedented technological change, human well-being in the United States has improved by virtually any objective measure. Figure 12.1 shows that life expectancy at birth—perhaps the single most important indicator of human well-being—increased by more than 30 years, from 47.3 years in 1900 to 77.0 years in 2000. The result would have been more or less the same had any of the other measures from chapter 2 been used to represent human well-being. Moreover, as shown in chapter 6, pollution levels did not keep pace with the growth in population or consumption of energy, other natural resources, and chemicals.[4]

This continual improvement in the human condition, for which life expectancy is a surrogate, indicates that economic growth and technological change have, for the past century or more, brought more good than harm to human health and well-being in the United States. This has been true whether pollution levels went up, as they did during the first few decades of the 20th century, or declined, as was the case in the latter part of that century.

Figure 12.2 also shows that despite a 100-fold increase in organic chemical usage, public health (for which life expectancy is a very good surrogate) has continued to improve. This is at odds with the popular view that life today is riskier because of pollution and chemicals. The inverse trends between chemical usage and public health is consistent with the notion that new technology does not, in fact, make matters worse. If anything, it replaces worse risks with risks that are not so bad, suggesting that in our obsession regarding each chemical's effects, we are overlooking the broader picture, namely, in the aggregate we are much safer now than we were a hundred years ago, even though there were fewer synthetic chemicals around and we used them much more sparingly.

The U.S. experience is not unique. Barring periods of war, human well-being has also improved more or less steadily during the past century in many of the other wealthy countries,[5] despite any ups and downs in their pollution levels during that period. This is also generally true for the bulk of the population in developing countries for the past half-century or so, with the notable exception of the inhabitants of sub-Saharan Africa in the past 15 or 20 years.

Because developing countries arrived late to the cycle of progress, they benefited from the transfer of technologies (which includes information, knowledge, and practices) that were first discovered or devised in today's developed countries. The most significant of these transferred technologies were those related to science- and technology-based agriculture, as well as to basic hygiene, public health, and medical technologies such as safe drinking water, sanitation, antibiotics, vaccinations, pasteurization, and establishment of clinics and dispensaries.[6] They also include information and knowledge about the importance and benefits of public health measures, universal public education, and greater participation of women in the workplace outside the home. Together, these technologies helped reduce hunger and malnourishment, as well as ensured healthier and longer-lived populations.

Thus, developed countries essentially served as the world's guinea pigs for urbanization and industrialization, as well as for most of those technologies.

Less obvious, but no less important, were improvements in transportation and communication networks, as well as increased trade within and between nations. These developments magnified the flow of inputs, products, and information related to medical, public health, and agricultural technologies from their points of generation to the points of use. The major innovations that have shaped these networks and stimulated trade worldwide also originated in today's richer countries. These innovations include the physical infrastructure needed for the networks (such as cables, wires, fiber optic networks, satellites, the Internet, rails, roads, and airports); the individual components that rely on or use that infrastructure (such as radios, TVs, phones, fax machines, computers, engines, trains, motor vehicles, and airplanes); and the "software" to manage and regulate the infrastructure and to improve the flow of the components. The software includes systems and rules for controlling the traffic flow of those components, whether they are locomotives, cars, planes, or information packets, as well as institutions such as the commodity and stock exchanges.

One consequence of the diffusion and transfer of these technologies is that human well-being in the developing countries (as measured by indicators such as mortality rates and life expectancy) is significantly more advanced than it was in the developed countries at equivalent levels of development. Notwithstanding urbanization and industrialization, most indicators of human well-being in the developing countries have improved since the 1950s. Even more remarkable is that these improvements occurred despite relatively long periods of stagnant or falling levels of per capita income in many developing countries caused, in large part, by poor policies and, often, a high tolerance for—or inability to address—corruption, sometimes exacerbated by natural calamities. For most countries, human well-being, as measured by the human development index (HDI), was higher in 2002 than in 1975 although, during the latter half of that period, HDIs dropped in many sub-Saharan countries and former communist countries in Eastern Europe and the former Soviet Union, in part because of deteriorating economic conditions brought about by poor policies, among other reasons.

Second, although many of today's developing countries haven't been on the cycle of progress for long, HDIs in their urban areas exceed those in rural areas. This might seem counterfactual to many casual observers given the obvious—and very visible—squalor and pollution in the cities of developing countries such as Mexico City; Teheran, Iran; and New Delhi, India. It is also a departure from the historical experience of the United States and the United Kingdom during their early periods of modern economic growth.[7] One reason for this departure is that prior to any significant urbanization in the developing countries, developed countries had already devised solutions to the most critical public health problems associated with urbanization, although in many parts of the developing world these solutions have not yet been fully implemented. Moreover, because rural areas are generally poorer, they lack access to many of the technologies that have improved human well-being in urban areas. In addition, because of lower population densities, rural areas cannot fully capture economies of scale for technologies such as sanitation, safe running water, piped natural gas, and electricity, which histori-cally helped reduce exposure to contaminated water and indoor air pollution. Today, contaminated water and indoor pollution are among the most significant environmental causes of public health problems (see table 11.2).[8]

Because developing countries were slow to get aboard the cycle of progress, during the latter part of the 19th century and the first half of the 20th century, gaps between developing and developed countries opened up for almost every objectively measurable indica-tor of human well-being (e.g., literacy rates, mortality rates, life expectancy, and access to safe water and sanitation). But transfer of technology during the latter half of the 20th century helped reduce virtually all those gaps. A possible exception to this rule is the gap in per capita income that expanded at least until the late 1970s. In a few instances, however, some late entrants to modern economic growth (e.g., Republic of Korea, Singapore, and Hong Kong) have shrunk the income gaps between themselves and many of the richest countries that commenced development earlier.

It is tempting to conclude from those trends in the gaps for various indicators that economic growth is less critical to improving human well-being and technology transfer is sufficient. Such a conclusion also draws support from the fact that HDIs improved in some developing countries even during periods of economic stagnation and shrinkage. However, this conclusion overlooks the fact that technology has first to be invented and, often, developed and made user-friendly, before it can be transferred and adopted successfully. But the majority of the technologies that improved human well-being in the past century and a half in both developed and developing countries are owed largely to the economic development of the richer countries and the factors underlying that development. First, being the first to advance economically, richer countries were also the first to stumble onto the problems associated with economic growth (including urbanization and industrialization). Second, being richer, they had—and continue to have—the wherewithal to expend resources on devising the required solutions, as well as on supporting research in general. Third, the factors that made them richer sooner were also instrumental in helping them identify and develop the needed solutions. These factors included development of human capital, a bias toward systematic problemsolving, independent thinking, and institutions that reward successful risktaking and technological innovation.

The case of sanitary reform in India also hints at the importance of economic growth and the institutions underlying such growth to the spread of technology. Sanitary reform came to India in 1870, well before it was introduced in Italy in 1890; to the countries that formed the old Austro-Hungarian Empire (where it came only after the Empire was dissolved) in 1918; to Japan in 1900; and to China in 1935.[9] However, even now, several decades later, large portions of the Indian population lack access to sanitation, while the latecomers are much better off in this regard. Clearly, neither technology transfer nor knowledge of a technology's potential is sufficient to stimulate technological change.

The world's experience with HIV/AIDS offers another example of the significance of economic development with respect to human well-being. The death rate due to AIDS has plunged in the United States since 1995 because of the development of new drugs and drug therapy regimes. However, because of the high cost of those solutions and their poverty, developing countries lag in their use of these technological advances. Accordingly, the United Nations established the Global Fund for AIDS, Tuberculosis, and Malaria, which, as of this writing, has been pledged $8.6 billion, with 99.2 percent of the funds coming from the governments and other entities from the rich nations.[10] Obviously, a poorer population, lacking resources, is more vulnerable, while a richer population is more resilient.[11] In addition, pharmaceutical companies, made rich by selling their life-lengthening pills and potions to clients in the wealthy countries, are importuned to give them at little or no cost to the people of the developing world. But without their rich clientele, pharmaceutical companies will have neither the incentive nor the fiscal ability to long continue developing—let alone transferring at large discounts—newer and better technologies to deal with AIDS, as well as a myriad of other diseases. Delivering on altruism comes easier with wealth.

Exceptions to the general trend of improving human well-being over time also testify to the importance of economic growth, openness to technological innovation, and the institutions that support them. The post-Communist era declines in the economic situation in Russia and many other former Communist bloc countries are also associated with increases in hunger, deterioration of public health services, increases in mortality, and declines in life expectancies. Life expectancies and other indicators of well-being have also declined in a number of sub-Saharan countries, which have had economic problems caused or aggravated by poor policies, AIDS, resurgence of malaria and tuberculosis, and civil and cross-border wars.

North Korea, long governed by one of the world's more dysfunctional regimes, offers one of the most visible examples of backsliding. Between 1993 and 1999, annual GDP per capita declined from $991 to $457. At the same time, life expectancy at birth dropped from 73.2 to 66.8 years, mortality for children under 5 years of age increased from 27 to 48 per 1,000, and infant mortality rates from 14 to 22.5 per 1,000 live births. Access to safe water decreased from 86 percent to 53 percent between 1994 and 1996, and vaccination coverage for diseases such as polio and measles declined from 90 percent of children in 1990 to 57 percent in 1997.[12]

In addition to the setbacks already noted, and notwithstanding the substantial progress in human well-being in the past century, about a billion people still live in absolute poverty, and 852 million people suffer from chronic hunger and undernourishment mostly in developing countries.[13] And still, 1.1 billion people lack access to improved water and 2.6 billion to improved sanitation. Diarrhea kills 1.8 million people each year; malaria—another preventable disease of poverty—annually claims 1.3 million lives; and indoor air pollution—because of burning of wood, dung, and coal inside homes—is estimated to cause 1.6 million premature deaths each year.[14]

Moreover, human demands on land and water for food, fiber, and timber are currently at their highest levels ever. Thirty-eight percent of the world's land area is now devoted to agricultural pursuits. The resulting deforestation and loss of habitat, combined with the withdrawal of prodigious amounts of water and other impacts of agricultural technologies, threaten to squeeze out the rest of nature and diminish biological diversity worldwide. In addition, many fear, rightly or wrongly, that the effects of greenhouse gas emissions on top of these threats could be devastating to the earth's ecosystems, landscapes, and biological diversity.

But these problems could have been worse. Without technological change and economic growth, it would have been impossible to sustain the world's current population at the rudimentary levels of 200 years ago, let alone advance human well-being to its current level. Malthus' fears were not borne out because, lacking any historical precedent, he could not have foreseen the unparalleled technological change that would occur in the following two centuries. Had technological change been frozen at, say, 1950 levels, the world would have needed to convert an additional 1,350 million hectares of forest and other habitat to cropland by 2002 merely to feed the current population at the wholly inadequate levels of the 1950s,[15] a time when hundreds of millions lived in countries chronically facing famines,[16] and even the United Kingdom still had food rationing;[17] United States emissions of particulate matter less than 10 micrometers (PM-10) would have been 21 times higher than they are today;[18]

and air pollution episodes, such as London's 5-day episodes in December 1952, which caused 4,000 "excess deaths" out of a population of 8.5 million, far from being an historical footnote, would have been all too real and frequent in urban areas in the United States and around the world.[19] And had technological change been halted in 1900, U.S. emissions from carbon dioxide from fossil fuel combustion and industrial sources would have been three times today's level, U.S. emissions of sulfur dioxide (SO_2) and volatile organic compounds would have been 15–20 times higher, and more than half a million more deaths would have occurred annually in the United States alone because of various water-related diseases (see table 8.1 and chapter 6).[20]

In fact, the air and water quality in the United States and the world's rich nations are better today than they have been in decades. The increase in their agricultural productivity has allowed them to reestablish forests and set habitat aside for biodiversity preservation. All this in a period when unprecedented population growth accompanied unmatched economic growth and technological change![21]

The long-term trajectories of most environmental indicators in the rich countries show that the effect of technological change and economic growth on the environment is much more complex than simply acting either as multipliers, as Neo-Malthusians convinced of the validity of the IPAT equation believe, or as divisors as many Cornucopians insist. Initially, economic growth and technology may cause environmental problems, but ultimately they contribute to the solutions. Thus, they eventually bring about environmental transitions. They are also instrumental in moving countries through their demographic transitions,[22] that is, in eventually bringing the population multiplier to heel.

Notably, the factors that have brought about environmental transitions are the same factors that reshaped society so that the anti-establishment environmentalists of the 1960s and 1970s are now part of the establishment—favored by billion dollar foundations, in the board room, and with their fingers on the levers of power inside and outside governments.

The Role of Technological Change

Just as yesterday's technology could not have sustained today's population, today's technology will be unable to sustain tomorrow's population.

Despite technological change, vast quantities of natural resources have been appropriated for human use in the past two centuries. Tomorrow's larger, and possibly more affluent, population will place ever greater demands on land, water, and other natural resources for food, energy, shelter, clothing, and other material goods. Human beings will resort to whatever technology is at hand to help meet these unprecedented demands. And if their basic demands are not sufficiently satisfied, today's technology gives them the ability to clear and convert even larger quantities of land, water, and other resources to human use, even if that use cannot be long sustained. The challenge for the future, therefore, is to meet human needs while containing impacts on the environment and other species.

Using the IPAT identity, it might be argued that if, over the next fifty years, global population increases by 50 percent and per capita GDP (a surrogate for per capita consumption) grows at the rate of 2 percent per year, then environmental impact on air, land, and water would quadruple, if all else is equal—that is, the impact per unit of GDP, or the technology factor (T-factor), is unchanged.

A popular suggestion for containing environmental impacts is to reduce population growth. But the population growth rate has declined dramatically in the past few decades. If current trends in fertility rates persist, then even without any heroic efforts, population will stabilize and, possibly, even decline later this century.[23] At the same time, given the large fraction of the current female population that is about to enter its childbearing years, it's doubtful that population growth rates can be brought down much faster without coercion (see box 12.1). Equally important, further reductions in fertility rates are probably not desirable in countries where they are below (or even close to) the replacement rate of about 2.1. That will only put additional pressure on old-age social security systems, many of which are struggling under the weight of their current load as a relatively greater number of retirees are supported for longer periods by a shrinking workforce.[24] As noted elsewhere, one method of helping alleviate the situation is to improve technology and the productivity of populations so that fewer working people can, in fact, support more retirees. Regardless, the assumption of a 50 percent increase in population by 2050 is not inconsistent with population stabilization in the next 50–100 years.

Neo-Malthusians—consistent with their faith in the IPAT identity in which *A* stands for affluence, a surrogate for consumption—also

Box 12.1
What about Population Growth?

Virtually no text on sustainable development is complete without the obligatory call to reduce population growth.[25] But I have eschewed such a call. Total fertility rates (TFRs), measured by the number of children per woman of childbearing age, have been dropping worldwide, and it is unlikely that these drops can be accelerated significantly unless societies are willing to sacrifice individual freedoms, as China has done.

Despite the disapproval of the Catholic Church, TFRs in mainly Catholic Latin America dropped 60 percent since 1962, and Catholic Spain and Italy have, at 1.3 births per woman, among the world's lowest TFRs. Similarly, pronatalist policies have had little success in increasing birth rates in Russia, Singapore, or Japan, and, so far, only moderate success in France, and their TFRs, ranging from 1.3 to 1.9, remain well below the replacement rate of 2.1.[26] Even China's TFR is below the replacement level. India's forced sterilization campaign of 1975–77 ultimately proved to be counterproductive.[27] Clearly, in matters as fundamental as the number of offspring a family should have, couples, especially in nontotalitarian nations, have shown that they are unlikely to heed the admonishments, entreaties, and inducements of their religious, political, or civic leaders or, for that matter, their own parents, friends, and acquaintances, to have more or fewer children. This decision is the one over all others that couples will make using their own calculus, based on their own economic circumstances, as well as hopes, aspirations, and opportunities for themselves and their offspring. China's experience is perhaps the exception that proves this rule.

Various estimates of "optimum population"[28] put out by scientists or environmental groups, even if accurate, are unlikely to be any more persuasive than the numerous theological or other civic leaders whose advice has apparently fallen on deaf ears.

(continued next page)

(continued)

More important determinants of TFR are economic development, as well as the desire for such development. In the short run, economic development and technological change increase the rate of population growth by reducing mortality rates. But in the long run, they moderate population growth by helping create the conditions for many families to voluntarily opt for fewer children. That is, just as economic development moves a society through an environmental transition, it—or the desire for it—also enables society to move through a demographic transition.[29]

First, because lower poverty means lower infant mortality rates and higher survival rates, that reduces pressures for more births. This is particularly important because in the poorer countries, children are about the only form of social security. Moreover, richer societies are more likely to be able to afford broader based social security programs, which can reduce the pressure for more children. Third, lower poverty levels also mean greater access to technology, which reduces the value of child labor whether on the farm or in urban areas. Moreover, wages are higher in richer societies, which also reduces pressures for children to participate in the work force. Fifth, richer societies offer greater educational and economic opportunities for women, which also increases the opportunity costs of their childbearing and child rearing years. Sixth, the time and cost of educating children to be competitive and productive in richer and more technologically advanced societies encourages small family sizes. Finally, many couples—arguably swayed by commercials and lifestyles depicted by a globalized and globalizing mass media (i.e., television and the movies)—defer child birth in favor of current consumption.

favor limiting consumption to reduce humankind's impacts on the environment (see box 12.2). Noting that it takes several times more land and water to produce a pound of food from hogs and cattle than from grain or vegetables, many analysts have espoused a switch

Box 12.2
What About Reducing Consumption?

Many environmentalists have identified human consumption as one of the root causes of environmental degradation.[30] Noting that consumption increases with affluence, some have likened it to a disease and labeled it "affluenza."[31] One remedy would be to lower the demand for land and water by switching to a mainly vegetarian diet. However, unless carefully qualified, such a diet could be counterproductive, particularly in developing nations (see table 11.2). Although overconsumption of meat and dairy products increases health risks for the affluent everywhere, underconsumption of animal products aggravates problems of malnutrition caused by micronutrient deficiencies, especially in developing nations. Technology may allow such micronutrients to be introduced into and absorbed by the human body through the consumption of grain, vegetables, and fruits that have been modified using traditional or bioengineering techniques or during processing (e.g., iodine in salt, folic acid in bread, or various vitamins and minerals in grains and processed cereals). Biotechnology might also help reduce meat consumption in traditionally nonvegetarian societies by developing GM crops that smell, taste, and have a texture and flavor akin to various meats. But until such products become more widely available, suggestions that would directly or indirectly reduce animal protein consumption need to be tempered with common sense.

Moreover, the efficacy of such calls is questionable unless populations already are predisposed toward vegetarianism, either because of religion or culture or because of concerns for a longer and healthier life. But if they are already predisposed, additional admonitions may be superfluous. Vanity and self-interested desires for personal health and longevity have altered many more diets than altruism or warnings that carrying capacity might be exceeded.

(continued next page)

(continued)

Perhaps even less effective than exhortations to modify diets are admonitions to reduce consumption of material goods and creature comforts. Although fertility rates might drop, in part because of the desire for consumption, there are few, if any, indications that consumption per capita will be limited any time soon, particularly in developing nations. Therefore, such consumption should be made as friendly as possible to the rest of nature. Technological progress makes that possible.

Just as the suit must be cut to fit the cloth, so must strategies and policies be designed to suit human nature. So we should eschew unrealistic calls to ingest foods that are less than appetizing and to reduce consumption patterns. Instead, we should attempt to harness individuals' selfish desires to improve their quality of life, and a call for greater economic development and technological change does exactly that.

to vegetarianism. But it's not clear how successful this can be among populations that are not already predisposed toward vegetarianism, such as Buddhists, Jains, and many Hindus. Anecdotal evidence suggests that many more people experiment with vegetarianism than persist with it over the long haul. But if vegetarianism were indeed to take hold, that could be counterproductive for populations that already suffer from certain micronutrient deficiencies, such as iron, zinc, and vitamin A deficiencies (see table 11.2). However, technology—if it were adopted—could come to the rescue. These examples include golden rice 2 developed by British scientists, which could provide 23 times as much vitamin A as the original golden rice developed by Swiss scientist Ingo Potrykus that still hasn't been commercialized; the International Rice Research Institute's "dream rice" that would produce higher quantities of essential micronutrients such as beta-carotene, lysine, and iron; and the Indian "protato," a potato with higher levels of protein. And in the future, bioengineered bananas might also be used to deliver vaccines for common diseases.

Another Neo-Malthusian favorite is to call for measures to reduce energy and material consumption (box 12.2). Such measures, particularly the former, are quite popular in the abstract but, as California's energy predicament of 2001 and the gas crunch of 2005 revealed, few consumers are driven to conserve unless by higher prices or a looming crisis. Fortunately, by its very nature, a market economy forces manufacturers to reduce prices to stay in business and maximize profits. This provides a built-in incentive to continually lower the energy and material content of their products so long as there is a cost attached to energy and materials, and the cost is allowed to be reflected in their prices. This translates into a constant striving for conservation and technological change and explains why the energy intensity of the economies of the rich countries (as measured by the energy use per unit of GDP) has dropped by 1 percent per year for the past century and a half. Also, we saw that because of market forces, air pollution in the United States began to be cleaned up decades before the federal government launched its command-and-control regulations. Nevertheless, despite the secular trend in technology, total energy, material, and chemical use continues to climb worldwide, and there are no signs that their use is about to decline any time soon. This is illustrated in figures 12.1 and 12.2 for the United States, which show the consumption of these substances growing more or less continually with economic growth punctuated by declines during recessions. These figures also show that there were fairly major drops in the consumption of metals and—hardly surprising—petroleum-derived organic chemicals during the recessions associated with the oil shocks of 1973 and 1979, as well as with a somewhat smaller drop during the recessions of the early 1990s.

Therefore, if we can't do much to significantly change population or consumption, by default we have to reduce the T-factor to limit the environmental impact. Tomorrow's technology must necessarily be even cleaner and more efficient than today's to avoid exacerbating current environmental problems. Just to maintain environmental impacts at current levels, the T-factor would have to decrease four-fold in 50 years, based on the scenario assumed earlier for population and economic growth. That is, overall "efficiency" would have to improve 75 percent merely to stay in place. And in areas where environmental quality is unacceptably poor today, overall efficiency would have to improve even further. For example, if reductions of

50 percent are currently necessary to get to an environmentally acceptable level, then in 50 years, the T-factor must improve eight-fold.

Some analysts have argued that technology can indeed reduce the T-factor eight- or even 10-fold.[32] Table 8.1 shows that improvements of comparable magnitude have indeed occurred for several environmental indicators, with the greatest reductions often occurring for those indicators that best reflect the quality of life. The exception in table 8.1 that proves this rule is the case of carbon dioxide (CO_2). First, as discussed in chapter 7, the perception that CO_2 might have untoward consequences is a relatively recent phenomenon, that is, the "period of perception" for CO_2 started late, and not enough time has elapsed to convert this perception into concrete actions. Another reason why T-factors for CO_2 emissions have not improved more is that in developing countries, in particular, penetration of fossil fuel energy usage is still in the growing stage.

Others believe, however, that technology is part of the problem, not the solution. Hence, the opposition to genetically modified (GM) crops, nuclear power plants, DDT, electromagnetic fields, and chemicals in general, to name just a few examples.[33]

Many technological skeptics have seized upon the precautionary principle to argue for severely restricting, if not banning, a technology if there are any doubts about its safety.[34] This principle has, for instance, been used to justify a ban on GM crops because such crops have not been shown to be absolutely safe for human consumption or for the environment.[35] But this justification for a GM crop ban is fundamentally flawed because while it takes credit for the uncertain—and so far, speculative—public health and environmental risks that a ban might reduce, it ignores the certain risks that such a ban would inevitably prolong (see chapter 9).[36] Such selective risk analysis is a perversion of the precautionary principle and can, in fact, increase risks to public health, the environment, or both, as we saw in chapter 9.[37]

Consider the public health consequences of a GM crop ban. Every year, hunger and malnutrition kill 6 million children under the age of 5 years worldwide (see table 9.1). If population increases by 50–100 percent during this century, then the numbers of deaths due to hunger and malnutrition will also increase by a like amount if all else, including food supplies per capita, remains equal. But relative to conventional crops, banning GM crops would, in fact, reduce options and decrease the quantity and the nutritional quality of food supplies that would otherwise be available in the future. Therefore, such a ban will increase future mortality and morbidity rates worldwide. In addition, pest-resistant and herbicide-tolerant GM crops could, by reducing the amounts, toxicity, or persistence of pesticides employed, lower the net health risks to farmers and the general public from the use of agricultural chemicals. Moreover, GM crops may also help diminish diet-related risks that contribute to about 19.7 million premature deaths annually due to cancers, heart disease, and strokes (see table 9.1). By contrast, the health effects of ingesting GM crops are unlikely to be as large and they are conjectural, at best. Hence, a GM crop ban is likely to increase the net harm to public health.

It should also be noted that given the level of scrutiny that GM crops receive, there is every chance that conventional crops have higher health-related risks. Consider, for example, that many people are allergic to natural peanuts. It is unlikely that a GM crop with a similar effect would ever be commercialized.

Moreover, by increasing productivity, GM crops would increase the amounts of land and water available for the rest of nature. Equally important, GM crops are likely to improve productivity while advancing no- or low-till agriculture; to lower reliance on chemical inputs, which would reduce global pollution burdens of fertilizers, pesticides, and carbon; and to further contain threats to the rest of nature. Lower agricultural demand for land and water would also decrease the socioeconomic costs of setting those resources aside for recreation, carbon sequestration, and other non-consumptive human uses. Thus, GM crops would be more protective of habitat, biological diversity, water quality, and the current climate than would conventional or organic agriculture.

Hence, contrary to conventional environmental wisdom, the precautionary principle, properly applied, with a more extensive consideration of the public health and environmental consequences of a ban, argues for a sustained effort to research, develop, and commercialize GM crops, provided reasonable caution is exercised. Corollaries to this conclusion are that a GM ban would be directly counter to the intents and purposes of the Convention on Biological Diversity and subsidiary agreements such as the Biosafety Protocol.

Some of the same groups that campaign most aggressively for the conservation of biodiversity and species are also the most vociferous about banning GM crops. For example, Greenpeace and Friends of the Earth (FOE) are in the vanguard of the opposition to GM crops not only on both sides of the Atlantic, but also in developing countries such as India and Thailand. With Friends like that, the Earth doesn't need another FOE.

Ironically, many of these groups are also quite enthusiastic about productivity-enhancing conservation technologies for energy, material, mineral, or even water use, but less keen on land use technologies that would produce more food, fiber, or timber per acre of land. As a consequence, while increasing efficiency as a conscious strategy to reduce environmental impacts is virtually an article of faith for the energy and materials sectors, for long it received short shrift for agriculture, forestry, and other land-based human activities.

This lack of enthusiasm for more efficient land use technologies can be traced to the fact that these groups—just as they did in their selective application of the precautionary principle to GM crops, for instance—have focused on the environmental downside of agricultural technologies, such as fertilizers and pesticides, but have overlooked their benefits because of past abuse of these technologies.[38] However, more recently, the notion that enhanced food productivity per unit of land and water through judicious means is good for the environment is gaining favor among conservation groups.

The potential of bioengineering extends well beyond agriculture. Any process, substance, or quality that can exist or is produced in or by a living organism can, in theory, be bioengineered into human-made food and forest crops. Armed with such traits, GM crops can be used to increase land and water use efficiency for forestry and timber production; produce colored cotton; manufacture bioplastics, biodiesel, and other biofuels; and eliminate pollution from contaminated soils and waters.

Once a better understanding is gained about how precisely genes help manufacture various proteins and control various processes in nature, it might be possible for bioengineering to develop products and confer traits that have no natural analogs, although it might be hard for a human being to imagine a trait that nature has not already tried sometime some place. In the future, many of today's chemical, pharmaceutical, and manufacturing factories might be supplanted by bioengineered crops, bioreactors, and biofactories. Biotechnology can also help conservation directly by helping propagate threatened, endangered, and, perhaps—*a la* Jurassic Park—even extinct species.

Bioengineering is but one example of science-based and market-driven technologies that could help meet human needs while limiting human demands on natural resources. Another example is precision agriculture, which uses combinations of high- and low-tech monitors, global positioning systems, computers, and process controllers to optimize the amounts and timing of the delivery of various inputs, such as water, fertilizers, and pesticides, depending on the specific crop variety, soil, and climatic conditions. Other examples include the numerous emerging technologies (e.g., photovoltaics, fuel cells, and hydrogen), which could displace fossil fuel combustion.

Of course, it is not enough to only rely on technologies that conserve natural resource use. Even the most efficient of technologies might have untoward environmental impacts. In such cases, additional controls may still need to be added on. For example, coal-fired power plants produce about 12 times as much electricity per unit of coal as compared to similar plants that existed in 1899.[39] Yet, despite the increase in efficiency, new coal-fired power plants are equipped with a variety of end-of-pipe (i.e., add-on) controls to reduce emissions of particulate matter, SO_2, and nitrogen oxides.

Nor is it sufficient to have technologies focused specifically on improving efficiency and environmental performance of the various polluting sectors of the economy; broad technological progress is also essential. The latter has given us ubiquitous, general-purpose hard technologies (e.g., electricity, calculators, computers, plastics, fiber optics, lasers, transistors, and photography) and soft technologies (e.g., patents, spreadsheets, inventory control, e-mail, insurance, risk management, and property rights), which contribute to the fabrication, manufacture, operation, and management of numerous other technologies that have helped reduce humanity's impacts on the rest of nature. Thus, it is important to stimulate research and development of science and technology across the board, so that, despite the fears of many Neo-Malthusians, affluence does not become synonymous with environmental degradation.

There is yet another reason for assuring technological change. Population growth rates are declining worldwide, which ought to help dampen emissions of greenhouse gases and relieve stresses on natural resources. However, this very success contains within it the seeds of another demographic challenge.[40] In the next several decades, fewer young people will have to support larger aging populations.[41] This will, among other things, increase pressures on changing the rules governing—and the generosity of—social security, thereby undermining one of the factors that help reduce fertility rates.[42] Decisionmakers in some developed countries and even the United States, where the birth rate is higher than for other Organisation for Economic Co-operation and Development (OECD) countries, have already begun to address these issues.[43] Although wisely eschewing targets for fertility and birth rates, a number of countries with below-replacement fertility rates such as Germany, Italy, and Japan, for instance, have instituted various policies—parental leave and additional health benefits for mother and child—that are implicitly pronatalist but so far with little effect on TFRs.[44] An alternative approach would be to foster conditions that would help boost productivity so that fewer workers can indeed support the many retired people without compromising social security benefits.[45] Thus, stimulating technological change could help ensure social stability and insure against a future resurgence in the population growth rates, thereby helping reduce one of the factors contributing to both global change and future vulnerability to its impacts.[46]

The Role of Economic Growth

Nowadays, there is a much better appreciation of the role of technology in improving the human condition while achieving and maintaining environmental quality. However, too many people in the environmental arena still view economic growth to be the problem, rather than a part of the solution, for sustainable development.[47] Some even equate it to a disease—affluenza, defined as the "excessive consumption by the world's wealthy"[48]—which, it is claimed, is in the process of devastating the world. Skepticism about economic growth also extends to some strong advocates of technological progress who recognize that technology can play a critical role in ensuring that the needs of a larger population are met in an environmentally sound manner.[49]

But without wealth, technological progress would occur much more slowly, if at all. This is because wealth can catalyze and accelerate each of the steps involved in technological progress. First, technology has to be invented, then it has to be improved and, possibly, modified for specific socioeconomic, cultural, and geographic situations. The wealthier a society, the more readily it can afford the research and development (R&D) activities that lead to the invention and innovation of new and improved technologies. This is true for R&D targeted at cleaner and more efficient natural resource and environmental technologies as well as for basic R&D. The latter is important because the course of scientific and technological progress is unpredictable and advances in different fields often buttress each other. For example, who would have thought that microprocessors, lasers, personal computers, electric motors, or synthetic materials would end up enhancing productivity and efficiency in areas as diverse as agriculture, pollution control, and human health? Today these inventions have revolutionized virtually every economic sector and sphere of human activity.

But as has been noted, the mere existence and development of new or improved technology is not sufficient. If a technology is not employed—for whatever reason—it cannot contribute to technological progress. Instead, it will be one more failed technology gathering dust on a shelf in the patent office, or elsewhere. So the next step is to acquire, operate, and maintain the technology. Wealth is pivotal to effecting each of these steps.

Consider that despite widespread and relatively longstanding knowledge of functioning alternatives to fossil fuel technologies, those alternatives are not yet widely used. Social and economic factors play a critical role in determining whether, and to what extent, a technology finds acceptance in the real world. Obviously, the cheaper a technology and richer the consumer (or society), the greater the likelihood that a technology will be adopted.

But wealth is not by itself enough; human capital is also critical. Wealth and human capital go hand in hand, as we saw in chapters 2 and 3. Wealthier societies are more able to develop their human capital. Affluence provides the funds for developing and nurturing the human capital that a technologically advanced society needs to sustain itself, that is, a more or less universal educational system that ultimately feeds the entire web of universities, laboratories, hospitals, banks, corporations, and even law firms that participate in the process of invention, innovation, and diffusion of technologies.[50] Equally important, wealthier societies can better afford to give their young the time and resources needed to develop their intellectual capital and to ready them for research at the frontiers of science, medicine, and technology.

Wealthier societies, moreover, serve as magnets for human capital from other societies. The attraction, however, isn't wealth alone but also the characteristics that enable a society to create wealth, namely, individual freedom, secure property rights, an ethic that rewards risk and effort, fewer class barriers, tolerance for immigrants, relatively honest government, and transparent regulations. And scientists and engineers, more likely than not, would prefer areas that are partial to, and have fewer barriers against, technological change. In all these respects, although the United States is not perfect, it stands head and shoulders above other societies. No wonder the best and the brightest of the world have, over the past century, gravitated to the United States. Germany's brain drain in the 1930s or India's in the past four decades, for instance, have not only been America's gain but, through the worldwide diffusion of ideas and knowledge, the world's as well.

When in the 1990s, India, for example, reduced its barriers against innovation and entrepreneurship, part of the brain drain reversed itself, bringing back more technology and greater human and social capital than had left India's shores to begin with. In fact, I would argue that India is benefiting more from this exchange than are the United States, the United Kingdom, or other countries that experienced the influx and efflux of Indian talent, in large part because the reverse diaspora brought with it a spirit of confident entrepreneurship that had been largely absent for the past several centuries.

Because technological change and economic development reinforce each other in a virtuous cycle of progress, it is hardly surprising that in almost every measurable aspect of human well-being, poorer countries do worse than the richer countries. Poorer people live shorter and unhealthier lives, their environment is more polluted, they get less education, and they have fewer opportunities to break out of the rigid strictures of caste and class. Diseases such as tuberculosis and diarrhea, which nowadays would merely sicken people in richer countries, still kill in poor ones. Similarly, individuals infected with HIV/AIDS are more likely to die prematurely in poor countries than in rich ones.

But the benefits of economic growth are not confined to improvements in direct indicators of human well-being. The richest countries are also the cleanest environmentally, because they have gone past their environmental transitions for most of their environmental problems. The richest countries are returning land to the rest of nature. They have the cleanest air in populated areas both outdoors and, more important, indoors, as well as the cleanest waters.

The gaps in the HDI between developing and developed countries, which have generally shrunk in the past half century, may grow once again as the currently developed countries address the various diseases of affluence (e.g., cancer, heart attacks, and strokes) and HIV/AIDS. Initially, at least, treatments for these diseases may be costly and unaffordable to most of their victims in the developing world. This is already obvious for HIV/AIDS, when treatments are available in the United States and Europe but beyond the reach of most inhabitants of Africa and Asia. Thus, in the future as it has been in the past, economic growth is necessary to generate the wealth to ensure that technology can be developed, afforded, and implemented.

Economic growth and the conditions conducive to such growth also help reduce fertility rate, which slows down population growth (see box 12.1), which ultimately advances environmental cleanup.

A more affluent society should be better able to cope with adversity in general, regardless of its cause, because it can mobilize the fiscal resources—and with that the human capital—needed to develop and bring online new or unused existing technologies, as well as the infrastructures needed to support them. Greater wealth also helps develop human capital, which is a catalyst for technological innovation and diffusion. In fact, as the easier problems of society are solved, the remaining problems are generally harder and costlier to address. Also, as the case of AIDS and drug-resistant tuberculosis illustrate, there is no guarantee that new diseases or variants of old diseases would not reverse decades of progress. The best way to cope with such eventualities is to amass the economic resources, human capital, and scientific and technological knowledge that might be needed to cope with them. Thus, continued progress will be aided by economic growth. It would, for example, increase purchasing power of individuals and societies, thereby improving their food and health security. Economic growth also helps ensure political support and funding for social safety nets for public health, food, and nutrition programs, which are particularly important for society's less fortunate.

In effect, just as someone suffering from AIDS is less immune to infectious disease no matter what the source of infection, so is a poorer society less immune to adversity no matter what its proximate cause, whether it is caused by disease, drought, floods, or other human-made or natural agency. Economic growth for a poor society is, in essence, like AZT for an HIV-infected individual: it boosts the immunity of the entire system and makes that society less vulnerable to adversity in general, except economic growth is more likely to be successful.

The Role of Free Trade

Trade, which is integral to globalization, involves not only the exchange of goods and services but also the transfer of ideas and knowledge. Trade is as old as nature itself, and international trade between nations is but one of its most recent manifestations.[51] The benefits of trade, which must be mutually realized for it to be sustained by any two parties, are based on the division of labor, specialization, and differential access to resources, commodities, and factors of production. An example of trade in nature is the symbiosis between corals and algae: the former provides protection and access to light, while the latter provides nutrients for their mutual growth. Similar mutual relationships between fungi and algae may have led to the formation of lichens. Another example includes that of mycorrhizae, which result from the symbiosis between roots and fungi such that the plants receive phosphate and water from the fungi in exchange for sugar. Also, in the symbiosis between nitrogen-fixing bacteria and legumes, the two exchange nitrogen for sugar. It has even been postulated that the eukaryotic cell—the basis for the protista (e.g., algae), fungi, plant, and animal kingdoms—might itself have evolved from the symbiosis between prokaryotic ancestors of mitochondria and chloroplasts starting, perhaps, about 1.5 billion years ago. Trade not only predates humanity, it is a critical part of what Paul Ehrlich has called "the machinery of nature."[52]

And long before there was a World Trade Organization (WTO), trade in goods and services made possible the family unit and the community itself. A family unit is viable because, through biological and cultural specialization, the female, who is also the primary caregiver, bears and rears children, and her contributions are complemented by the male's efforts to feed, clothe, shelter, and protect the family. Similarly, without trade with its "environs," an urban population would be unsustainable. Most of the food, clothing, and materials needed to build houses are generally imported from elsewhere.

The extent of an urban area's environs is determined by the range over which essential goods are traded for it to survive and function. This has always been limited by the distance over which those goods could be moved profitably relative to the risk assumed and without spoilage. Successive technological revolutions have expanded this distance. They have increased the volume and weight of shipments and the speed of transportation by orders of magnitude as human locomotion was supplanted, first, by the ox-drawn cart, then the sail-powered ship, the steam-driven locomotive, the diesel-fueled truck, and, now, the jet-powered aircraft.[53] Software technologies, such as paper currency, letters of credit, insurance to reduce risk, and commodity brokerage, also helped boost trade within and outside individual political jurisdictions.

As is evident from Jared Diamond's examples of societal collapse, inability to trade can contribute to marginal societies withering or dying. For example, the Norse in Greenland perished once the difficulties of trading with the home country (or its colonies) and other countries became insurmountable with the advance of the Little Ice Age. However, Iceland, the Orkneys, and the Shetlands survived.[54] And who knows whether the original inhabitants of Easter Island may not have done better if they had been less geographically isolated and more able to trade with other islands for critical resources, such as timber, that they needed for sea-going boats.

Because of trade, today we have the global village with all parts sustaining one another. It is possible to go to a grocery store in Washington, D.C., for instance, and find products from all corners of the globe: grapes from Chile, salmon from Norway, rice from India, and lamb from New Zealand. Because of trade and technology, an individual family unit, community, or country no longer needs to be self-sufficient in basic necessities, so long as it can obtain them through either direct purchase or exchange for their goods or services, or failing that, through assistance from others who either have access to or are wealthy enough to afford such assistance. In effect, trade has globalized sustainability.[55]

Although many governments, policymakers, and anti-globalization nongovernmental organizations pursue self-sufficiency, one can debate whether that is worth its economic and environmental price. Consider the trade in agricultural commodities. Most developing countries—119 out of the 130 developing countries for which data were readily available for 1998–2000—are net importers of cereals.[56] More than 10 percent of the cereals consumed by the developing countries are imported. In the absence of trade, food deficit countries would have had even lower supplies, higher prices, or both. In either case, levels of hunger and malnutrition would have been higher. Not only is such an outcome intrinsically undesirable because it aggravates hunger—an unenviable human condition—and, therefore, human suffering, it also retards improvements in public health, increases mortality rates, and reduces life expectancy in the importing countries.

Trade also reduces the pressure to exploit marginal land resources, which helps avoid additional, and unnecessary, environmental degradation. If in 1997 there had been no trade in cereals and if each country increased (or reduced) cereal production by an amount equal to its net imports (or exports), then *at least* an additional 26 million hectares (Mha) more would have had to be harvested worldwide.[57] This breaks down into an increase of 55 Mha in the developing nations (who are net importers), partially offset by a reduction of 29 Mha in developed nations (who are net exporters). In the absence of trade in cereals, not only would the quantity of habitat lost to cropland have increased, the extra lost habitat would probably have been of a higher quality. This is because developing nations are concentrated in the tropics, their ecosystems are particularly at risk, and terrestrial species' richness generally seems to increase as we move toward the tropics.[58] Hence, the net effect of trade in cereals on global biological diversity and the environment are, most likely, positive.

Given these benefits and the fact that trade is part and parcel of the machinery of nature, one would think that environmentalists would be favorably disposed toward trade. But, in fact, many environmentalists contend that trade and environmental quality are antithetical.[59] First, they argue, trade allows richer nations to continue their excess consumption of timber products and beef, for instance, by despoiling tropical forests in developing nations. Moreover, roads built to move products to markets further destroy or degrade forests by enabling easier colonization and exploitation. There is, indeed, some truth to these claims, but international trade-related activities—timber harvesting, converting natural forests to plantations for agricultural and forest crops, and large-scale cattle ranching—do not seem to be principle causes of changes in the quality and quantity of forest cover.

In 1998, exports from developing nations (where most tropical and subtropical forests are located) accounted for 4.2 percent of the industrial roundwood production. If the figures for industrial roundwood are combined with fuelwood, their exports' share of production declines to less than 1 percent. Net exports were even lower (below 0.3 percent and 0.05 percent, respectively).[60] In fact, according to the *Global Forest Resource Assessment 2000* from the Food and Agriculture Organization, between 1990 and 2000, forest plantations were responsible for less than 10 percent of natural forests that were converted to other types of land cover. In fact, the proximate cause of most (about three-fourths) of the conversion of natural forests worldwide during the 1990s was agriculture.[61]

The underlying causes of such conversion could range from poor government policies (e.g., subsidies, resettlement schemes, and creation of water reservoirs), domestic demand, uncertain land tenure and property rights systems, social structures that displace various populations who then have to resort to deforestation, and corrupt political structures.[62] Although ranching may be a factor in some Latin American deforestation, its effects are magnified by poor policies favoring land clearance.[63] Moreover, despite a 74 percent increase in Brazilian beef production between 1980 and 1996, for instance, its beef exports peaked at 15 percent of production in the mid 1980s and dropped to 5 percent by 1996, indicating that most increased production went to meet domestic needs.[64] Similarly, increased production of palm oil, rice, pulp, and paper in tropical countries—activities that often occur on forested or previously forested areas—seems to have mainly gone toward satisfying domestic demand, although there might be exceptions for specific products in individual countries.[65] All of this suggests that international trade is not a primary driver of tropical deforestation. Somewhat surprisingly, the relationships between population density and population growth with deforestation seem to be relatively weak.[66]

Another argument against trade is its potential effects on endangered species (or their parts). The Convention on International Trade of Endangered Species of Wild Flora and Fauna deals with various facets of the complex issue of trade with respect to a variety of wild species, such as elephants, minke whales, and mahogany. Skeptics of trade argue that trade in these species (and their parts) would accelerate the demise of various species. Proponents of trade, however, counter that regulated trade would provide local communities and nations that host the endangered species with much-needed funds for social and conservation needs, thereby provide the incentive necessary for conservation. Otherwise, they argue, endangered species may become the proverbial white elephants whose owners would welcome their extinction.[67]

Third, skeptics note that trade, by increasing economic development and associated transportation would result in greater local, regional, and global emissions. It is also claimed that trade between nations with unequal income levels may create "pollution havens" with dirty industry relocating from cleaner, richer countries to poorer ones with laxer environmental standards, which, in turn, may lead to a "race to the bottom."[68] The difference between the two is that under a race-to-the-bottom hypothesis, nations would opt for less-than-optimal environmental standards so as to improve their competitive position and thereby collectively reduce international welfare, while under the pollution haven hypothesis, international welfare might be optimal if countries with a lower demand for environmental quality adopt less stringent standards while others with a higher demand adopt higher standards.[69] Substantial work has gone into trying to identify whether empirical data across countries or political jurisdictions indicate that openness to trade supports either hypothesis. These studies indicate virtually no support for the race-to-the-bottom hypothesis and weak support for the existence of pollution havens.[70] The problem with most of these studies, however, is that they tend to equate higher pollution levels with improved well-being. As we have seen, this isn't always the case, which is why environmental transitions occur in the first place. The transition occurs because at a sufficiently high level of human well-being, societies equate well-being with better environmental quality rather than additional economic development. A race to the bottom or a pollution haven is only deplorable if they are imposed by force, other nondemocratic means, or methods that violate human rights. However, if a society decides on its own to trade economic development for environmental quality or vice versa, that is their right.

China, arguably, does not fall into this category. Had it been a democracy, it—or rather its population—may have willingly traded some economic development for a better quality of the environment. It's conceivable, however, that the redistributionist impulses in a democracy would have substantially slowed down economic growth, as it did in India. Nevertheless, because of its pluralistic democracy, India's progress is probably more robust, and the Indian tortoise may yet catch the Chinese hare. But even if it doesn't, the former's achievement should be deemed a bigger success because the means are at least as important as the ends, and whether one lives in a democracy is itself a factor in determining human well-being.

Trade is also an important contributor to economic development. In 2003, for instance, about 21.5 percent of the GDP of the least developed countries (LDCs) was derived from exports.[71] For low-income countries, which includes LDCs, exports accounted for 20.8 percent of GDP. The corresponding figure for middle-income countries was 32.3 percent. Certainly, the increased economic activity might well have increased emissions of pollutants for which the country in question had not yet gone through its various environmental transitions. However, if the country was at or beyond its transitions, then emissions might have been diminished. Thus, because of increased wealth, the first rank indicators of well-being—access to food, safe water and sanitation, infant mortality, and life expectancy—are more likely to have improved because the transitions for those indicators are either nonexistent or occur at relatively low levels of income (see, e.g., figures 6.4, 6.13, and 6.14) while pollutant concentrations—lower ranked indicators, which, therefore, have their transitions at higher levels of economic development—may or may not have increased. Hence, the well-being of the population in the poorer country might well have improved, despite an increase in certain pollutant levels.

But more important, those arguments against trade are fundamentally flawed: they assume that the basic objective of public policy is to minimize pollution and environmental degradation rather than to maximize social welfare. Greater economic growth is, in fact, the objective not because it is an end in itself but because it provides societies the wherewithal to improve their quality of life—richer is virtually always better fed, healthier, longer lived, and, ultimately, cleaner.[72] And the institutions that advance economic development and economic freedom are by and large the same institutions that advance political freedom and equality of opportunity.

We have seen throughout this book that human well-being (and social welfare) of a society can be improved even as some aspects of environmental quality are degraded. In fact, it is the divergence between human well-being and environmental quality at lower levels of per capita income that is responsible for environmental transitions. Because of this divergence, it is possible that differential standards can improve human well-being for both the exporter and the importer. An example of this is that of the ship recycling industry in India and Pakistan, which exists only because rich countries are unwilling to take on the unpleasant, if not dangerous, task of disposing of ships at the end of their lifespans.[73] Thus, trade in such waste commodities brings benefits to both the exporter and the importer, and one nation's hazardous waste becomes another's valuable resource.

Trade advocates also note that the role of environmental laws in locating industries is more often than not minor compared to labor costs; confidence in, and stability of, legal and economic institutions; ability to repatriate profits; access to reliable and robust commercial and communications infrastructure; and the potential magnitude of local markets.[74] Moreover, they note that trade diffuses technologies, including environmental technologies, effectively and efficiently. For example, waste water technologies are exported by the United States to Indonesia, while improved air pollution control technologies are imported by the United States from Japan and Germany.

Trade skeptics also argue that the institutions for monitoring international trade (e.g., the WTO) can exert pressure to relax environmental laws by ruling they are nontariff barriers to trade. For example, a WTO panel rejected the European Union's ban on beef treated with growth hormones because it was not based on scientific evidence.[75] But this ruling may yet have a net positive environmental impact because the use of such hormones, by increasing feed efficiency, may reduce the resources needed to produce a pound of beef. Finally, skeptics point out that trade, through accident or design, has helped transplant several invasive nonnative species to new locations to the detriment of native species, as well as spread various epidemics around the world.[76]

Several of the arguments made by trade skeptics have some validity, but they should be considered in the wider context of overall

404

sustainability. Trade, as we have seen, is not only critical for reducing malnutrition and hunger worldwide, it also helps limit exploitation of marginal lands and overexploitation of productive lands for growing crops, grazing, and felling timber, provided neither trade nor the activities themselves are subsidized, and prices account for market failures. In fact, free trade is an argument against the idea that a country needs to be self-sufficient in food, oil, or other basic commodities—an idea often used to justify environmentally and economically unsound subsidies.[77]

Trade also helps poorer nations raise capital in richer nations. Net private capital flows from developed to developing nations increased from around $50 billion in 1990 to $285 billion in 1997, the year of the Asian Financial Crisis, after which they dropped but have since picked up once again. Since 2004, they have exceeded $300 billion.[78]

Globalization has also helped increase remittances to developing countries from workers in the developed countries. These remittances amounted to $126 billion in 2004. By contrast, official development aid in 2004 amounted to $79 billion, a record amount due to increased aid to Iraq and the Asian tsunami.[79] Together, private capital flows, remittances, and aid were equivalent to about 7 percent of developing countries' GDP.[80]

Recent history illustrates that civil and cross-border conflicts, by disrupting commerce and movement of goods, and poor public policies are today among the major causes of famine and unsustainable resource use.[81] But free trade and war don't mix well. By creating mutual dependencies, increasing wealth, and allowing access to natural resources that one group lacks but may need, trade reduces the incentives for people to garnish those resources by force or by migration. Free trade, particularly in basic commodities, such as food crops, fuels, and energy, and other natural resources, also gives countries incentives to live in harmony rather than obtain them through force. With today's technology, education, and new institutions, free trade can be a force for peace and prosperity rather than an excuse for war and oppression. The contrast between Japan's quest to establish a greater coprosperity sphere through force before and during World War II in order to take the natural resources it lacked, as well as its post-war experience in gaining access to these very resources through trade, argues for optimism on this score.[82]

That perpetual pessimist, Lester Brown, once asked, "Who will feed China?"[83] Initially, it seemed that the correct answer was that with free trade both America and the European Union (EU) could help fulfill China's food needs. Currently, though, with improvements in technology, China has increased its cereal yield so that it is today more than four-fold what it was in 1961.[84] In fact, in 2001–03 it was a net exporter of cereals, pulses (legumes), vegetables, and fruits (but a net importer for the other remaining groups of major food commodities, for example, starch roots, sugar crops, and oil crops).[85] Although China might become more dependant on food imports over the next few years because of increase in demand due to its increasing population and skyrocketing economic growth, it should be noted that China has one of the most active programs to study, adopt, and commercialize GM crops. This approach is already providing benefits in terms of higher yields, lower reliance on pesticides, and increased profits to farmers, as we saw in chapter 9.

In any case, should China's food production fail to keep pace with domestic demand or otherwise falter, the United States and the EU would be waiting in the wings, unless all their surplus cropland ends up being dedicated to ethanol or carbon sequestration in pursuit of the subsidies being handed out (see later in this section). In some ways that would be a shame. A food importer is unlikely to bite the hand that feeds it, nor is an exporter eager to lose its livelihood by fighting its customers. And mutual dependence between these trade giants—China, the United States, and the EU—would reduce the risk of conflict between them, which not very long ago was feared might break out some day.[86] It would also help save China's environment, itself a worthy environmental goal.

An ancillary benefit of trade is that by helping increase economic growth in developing countries, it creates jobs and reduces the pressure to emigrate to developed countries. In turn, this would result in a net reduction in global energy usage, all else being equal. The average American emits 5.5 times as much CO_2 from fossil fuel-burning and industrial sources as the average Mexican, who in turn emits 16 times as much as the average Haitian.[87]

Despite the importance of trade to global sustainability, however, there is a danger that the developed countries may refrain from producing surpluses, which, then, have to be exported or destroyed. Having met their own needs, many in the richer countries are unwilling to risk their environmental well-being for producing surpluses for export elsewhere.[88] Thus, one of the arguments against GM crops is that the developed world is already saturated with surpluses and, therefore, can forego the added gains in productivity that such crops would bring. Similarly, there are efforts in North America and the EU to mitigate carbon emissions by, among other things, subsidizing land for fuel farms or carbon sequestration even as subsidies for the production of food crops are removed. Such actions would reduce food surpluses, increase food costs globally, and decrease food security in many developing countries, providing them with a powerful incentive to overexploit marginally productive lands, which would increase environmental degradation. Ironically, the desire to reduce hunger in developing countries and environmental damage in general are among the reasons advanced for reducing carbon emissions. So here not only do we have a policy for developed countries that might aggravate the problems of the developing countries, but also one that could well be counterproductive to its stated goals.

Notably, controversy over globalization has focused largely on whether it exacerbates income inequality between the rich and the poor. But although human well-being generally improves with wealth, the two are not synonymous. The central issue, therefore, is not whether income gaps are growing but whether globalization advances well-being and, if inequalities in well-being have expanded, whether that is because the rich have advanced at the expense of the poor. And, in fact, inequalities between rich and poor with respect to the more direct measures of human well-being, such as freedom from hunger, mortality rates, child labor, education, access to safe water, and life expectancy, have generally shrunk dramatically since the mid 1990s irrespective of trends in income inequality. However, where those gaps have shrunk the least or even expanded recently, as in sub-Saharan Africa or in the erstwhile Communist states of Eastern Europe and the former Soviet Union, the problem is too little, rather than too much, globalization.

The rich are not better off because they have taken something away from the poor; rather, the poor are better off because through globalization they benefit from the technologies developed by the rich, and their situation would have improved further had they been better able to capture the benefits of globalization. A certain level of global inequality may even benefit the poor as rich countries develop and invest in more expensive medicines and technologies that can then become affordable to the poor. In fact, if the rich can be faulted at all, it is that by subsidizing favored economic sectors and maintaining import barriers they have retarded globalization and made it harder for many developing countries to capture its benefits.

However, although globalization has been critical for the improvements in well-being during the past several decades, a word of caution is warranted regarding trade in knowledge and ideas. Such trade not only globalizes good concepts such as basic hygiene, nutrition, and human rights, but it can also globalize bad ideas. Some of the worst ideas to ever be globalized include public ownership of the means of production and its stepchild, the command-and-control economy. Global demonization of DDT following Rachel Carson's *Silent Spring* contributed to the resurgence of malaria. How terrible an idea this was can be gauged by the fact that reinstituting indoor spraying of DDT in parts of South Africa and Zambia reduced cases of malaria by 80 percent and 50 percent, respectively.[89] More recently, the notion fervently held by some who have never starved except out of free choice—that GM crops could be more dangerous than no food at all—was transplanted to Zambia with tragic consequences and to the eternal shame of those who raised their voices against the alleged dangers of GM crops but kept their council when they refused food for the starving millions.

In summary, although free and unsubsidized trade has its drawbacks and foes, it is part of the web of institutions necessary for helping to satisfy the needs and wants of a larger and more affluent global population while limiting environmental impacts. Such trade in goods, services, ideas, and knowledge enhances economic growth; helps diffuse technology worldwide; ensures efficient movement of food, natural resources, and capital from surplus to deficit areas; reduces pressures on marginal lands and other natural resources; and whether or not it can reduce income gaps between the rich and poor, it reduces gaps with respect to the more critical measures of human well-being, which is the fundamental reason for acquiring wealth in the first place.

Can the Planet Survive Progress?

Thanks to the cycle of progress, humanity, though more populous and still imperfect, has never been in better condition.

The next few decades will see a world that will almost certainly be more populated than it is today. If the cycle of progress is unable to advance this additional burden or is slowed significantly for whatever reason, our children will inherit a world where hunger, poverty, and infectious and parasitic diseases claim ever greater numbers, as well as where humanity's quest for food, clothing, and shelter diverts even larger shares of land and water away from the rest of nature.

Alternatively, the cycle of progress could continue to move farther and faster giving us a world where the population has stabilized; where hunger and malnutrition have been virtually banished; where malaria, tuberculosis, AIDS, and other infectious and parasitic diseases are distant memories; and where humanity meets its needs while ceding land and water back to the rest of nature. And although there will no doubt be some environmental degradation and the climate might be somewhat warmer, they need not be catastrophically so. Almost everyone could have access to adequate sanitation and clean water. The air and water could be cleaner even if "code red" days were to still occur occasionally in Mexico City, Beijing, and New Delhi. And even in sub-Saharan Africa infant mortality could be as low as it is today in the United States and life expectancies as high.

Perhaps the most hopeful sign that the further improvements in the human condition are possible and that the second vision of the world is within grasp is that although today's developing countries lag the developed countries in virtually every indicator of human and environmental well-being, the former are ahead of where the latter used to be at equivalent levels of economic and social development. This is indeed the case for every critical indicator examined here, such as infant mortality, life expectancy, literacy, and access to safe water. Profiting further from the experience of today's developed world, developing countries have also started addressing their pollution problems at much earlier levels of economic development.

But if the past two centuries' progress in human welfare is to be more than a fleeting memory in the long history of mankind and if the level of human well-being that currently exists in today's richer nations is to permeate to other parts of the globe, we will need continued technological progress.

But technology, by itself, is insufficient for technological progress. We also need economic growth because it catalyzes the creation, diffusion, and utilization of technology. We also need to pay attention to other components of the cycle: free trade in ideas, knowledge, goods, and human and fiscal capital; education; and public health. But most important, we need to ensure that the cycle does not run out of power.

Fueling the cycle of progress is not inevitable. Rarely have the conditions responsible for technological change and economic growth come together at any place for too long. The life span of virtually every empire, civilization, or political and economic system can be measured in terms of a few centuries and sometimes even decades. In fact, long-lasting entities such as the ancient Egyptian civilization or the Roman or Byzantine empires are characterized more by their stability (before their eventual demise) than by long-term gains in the average person's lot. To ensure that the cycle of progress keeps moving forward, the institutions underlying that cycle need to be nurtured and, in many places, strengthened.

These institutions that power technological progress include free markets; secure property rights to both tangible and intellectual products; fair, equitable, and relatively transparent rules to govern those markets and enforce contracts; institutions for accumulating and converting knowledge into useful and beneficial products; and honest and predictable bureaucracies and governments. These institutions also underpin a strong civil society. However, building and strengthening these institutions may not be enough if society is hostile to change and if richer societies—in their quest for zero risk—reject imperfect ("second best") solutions. The quest for perfection in an imperfect world should lead to progress, not paralysis. In fact, the history of the progress in human well-being during the past two centuries is one in which higher-risk technologies are progressively replaced by technologies that, while not risk-free, carry lower risks. If through a misapplication of the precautionary principle, humanity had waited for the perfect energy source, it would still be living in the dark, shivering from the cold, starving from hunger, and lucky to live beyond 40.

Jared Diamond's retelling of the extinction of the Norse civilization in Greenland provides us with a powerful parable of the perils of shunning technological change.[90] As the Medieval Warming Period gave way to the Little Ice Age, the Vikings stuck to their time-honored ways. Survival wasn't made easier by the fact that they apparently had a taboo against eating fish.[91] Even though they were isolated from their traditional trading partners and despite having the successful example of the Inuits to learn from, they did not adopt the latter's fishing and hunting techniques for reasons that cannot be fathomed (perhaps that was because of inflexible social institutions—or a Viking version of the precautionary principle). We saw shades of a similar dynamic play out, fortunately not to its bitter end, when, in 2002, Zambia refused food aid because it contained GM corn from the United States.[92] Whatever the reason, because the Vikings were not open to technological change, they failed to adapt—and perished.

As Diamond observes, "A society's fate lies in its own hands and depends substantially on its own choices."[93] I contend that one of society's critical choices is its attitude toward and openness to technological change.

Of course, it is possible that with sufficient economic growth and technological change, the general pattern that we see today with respect to human well-being, namely, matters improving with income, will be less obvious in the future. Consider, for example, the curve depicting access to safe water versus per capita income (illustrated in figure 6.13). Conceivably, with constant technological change, the knee in the curve would shift further toward the left as more cost-effective technologies are developed. At the same time, further economic growth could push virtually all countries to the right of the knee. Because of the combination of these two trends, a few decades from now virtually everyone should have access to safe water. Similarly, a few decades from now one may no longer be able to determine a strong dependence of life expectancy on the level of economic development. Accordingly, some people might conclude that economic growth, having served its purpose as the midwife for technological change, had become superfluous. Others might conclude that further technological change itself is unnecessary.

Shades of these arguments are already evident in the opposition to GM foods and the use of DDT. Notably, most of the opposition to these technologies comes from people who are quite comfortably off, that is, they come from societies where incomes are beyond the knee of the well-being versus income curves, and they see little or no utility in enhancing the quantity and quality of food, or in cost-effective vector control. Although I have shown that these arguments are invalid today because of the large numbers worldwide who would—and, indeed, do—benefit from such technologies, is it possible that, after the evident problems of today are more or less solved, these arguments would carry much greater weight? Could we then eschew further economic growth and technological change?

We dare not do so. First, as noted, there are no perfect solutions. Every solution contains within it the germs of another problem. Thus, horse-drawn transportation—the polluter of the city a century ago[94]—was replaced by the internal combustion engine. But today it is that engine that pollutes the city. Tomorrow's solutions will no doubt have their own problems. But that's progress—continually replacing bigger problems with smaller ones, and the problems that are left over will always be harder to solve. Second, even if humanity rests on its laurels, the rest of nature will go on automatically probing its defenses and launching new offenses. Inevitably, humankind will be exposed to new and more virulent forms of old diseases. And to cope with those too, we will need to muster all our resources and ingenuity.

In a celebrated article half-a-century ago, the eminent mathematician, John von Neumann, asked whether humankind can survive technology.[95] We now know the answer: We cannot survive without it—certainly not if we want to maintain the quality of our lives or the environment, considering the numbers that exist today or will exist in the future. But technology is not enough; we also need economic development. Although there are no guarantees, acting together, they—more than anything else—offer the best hope for technological progress, without which we cannot expand current limits to growth.

Appendix A

Regression Results

The following methodology was used in the regression analyses used to generate the relationships between various indicators (represented by y), income (x = per capita income [PCI]), and time. First, unless otherwise noted, data for y and PCI were obtained for various countries for two separate years for which there seemed to be sufficient data. Ideally, the two years selected should be as wide apart as possible. Since I used purchasing parity power-adjusted international dollars for PCI and data for that series in World Bank's *World Data Indicators*,[1] started in 1975, which meant the earliest year that I could employ was 1975. Frequently, in the early years, data for an indicator (y) were relatively sparse. Accordingly, a later start date had to be used for that particular indicator. Similarly, the second year was selected to be as late as possible, assuming sufficient data. Thus, for life expectancy, I used the years 1977 and 2003, while for access to sanitation and safe water, I used 1990 and 2002. Second, the relationship that best fit these data was determined using linear, log-linear, and log-log regression analyses (employing ordinary least squares) per the following equation:

$$F(y) = A + B \times \Delta i + C \times F(x),$$

where $F(y) = y$ for linear and log-linear analyses and log y for log-log analysis; $F(x) = x$ for linear analysis, or log x for log-linear and log-log analyses; Δi is a dummy variable, 0 for the first year and 1 for the second year; and A, B, and C are constants. Thus, for the linear or log-linear cases, B provides an estimate for the displacement of the indicator (y) going from the first year to the second year (i.e., the displacement of the curve if PCI is kept constant). As noted, it provides an indication of technological change.

Results are shown in table A only for the "best fit" equation defined as the equation that explained the greatest amount of the variation in $F(y)$ provided the coefficients C and B (if relevant) had

413

p values < 0.05. There are, however, two exceptions. First, for malnutrition prevalence, p for the coefficient B was 0.052, that is, it wasn't significant at the 0.05 level. The second exception was for access to sanitation (see later text).

For indicators for which theoretical upper or lower limits (e.g., malnutrition and access to safe water and sanitation) had been reached for certain countries, best fit lines were generated, where appropriate, using a Tobit regression model. In these cases, R^2 shown are for the normal (non-Tobit) model. The pseudo R^2 for the Tobit model are also shown. The values of A, B, and C used to generate the figures in the book are based on the latter model.

For access to sanitation, the coefficients of B and C for the log-log formulation per the earlier equation were significant at the 0.05 level without any truncation using the Tobit model. However, p exceeded 0.05 when the Tobit model was employed. Accordingly, the following equation was used in a Tobit regression model to generate the figure for access to sanitation:

$$\log y = A + B \times \Delta i + (C + D \times \Delta s)A \log x,$$

where Δs is a dummy variable, which allows the slope of $\log x$ to vary with the year (with $\Delta s = 0$ for the first year and 1 for the second year), and all the other symbols are as defined earlier.

Years	N	R²	Adjusted R²	Regression Equation	p-values for A	B	C	D
				Cereal Yield (CY); Linear Regression: World Bank (2005)				
1975, 2003	258	0.4748	0.4707	$CY = 1131\,371 + 525.8823\Delta i + 0.1171533\ PCI$	*	*	*	
				Food Supplies per Capita per Day; Log-Linear Regression; World Resources Institute (2005); World Bank (2005)				
1975, 2002	263	0.6487	0.646	$FS = -438.0738 + 166.2341\Delta i + 815.6498\log PCI$	0.002	*	*	
				Malnutrition Prevalence (MP), by weight, in children < 5 YEARS (%); Log-Log Regression; World Bank (2005)				
1987, 2000	63	0.5761	0.5619	$\log MP = 3.783343 - 0.1320072\Delta i - 0.7349484\log PCI$	*	0.052	*	
				Infant Mortality (IM) Rate (deaths per 1,000 live births) for children < 1 year; Log-Log Regression; World Bank (2005)				
1980, 2003	271	0.7736	0.7719	$\log IM = 4.680324 - 0.2337074\Delta i - 0.8314025\log PCI$	*	*	*	
				Life Expectancy at Birth (years); Log-Linear Regression; World Bank (2005)				
1977, 2003	268	0.5656	0.5623	$LE = -6.709606 + 3.976114\Delta i + 18.48417\log PCI$	0.08	*	*	
				Health Adjusted Life Expectancy (HALE); Log-Linear Regression; WRI (2005), Based on WHO (2004)				
2002	159	0.703	0.7011	$HALE = -12.35814 + 19.01701\log FCI$	0.001	*		

Years	N	R^2	Adjusted R^2	Regression Equation	p-values for A	B	C	D
Child Labor (CL), in % of children between 10 and 14 years; Log-Linear Regression; World Bank (2005)								
1975, 2003	262	0.6114	0.6084	CL = 102.4058 − 5.197959Δi − 23.73023 log PCI	*	*	*	
1975, 2003 (Tobit)	262	(65)* censored	0.1584 pseudo R^2	CL = 129.5907 − 10.31326Δi − 31.31774 log PCI	*	*	*	
Access to Safe Water; Log-Log Regression; World Bank (2005)								
1990, 2002	241	0.5254	0.5214	log SW = 1.127999 + 0.0301873Δi + 0.2039912 log PCI	*	0.015	*	
1991, 2002 (Tobit)	241	(48)*	−3.6459 pseudo R^2	log SW = 0.8560358 + 0.0280466Δi + 0.2872922 log PCI	*	0.046	*	
Access to Sanitation (SAN); Log-Log Regression; Tobit; World Bank (2005)								
1990, 2002	222	0.5462	0.542	log SAN = 0.0245611 + 0.587957Δi + 0.466124 log PCI	0.815	0.027	*	
1990, 2002	222	1.2718		log SAN = −0.399022 + 0.0516132Δi + 0.5971093 log PCI	0.002	0.072	*	
1990, 2002 (Tobit)	222	0.553	0.5469	log SAN = −0.1806921 + 0.4335174Δi + (0.5245442 − 0.1058688Δs) log PCI	0.239	0.037	*	0.069
1990, 2002 (Tobit)	222	(30)*	1.3005 pseudo R^2	log SAN = −0.7022743 + 0.5960962Δi + (0.6847152 − 0.1570265Δs) log PCI	*	0.017	*	0.028

Years	N	R²	Adjusted R²	Regression Equation	p-values for A	B	C	D
				Health Expenditures (HE) per Capita (current US$); PCI (in PPP-adjusted, 2000 international $); World Bank (2005)				
2002	161	0.8079	0.8066	$HE = -243.6299 + 0.084729 PCI$	*			
				Total Fertility Rate (TFR); Log-Log Regression; World Bank (2005)				
1977, 2003	270	0.6301	0.6274	$\log TFR = 1.907929 - 0.1751518 \Delta i - 0.3553777 \log PCI$	*	*	*	
				R&D Expenditures (IN % OF GDP); Linear Regression; World Bank (2005)				
2002	55	0.5223	0.5133	$R\&Dexp = 0.1176272 + 0.0000789 PCI$	0.493	*		
				Tertiary Schooling (TS); Log-Log Regression; World Bank (2005)				
1990, 2002	180	0.5804	0.5757	$\log TS = -2.419272 + 0.2061107 \Delta i + 0.9291942 \log PCI$	*	0.001	*	

a. Number of censored observations. * indicates p-value < 0.001

SOURCE: World Bank, *World Development Indicators*, http://devdata.worldbank.org/dataonline (accessed July 12, 2005); World Resources Institute, EarthTrends, www.wri.org (accessed June 23, 2005); WHO, *World Health Report 2004* (Geneva: WHO, 2004).

Appendix B

Instead of education per se, I, for long-term HDI trends for the United States, use literacy data because they are more readily available. Similar to the UNDP's approach, I calculate the composite HDI as the average of its three components, HDI_i, with each component being estimated using,

$$HDI_i = \frac{actual_i - min_i}{max_i - min_i}$$

where $actual_i$ is the actual value of ith component of the HDI (that is, life expectancy, literacy or GDP per capita), and max_i and min_i are the maximum and minimum values that the ith component might take, respectively. As noted, HDI_3, the component related to GDP per capita, are estimated using the log of the GDP per capita instead of GDP per capita. That is,

$$HDI_3 = \frac{\log(actualGDP / capita) - \log(minGDP / capita)}{\log(maxGDP / capita) - \log(minGDP / capita)}$$

Thus the human development index can be calculated as

$$HDI = \frac{1}{3}\sum_i HDI_i$$

and by definition, the HDI scale tops out at one unit.

In order to construct a long-term trend in HDI for the United States, I assume that for each of the three components the minimum value ought to correspond to what it was around 1820, approximately at the start of its industrialization i.e., 30 years for life expectancy, 73.7 percent for literacy, and $1,257 (in 1990 international PPP-adjusted dollars) for GDP per capita.[1] For the maximum values, I assume 85 years, 100 percent, and $40,000, respectively, similar to what UNDP assumes.[2] I also assume that literacy stays at 99 percent after 1970. This understates the level of improvement in human well-being because it does not account for the increases in the educational level of the average American in the long term.

Notes

Chapter 1

1. Charles Dickens, *The Old Curiosity Shop* (Pleasantvill, NY: Reader's Digest Association, 1988), pp. 316–18. Note this was originally published in serial form in 1840–1841. The first book edition apparently appeared in 1841.

2. Analysis by Roderick Floud and Bernard Harris of human development in Britain from 1756 to 1980 indicates that its level commenced a long-term increase in the latter part of the 18th century. The level faltered slightly in the late 1830s, but it has been climbing since the 1840s. To measure the level of human development, they used a human development index (HDI) composed of life expectancy at birth, percent literacy, and the logarithm of the gross domestic product per capita. The HDI is described in greater detail in chapter 2. Other measures of human welfare (e.g., heights and life expectancy) indicate a slight retrenchment during the 1830s and 1840s. However, all those measures indicate a sustained improvement in human welfare since that time. See Roderick Floud and Bernard Harris, "Health, Height, and Welfare: Britain, 1700–1980," in *Health and Welfare During Industrialization*, ed. Richard H. Steckel and Roderick Floud (Chicago: University of Chicago Press, 1997), pp. 91–126. In particular, see pages 116 and 118.

3. Indur M. Goklany, "The Future of Industrial Society" (paper presented at the International Conference on Industrial Ecology and Sustainability, University of Technology of Troyes, Troyes, France, September 22–25, 1999); Goklany, "Economic Growth and the State of Humanity," Policy Study no. 21, Political Economy Research Center, Bozeman, MT, 2001.

4. Indur M. Goklany, "Saving Habitat and Conserving Biodiversity on a Crowded Planet," *BioScience* 48 (1998): 941–53; Indur M. Goklany, "Potential Consequences of Increasing Atmospheric CO_2 Concentration Compared to Other Environmental Problems," *Technology* 7S (2000):189–213.

5. For example, civil war, aggravated by droughts, caused famines in Ethiopia, Somalia, and Sudan in the 1990s. Similarly, a dysfunctional regime converted a food problem into a full-scale famine in North Korea. See Goklany, "Strategies to Enhance Adaptability: Technological Change, Economic Growth, and Free Trade," *Climatic Change* 30 (1995): 427–49.

6. E. A. Wrigley and R. S. Schofield, *The Population History of England 1541–1871: A Reconstruction* (Cambridge, MA: Harvard University Press, 1981), p. 529; Michael R. Haines, *Estimated Life Tables for the United States, 1850–1900*, Historical Paper no. 59 (Cambridge, MA: National Bureau of Economic Research, 1994); Roderick Floud and Bernard Harris, "Health, Height, and Welfare: Britain, 1700–1980."

7. Paul Harrison, *The Third Revolution* (London: I. B. Tauris, 1992); Atiq Rahman, Nick Robins, and Anne Roncerel, eds., *Exploding the Population Myth: Consumption versus Population: Which Is the Climate Bomb?* (Brussels, Belgium: Climate Network Europe, 1993); Stephen Boyden and Stephen Dover, "Natural-Resource Consumption

NOTES TO PAGES 5–8

and Its Environmental Impacts in the Western World: Impacts of Increasing per Capita Consumption," *Ambio* 21 (1992): 63–69; Norman Myers, "Consumption: Challenge to Sustainable Development," *Science* 276 (April 4, 1997): 53–55; and Robert Engelman, *Stabilizing the Atmosphere: Population, Consumption, and Greenhouse Gases* (Washington, DC: Population Action International, 1994).

8. Henceforth, I will use the term "environmental" to pertain to the environment as well as natural resources.

9. Paul R. Ehrlich, *The Population Bomb* (New York: Ballantine Books, 1968).

10. Paul R. Ehrlich and Richard L. Harriman, *How to Be a Survivor: A Plan to Save Planet Earth* (New York: Ballantine, 1971), pp. 166–203.

11. Ibid., pp. 14–15.

12. Ibid. p. 21.

13. Lester R. Brown, *World Without Borders* (New York: Random House, 1972), p. 18.

14. Donella H. Meadows, Dennis L. Meadows, Jorgen Randers, and William W. Behrens III, *The Limits to Growth: A Report for the Club of Rome's Project on the Predicament of Mankind* (New York: Universe Books, 1972).

15. Gerald O. Barney, ed., *Global 2000 Report to the President* (New York: Pergamon Press, 1980). See also James Gustave Speth, *Red Sky at Morning: America and the Crisis of the Global Environment* (New Haven, CT: Yale University Press, 2004), pp. 1–9.

16. Donella H. Meadows, Dennis L. Meadows, and Jorgen Randers, *Beyond the Limits: Confronting Global Collapse, Envisioning a Sustainable Future* (Post Mills, VT: Chelsea Green, 1992); Garrett Hardin, *Living Within Limits: Ecology, Economics, and Population Taboos* (New York: Oxford University Press, 1993), pp. 202–03.

17. Barry Commoner, "The Environmental Cost of Economic Growth," *Chemistry in Britain* 8 (1972): 52–65.

18. Wilfred Beckerman, *In Defence of Economic Growth* (London: Jonathan Cape, 1974); Wilfred Beckerman, *Through Green-Colored Glasses: Environmentalism Reconsidered* (Washington, DC: Cato Institute, 1996); Julian L. Simon and Herman Kahn, eds., *The Resourceful Earth: A Response to Global 2000* (New York: Blackwell, 1984); Julian L. Simon, E. Calvin Beisner, and John Phelps, eds., *The State of Humanity* (Cambridge, MA: Blackwell, 1994); Ronald Bailey, ed., *The True State of the Planet* (New York: Free Press, 1995); Ronald Bailey, ed., *Earth Report 2000: Revisiting the True State of the Planet* (New York: McGraw-Hill, 1999); Gregg Easterbrook, *A Moment on the Earth: The Coming Age of Environmental Optimism* (New York: Viking, 1995); Bjørn Lomborg, *The Skeptical Environmentalist: Measuring the Real State of the World* (Cambridge: Cambridge University Press, 2001).

19. See, for example, Jim Norton, "Correcting Myths from Gregg Easterbrook," http://info-pollution.com/easter.htm (accessed February 27, 2006); "Correcting Myths from Bjørn Lomborg," http://info-pollution.com/lomborg.htm (accessed February 27, 2006); Paul R. Ehrlich and Anne H. Ehrlich, "Betrayal of Science and Reason: How Anti-environmental Rhetoric Threatens Our Future (Washington, DC: Island Press, 1996); John Rennie, Stephen Schneider, John P. Holdren, John Bongaarts, and Thomas Lovejoy, "Misleading Math about the Earth," *Scientific American* (January 2002): 61–71.

20. Danish Committee on Scientific Dishonesty, *2003 Annual Report* (Copenhagen: Danish Research Asgency, 2004), pp. 26–28, http://forsk.dk/pls/portal/docs/ PAGE/FORSKNINGSSTYRELSEN/FORSKNINGSSTYRELSEN_FORSIDE/ UDVALGENE_VIDENSKABELIG_UREDELIGHED/NYT_FRA_UVVU/ PRESSEMEDDELELSER/DCSD_REPORT_2003/UVVU_2003_EN.PDF (accessed

March 2, 2006); Environmental Assessment Institute, "Lomborg Decision Overturned by Danish Ministry of Science," December 17, 2003, http://www.imv.dk/Default. aspx?ID=233; Martin Agerup, "Something's (No Longer) Rotten in Denmark," December 18, 2003, http://www. policynetwork.net/main/article.php? article_id=562 (accessed March 2, 2006). See also John Kay, "Previous Convictions: Physics Envy," *Prospect* 85 (April 2003), http//www.prospect-magazine.co.uk/print article.php?id=5552&category=143&issue=o&author= (accessed March 2, 2006).

21. For example, Donella H. Meadows, Jorgen Randers, and Dennis L. Meadows, *Limits to Growth: The 30-Year Update* (White River Junction, VT: Chelsea Green, 2004); Paul R. Ehrlich and Anne H. Ehrlich, *One With Nineveh: Politics, Consumption, and the Human Future* (Washington, DC: Island Press, 2004); James Gustave Speth, *Red Sky at Morning: America and the Crisis of the Global Environment* (New Haven, CT: Yale University Press, 2004); Lester R. Brown, *Plan B: Rescuing a Planet under Stress and a Civilization in Trouble* (New York: W. W. Norton, 2003); Jared Diamond, *Collapse: How Societies Choose to Fail or Succeed* (New York: Viking, 2005).

22. Barry Commoner fully developed this identity. See "The Environmental Cost of Economic Growth," *Chemistry in Britain* 8 (1972): 52–65—but it was popularized in its present form by Ehrlich and his collaborators in Anne H. Ehrlich and Paul R. Ehrlich, *Earth* (New York: Franklin Watts, 1987), pp. 109–12; and Paul R. Ehrlich and Anne H. Ehrlich, *The Population Explosion* (New York: Simon and Schuster, 1990), pp. 58, 273.

23. Jesse H. Ausubel, "Does Climate Still Matter?" *Nature* 350 (1991): 649–52; See also Goklany, "Strategies to Enhance Adaptability: Technological Change, Economic Growth, and Free Trade."

24. Barry Commoner, "The Environmental Cost of Economic Growth"; Paul R. Ehrlich and John P. Holdren, "Impact of Population Growth," *Science* 171 (1971): 1212–17; Paul R. Ehrlich and Anne H. Ehrlich, *Healing the Planet* (Reading, MA: Addison-Wesley 1991), p. 7.

25. John R. Ehrlich and Anne H. Ehrlich, *Healing the Planet*, p. 7.

26. Norman Myers, "Consumption: Challenge to Sustainable Development."

27. Carolyn Raffensperger and Joel Tickner, eds., *Protecting Public Health and the Environment: Implementing the Precautionary Principle* (Washington, DC: Island Press, 1999).

28. Jared Diamond, *Collapse*, p. 504.

29. Ibid., p. 505.

30. Paul R. Ehrlich and John P. Holdren, "Impact of Population Growth"; Jared Diamond, *Collapse*, p. 490.

31. Indur M. Goklany, *The Precautionary Principle: A Critical Appraisal of Environmental Risk Assessment* (Washington, DC: Cato Institute, 2001).

32. Ibid.

33. William J. Clinton, State of the Union Address, 1998, www.pub.whitehouse.gov/uri-res/I2R?pdi://oma.eop.gov. us/1998/01/27/11.text.1 (accessed on September 18, 1998); William J. Clinton, State of the Union Address, 1999, www.pub.whitehouse.gov/uri-res/I2R?pdi://oma.eop.gov.us/1999/1/20/1.text.1 (accessed on July 7, 1999).

34. Indur M. Goklany, *The Precautionary Principle*.

35. Indur M. Goklany, "From Precautionary Principle to Risk-Risk Analysis," *Nature Biotechnology* 20 (2002): 1075.

36. Indur M. Goklany, *The Precautionary Principle*.

37. Jesse H. Ausubel, "Resources and Environment in the 21st Century: Seeing Past the Phantoms," *World Energy Council Journal* (July 1998): 8–16; David S. Landes, *The Wealth and Poverty of Nations: Why Some Are So Rich and Some So Poor* (New York: W. W. Norton, 1998).

38. Indur M. Goklany, "Strategies to Enhance Adaptability: Technological Change, Economic Growth, and Free Trade," 427–49; Goklany, "Richer Is Cleaner: Long Term Trends in Global Air Quality," in *The True State of the Planet*, ed. Ronald Bailey (New York: Free Press, 1995), pp. 339–77; Indur M. Goklany, *Clearing the Air: The True Story of the War on Air Pollution* (Washington, DC: Cato Institute, 1999).

39. Simon Kuznets, "Economic Growth and Income Inequality," *American Economic Review* 45 (1955): 1–28.

40. Nemat Shafik and Sushenjit Bandhopadhyaya, "Economic Growth and Environmental Quality: Time Series and Cross-Country Evidence," World Bank Policy Research Working Paper no. 904, Washington, DC, 1992; Gene M. Grossman and Alan B. Krueger, "Economic Growth and the Environment," *Quarterly Journal of Economics* 110 (1995): 353–77; Thomas M. Selden and Daqing Song, "Environmental Quality and Development: Is There a Kuznets Curve for Air Pollution Emissions?" *Journal of Environmental Economics and Management* 27 (1994): 147–62.

41. Intergovernmental Panel on Climate Change, *Summary for Policymakers: IPCC WGI Third Assessment Report* (Cambridge, UK: Cambridge University Press, 2001).

Chapter 2

1. Colin McEvedy and Richard Jones, *Atlas of World Population History* (New York: Penguin, 1978), p. 342; United Nations Population Division (UNPD), World Population Prospects: The 2004 Revision Database, http://esa.un.org/unpp (accessed August 27, 2005), henceforth WPP (2004). Food and Agriculture Organization (FAO), *FAOSTAT 2002*, http://apps.fao.org, henceforth FAO (2002).

2. Paul Bairoch, "International Industrialization Levels from 1750 to 1980," *Journal of European Economic History* 11 (1982): 269–333. Bairoch defines manufacturing industry as industry in general except mining, construction, electricity, gas, and water.

3. G. Gregg Marland, Thomas A. Boden, and Robert J. Andres, "Global, Regional, and National CO_2 Emissions," in *Trends: A Compendium of Data on Global Change* (Oak Ridge, TN: Carbon Dioxide Information Analysis Center, Oak Ridge National Laboratory, and U.S. Department of Energy, 2005).

4. This is calculated from GDPs provided by Angus Maddison, *The World Economy: Historical Statistics* (Paris: Organisation for Economic Co-operation and Development [OECD], 2003), www.ggdc.net/~maddison/ (accessed July 30, 2005), hereafter Angus Maddison (2003).

5. This chapter draws upon, and updates information contained in Goklany, "Economic Growth and the State of Humanity," Policy Study no. 21, Political Economy Research Center, Bozeman, MT, 2001.

6. See, for example, Jasper Becker, *Hungry Ghosts: Mao's Secret Famine* (New York: Free Press, 1996).

7. World Health Organization (WHO), *The World Health Report 1999* (Geneva: WHO, 1999), henceforth WHO (1999); Indur M. Goklany, "The Future of Industrial Society" (paper presented at the International Conference on Industrial Ecology and Sustainability, University of Technology of Troyes, Troyes, France, September 22–25, 1999).

8. WHO (1999); Indur M. Goklany, "The Future of Industrial Society."

9. World Bank, *World Development Indicators CD-ROM* (Washington, DC: 2001).

10. The GDP of a country, say the United States, in a given year is a measure of the economic value that is produced within that country's borders during that year. However, some of this product might leave the country, for example, as profits generated by a foreign company or wages paid to a foreigner. By the same token, profits and wages generated abroad by U.S. companies and U.S. labor could flow into the United States. Thus, to calculate the gross national product (GNP), the GDP has to be adjusted for these flows in and out of the United States (i.e., GNP = GDP − outflows + inflows). To obtain the gross national income (GNI), one subtracts the amount by which capital has depreciated from the GNP. For most countries, the GDP and GNP are generally within 1 percent or so of each other. For the United States, for example, between 1999 and 2004, the GNP was about 0.5 percent less than GDP, while the GNI varied from 11 to 12 percent below the GDP. U.S. Bureau of the Census (USBOC) *Statistical Abstract of the United States 2006* (Washington, DC: Government Printing Office, 2006), p. 448. However, for some countries the difference between these measures can be substantial. For example, in Luxembourg, which is generally at the top of the world's GDP per capita table, the GDP is substantially larger than GNP because 90,000 people in its labor force (equivalent to a fifth of its entire population) commute across the border every day from Belgium, France, Germany, and the Netherlands to work largely in its lucrative financial service sector. Anonymous, "GDP and GNI," OECD Observer no. 246–247, December 2004–January 2005, www.oecdobserver.org/news/fullstory.php/aid/1507/GDP_and_GNI.html. Because those workers are not counted as part of Luxembourg's population of 450,000, Luxembourg's GDP per capita seems formidably large. Similarly, Ireland also has a very high GDP per capita, while GNI per capita, although still very high, was more than 17 percent lower in 2003 in part because of profits repatriated by foreign investors. Anonymous, "GDP and GNI"; World Resources Institute, Earth Trends, http://earthtrends.wri.org/searchable_db/index.php?theme=5 (accessed July 30, 2006).

11. See, for example, Richard A. Easterlin, *Growth Triumphant: The Twenty-First Century in Historical Perspective* (Ann Arbor, MI: University of Michigan Press, 1996).

12. See, for example, UNDP, *Human Development Report 2000* (New York: Oxford University Press, 2000).

13. William Paddock and Paul Paddock, *Famine 1975! America's Decision: Who Will Survive?* (Boston, MA: Little, Brown, 1967); Paul R. Ehrlich, *The Population Bomb* (New York: Ballantine Books, 1968).

14. WPP (2004).

15. Angus Maddison (2003).

16. Donald O. Mitchell and Merlinda D. Ingco, "The World Food Outlook," *Hunger Notes* 19 (Winter 1993–1994): 20–25; World Resources Institute (WRI), *World Resources 2000–01* (Washington, DC: WRI, 2000); Commodity Prices Pink Sheet, July 2005, http://siteresources.worldbank.org/INTPROSPECTS/Resources/Pnk_0705.pdf (accessed July 12, 2005).

17. Indur M. Goklany, "Meeting Global Food Needs: The Environmental Trade-Offs Between Increasing Land Conversion and Land Productivity," *Technology* 6 (1999): 107–30.

18. FAO, *FAOSTAT 2005*, http://apps.fao.org, henceforth FAO (2005).

19. Ibid.

20. FAO, *Assessment of Feasible Progress in Food Security, Technical Background Documents 12–15*, vol. 3 (Rome, Italy: FAO, 1996).

21. Ibid.

22. Robert W. Fogel, "The Contribution of Improved Nutrition to the Decline of Mortality Rates in Europe and America," in *The State of Humanity*, ed. Julian L. Simon, E. Calvin Beisner, and John Phelps (Cambridge, MA: Blackwell, 1995), pp. 61–71; Robert W. Fogel, *The Fourth Great Awakening and the Future of Egalitarianism* (Chicago: University of Chicago Press, 2000).

23. FAO, *Assessment of Feasible Progress in Food Security*.

24. FAO (2005).

25. Indur M. Goklany, "Meeting Global Food Needs: The Environmental Trade-Offs Between Increasing Land Conversion and Land Productivity," 107–30; FAO (2005).

26. The 2000–02 figure for food supply is from FAO, *The State of Food Insecurity in the World 2004* (Rome, Italy: FAO, 2004), available at www.fao.org/documents/show_cdr.asp?url_file/docrep/007/y5650e/y5650e00.htm (accessed July 12, 2005). The 1969–71 food supply estimate is from FAO, *State of Food Insecurity in the World 2001* (Rome, Italy: FAO, 2001), p. 8. Population estimates are from FAO (2005).

27. WPP (2004).

28. Jasper Becker, *Hungry Ghosts*.

29. Data for daily food supplies per capita are from World Resources Institute's EarthTrends database online at www.wri.org (accessed July 12, 2005), henceforth WRI (2005). Data on GDP per capita are from the World Bank's *World Development Indicators*, http://devdata.worldbank.org/dataonline/ (accessed July 12, 2005), henceforth World Bank (2005). This particular data set uses international (PPP-adjusted) dollars, which are obtained using a special conversion methodology that uses "purchasing power parity" and is designed to reflect more accurately the purchasing powers of different currencies. Conversion is based on the number of units of a country's currency required to buy the same amounts of goods and services in the domestic market as a dollar would buy in the United States. In contrast, the market exchange rate of a currency in U.S. dollars is the amount of the currency one can buy with one U.S. dollar on the open currency market.

30. The smoothed curves in this figure were generated by regressing FS against the logarithm of income (or PCI) based on the following "log-linear" relationship:

$$FS = A + B \times D + C \times \log(PCI)$$

where D is a dummy variable to represent observations for different years ($D = 0$ for 1975, and 1 for 2002), and A, B, and C are constant coefficients. Under this formulation, C is the slope of the food supply curves for either 1975 or 2002 when they are plotted against $\log(PCI)$. Per the log-linear equation, this slope is the same for both curves. B, the coefficient of the dummy variable, is the shift in the FS curve as one goes from 1975 to 2002. A total of 263 observations were used for the two years (i.e., N = 263), the adjusted $R^2 = 0.65$, and the coefficients of the $\log(PCI)$ term and the dummy variable are positive and significant at the 99.9 percent level (i.e., p < 0.001). In other words, the dependence of FS on GDP per capita is significant, as is the upward shift in this indicator as we go from 1975 to 2002. Details on the coefficients A, B, and C are provided in appendix A.

31. Ibid.

32. The two cereal yield (CY) curves in figure 2.3 have been fitted using an approach similar to that used to generate figure 2.2, with the exception that a linear equation is used to estimate the intercept for the initial year, the change in the intercept between

the initial and final years, and the common slope. As indicated in appendix A, the common slope for the two CY curves is positive, that is, CY increases with wealth. This increase is statistically significant at the 99.9 percent confidence level, as is the change in intercept (on the CY axis) going from 1975 to 1999. The latter indicates that CY improved significantly with technological change between those two years. For this figure, the combined N = 258 and adjusted R^2 = 0.47. See appendix A for further details.

33. Indur M. Goklany, "Saving Habitat and Conserving Biodiversity on a Crowded Planet," 941–53.

34. Indur M. Goklany, "Strategies to Enhance Adaptability: Technological Change, Sustainable Growth, and Free Trade," *Climatic Change* 30 (1995): 427–49.

35. The best fit curve, based on data from World Bank (2005), was generated using the following log-log equation:

$$\log(\text{malnutrition}) = A + B \times D + C \times \log(\text{PCI}),$$

where D is a dummy variable used to distinguish observations for different years (D = 0 for 1987, and 1 for 2000), and A, B, and C are constant coefficients, N = 63, and the adjusted R^2 = 0.56. The coefficient of the log(PCI) term is positive and significant at the 99.9 percent level (i.e., $p < 0.001$). However, the coefficient of the dummy variable, while positive, is significant at the 90 percent level but not the 95 percent level (p = 0.052). In other words, the dependence of malnutrition on income is significant, but not necessarily the downward shift in this indicator from 1987 to 2000. See appendix A for further details.

36. The World Bank's estimates of absolute poverty are based on an income of a dollar per day in 1993 international dollars. See Martin Ravallion, "Pessimistic on Poverty?" *Economist*, April 7, 2004, www.columbia.edu/~xs23/papers/worlddistribu tion/ravallion.htm (accessed August 29, 2005).

37. Kenneth Hill, "The Decline in Childhood Mortality," in *The State of Humanity*, ed. Julian L. Simon, E. Calvin Beisner, and John Phelps (Cambridge, MA: Blackwell, 1995), pp. 37–50.

38. World Bank (2005).

39. WRI, *World Resources 2000–01*.

40. U.S. Bureau of the Census (USBOC), *Historical Statistics of the United States, Colonial Times to 1970* (Washington, DC: GPO, 1975), p. 60, henceforth USBOC (1975); National Center for Health Statistics, *National Vital Statistics Report: Births, Marriages, Divorces, and Deaths: Provisional Data for 2004*, vol. 53 (no. 21), June 28, 2005.

41. WPP (2004); World Bank (2005).

42. See World Bank, *World Development Report: Investing in Health* (New York: Oxford University Press, 1993); Lant Pritchett and Lawrence H. Summers, "Wealthier Is Healthier," *Journal of Human Resources* 31 (1996): 841–68.

43. The curves in figure 2.5 were fitted using a log-log relationship that uses a procedure similar to that described in note 35. N = 271 and adjusted R^2 = 0.77 with a dummy variable to distinguish data for the different years. The lowering of the curve over time is consistent with the creation and diffusion of new and existing-but-underused technologies. The lowering of the infant mortality with both the passage of time and with the increase of income is significant at the 99.9 percent level. See appendix A for further details.

44. Figure 2.6, which shows the dependence of health expenditures in 2002 on the level of economic development, was generated using linear regression analysis. For

427

this figure, N = 161 and adjusted R^2 = 0.81. The slope is statistically significant at the 99.9 percent confidence level. See appendix A for further details.

45. Figure 2.7 illustrates the dependence of access to safe water on per capita income for 1990 and 2002. It was generated using a tobit model with the upper limit for access to safe water constrained to 100 percent. The regression analysis used a log-log equation. (See also note 35.) The coefficient of log(PCI), that is, the common slope for the two years, is positive and statistically significant at the 99.9 percent confidence level. The coefficient of the dummy variable, which describes the shift in the curve with time, is positive and significant at the 95 percent level. For this figure, N = 241 and pseudo R^2 = –3.65. See appendix A for further details.

46. Figure 2.8 shows the dependence of access to sanitation (SAN) on per capita income for 1990 and 2002. It was generated using a tobit model with the upper limit for access to sanitation constrained to 100 percent. The regression analysis used the following log-log equation:

$$\log(SAN) = A + B \times D + C \times (1 + d \times E/C) \times \log(PCI),$$

where A, B, C, and E are constants, and D and d are dummy variables taking the value of 0 for 1990 and 1 for 2000. This formulation allows the intercept on both the log(SAN) axis and the slope, that is, the coefficient of the log(PCI) term, to vary with the year. C, the slope for log(PCI) in 1990, is positive and significant at the 99.9 percent level indicating that access to sanitation increases with income. B, the intercept on the log(SAN) axis, is positive and significant at the 95 percent level, which indicates that the upward displacement of sanitation with time is significant. E, although also significant at the 95 percent level, is negative. This decline in the sensitivity of access to sanitation to income is consistent with the notion that the merits of sanitation are better recognized now and more likely nowadays to be implemented at lower levels even in poorer countries, perhaps because the costs of improving such access are affordable (for whatever reason). For this figure, N = 222 and pseudo R^2 = 1.30. See appendix A for further details.

47. Robert W. Fogel, "The Contribution of Improved Nutrition to the Decline of Mortality Rates in Europe and America," 61–71.

48. Angus Maddison, *The World Economy: A Millennial Perspective* (Paris: OECD, 2001), henceforth Angus Maddison (2001).

49. World Bank (2005).

50. Samuel H. Preston, "Human Mortality Throughout History and Prehistory," in *The State of Humanity*, ed. Julian L. Simon, E. Calvin Beisner, and John Phelps (Cambridge, MA: Blackwell, 1995), pp. 30–36.

51. Maddison (2001).

52. See table 2.4, World Bank (2005).

53. Ibid.

54. Roderick H. Floud and Bernard Harris, "Health, Height, and Welfare: Britain, 1700–1980," in *Health and Welfare during Industrialization*, ed. Richard H. Steckel and Roderick Floud (Chicago: University of Chicago Press, 1997), pp. 91–126.

55. Michael R. Haines, "Estimated Life Tables for the United States, 1850–1900," Historical Paper no. 59, National Bureau of Economic Research, Cambridge, MA, 1994.

56. Robert W. Fogel, "The Contribution of Improved Nutrition to the Decline of Mortality Rates in Europe and America," 63.

57. Improvements in sanitation in the United States and the United Kingdom, for example, preceded the knowledge of germ theory.

58. World Bank, *World Development Report: Investing in Health* (New York: Oxford University Press, 1993); Barry R. Bloom, "The Future of Public Health," *Nature* 402 (1999, Supplement): C63–64.

59. Figure 2.10, constructed using data from World Bank (2005), uses the same methodology as is used for figure 2.2 for food supplies per capita. See note 29. The smoothed curves in this figure are based on log-linear regression analysis—N = 268 for 1977 and 2003 cumulatively and adjusted R^2 = 0.56. The increase in life expectancy due to increase in income and the passage of time is significant at the 99.9 percent level. Additional details are contained in appendix A.

60. Angus Maddison (2001).

61. USBOC (1975).

62. GDP per capita data are from Angus Maddison (2001); life expectancy data are from World Bank (2005).

63. Data for the United States are from Angus Maddison (2003) for GDP per capita and Michael R. Haines, *Estimated Life Tables for the United States, 1850–1900*, for life expectancy. Data for sub-Saharan Africa are from World Bank (2005).

64. Figure 2.11 uses data from WRI (2005) for 1950–55 and 1955–60 (plotted as 1952.5 and 1957.5, respectively). For Russia, it plotted the WRI data for 1960–65 and 1965–70 as 1962 and 1967 data. The multiple years reflect five-year averages. The rest of the data are from World Bank (2005).

65. World Bank (2005).

66. Groningen Growth and Development Centre (GGDC), 2005, Total Economy database, http://www.ggdc.net, henceforth GGDC (2005).

67. Charles Becker and David Bloom, "The Demographic Crisis in the Former Soviet Union: Introduction," *World Development* 26 (1998): 1913–19.

68. World Bank (2005).

69. UNDP (2000).

70. World Bank (2005).

71. In the 2005 online version of the World Bank's *World Development Indicators*, Zimbabwe had a higher life expectancy than Zambia in 2003 (38.5 years vs. 36.5 years). However, the July 2006 version shows the reverse (Zimbabwe at 37.2 years and Zambia at 37.7 years for 2003). Also the 2006 version indicates a slight increase in 2004 for Zambia (38.1) but no change for Zimbabwe. These trends, if real, partly reflect the fact that the economic situation in Zimbabwe has deteriorated while Zambia's situation has apparently improved, and that the former has instituted a more aggressive HIV/AIDS control program since around 2000.

72. WPP (2004); World Bank (2005).

73. OECD, "Maintaining Prosperity in an Aging Society," Policy Brief no. 5-1998, OECD, Paris, 1998; Donna E. Shalala, "Eliminating Racial and Ethnic Health Disparities [sic]" (speech delivered at the Patricia Harris Public Affairs Program, Howard University, March 13, 1998), http://www.hhs.gov/news/speeches/HOWARDPH.html (accessed February 3, 2001).

74. U.S. Department of Health and Human Services, "Active Aging: A Shift in the Paradigm," Office of Disability, Aging, and Long-Term Care, May 1997, http://aspe.hhs.gov/daltcp/reports/actaging.htm (accessed August 7, 2000).

75. Robert W. Fogel, *Changes in the Process of Aging during the Twentieth Century: Findings and Procedures of the Early Indicators Project*, Working Paper no. 9941, National Bureau of Economic Research, Cambridge, MA, 2003.

76. WHO, *World Health Report 2004* (Geneva: WHO, 2004). Health-adjusted life expectancy is the life expectancy adjusted downward to account for the degradation in the quality of life due to ill health. It is calculated by subtracting a portion of years of ill health (weighted according to severity) from the expected (unadjusted) life expectancy to give the equivalent years of healthy life.

77. Figure 2.12 is based on data from WHO (2004) through WRI (2005) using a log-linear equation. $N = 159$, adjusted $R^2 = 0.70$. The increase in HALE with the log of income is significant at the 99.9 percent level. See appendix A for further details.

78. Angus Maddison (2001) and GGDC (2005).

79. Angus Maddison (2001), p. 322.

80. Ibid., p. 265.

81. Updated from Indur M. Goklany, "Meeting Global Food Needs: The Environmental Trade-Offs Between Increasing Land Conversion and Land Productivity," 107–30, based on USBOC (1975) and USBOC, *Statistical Abstract of the United States 2004–2005* (Washington, DC: Government Printing Office, 2004), henceforth USBOC (2004).

82. Jesse H. Ausubel and Arnulf Grübler, "Working Less and Living Longer," *Technological Forecasting and Social Change* 50 (1995): 113–31.

83. Jesse H. Ausubel and Arnulf Grübler estimated disposable hours by subtracting 10 years for childhood and first elementary education and assuming 10 hours per day for sleep, eating, and personal hygiene for both genders. Total life hours of work were estimated as the product of years in a career, weeks worked per year, and hours worked per week on paid and "socially obligatory activities" including unpaid, informal work; child care; housework; and voluntary activities.

84. World Bank (2005); United Nations Educational, Scientific, and Cultural Organization, http://www.uis.unesco.org/ev.php?ID = 6057_201&ID2 = DO_TOPIC (accessed July 7, 2005).

85. The curves for 1990 and 2002 were fitted using log-log regression on data from World Bank (2005). See note 35. $N = 180$ and adjusted $R^2 = 0.58$. The slope of the curves plotted against log(PCI) is positive and statistically significant at the 99.9 percent confidence level, as is the increase in tertiary enrolment over time, that is, the coefficient of the dummy variable (*D*). See appendix A for further details.

86. World Bank (2005); World Bank, *World Development Indicators 1999*.

87. Angus Maddison, *Monitoring the World Economy, 1820–1992* (Paris: OECD, 1995); and Angus Maddison, *Chinese Economic Performance in the Long Run* (Paris: OECD, 1998).

88. Data are from World Bank, *World Development Indicators 2001*; and World Bank (2005).

89. The curves in figure 2.17, based on data from World Bank (2005), are fitted using information derived from log-linear regression using a tobit model with the data truncated at child labor = 0. The decline in child labor with the passage of time and with increasing GDP per capita are statistically significant at the 99.9 percent confidence level, $N = 262$, and pseudo $R^2 = 0.16$. Details of the regression analysis are provided in appendix A.

90. Freedom House, *Democracy's Century* (New York: Freedom House, 2002).

91. Freedom House, *Freedom in the World* (New York: Freedom House, 2005).

92. UNDP, *Human Development Report 2000*.

93. James Gwartney, Robert Lawson, and Dexter Samida, *Economic Freedom of the World: 2000 Annual Report* (Vancouver, BC: Fraser Institute, 2000). The degree of

economic freedom is characterized by a measure called the economic freedom of the world index (or the economic freedom index, for short), which will be addressed in greater detail in chapter 4.

94. James Gwartney and Robert Lawson, with Chris Edwards, Walter Park, Veronique de Rugy, and Smita Wagh, *Economic Freedom of the World: 2002 Annual Report* (Vancouver, BC: Fraser Institute, 2002), www.cato.org/ economicfreedom/2002/efw-2002.ppt (accessed June 26, 2002).

95. James Gwartney and Robert Lawson, *Economic Freedom of the World: 2004 Annual Report* (Vancouver, BC: Fraser Institute, 2004).

96. Ibid.

97. Ibid.

98. James Gwartney and Robert Lawson, *Economic Freedom of the World: 2002 Annual Report* (Vancouver, BC: Fraser Institute, 2002), pp. 17–19, www.cato.org/economic-freedom/ (accessed June 26, 2002).

99. In Dora L. Costa and Richard H. Steckel "Long-Term Trends, Health, Welfare, and Economic Growth in the United States," in *Health and Welfare during Industrialization*, ed. Richard H. Steckel and Rodrick Floud (Chicago: University of Chicago Press, 1997), p. 72.

100. Ibid.

101. Michael R. Haines, *Estimated Life Tables for the United States, 1850–1900* (1994).

102. Roderick Floud and Bernard Harris, "Health, Height, and Welfare: Britain, 1700–1980," pp. 91–126.

103. Lars G. Sandberg and Richard H. Steckel, "Was Industrialization Hazardous to Your Health? Not in Sweden," in *Health and Welfare during Industrialization*, ed. Richard H. Steckel and Roderick Floud (Chicago: University of Chicago Press, 1997), pp. 127–59.

104. Sophia Twarog, "Heights and Living Standards in Germany, 1850–1939: The Case of Württemberg," in *Health and Welfare during Industrialization*, ed. Richard H. Steckel and Roderick Floud (Chicago: University of Chicago Press, 1997), pp. 285–330.

105. UNDP (2004).

106. GDP per capita trends are based on constant, PPP-adjusted international dollars (World Bank 2005).

107. "Zim Commander 'Not Killed in DRC'," *Daily Mail and Guardian*, December 15, 1998, www.mg.co.za/mg/za/archive/98dec/15decpmnews.html (accessed July 26, 2000); United Nations High Commission on Refugees (UNHCR), "UNHCR Appeals for Funds for Great Lakes Operations," press release, March 2, 1998, http://www.unhcr.ch/news/pr/pr980302.htm (accessed July 25, 2000); UNHCR, "1999 Global Appeal/Great Lakes," www.unhcr.ch/fdrs/ga99/overlake.htm (accessed February 2, 2001); UNHCR, "Global Appeal/Southern Africa," www.unhcr.ch/fdrs/ga99oversaf.htm (accessed February 2, 2001).

108. The decline in their GDP per capita was largely due to a drop in the price of oil during this period.

109. Centers for Disease Control and Prevention (CDC), *HIV/AIDS Surveillance Report* 13, no. 2 (2002): table 31; CDC *HIV/AIDS Surveillance Report* 14, no. 2 (2003): table 7; CDC, "Cases of HIV Infection and AIDS in the United States, 2003," *HIV/AIDS Surveillance Report* 15: table 7, www.cdc.gov/hiv/stats/2003 SurveillanceReport.htm; Joyce A. Martin, Betty L. Smith, T. J. Mathews, and Stephanie J. Ventura, "Births and Deaths: Preliminary Data for 1998," *National Vital Statistics* 47, no. 25 (1999): 28.

Chapter 3

1. This chapter draws upon, and updates information contained in, Indur M. Goklany, "The Globalization of Human Well-Being," Cato Institute Policy Analysis no. 447, August 22, 2002.

2. See, for example, Kevin Watkins, Aart Kraay, and David Dollar, "Point/Counterpoint: Making Globalization Work for the Poor," *Finance and Development* 39, no.1 (March 2002), www.imf.org/external/pubs/ft/fandd/2002/03/watkins.htm (accessed August 8, 2002); Martin Khor, "Backlash Grows Against Globalization," 1996, www.globalpolicy.org/globaliz/bcklash1.htm; W. Bowman Cutter, Joan E. Spero, and Laura D'Andrea Tyson, "New World, New Deal," *Foreign Affairs* (March/April 2000), www.foreignpolicy2000.org/library/issuebriefs/readingnotes/fa_tyson.html; Bernard Wasow, "New World, Bum Deal?" *Foreign Affairs* (July/August 2000), www.tcf.org/Opinions/In_the_News/Wasow-NewWorld_BumDeal.html; Jay Mazur, "Labor's New Internationalism, *Foreign Affairs* (January/February 2000); "The FP Interview: Lori's War," interview originally published in *Foreign Policy* (Spring 2000), www.foreignpolicy.com/best_of_fp/articles/wallach.html; United Nations Development Programme (UNDP), *Human Development Report 1999* (New York: UNDP, 1999), pp. 3, 11.

3. W. Bowman Cutter, Joan E. Spero, and Laura D'Andrea Tyson, "New World, New Deal."

4. UNDP, *Human Development Report 1999*.

5. UNDP, *Human Development Report 2000* (New York: Oxford University Press, 2000).

6. Also reported in 1990 international dollars; Angus Maddison, *The World Economy: Historical Statistics* (Paris: Organisation for Economic Co-operation and Development, 2003), data available at www.ggdc.net/~maddison/ (accessed July 30, 2005), henceforth Angus Maddison (2003). Today's dollar (in real terms) buys a lot more than the same dollar would have even half a century ago, let alone a millennium ago, as discussed in chapter 2.

7. Groningen Growth and Development Centre (GGDC), Total Economy database, www.ggdc.net, henceforth GGDC (2005).

8. World Bank, *World Development Indicators 2005*, table 2.5a, http://www.dev data.worldbank.org/wdipdfs/table2_5.pdf (accessed July 25, 2006). See also Shaohua Chen and Martin Ravallion, "How Have the World's Poorest Fared since the Early 1980s?" World Bank Policy Research Working Paper WPS no. 3341, Washington, DC.

9. UNDP, *Human Development Report 2002* (New York: Oxford University Press, 2002), p.19.

10. See, for example, Indur M. Goklany, "The Globalization of Human Well-Being."

11. UNDP, *Human Development Report 2002*, p. 19.

12. Ibid., p. 19.

13. David Dollar and Aart Kraay, "Growth Is Good for the Poor," World Bank Policy Research Working Paper no. 2587, 2000, www.worldbank.org/research/growth/absdollakray.htm.

14. François Bourguignon and Christian Morrisson, "Inequality Among World Citizens, 1820–1992" (Paris: Département et Laboratoire d'Economie Théorique et Appliquée, Ecole Normale Superieure, 2001), www.delta. ens.fr/XIX/paper_WD19.pdf. Note that figure 3.1, which does not have any data from 1929 to 1950, washes out the effects of both the Great Depression and World War II.

15. World Bank, *World Development Indicators 2005*, table 2.5a. See also Shaohua Chen and Martin Ravallion, "How Have the World's Poorest Fared since the Early 1980s?"; World Bank, *Global Economic Prospects, and the Developing Countries 2002* (Washington, DC: World Bank, 2002), pp. 30–31.

16. Xavier Sala-i-Martin, *The World Distribution of Income (Estimated from Individual Country Distributions)*, May 2002, p. 2, www.columbia.edu/~xs23/papers/pdfs/WorldIncomeDistribution.pdf (accessed August 8, 2002).

17. Food and Agriculture Organization (FAO), *FAOSTAT 2002*, http://apps.fao.org.

18. Xavier Sala-i-Martin, *The World Distribution of Income*, p. 36.

19. Surjit S. Bhalla, *Imagine There's No Country: Poverty, Growth, and Inequality in the Era of Globalization* (Washington, DC: Institute for International Economics, 2002), pp. 174–78.

20. Ibid., pp. 10, 174–78.

21. Ibid, pp. 182–86. The Gini coefficient—named after the Italian economist Corrado Gini, who formulated this measure in 1912—is a number between 0 and 100, where 0 corresponds to perfect equality (i.e., everyone has the same income) and 100 corresponds to absolute inequality (i.e., one person has all the income, while everyone else has zero income). Wikipedia, http://en.wikipedia.og/wiki/Gini_coefficient (accessed August 2, 2006). Thus, the higher the number, the greater the inequality. However, the scale is highly nonlinear.

22. For instance, Stephen Lewis, a leading Canadian New Democrat Party politician, former Canadian ambassador to the United Nations, and erstwhile deputy executive director of United Nations Children's Fund, is quoted as having said that "there is something profoundly wrong with globalization. . . . There is more to the world than creating bigger markets. We can't ignore the human dimension": in Ryan Smith, "Lewis Flays Globalization," *University of Alberta Express News*, January 29, 2001, http://www.expressnews.ualberta.ca/article.cfm?id = 393 (accessed July 25, 2006). Similarly, Lori Wallach, an anti-globalization organizer who came to prominence during the Seattle protests, notes that "[t]he question is, what is going on in real measures of well-being? So, while the volume, the flow of goods, may be up, and in some countries gross national product may be up, those macroeconomic indicators don't represent what's happening for the day-to-day standard of living for an enormous number of people in the world. That gets to one of the biggest critiques of the World Trade Organization in its first five years, which is that while the overall global flow of trade continues to grow, the share of trade flows held by developing countries has declined steadily. Similarly, over that five-year period, while the macroeconomic indicators have often looked good, real wages in many countries have declined, and wage inequality has increased both within and between countries"; see "The FP Interview: Lori's War," in *Foreign Policy* (Spring 2000): 44.

23. Zach Dubinsky, "Amid the Tears: Protesters, Police, Politics, and the People of Quebec," *Cleveland FreeTimes* (April 25–May 1, 2001), on file with author. This slogan is reminiscent of the title of a book by Eric A. Davidson, *You Can't Eat GNP: Economics as If Ecology Mattered* (Cambridge, MA: Perseus, 2000).

24. Indur M. Goklany, *Economic Growth and the State of Humanity* (Bozeman, MT: Political Economy Research Center, 2001); and Goklany, "The Future of the Industrial System," (invited paper, International Conference on Industrial Ecology and Sustainability, University of Technology of Troyes, Troyes, France, September 22–25, 1999).

25. James Gwartney and Robert Lawson with Walter Park and Charles Skipton, *Economic Freedom of the World: Annual Report 2001* (Vancouver, BC: Fraser Institute, 2001); David Dollar and Aart Kraay, "Growth Is Good for the Poor," World Bank Policy Research Working Paper no. 2587, 2000, www.worldbank.org/research/growth/absdollakray.htm.; James Gwartney, Randall Holcombe, and Robert Lawson, "The Scope of Government and the Wealth of Nations," *Cato Journal* 18 (1998): 163–90; Seth W. Norton, "Poverty, Property Rights, and Human Well-Being: A Cross-National Study," *Cato Journal* 18, no. 2 (1998): 233–45; Robert J. Barro, *The Determinants of Economic Growth: A Cross-Country Empirical Study* (Cambridge, MA: MIT Press, 1997). With respect to democracy and economic growth, Robert J. Barro's *The Determinants of Economic Growth* suggests that increased economic growth tends to increase democracy (the so-called Lipset hypothesis) but democracy's effect on economic growth is mixed; apparently growth increases with democracy at low levels of democracy but declines at high levels, perhaps because redistribution impulses are harder to contain in democracies. This is echoed in William Easterly, *The Elusive Quest for Growth: Economists' Adventures and Misadventures in the Tropics* (Cambridge, MA: MIT Press, 1991): 265–67. See also, Dani Rodrik, "Democracy and Economic Performance," Kennedy School of Government, Harvard University, December 14, 1997, http://ksghome.harvard.edu/~drodrik.academic.ksg/demoecon.PDF; Francisco L. Rivera-Batiz, "Democracy, Governance, and Economic Growth: Theory and Evidence," undated, www.columbia.edu/cu/economics/discpapr/DP0102-57.pdf.

26. Paul Ehrlich, *The Population Bomb* (New York: Ballantine Books, 1968).

27. William Paddock and Paul Paddock, *Famine 1975! America's Decision: Who Will Survive?* (Boston, MA: Little, Brown, 1967).

28. FAO, *The State of Agriculture 1996* (Rome: FAO, 1996); FAO, *The State of Food Insecurity in the World 2002* (Rome: FAO, 2002), p. 31.

29. FAO, *The State of Food Insecurity in the World 2002*, p. 32; FAO, *The State of Food Insecurity in the World 2004* (Rome: FAO, 2004).

30. FAO, *FAOSTAT 2005*, http://apps.fao.org. This is over and above their level of production and stocks at hand.

31. Indur M. Goklany, "Strategies to Enhance Adaptability: Technological Change, Sustainable Growth, and Free Trade," *Climatic Change* 30 (1995): 427–49.

32. Kenneth Hill, "The Decline in Childhood Mortality," in *The State of Humanity*, ed. Julian L. Simon (Cambridge, MA: Blackwell, 1995), pp. 37–50.

33. United Nations Population Division, *World Population Prospects: The 2004 Revision Database*, http://esa.un.org/unpp/ (accessed August 27, 2005), hereinafter WPP (2004).

34. World Bank, *World Development Indicators*, http://devdata.worldbank.org/dataonline (accessed July 12, 2005).

35. The country groupings in this—and the following three—figures are taken from the classifications used in the World Bank's *World Development Indicators 2005*, http://devdata.worldbank.org/dataonline (accessed July 12, 2005).

36. Angus Maddison, *The World Economy: Historical Statistics* (Paris: OECD, 2003), www.ggdc.net/~maddison (accessed July 30, 2005).

37. UN Population Division, *World Population Prospects: The 2004 Revision Database*, http://esa.un.org/unpd (accessed August 27, 2005).

38. World Bank, *World Development Indicators 2002*.

39. Ibid.

40. For example, in 1998, Zambia lost more than twice as many disability adjusted life years to malaria than to HIV/AIDS (Richard Tren, personal communication, May 14, 2002, based on statistics from Zambia's Board of Health). The malaria mortality rate in sub-Saharan Africa, which had been 184 per 100,000 in 1950, declined to 107 per 100,000 in 1970. After continuing its decline until the 1980s, it began to rebound in the late 1980s. By 1997, it had increased to 165. By contrast, in the rest of the world it declined from 7 per 100,000 in 1970 to 1 per 100,000 in 1997; World Health Organization (WHO), *World Health Report 1999* (Geneva: WHO, 1999), p. 50.

41. Centers for Disease Control and Prevention (CDC), *HIV/AIDS Surveillance Report* 13, no. 2 (2002): table 31; CDC, *HIV/AIDS Surveillance Report* 14, no. 2 (2003): table 7; CDC, "Cases of HIV Infection and AIDS in the United States, 2003," *HIV/AIDS Surveillance Report* 15: table 7, www.cdc.gov/hiv/stats/2003 SurveillanceReport.htm; Joyce A. Martin, Betty L. Smith, T. J. Mathews, and Stephanie J. Ventura, "Births and Deaths: Preliminary Data for 1998," *National Vital Statistics* 47, no. 25 (1999): 28.

42. World Bank, *World Development Indicators 2002*.

43. Data chart, *The Economist*, March 23–30, 2002, p. 102.

44. Stephen Moore and Julian L. Simon, *It's Getting Better All the Time: 100 Greatest Trends of the Last 100 Years* (Washington, DC: Cato Institute, 2000), p. 79.

45. Data for 1947 is from the U.S. Bureau of the Census (USBOC), *Historical Statistics of the United States: Colonial Times to 1970* (Washington, DC: GPO, 1975), p. 297, henceforth USBOC (1975). The data for 1947 for blacks includes data on other nonwhite races. For 2003, data is from USBOC, *Current Population Survey: 2003 and 2004 Annual Social and Economic Suppplements*, www.census. gov/hhes/www/img/incpov03/fig07.jpg (accessed August 7, 2005). 2003 data for whites is for non-Hispanic whites.

46. Carmen DeNavas-Walt, Robert W. Cleveland, and Marc L. Roemer, *Money Income in the United States, 2000* (Washington, DC: USBOC, 2001), p. 2.

47. USBOC (1975), p. 55; Donna L. Hoyert, Hsiang Ching Kung, and Betty L. Smith, "Deaths: Preliminary Data for 2003," *National Vital Statistics Reports* 53, no. 15 (Hyattsville, MD: National Center for Health Statistics, 2005). The data for 1940 for "blacks" includes data on other nonwhite races, while the 2003 data for whites does not include Hispanics.

48. USBOC (1975), pp. 14, 380; USBOC, *Statistical Abstract of the United States 2004–2005* (Washington, DC: GPO, 2004). The data for 1940 for blacks includes data on other nonwhite races, while the 2003 data for whites does not include Hispanics.

49. Robert W. Fogel, *The Fourth Great Awakening and the Future of Egalitarianism* (Chicago: University of Chicago Press, 2000); Richard A. Easterlin, *Growth Triumphant: The Twenty-First Century in Historical Perspective* (Ann Arbor, MI: University of Michigan Press, 1996); and Monroe Lerner and Odin W. Anderson, *Health Progress in the United States, 1900–1960* (Chicago: University of Chicago Press, 1963).

50. Robert W. Fogel, *The Fourth Great Awakening and the Future of Egalitarianism*, p. 149.

51. UNDP, *Human Development Report 2000*, p. 152.

52. Peter H. Gleick, *The World's Water: The Biennial Report on Freshwater Resources* (Washington, DC: Island Press, 1998).

53. Amartya Sen, "A World of Extremes: Ten Theses on Globalization," *Los Angeles Times*, July 17, 2001, www.globalpolicy.org/globaliz/define/0717amrt.htm.

Chapter 4

1. This is one of the major reasons why, whether income inequalities between nations are widening or not, by and large the gaps in human well-being are diminishing. See Indur M. Goklany, "The Globalization of Human Well-Being," Cato Institute Policy Analysis no. 447, August 22, 2002.

2. See, e.g., Indur M. Goklany, "Strategies to Enhance Adaptability: Technological Change, Economic Growth, and Free Trade," *Climatic Change* 30 (1995): 427–49.

3. Richard A. Easterlin, *Growth Triumphant: The Twenty-First Century in Historical Perspective* (Ann Arbor, MI: University of Michigan Press, 1996).

4. Indur M. Goklany, "Saving Habitat and Conserving Biodiversity on a Crowded Planet," *BioScience* 48 (1998); 941–53; Goklany, "The Future of the Industrial System" (invited paper, International Conference on Industrial Ecology and Sustainability, University of Technology of Troyes, Troyes, France, September 22–25, 1999).

5. Indur M. Goklany, "Strategies to Enhance Adaptablity."

6. Robert W. Fogel, "The Contribution of Improved Nutrition," in *The State of Humanity,* ed. Julian L. Simon, E. Calvin Beisner, and John Phelps (Cambridge, MA: Blackwell, 1995), pp. 61–71; Robert W. Fogel, *The Fourth Great Awakening and the Future of Egalitarianism* (Chicago: University of Chicago Press, 2000), pp. 74–79; World Health Organization (WHO), *World Health Report 1999* (Geneva: WHO, 1999); Richard A. Easterlin, *Growth Triumphant,* pp. 46, 89–91; Goklany, "Saving Habitat and Conserving Biodiversity."

7. Robert W. Fogel, *The Fourth Great Awakening*; Richard A. Easterlin, *Growth Triumphant.*

8. Food and Agriculture Organization (FAO), *The State of Food Insecurity in the World 2002* (Rome: FAO, 2002), p. 6.

9. Ibid.

10. Indur M. Goklany, "Saving Habitat and Conserving Biodiversity." See also Lant Pritchett and Lawrence H. Summers, "Wealthier Is Healthier," *Journal of Human Resources* 31 (1996): 841–68.

11. Indur M. Goklany, "Economic Growth and the State of Humanity," Policy Study no. 21, Political Economy Research Center, Bozeman, MT, 2001.

12. See also Lant Pritchett and Lawrence H. Summers, "Wealthier Is Healthier."

13. World Bank, *World Development Report 1993: Investing in Health* (New York: Oxford University Press, 1993), pp. 17–21; Robert W. Fogel, "The Contribution of Increased Nutrition"; Richard A. Easterlin, *Growth Triumphant,* pp. 89–91; WHO, *World Health Report 1999*; Barry Bloom, "The Future of Public Health," *Nature* 402 (Supplement 1999): C63–64.

14. Robert W. Fogel, "The Contribution of Increased Nutrition," p. 65.

15. Richard A. Easterlin, *Growth Triumphant,* pp. 89–91.

16. World Bank, *World Development Report 1993,* p. 18.

17. Shirley R. Watkins, "Historical Perspective on the School Meals Programs: The Case for Strong Federal Programs" (paper presented at Ceres Forum on School Meals Policy, Georgetown University Center for Food and Nutrition Policy, Washington, DC, November 24, 1997, cited August 15, 2000) www.fns.usda.gov/fncs/shirley/speeches/support/sw971124.htm.

18. WHO, *World Health Report 1999*; Robert W. Fogel, "The Contribution of Increased Nutrition."

19. Indur M. Goklany, "The Globalization of Human Well-Being."

20. Richard A. Easterlin, *Growth Triumphant*, p. 161.

21. World Bank, *World Development Report 1993*, p. 19.

22. *Guardian*, "Malaria Impedes Development in Africa," May 12, 2000, cited October 2, 2000; www.newafrica.com/newsarchivesq220000/may/socialnews.asp; Harvard University Center for International Development and the London School of Hygiene and Tropical Medicine, "Economics of Malaria: Executive Summary (2000)," www.malaria.org/jdsachseconomic.html (accessed October 2, 2000).

23. The cycle of progress is briefly described in Goklany, *Economic Growth and the State of Humanity*, pp. 26–31. See also, Indur M. Goklany, "The Future of the Industrial System."

24. Robert J. Barro, *The Determinants of Economic Growth: A Cross-Country Empirical Study* (Cambridge, MA: MIT Press, 1997); Indur M. Goklany, "Strategies to Enhance," pp. 427–49.

25. Using data for 2002, linear regression analysis of cross-country data from *World Development Indicators 2005* shows that the slope is significant at the 99.9 percent level (N = 55, adjusted R^2 = 0.513). This analysis used GDP per capita adjusted for purchasing power parity.

26. Richard A. Easterlin, *Growth Triumphant*, p. 46. "Generally," because as Joel Mokyr, *The Lever of Riches: Technological Creativity and Economic Progress* (New York: Oxford University Press, 1990), pp. 174–75, has pointed out, this may not always be the case. See also William Easterly, *The Elusive Quest for Growth: Economists' Adventures and Misadventures in the Tropics* (Cambridge, MA: MIT Press, 2001), pp. 71–84.

27. United Nations Development Programme (UNDP), *Human Development Report 1999* (New York: Oxford University Press, 1999).

28. Indur M. Goklany, "Saving Habitat and Conserving Biodiversity."

29. Jeffrey A. Frankel and David Romer, "Does Trade Cause Growth?" *American Economic Review* 89 (June 1999): 379–99; Robert J. Barro, *The Determinants of Economic Growth*; David Dollar and Aart Kraay, "Growth Is Good for the Poor."

30. Indur M. Goklany, "Strategies to Enhance Adaptability."

31. Ibid.

32. United Nations, "Security Council Extends Iraq 'Oil-for-Food' Programme for Further 186 Days," press release SC/6872, June 8, 2000, www.un.org/News/Press/docs/2000/20000608.sc6872.doc.html.

33. Nathan Rosenberg and Luther E. Birdzell Jr., *How the West Grew Rich: The Economic Transformation of the Industrial World* (New York: Basic Books, 1985); Joel Mokyr, *The Lever of Riches*, pp. 174–75; Fernand Braudel, *The Perspective of the World: Volume III. Civilization and Capitalism 15th–18th Century*, English edition, trans. Sîan Reynolds (New York: Harper & Row, 1984); Richard A. Easterlin, *Growth Triumphant*; David S. Landes, *The Wealth and Poverty of Nations: Why Some Are So Rich and Some So Poor* (New York: W. W. Norton, 1998).

34. Jesse H. Ausubel, "Does Climate Still Matter?" *Nature* 350 (1991): 649–52.

35. Robert W. Fogel, *The Fourth Great Awakening*, p. 73.

36. Jared Diamond, *Guns, Germs, and Steel* (New York: W. W. Norton, 1998).

37. See, for example, Robert J. Barro, *The Determinants of Economic Growth*; David Dollar and Aart Kraay, *Growth Is Good for the Poor* (Washington, DC: Development Research Group, World Bank, 2000), www.worldbank.org/research/growth/absdollakray.htm; James Gwartney and Robert Lawson, *Economic Freedom of the World: 2005 Annual Report* (Vancouver, BC: Fraser Institute, 2005); James Gwartney, Randall

Holcombe, and Robert Lawson, "The Scope of Government and the Wealth of Nations," *Cato Journal* 18, no. 2 (1998): 163–90.

38. Fernand Braudel, *The Perspective of the World*; Joel Mokyr, *The Lever of Riches*; David S. Landes, *The Wealth and Poverty of Nations*; Nathan Rosenberg and Luther E. Birdzell, *How the West Grew Rich*.

39. James Gwartney, et al., "The Scope of Government and the Wealth of Nations."

40. William Easterly and Sergio T. Rebelo, "Fiscal Policy and Economic Growth: An Empirical Investigation," *Journal of Monetary Economics* 32, no. 3 (1993): 417–58; Robert J. Barro, "Economic Growth in a Cross Section of Countries," *Quarterly Journal of Economics* 106 (1991): 407–33; Robert J. Barro, *The Determinants of Economic Growth*; David Dollar and Aart Kraay, *Growth Is Good for the Poor*.

41. James Gwartney, et al., "The Scope of Government and the Wealth of Nations."

42. Stephen Knack and Phillip Keefer, "Institutions and Economic Performance: Cross-Country Tests Using Alternative Institutional Measures," *Economics and Politics* 7, no. 3 (1995): 207–27; Robert J. Barro, *The Determinants of Economic Growth*; David Dollar and Aart Kraay, *Growth Is Good for the Poor*.

43. Jeffrey A. Frankel and David Romer, "Does Trade Cause Growth?" *The American Economic Review* 89 (June 1999): 379–99.

44. Stanley Fischer, "The Role of Macroeconomic Factors in Growth," *Journal of Monetary Economics* 32, no. 3: 485–12; Robert J. Barro, *The Determinants of Economic Growth*; David Dollar and Aart Kraay, *Growth Is Good for the Poor*.

45. Robert J. Barro, *The Determinants of Economic Growth*.

46. James Gwartney, et al., *Economic Freedom of the World: 2001 Annual Report*, p. 5.

47. James Gwartney, et al., *Economic Freedom of the World: 2001 Annual Report*, pp. 8–9.

48. James Gwartney, et al., *Economic Freedom of the World: 2001 Annual Report*, pp. 16, 20.

49. Ibid.

50. The European Monetary Union countries consists of Austria, Belgium, Denmark, Finland, France, Germany, Greece, Ireland, Italy, Luxembourg, Netherlands, Portugal, Spain, Sweden, and United Kingdom.

51. World Bank, *World Development Indicators*, http://devdata.worldbank.org/dataonline (accessed July 12, 2005). Sweden's infant mortality rate, which is the world's lowest, was 2.8 per 1,000 births in 2003.

52. John G. Myers, Stephen Moore, and Julian L. Simon, "Trends in Availability of Non-Fuel Minerals," in *The State of Humanity*, ed. Julian L. Simon, E. Calvin Beisner, and John Phelps (Cambridge, MA: Blackwell, 1995), pp. 303–12; Stephen Moore, "The Coming Age of Abundance," in *The True State of the Planet*, ed. Ronald Bailey (New York: Free Press, 1995), pp. 109–39; Jesse H. Ausubel and H. Dale Langford, eds., *Technological Trajectories and the Environment* (Washington, DC: National Academy Press, 1997); Jesse H. Ausubel, "Resources and Environment in the 21st Century: Seeing Past the Phantoms," *World Energy Council Journal* (July 1998): 8–16; Nebojsa Nakicenovic, Arnulf Grübler, and Alan McDonald, eds., *Global Energy Perspectives* (Cambridge, UK: Cambridge University Press, 1998); Bjørn Lomborg, *The Skeptical Environmentalist* (Cambridge, UK: Cambridge University Press, 2001); John E. Tilton, *On Borrowed Time? Assessing the Threat of Mineral Depletion* (Washington, DC: Resources for the Future, 2002).

53. Paul Glader, "Hot Metal with Steel Soaring, a Ghost Fleet Is in High Demand," *Wall Street Journal*, January 10, 2006, p. A1.

54. Bjørn Lomborg, "Running on Empty," *Guardian Unlimited*, August 16, 2001, www.guardian.co.uk/Archive/Article/0,4273,4239923,00.html (accessed March 18, 2006).

55. Doug Mellgren, "Delay in Controversial Exports Leads to Price Collapse for Norwegian Whale Blubber," *Associated Press*, May 23, 2002; Doug Mellgren, "Blubber's Price Sinks after Norway Bans Export of Whale Products," *Associated Press*, June 5, 2000.

56. Stephen Moore, "The Coming Age of Abundance"; John Myers, Stephen Moore, and Julian L. Simon, "Trends in Availability of Non-Fuel Minerals"; Stephen Moore and Julian L. Simon, *It's Getting Better All the Time: 100 Greatest Trends of the Last 100 Years* (Washington, DC: Cato Institute, 2000).

57. In figure 4.4, data up to 1990 are from Stephen Moore, "The Coming Age of Abundance." To construct the figure from 1990 onward, the following data sources were used. Metal price data for 1990 are from United States Geological Survey (USGS), *Metal Prices in the United States through 1998* (Reston, VA: USGS, 2004), http://minerals.usgs.gov/minerals/pubs/metal_prices/; price data for 2000 and 2005 for all metals except tungsten are from USGS, *Mineral Commodity Summaries*, http://minerals.usgs.gov/minerals/pubs/mcs/; for tungsten, the price data are from 1990 through 2004 and based on the price of ammonium paratungstate; for 2000 and 2004, tungsten price data are from USGS, *Minerals Yearbook 2004*, http://minerals.usgs.gov/minerals/pubs/commodity/tungsten/index.html#mcs; and data for hourly wages from 1990 through 2005 are for the nonfarm private sector, taken from Bureau of Labor Statistics, *Establishment Data: Historical Hours and Earnings*, ftp://ftp.bls.gov/pub/suppl/empsit.ceseeb2.txt. All sites were accessed on March 19, 2006.

58. Paul Roberts, *The End of Oil: On the Edge of a Perilous New World* (New York: First Mariner Books, 2005); Kenneth S. Deffeyes, *Beyond Oil: The View from Hubbert's Peak* (New York: Hill and Wang, 2005).

59. Jerry Taylor, "Debate Over Depletion Is Silly," *Peak Oil News*, July 12, 2005, http://peakoil.blogspot.com/005/07/debate-over-depletion-is-silly.html (accessed March 18, 2006).

Chapter 5

1. Paul Harrison, *The Third Revolution* (London: I. B. Tauris, 1992); Atiq Rahman, Nick Robins, and Anne Roncerel, eds., *Exploding the Population Myth: Consumption versus Population: Which Is the Climate Bomb?* (Brussels, Belgium: Climate Network Europe, 1993); Stephen Boyden and Stephen Dover, "Natural-Resource Consumption and Its Environmental Impacts in the Western World: Impacts of Increasing per Capita Consumption," *Ambio* 21 (1992): 63–69; Norman Myers, "Population/Environment Linkages: Discontinuities Ahead," *Ambio* 21 (1992): 116–18; Robert Engelman, *Stabilizing the Atmosphere: Population, Consumption, and Greenhouse Gases* (Washington, DC: Population Action International, 1994).

2. Indur M. Goklany, *The Precautionary Principle: A Critical Appraisal of Environmental Risk Assessment* (Washington, DC: Cato Institute, 2001), chapter 3.

3. See, for example, Ann Gibbons, "Biotech Pipeline: Bottleneck Ahead," *Science* 254 (1991): 369–70; Peter Huber, "Exorcists vs. Gatekeepers in Risk Regulation," *Regulation* 7 (November–December 1983): 23–32; Michael Shapiro, "Toxic Substances Policy," in *Public Policies for Environmental Protection*, ed. Paul R. Portney (Washington, DC: Resources for the Future, 1990), pp. 195–241; and Environmental Protection

Agency, *Clean Air Act of 1990*, 42 USC 7401-7671q, P.L. 101-549, 104 Stat. 2399 (Washington, DC).

4. Indur M. Goklany, *Clearing the Air: The Real Story of the War on Air Pollution* (Washington, DC: Cato Institute, 1999), pp. 37–38.

5. As noted previously, I use the term "environmental" to pertain to both the environment and natural resources.

6. Barry Commoner, "The Environmental Cost of Economic Growth," *Chemistry in Britain* 8 (1972): 52–65.

7. Paul R. Ehrlich and Anne H. Ehrlich, *Healing the Planet* (Reading, MA: Addison-Wesley, 1991), p. 7, state that T increases with P; however, the logic employed for this contention would also lead to the conclusion that it ought to increase with time. See Paul R. Ehrlich and John P. Holdren, "Impact of Population Growth," *Science* 171 (1971): 1212–17.

8. Paul R. Ehrlich and John P. Holdren, "Impact of Population Growth," pp. 1212–17; Paul R. Ehrlich, Gary Wolff, Gretchen C. Daily, Jennifer B. Hughes, et al., "Knowledge and the Environment," *Ecological Economics* 30, no. 2 (1999): 267–84.

9. Jesse H. Ausubel, "Resources and Environment in the 21st Century: Seeing Past the Phantoms," *World Energy Council Journal* (July 1998): 8–16; Chris Ryan, "Information Technology and DfE: From Support Tool to Design Principle," *Journal of Industrial Ecology* 3, no. 1 (1999): 5–8.

10. Jesse H. Ausubel, "Resources and Environment in the 21st Century: Seeing Past the Phantoms." See also David S. Landes, *The Wealth and Poverty of Nations: Why Some Are So Rich and Some So Poor* (New York: W. W. Norton, 1998).

11. Indur M. Goklany, "Strategies to Enhance Adaptability: Technological Change, Economic Growth, and Free Trade," *Climatic Change* 30 (1995): 427–44; Indur M. Goklany, "Richer Is Cleaner: Long-Term Trends in Global Air Quality," in *The True State of the Planet*, ed. Ronald Bailey (New York: Free Press, 1995), pp. 339–77.

12. This section draws heavily from Goklany, *Clearing the Air*, chapter 5.

13. Simon Kuznets, "Economic Growth and Income Inequality," *American Economic Review* 45 (1955): 1–28.

14. Indur M. Goklany, "Factors Affecting Environmental Impacts: The Effects of Technology on Long-Term Trends in Cropland, Air Pollution, and Water-Related Diseases," *Ambio* 25 (1996): 497–503.

15. Goklany, *Clearing the Air*, pp. 24–25.

16. U.K. Meteorological Office, "The Great Smog of 1952," www.metoffice.com/education/secondary/students/smog.html (accessed July 30, 2006).

17. Indur M. Goklany, *Clearing the Air*, pp. 24–25.

18. In this figure, GDP per capita is based on PPP-adjusted current (international) dollars. Figure 5.2 is based on a linear regression using data from World Bank, *World Development Indicators*, http://devdata.worldbank.org/dataonline (accessed July 12, 2005). N and R^2 are 55 and 0.513, respectively. The slope is statistically significant at the 99.9 percent confidence level.

19. Indur M. Goklany, "Strategies to Enhance Adaptability: Technological Change, Economic Growth, and Free Trade."

20. Indur M. Goklany, *Clearing the Air*, pp. 24–25.

21. U.S. Bureau of Commerce (USBOC), *Historical Statistics of the United States, Colonial Times to 1970* (Washington, DC: Government Printing Office, 1975).

22. USBOC, *Historical Statistics of the United States, Colonial Times to 1970*; USBOC, *Statistical Abstract of the United States 1998* (Washington, DC: Government Printing Office, 1998).

23. Indur M. Goklany, "The Environmental Transition to Air Quality," *Regulation* 21 (1998): 36–46.

24. Indur M. Goklany, "Strategies to Enhance Adaptability: Technological Change, Economic Growth, and Free Trade."

25. Sander M. de Bruyn, J. C. J. M. van den Bergh, and J. B. Opschoor, "Economic Growth and Emissions: Reconsidering the Empirical Basis of Environmental Kuznets Curves," *Ecological Economics* 25, no. 2 (1998): 161–75.

26. Note that the distance along the affluence axis between points T_B and T_A on the curve for country A depends on its rate of economic growth, and it does not have to be equal to the corresponding distance for country B.

27. Several international agreements have differential obligations for nations, for example, the Montreal Protocol for chlorofluorocarbons or the Kyoto Protocol for greenhouse gases.

28. In applying this identity, affluence will be measured as GDP per capita. If GDP data are unavailable, gross national product (GNP) may be used. For the United States the difference between these two measures is slight. According to the Bureau of Economic Analysis 1929–97 series, annual GNP, on average, is 0.54 percent greater than the corresponding year's GDP, with the maximum and minimum differences ranging from $+1.21$ to -0.05 percent. Accordingly, for the United States, I will use GNP and GDP interchangeably.

Assuming GDP data are available, the identity may be rewritten as the following:

$$I \equiv \text{population} \times (\text{GDP/population}) \times T \qquad (5\text{-}1)$$

which can be simplified to,

$$I \equiv \text{GDP} \times T \qquad (5\text{-}2)$$

Thus, the technology factor, T, is equivalent to impact per unit of GDP. Notably, a decline in T denotes an improvement in technology, which would reduce I.

If we want to characterize technological change (ΔT) from an initial time (t_i) to final time (t_f) then,

$$\Delta T = \Delta(I/\text{GDP}) \qquad (5\text{-}3)$$

In the analysis of trends, I will normalize population, affluence, their product (GDP), and the technology factor so that they take the value of unity at the beginning of the period. Accordingly,

$$T_f \equiv I_f/\text{GDP}_f \qquad (5\text{-}4)$$

and

$$\Delta T \equiv (I_f/\text{GDP}_f) - 1 \qquad (5\text{-}5)$$

where the subscript f (for final) denotes the value at the end of the period, that is, at time t_f.

In many cases, for example, for air or water pollution, emissions (E) are used to characterize the environmental impact. In such cases,

$$\Delta T \equiv \Delta(\text{emissions/GDP}) \equiv \Delta(E/\text{GDP}) \equiv (E_f/\text{GDP}_f) - 1 \qquad (5\text{-}6)$$

That is, the change in emissions per GDP is a measure of technological change over the period examined.

Chapter 6

1. See, for example, Paul R. Ehrlich and Edward O. Wilson, "Biodiversity Studies: Science and Policy," *Science* 253 (1991): 758–62; David S. Wilcove, David Rothstein, and Jason Dubow, "Quantifying Threats to Imperiled Species in the United States," *BioScience* 48, no. 8 (1998): 607–15.

2. Jonathan E. M. Baillie, Craig Hilton-Taylor, and Simon N. Stuart, *2004 IUCN Red List of Threatened Species: A Global Species Assessment* (Gland, Switzerland: World Conservation Union, 2004), www.iucn.org/themes/ssc/red_list_2004/GSA_book/Red_List_2004_book.pdf (accessed December 20, 2005).

3. John F. Richards, "Transformations of the Global Environment," in *The Earth as Transformed by Human Action: Global and Regional Changes in the Biosphere Over the Past 300 Years*, ed. B. L. Turner II, William C. Clark, Robert W. Kates, John F. Richards, et al. (Cambridge, UK: Cambridge University Press, 1988), p. 164.

4. Data on cropland harvested are from the U.S. Department of Agriculture (USDA). USDA, "USDA Data on Major Land Uses," www.ers.usda.gov/data/Major LandUses/spreadsheets/c1910_00.xls (accessed December 20, 2005), henceforth USDA (2005a); for 1996–2004, "Agricultural Statistics 2005," pp. ix–17, henceforth USDA (2005b). U.S. population data are from the U.S. Bureau of the Census (USBOC). for 1900–59, "Historical National Population Estimates, 1900 to 1999" www.census.gov/popest/archives/pre-1980/ (accessed August 14, 2005), henceforth USBOC (2000); for 1960–99, "Statistical Abstract 2004–2005," henceforth USBOC (2004a); and for 2000–04," "National and State Population Estimates: Annual Population Estimates 2000 to 2004," www.census.gov/popest/states/NST-ann-est.html, (accessed August 14, 2005), henceforth USBOC (2005a). Data on GDP are from the U.S. Department of Commerce (DOC). For real GDP (in chained 2000 dollars) for 1929–2004, Bureau of Economic Analysis (BEA) "National Income and Products Accounts," table 1.1.6, www.bea.gov/bea/dn/nipaweb/SelectTable.asp?Popular = Y (accessed August 13, 2005), henceforth BEA (2005); and for 1900–28, data derived from USBOC, *Historical Statistics of the United States, Colonial Times to 1970* (Washington, DC: Government Printing Office, 1975), henceforth USBOC (1975)—using the method employed in Indur M. Goklany, *Clearing the Air* (Washington, DC: Cato Institute, 1999), pp. 68–69.

5. As a first order approximation, one would expect food consumption to increase directly with population, if all else remains the same. However, as populations grow richer, their dietary habits also change. There is often greater emphasis on meat and milk-based foods, which further increases demand on grains and, therefore, cropland. Also, arguably, wastage may also increase. This assumption of no technological change is often made if for no reason other than the fact that, in the absence of any method of modeling such change in the future, it is convenient. Indur M. Goklany, "Factors Affecting Environmental Impacts: The Effects of Technology on Long-Term Trends in Cropland, Air Pollution, and Water-Related Diseases," *Ambio* 25 (1996): 497–503.

6. In 1910–12, 17 percent of cropland was devoted to exports on the average, compared to 33 percent in 1988–90, the last years for which such data were apparently estimated. See USBOC, *Statistical Abstract of the United States 1993* (Washington, DC: Government Printing Office, 1993) and *U.S. Bureau of the Census, Statistical Abstract of the United States 1994* (Washington, DC: Government Printing Office, 1994).

7. Indur M. Goklany, "Strategies to Enhance Adaptability: Technological Change, Economic Growth, and Free Trade," *Climatic Change* 30 (1995): 427–44.

8. This calculation uses the methodology employed by Indur M. Goklany and Merritt W. Sprague, which substantially underestimates cropland requirements in the absence of technological change. It assumes that new lands brought into production will be just as productive as existing cropland. This is unlikely because the most productive lands are probably already being used as cropland. The calculation also assumes that no technological change would have been necessary to maintain the productivity of existing cropland at 1910 levels. The calculation also assumes no change in the fraction of produce exported between 1910 and 1998. Indur M. Goklany and Merritt W. Sprague, *An Alternative Approach to Sustainable Development: Conserving Forests, Habitat, and Biological Diversity by Increasing the Efficiency and Productivity of Land Utilization* (Washington, DC: Office of Program Analysis, Department of the Interior, 1991).

9. Natural Resources Conservation Service (NRCS), "Summary Report: 1997 National Resources Inventory, revised December 2000" (USDA-NCRS 2000), www.nhq.nrcs.usda.gov/NRI/1997/summary_report/original/contents.html (accessed October 11, 2001).

10. This estimate includes all nonfederal rural lands classified by the Department of Agriculture as (a) classes I through V except for those in forests or "other rural lands" (including 139 million acres that could be used as cropland with "very careful management" or reduction in the choice of crops) and (b) 21 million acres in classes VI and VII that were in crops or in the Conservation Reserve Program in 1997. "Other rural lands" includes farmsteads and other farm structures, field windbreaks, barren land such as salt flats or exposed rock, and marshland. Class IV soils have very severe limitations that reduce the choice of plants, require very careful management, or both. Class V soils are not likely to erode but have other limitations, impractical to remove, that limit their use largely to pasture or range and woodland or wildlife. Classes VI and VII soils have severe limitations that make them generally unsuitable for cultivation. See NRSC, "Summary Report: 1997 National Resources Inventory, revised December 2000."

11. Indur M. Goklany, et al., *America's Biodiversity Strategy: Actions to Conserve Species and Habitats* (Washington, DC: U.S. Departments of Agriculture and the Interior, 1992), p. 70; Indur M. Goklany, "Saving Habitat and Conserving Biodiversity on a Crowded Planet," *BioScience* 48 (1998): 941–53.

12. Paul Faeth, *Growing Green: Enhancing the Economic and Environmental Performance of United States Agriculture* (Washington, DC: World Resources Institute, 1995).

13. Roger E. Meiners and Andrew P. Morris, "Silent Springs and Silent Villages: Pesticides and the Trampling of Property Rights," in *Government vs. Environment*, ed. Donald R. Leal and Roger E. Meiners (Lanham, MD: Rowman and Littlefield, 2001), p. 18.

14. The following sources are used for the data in figure 6.2: cropland from 1700–1950, Indur M. Goklany, "Meeting Global Food Needs: The Environmental Trade-Offs Between Increasing Land Conversion and Land Productivity," *Technology* 6 (1999): 107–30; cropland from 1961–2002, Food and Agriculture Organization (FAO), *FAOSTAT 2005*, http://aaps.fao.org (accessed July 12, 2005), henceforth FAO (2005); population from 1700–1950, Colin McEvedy and Richard Jones, *Atlas of World Population History* (New York: Penguin, 1978); population from 1961–2002, FAO (2005).

15. For cropland and population, these calculations used the data sources listed in the previous note. GDP data were obtained from Angus Maddison, *The World Economy: Historical Statistics* (Paris: Organisation for Economic Co-operation and

Development [OECD], 2003), www.ggdc.net/~maddison (accessed July 30, 2005), henceforth Angus Maddison (2003).

16. Indur M. Goklany, "Agricultural Technology and the Precautionary Principle," in *Environmental Policy and Agriculture: Conflicts, Prospects, and Implications*, ed. Roger E. Meiners and Bruce Yandle (Lanham, MD: Rowman and Littlefield, 2003).

17. FAO (2005).

18. World Resources Institute (WRI), *World Resources 1998–99 Database* (Washington, DC: WRI, 1998).

19. FAO (2005).

20. Nikos Alexandratos, *World Agriculture: Towards 2010* (Chichester, UK: FAO and John Wiley, 1995).

21. WRI, EarthTrends, www.wri.org (accessed February 24, 2006).

22. Paul R. Ehrlich, Anne H. Ehrlich, and Gretchen C. Daily, "Food Security, Population, and Environment," *Population and Development Review* 19 (1993): 1–32; Lester R. Brown and Hal Kane, *Full House: Reassessing the World's Population Carrying Capacity* (New York: W. W. Norton, 1994); David Pimentel, Rebecca Harman, and Matthew Pacenza, "Natural Resources and an Optimum Human Population," *Population and Environment* 15 (1994): 347–69.

23. Figure 6.3 is based on data from World Bank, *World Development Indicators 2005*, http://devdata.worldbank.org/ wdipdfs/table2-5.pdf (accessed July 25, 2006). See chapter 2.

24. E.-C. Oerke, A. Weber, H.-W. Dehne, and F. Schonbeck, "Conclusion and Perspectives," in *Crop Production and Crop Protection: Estimated Losses in Food and Cash Crops*, ed. E.-C. Oerke, A. Weber, H.-W. Dehne, and F. Schonbeck (Amsterdam: Elsevier, 1994), pp. 742–70.

25. FAO, *Global Forest Resource Assessment 2000* (Rome: FAO, 2000), p. 9, henceforth GFRA (2000).

26. FAO (2005).

27. Indur M. Goklany, "The Importance of Climate Change Compared to Other Global Changes," 1024–41.

28. Jasper Becker, *Hungry Ghosts: Mao's Secret Famine* (New York: Free Press, 1997).

29. FAO (2005).

30. Indur M. Goklany, *Air and Inland Surface Water Quality: Long-Term Trends and Relationship to Affluence* (Washington, DC: Office of Program Analysis, U.S. Department of the Interior, 1994); Indur M. Goklany, "Factors Affecting Environmental Impacts: The Effects of Technology on Long-Term Trends in Cropland, Air Pollution, and Water-Related Diseases"; Indur M. Goklany, "The Importance of Climate Change Compared to Other Global Changes"; and Council on Environmental Quality (CEQ), *Environmental Quality Statistics* (Washington, DC: CEQ, 1996).

31. Robert J. Gilliom, Jack E. Barbash, Charles G. Crawford, et al., "The Quality of Our Nation's Waters: Pesticides in the Nation's Streams and Ground Water, 1992–2001," U.S. Geological Survey Circular 1291, Reston, VA, 2006, p. 128. See also C. J. Schmitt, J. L. Zajicek, and P. H. Peterman, "National Pesticide Monitoring Program," *Archives of Environmental Contamination and Toxicology* 19 (1990): 748–81. The half-life is the period of time over which the concentration is reduced to half its original level. Thus with a half-life of 7 years, DDT levels would drop to a half in 7 years, to a quarter in 14, and to an eighth in 21 years.

32. CEQ, *Environmental Quality Statistics* (Washington, DC: CEQ, 1999), http:// ceq.eh.doe.gov/nepa/reports/statistics/ (accessed November 10, 2002).

33. CEQ, *Environmental Quality* (Washington, DC: CEQ, 1992).

34. If substance A is present in substance B at very low concentrations, the concentration of the former will often be specified in term of parts per million. A concentration of 1 part per million of DDE in waterfowl means that there is one molecule of DDE in a million molecules that form the waterfowl.

35. CEQ, *Environmental Quality* (Washington, DC: CEQ, 1993).

36. Indur M. Goklany, "The Importance of Climate Change Compared to Other Global Changes."

37. Mats Olsson, Anders Bignert, Jan Eckhell, and Per Jonsson, "Comparison of Temporal Trends (1940s–1990s) of DDT and PCB in Baltic Sediment and Biota in Relation to Sediment," *Ambio* 29 (2000): 195–201; and Jens Skei, Per Larsson, Rutger Rosenberg, Per Jonsson, et al., "Eutrophication and Contaminants in Aquatic Ecosystems," *Ambio* 29 (2000): 184–94.

38. CEQ, *Environmental Quality Statistics.*

39. USBOC, *Statistical Abstract of the United States* (Washington, DC: Government Printing Office, 1987).

40. United Nations Environment Program/Global Environmental Monitoring System, *Environmental Data Report 1991–92* (Cambridge, UK: Blackwell, 1991).

41. Daniel Smith, "Worldwide Trends in DDT Levels in Human Breast Milk," *International Journal of Epidemiology* 28, no. 2 (1999): 179–88.

42. Dissolved oxygen is oxygen that is dissolved in the water; the higher the concentration of dissolved oxygen in the water the more fish and other oxygen-dependent life it can support.

43. CEQ, *Environmental Quality Statistics* (Washington, DC: CEQ, 2002), http://ceq.eh.doe.gov/nepa/reports/statistics/ (accessed November 10, 2002).

44. Ibid.

45. FAO, *Global Forest Resource Assessment 2000.*

46. Richard A. Smith, Richard B. Alexander, and Kenneth J. Lanfear, "Stream Water Quality in the Conterminous United States: Status and Trends of Selected Indicators during the 1980s," National Water Summary 1990–91: Stream Water Quality, Water Supply Paper no. 2400, U.S. Geological Survey, Reston, VA, 1993. A portion of the decline in nitrates could be attributable to NO_x controls for air pollution. Indur M. Goklany, "Richer Is Cleaner: Long-Term Trends in Global Air Quality," in *The True State of the Planet*, ed. Ronald Bailey (New York: Free Press, 1995), pp. 339–77.

47. Indur M. Goklany, *Air and Inland Surface Water Quality: Long-Term Trends and Relationship to Affluence;* CEQ, *Environmental Quality Statistics* (1996).

48. CEQ, *Environmental Quality Statistics.*

49. Indur M. Goklany, *Air and Inland Surface Water Quality: Long-Term Trends and Relationship to Affluence.*

50. This section draws from—and updates—information contained in Indur M. Goklany, *Clearing the Air: The Real Story of the War on Air Pollution* (Washington, DC: Cato Institute, 1999).

51. The methodology for developing estimates of indoor air quality is described in Goklany, "Factors Affecting Environmental Impacts."

52. Indur M. Goklany, *Clearing the Air.*

53. Ibid.

54. See, for example, *New York Times, The New York Times Index 1940* (New York: New York Times, 1941), p. 6.

55. Air emissions data for VOC and NO$_x$ were obtained from the following sources. For 1900–39, used data from Goklany, *Clearing the Air*, p. 68; for 1940–50, used data from Environmental Protection Agency (EPA), *National Air Pollutant Emission Trends, 1900–1998*, (henceforth ET1998); for 1960, used the average of the data from ET1998 (or ET2000) and ET2001 (or ET2002 or ET2003); for 1970–2003, used ET2003. For SO$_2$ emissions data; for 1900–39, used data from Indur M. Goklany, *Clearing the Air, p.*68; for 1940–69, used data from ET1998; for 1970–89, used ET2002; for 1990–2003, used ET2003. Note that ETxxxx refer to EPA's annual emission trends reports that provide data to the year xxxx. Note that ET2001 raised estimates of VOC, NOx, and CO emissions from 1940 onward to account for more realistic driving behavior than had been assumed by EPA until then. In particular, the new estimates used higher driving speeds. Based on conversations with EPA engineers at their Ann Arbor, MI, laboratory, it is apparent that such adjustments are increasingly less relevant as one goes back in time because the roadways in the 1940s did not allow for the higher speeds that were possible in the 1970s (David Brzezinski and Harvey Michaels, personal communications, August 2005). Accordingly, to reconcile data from earlier and later versions of the emission trends reports, it was agreed that one could reasonably assume that the amount of the adjustment would grow linearly from zero for 1940 to 100 percent for 1970. U.S. population data are from USBOC. For 1900–59, USBOC (2000); for 1960–99, USBOC (2004a); and for 2000–04, USBOC (2005a). Data on GDP are from the U.S. Department of Commerce. Real GDP (in chained 2000 dollars) for 1929–2004 from BEA (2005); and for 1900–28, data derived from USBOC (1975) using the method employed in Indur M. Goklany, *Clearing the Air*, pp. 68–69.

56. CO emissions data are from the following sources. For 1940–1950, *ET1998*; for 1960, used the average of the data from ET1998 (or ET2000) and ET2001 (or ET2002 or ET2003); for 1970–2003, used ET2003.

57. PM-10 data excluded emissions from geogenic, agricultural, from and forestry sources, as well as from fugitive dust sources. Data for 1940–74 came from ET1998; data for 1975–2002 was from ET2002.

58. They might have commenced earlier but the improvements might have been swamped by increases in population or GDP.

59. Indur M. Goklany, *Clearing the Air*.

60. Figure 6.7 is based on Indur M. Goklany, *Clearing the Air*, and EPA, *National Air Quality and Emissions Trends Report, 2003: Special Studies Edition*, table A-11, www.epa.gov/air/airtrends/aqtrnd03/ (accessed August 15, 2005).

61. EPA, *National Air Quality and Emissions Trends Report 1999*, www.epa.gov/air/ aqtrnd99/PDF%20Files/tables/a_16.pdf (accessed November 13, 2002), henceforth AQ & ETR (1999).

62. Goklany, *Clearing the Air*; EPA, *National Air Quality and Emissions Trends Report 2000*, www.epa.gov/oar/aqtrnd00/appenda.pdf (accessed November 12, 2002).

63. AQ & ETR (1999).

64. Indur M. Goklany, *Clearing the Air*.

65. An additional 23 percent is spent indoors elsewhere (e.g., in their place of work).

66. The following data sources were used. Residential emissions, ET1998 for 1940, 1950, and 1960, and ET2002 for 1970–89 and 2000–02; number of houses occupied, *Statistical Abstract 1995,* p. 733 for 1940–1960; for 1970–2002, U.S. Bureau of the Census, "Housing Vacancies and Homeownership," www.census.gov/hhes/www/ housing/hvs/historic/histtab7.html (accessed August 14, 2005). No residential emissions data were used for 1990 through 1999, because ET2002's estimates for that

period are suspect. Between 1989 and 1990, it shows a doubling of NOx emissions from natural gas and distillate (from 347,000 tonnes to 780,000 tonnes). However, Energy Information Administration's *Annual Energy Review 2004* indicates that consumption of both fuels actually dropped between 1989 and 1990. Energy Information Administration (EIA), *Annual Energy Review 2004*, www.eia.doc.gov/emeu/aer/contents.html (accessed December 20, 2004). Then going from 1998 to 1999, these emissions are halved (from 688,000 tons to 326,000 tons), but *Annual Energy Review* (2004) indicates that gas and distillate usage increased by between 5 percent and 7 percent. A plausible interpretation is that the earlier error was corrected by the later error. There is also an unexplained discontinuity in the VOC data going from 1999 to 2000. Accordingly, the figure ignores all data from 1990 through 1999. See EIA, *Annual Energy Review 2004*.

67. Trends in VOC emissions from residential combustion emissions per occupied housing unit may not be a good proxy for VOC concentrations indoors because they ignore emissions from solvents and other liquids that are often stored at home.

68. Specifically, pre-1970 reductions contributed approximately 95, 92, 91, and 98 percent of the 1940–2002 reductions for PM-10, CO, SO_2, and VOC, respectively.

69. Indur M. Goklany, "Factors Affecting Environmental Impacts."

70. EIA, *Annual Energy Review 2004*.

71. Indur M. Goklany, *Clearing the Air*.

72. USBOC (1975).

73. Indur M. Goklany, *Clearing the Air*; EIA, *Annual Energy Review 2004*.

74. USBOC (1975).

75. EIA, *Annual Energy Review 2004*.

76. USBOC (1975).

77. Ibid.; USBOC (2004a), pp. 7, 674.

78. USBOC (1975); EIA, *Annual Energy Review 2004*.

79. Indur M. Goklany, "Factors Affecting Environmental Impacts."

80. Indur M. Goklany, "Factors Affecting Environmental Impacts"; EIA, *Annual Energy Review 2004*.

81. Indur M. Goklany, *Clearing the Air*; EIA, *Annual Energy Review 2004*.

82. Indur M. Goklany, *Clearing the Air*.

83. A *multicyclone* is a device composed of several smaller "cyclones" operating in parallel to collect solid or liquid particles from a stream of gas (e.g., exhaust gas from a coal-fired boiler). Each cyclone is a conical device designed to knock out solid or liquid particles from the gas stream. This stream is introduced tangentially into the cyclone, which spins the gas stream along the inside wall of the cyclone. Because particles are heavier than the gas and have greater inertia, they are forced on to the cyclone's inside wall, and then they drop to the bottom of their own weight. An *electrostatic precipitator* is a larger version of the electric devices that are used nowadays to purify air indoors. They consist of arrays of "discharge electrodes" and "plate collectors." The electrodes impart a negative charge to the particles in the incoming gas stream. Then, as the gas stream goes past the positively charged plates, these negatively charged particles are attracted to and collected on the plates. These plates are then rapped or vibrated periodically so that the particles then drop from the plates into hoppers below. Baghouses, also known as *fabric filters*, are larger versions of the home vacuum cleaner. The particle-laden gas stream is introduced into a large compartment containing numerous bags made of tightly woven fabric, hence the term *baghouse*. The gas stream deposits particles on one side of the fabric and goes

through to the other side, where the clean stream is collected and discharged. As is the case for electrostatic precipitators, these bags are rapped or vibrated periodically so that the particles then drop into hoppers below.

84. EIA, *Annual Energy Review 2004*.

85. Indur M. Goklany, *Clearing the Air*.

86. Ibid.

87. EIA, *Annual Energy Review 2004*.

88. CO_2 emissions data are from Gregg Marland, Thomas J. Boden, and Robert J. Andres, *National CO_2 Emissions from Fossil-Fuel Burning, Cement Manufacture, and Gas Flaring: 1751-2002* (Oak Ridge, TN: Carbon Dioxide Information Analysis Center, Oak Ridge National Laboratory, 2005), http://cdiac.esd.ornl.gov/ftp/trends/emissions/usa.dat (accessed December 21, 2005). Data on GDP and population are from Angus Maddison (2003).

89. Figure 6.11 is constructed using data from OECD, *OECD Environmental Data Compendium 1997* (Paris: OECD, 1997); OECD, *OECD Environmental Data Compendium 1999* (Paris: OECD, 1999).

90. The 30 states include the three North American nations (the United States, Canada, and Mexico), Australia, New Zealand, Japan, South Korea, and 23 of 25 members of the European Union (i.e., all except Cyprus and Slovenia).

91. OECD, *OECD Environmental Data Compendium 2004* (Paris: OECD, 2005), henceforth OECD (2005).

92. European Environment Agency (EEA), *The European Environment: State and Outlook 2005* (Copenhagen: EEA, 2005), pp. 94–95, henceforth EEA (2005).

93. The EU-15 comprised the following 15 countries: Austria, Belgium, Denmark, Finland, France, Germany, Greece, Ireland, Italy, Luxembourg, the Netherlands, Portugal, Spain, Sweden, and the United Kingdom.

94. EEA (2005), p. 266.

95. OECD (2005).

96. OECD (2005).

97. EEA (2005), p. 96; OECD (2005).

98. OECD (2005).

99. EEA (2005), supporting material available at http://dataservice.eea.eu.int/atlas/viewdata/viewpub.asp?id=1080 (accessed January 4, 2006).

100. Ibid.

101. Ibid, p. 99.

102. EEA (2005), supporting material available at http://dataservice.eea.eu.int/atlas/viewdata/viewpub.asp?id=1092 (accessed January 4, 2006).

103. Ibid.

104. On the same basis; World Bank, *World Development Indicators* (Washington, DC: World Bank, 1999).

105. International Fuel Quality Center, "Overview of Leaded Gasoline and Sulfur Levels in Gasoline and Diesel," www.un.org/esa/gite/cleanfuels/ifqc-globaloverview.pdf (accessed July 26, 2006).

106. Ibid.

107. Craig Timberg, "Era of Leaded Gas Comes to an End in Most of Africa," *Washington Post,* January 1, 2006, www.washingtonpost.com/wp-dyn/content/article/2005/12/31/AR2005123100957.html (accessed July 26, 2006).

108. *Times of India*, "Delhi Air Cleaner But There Is Scope for Improvement," June 6, 2000, http://sdnp.delhi.nic.in/ node/jnu/news/jun2000/jun6.html (accessed February 4, 2003).

109. Ibid.

110. Steven F. Hayward, *Index of Leading Environmental Indicators: The Nature and Sources of Ecological Progress in the U.S. and the World* (San Francisco, CA: Pacific Research Institute, 2006), p. 89.

111. Jiming Hao and Litao Wang, "Improving Urban Air Quality in China: Beijing Case Study," *Journal of the Air & Waste Management Association* 55 (2005): 1298–1305, 1300 and figure 7.

112. Ibid., figure 17.

113. David Wheeler, *Racing to the Bottom? Foreign Investment and Air Pollution in Developing Countries* (Washington, DC: World Bank, 2001), pp. 4–5, http://netec.mcc.ac.uk/WoPEc/data/Papers/wopwobaed2524.html, (accessed November 10, 2002).

114. Petros Koutrakis, Sonja N. Sax, Jeremy A. Sainat, Brent Coull, et al., "Analysis of PM10, PM2.5, and PM2.5-10 Concentrations in Santiago, Chile, from 1989 to 2001," *Journal of the Air & Waste Management Association* (March 2005).

115. Jiming Hao and Litao Wang, "Improving Urban Air Quality in China: Beijing Case Study," 1300 and figure 7.

116. Ibid., figure 15.

117. Steven F. Hayward, *Index of Leading Environmental Indicators: The Nature and Sources of Ecological Progress in the U.S. and the World* (San Francisco, CA: Pacific Research Institute, 2006), p. 89.

118. Jerome O. Nriagu, "Tales Told in Lead," *Science* 281 (1998): 1622–23. See also William Shotyk, et al.,"History of Atmospheric Lead Deposition since 12,370 14C yr BP from a Peat Bog, Jura Mountains, Switzerland," *Science* 281 (1998): 1635–40.

119. WHO, *World Health Report 2002* (Geneva: WHO, 2002), pp. 69–70, www.who.int/whr/en/ (accessed November 14, 2002).

120. WHO, *Global Burden of Disease 2000, Version 2 Estimates*, www3.who.int/who sis/menu.cfm?path = evidence, burden,burden_estimates,burden_estimates_2000V2, burden_estimates_2000V2_region&language = english, (accessed November 14, 2002); WHO, *World Health Report 2002*, annex 11 and 12 tables, www.who.int/whr/en/ (accessed November 14, 2002). Other WHO sources, based on different but older analyses, place the total number of premature deaths due to air pollution at about 3 million with 2.8 million due to indoor air pollution. See, for example, WHO, *WHO Strategy on Air Quality and Health: Revised Final Draft* (Geneva: WHO, 2001), www.who.int/peh/air/Strategy.pdf (accessed November 1, 2002); Nigel Bruce, Rogelio Perez-Padilla, and Rachel Albalak "Indoor Air Pollution in Developing Countries: A Major Environmental and Public Health Challenge," *Bulletin of the World Health Organization* 78 (2000): 1078–92.

121. One lost DALY is equal to the loss of one healthy life year.

122. WHO, *The World Health Report 1999* (Geneva: WHO, 1999).

123. WHO, *Global Water Supply and Sanitation Assessment 2000 Report*, www.who.int/water_sanitation_health/Globassessment/Global1.htm#1.1 (accessed November 14, 2002).

124. Ibid.

125. Ibid.

126. WHO, *Global Burden of Disease 2000, Version 2 Estimates*; WHO, *World Health Report 2002*, annex 11 and 12 tables.

127. Ibid., pp. 67, 71–72.

128. World Bank, *World Development Indicators 1999*.

129. World Resources Institute, EarthTrends, http://earthtrends.wri.org/search able_db/index.php?theme=2 (accessed July 30, 2006).

130. WHO/UNICEF, *Global Water Supply.*

131. USBOC, *Statistical Abstract of the United States 1999* (Washington, DC: Government Printing Office, 1999).

132. Randall Lutter and John F. Morrall III, "Health-Health Analysis: A New Way to Evaluate Health and Safety Regulations," *Journal of Risk and Uncertainty* 8 (1994): 43–66.

133. USBOC (1975), p. 63; Abel Wolman, in *Water, Health and Society—Selected Papers by Abel Wolman*, ed. Gilbert F. White (Bloomington, IN: Indiana University Press, 1969).

134. Morbidity also dropped. Between 1912 and 1970, typhoid and paratyphoid cases decreased from 818 per million to 2 per million USBOC (1975), pp. 58, 77.

135. Data for 1997 are based on mortality corresponding to the International Classification of Diseases, Ninth Revision (ICD-9), code 002, from Centers for Disease Control and Prevention (CDC), WONDER Compressed Mortality Data Base, http://wonder.cdc.gov/mortSQL.shtml (accessed January 14, 2003).

136. USBOC, *Statistical Abstract of the United States 1958* (Washington DC: USBOC, 1958), p. 68; and WONDER database CDC 2002, http://wonder.cdc.gov. These figures exclude deaths due to diarrhea in the newborn from 1900 to 1920. Many of these diseases are caused by consuming foods contaminated by wastewater. Data for 1998 are from CDC, WONDER Compressed Mortality Data Base.

137. Gunther F. Craun, "Statistics of Waterborne Outbreaks in the United States (1920–1980)," in *Waterborne Diseases in the United States*, ed. Gunther F. Craun (Boca Raton, FL: CRC Press, 1986), pp. 73–159.

138. Rachel S. Barwick, Deborah A. Levy, Gunther F. Craun, Michael J. Beach, et al., "Surveillance for Waterborne-Disease Outbreaks—United States, 1997–1998," *CDC Surveillance Summaries, Mortality, and Morbidity Weekly Report* 49, no. SS-4 (May 26, 2000): 1–35; Sherline H. Lee, Deborah A. Levy, Gunther F. Craun, Michael J. Beach, et al., "Surveillance for Waterborne-Disease Outbreaks—United States, 1999–2000," *CDC Surveillance Summaries, Mortality, and Morbidity Weekly Report* 51 no. SS08 (November 22, 2002): 1–29.

139. Earth Changes TV, "Coroner Confirms Six *E. coli* Deaths . . . 07/28/00," www.earthchangestv.com/biology/July 2000/0728coroner.htm (accessed February 4, 2003); American Water Works Association, "Walkerton Coroner's Office Investigating Deaths," (2000), www.awwa.org/communications/mainstream/archives/2000/July/ms0700 walker.cfm (accessed February 4, 2003); Canoe, "Excerpts from Summary of Walkerton Report," January 17, 2002, www.canoe.ca/EcoliTragedy/020118_excerpts-cp.html (accessed February 4, 2003); Canadian Broadcasting Corporation, "2002 Ottawa News in Review," January 18, 2002, www.canoe.ca/Ecoli Tragedy/020118_excerpts- cp.html (accessed February 5, 2003).

140. See also Rachel S. Barwick, et al., "Surveillance for Waterborne-Disease Outbreaks—United States, 1997–1998" (2000); Gunther F. Craun, "Causes of Waterborne Outbreaks in the United States," *Water Science and Technology* 24 (1991): 17–20.

141. The derivation of the best fit lines for these figures is presented in chapter 2.

142. G. Gregg Marland, Robert J. Andres, and Thomas A. Boden, "Global, Regional, and National CO_2 Emissions," in *Trends: A Compendium of Data on Global Change* (Oak Ridge, TN: Carbon Dioxide Information Analysis Center, Oak Ridge National

Laboratory, 2005), http://cdiac.esd.ornl.gov/trends/emis/tre_glob.htm (accessed on December 22, 2005).

143. A. Neftel, H. Friedli, E. Moor, H. Lötscher, et al., "Historical Carbon Dioxide Record from the Siple Station Ice Core," in *Trends: A Compendium of Data on Global Change* (Oak Ridge, TN: Carbon Dioxide Information Analysis Center, Oak Ridge National Laboratory, U.S. Department of Energy, 2004), http://cdiac.esd.ornl.gov/trends/co2/siple.htm (accessed December 29, 2005); C. D. Keeling and T. P. Whorf, note 163.

144. Philip D. Jones, D. E. Parker, Tim J. Osborne, Keith R. Briffa, et al., "Global and Hemispheric Temperature Anomalies—Land and Marine Instrumental Records," in *Trends: A Compendium of Data on Global Change* (Oak Ridge, TN: Carbon Dioxide Information Analysis Center, Oak Ridge National Laboratory, U.S. Department of Energy, 2004), http://cdiac.esd.ornl.gov/ftp/ trends/temp/jonescru/global.dat (accessed December 29, 2005).

145. The Intergovernmental Panel on Climate Change (IPCC) estimates a 0.4°C to 0.8°C increase in the global temperature during the past century. See IPCC, *Climate Change 2001: The Scientific Basis* (New York: Cambridge University Press, 2001), pp. 2–3. The IPCC's estimates are based on surface measurements, but it is not clear how geographically representative surface stations used to estimate trends are of conditions averaged over the globe, nor is it clear that the surface measurements are not unduly influenced by local factors such as the urban heat island effect and other land use and land cover factors. See, John R. Christy, "The Global Warming Fiasco," in *Global Warming and Other Eco Myths*, ed. Ronald Bailey (Roseville, CA: Prima Publishing, 2002), chapter 1.

146. Kevin Trenberth and George Taylor, "Does Climate Change Cause More Extreme Weather? YES. Economic Effects of Weather Disasters Warrant Action on Warming, NO. Blaming Disasters on Global Warming Doesn't Help," Washington Post Issues Forum: Global Climate Change, www.washingtonpost.com/wp-adv/specialsales/nei/global/article9.htm (accessed February 4, 2003); Frank McDonald, "Economies at Risk Unless Global Warming Is Tackled," *The Irish Times*, 1998, www.energyaction.ie/news_environ.htm (accessed February 4, 2003); Bob Reiss, *The Coming Storm: Extreme Weather and Our Terrifying Future* (New York: Hyperion, 2001); Ross Gelbspan, *The Heat Is On: The High Stakes Battle over Earth's Threatened Climate* (Reading, MA: Addison-Wesley, 1997).

147. William J. Clinton, State of the Union Address, 1998, www.pub.white house.gov/uri-res/I2R?pdi://oma.eop.gov.us/1998/01/27/11.text.1 (accessed June 15, 2000); William J. Clinton, State of the Union Address, 1999, www.pub.whitehouse.gov/uri-res/I2R?pdi://oma.eop.gov.us/1999/1/20/1.text.1 (accessed June 15, 2000); George M. Woodwell, "Exaggeration or Underestimate," *Nature* 390 (1997): 547; and Greenwire, *Worldview—Climate Change II: Scientists Fear Warming* (February 5, 1998) available through search engine at http://national journal.com/pubs/greenwire/extra/search.htm.

148. UN Framework Convention on Climate Change (UNFCCC), *The Kyoto Protocol to the United Nations Framework Convention on Climate Change*, 1999, www.unfccc.de/resource/docs/convkp/kpeng.html (accessed September 12, 2006).

149. See, for example, Henry W. Kendall and David Pimentel, "Constraints on the Expansion of the Global Food Supply," *Ambio* 23 (1998): 198–205.

150. Michael E. Mann, Raymond S. Bradley, and Malcolm K. Hughes, "Global-Scale Temperature Patterns and Climate Forcing over the Past Six Centuries," *Nature*

392 (1998): 779–87; Michael E. Mann, Raymond S. Bradley, and Malcolm K. Hughes, "Northern Hemisphere Temperatures during the Past Millennium: Inferences, Uncertainties, and Limitations," *Geophysical Research Letters* 26 (1999): 759–62; Michael E. Mann and Philip D. Jones, "Global Surface Temperatures over the Past Two Millennia," *Geophysical Research Letters* 30 (2003): 10.1029/2003GL017814.

151. Aiguo Dai, Kevin E. Trenberth, and Taotao Qian, "A Global Data Set of Palmer Drought Severity Index for 1870–2002: Relationship with Soil Moisture and Effect of Surface Warming," *Journal of Hydrometeorology* 5 (2004): 1117–30; Kevin E. Trenberth, John Overpeck, and Susan Solomon, "Exploring Drought and Its Implications for the Future," *Eos: Trans. American Geophysical Union* 85 (January 20, 2004): 27; Aiguo Dai, Kevin E. Trenberth, and T. R. Karl, "Global Variations in Droughts and Wet Spells," *Geophysical Research Letters* 25 (1998): 3367–70.

152. Neville Nicholls, "Increased Australian Wheat Yield due to Recent Climate Trends," *Nature* 387 (1997): 484–85.

153. David B. Lobell and Gregory P. Asner, "Climate and Management Contributions to Recent Trends 6 in the United States Agricultural Yields," *Science* 299 (2003): 1032.

154. Graciela O. Magrin, María I. Travasso, and Gabriel R. Rodríguez, "Changes in Climate and Crop Production during the 20th Century in Argentina," *Climatic Change* 72 (2005): 229–49.

155. Ranga B. Myneni, C. D. Keeling, C. J. Tucker, G. Asrar, et al., "Increased Plant Growth in the Northern High Latitudes from 1981 to 1991," *Nature* 386 (1997): 698–702; Annette Menzel and Peter Fabian, "Growing Season Extended in Europe," *Nature* 397 (1999): 659; D. S. Schimel, J. I. House, K. A. Hibbard, P. Bousquet, et al., "Recent Patterns and Mechanisms of Carbon Exchange by Terrestrial Ecosystems," *Nature* 414 (2001): 169–72; Gian-Reto Walther, Eric Post, Peter Convey, Annette Menzel, et al., "Ecological Responses to Recent Climate Change," *Nature* 416 (2002): 389–95. Some researchers note that the recent increase in the length of the growing season might be the result of natural variation, which might cause the length to vary by ± 10 days. See, Michael A. White, Steven W. Running, and Peter E. Thornton, "The Impact of Growing-Season Length Variability on Carbon Assimilation and Evapotranspiration over 88 Years in the Eastern US Deciduous Forest," *International Journal of Biometeorology* 42 (1999): 139–45. See also Paolo D'Odorico, JaeChan Yoo, and Siegfried Jaeger, "Changing Seasons: An Effect of the North Atlantic Oscillation?" *Journal of Climate* 15 (2002): 435–45, whose analysis suggests that the North Atlantic Oscillation might be responsible for the variations.

156. Annette Menzel, Gert Jakobi, Rein Ahas, Helfried Scheifinger, et al., "Variations of the Climatological Growing Season (1951–2000) in Germany Compared with Other Countries," *International Journal of Climatology* 23, no. 7 (2003): 793–812.

157. Ibid.

158. Camille Parmesan and Gary Yohe, "A Globally Coherent Fingerprint of Climate Change Impacts across Natural Systems," *Nature* 421 (2003): 37–42.

159. Terry L. Root, Jeff T. Price, Kimberly R. Hall, Stephen H. Schneider, et al., "Fingerprints of Global Warming on Wild Animals and Plants," *Nature* 421 (2003): 57–60.

160. John Reilly, Walter Baethgen, F. E. Chege, Siebe C. van de Greijn, et al., "Agriculture in a Changing Climate: Impacts and Adaptations," in *Climate Change 1995: Impacts, Adaptations, and Mitigation of Climate Change*, ed. Robert T. Watson,

Marufu C. Zinyowera, Richard H. Moss, and David J. Dokken (Cambridge, UK: Cambridge University Press; 1996), pp. 427–67.

161. Sylvan H. Wittwer, *Food, Climate, and Carbon Dioxide: The Global Environment and World Food Production* (Boca Raton, FL: Lewis Publishers, 1995), pp. 56–57.

162. FAO (2005).

163. Based on CO_2 concentrations at Mauna Loa; C. D. Keeling and T. P. Whorf, "Atmospheric CO_2 Concentrations (ppmv) Derived from in situ Air Samples Collected at Mauna Loa Observatory, Hawaii," www.cdiac.esd.ornl. gov/ftp/maunaloa-co2/maunaloa.co2 (accessed December 22, 2005).

164. Philip D. Jones, David E. Parker, Timothy J. Osborn, and Keith R. Briffa, "Global Monthly and Annual Temperature Anomalies (degrees C), 1856–2000," July 2001, http://.cdiac.esd.ornl.gov/ftp/trends/temp/jonescru/global.dat (accessed December 22, 2005).

165. Indur M. Goklany and Merritt W. Sprague, *A Different Approach to Sustainable Development: Conserving Forests, Habitat, and Biological Diversity by Increasing the Efficiency and Productivity of Land Utilization* (Washington, DC: Office Program Analysis, U.S. Department of the Interior, 1991); Indur M. Goklany, "Meeting Global Food Needs: The Environmental Trade-Offs Between Increasing Land Conversion and Land Productivity," *Technology* 6 (1999): 107–30.

166. Indur M. Goklany, "Strategies to Enhance Adaptability," 427–49; Goklany, "Meeting Global Food Needs," 107–30.

167. FAO (2005).

168. Ibid.; see FAO, *Global Forest Resource Assessment 2005: 15 Key Findings* (Rome: FAO, 2005).

169. FAO, *Global Forest Resource Assessment 2000* (Rome: FAO, 2000). According to the 2000 assessment, net losses in forest area between 1990 and 2000 were somewhat larger at 94 Mha. This resulted from a loss of 123 Mha in tropical and subtropical areas and a gain of 29 Mha elsewhere in the world. Detailed results from the latest 2005 assessment were not available as of this writing.

170. Ibid.

171. R. C. Myneni, C. D. Keeling, C. J. Tucker, G. Asrar, et al., "Increased Plant Growth in the Northern High Latitudes from 1981 to 1991," *Nature* 386 (1997): 698–702; Pieter P. Tans and James W. C. White, "The Global Carbon Cycle: In Balance, with a Little Help from the Plants," *Science* 281 (1998): 183–84; S. Fan, M. Gloor, J. Mahlman, S. Pacala, et al., "A Large Terrestrial Carbon Sink in North America Implied by Atmospheric and Oceanic Carbon Dioxide Data and Models," *Science* 282 (1998): 442–46; Hanqin Tian, Jerry M. Melillo, David W. Kicklighter, A. David McGuire, et al., "Effect of Interannual Climate Variability on Carbon Storage in Amazonian Ecosystems," *Nature* 396 (1998): 664–67; D. S. Schimel, J. I. House, K. A. Hibbard, P. Bousquet, et al., "Recent Patterns and Mechanisms of Carbon Exchange by Terrestrial Ecosystems," *Nature* 414 (2001): 169–72.

172. R. R. Nemani, C. D. Keeling, H. Hashimoto, W. M. Jolly, et al., "Climate-Driven Increases in Global Terrestrial Net Primary Production from 1982 to 1999," *Science* 300 (2003): 1560–63.

173. Michael A. White, Steven W. Running, and P. E. Thornton, "The Impact of Growing-Season Length Variability on Carbon Assimilation and Evapotranspiration over 88 Years in the Eastern US Deciduous Forest," *International Journal of Biometeorology* 42 (1999): 139–45.

174. D. S. Schimel et al., "Recent Patterns and Mechanisms of Carbon Exchange by Terrestrial Ecosystems."

175. FAO, *The State of the World's Forests 1997* (Rome: FAO, 1997); Jeffrey R. Vincent and Theodore Panayotou, ". . . Or Distraction," *Science* 276 (1997): 55–57.

176. These estimates are based on data from FAO (2005). They assume that between 1990 and 2000, the areas of agricultural land and cropland would expand in proportion to the increase in food production and that agricultural productivity would be frozen at 1990 levels (i.e., the increased food production would be met through an increase in agricultural land rather than any technological change).

177. Estimates provided in table 6.6 assume that crop production in 2002 would be maintained at its actual 2002 production level.

178. Indur M. Goklany, "Saving Habitat and Conserving Biodiversity on a Crowded Planet." *BioScience* 48 (1998): 941–53.

179. Gian-Reto Walther, Eric Post, Peter Convey, Annette Menzel, et al., "Ecological Responses to Recent Climate Change," *Nature* 416 (2002): 389–95.

180. Camille Parmesan and Gary Yohe, "A Globally Coherent Fingerprint" (2003). See also Terry L. Root, Jeff T. Price, Kimberly R. Hall, Stephen H. Schneider, et al., "Fingerprints of Global Warming" (2003).

181. Camille Parmesan and Gary Yohe, "A Globally Coherent Fingerprint."

182. World Wildlife Fund-Finland, "Climatic Change Has Altered Finnish Flora and Fauna," press release, May 17, 2002, on file with author.

183. Royal Society for the Protection of Birds (RSPB), *The State of the UK's Birds 2000* (Bedfordshire, UK: RSPB, 2001); RSPB, *The State of the UK's Birds 2001* (Bedfordshire, UK 2002); RSPB, *The State of the UK's Birds 2004* (Bedfordshire, UK, 2005); Wildlife News, "Climate Change Turns Up the Heat on UK's Threatened Birds," August 10, 2002, www.naturalworldtours.co.uk/articles2002/August/aug1002l.htm (accessed on December 8, 2002).

184. Richard Fox, "Millennium Atlas of Butterflies in Britain and Ireland," Butterfly Conservation press release, March 2, 2001, www.butterfly-conservation.org/ne/news/bnm/english.html (accessed on December 8, 2002); Richard Fox, "A Butterfly's Map of Climate Change," October 9, 2001, www.changingclimate.org/content/articles/article/data/section_3/article_7/part_18/ (accessed on December 8, 2002).

185. Ranga B. Myneni, C. D. Keeling, C. J. Tucker, G. Asrar, et al., "Increased Plant Growth in the Northern High Latitudes from 1981 to 1991," *Nature* 386 (1997): 698–702; Annette Menzel and Peter Fabian, "Growing Season Extended in Europe," *Nature* 397 (1999): 659; D. S. Schimel, K. A. Hibbard, P. Bousquet, P. Ciais, P. Peylin, et al., "Recent Patterns and Mechanisms of Carbon Exchange by Terrestrial Ecosystems," *Nature* 414 (2001): 169–72; Gian-Reto Walther, Eric Post, Peter Convey, Annette Menzel, et al., "Ecological Responses to Recent Climate Change," *Nature* 416 (2002): 389–95. Some researchers note that the recent increase in the length of the growing season might be the result of natural variation, which might cause the length to vary by "10 days. See, Michael A. White, Steven W. Running, and Peter E. Thornton, "The Impact of Growing-Season Length Variability on Carbon Assimilation and Evapotranspiration over 88 Years in the Eastern US Deciduous Forest," *International Journal of Biometeorology* 42 (1999): 139–45. See also Paolo D'Odorico, JaeChan Yoo, and Siegfried Jaeger, "Changing Seasons: An Effect of the North Atlantic Oscillation?" *Journal of Climate* 15 (2002): 435–45, whose analysis suggests that the North Atlantic Oscillation might be responsible for the variations.

186. Rachael Hickling, David B. Roy, Jane K. Hill, and Chris D. Thomas, "A Northward Shift of Range Margins in British Odonata," *Global Change Biology* 11, no. 3 (March 2005): 502–06. See also Arndt Hampe and Remy J. Petit, "Conserving Biodiversity under Climate Change: the Rear Edge Matters," *Ecology Letters* 8 (2005): 461–67.

187. David G. Vaughan, Garth J. Marshall, William M. Connolley, John C. King, et al., "Climate Change: Devil in the Detail," *Science* 293 (2001): 1777–79.

188. J. Alan Pounds, Martin R. Bustamante, Luis A. Coloma, Jamie A. Consuegra, et al., "Widespread Amphibian Extinctions from Epidemic Disease Driven by Global Warming," *Nature* 439 (2006): 161–67.

189. Patrick J. Michaels, "Jumping to Conclusions: Frogs, Global Warming, and Nature (Revised)," *World Climate Report*, January 11, 2006, www.worldclimate report.com/index.php/2006/01/11/jumping-to-conclusions-frogs-global-warming-and-nature/ (accessed January 26, 2006).

190. Alastair H. Fitter and Richard S. R. Fitter, "Rapid Changes in Flowering Time in British Plants," *Science* 296 (2002): 1689–91.

191. Gian-Reto Walther, Eric Post, Peter Convey, Annette Menzel, et al., "Ecological Responses to Recent Climate Change," *Nature* 416 (2002): 389–95; David G. Vaughan, Garth J. Marshall, William M. Connolley, John C. King, et al., "Climate Change."

192. Gian-Reto Walther, et al., "Ecological Responses to Recent Climate Change."

193. Wil L. M. Tamis, Maarten Van't Zelfde, Ruud Van Der Meijden, and Helias A. Udo De Haes, "Changes in Vascular Plant Biodiversity in the Netherlands in the 20th Century Explained by Their Climatic and Other Environmental Characteristics," *Climatic Change* 72 (2005): 37–56.

194. Gian-Reto Walther, et al., "Ecological Responses to Recent Climate Change."

195. Fabrizio Grieco, Arie J. van Noordwijk, and Marcel E. Visser, "Evidence for the Effect of Learning on Timing of Reproduction in Blue Tits," *Science* 296 (2002): 136–38.

196. Jay Withgott, "Last Year's Food Guides This Year's Brood," *Science* (2002): 29–31.

197. National Oceanic and Atmospheric Administration (NOAA), National Environmental Satellite Data Information Service (NESDIS) and National Climatic Data Center (NCDC), *2003 Annual Summaries* (Asheville, NC: National Climatic Data Center, 2004); National Weather Service (NWS), *Natural Hazard Statistics*, www.nws.noaa.gov/om/hazstats.shtml (accessed October 15, 2005).

198. Hydrologic Information Center (HIC), *Flood Fatalities*, www.nws.noaa.gov/oh/hic/flood_stats/recent_individual_deaths.shtml (accessed August 22, 2005). For example, the HIC lists 66 and 99 fatalities for the years 2001 and 2003, respectively, while the *2003 Annual Summaries* list them as 48 and 86.

199. Eric S. Blake, Paul J. Hebert, Jerry D. Jarrell, and Max Mayfield, "The Deadliest, Costliest, and Most Intense United States Hurricanes of This Century (and Other Frequently Requested Hurricane Facts)," *NOAA Technical Memorandum NWS TPC-1* (Miami, FL: National Weather Service, 2005). Eric S. Blake, Paul J. Hebert, Jerry D. Jarrell, and Max Mayfield list 60 and 24 fatalities due to hurricanes in 2004 and 2003, respectively. By contrast, the *2003 Annual Summaries* list 34 and 14 for these years.

200. CDC, WONDER database, http://wonder.cdc.gov.

201. See Indur M. Goklany, "Richer Is More Resilient."

202. In the WONDER database, mortality data for 1979–98 are coded using the International Classification of Disease, version 9 (i.e., ICD-9), and ICD-10 for 1999

onward. To identify deaths due to extreme heat, I used codes E900.0 and E900.9 for ICD-9 per Indur M. Goklany and Soren R. Straja, "United States Death Rates due to Extreme Heat and Cold Ascribed to Weather, 1979–1997," *Technology* 7S (2000): 165–73, and X30 for ICD-10. The corresponding codes used for extreme cold were E901.0 and E901.9 and X31, respectively.

203. Anthony J. McMichael, Andrew Haines, Rudi Slooff, and Sari Kovats, eds., *Climate Change and Human Health* (Geneva: WHO, 1996); Edwin M. Kilbourne, "Cold Environments," in *The Public Health Consequences of Disasters*, ed. Eric K. Noji (New York: Oxford University Press, 1997), pp. 270–86; Edwin M. Kilbourne, "Heat Waves and Hot Environments," in *The Public Health Consequences of Disasters*, ed. Eric K. Noji (New York: Oxford University Press, 1997), pp. 245–69.

204. Christopher J. L. Murray and Alan D. Lopez, *The Global Burden of Disease* (Geneva: WHO, 1996).

205. Anthony J. McMichael, et al., eds., *Climate Change and Human Health*; Edwin M. Kilbourne, "Cold Environments"; Edwin M. Kilbourne, "Heat Waves and Hot Environments."

206. This includes 75 deaths per year due to miscellaneous categories such as drought, mud slides, winter storms, and avalanches. This is based on National Weather Service (NWS), *Natural Hazard Statistics*, www.nws.noaa.gov/om/hazstats.shtml (accessed December 28, 2005).

207. USBOC (2006), p. 97.

208. Hurricane-related fatalities in 2004 were around 1,500. This is based on an estimate of 1,336 fatalities due to Hurricane Katrina, per Richard D. Knabb, Jamie R. Rhome, and Daniel P. Brown, "Tropical Cyclone Report, Hurricane Katrina, August 23–30, 2005," National Hurricane Center, December 20, 2005; and 119 fatalities due to Hurricane Rita, per The Weather Page, "2005 Hurricane Season Summary" (updated December 2, 2005), http://primera.tamu.edu/kcchome/weather.html (accessed December 22, 2005). It is conceivable that many Katrina-related fatalities will eventually be assigned to floods, because their proximate cause was flooding due to the levee breaks in New Orleans in Katrina's aftermath. As of this writing, an official report on Hurricane Rita had not been released.

209. USBOC (2006), p. 87.

210. Indur M. Goklany and Soren R. Straja, "United States Death Rates due to Extreme Heat and Cold Ascribed to Weather, 1979–1997"; R. E. Davis, P. C. Knappenberger, W. M. Novicoff, and P. J. Michaels, "Decadal Changes in Heat-Related Human Mortality in the Eastern United States," *Climate Research* 22 (2002): 175–84.

211. National Climatic Data Center (NCDC), *Annual Summaries* (Asheville, NC: NCDC, 2004); S. Hinton, personal communication, August 2005; NWS, *National Hazard Statistics*, www.nws.noaa.gov/om/hazstats.shtml (accessed October 15, 2005).

212. Ibid.

213. Thomas R. Karl and Richard W. Knight, "Secular Trends of Precipitation Amount, Frequency, and Intensity in the United States," *Bulletin of the American Meteorological Society* 79 (1998): 231–41; and Harry F. Lins and James R. Slack, "Streamflow Trends in the United States," *Geophysical Research Letters* 26 (1999): 227–30. See, also, Jurgen D. Garbrecht, and Frederic E. Rossel, "Decade-scale Precipitation Increase in Great Plains at End of 20th Century," *Journal of Hydrologic Engineering* 7 (2002): 64–75; C. Emdad Haque, "Risk Assessment, Emergency Preparedness and Response to Hazards: The Case of the 1997 Red River Valley Flood, Canada," *Natural Hazards* 21 (2000): 225–45; J. Rolf Olsen, Jery R. Stedinger, Nicholas C. Matalas, and Eugene

Z. Stakhiv, "Climate Variability and Flood Frequency Estimation for the Upper Mississippi and Lower Missouri Rivers," *Journal of the American Water Resources Association* 35 (1999): 1509–23.

214. HIC, *Flood Losses: Compilation of Flood Loss Statistics*, 2005, www.nws.noaa.gov/oh/hic/flood_stats/Flood_loss_time_series.htm, as adjusted per Goklany, "Potential Consequences of Increasing Atmospheric CO_2 Concentration Compared to Other Environmental Problem," *Technology* 7S (2000): 189–213. Notably, there were several discrepancies between the flood fatalities data from NOAA's HIC and its NCDC, and both differ from data in the Bureau of the Census' Statistical Abstracts and the Historical Statistics (USBOC [1975]). Because HIC was supposedly the original source for the flood data for the other groups as well, it was decided to use the HIC data set. However, in the earlier years, even the HIC data set may be prone to error, possibly undercounting fatalities. For instance, in 1911, that data set shows zero fatalities; however, the *New York Times* indicates that there were at least 55 fatalities that flood year. Similarly, the *Times* indicates at least 244 fatalities in 1928 and 42 in 1931 compared to 15 and zero, respectively, in the HIC data set. However, the corrected values may themselves be lower bounds. The keeper of the HIC's data set expresses greater confidence in the data after the mid 1960s on fatalities and mid 1950s on property losses.

215. In Eric S. Blake, Jerry D. Jarrell, and Max Mayfield, "The Deadliest, Costliest, and Most Intense United States Hurricanes of This Century."

216. Christopher W. Landsea, Neville Nicholls, William M. Gray, and Lixion A. Avila, "Downward Trends in the Frequency of Intense Atlantic Hurricanes during the Past Five Decades," *Geophysical Research Letters* 23 (1996): 1697–1700; Christopher W. Landsea, Roger A. Pielke Jr., Alberto M. Mestas-Nuñez, and John A. Knaff, "Atlantic Basin Hurricanes: Indices of Climatic Changes," *Climatic Change* 42 (1999): 89–129. See also D. R. Mestas-Nuñez and John A. Knaff, "Atlantic Basin Hurricanes: Indices of Climatic Changes," and P. Ambenje, "Observed Variability and Trends in Extreme Climate Events: A Brief Review," *Bulletin of the American Meteorological Society* 81 (2000): 417–25.

217. Indur M. Goklany, "Potential Consequences of Increasing Atmospheric CO_2 Concentration Compared to Other Environmental Problems."

218. U.S. population data are from USBOC (2000, 2004a, 2005a) for 1900–59, 1960–99, and 2000 to 2004, respectively.

219. See, for example, Indur M. Goklany, "Richer Is More Resilient."

220. Spiegel Online, "Katrina Should Be a Lesson to US on Global Warming," August 30, 2005, on file with author, quotes from an editorial written by then-minister Jürgen Trittin: "There is only one possible route of action. . . . Greenhouse gases have to be radically reduced and it has to happen worldwide. Until now, the US has kept its eyes shut to this emergency. (Americans) make up a mere 4 percent of the population, but are responsible for close to a quarter of emissions. . . . The Bush government rejects international climate protection goals by insisting that imposing them would negatively impact the American economy. The American president is closing his eyes to the economic and human costs his land and the world economy are suffering under natural catastrophes like Katrina and because of neglected environmental policies."

221. NOAA, "NOAA Reviews Record-Setting 2005 Atlantic Hurricane Season: Active Hurricane Era Likely to Continue," news release, November 29, 2005; Quirin Schiermeier, "Trouble Brews over Contested Trend in Hurricanes," *Nature* 435 (2005): 1008–09; Kenneth Chang, "Storms Vary with Cycles, Experts Say," *New York Times*,

August 30, 2005, on file with author. For an extremely useful discussion on hurricanes and global warming, see Roger A. Pielke Jr., Christopher Landsea, Max Mayfield, Jim Laver, et al., "Hurricanes and Global Warming," *Bulletin of the American Meteorological Society* 86 (November 2005): 1571–75.

222. EM-DAT, Emergency Disaster database, Office of Foreign Disaster Aid and Center for Research on the Epidemiology of Disasters at the Université Catholique de Louvain, Brussels, Belgium, www.em-dat.net/disasters/statisti.htm (accessed September 6, 2005), henceforth EM-DAT (2005).

223. Figure 6.17 is constructed using data from the following sources. For deaths, EM-DAT (2005). For population from 1900–25, Colin McEvedy and Richard Jones, *Atlas of World Population History* (New York: Penguin, 1978). For population from 1950–2004, World Resources Institute, Earth Trends database, www.wri.org (accessed July 12, 2005). For population from 1926–49, estimates were based on interpolation for each year using the 1925 estimate from Colin McEvedy and Richard Jones and the 1950 WRI estimate, assuming exponential population growth. For 2004, I excluded the deaths due to the Boxing Day Tsunami disaster (which, according to EM-DAT, killed 226,435 people). Death estimates, in particular, are approximate and, possibly, more prone to error as we go further into the past. Note that EM-DAT is not quite complete, but it should have captured the major natural disasters, particularly in recent years. EM-DAT contains data on the occurrence and effects of more than 12,800 mass disasters in the world from 1900 to present. The data are compiled from various sources, including UN agencies, nongovernmental organizations, insurance companies, research institutes, and press agencies. For a disaster to be entered into the database one or more of the following criteria must be met: (a) at least 10 people must have been reported killed, (b) at least 100 people must have been reported as affected, (c) a state of emergency must have been declared, or (d) there should have been a call for international assistance.

224. Christoph Schär and Gerd Jendritzky, "Climate Change: Hot News from Summer 2003," *Nature* 432 (December 2, 2004): 559–60| doi: 10.1038/432559a; Peter A. Stott, Daithi A. Stone, and Myles R. Allen, "Human Contribution to the European Heatwave of 2003," *Nature* 432 (December 2, 2004): 610–14.

225. WHO, *World Health Report 2004* (Geneva: WHO, 2004).

226. Jonathan A. Patz, Diarmid Campbell-Lendrum, Tracey Holloway, and Jonathan A. Foley, "Impact of Regional Climate Change on Human Health," *Nature* 438 (November 17, 2005): 310–17.

227. Anthony J. McMichael, Diarmid Campbell-Lendrum, Sari Kovats, Sally Edwards, et al., "Global Climate Change," in *Comparative Quantification of Health Risks: Global and Regional Burden of Disease due to Selected Major Risk Factors*, ed. Majid Ezzati, Alan D. Lopez, Anthony Rodgers, and Christopher J. L. Murray (Geneva: WHO, 2004), pp. 1543–1649.

228. Ibid., p. 1546.

229. Moreover, the estimates were based on modeling studies, with quantification based on anecdotal information. The temperature-disease relationship used to develop the estimate for diarrhea, for example, was based on 6 years worth of data from Lima, Peru, and 20 years of data from Fiji. In addition, the amount of climate change estimated for 2000 was based on the results of a general circulation model at resolution of 3.750 longitude and 2.50 latitude. The results of such models, which are inexact at best at the global level, tend to greater uncertainty as the resolution gets finer.

230. Mary W. Downton, J. Zoe Miller, and Roger A. Pielke Jr., "Reanalysis of United States National Weather Service Flood Loss Database," *Natural Hazards Review* 6 (2005): 13–22.

231. Indur M. Goklany, "Potential Consequences of Increasing Atmospheric CO_2 Concentration Compared to Other Environmental Problems," 189–213. The latter calculation commenced in 1925 because that was the first year for which data was available from the Bureau of Economic Affairs on fixed tangible reproducible assets.

232. Roger A. Pielke Jr. and Christopher W. Landsea, "Normalized Hurricane Damage in the United States: 1925–1995," *Weather and Forecasting* 13 (1998): 621–31.

233. The following data sources were used to construct figure 6.18: for property losses and frequency of hurricane strikes, Erik S. Blake, Paul J. Hebert, Jerry D. Jarrell, Max Mayfield, et al., "The Deadliest, Costliest, and Most Intense United States Hurricanes from 1851 to 2004"; and for state incomes over time, Bureau of Economic Affairs, www.bea.gov/bea/dn/FA2004/SelectTable.asp (accessed August 22, 2005). Each state's income was weighted by the frequency with which hurricanes scored a direct hit on them during this period. This helps account for the fact that if a hurricane hits a rich state, one should expect damages to be higher. I used personal income for each affected state rather than wealth because of the unavailability of time series for the wealth in the various states.

234. At the national level, the R^2 for the correlation between personal income and wealth (i.e., fixed assets and consumer durable goods) is 0.997 for 1929–2004. The correlation coefficient is 0.260 (with a 95 percent confidence interval extending from 0.256 to 0.265).

235. An alternate approach would have been to explicitly use population growth for each state and a national average of wealth per capita. However, that would not capture the fact that on a per capita basis the affected states might be wealthier now relative to the average U.S. person than they used to be (which I suspect to be the case).

236. Bureau of Transport Economics, *2001 Economic Costs of Natural Disasters in Australia*, chapter 3, www.bte.gov.au/docs/r103_index.htm (accessed December 12, 2002).

237. IPCC, *Climate Change 2001: The Synthesis Report* (Cambridge, UK: Cambridge University Press, 2001), p. 256.

238. Anthony J. McMichael, et al., "Human Health," in *Climate Change 2001: Impacts, Adaptation, and Vulnerability* (New York: Cambridge University Press, 2001), p. 463.

239. WHO, *World Health Report 1997* (Geneva: WHO, 1997); WHO, *World Health Report 2004* (Geneva: WHO, 2004).

240. See, for example, Anthony J. McMichael, et al., "Human Health." Jonathan A. Patz, et al., "Impact of Regional Climate Change on Human Health."

241. Paul Reiter, "Global Warming and Mosquito-Borne Disease in USA," *Lancet* 348 (1996): 622; Joan H. Bryan, Desmond H. Foley, and Robert W. Sutherst, "Malaria Transmission and Climate Change in Australia," *Medical Journal of Australia* 164 (1996): 345–47; Paul Reiter, Christopher J. Thomas, Peter M. Atkinson, Simon I. Hay, et al., "Global Warming and Malaria: A Call for Accuracy," *Lancet Infectious Disease* 4 (2004): 323–24; Indur M. Goklany, "Potential Consequences of Increasing Atmospheric CO_2 Concentration."

242. Lyman O. Howard, "Economic Loss to the People of the United States through Insects That Carry Disease," *National Geographic* 20 (1909): 735–49; Roy Porter, ed., *The Cambridge Illustrated History of Medicine* (New York: Cambridge University Press, 1996), pp. 32–34, 40–43, 104–05, 318–19; Paul Reiter, "Would Malaria Spread to

Europe in a Warmer Climate?" in *The Impacts of Climate Change: An Appraisal for the Future* (London: International Policy Press, 2004), pp. 37–43.

243. Wilson G. Smillie, "The Period of Great Epidemics in the United States (1800–1875)," in *The History of American Epidemiology*, ed. Franklin H. Top (St. Louis, MO: C. V. Mosby, 1952), pp. 52–73.

244. World Bank, *World Development Indicators 2002*.

245. Indur M. Goklany, "Factors Affecting Environmental Impacts."

246. Harry M. Rosenberg, Stephanie J. Ventura, Jeffrey D. Mauerer, Robert L. Heuser, et al., "Births and Deaths: United States, 1995," *Monthly Vital Statistics Report* 45, no. 3 (Supp. 2, 1996): 31.

247. World Resources Institute, EarthTrends, http://earthtrends.wri.org/ (accessed August 5, 2006).

248. Indur M. Goklany, "Potential Consequences of Increasing Atmospheric CO_2 Concentration."

249. Anthony J. McMichael, Andrew Githeko, et al., "Human Population Health," in *Climate Change 1995: Impacts, Adaptations and Mitigation of Climate Change*, ed. Robert T. Watson, Mafuru C. Zinyowera, and Richard H. Moss (Cambridge, UK: Cambridge University Press, 1996), pp. 561–84; Robert T. Watson, Mafuru C. Zinyowera and Anthony J. McMichael, eds., *Climate Change and Human Health* (Geneva: WHO 1996).

250. Simon I. Hay, Jonathan Cox, David J. Rogers, Sarah E. Randolph, et al., "Climate Change and the Resurgence of Malaria in the East African Highlands," *Nature* 415 (2002): 905–09; David J. Rogers, Sarah E. Randolph, Robert W. Snow, and Simon I. Hay, "Satellite Imagery in the Study and Forecast of Malaria," *Nature* 415 (2002): 710–15. See also the exchange of letters between Simon I. Hay, Jonathan Cox, David J. Rogers, Sarah E. Randolph, et al., "Climate Change (Communication Arising): Regional Warming and Malaria Resurgence," *Nature* 420 (2002): 627–28.

251. Gary Taubes, "Global Warming: Apocalypse Not," *Science* 278 (1997): 1004–06; Francisco P. Pinheiro and Roberto Chuit, "Emergence of Dengue Hemorrhagic Fever in the Americas," *Infections in Medicine* 15, no. 4 (1998): 244–51; Adrian C. Sleigh, Xi-Li Liu, Sukhan Jackson, Peng Li, et al., "Resurgence of Vivax Malaria in Henan Province, China," *Bulletin of the World Health Organization* 76 (1998); R. E. Besser, Rojas B. Moscoso, Angulo O. Cabanillas, Venero L. González, et al., "Prevention of Cholera Transmission: Rapid Evaluation of the Quality of Municipal Water in Trujillo, Peru," *Bol Oficina Sanit Panam* 119, no. 3 (1995): 189–94; Donald R. Roberts, Larry L. Laughlin, Paul Hsheih, and Llewellyn J. Legters, "DDT, Global Strategies, and a Malaria Control Crisis in South America," *Emerging Infectious Diseases* 3 (1997): 295–301; Donald R. Roberts, S. Manguin, and J. Mouchet, "A Probability Model of Vector Behavior: Effects of DDT Repellency, Irritancy, and Toxicity in Malaria Control," *Journal of Vector Control* 25 (2000): 48–61; Indur M. Goklany, "Potential Consequences of Increasing Atmospheric CO_2 Concentration Compared to Other Environmental Problems," 189–213; David J. Rogers, et al., "Satellite Imagery in the Study and Forecast of Malaria."

252. Donald R. Roberts, Larry L. Laughlin, Paul Hsheih, and Llewellyn J. Legters, "DDT, Global Strategies, and a Malaria Control Crisis in South America"; Donald R. Roberts, S. Manguin, and J. Mouchet, "A Probability Model of Vector Behavior: Effects of DDT Repellency, Irritancy, and Toxicity in Malaria Control"; Karen I. Barnes, David N. Durrheim, Francesca Little, Amanda Jackson, et al., "Effect of Artemether-Lumefantrine Policy and Improved Vector Control on Malaria Burden in KwaZulu-Natal, South Africa," *Public Library of Science Medicine* (2005): doi 10.1371/

journal.pmed.0020330; Patrick E. Duffy and Theonest K. Mutabingwa, "Rolling Back a Malaria Epidemic in South Africa," *Public Library of Science Medicine* (2005): doi: 10.1371/journal.pmed.0020368; Richard Tren, "IRS & DDT in Africa—Past and Present Successes," *54th Annual Meeting, American Society of Tropical Medicine and Hygiene (ASTMH)*, Washington, DC, December 11–15, 2005; Donald R. Roberts, "Policies to Stop/Prevent Indoor Residual Spraying for Malaria Control," *54th Annual Meeting, ASTMH*, Washington, DC, December 11–15, 2005.

253. Richard Tren, "IRS & DDT in Africa."

254. Ibid.

255. The following timeline has been pieced together based on Richard Tren, "IRS & DDT in Africa"; M. H. Craig, I. Kleinschmidt, J. B. Nawn, D. Le Sueur, and B. L. Sharp, "Exploring Thirty Years of Malaria Case Data in KwaZulu-Natal, South Africa: Part II. The Impact of Non-Climatic Factors," *Tropical Medicine and International Health* 9 (2004): 1258–66; Karen I. Barnes, et al., "Effect of Artemether-Lumefantrine Policy and Improved Vector Control on Malaria Burden in KwaZulu-Natal, South Africa."

256. M. H. Craig, I. Kleinschmidt, J. B. Nawn, D. Le Sueur, and B. L. Sharp, "Exploring Thirty Years of Malaria Case Data in KwaZulu-Natal, South Africa: Part I. The Impact of Climatic Factors," *Tropical Medicine and International Health* 9 (2004): 1247–57; M. H. Craig, et al., "Impact of Non-Climatic Factors."

257. Ibid.

258. M. H. Craig, et al., "Impact of Non-Climatic Factors"; Karen I. Barnes, et al., "Effect of Artemether-Lumefantrine Policy and Improved Vector Control on Malaria Burden in KwaZulu-Natal, South Africa"; Patrick E. Duffy and Theonest K. Mutabingwa, "Rolling Back a Malaria Epidemic in South Africa"; Richard Tren, "IRS & DDT in Africa."

259. Indur M. Goklany, "From Precautionary Principle to Risk-Risk Analysis," *Nature Biotechnology* 20 (November 2002): 1075; Indur M. Goklany, *The Precautionary Principle: A Critical Appraisal of Environmental Risk Assessment* (Washington, DC: Cato Institute, 2001).

260. John A. Church, "Changes in Sea Level," in *Climate Change 2001: The Scientific Basis, Contribution of Working Group I to the Third Assessment Report of the Intergovernmental Panel on Climate Change*, ed. J. T. Houghton, Y. Ding, D. J. Griggs, M. Noguer, et al. (Cambridge, UK: Cambridge University Press, 2001), p. 881.

261. John A. Church and Neil J. White, "A 20th Century Acceleration in Global Sea-Level Rise," *Geophysical Research Letters* 33 (2006): L01602, doi:10.1029/2005GL024826.

262. Anny Cazenave and R. S. Nerem, "Present-Day Sea Level Change: Observations and Causes," *Review of Geophysics* 42 (2004): RG3001, doi: 10.1029/2003RG000139.

263. Ibid.

264. Alix Lombard, Anny Cazenave, Pierre-Yves Le Traon, and Masayoshi Ishii, "Contribution of Thermal Expansion to Present-Day Sea Level Rise Revisited," *Global and Planetary Change* 47 (2005): 1–16.

265. Jeffrey A. McNeely, Madhav Gadgil, C. Leveque, C Padoch, et al., "Human Influences in Biodiversity," in *Global Biodiversity Assessment*, ed. Vernon H. Heywood (Cambridge, UK: Cambridge University Press, 1995), pp. 755–57.

266. Michael N. Tsimplis and Michael Rixen, "Sea Level in the Mediterranean Sea: The Contribution of Temperature and Salinity Changes," *Geophysical Research Letters* 10.1029/2002GL015870, http://modb.oce.ulg.ac.be/mare/grlrixen2.pdf (accessed December 13, 2002).

267. Curt H. Davis, Yonghong Li, Joseph R. McConnell, Markus M. Frey, et al., "Snowfall-Driven Growth in East Antarctic Ice Sheet Mitigates Recent Sea-Level Rise," *Science* 308 (2005): 1898–1901. Note that H. Jay Zwally, Mario B. Giovinetto, Jun Li, Helen G. Cornejo, et al., using a slightly shorter record (9 years), estimated a positive contribution to sea level rise for the Antarctica of 0.08 mm year. See H. Jay Zwally, Mario B. Giovinetto, Jun Li, Helen G. Cornejo, et al., "Mass Changes of the Greenland and Antarctic Ice Sheets and Shelves and Contributions to Sea-Level Rise: 1992–2002," *Journal of Glaciology* 51 (2005): 509–27.

268. Ola M. Johannessen, Kirill Khvorostovsky, Martin W. Miles, and Leonid P. Bobylev, "Recent Ice-Sheet Growth in the Interior of Greenland," *Science* 310 (2005): 1013–16.

269. I. Velicogna and J. Wahr, "Measurements of Time-Variable Gravity Show Mass Loss in Antarctica," *Sciencexpress* (2006): 10.1126science.1123785.

270. E. Rignot and P. Kanagaratnam, "Changes in the Velocity Structure of the Greenland Ice Sheet," *Science* 311 (2006): 986–90.

271. WHO, *World Health Report 2002*; p. 72, and annex 11 and 12 tables; WHO, *Global Burden of Disease 2000, Version 2 Estimates*.

272. Jonathan A. Patz, Diarmid Campbell-Lendrum, Tracey Holloway, and Jonathan A. Foley, "Impact of Regional Climate Change on Human Health," *Nature* 438 (2005): 310–17; M. Ezzati, A. D. Lopez, A. Rodgers, and C. J. L. Murray, *Comparative Quantification of Health Risks: Global and Regional Burden of Disease due to Selected Major Risk Factors* (Geneva: WHO, 2004).

273. WHO, *World Health Report 2002—Reducing Risks, Promoting Healthy Life: Methods Summaries for Risk Factors Assessed in Chapter 4*, pp. 26–27, www.who.int/whr/2002/summary_riskfactors_chp4.pdf (accessed January 22, 2006).

274. WHO, *World Health Report 2002*, p. 72.

275. WHO, *World Health Report 2002*, pp. 67, 71–72.

276. Ibid., Annex tables 11–12.

Chapter 7

1. Indur M. Goklany, "Richer is Cleaner: Long-Term Trends in Global Air Quality," in *The True State of the Planet*, ed. Ronald Bailey (New York: Free Press, 1995), pp. 339–77.

2. Indur M. Goklany, *Clearing the Air: The True Story of the War on Air Pollution* (Washington, DC: Cato Institute, 1999), pp. 91–95.

3. The "time of federalization" indicates when responsibility and oversight of control for the pollutant was taken over by the federal government. Ibid., pp. 3, 91–96.

4. Ibid., 73–86.

5. Complicating the situation even further is that Goklany, *Clearing the Air*, presents U.S. emissions for PM-10 (i.e., particulate matter less than 10 micrometers in diameter) rather than PM per se. Although PM per se has been generally regarded as an air pollutant at least since the beginning of this century, if not earlier, it wasn't until the 1970s that smaller particles of particulate matter, such as PM-10, became an issue.

6. Goklany, *Clearing the Air*, pp. 52–65.

7. Goklany, "Factors Affecting Environmental Impacts."

8. As late as December 1998, a joint report of the New Zealand Ministry for the Environment and the Ministry of Transport noted, "The limited monitoring data for New Zealand of both photochemical oxidants and their precursors makes it difficult

to assess the degree of risk posed by current levels, and therefore to estimate the emission reductions required." See New Zealand Ministry for the Environment and the Ministry of Transport, *Ambient Air Quality and Pollution Levels in New Zealand; Targets for Vehicle Emissions Control*, p. 69, www.mfe.govt.nz/publications/air/targets-for-vehicle-emissions-dec98.pdf (accessed January 3, 2006).

9. New Zealand Ministry for the Environment (MfE), "Monitoring of CO, NO_2, SO_2, Ozone, Benzene and Benzo(a)pyrene in New Zealand," Air Quality Technical Report no. 42, Wellington, NZ, 2004, p. 69.

10. In figure 7.1, the GEP and the U.S. GDP are measured in terms of purchasing power parity-adjusted international dollars. The economic data used here are taken from Angus Maddison, *The World Economy: Historical Statistics* (Paris: Organisation for Economic Co-operation and Development, 2003), www.ggdc.net/~maddison (accessed July 30, 2005), henceforth Angus Maddison (2003); and Groningen Growth and Development Centre, Total Economy database, www.ggdc.net, henceforth GGDC (2005). Emissions data are from Gregg Marland, Thomas A. Boden, and Robert J. Andés, "Global, Regional, and National CO_2 Emissions," in *Trends: A Compendium of Data on Global Change* (Oak Ridge, TN: Carbon Dioxide Information Analysis Center, Oak Ridge National Laboratory and U.S. Department of Energy, 2005).

11. Nebojsa Nakicenovic, Arnulf Grübler, and Alan McDonald, eds., *Global Energy Perspectives* (New York: Cambridge University Press, 1998).

12. Based on Angus Maddison (2003) and Gregg Marland, Thomas A. Boden, and Robert J. Andés, "Global, Regional, and National CO_2 Emissions," in *Trends: A Compendium of Data on Global Change* (Oak Ridge, TN: Carbon Dioxide Information Analysis Center, Oak Ridge National Laboratory and U.S. Department of Energy, 2005).

13. Gregg Marland, Thomas J. Boden, and Robert J. Andres, *National CO_2 Emissions from Fossil-Fuel Burning, Cement Manufacture, and Gas Flaring: 1751–2002* (Oak Ridge, TN: Carbon Dioxide Information Analysis Center, Oak Ridge National Laboratory, 2005), http://cdiac. esd.ornl.gov/trends/emis/em_cont.htm (accessed January 2, 2006).

14. World population growth peaked around 2.06 percent per year between 1965 and 1970, according to data from United Nations Population Division, *World Population Prospects: The 2004 Revision Population Database*, http://esa.un.org/unpp/ (accessed January 5, 2005). This had dropped to 1.22 percent per year between 2000 and 2005.

15. Intergovernmental Panel on Climate Change (IPCC), *Climate Change 1995: The Science of Climate Change* (Cambridge, UK: Cambridge University Press, 1996).

16. Frederick Seitz, and 17,000 others, *Global Warming Petition*, www.oism.org/pproject/s33p428.htm (accessed February 5, 2003); Patrick Michaels and Robert Balling, *The Satanic Gases: Clearing the Air about Global Warming* (Washington, DC: Cato Institute, 2000).

17. "The greatest environmental challenge of the new century is global warming," according to William J. Clinton, State of the Union Address, 2000, C-Span, January 27, 2000, on file with author. "Global climate disruption represents one of the single greatest threats to our future," according to Albert Gore, quoted in "'U' Broadcasts Global Summit," *The Michigan Daily*, www.pub.umich.edu/daily/1997/oct/10-07-97/news/news3.html (accessed February 5, 2003). See also Greenwire, *Worldview— Climate Change II: Scientists Fear Warming*, February 5, 1998, http://nationaljournal.com/pubs/greenwire/extra/search.htm (accessed January 15, 2000).

18. Indur M. Goklany, "The Importance of Climate Change Compared to Other Global Changes," Proceedings of the Second International Specialty Conference: Global Climate Change—Science, Policy, and Mitigation/Adaptation Strategies, Crystal City, Virginia, October 13–16, 1998 (Sewickley, PA: Air and Waste Management Association, 1999), pp. 1024–41; Indur M. Goklany, "Richer Is More Resilient: Dealing with Climate Change and More Urgent Environmental Problems," in Earth Report 2000, Revisiting the True State of the Planet, ed. Ronald Bailey (New York: McGraw-Hill, 1999): 155–87; Indur M. Goklany, "Potential Consequences of Increasing Atmospheric CO_2 Concentration Compared to Other Environmental Problems," Technology 7S (2000): 189–213; Indur M. Goklany, "A Climate Policy for the Short and Medium Term: Stabilization or Adaptation?" Energy and Environment 16 (2005): 667–80; Indur M. Goklany, "Is a Richer-but-Warmer World Better than Poorer-but-Cooler Worlds?" 25th Annual North American Conference of the U.S. Association for Energy Economics/International Association of Energy Economics, September 21–23, 2005; Indur M. Goklany, "Is Climate Change the 21st Century's Most Urgent Environmental Problem?" Lindenwood University, Economic Policy Lecture no. 7, St. Charles, MO 2005.

19. Indur M. Goklany, Clearing the Air, pp. 91–93.

20. Molly Villamana, "Shareholders Gaining More Leverage for Environmental Concerns," Greenwire, March 18, 2002, http://80-www.eenews.net.proxygw.wrlc.org/subscriber/search/swishe-search.cgi; Greenpeace, "New Nuclear Power Stations on Government Agenda," www.greenpeace.org.uk/contentlookup.cfm?CFID=377125&CFTOKEN=18513916&SitekeyParam=D-E-D (accessed February 5, 2003); Greenpeace, "Global Warming Campaign," www.green-peace.org.uk/contentlookup.cfm?CFID=377125&CFTOKEN=18513916&SitekeyParam=D-A (accessed February 5, 2003); Sierra Club Miami Group, "It Ain't Over Until the Leases Are Cancelled," http://florida.sierraclub.org/miami/cons_offshore.htm (accessed February 5, 2003).

21. Indur M. Goklany, "Do We Need the Federal Government to Protect Air Quality?" Policy Study no. 150, Center for the Study of American Business, Washington University, St. Louis, MO, 1998, pp. 30–31; Mariano Torras and James K. Boyce, "Income, Inequality, and Pollution: A Reassessment of the Environmental Kuznets Curve," Ecological Economics 25 (1998): 147–60. However, the precise pace of progress may be modulated by the attitudes of the ruling elites. Whether—and when—it occurs in nondemocratic societies is entirely idiosyncratic because it depends on the ideologies or whims of their ruler(s) or ruling group(s).

22. Indur M. Goklany, "Factors Affecting Environmental Impacts"; Indur M. Goklany, Clearing the Air, pp. 52–65, 111–13.

23. Indur M. Goklany, "Adaptation and Climate Change" (paper presented at the Annual Meeting of the American Association for the Advancement of Science, Chicago, February 6–11, 1992); Indur M. Goklany, "Integrated Strategies to Reduce Vulnerability and Advance Adaptation, Mitigation, and Sustainable Development," forthcoming in Mitigation and Adaption Strategies for Global Change (2006).

24. Sander M. de Bruyn, J. C. J. M. van den Bergh, and J. B. Opschoor, "Economic Growth and Emissions: Reconsidering the Empirical Basis of Environmental Kuznets Curves," Ecological Economics 25 (1998): 161–75.

25. Indur M. Goklany, "Factors Affecting Environmental Impacts: The Effects of Technology on Long-Term Trends in Cropland, Air Pollution, and Water-Related Diseases," Ambio 25 (1996): 497–503.

Chapter 8

1. Both affluence and GDP are measured in terms of constant (or real) dollars.

2. It might be argued that in order to estimate ΔT for agriculture, it might also be appropriate to use population rather than GDP ($= P \times A$) on the ground that demand for food would not increase linearly with affluence. However, that would ignore the fact that with greater affluence the demand for meat and other protein goes up, as does the propensity for wastage. Perhaps, the correct measure would be to use the product of population and the logarithm of affluence. Notably, if only population is used, ΔT would be -69 percent for the United States between 1910 and 2000.

3. Paul R. Ehlich, Gary Wolff, Gretchen C. Dailey, Jennifer B. Hughes, et al., "Knowledge and the Environment," *Ecological Economics* 30, no. 2 (1999): 267–84.

4. Indur M. Goklany, "Strategies to Enhance Adaptability: Technological Change, Economic Growth, and Free Trade," *Climatic Change* 30 (1995): 427–49.

5. Mariano Torras and James K. Boyce, "Income, Inequality, and Pollution: A Reassessment of the Environmental Kuznets Curve," *Ecological Economics* 25 (1998): 147–60; Dale S. Rothman and Sander M. De Bruyn,"Probing into the Environmental Kuznets Curve Hypothesis," *Ecological Economics* 25 (1998): 143–45.

6. Figure 6.11 is based on trend data in Organisation for Economic Co-operation and Development (OECD) *Environmental Data Compendium 1999* (Paris: OECD, 1999). In 1995, based on data from the World Bank, *World Development Indicators* (Washington, DC: World Bank, 1999), the PPP-adjusted GDP per capita (in current international dollars) for 10 of these nations (among the world's richest and most industrialized) were more than above $15,000, and between $4,000 and $10,000 for the remaining 4 (the Czech Republic, Poland, the Slovak Republic, and Russia).

7. $R^2 < 0.006$, $p \gg 0.1$ (Indur M. Goklany, *Clearing the Air: The True Story of the War on Air Pollution* [Washington, DC: Cato Institute, 1999], p. 103). This analysis used data for Canada, the United States, Japan, Belgium, France, Germany, Luxembourg, Norway, and the United Kingdom, i.e., $n = 9$). The year 1993 was used because n shrinks to 6 in 1994 and 4 in 1995. The GDP per capita data were obtained from Organisation for Economic Co-operation and Development (OECD), *OECD in Figures 1998* (Paris: OECD, 1998).

8. Environmental Protection Agency (EPA), *America's Children and the Environment* (Washington, DC: EPA, 2001): and EPA, *America's Children and the Environment* (Washington, DC: EPA, 2003), hereinafter ACE (2000) and ACE (2003).

9. Based on key findings of ACE (2003), http://www.epa.gov/envirohealth/children/findings/index.htm (accessed January 6, 2006).

10. Ibid.

11. Ibid.

12. Ibid.

13. ACE (2000).

14. Based on key findings of ACE (2003), http://www.epa.gov/envirohealth/children/findings/index.htm (accessed January 6, 2006).

15. In figure 8.1, which is based on data from World Bank, *World Development Indicators 2005*, the continuous curves are fitted using a log-linear model similar to the one used for food supply and life expectancy in chapter 2. For this figure, $N = 270$, adjusted $R^2 = 0.63$. The dependence of total fertility rate on GDP per capita is significant, as is the downward shift in this indicator as we go from 1977 to 2002. See appendix A. World Bank, *World Development Indicators*, http://devdata.worldbank.org/dataonline (accessed July 12, 2005), henceforth World Bank (2005).

16. The average per capita income for the "high-income countries" increased from $15,719 in 1977 to $26,121 in 2003 in PPP-adjusted 2000 international dollars (World Bank [2005]).

17. Parts of the material in this section have appeared in Indur M. Goklany, "Comparing 20th Century Trends in United States and Global Agricultural Land and Water Use," *Water International* 27, no. 3 (2002): 321–29.

18. Food and Agriculture Organization (FAO) *FAOSTAT 2002,* http://apps.fao.org, henceforth FAO (2002); and Igor A. Shiklomanov, "Appraisal and Assessment of World Water Resources," *Water International* 25, no. 1 (2000): 11–32.

19. Edward O. Wilson, *The Diversity of Life* (Cambridge, MA: Belknap, 1992); Indur M. Goklany, "Saving Habitat and Conserving Biodiversity on a Crowded Planet," *BioScience* 48 (1998): 941–53; Indur M. Goklany, "The Future of Industrial Society" (paper presented at the International Conference on Industrial Ecology and Sustainability, University of Technology of Troyes, Troyes, France, September 22–25, 1999); International Union for the Conservation of Nature and Natural Resources (IUCN), "The Freshwater Biodiversity Crisis," *World Conservation* 2 (1999), www.iucn.org/bookstore/bulletin/1999/wc2/content/freshwaterbio.pdf

20. IUCN, "The Freshwater Biodiversity Crisis"; Wilson, *The Diversity of Life.*

21. IUCN, "The Freshwater Biodiversity Crisis"; Carmen Revenga and Greg Mock, "Freshwater Biodiversity in Crisis," in *EarthTrends: Featured Topic* (Washington, DC: World Resources Institute, 2001).

22. Jonathan E. M. Baillie, Craig Hilton-Taylor, and Simon N. Stuart, *2004 IUCN Red List of Threatened Species: A Global Species Assessment* (Gland, Switzerland: World Conservation Union, 2004), www.iucn.org/themes/ssc/red_2list_2004/GSA_book/Red_List_2004_book.pdf (accessed December 20, 2005), p. 21.

23. Wayne B. Solley, Robert R. Pierce, and Howard A. Perlman, "Estimated Use of Water in the United States in 1995," U.S. Geological Survey Circular 1200, Denver, CO (1998).

24. Ibid.

25. Data for figure 8.2 are from the following sources. For irrigated land, from 1910–55, U.S. Bureau of the Census (USBOC), *Historical Statistic of the United States, Colonial Times to 1970* (Washington, DC: Government Printing Office, 1975), p. 433, henceforth USBOC (1975); from 1960–95, U.S. Department of Agriculture (USDA), *Agricultural Statistics 2001,* pp. ix–7, www.nass.usda.gov/Publications/Ag_Statistics/index.asp (interpolated, as necessary); for 2000, Noel Gollehon, William Quinby, and Marcel Aillery, "Agricultural Resources and Indicators: Water Use and Pricing in Agriculture," in *Agricultural Resources and Environmental Indicators 2003,* ed. Ralph Heimlich, www.ers.usda.gov/publications/arei/ah722/ (accessed August 19, 2005). For irrigation water, USBOC (1975), p. 434; for 1950–2000, Wayne B. Solley, Robert R. Pierce, and Howard A. Perlman, "Estimated Use of Water in the United States in 1995"; and Susan S. Hutson, Nancy L. Barber, Joan F. Kenny, Kristin S. Linsey, et al., "Estimated Use of Water in the United States in 2000," U.S. Geological Survey Circular 1268, released March 2004, revised April 2004, May 2004, February 2005, http://pubs.usgs.gov/ circ/2004/circ1268/. For population, for 2000–04: "National and State Population Estimates: Annual Population Estimates 2000 to 2004," http://www.census. gov/popest/states/NST-ann-est.html (accessed August 14, 2005); for 1900–59, *Historical National Population Estimates, 1900 to 1999,* www.census.gov/popest/archives/pre-1980/ (accessed August 14, 2005); for 1960–99, USBOC, *Statistical Abstract of the United States 2004–2005* (Washington, DC: Government Printing

Office, 2004). For cropland, for 1910–95, *USDA Data on Major Land Uses,* www.ers.usda.gov/data/MajorLandUses/spreadsheets/c1910_00.xls (accessed December 20, 2005); for 1996–2004, from *Agricultural Statistics 2005,* www. nass.usda.gov/Publications/Ag_Statistics/index.asp, pp. ix–17. Some caution is warranted regarding the data on irrigated land. First, the data are interpolated from the periodic Censuses of Agriculture. Second, until 1997 these data were collected by the Department of Commerce. The latest (1997) Census was collected by the U.S. Department of Agriculture (USBOC [1975]); U.S. Department of Agriculture, *Agricultural Statistics 2001,* and it shows a very rapid increase since the early 1990s in the amount of irrigated land. But another data set collected by the U.S. Geological Survey (USGS) Wayne B. Solley, Robert R. Pierce, and Howard A. Perlman, "Estimated Use of Water in the United States in 1995," shows a much smaller increase. A comparison of the Census of Agriculture (interpolated) estimates with the USGS's, estimates from 1960 through 1995 show that the latter's figures are consistently higher by 10–25 percent. See Indur M. Goklany, "Comparing Twentieth Century Trends in U.S. and Global Agricultural Water and Land Use," *Water International* 27 (2002): 321–29 .

26. USDA, "Crops: United States Estimate Track (Series) Record, 1866–Current," National Agricultural Statistics Service (NASS) Stock no. 96120, 2000, www.ers. usda.gov/prodsrvs/dp-fc.htm (accessed July 27, 2000); USDA, *Agricultural Statistics 2005,* chapter I.

27. Figure 8.3 is based on water and irrigated land data from Igor A. Shiklomanov, "Appraisal and Assessment of World Water Resources," *Water International* 25, no. 1 (2000): 11–32. Cropland data are from Indur M. Goklany, "Meeting Global Food Needs," and FAO (2002); and population data are from Colin McEvedy and Richard Jones, *Atlas of World Population History* (New York: Penguin, 1978). Because FAO's data commence in 1961, 1960 data for cropland, population, and irrigated land are extrapolated using data for 1961 and 1962 from FAO (2002).

28. Igor A. Shiklomanov, "Appraisal and Assessment of World Water Resources."

29. Marie Leigh Livingston, "Institutional Requisites for Efficient Water Markets," in *Markets for Water: Potential and Performance,* ed. K. William Easter, Mark W. Rosegrant, and Ariel Dinar (Norwell, MA: Kluwer Academic Publishers, 1998), pp. 19–33.

30. Indur. M. Goklany and Merritt W. Sprague, *An Alternative Approach to Sustainable Development: Conserving Forests, Habitat and Biological Diversity by Increasing the Efficiency and Productivity of Land Utilization* (Washington, DC: Office of Program Analysis, U.S. Department of the Interior, 1991).

31. Based on Natural Resources Conservation Service (NRCS), *Summary Report: 1997 National Resources Inventory, Revised December 2000,* 2001, www.nhq.nrcs. usda.gov/NRI/1997/summary_report/original/contents.html.

32. USBOC (1975), p. 240.

33. Ibid., p. 240.

34. Ibid., p. 11.

35. Wayne B. Solley, Robert R. Pierce, and Howard A. Perlman, "Estimated Use of Water in the United States in 1995"; Sandra Postel, *Pillar of Sand: Can the Irrigation Miracle Last?* (New York: W. W. Norton, 1999).

36. Wayne B. Solley, Robert R. Pierce, and Howard A. Perlman, "Estimated Use of Water in the United States in 1995," pp. 62–63.

37. Indur M. Goklany, "Comparing 20th Century Trends in United States and Global Agricultural Land and Water Use."

38. FAO, FAOSTAT database, 2001, http://apps.fao.org; and Indur M. Goklany, "Precaution without Perversity: A Comprehensive Application of the Precautionary Principle to Genetically Modified Crops."

39. FAO, *The State of Food and Agriculture 1996* (Rome: FAO, 1996); David J. Pimentel, James Houser, Erika Preiss, Omar White, et al., "Water Resources: Agriculture, the Environment, and Society," *BioScience* 47, no. 2 (1997): 97–106; Sandra L. Postel, Gretchen C. Daily, and Paul R. Ehrlich, "Human Appropriation of Renewable Fresh Water," *Science* 271 (1996): 785–88; Postel, *Pillar of Sand: Can the Irrigation Miracle Last?*

40. Mark I. L'Vovich, Gilbert F. White, A. V. Belyaev, Janasz Kindler, et al., "Use and Transformation of Terrestrial Water Systems," in *The Earth as Transformed by Human Action*, ed. Billie L. Turner II, William C. Clar, Robert W. Kates, John F. Richards, et al. (New York: Cambridge University Press, 1990), pp. 235–52; Indur M. Goklany, "Saving Habitat and Conserving Biodiversity on a Crowded Planet," 941–53; Gleick, *The World's Water: The Biennial Report on Freshwater Resources.*

41. Terry L. Anderson, "Water, Water Everywhere But Not a Drop to Sell," in *The State of Humanity*, ed. Julian Simon, E. Calvin Beisner, and John Phelps (Cambridge, MA: Blackwell, 1995), pp. 425–33.

42. Goklany and Merritt W. Sprague, *An Alternative Approach to Sustainable Development*; Intergovernmental Panel on Climate Change [IPCC], "Resource Use and Management," in *Climate Change: The IPCC Response Strategies* (Washington, DC: Island Press, 1991), pp. 163–202; Caroline Taylor, "The Challenge of African Elephant Conservation," *Conservation Issues* 4, no. 2 (1997): 1, 3–11.

43. Roy L. Prosterman, Tim Hanstad, and Li Ping, "Can China Feed Itself?" *Scientific American* 275, no. 5 (1996): 90–96.

44. James Gwartney, Robert Lawson, and, Dexter Samida, *Economic Freedom of the World: 2000 Annual Report* (Vancouver, BC: Fraser Institute, 2000), p. 76.

45. Seth W. Norton, "Poverty, Property Rights, and Human Well-Being: A Cross-National Study," *Cato Journal* 18, no. 2 (1998): 242.

46. Indur M. Goklany and Merritt W. Sprague, *An Alternative Approach to Sustainable Development: Conserving Forests, Habitat, and Biological Diversity by Increasing the Efficiency and Productivity of Land Utilization* (Washington, DC: Office of Program Analysis, U.S. Department of the Interior, 1991); IPCC, "Resource Use and Management," pp. 163–202; Indur M. Goklany, "Saving Habitat and Conserving Biodiversity on a Crowded Planet," 941–53.

47. Terry L. Anderson, "Water, Water Everywhere But Not a Drop to Sell," 425–33; David J. Pimentel, et al., "Water Resources: Agriculture, the Environment, and Society."

48. Ismail Serageldin, *Toward Sustainable Management of Water Resources* (Washington, DC: World Bank, 1995).

49. Terry L. Anderson, "Water, Water Everywhere But Not a Drop to Sell"; Mark W. Rosegrant, Renato Gazmuri Schleyer, and Satya N. Yadav, "Water Policy for Efficient Agricultural Diversification: Market-based Approaches," *Food Policy* 20 (1995): 203–23; Ismail Serageldin, *Toward Sustainable Management of Water Resources*; K. William Easter, Mark W. Rosegrant, and Ariel Dinar, *Markets for Water: Potential and Performance* (Norwell, MA: Kluwer Academic Publishers, 2000).

50. Mark W. Rosegrant, Renato Gazmuri Schleyer, and Satya N. Yadav, "Water Policy for Efficient Agricultural Diversification: Market-based Approaches."

51. R. Maria Saleth, "Water Markets in India: Economic and Institutional Aspects," in *Markets for Water: Potential and Performance*, ed. K. William Easter, Mark W. Rosegrant, and Ariel Dinar (Norwell, MA: Kluwer Academic Publishers, 1998): pp.

187–205; Ruth S. Meinzen-Dicks, "Groundwater Markets in Pakistan: Institutional Development and Productivity Impacts," in *Markets for Water: Potential and Performance,* ed. K. William Easter, Mark W. Rosegrant, and Ariel Dinar (Norwell, MA: Kluwer Academic Publishers, 1998), pp. 207–22.

52. These estimates are based on 1999–2000 data from FAOSTAT's Food Balance Sheet for the world. FAO (2002) (accessed December 18, 2002). It includes estimates for milk, butter, and eggs.

53. FAO, *The State of World Fisheries and Aquaculture (SOFIA) 2000,* www.fao.org/DOCREP/003/X8002E/X8002E00.htm (accessed December 1, 2002).

54. Ibid.

55. Donald R. Leal, *Homesteading the Oceans: The Case for Property Rights in United States Fisheries* (Bozeman, MT: Political Economy Research Center, 2000); Indur M. Goklany, "Meeting Global Food Needs: The Environmental Trade-offs Between Increasing Land Conversion and Land Productivity," *Technology* 6 (1999): 107–30.

56. Terry Anderson and Donald R. Leal, *Free Market Environmentalism* (New York: Palgrave, 2001), chapter 8.

57. FAO, *The State of World Fisheries and Aquaculture (SOFIA) 2000.*

58. Indur M. Goklany, *Clearing the Air,* pp. 22–24, 91–95.

59. Ibid.

60. Nebojsa Nakicenovic, Arnulf Grübler, and Alan McDonald, eds., *Global Energy Perspectives* (Cambridge, UK: Cambridge University Press, 1998).

61. Indur M. Goklany, "Adaptation and Climate Change" (paper presented at the Annual Meeting of the American Association for the Advancement of Science, Chicago, February 6–11, 1992); Indur M. Goklany, "Strategies to Enhance Adaptability: Technological Change, Economic Growth, and Free Trade," *Climatic Change* 30 (1995): 427–49.

62. James Gwartney, Robert Lawson, and Dexter Samida, *Economic Freedom of the World 2000* (Vancouver, BC: Fraser Institute, 2000).

63. Seth W. Norton, "Poverty, Property Rights, and Human Well-Being: A Cross-National Study," 233–45.

64. Goklany, *Clearing the Air,* pp. 133–37.

65. Martin V. Melosi, *Effluent America: Cities, Industry, Energy, and the Environment* (Pittsburgh: University of Pittsburgh Press, 2001).

66. Indur M. Goklany, *Air and Inland Surface Water Quality: Long-Term Trends and Relationship to Affluence* (Washington, DC: Office of Program Analysis, Department of the Interior, 1994).

67. Paul Faeth, *Growing Green: Enhancing the Economic and Environmental Performance of United States Agriculture* (Washington, DC: World Resources Institute, 1995); Kenneth D. Frederick, "Water Resources: Increasing Demand and Scarce Supplies," in *America's Renewable Resources: Historical Trends and Current Challenges,* ed. Kenneth D. Frederick and Roger A. Sedjo (Washington, DC: Resources for the Future, 1991), pp. 23–78.

68. Jon H. Goldstein, Joan R. Hartmann, et al., *The Impacts of Federal Programs on Wetlands, Volume II: A Report to Congress by the Secretary of the Interior* (Washington, DC: Department of the Interior, 1994).

69. Roger E. Meiners and Andrew P. Morris, "Silent Springs and Silent Villages: Pesticides and the Trampling of Property Rights," in *Government vs. Environment,* ed. Donald R. Leal and Roger E. Meiners (Lanham, MD: Rowman and Littlefield, 2001), pp. 15–37.

70. Indur M. Goklany, "Strategies to Enhance Adaptability: Technological Change, Economic Growth, and Free Trade"; Indur M. Goklany, *Clearing the Air*, pp. 87–109.

Chapter 9

1. This chapter is a revised and updated version of a policy study first published by the Weidenbaum Center, Washington University in St. Louis, Missouri. See Indur M. Goklany, "Applying the Precautionary Principle to Genetically Modified Crops," Policy Study no. 157, Center for the Study of American Business, Washington University, St. Louis, MO, 2000.

2. Carolyn Raffensperger and Joel Tickner, *Protecting Public Health and the Environment: Implementing the Precautionary Principle* (Washington DC: Island Press, 1999), p. 8.

3. See Julian Morris, ed., *Rethinking Risk and the Precautionary Principle* (Oxford: Butterworth-Heinemann, 2000), pp. 1–21.

4. See, for example, Jonathan Adler, "More Sorry Than Safe: Assessing the Precautionary Principle and the Proposed International Biosafety Protocol," *Texas International Law Journal* 35 (2000): 194–204.

5. See United Nations (UN), *Agenda 21: The UN Programme of Action From Rio* (New York: United Nations, 1992), p. 10; UN Framework Convention on Climate Change (UNFCCC), *UN Framework on Climate Change* (New York: United Nations, 1992), article 3.3; Lyle Glowka, Francoise Burhenne-Guilmin, and Hugh Synge, *A Guide to the Convention on Biological Diversity* (Gland, Switzerland: World Conservation Union, 1994), p. 11.

6. Convention on Biological Diversity (CBD), "Cartagena Protocol on Biosafety to the Convention on Biological Diversity," 2000, www.biodiv.org/biosafe/Protocol/html/Biosafe-Prot.html.

7. Frances B. Smith, "The Biosafety Protocol: The Real Losers are Developing Countries," *Briefly . . . Perspectives on Legislation, Regulation, and Litigation* 4 (March 2000), National Legal Center for the Public Interest, Washington, DC.

8. Indur M. Goklany, "Applying the Precautionary Principle to Genetically Modified Crops."

9. Friends of the Earth (FOE), "FoE Supports Tory GM Moratorium Call: What about the Precautionary Principle Mr. Blair," press release, 1999, www.foe.co.uk/upsinfo/infoteam/pressrel/1999/19990203170456.html (accessed May 15, 2000); and Indur M. Goklany, "Applying the Precautionary Principle in a Broader Context," in *Rethinking Risk and the Precautionary Principle*, ed. Julian Morris (Oxford: Butterworth-Heinemann, 2000), pp. 189–228.

10. Indur M. Goklany, Roger Bate, and Kendra Okonski, "Will Children Eat GM Rice, or Risk Blindness from Vitamin A Deficiency?" *British Medical Journal* (2001), www.bmj.com/cgi/eletters/3227279/126/b#EL1 (accessed February 9, 2001); Indur M. Goklany, "From Precautionary Principle to Risk-Risk Analysis," *Nature Biotechnology* 20 (November 2002): 1075.

11. Maureen L. Cropper and Paul R. Portney, "Discounting Human Lives," *Resources* 108 (Summer 1992): 1–4.

12. Centers for Disease Control and Prevention (CDC), "U.S. HIV and AIDS cases reported through June 2000," HIV/AIDS Surveillance Report no. 12, 2000, www.cdc.gov/hiv/stats/hasr1201.htm (accessed February 21, 2001).

13. See Food and Agriculture Organization (FAO), FAOSTAT database, 2001, http://apps.fao.org; and Igor A. Shiklomanov, "Appraisal and Assessment of World Water Resources," *Water International* 25, no. 1 (2000): 11-32.

14. This is based on an estimated annual loss of (a) 13.0 Mha between 1980 and 1990, (b) 8.9 Mha between 1990 and 2000, and (c) 7.3 Mha between 2000 and 2005. See FAO, *Global Forest Resource Assessment 2000* (Rome: FAO, 2000), p. 11; FAO, *Global Forest Resource Assessment 2005: 15 Key Findings* (Rome: FAO, 2005).

15. UN Population Division (UNPD), *World Population Prospects: The 2004 Revision Database*, http://esa.un.org/unpp/ (accessed January 7, 2006).

16. Not only do richer populations consume more, they are more likely to consume meat and milk products, which means greater demand for feed for animals. In general, it requires several pounds of grain to produce one pound of meat. For example, the feed conversion ratio for pork is estimated to range from 2.2 kg to 5.9 kg of feed for each kg of live-body weight gained during the grower/finisher phase, with a mean of 3.2; beef cattle take 7-10 pounds of feed to produce a pound of live weight; and broiler chickens require about 2 pounds of feed per pound of live weight produced. See Williard C. Losinger, "Feed-Conversion Ratio of Finisher Pigs in the USA," *Preventive Veterinary Medicine* 36, no. 4 (1998): 287-305; Minnesota Pork Board, "Value Added," www.mnpork.com/ValueAdded.php (accessed January 7, 2006).

17. See also Indur M. Goklany, "The Future of Industrial Society" (invited paper, International Conference on Industrial Ecology and Sustainability, University of Technology of Troyes, Troyes, France, September 22-25, 1999), published in *Perspectives on Industrial Ecology*, ed. Dominique Bourg and Suren Erkman (Sheffield, UK: Greenleaf Publishing, 2003), pp. 194-222; Indur M. Goklany, "Is Climate Change the 21st Century's Most Urgent Environmental Problem?" Lindenwood University Economic Policy Lecture 7, St. Charles, MO, 2005; Indur M. Goklany, "A Climate Policy for the Short and Medium Term: Stabilization or Adaptation?" *Energy and Environment* 16 (2005): 667-80.

18. This figure is updated from Indur M. Goklany, "Meeting Global Food Needs: The Environmental Trade-Offs Between Increasing Land Conversion and Land Productivity,"189-213, using data from UNPD, *World Population Prospects*, and FAO, FAO (2006), http://apps.fao.org (accessed January 7, 2006), henceforth FAO (2006).

19. UNPD, *World Population Prospects: The 2004 Revision*.

20. FAO (2006).

21. Indur M. Goklany, "Meeting Global Food Needs: The Environmental Trade-Offs Between Increasing Land Conversion and Land Productivity," 189-213.

22. FAO (2006).

23. Goklany, "Meeting Global Food Needs: The Environmental Trade-Offs Between Increasing Land Conversion and Land Productivity," 189-213.

24. Calculated from FAO (2006).

25. See Hans Linnemann, J. De Hoogh, M. A. Keyzer, H. D. J. Van Heemst, et al., *MOIRA: Model of International Relations in Agriculture* (Amsterdam: North Holland, 1979), pp. 48-53.

26. E.-C. Oerke, A. Weber, H.-W. Dehne, and F. Schonbeck, eds., *Crop Production and Crop Protection: Estimated Losses in Food and Cash Corps* (Amsterdam: Elsevier, 1994), pp. 742-70.

27. Gordon Conway and Gary Toenniesen, "Feeding the World in the Twenty-First Century," *Nature* 402 (suppl. 1999): C55-C58; Charles C. Mann, "Crop Scientists Seek a New Revolution," *Science* 283 (1999): 310-14.

28. Indur M. Goklany and Merritt W. Sprague, *An Alternative Approach to Sustainable Development: Conserving Forests, Habitat and Biological Diversity by Increasing the Efficiency and Productivity of Land Utilization* (Washington, DC: Office of Program Analysis, Department of Interior, 1991).

29. William H. Bender, "An End Use Analysis of Global Food Requirements," *Food Policy* 19 (1994): 381–95.

30. World Bank, *New & Noteworthy in Nutrition* 24 (1994), www.worldbank.org/html/extdr/hnp/nutrition/nnn/nnn24.htm (accessed January 5, 2000).

31. Wolf B. Frommer, Uwe Ludewig, and Doris Rentsch, "Taking Transgenic Plants with a Pinch of Salt," *Science* 285 (1999): 1222–23.

32. See, for example, Juan Manuel de la Fuente, Verenice Ramírez-Rodríguez, Jose Luis Cabrera-Ponce, and Luis Herrera-Estrella, "Aluminum Tolerance in Transgenic Plants by Alteration of Citrate Synthesis," *Science* 276 (1997): 1566–68; Maris P. Apse, Gilad S. Aharon, Wayne A. Snedden, and Eduardo Blumwald, "Salt Tolerance Conferred by Overexpression of a Vacuolar Na + /H + Antiport in *Arabidopsis*," *Science* 285 (1999): 1256–58; Hong-Xia Zhang and Eduardo Blumwald, "Transgenic Salt-Tolerant Tomato Plants Accumulate Salt in Foliage But Not in Fruit," *Nature Biotechnology* 19 (2001): 765–68; Mie Kasuga, Qiang Liu, Setsuko Miura, Kazuko Yamaguchi-Shinozaki, et al., "Improving Plant Drought, Salt, and Freezing Tolerance by Gene Transfer of a Single Stress-Inducible Transcription Factor," *Nature Biotechnology* 17 (1999): 287–91; Monkombu Sambasivan Swaminathan, "Genetic Engineering and Food, Ecological and Livelihood Security in Predominantly Agricultural Developing Countries" (paper presented at CGIAR/NAS Biotechnology Conference, October 21–22, 1999, Washington, DC), www.cgiar.org/biotechc/swami.htm (accessed November 11, 1999); Gordon Conway and Gary Toenniesen, "Feeding the World in the Twenty-First Century"; Anne S. Moffat, "Crop Engineering Goes South," *Science* 285 (1999): 370–71; Qifa Zhang, "Meeting the Challenges of Food Production: The Opportunities of Agricultural Biotechnology in China" (paper presented at CGIAR/NAS Biotechnology Conference, October 21–22, 1999, Washington, DC), www.cgiar.org/biotechc/zhang.htm (accessed November 11, 1999); Elizabeth Pennisi, "Plant Biology: Transferred Gene Helps Plants Weather Cold Snaps," *Science* 280 (1998): 36; C. Sanjeev Prakash, "Engineering Cold Tolerance Takes a Major Step Forward," *ISB News* (May 1998), www.isb.vt.edu/news/1998 news98.may.html# may9802 (accessed January 15, 2000). See also Kirsten R. Jaglo-Ottosen, Sarah J. Gilmour, Daniel G. Zarka, Oliver Schabenberger, et al., "*Arabidopsis* CBF-1 Overexpression Induces COR Genes and Enhances Freezing Tolerance," *Science* 280 (1998): 104–06.

33. Basia Vinocur and Arie Altman, "Recent Advances in Engineering Plant Tolerance to Abiotic Stress: Achievements and Limitations," *Current Opinion in Biotechnology* 16 (2005): 123–32.

34. Apse, et al., "Salt Tolerance Conferred by Overexpression of a Vacuolar Na + / H + Antiport."

35. Hong-Xia Zhang and Eduardo Blumwald, "Transgenic Salt-Tolerant Tomato Plants"; EurekAlert, "Genetically Engineered Tomato Plant Grows in Salty Water," press release, University of California–Davis, July 30, 2001, www.eurekalert.org/pub_releases/2001-07/uoc—get072501.php (accessed January 9, 2006).

36. Ibid.

37. Lincoln Taiz and Eduardo Zeigler, *Plant Physiology*, 3rd ed. (Sunderland, MA: Sinauer Associates, 2002).

38. Cixin He, Juqiang Yan, Guoxin Shen, Lianhai Fu, et al., "Expression of an *Arabidopsis* Vacuolar Sodium/Proton Antiporter Gene in Cotton Improves Photosynthetic Performance under Salt Conditions and Increases Fiber Yield in the Field," *Plant and Cell Physiology* 46 (2005): 1848–54.

39. Viswanathan Chinnusamy, Andre Jagendorf, and Jian-Kang Zhu, "Understanding and Improving Salt Tolerance in Plants," *Crop Science* 45 (2005): 437–48.

40. Ajay K. Garg, Ju-Kon Kim, Thomas G. Owens, Anil P. Ranwala, et al., "Trehalose Accumulation in Rice Plants Confers High Tolerance Levels to Different Abiotic Stresses," *Proceedings of the National Academy of Sciences* 99 (2002): 15898–903.

41. Yan Jin, Song Weining, and Eviatar Nevo, "A MAPK Gene from Dead Sea Fungus Confers Stress Tolerance to Lithium Salt and Freezing-Thawing: Prospects for Saline Agriculture," *Proceedings of the National Academy of Sciences* 102 (2005): 18992–997.

42. Neeti Sanan-Mishra, Xuan Hoi Pham, Sudhir K. Sopory, and Narendra Tuteja, "Pea DNA Helicase 45 Overexpression in Tobacco Confers High Salinity Tolerance without Affecting Yield," *Proceedings of the National Academy of Sciences* 102 (2005): 509–14. See also Arnab Mukhopadhyay, Shubha Vij, and Akhilesh K. Tyagi, "Overexpression of a Zinc-Finger Protein Gene from Rice Confers Tolerance to Cold, Dehydration, and Salt Stress in Transgenic Tobacco," *Proceedings of the National Academy of Sciences* 101 (2004): 6309–631; Sneh L. Singla-Pareek, M. K. Reddy, and S. K. Sopory, "Genetic Engineering of the Glyoxalase Pathway in Tobacco Leads to Enhanced Salinity Tolerance," *Proceedings of the National Academy of Sciences* 100 (2004): 14672–677.

43. Mary Lou Guerinot, "Improving Rice Yields: Ironing Out the Details," *Nature Biotechnology* 19 (2001): 417–18.

44. Michiko Takahashi, Hiromi Nakanishi, Shinji Kawasaki, Naoko K. Nishizawa, et al., "Enhanced Tolerance of Rice to Low Iron Availability in Alkaline Soils Using Barley Nicotianamine Aminotransferase Genes," *Nature Biotechnology* 19 (2001): 466–69; Mary Lou Guerinot, "Improving Rice Yields"; Michael A. Grusak, "Enhancing Mineral Content in Plant Food Products," *Journal of the American College of Nutrition* 21 (2002): 178S–83S.

45. Mary Lou Guerinot, "Improving Rice Yields."

46. Gordon Conway and Gary Toenniesen, "Feeding the World in the Twenty-First Century."

47. West Africa Rice Development Association, *Bintu and Her New Rice for Africa: Breaking the Shackles of Slash-and-Burn Farming in the World's Poorest Region*, p. 7, www.warda.cgiar.org/publications/KBtext.pdf (accessed November 19, 2002).

48. Charles C. Mann, "Crop Scientists Seek a New Revolution," 310–14; see also Julian I. Schroeder and Josef M. Kuhn, "Abscisic Acid in Bloom," *Nature* 439 (2006): 277–78; Fawzi A. Razem, Ashraf El-Kereamy, Suzanne R. Abrams, and Robert D. Hill, "The RNA-Binding Protein FCA is an Abscisic Acid Receptor," *Nature* 439 (2006): 290–94.

49. Maurice S. B. Ku, Sakae Agarie, Mika Nomura, Hiroshi Fukayama, et al, "High-level Expression of Maize Phosphoenolpyruvate Carboxylase in Transgenic Plants," *Nature Biotechnology* 17 (1999): 76–80; Gerald Edwards, "Tuning up Crop Photosynthesis," *Nature Biotechnology* 17 (1999): 22–23; Gordon Conway and Gary Toenniesen, "Feeding the World in the Twenty-First Century." See also Christopher Surridge, "Agricultural Biotech: The Rice Squad," *Nature* 416 (2002): 576–78.

50. When plants first evolved, photorespiration was not a problem because the atmosphere then was high in CO_2 and low in oxygen. Because of photosynthesis, oxygen accumulated in the atmosphere and reached the present level a million years ago and today's atmospheric CO_2 levels limit photosynthesis in C3 plants.

51. Maurice S. B. Ku, D. Cho, X. Li, D. M. Jiao, M. Pinto, M. Miyao, and M. Matsuoka, "Introduction of Genes Encoding C4 Photosynthesis Enzymes into Rice Plants: Physiological Consequences," *Novartis Foundation Symposium* 236 (2001): 100–11; ISB News Report, "Metabolically Modified Rice Exhibits Superior Photosynthesis and Yield," May 2000, http://131.104.232.9/agnet/2000/5-2000/ag-05-03-00-02.txt, (accessed November 19, 2002).

52. Christopher Surridge, "Agricultural Biotech."

53. Charles C. Mann, "Genetic Engineers Aim to Soup Up Crop Photosynthesis," *Science* 283 (1999): 314–16.

54. Centro Internacional de Mejoramiento de Maíz y Trigo (CIMMYT), *Striga Weed Control with Herbicide-Coated Maize Seed*, July 29, 2002, http://www.cimmyt.org/Research/Maize/results/striga/control.htm (accessed November 20, 2002). See also Charles C. Mann, "Biotech Goes Wild," *Technology Review* 12, no. 4 (July/August 1999): 36–43; Colin MacIlwain, "Access Issues May Determine Whether Agri-Biotech Will Help the World's Poor," *Nature* 402 (1999): 341–45; Gordon Conway and Gary Toenniesen, "Feeding the World in the Twenty-First Century."

55. African Agricultural Technology Foundation, *A New Bridge to Sustainable Agricultural Development in Africa: May 2002–December 2004, Inaugural Report*, p. 34, www.aatf-africa.org/publications/AATF_Annual_Report.pdf (accessed January 14, 2006).

56. Martin Parniske, "Plant-Fungal Associations: Cue for the Branching Connection," *Nature* 435 (2005): 750–51; Kohki Akiyama, Ken-ichi Matsuzaki, and Hideo Hayashi, " Plant Sesquiterpenes Induce Hyphal Branching in Arbuscular Mycorrhizal Fungi," *Nature* 435 (2005): 824–27.

57. International Rice Research Institute (IRRI), "Nitrogen-Fixing Rice Moves Closer to Reality," *IRRI Science Online*, December 21, 1999, www.iclarm.org/irri/Science.html (accessed February 1, 2000).

58. Gordon Conway and Gary Toenniesen, "Feeding the World in the Twenty-First Century"; C. Sanjeev Prakash, "A First Step Towards Engineering Improved Phosphorus Uptake," *ISB News*, May 1998, www.isb.vt.edu/news/1998/news98.may.html#may9802 (accessed January 15, 2000); and Inside Purdue, *Raghothama: Phosphorus Uptake Gene Discovered*, 1998, www.purdue.edu/PER/1.13.98.IP.html (accessed January 19, 2000).

59. Francis Galibert, Turlough M. Finan, Sharon R. Long, Alfred Pühler, et al., "The Composite Genome of the Legume Symbiont *Sinorhizobium meliloti*" *Science* 293 (2001): 668–72.

60. Manjula Govindarajulu, Philip E. Pfeffer, Hairu Jin, Jehad Abubaker, et al., "Nitrogen Transfer in the Arbuscular Mycorrhizal Symbiosis," *Nature* 435 (2005): 819–23; Martin Parniske, "Plant-Fungal Associations: Cue for the Branching Connection," *Nature* 435 (2005): 750–51.

61. Gordon Conway and Gary Toenniesen, "Feeding the World in the Twenty-First Century" Dan Ferber, "Risks and Benefits: GM Crops in the Cross Hairs," *Science* 286 (1999): 1662–66; Agbros, Agbios Database, www.agbios.com/dbase.php (accessed November 20, 2002).

62. Dennis Gonsalves, "Transgenic Papaya in Hawaii and Beyond," *AgBioForum: The Journal of Agrobiotechnology Management and Economics* 7, no. 1 and 2 (2004), http://www.agbioforum.org/v7n12/v7n12a07-gonsalves.htm, (accessed January 19, 2006); Sujatha Sankula, Gregory Marmon, and Edward Blumenthal, *Biotechnology-Derived Crops Planted in 2004—Impacts on US Agriculture* (Washington, DC: National Center for Food and Agricultural Policy, 2005), pp.11–13, www.ncfap.org/whatwedo/pdf/2004biotechimpacts.pdf (accessed January 19, 2006).

63. C. Ford Runge and Barry Ryan, *The Global Diffusion of Plant Biotechnology: International Adoption and Research in 2004* (Washington, DC: Council on Biotechnology Information, 2004), p. 18.

64. Piyaporn Wongruang, "Papaya Farmers Rally for End to Ban on GMO Field Trials," *Bangkok Post*, January 13, 2006, www.checkbiotech.org/root/index.cfm?fuseaction=news&doc_id=12027&start=1&control=161&page_start=1&page_nr=101&pg=1 (accessed January 14, 2006).

65. Linda McCandless, "Dennis Gonsalves Receives the 2002 von Humboldt Award for Agriculture," press release, New York State Agricultural Experiment Station, Cornell University, November 6, 2002, www.nysaes.cornell.edu/pubs/press/current/vonhumboldtnov4.html, (accessed November 21, 2002).

66. International Center for Tropical Agriculture (CIAT), *Improved Cassava for the Developing World: Project IP3 Annual Report 2001*, p.168, www.ciat.cgiar.org/yuca/pdf/annualrep_2001_output8.pdf (accessed November 20, 2002); Katie Mantell, "Global Partnership to Boost Cassava Research," *SciDev.Net*, November 11, 2002, www.scidev.net/News/index.cfm? fuseaction=readNews & itemid=288 & language=1 (accessed January 14, 2006). See also Anne S. Moffat, "Crop Engineering Goes South," *Science* 285 (1999): 370–71.

67. Gordon Conway and Gary Toenniesen, "Feeding the World in the Twenty-First Century."

68. Eric Hand, "Hungry African Nations Balk at Biotech Cassava," *St. Louis Post-Dispatch*, August 29, 2005.

69. Peggy G. Lemaux, *Plant Growth Regulators and Biotechnology* (paper presented at the Western Plant Growth Regulator Society, January 13, 1999, Anaheim, CA), http://plantbio.berkeley.edu/~outreach/REGULATO.HTM (accessed January 19, 2000).

70. Runge and Ryan, *The Global Diffusion of Plant Biotechnology*, p. 30.

71. Ibid., p. 36

72. Ibid., p. 34.

73. T. M. Manjunath, "A Decade of Commercialized Transgenic Crops—Analyses of Their Global Adoption, Safety and Benefits," *The Sixth Dr. S. Pradhan Memorial Lecture, Indian Agricultural Research Institute* (IARI), New Delhi, March 23, 2005.

74. Sarah J. Liljegren, Gary S. Ditta, Yuval Eshed, Beth Savidge, et al., "*SHATTER-PROOF* MADS-Box Gene Control Seed Dispersal in *Arabidopsis*," *Nature* 404 (2000): 766–70.

75. Bruce R. Thomas and Kent J. Bradford, "Crop Biotechnology: Feeds for Livestock," Seed Biotechnology Center, University of California–Davis, April 25, 2001, http://sbc.ucdavis.edu/outreach/lecture/livestock_feeds.htm (accessed November 20, 2002); Barbara Mazur, Enno Krebbers, and Scott Tingey, "Gene Discovery and Product Development for Grain Quality Traits," *Science* 285 (1999), 372–75; Gordon Conway and Gary Toenniesen, "Feeding the World in the Twenty-First Century."

76. Rachel Melcer, "Corn Genetically Engineered for Animal Feed Ready to Market," *St. Louis Post-Dispatch*, November 20, 2005.

77. Yasuhiko Toride, "Lysine and Other Amino Acids for Feed: Production and Contribution to Protein Utilization in Animal Feeding," FAO Corporate Document Repository, 2002, www.fao.org/documents/show_cdr.asp?url_file/docrep/007/y5019e/y5019e0a.htm (accessed January 15, 2006). See also FAO Animal Production and Health, *Protein Sources for the Animal Feed Industry: Expert Consultation and Workshop, Bangkok, April 29–May 3, 2002* (Rome: FAO, 2004).

78. EurekAlert, "Growing Crops to Cope with Climate Change," January 19, 2006, www.eurekalert.org/pub_releases/2006-01/babs-gct011906.php (accessed January 20, 2006).

79. Indur M. Goklany, "Applying the Precautionary Principle in a Broader Context," in *Rethinking Risk and the Precautionary Principle*, ed. Julian Morris (Oxford: Butterworth-Heinemann 2000), pp. 189–228.

80. Sujatha Sankula, Gregory Marmon, and Edward Blumenthal, *Biotechnology-Derived Crops Planted in 2004—Impacts on US agriculture: Executive Summary* (Washington, DC: National Center for Food and Agricultural Policy, 2005), p. 1, henceforth Sankula et al., *Executive Summary* (2005).

81. Ibid.; USDA, *Agricultural Statistics 2005*, pp. ix–17.

82. Sankula et al., *Executive Summary* (2005), pp. 4–5.

83. Environmental Protection Agency (EPA), *"Bacillus thuringiensis Plant-Incorporated Protectants," Biopesticides Registration Action Document* (October 16, 2001): IIE42.

84. Ibid., IIE36.

85. Ibid., IIE38–40.

86. Ronald Smith and Roger Leonard, "Farmers and Public Benefit from Insect-Protected Cotton," Alabama Cooperative Extension System Newsline, July 9, 2001, www.aces.edu/dept/extcomm/newspaper/july9a01_op-ed.html (accessed November 23, 2002).

87. C. Sanjeev Prakash, *Relevance of Biotechnology to Indian Agriculture*, 1999, www.teriin.org/discuss/biotech/abstracts.htm (accessed January 15, 2000).

88. Hindu Business Line, *Bt Cotton Trials Show Yield Rise*, 2000, www.indiaserver.com/bline/2000/01/19/stories/071903a1.htm (accessed January 19, 2000).

89. Financial Express (New Delhi), "Bt Cotton Goes up in Smoke—Farmers Should Not Have to Pay for Centre's Folly," October 20, 2001, http://sdnp.delhi.nic.in/headlines/oct01/25-10-2001-news5.html (accessed November 22, 2002).

90. R. Ramchandran, "Green Signal for Bt-cotton," *Frontline*, April 13–26, 2002, www.flonnet.com/fl1908/19080770htm (accessed November 22, 2002).

91. T. M. Manjunath, "A Decade of Commercialized Transgenic Crops."

92. Clive James, *CropBiotech Update Special Edition: Highlights of ISAAA Briefs No. 34–2005 Global Status of Commercialized Biotech/GM Crops: 2005*, www.isaaa.org (accessed January 14, 2006); Economic Research Service, *Cotton and Wool Yearbook (89004)*, www.ers.usda.gov/Data/sdp/view.asp?f = crops/89004/ (accessed January 14, 2006).

93. T. M. Manjunath, "A Decade of Commercialized Transgenic Crops." See also Matin Qaim and David Zilberman, "Yield Effects of Genetically Modified Crops in Developing Countries," *Science* 299 (2003): 900–02.

94. Julie M. Edge, John H. Benedict, John P. Carroll, and H. Keith Reding, "Bollgard Cotton: An Assessment of Global Economic, Environmental, and Social Benefits," *Journal of Cotton Science* 5 (2001): 1–8; Yousouf Ismael, Richard Bennett, and Stephen

Morse, "Farm Level Impact of Bt Cotton in South Africa," *Biotechnology and Development Monitor* 48 (2001): 15–19, www.biotech-monitor.nl/4806.htm (accessed March 17, 2002); Jikun Huang, Scott Rozelle, Carl Pray, and Qinfang Wang, "Plant Biotechnology in China," *Science* 295 (2002): 674–77.

95. See table 4 in Jikun Huang, et al., "Plant Biotechnology in China," 674–77.

96. Carl E. Pray, Jikun Huang, Ruifa Hu, and Scott Rozelle, "Five Years of Bt Cotton in China—The Benefits Continue," *The Plant Journal* 31, no. 4 (2002): 423–30.

97. Yousouf Ismael, Richard Bennett, and Stephen Morse, "Farm Level Impact of Bt Cotton in South Africa," 15–19.

98. Sankula et al., *Executive Summary* (2005), p. 5.

99. J .E. Carpenter and L. P. Gianessi, *Agricultural Biotechnology: Updated Benefits Estimates* (Washington, DC: National Center for Food and Agricultural Policy, 2001), p. 4. It is conceivable that use of Bt corn for a few years may reduce insect pressure in subsequent years. Also, because of the highly specific action of Bt, populations of nontargeted insects (e.g., natural predators of the targeted insect or other pests) may be enhanced, allowing them to do the work of pesticides. See, for example, P. J. Dale, B. Clarke, and E. M. G. Fontes, "The Potential for the Environmental Impact of Transgenic Crops," *Nature Biotechnology* 20 (2002): 567–74. Farmers may lose money if they bought more expensive Bt seeds but insect pressure turned out to be low because then it might have been cheaper to stay with traditional seeds. But this argument only works with the benefit of hindsight. It overlooks the fact that Bt seed is also an insurance policy—just in case insect pressure turns out to be high.

100. Carpenter and Gianessi, *Agricultural Biotechnology*, p. 4.

101. Jikun Huang, Ruifa Hu, Scott Rozelle, and Carl Pray, "Insect-Resistant GM Rice in Farmers' Fields: Assessing Productivity and Health Effects in China," *Science* 308 (2005): 68–90.

102. Philip Brasher, "Brasher: Iran Takes Rice Biotech Lead," DesMoinesRegister. com, January 22, 2006, http://desmoinesregister.com/apps/pbcs.dll/article?AID/ 20060122/BUSINESS01/601220322/1030 (accessed January 23, 2006).

103. Jikun Huang, Ruifa Hu, Scott Rozelle, and Carl Pray, "Insect-Resistant GM Rice in Farmers' Fields: Assessing Productivity and Health Effects in China," *Science* 308 (2005): 68–90.

104. Leonard P. Gianessi, Cressida S. Silvers, Sujatha Sankula, and Janet E. Carpenter, *Plant Biotechnology: Current and Potential Impact for Improving Pest Management in United States Agriculture: An Analysis of 40 Case Studies* (Washington, DC: National Center for Food and Agricultural Policy, 2002).

105. Sankula et al., *Executive Summary* (2005).

106. Ibid.

107. Sujatha Sankula, Gregory Marmon, and Edward Blumenthal, *Biotechnology-Derived Crops Planted in 2004—Impacts on US agriculture: Full Report* (Washington, DC: National Center for Food and Agricultural Policy, 2005).

108. American Soybean Association (ASA), "ASA Study Confirms Environmental Benefits of Biotech Soybeans," November 12, 2001, www.soygrowers.com/newsroom/ releases/2001%20releases/r111201.htm, (accessed November 22, 2002).

109. Richard Fawcett and Dan Towery, *Conservation Tillage and Plant Biotechnology* (West Lafayette, IN: Conservation Technology Information Center, 2002).

110. Ibid., pp. 6–7.

111. Stephen Carpenter, Nina F. Caraco, David L. Correll, Robert W. Howarth, et al., "Nonpoint Pollution of Surface Waters with Phosphorus and Nitrogen," *Issues*

in Ecology 3 (Summer 1998), www.esa.sdsc.edu/carpenter.htm (accessed February 10, 2000).

112. Intergovernmental Panel on Climate Change (IPCC), *Climate Change 1995: The Economic and Social Dimensions of Climate Change* (Cambridge, UK: Cambridge University Press, 1996).

113. Grabau Laboratory, "Improving Phosphorus Utilization in Soybean Meal Through Phytase Gene Engineering," February 19, 1998, www.biotech.vt.edu/plants/grabau/projects.html (accessed February 9, 2000); Libby Mikesell, "Ag Biotech May Help Save the Bay," www.bio.org/food&ag/cbf.html (accessed February 21, 2000); CeresNet, *Environmental Benefits of Agricultural Biotechnology*, February 2, 1999, www.ceresnet.org/Cnetart/990202_Environ_Benefits-AgBio.txt (accessed February 10, 2000); Bruce R. Thomas and Kent J. Bradford, "Crop Biotechnology: Feeds for Livestock," April 25, 2001, Seed Biotechnology Center, University of California–Davis, http://groups.ucanr.org/sbc/Events/Lecture/livestock_feeds.htm (accessed January 14, 2006).

114. Serguei P. Golovan, "Pigs Expressing Salivary Phytase Produce Low-phosphorus Manure," *Nature Biotechnology* 19 (2001): 741–45.

115. Om Parkash Dhankher, Yujing Li, Barry P. Rosen, Jin Shi, et al., "Engineering Tolerance and Hyperaccumulation of Arsenic in Plants by Combining Arsenate Reductase and γ-Glutamylcysteine Synthetase Expression," *Nature Biotechnology* 20 (2002): 1140–45; Myrna E. Watanabe, "Can Bioremediation Bounce Back?" *Nature Biotechnology* 19 (2001): 1111–15; Anne S. Moffat, "Engineering Plants to Cope with Metals," *Science* 285 (1999): 369–70.

116. Ayalew Mentewab, Vinitha A. Cardoza, and C. Neal Stewart Jr., "Genomic Analysis of the Response of *Arabidopsis thaliana* to trinitrotoluene as Revealed by cDNA Microarrays," *Plant Science* 168 (2005): 1409–24; Rekha Seshadri, Lorenz Adrian, Derrick E. Fouts, Jonathan A. Eisen, et al., "Genome Sequence of the PCE-Dechlorinating Bacterium *Dehalococcoides ethenogenes*." *Science* 307 (2005): 105–08; Nerissa Hannink, Susan J. Rosser, Christopher E. French, Amrik Basran, et al., "Phytodetoxification of TNT by Transgenic Plants Expressing a Bacterial Nitroreductase," *Nature Biotechnology* 19 (2001): 1168–72; Watanabe, "Can Bioremediation Bounce Back?"

117. Michigan Technological University (MTU), *New Aspen Could Revolutionize Pulp and Paper Industry*, October 11, 1999, www.admin.mtu.edu/urel/breaking/1999/aspen.htm (accessed January 10, 2000).

118. Eleanor Lawrence, "Biotechnology: Plastic Plants," *Nature Science Update*, September 28, 1999, http://helix.nature.com/nsu/990930-5.html (accessed January 11, 2000).

119. See chapter 2.

120. FAO, *State of Food Insecurity in the World 2004* (Rome: FAO, 2004), pp. 32–33.

121. United Nations Population Division, *World Population Prospects* (2001), tables available at http://esa.un.org/unpp/ (accessed November 22, 2002).

122. WHO, *The World Health Report 2002* (Geneva: WHO, 2002); FAO, *The State of Food Insecurity in the World* (Rome: FAO, 1999).

123. WHO, *Micronutrient Deficiencies: Battling Iron Deficiency Anemia*, 2003, www.who.int/nut/vad.htm (accessed January 16, 2006).

124. S. Datta, quoted in Vissuta Pothong, "Asian Scientists Work to Develop Waterless 'Aerobic' Rice," *Reuters*, November 18, 2002.

125. WHO, *Micronutrient Deficiencies: Battling Vitamin A Deficiency*, 2003, www.who.int/nut/vad.htm (accessed January 16, 2006).

126. Ibid.

127. WHO, *World Health Report 2002*, p. 54.

128. Jennifer Bryce, Cynthia Boschi-Pinto, Kenji Shibuya, and Robert E. Black, "WHO Estimates of the Causes of Death in Children," *Lancet* 365 (March 26, 2005): 1147–52; WHO, *World Health Report 2002*, Annex table 11.

129. Mercedes de Onis, Edward A. Frongillo, and Monika Blossner, "Is Malnutrition Declining? An Analysis of Changes in Levels of Child Malnutrition since 1980," *Bulletin of the World Health Organization* 78, no. 10 (2000): 1222–33.

130. WHO, *World Health Report 2002*, pp. 53–56.

131. Ibid., pp. 57–61.

132. WHO, *World Health Report 2002*, Annex table 2. "Highest-income countries," as used here, is roughly equivalent to the WHO's "stratum A" countries (i.e., countries with both low child mortality and low adult mortality). In general, stratum A countries include the richest countries, except that it also includes Cuba. Other stratum A countries are Australia, Brunei, Canada, Japan, New Zealand, Singapore, the United States, and the Western European countries.

133. WHO, *Global Burden of Disease 2000, Version 2 Estimates*, www3.who.int/whosis/menu.cfm?path = evidence,burden,burden_estimates,burden_estimates_2000V2,burden_estimates_2000V2_region&language = english (accessed November 14, 2002); WHO, *World Health Report 2002*, Annex 11 and 12 tables, www.who.int/whr/en/ (accessed November 14, 2002).

134. S. Datta, quoted in Vissuta Pothung, "Asian Scientists Work to Develop Waterless 'Aerobic' Rice," *Reuters*, November 18, 2002.

135. Trisha Gura, "New Genes Boost Rice Nutrients," *Science* 285 (1999): 994–95; Mary Lou Guerinot, "The Green Revolution Strikes Gold," *Science* 287 (2000): 241–43; Xudong Ye, et al., "Engineering the Provitamin A (â-Carotene) Biosynthetic Pathway into (Carotenoid-Free) Rice Endosperm," *Science* 287 (2000): 303–05. See also F. Goto, et al., "Iron Fortification of Rice Seed by the Soybean Ferritin Gene," *Nature Biotechnology* 17 (1999): 282–86.

136. Jacqueline A. Paine, Catherine A. Shipton, Sunandha Chaggar, Rhian M. Howells, et al., "Improving the Nutritional Value of Golden Rice through Increased Pro-Vitamin A Content," *Nature Biotechnology* 23 (2005): 482–87.

137. S. Datta quoted in Vissuta Pothung, " Asian Scientist Work to Develop Waterless 'Aerobic' Rice," *Reuters*, November 18, 2002.

138. Anne S. Moffet, "Crop Engineering Goes South," 369–70; Paul Smaglik, "Success of Edible Vaccine May Depend on Picking Right Fruit," *The Scientist* 12, August 17, 1998, www.thescientist.library.upenn.edu/yr1998/August/pg4_story2_980817.html, (accessed January 7, 2000).

139. Z. Huang, I. Dry, D. Webster, R. Strugnell, and S. Wesselingh, "Plant-Derived Measles Virus Hemagglutinin Protein Induces Neutralizing Antibodies in Mice," *Vaccine* 19 (2001): 2163–171.

140. *World Health Report 2002*, annex table 2.

141. Babette Regierer, Alisdair R. Fernie, Franziska Springer, Alicia Perez-Melis, et al., "Starch Content and Yield Increase as a Result of Altering Adenylate Pools in Transgenic Plants," *Nature Biotechnology* 20 (2002): 1256–60.

142. International Food Information Council, *Backgrounder—Food Biotechnology*, 1999, http://ificinfo.health.org/ backgrnd/BKGR14.htm (accessed January 12, 2000).

143. G. P. Munkvold and R. L. Hellmich, "Genetically Modified, Insect Resistant Corn: Implications for Disease Management," *APSnet Plant Pathology Online*, 1999, www.scisoc.org/feature/BtCorn/Top.html (accessed February 19, 2000).

144. R. Morton, "One More Reason Why Bt Crops More Safe than Bt Sprays," *Agbioview*, February 16, 2001, www.agbioview.org.

145. Stacey A. Missmer, Lucina Suarez, Marilyn Felkner, Elaine Wang, et al., "Exposure to Fumonisins and the Occurrence of Neural Tube Defects along the Texas–Mexico Border," *Environmental Health Perspectives* 114 (2006): 237–41.

146. Thomas and Bradford, *Crop Biotechnology*.

147. F. Bolin, "Leveling Land Mines with Biotechnology," *Nature Biotechnology* 17 (1999): 732; C. F. French, S. J. Rosser, G. J. Davies, S. Nicklin, et al., "Biodegradation of Explosives by Transgenic Plants Expressing Pentaerythritol Tetranitrate Reductase," *Nature Biotechnology* 17 (1999): 491–94.

148. R. Morton, "One More Reason Why Bt Crops More Safe than Bt Sprays."

149. P. J. Dale, B. Clarke, and E. M. G. Fontes, "The Potential for the Environmental Impact of Transgenic Crops," *Nature Biotechnology* 20, no. 6 (2002): 567–74.

150. Fred Gould, "Sustaining the Efficacy of Bt Toxins," in *Agricultural Biotechnology and Environmental Quality: Gene Escape and Pest Resistance*, ed. R. W. F. Hardy and J. B. Segelken (Ithaca, NY: National Agricultural Biotechnology Council, 1998).

151. Bruce E. Tabashnik, Timothy J. Dennehy, and Yves Carrière, "Delayed Resistance to Transgenic Cotton in Pink Bollworm," *Proceedings of the National Academy of Sciences* 102 (2005): 15389–393; Y.-B. Liu, B. E. Tabashnik, T. J. Dennehy, A. J. Patin, et al., "Development Time and Resistance to Bt Crops," *Nature* 400 (1999): 519; Agbiotechnet, *Hot Topic: Bt Plants: Resistance and Other Issues*, July 1999, www.agbiotechnet.com/topics/hot.asp, (accessed February 4, 2000); Jeffrey L. Fox, "Resistance to Bt Toxin Surprisingly Absent from Pests," *Nature Biotechnology* 21 (2003): 958–59.

152. Y.-B. Liu, B. E. Tabashnik, T. J. Dennehy, A. J. Patin, et al., "Development Time and Resistance to Bt Crops"; Agbiotechnet, *Hot Topic: Bt Plants: Resistance and Other Issues*.

153. EPA, "Bt Corn Insect Resistance Management Announced for 2000 Growing Season," EPA Headquarters Press Release, January 14, 2000.

154. Fred Gould, "Sustaining the Efficacy of Bt Toxins."

155. Gordon Conway, "Food for All in the Twenty-First Century," *Environment* 42 (2000): 9–18.

156. Henry Daniell, "The Next Generation of Genetically Engineered Crops for Herbicide and Insect Resistance: Containment of Gene Pollution and Resistant Insects," *AgBiotechNet* 1, August, 1999, www.agbiotechnet.com/reviews/aug99/html/Daniell.htm (accessed February 12, 2000); M. Kota, H. Daniell, S. Varma, F. Garczynski, "Overexpression of the *Bacillus Thuringiensis* (Bt) CRY2A2 Protein in Chloroplasts Confers Resistance to Plants against Susceptible and Bt-Resistant Insects," *Proceeding of the National Academy of Sciences* (1996): 1840–45; Guang-Ning Ye, Peter T. J. Hajdukiewicz, Debra Broyles, Damian Rodriguez, et al., "Plastid-Expressed 5-enolpyruvylshikimate-3-phosphate Synthase Genes Provide High Level Glyphosate Tolerance in Tobacco," *The Plant Journal* 25, no. 3 (2001): 261–70; B. De Cosa, W. Moar, S.-B. Lee, M. Miller, et al., "Overexpression of the Bt Cry2Aa2 Operon in Chloroplasts Leads to Formation of Insecticidal Crystals," *Nature Biotechnology* 19 (2001): 71–74; "Stable Genetic Transformation of Tomato Plastids and Expression of a Foreign Protein in Fruit," *Nature Biotechnology* 19 (2001): 870–75.

157. Yves Carrière, Christa Ellers-Kirk, Mark Sisterson, Larry Antilla, et al., "Long-Term Regional Suppression of Pink Bollworm by *Bacillus thuringiensis* Cotton," *Proceedings of the National Academy of Sciences*, published online February 5, 2003,

www.pnas.org/cgi/doi:10.1073/pnas.0436708100 (2003); Fox, "Resistance to Bt Toxin Surprisingly Absent from Pests"; Bruce E. Tabashnik, "Frequency of Resistance to Bacillus thuringiensis in Field Populations of Pink Bollworm," *Proceedings of the National Academy of Sciences* 97, no. 24 (2000): 12980–984; Drew L. Kershen, "The Risks of Going Non-GMO," *Oklahoma Law Review* 53, no. 4 (2001).

158. Bruce E. Tabashnik, et al.,"Delayed Resistance to Transgenic Cotton in Pink Bollworm."

159. Yves Carrière, et al., "Long-Term Regional Suppression of Pink Bollworm by *Bacillus thuringiensis* Cotton."

160. John E. Losey, Linda S. Rayor, and Maureen E. Carter, "Transgenic Pollen Harms Monarch Larvae," *Nature* 399 (1999): 214; T. Walliman, "Bt Toxin: Assessing GM Strategies," *Science* 287 (2000): 41; D. Saxena, S. Flores, and G. Stotzky, "Transgenic Plants: Insecticidal Toxin in Root Exudates from Bt Corn," *Nature* 402 (1999): 480; P. J. Dale, B. Clarke, and E. M. G. Fontes, "The Potential for the Environmental Impact of Transgenic Crops," *Nature Biotechnology* 20 (2002): 567–74.

161. John E. Losey, et al., "Transgenic Pollen Harms Monarch Larvae," 214.

162. L. C. H. Jesse and J. J. Obrycki, "Field Deposition of Bt Transgenic Corn Pollen: Lethal Effects on the Monarch Butterfly," *Oecologia* 125 (2000): 241–48.

163. Mark K. Sears, Richard L. Hellmich, Dian E. Stanley-Horn, Karen S. Oberhauser, et al., "Impact of Bt Corn Pollen on Monarch Butterfly Populations: A Risk assessment," *Proceedings of the National Academy of Sciences* 98 (2001): 11937–942; A. R. Zangerl, D. McKenna, C. L. Wraight, M. Carroll, P. Ficarello, et al., "Effects of Exposure to Event 176 *Bacillus thuringiensis* Corn Pollen on Monarch and Black Swallowtail Caterpillars under Field Conditions," *Proceedings of the National Academy of Sciences* 98 (2001): 11908–912; R. L. Hellmich, Blair D. Siegfried, Mark K. Sears, Diane E. Stanley-Horn, et al., "Monarch Larvae Sensitivity to *Bacillus thuringiensis*-Purified Proteins and Pollen," *Proceedings of the National Academy of Sciences* 98 (2001): 11925–930.

164. R. Lewis and B. A. Palevitz, "Science vs. P.R.: GM Crops Face Heat of Debate," *The Scientist* 13 (1999), www.the-scientist.library.upenn.edu/yr1999/oct/lewis_p1_991011.html (accessed January 19, 2000). See also Mary Beth Sheridan, "A Delicate Balancing Act in Mexico," *Los Angeles Times*, February 29, 2000.

165. NASA Earth Observatory, "Mass Mortality of Monarchs in Mexico," http://earthobservatory.nasa.gov/Newsroom/NewImages/images.php3?img_id = 7767 (accessed November 26, 2002).

166. P. J. Dale, B. Clarke, and E. M. G. Fontes, "The Potential for the Environmental Impact of Transgenic Crops."

167. A. Hilbeck, M. Baumgartner, P. M. Fried, and F. Bigler, "Effects of Transgenic *Bacillus Thuringiensis* Corn-Fed Prey on Mortality and Development Time of Immature *Chysoperla Carnea (Neuroptera: Chrysopidae)*," *Environmental Entomology* 27, no. 2 (1998): 480–87.

168. Dan Ferber, "Risks and Benefits: GM Crops in the Cross Hairs," *Science* 286 (1999): 1662–66; Cindy Lynn Richard, *CBS News Covers Iowa Researcher's Study on Bt Corn Pollen and Monarch Butterfly Larvae* (Ames, IA: Council for Agricultural Science and Technology, 2000), www.cast-science.org/biotechnology/20000821.htm (accessed February 13, 2001); EPA, "*Bacillus thuringiensis* Plant-Incorporated Protectants," *Biopesticides Registration Action Document* (October 16, 2001): IIC39–IIC40.

169. A. Gray, *Nature Debates: Be Careful What You Wish . . .*, October 15, 1998, www.biotech-info.net/monarch_Q&A.html (accessed February 12, 2000); C. L.

Wraight, A. R. Zangerl, M. J. Carroll, and M. R. Berenbaum, "Absence of Toxicity of *Bacillus thuringiensis* Pollen to Black Swallowtails under Field Conditions," *Proceedings of the National Academy of Sciences* 97 (2000): 7700–703.

170. EPA, *October 18–20, 2000 FIFRA SAP Meeting: Bt Plant Pesticides Risk and Benefits Assessment*, 2000, www.epa.gov/scipoly/sap/2000/october/questions.pdf (accessed March 3, 2001).

171. Mike Mendelsohn, John Kough, Zigfridais Vaituzis, and Keith Matthews, "Are Bt Crops Safe?" *Nature Biotechnology* 21 (2003): 1003–09; EPA, "*Bacillus thuringiensis* Plant-Incorporated Protectants," I1–2, I18–19.

172. M. Kota, et al., "Overexpression of the *Bacillus Thuringiensis* (Bt) CRY2A2 Protein in Chloroplasts Confers Resistance to Plants Against Susceptible and Bt-resistant Insects"; S. E. Scott and M. J. Wilkinson, "Low Probability of Chloroplast Movement from Oilseed Rape (*Brassica Napus*) into Wild *Brassica Rapa*," *Nature Biotechnology* 17 (1999): 390–92; D. Chamberlain and C. N. Stewart, "Transgene Escape and Transplastomics," *Nature Biotechnology* 17 (1999): 330–31; Chun Y. Huang, Michael A. Ayliffe, and Jeremy N. Timmis, "Direct Measurement of the Transfer Rate of Chloroplast DNA into the Nucleus," *Nature*, advance online publication, February 5, 2003, doi:10.1038/nature01435. Chun Y. Huang et al. showed that in 1 out of 16,000 seedlings, the gene had jumped from the chloroplast to the gene. This indicates that the probability of gene flow can, indeed, be substantially diminished through engineering the gene into the chloroplasts as opposed to the nucleus. Note that the estimated probability of a seed making it to a neighboring (non-GM) field is of the order of 1 in 10,000, so the combined probability of a gene in the chloroplast making it into a non-GM field is 1 in 160,000,000. See Stephen Cauchi, "New Fears Raised about GM Plants," *The Age*, February 6, 2003, www.theage.com.au/articles/2003/02/05/1044318670302.html (accessed February 6, 2003).

173. A. A. Snow, "Transgenic Crops—Why Gene Flow Matters," *Nature Biotechnology* 20, no. 6 (2002): 542.

174. A. J. Gray and A. F. Raybould, "Reducing Transgene Escape Routes," *Nature* 392 (1998): 653–54.

175. Charles C. Mann, "Biotech Goes Wild," *Technology Review* (July/August 1999); Philip J. Regal, "Scientific Principles for Ecologically Based Risk Assessment of Transgenic Organisms," *Molecular Ecology* 3 (1994): 5–13; Peggy G. Lemaux, "Plant Growth Regulators and Biotechnology" (paper presented at the Western Plant Growth Regulator Society, Anaheim, CA, January 13, 1999).

176. David Quist and Ignacio H. Chapela, "Transgenic DNA Introgressed into Traditional Maize Landraces in Oaxaca, Mexico," *Nature* 414 (2001): 541–43.

177. Paul Christou, "No Credible Scientific Evidence Is Presented to Support Claims That Transgenic DNA was Introgressed into Traditional Maize Landraces in Oaxaca, Mexico," *Transgenic Research* 11 (2002): iii–v.

178. For a more detailed account of events surrounding this affair, see Barry A. Palevitz, "Corn Goes Pop, Then Kaboom," *The Scientist* 16, no. 18 (April 29, 2002): 18.

179. Peter H. Raven, "Transgenes in Mexican Maize: Desirability or Inevitability?" *Proceedings of the National Academy of Sciences* 102 (2005): 13003–04.

180. S. Ortiz-Garcia, E. Ezcurra, B. Schoel, et al., "Absence of Detectable Transgenes in Local Landraces of Maize in Oaxaca, Mexico (2003–2004)," *Proceedings of the National Academy of Sciences* 102 (2005): 12338–343.

181. Peter H. Raven, "Transgenes in Mexican Maize."

182. See ibid.; A. A. Snow, "Transgenic Crops—Why Gene Flow Matters."

183. Peter H. Raven, "Transgenes in Mexican Maize"; Gregory Conko and C. S. Prakash, "Report of Transgenes in Mexican Corn Called into Question," *ISB News Report*, March 2002, www.isb.vt.edu/news/2002/news02.mar.html (accessed February 5, 2003); Ronald Bailey, "Environmentalist Biofraud?" *Reason Online*, February 12, 2002, http://reason.com/rb/rb021202.shtml (accessed February 5, 2003). See also Mark Sagoff, "What's Wrong with Exotic Species?" *Report from the Institute for Philosophy and Public Policy* 19 (Fall 1999): 16–23; Indur M. Goklany, "Applying the Precautionary Principle in a Broader Context," in *Rethinking Risk and the Precautionary Principle*, ed. Julian Morris (Oxford, UK: Butterworth-Heinemann, 2000), pp. 189–228.

184. Peter H. Raven, "Transgenes in Mexican Maize."

185. Royal Society, *Genetically Modified Plants for Food Use*, 1998, www.royalsoc. ac.uk/st_po140.htm (accessed January 11, 2000).

186. Ibid.

187. Philip J. Regal, "Scientific Principles for Ecologically Based Risk Assessment of Transgenic Organisms."

188. M. J. Crawley, S. L. Brown, R. S. Hails, D. D. Kohn, et al., "Biotechnology: Transgenic Crops in Natural Habitats," *Nature* 409 (2001): 682–83.

189. See also P. J. Dale, B. Clarke, and E. M. G. Fontes, "Potential for the Environmental Impact of Transgenic Crops."

190. R. James Cook, "Toward Science-Based Risk Assessment for the Approval and Use of Plants in Agriculture and Other Environments" (paper presented at Consultative Group on International Agricultural Research/National Academy of Sciences Biotechnology Conference, October 21–22, 1999), www.cgiar.org/biotechc/ mccalla.htm (accessed November 11, 1999); Mann, "Biotech Goes Wild."

191. Indur M. Goklany, "Precaution without Perversity: A Comprehensive Application of the Precautionary Principle to Genetically Modified Crops," *Biotechnology Law Report* 20, no. 3 (2001): 377–96. See also Sagoff, "What's Wrong with Exotic Species?" 16–23; A. J. S. Rayl, "Are All Alien Invasions Bad?" *The Scientist* 14, 2000, www.the-scientist.com/yr2000/mar/rayl_p15_000320.html (accessed March 21, 2000); and, for a different viewpoint, B. Johnson, "Conserving Our Natural Environment," *Nature Biotechnology* 17 (1999): BV29–BV30.

192. Royal Society, *Genetically Modified Plants for Food Use*.

193. Henry Daniell, "The Next Generation of Genetically Engineered Crops for Herbicide and Insect Resistance: Containment of Gene Pollution and Resistant Insects"; Henry Daniell, "Molecular Strategies for Gene Containment in Transgenic Crops," *Nature Biotechnology* 20, no. 6 (2002): 581–86; Royal Society, *Genetically Modified Plants for Food Use*; Chun Y. Huang, Michael A. Ayliffe, and Jeremy N. Timmis, "Direct Measurement of the Transfer Rate of Chloroplast DNA into the Nucleus."

194. National Center for Health Statistics, *Health, United States, 2002*, table 28, www.cdc.gov/nchs/products/pubs/pubd/hus/02tables.htm (accessed November 23, 2002).

195. Royal Society, *Genetically Modified Plants for Food Use*; Royal Society, "Genetically Modified Plants for Food Use and Human Health—An Update," Policy Document 4, London, 2002.

196. Trudy Netherwood, Susana M Martín-Orúel, Anthony G. O'Donnell, Sally Gockling, et al., "Assessing the Survival of Transgenic Plant DNA in the Human Gastrointestinal Tract," *Nature Biotechnology* 22 (2004): 204–09.

197. John Heritage, "The Fate of Transgenes in the Human Gut," *Nature Biotechnology* 22 (2004): 170–72.

198. Robert Buchanan, Statement to the Senate Committee on Agriculture, Nutrition, and Forestry, October 6, 1999, www.senate.gov/~agriculture/buc99106.htm, (accessed January 11, 2000).

199. Emma Young, "GM Pea Causes Allergic Damage in Mice," NewScientist.com News, November 20, 2005, www.newscientist.com/channel/health/dn8347 (accessed January 15, 2006).

200. Royal Society, *Genetically Modified Plants for Food Use*; and S. Gendel, *The Biotechnology Information for Food Safety Database*, 1999, www.iit.edu/~sgendel/fa.htm (accessed January 11, 2000).

201. See, for example, Goklany, *Applying the Precautionary Principle to Genetically Modified Crops*, and Young, "GM Pea causes Allergic Damage in Mice."

202. Buchanan, Statement to the Senate Committee on Agriculture, Nutrition, and Forestry; Kathleen Scalise, "UC Researchers Discover New Solution for Food Allergies Effective with Milk, Wheat Products, Maybe Other Foods," University of California, *Berkeley News Release*, October 19, 1997, www.urel.berkeley.edu/urel_1/CampusNewsPressReleases/releases/10_19_97a.html (accessed January 5, 2000).

203. Stephen Day, "Crumbs of Comfort," *The Guardian*, May 24, 2001; Keith Mulvihill, "Hypoallergenic Peanut May Be on the Horizon," *Reuters Health*, March 6, 2002, www.reuters.com/news_article.jhtml?type=search&StoryD=70463 (accessed March 17, 2002).

204. Kurt Kleiner, "Biotech Researchers Create Safer Soybeans," *New Scientist Online News*, September 2, 2002, www.newscientist.com/hottopics/gm/gm.jsp?id=ns99992782.

205. Royal Society, *Genetically Modified Plants for Food Use*; see also FAO/WHO, "Biotechnology and Food Safety" (report of a Joint FAO/WHO Consultation, Rome, Italy, September 30–October 4, 1996), www.fao.org/es/ESN/food/pdf/biotechnology.pdf (accessed February 6, 2003); WHO/FAO, *Safety Aspects of Genetically Modified Foods of Plant Origin, Report of a Joint FAO/WHO Expert Consultation on Foods Derived from Biotechnology* (Geneva: WHO, 2000), p.14; Dan Ferber, "Superbugs on the Hoof," *Science* 288 (2000): 792–94; *Science*, "Corrections and Clarifications," *Science* 288 (2000): 1751.

206. Brian Miki and Sylvia McHug, "Selectable Marker Genes in Transgenic Plants: Applications, Alternatives and Biosafety," *Journal of Biotechnology* 107 (2004): 193–232; Andrew Coghlan, "On Your Markers," *New Scientist*, 1999, www.newscientist.com/nsplus/insight/gmworld/gmfood/gmnews97.html (accessed November 20, 1999).

207. Brian Miki and Sylvia McHug, "Selectable Marker Genes in Transgenic Plants"; P. D. Hare, and N. H. Chua, "Excision of Selectable Marker Genes from Transgenic Plants," *Nature Biotechnology* 20, no. 6 (2002): 575–80. See also A. Mentewab and C. N. Stewart Jr., "Overexpression of an *Arabidopsis thaliana* ABC Transporter Confers Kanamycin Resistance to Transgenic Plants," *Nature Biotechnology* 23 (2005): 1177–80; C. Neal Stewart Jr. and Ayalew Mentewab, "Horizontal Gene Transfer: Plant vs. Bacterial Genes for Antibiotic Resistance Scenarios—What's the Difference?" *ISB News Report*, October 2005, www.isb.vt.edu/news/2005/news05.Oct.htm (accessed January 15, 2006).

208. Coghlan, "On Your Markers."

209. Royal Society, *Genetically Modified Plants for Food Use*; Keith Harding, "Biosafety of Selectable Marker Genes," BINAS On-line, United Nations Industrial Development Organization, 1998, www.bdt.org.br/binas/index. html (accessed June 12, 2000); Hare and Chua, "Excision of Selectable Marker Genes."

210. See, for example, Jonathan Williams, "Organic Farming in the Uplands of Mid Wales," Statement at Earth Options, Second "Look Out Wales" Environmental Forum, May 1998, www.wyeside.co.uk/expotec/earth_options.htm (accessed March 19, 2000).

211. *FAOSTAT 2005*.

212. Indur M. Goklany, "Meeting Global Food Needs: The Environmental Trade-Offs Between Increasing Land Conversion and Land Productivity," 107–30.

213. Colin MacIlwain, "Access Issues May Determine Whether Agri-Biotech Will Help the World's Poor," *Nature* 402 (1999): 341–45.

214. Indur M. Goklany, "Meeting Global Food Needs: The Environmental Trade-Offs Between Increasing Land Conversion and Land Productivity," 107–30.

215. Ibid.

216. Lyle Glowka, Francoise Burhenne-Guilmin, and Hugh Synge, *A Guide to the Convention on Biological Diversity* (Gland, Switzerland: World Conservation Union, 1994), p. 11.

217. Maria Burke, *Farm Scale Evaluations—Managing GM Crops with Herbicides: Effects on Farmland Wildlife* (2005), www.defra.gov.uk/environment/gm/fse/results/fse-summary-05.pdf (accessed January 18, 2006). The discussion on FSEs is taken from Burke, *Farm Scale Evalutions*, and Indur M. Goklany, Testimony on Farm Scale Evaluations of Genetically Modified Herbicide Tolerant Crops to Advisory Committee on Releases to the Environment, November 15, 2003, http://members.cox.net/imgrant/Testimony%20to%20ACRE%20on%20Farm%20Scale%20Evaluations.pdf (accessed January 18, 2006).

218. Indur M. Goklany, "Nature," *Biotechnology* 20 (2002): 1075; Indur M. Goklany, *The Precautionary Principle: A Critical Appraisal of Environmental Risk Assessment* (Washington, DC: Cato Institute, 2001).

219. L. G. Firbank, J. N. Perry, G. R. Squire, D. R. Brooks, et al., "The Implications of Spring-Sown Genetically Modified Herbicide-Tolerant Crops for Farmland Biodiversity: A Commentary on the Farm Scale Evaluations of Spring Sown Crops," www.defra.gov.uk/environment/gm/fse/results/fse-commentary.pdf (accessed January 17, 2006).

220. Cabinet Office Strategy Unit, "Field Work: Weighing Up the Costs and Benefits of GM Crops," Analysis papers, p. 47, www.pm.gov.uk/files/pdf/GManalysis1234.pdf (accessed November 12, 2003); M. J. May, "Economic Consequences for UK Farmers of Growing GM Herbicide Tolerant Sugar Beet," *Journal of Applied Biology* 142 (2003): 41–48; A. M. Dewar, "A Novel Approach to the Use of Genetically Modified Herbicide Tolerant Crops for Environmental Benefit," *Proceedings of the Royal Society B* 270 (2003): 335–40.

221. Cabinet Office Strategy Unit, "Field Work," p. 45; Serecon Management Consulting Inc. and Koch Paul Associates, "An Agronomic and Economic Assessment of Transgenic Canola" (prepared for the Canola Council of Canada), www.canolacouncil.org/ (accessed November 12, 2003).

222. Cabinet Office Strategy Unit, "Field Work," p. 48.

223. Henry Daniell, "The Next Generation of Genetically Engineered Crops for Herbicide and Insect Resistance: Containment of Gene Pollution and Resistant Insects"; Henry Daniell, "Molecular Strategies for Gene Containment in Transgenic Crops"; Chun Y. Huang, Michael A. Ayliffe, and Jeremy N. Timmis, "Direct Measurement of the Transfer Rate of Chloroplast DNA into the Nucleus."

224. Greenpeace, *Stop Monsanto's Terminator Technology*, 1998, www.greenpeace.org/~geneng/highlights/pat/98_09_20.htm (accessed January 12, 2000).

225. Graham Brookes and Peter Barfoot, *GM Crops: The Global Socioeconomic and Environmental Impact—The First Nine Years, 1996–2004* (Dorchester, UK: PG Economics Ltd., 2005).

226. Energy Information Administration, "Annual Energy Review 2004," Report No. DOE/EIA-0384, 2004, http://www.eia.doe.gov/emeu/aer/overview.html (accessed January 20, 2006).

227. Glowka, Burhena-Guilmin, and Synge, *A Guide to the Convention on Biologoical Diversity*, p. 11.

228. Ibid., pp. 39–41.

229. Ibid., p. 39.

230. Indur M. Goklany, "The Importance of Climate Change Compared to Other Global Changes," 1024–41.

231. CBD, *Cartagena Protocol on Biosafety to the Convention on Biological Diversity*, 2000, www.biodiv.org/biosafe/Protocol/html/Biosafe-Prot.html (accessed March 3, 2001).

232. UN, *AGENDA 21:The UN Programme of Action From Rio* (New York: United Nations, 1992).

233. Glowka, Burhena-Guilmin, and Synge, *A Guide to the Convention on Biological Diversity*, p. 97; CBD, *Cartagena Protocol on Biosafety to the Convention on Biological Diversity*.

234. See, for example, FOE, "FoE Supports Tory GM Moratorium Call: What about the Precautionary Principle Mr. Blair," press release, 1999, www.foe.co.uk/pubsinfo/infoteam/pressrel/1999/19990203170456.html (accessed May 15, 2000); and FOE, "FoE Remains Sceptical about Monsanto's Terminator Pledge," press release October 5, 1999, www.foeeurope.org/press/foe_remains_sceptical.htm (accessed February 21, 2000).

Chapter 10

1. See, for example, William J. Clinton, State of the Union Address, 1998, www.washingtonpost.com/wp-srv/politics/special/states/docs/sou98.html (accessed January 26, 2006); William J. Clinton, State of the Union Address, 1999, www.washingtonpost.com/wp-srv/politics/special/states/docs/sou99.html1 (accessed January 26, 2006); and Greenwire, *Worldview—Climate Change II: Scientists Fear Warming*, February 5, 1998, available through search engine at http://nationaljournal.com/pubs/greenwire/extra/search.htm.

2. Organisation for Economic Co-operation and Development (OECD), *Toward a Sustainable Future*, www.oecd.org/document/25/0,2340,en_2649_34495_1914137_1_1_1_1,00.html (accessed January 26, 2006).

3. Cordis News, *Reducing Global Warming is Our Priority, Say Chirac and Blair*, November 19, 2004, on file with author.

4. David King, "Climate Change Science: Adapt, Mitigate, or Ignore?" *Science* 303 (2004): 176–77.

5. Robert May, "Threats to Tomorrow's World," Anniversary Address, Royal Society, November 30, 2005, www.royalsoc.ac.uk/publication.asp?id=2181 (accessed January 22, 2006).

6. "No-regret" actions include the elimination of unjustified subsidies that would directly or indirectly increase energy or land use that might contribute to greenhouse gas emissions, letting secular technological change run its usual course, and actions that would be undertaken to solve more critical social, public health, and environmental problems while incidentally reducing greenhouse gas emissions. The last category could include, for instance, actions to reduce coal burning inside homes to limit indoor air pollution.

7. Indur M. Goklany, "The Future of Industrial Society" (paper presented at the International Conference on Industrial Ecology and Sustainability, University of Technology of Troyes, Troyes, France, September 22–25, 1999); Goklany, "Potential Consequences of Increasing Atmospheric CO_2 Concentration Compared to Other Environmental Problems," *Technology* 7S (2000): 189–213.

8. World Health Organization (WHO), *World Health Report 2002* (Geneva: WHO, 2002), Annex tables 11 and 12. See also the discussion in chapter 11, which, however, excludes risk factors related to occupational health and safety.

9. WHO, *World Health Report 2002*; WHO, *Global Burden of Disease 2000, Version 2 Estimates*, www3.who.int/whosis/menu.cfm?path = evidence,burden,burden_estimates, burden_estimates_2000V2,burden_estimates_2000V2_region&language = english (accessed November 14, 2002).

10. Intergovernmental Panel on Climate Change (IPCC), *Climate Change 1995: The Economic and Social Dimensions of Climate Change* (Cambridge, UK: Cambridge University Press, 1995).

11. Thomas R. Knutson and Robert E. Tuleya, "Impact of CO_2-Induced Warming on Simulated Hurricane Intensity and Precipitation: Sensitivity to the Choice of Climate Model and Convective Parameterization," *Journal of Climate* 17 (2004): 3477–95.

12. C. D. Keeling and T. P. Whorf, "Atmospheric CO_2 Concentrations (ppmv) Derived from *in situ* Air Samples Collected at Mauna Loa Observatory, Hawaii," http://cdiac.esd.ornl.gov/ftp/maunaloa-co2/maunaloa.co2 (accessed December 22, 2005). Note that a constant year-to-year increase results in an exponential increase.

13. CO_2 Science, *Effects of Atmospheric CO_2 Enrichment on Methane Emissions from Leaves of Wetland Plants*, www.co2science.org/scripts/CO2ScienceB2C/articles/V8/ N36/B2.jsp (accessed March 11, 2006). This speculation is based on a review of an empirical study of methane emissions from wetland plants. See Kristy N. Garnet, J. Patrick Megonigal, Carol Litchfield, and George E. Taylor Jr., "Physiological Control of Leaf Methane Emission from Wetland Plants," *Aquatic Botany* 81 (2005): 141–55.

14. Langenfelds P. Steele, Paul B. Krummel, and Ray L. Langenfelds, *Atmospheric CH4 Concentrations from the CSIRO GASLAB Flask Sampling Network*, http://cdiac.ornl.gov/trends/atm_meth/csiro/csiro_gaslabch4.html (accessed February 5, 2006).

15. Ahilleas Maurellis and Jonathan Tennyson, "The Climatic Effects of Water Vapour," *Physics World*, May 2003, http://physicsweb.org/articles/world/16/5/7/ 3 (accessed February 16, 2006); National Research Council, *Radiative Forcing of Climate Change: Expanding the Concept and Addressing Uncertainties* (Washington, DC: Joseph Henry Press, 2005).

16. M. H. Zhang, W. Y. Lin, S. A. Klein, J. T. Bacmeister, et al., "Comparing Clouds and Their Seasonal Variations in 10 Atmospheric General Circulation Models with Satellite Measurements," *Journal of Geophysical Research* 110 (2005): D15S02,

doi:10.1029/2004JD005021; A. Pier Siebesma, et al., "Cloud Representation in General-Circulation Models Over the Northern Pacific Ocean: A EUROCS Intercomparison Study," *Quarterly Journal of the Royal Meteorological Society* 130 (2004): 3245–67; David Randall, Marat Khairoutdinov, Akio Arakawa, and Wojciech Grabowski, "Breaking the Cloud Parameterization Deadlock," *Bulletin of the American Meteorological Society* 84 (2003): 1547–64.

17. Andrew D. Friend and Nancy Y. Kiang, "Land Surface Model Development for the GISS GCM: Effects of Improved Canopy Physiology on Simulated Climate," *Journal of Climate* 18 (2005): 2883–902; Joseph L. Eastman, Michael B. Coughenour, and Roger A. Pielke Sr., "The Regional Effects of CO_2 and Landscape Change Using a Coupled Plant and Meteorological Model," *Global Change Biology* 7 (2001): 797–815. See also Curtis H. Marshall, Roger A. Pielke Sr., and Louis T. Steyaert, "Has the Conversion of Natural Wetlands to Agricultural Land Increased the Incidence and Severity of Damaging Freezes in South Florida?" *Monthly Weather Review* 132 (2004): 2243–58; Andrew J. Pitman, Gemma T. Narisma, Roger A. Pielke Sr., and N. J. Holbrook, "The Impact of Land Cover Change on the Climate of Southwest Western Australia," *Journal of Geophysical Research* 109 (2004): D18109, doi:10.1029/2003JD004347.

18. Mark Z. Jacobson, "Climate Response of Fossil Fuel and Biofuel Soot, Accounting for Soot's Feedback to Snow and Sea Ice Albedo and Emissivity," *Journal of Geophysical Research* 109 (2004): D21201, doi:10.1029/2004JD004945; Mark Z. Jacobson, "Strong Radiative Heating Due to Mixing State of Black Carbon in Atmospheric Aerosols," *Nature* 409 (2001): 695–97; Colin D. O'Dowd, Maria Cristina Facchini, Fabrizia Cavalli, Darius Ceburnis, et al., "Biogenically Driven Organic Contribution to Marine Aerosol," *Nature* 431 (2004): 676–80; S. K. Idso, "Aerosols (Biological-Aquatic)—Summary," CO_2 Science, www.co2science.org/scripts/CO2ScienceB2C/subject/a/summaries/aerosolsbioaqua.jsp (accessed January 8, 2006); R. J. Charlson, J. E. Lovelock, M. O. Andrea, and S. G. Warren, "Oceanic Phytoplankton, Atmospheric Sulfur, Cloud Albedo, and Climate" *Nature* 326 (1987): 655–61.

19. See, for example, D. Cziczo, R. Posselt, U. Lohmann, and D. Murphy, "The Indirect Effects of Aerosols on Climate," *Newsletter of the International Global Atmospheric Chemistry Project* 32 (November 2005): 23–28; U. Lohmann, "Workshop Highlight: 'Can We Improve Model Estimates of the Anthropogenic Indirect Aerosol Effect?'" *Newsletter of the International Global Atmospheric Chemistry Project* 32 (November 2005), 28–30; R. McFiggans, "Workshop Highlight: 'The Indirect Effect in Warm Clouds,'" *Newsletter of the International Global Atmospheric Chemistry Project* 32 (November 2005): 30–31; National Research Council, *Radiative Forcing of Climate Change: Expanding the Concept and Addressing Uncertainties* (Washington, DC: Joseph Henry Press, 2005). For anyone eager to learn about these issues in greater depth, an excellent place to start is the Climate Science blog established and maintained by Roger A. Pielke Sr. of the University of Colorado, http://climatesci.atmos.colostate.edu/.

20. Joseph L. Eastman, Michael B. Coughenour, and Roger A. Pielke Sr., "The Regional Effects of CO_2 and Landscape Change Using a Coupled Plant and Meteorological Model."

21. Roger A. Pielke Sr., "Overlooked Issues in the National Climate and IPCC Assessments," *Climatic Change* 52 (2002): 1–11.

22. John Turner, Steve R. Colwell, Gareth J. Marshall, Tom A. Lachlan-Cope, et al., "Antarctic Climate Change during the Last 50 Years," *International Journal of*

Climatology 25 (2005): 279–94; Nathan P. Gillett and David W. J. Thompson, "Simulation of Recent Southern Hemisphere Climate Change," *Science* 302 (2003): 273–75; David G. Vaughan, Gareth J. Marshall, William M. Connolley, John C. King, et al., "Climate Change: Devil in the Detail," *Science* 293 (2001): 1777–79.

23. Jiping Liu, Judith A. Curry, and Doug G. Martinson, "Interpretation of Recent Antarctic Sea Ice Variability," *Geophysical Research Letters* 31 (2004): 10.1029/ 2003GL018732; Donald J. Cavalieri, Claire L. Parkinson, and Konstantin Y. Vinnikov, "30-Year Satellite Record Reveals Contrasting Arctic and Antarctic Decadal Sea Ice Variability," *Geophysical Research Letters* 30 (2003): 10.1029/2003GL018031; Peter T. Doran, John C. Priscu, W. Berry Lyons, John E. Walsh, et al., "Antarctic Climate Cooling and Terrestrial Ecosystem Response," *Nature* 415 (2002): 517–20; Andrew B. Watkins and Ian Simmonds, "Current Trends in Antarctic Sea Ice: The 1990s Impact on a Short Climatology," *Journal of Climate* 13 (2000): 4441–51; H. Jay Zwally, Josefino C. Comiso, Claire L. Parkinson, Donald J. Cavalieri, et al., "Variability of Antarctic Sea Ice, 1979–1998," *Journal of Geophysical Research* 107 (2002): 8755–56; Josefino C. Comiso, "Variability and Trends in Antarctic Surface Temperatures from in situ and Satellite Infrared Measurements," *Journal of Climate* 13 (2002): 1674–96.

24. Atsumu Ohmura and Martin Wild, "Is the Hydrological Cycle Accelerating?" *Science* 298 (2002): 1345–46; Michael L. Roderick and Graham D. Farquhar, "The Cause of Decreased Pan Evaporation Over the Past 50 Years," *Science* 298 (2002): 1410–11; Michael L. Roderick and Graham D. Farquhar, "Changes in Australian Pan Evaporation from 1970 to 2002," *International Journal of Climatology* 44 (2004): 1077–90. A recent paper indicates that evaporotranspiration may have decreased worldwide due to higher water use efficiency in the plant world because of higher CO_2 concentrations. See Nicola Gedney, P. M. Cox, R. A. Betts, O. Boucher, et al., "Detection of a Direct Carbon Dioxide Effect in Continental River Runoff Records," *Nature* 439 (2006): 835–38.

25. Autonomous or automatic responses refer to actions that would or could be undertaken by individual actors or through collective actions to reduce damages or capture gains from climate change without requiring explicit changes in laws and policies.

26. Indur M. Goklany, "Integrated Strategies to Reduce Vulnerability and Advance Adaptation, Mitigation, and Sustainable Development," forthcoming in *Mitigation and Adaption Strategies for Global Change* (2006); Indur M. Goklany, "A Climate Policy for the Short and Medium Term: Stabilization or Adaptation?" *Energy and Environment* 16 (2005): 667–80; Indur M. Goklany, "Is a Richer-but-Warmer World Better than Poorer-but-Cooler Worlds?" 25th Annual North American Conference of the US Association for Energy Economics/International Association of Energy Economics, September 21–23, 2005, available on CD-Rom, *Fueling the Future: Prices, Productivity, Policies, and Prophecies.*

27. IPCC, *Summary for Policymakers: IPCC WGI Third Assessment Report* (Cambridge, UK: Cambridge University Press, 2001), p. 8.

28. Ibid.

29. James E. Hansen and Makiko Sato, "Trends of Measured Climate Forcing Agents," *PNAS* 19 (2001): 14778–783.

30. James E. Hansen, "Is There Still Time to Avoid 'Dangerous Anthropogenic Interference' with Global Climate? A Tribute to Charles David Keeling" (presentation, American Geophysical Union, San Francisco, California, December 6, 2005). Notably, linear extrapolation of past trends into the future is valid if emissions and, more

important, greenhouse gas concentrations increase exponentially because changes in temperature increase should increase with the logarithm of the concentration. (Multiplying an exponential increase with a logarithmic increase results in a linear increase.)

31. IPCC, *Summary for Policymakers*, 2; World Climate Report, "Satellite 'Warming' Vanishes," *World Climate Report* 6, no. 9 (2001).

32. John R. Christy, David E. Parker, Simon J. Brown, Ian Macadam, et al., "Differential Trends in Tropical Sea Surface and Atmospheric Temperatures since 1979," *Geophysical Research Letters* 28 (2001): 183–86.

33. IPCC, *Summary for Policymakers*, p. 1.

34. It is not clear how geographically representative surface stations used to estimate trends are of conditions averaged over the globe.

35. Data available at http://climate.uah.edu/jan2006.htm (accessed March 9, 2006).

36. Goddard Space Flight Center, "Keeping New York City 'Cool' is the Job of NASA's 'Heat Seekers,'" press release, January 30, 2006, www.nasa.gov/centers/goddard/news/topstory/2005/nyc_heatisland.html; Jorge E. Gonzalez, Jeffrey C. Luvall, Douglas Rickman, Daniel Comarazamy, et al., "Urban Heat Islands Developing in Coastal Tropical Cities," *EOS, Transactions, American Geophysical Union* 86 (2005): 397, 403; A. T. J. De Laat and A. N. Maurellis, "Industrial CO_2 Emissions as a Proxy for Anthropogenic Influence on Lower Tropospheric Temperature Trends," *Geophysical Research Letters* 31 (2004): 10.1029/2003GL019024; L. Liming Zhou, Robert E. Dickinson, Yuhong Tian, Jingyun Fang, et al., "Evidence for a Significant Urbanization Effect on Climate in China," *PNAS* 101 (2004): 9540–44; Longxun Chen, Wenqin Zhu, Xiuji Zhou, and Zijiang Zhou, "Characteristics of the Heat Island Effect in Shanghai and Its Possible Mechanism," *Advances in Atmospheric Sciences* 20 (2003): 991–1001; Eugenia Kalnay and Ming Cai, "Impact of Urbanization and Land Use Change on Climate," *Nature* 423 (2003): 528–31; Ross McKitrick and Patrick J. Michaels, "A Test of Corrections for Extraneous Signals in Gridded Surface Temperature Data," *Climate Research* 26 (2004): 159–73.

37. Curtis H. Marshall, Roger A. Pielke Sr., and Louis T. Steyaert, "Has the Conversion of Natural Wetlands to Agricultural Land Increased the Incidence and Severity of Damaging Freezes in South Florida?" Andrew J. Pitman, Gemma T. Narisma, Roger A. Pielke Sr., and N. J. Holbrook, "The Impact of Land Cover Change on the Climate of Southwest Western Australia."

38. See Patrick J. Michaels and Robert Balling, *The Satanic Gases* (Washington, DC: Cato Institute, 2000), for a blow-by-blow description of these arguments.

39. IPCC, *Summary for Policymakers*.

40. Mark Jacobson "Strong Radiative Healing Due to Mixing State of Black Carbon in Atmospheric Aerosols"; Mark Jacobson "Climate Response of Fossil Fuel and Biofed Soot."

41. Martin L. Parry, ed., *Global Environmental Change, Part A: Special Issue: An Assessment of the Global Effects of Climate Change under SRES Emissions and Socioeconomic Scenarios* 14 (2004): 1–99. This collection includes the following papers: P. E. Levy, M. G. R. Cannell, and A. D. Friend, "Modeling the Impact of Future Changes in Climate, CO_2 Concentration and Land Use on Natural Ecosystems and the Terrestrial Carbon Sink," *Global Environmental Change, Part A* 14 (2004): 21–30; Robert J. Nicholls, "Coastal Flooding and Wetland Loss in the 21st Century: Changes Under the SRES Climate and Socio-economic Scenarios," *Global Environmental Change, Part A* 14 (2004): 69–86; Martin L. Parry, Cynthia Rosenzweig, Ana Iglesias, Matthew

Livermore, et al., "Effects of Climate Change on Global Food Production under SRES Emissions and Socio-economic Scenarios," *Global Environmental Change, Part A* 14 (2004): 53–67; Nigel W. Arnell, "Climate Change and Global Water Resources: SRES Emissions and Socio-economic Scenarios," *Global Environmental Change, Part A* 14 (2004): 31–52; M. Van Lieshout, R. S. Kovats, M. Livermore, and P. Marten, "Climate Change and Malaria: Analysis of the SRES Climate and Socio-economic Scenarios," *Global Environmental Change, Part A* 14 (2004): 87–99.

42. Nigel W. Arnell, M. G. R. Cannell, M. Hulme, R. S. Kovats, et al., "The Consequences of CO_2 Stabilization for the Impacts of Climate Change," *Climatic Change* 53 (2002): 413–46; Martin L. Parry and Matthew Livermore, *Global Environmental Change, Part A, Special Issue* 9 (1999).

43. David King, "Climate Change Science: Adapt, Mitigate, or Ignore?" 176. This statement is apparently based on Martin L. Parry, Nigel Arnell, A. McMichael, Robert Nicholls, et al., "Viewpoint. Millions at Risk: Defining Critical Climate Change Threats and Targets," *Global Environmental Change, Part A* 11 (2001): 181–83.

44. Nigel Arnell, M. G. R. Cannell, M. Hulme, and R. S. Kovats, "The Consequences of CO_2 Stabilization for the Impacts of Climate Change," p. 418.

45. IPCC, *Summary for Policymakers*, pp. 10–11.

46. DEFRA (U.K. Department of Environment, Food, and Rural Affairs), *Scientific and Technical Aspects of Climate Change, including Impacts and Adaptation and Associated Costs*, September 2004, www.defra.gov.uk/environment/climatechange/pdf/cc-science-0904.pdf (accessed February 14, 2005); Robert J. Nicholls and Jason A. Lowe, "Benefits of Mitigation of Climate Change for Coastal Areas," *Global Environmental Change, Part A* 14 (2004): 229–244.

47. IPCC, *Special Report on Emission Scenarios* (Cambridge, UK: Cambridge University Press, 2000), henceforth SRES (2000).

48. N. W. Arnell, M. J. L. Livermore, S. Kovats, P. E. Levy, et al., "Climate and Socio-economic Scenarios for Global-Scale Climate Change Impacts Assessments: Characterizing the SRES Storylines," *Global Environmental Change, Part A* 14 (2004): 3–20.

49. Richard A. Kerr, "Confronting the Bogeyman of the Climate System," *Science* 310 (2005): 432–33; Andrew J. Weaver and Claude Hillaire-Marcel, "Ice Growth in the Greenhouse: A Seductive Paradox but Unrealistic Scenario," *Geoscience Canada* 31 (2004): 77–85; Carl Wunsch, "Gulf Stream Safe if Wind Blows and Earth Turns," *Nature* 428 (2004): 601.

50. Richard Seager, D. S. Battisti, J. Yin, P. N. Leiby, et al. "Is the Gulf Stream Responsible for Europe's Mild Winters?" *Quarterly Journal of the Royal Meteorological Society* 128 (2002): 2563–86.

51. Harry L. Bryden, Hannah R. Longworth, and Stuart A. Cunningham, "Slowing of the Atlantic Meridional Overturning Circulation at 25°N," *Nature* 438 (2005): 655–57. See also Richard A. Kerr, "The Atlantic Conveyor May Have Slowed, But Don't Panic Yet," *Science* 310 (2005): 1403–04.

52. Richard Kerr, "The Atlantic Conveyor May Have Slowed, But Don't Panic Yet," 1404.

53. J. M. Gregory, K. W. Dixon, R. J. Stouffer, A. J. Weaver, et al., "A Model Intercomparison of Changes in the Atlantic Thermohaline Circulation in Response to Increasing Atmospheric CO_2 Concentration," *Geophysical Research Letters* 32 (2005): L12703, doi:10.1029/2005GL023209. See also Andreas Schmittner, Mojib Latif, and B. Schneider, "Model Projections of the North Atlantic Thermohaline Circulation for

the 21st Century Assessed by Observations," *Geophysical Research Letters* 32 (2005): L23710, 10.1029/2005GL024368, which reports that 28 projections from 9 different coupled global climate models of a scenario of future CO_2 increase projected a gradual weakening of the North Atlantic thermohaline circulation by 25 ($\pm$25) percent until 2100.

54. Stefan Lovgren, "Greenland Melt May Swamp LA, Other Cities, Study Says," National Geographic News, April 8, 2004, http://news.nationalgeographic.com/news/2004/04/0408_040408_greenlandicemelt.html (accessed March 11, 2006); Michael Oppenheimer, "Polar Ice Sheets, Melting, and Sea Level Change," American Association for the Advancement of Science, June 15, 2004, www.aaas.org/news/releases/2004/0615Oppenheimer.pdf (accessed March 11, 2006).

55. Indur M. Goklany, "Saving Habitat and Conserving Biodiversity on a Crowded Planet."

56. David King, "Climate Change Science"; Martin L. Parry et al. "Viewpoint. Millions at Risk" Martin L. Parry, *Global Environmental Change, Part A: Special Issue.*

57. Martin L. Parry et al., *Global Environmental Change, Part A: Special Issue.*

58. Ibid.

59. Ibid., p 57.

60. Indur M. Goklany, "Is a Richer-but-Warmer World Better than Poorer-but-Cooler Worlds?"; Indur M. Goklany, "Integrated Strategies to Reduce Vulnerability and Advance Adaptation, Mitigation, and Sustainable Development."

61. Indur M. Goklany, "Is a Richer-but-Warmer World Better than Poorer-but-Cooler Worlds?"

62. Martin L. Parry et al., *Global Environmental Change, Part A: Special Issue.*

63. CO_2 Science, Plant Growth, www.co2science.org/scripts/CO2ScienceB2C/data/data.jsp (accessed February 4, 2006). This website maintains a register of experimental results on the growth of hundreds of crops and other plants under greater-than-ambient CO_2 concentrations. For the major crops, the vast majority of entries indicate a positive growth response at high CO_2 conditions. See also chapter 6. Ironically, a recent study suggests that higher water-use efficiency in plants because of higher CO_2 concentrations may have contributed to a worldwide increase in runoff during the 20th century. See Nicola Gedney, P. M. Cox, R. A. Betts, O. Boucher, et al., "Detection of a Direct Carbon Dioxide Effect in Continental River Runoff Records."

64. Indur M. Goklany, "Relative Contributions of Global Warming to Various Climate-Sensitive Risks, and Their Implications for Adaptation and Mitigation," *Energy and Environment* 14 (2003): 797–822.

65. Nigel Arnell, "Climate Change and Global Water Resources."

66. Nigel Arnell, et al., "The Consequences of CO_2 Stabilization for the Impact of Climate Change."

67. Martin L. Parry, et al., "Viewpoint: Millions at Risk."

68. See Indur M. Goklany, "Relative Contributions of Global Warming to Various Climate-Sensitive Risks."

69. WHO, *World Health Report 1999* (Geneva: WHO, 1999), chapter 4.

70. Richard S. J. Tol and Hadi Dowlatabadi, "Vector-Borne Diseases, Development, and Climate Change," *Integrated Assessment* 2 (2001): 173–81.

71. See also Indur M. Goklany, *The Precautionary Principle: A Critical Appraisal of Environmental Risk Assessment* (Washington, DC: Cato Institute, 2001), pp. 13–27.

72. ReliefWeb, "EU Cautions over Plans to use DDT to Fight Malaria," February 2, 2005, www.reliefweb.int/rw/RWB.NSF/db900SID/DDAD-699MXX?OpenDocument

(accessed February 18, 2006); UN Office for the Coordination of Humanitarian Affairs, "UGANDA: Anti-DDT Lobby Could Slow Fight Against Malaria, Minister Says," IRIN News, April 25, 2005, www.irinnews.org/report.asp?ReportID = 46790& SelectRegion = East_Africa &SelectCountry = UGANDA (accessed February 18, 2006); Richard Tren and Roger Bate, "Wolfowitz's Challenge: The World Bank's New Head Could Save Many Lives," National Review Online, March 29, 2005, www.national review.com/comment/tren_bate200503290754.asp (accessed February 18, 2006).

73. Robert Nicholls, "Coastal Flooding and Wetland Loss in the 21st Century."

74. Ibid., 74.

75. See ibid., table 7.

76. This estimate excludes an estimated 0.51 million people who died from malaria but whose deaths were attributed to underweight in the report. WHO, *World Health Report 2002* (Geneva: WHO, 2002).

77. EM-DAT, Emergency Disaster Database, Office of Foreign Disaster Aid and Center for Research on the Epidemiology of Disasters at the Université Catholique de Louvain, Brussels, Belgium, www.em-dat.net/disasters/statisti.htm (accessed on September 6, 2005), henceforth EM-DAT (2005).

78. A *biome* is defined as a major ecological community such as grassland, tropical rain forest, or desert. Specific biomes correspond to divisions of the world"s vegetation characterized by a defined climate and composed of specific types of plants and animals (e.g., tropical rain forest or desert). *Net biome productivity* is a measure of the biome's productivity in terms of the net amount of carbon it moves from the atmosphere into the biome. It includes the amount of carbon that is sequestered in the plants above ground (in tree trunks, shoots, and leaves), below ground (in the roots), and in soils, minus carbon that is lost from the biome to the atmosphere through respiration or through changes in land cover (e.g., deforestation).

79. This table is based on N. W. Arnell, M. J. L. Livermore, S. Kovats, P. E. Levy, et al., "Climate and Socio-economic Scenarios for Global-Scale Climate Change Impacts Assessments: Characterizing the SRES Storylines," *Global Environmental Change, Part A* 14 (2004): 3–20; P. E. Levy, M. G. R. Cannell, and A. D. Friend, "Modeling the Impact of Future Changes," and Robert Nicholls, "Coastal Flooding and Wetland Loss in the 21st Century."

80. P. E. Levy, M. G. R. Cannell, and A. D. Friend, "Modeling the Impact of Future Changes."

81. Indur M. Goklany and David A. King, "Climate Change and Malaria," *Science* 306 (2004): 55–57.

82. Indur M. Goklany, "Potential Consequences of Increasing Atmospheric CO_2 Concentration Compared to Other Environmental Problems"; Indur M. Goklany, "A Climate Policy for the Short to Medium Term."

83. "No regret" policies or actions are those can be justified on their own merits without reference to climate change or are not associated with measures that would advance sustainable development or adaptive capacities (through focused or broad development).

84. This table excludes malaria, because the results for the Fast Track Assessment reported in van Lieshout et al. in 2004 provided data for PAR but not enough information to estimate TPAR, which makes it impossible to use their results to estimate the impacts of malaria on well-being. But as we saw in the foregoing, richer countries are unlikely to succumb to malaria to the same degree as poorer ones, van Lieshout et al., "Climate Change and Malaria."

85. Indur M. Goklany, "Is a Richer-but-Warmer World Better than Poorer-but-Cooler Worlds?"

86. Table 10.7 is based on Indur M. Goklany, "A Climate Policy for the Short and Medium Term," which compiled results from Nigel W. Arnell, "Climate Change and Global Water Resources," *Global Environmental Change, Part A* 9 (1999): S31–S49, and Nigel Arnell, M. G. R. Cannell, M. Hulme, R. S. Kovats, et al., "The Consequences of CO_2 Stabilization for the Impact of Climate Change," to allow a comparison between various scenarios for mitigation and adaptation.

87. Martin L. Parry, et al., "Viewpoint: Millions at Risk."

88. Indur M. Goklany, "Relative Contributions of Global Warming to Various Climate-Sensitive Risks, and Their Implications for Adaptation and Mitigation," *Energy and Environment* 14 (2003): 797–822.

89. Indur M. Goklany, "A Climate Policy for the Short to Medium Term." The cumulative GDP of Annex I countries in 2003 was $29 trillion (in 2003 dollars; World Bank, *World Development Indicators*, http://devdata.worldbank.org/dataonline (accessed July 12, 2005). By 2010, their GDP should be $33 trillion (also in 2003 dollars), assuming that it continues to grow at the same rate as it did between 1996 and 2003.

90. UN Millennium Project, *Investing in Development: A Practical Plan to Achieve the Millennium Development Goals* (New York: EarthScan and UN Millennium Project, 2005).

91. WHO, *World Health Report 1999* (Geneva: WHO, 1999), Chapter 4; UN Millennium Project, *Coming to Grips with Malaria in the New Millennium*, Task Force on HIV/AIDS, Malaria, TB, and Access to Essential Medicines, Working Group on Malaria.

92. Indur M. Goklany, "Potential Consequences of Increasing Atmospheric CO_2 Concentration Compared to Other Environmental Problems"; Indur M. Goklany, *The Precautionary Principle*.

93. This calculation assumes that changes in food production would be achieved through changes in productivity (i.e., "effective" yields) rather than in the area under cultivation.

94. Indur M. Goklany, "Relative Contributions of Global Warming to Various Climate-Sensitive Risks"; Indur M. Goklany, "Integrated Strategies."

95. Ibid.

96. Nigel Arnell, et al., "The Consequences of CO_2 Stabilization for the Impact of Climate Change."

97. Indur M. Goklany, "Potential Consequences of Increasing Atmospheric CO_2 Concentration Compared to Other Environmental Problems"; Indur M. Goklany, "Integrated Strategies."

98. Ibid.; Indur M. Goklany, "Comparing 20th Century Trends in United States and Global Agricultural Land and Water Use," *Water International* 27 (2002): 321–29.

99. Indur M. Goklany, "Comparing 20th Century Trends in the United States."

100. Robert Nicholls, *The Impacts of Sea Level Rise*, www.metoffice.com/research/hadleycentre/pubs/brochures/B1999/imp_sea_rise.html (accessed February 12, 2006).

101. David W. Pearce, W. Cline, A. Achanta, S. Fankhauser, et al., "The Social Costs of Climate Change: Greenhouse Damage and the Benefits of Control," in *Climate Change 1995: Economic and Social Dimensions of Climate Change* (New York: Cambridge University Press, 1996), p. 191.

102. Indur M. Goklany, "Richer Is More Resilient: Dealing with Climate Change and More Urgent Environmental Problems," in *Earth Report 2000, Revisiting the True State of the Planet*, ed. Ronald Bailey (New York: McGraw-Hill, 1999), pp. 155–87.

103. James Wolfensohn, "Climate change," quote available at http://lnweb18. worldbank.org/ESSD/essdext.nsf/46ByDocName/ClimateChange (accessed May 12, 2003).

104. Ibid.; Robert T. Watson and I. Johnson, "Developing Countries Face Worst in Global Warming," *Business Day* (Johannesburg), July 23, 2001, http://allafrica.com/stories/200107230695.html (accessed May 12, 2003); Working Group on Climate Change and Development, *Up in Smoke: Threats from, and Responses to, the Impact of Global Warming on Human Development* (London: New Economic Foundation, 2004).

105. A second estimate places the additional cost of attaining the MDGs by 2015 at $40–$60 billion annually. World Bank, *The Costs of Attaining the Millennium Development Goals*, 2002, www.worldbank.org/html/extdr/mdgassessment.pdf (accessed December 10, 2002).

106. Robert T. Watson and I. Johnson, "Developing Countries Face Worst in Global Warming"; Working Group on Climate Change and Development, *Up in Smoke: Threats from, and Responses to, the Impact of Global Warming on Human Development*.

107. Julian Morris, *Sustainable Development: Promoting Progress or Perpetuating Poverty* (London: Profile Books, 2002); Indur M. Goklany, "Richer is More Resilient: Dealing with Climate Change and More Urgent Environmental Problems," in *Earth Report 2000, Revisiting the True State of the Planet*, ed. Ronald Bailey (New York: McGraw-Hill, 1999), pp. 155–87; Indur M. Goklany, "Integrated Strategies."

108. This section is adapted from Indur M. Goklany, "Integrated Strategies to Reduce Vulnerability and Advance Adaptation, Mitigation, and Sustainable Development."

109. Indur M. Goklany, "Adaptation and Climate Change"; Sally M. Kane and Jason F. Shogren, "Linking Adaptation and Mitigation in Climate Change Policy," *Climatic Change* 45 (2000): 75–102; Thomas J. Wilbanks, S. M. Kane, P. N. Leiby, R. D. Perlack, et al., "Possible Responses to Global Climate Change: Integrating Mitigation and Adaptation," *Environment* 45 (2003): 28–38.

110. Indur M. Goklany, "Strategies to Enhance Adaptability"; Indur M. Goklany, "Integrated Strategies."

111. Hanh H. Dang, Axel Michaelowa, and Dao D. Tuan, "Synergy of Adaptation and Mitigation Strategies in the Context of Sustainable Development: The Case of Vietnam," *Climate Policy* 3S1 (2003): S81–S96; Saleemul Huq and Michael Grubb, "Scientific Assessment of the Inter-relationships of Mitigation and Adaptation," 2003, www.ipcc.ch/activity/cct2a.pdf (accessed June 1, 2004).

112. IPCC, *Climate Change 2001: Impacts, Adaptation, and Vulnerability* (New York: Cambridge University Press, 2001).

113. Sam Hitz and Joel Smith, "Estimating Global Impacts from Climate Change," *Global Environmental Change, Part A* 14 (2004): 201–18.

114. Hanh H. Dang, Axel Michaelowa, and Dao D. Tuan, "Synergy of Adaptation and Mitigation Strategies."

115. Indur M. Goklany, "Strategies to Enhance Adaptability."

116. Indur M. Goklany, "A Climate Policy for the Short and Medium Term."

117. Indur M. Goklany, "Relative Contributions of Global Warming to Various Climate-Sensitive Risks."

118. Indur M. Goklany, "Adaptation and Climate Change"; Indur M. Goklany, "Potential Consequences of Increasing Atmospheric CO_2 Concentration Compared to Other Environmental Problems"; Indur M. Goklany, "Integrated Strategies."

119. See also Thomas C. Schelling, "Intergenerational Discounting," *Energy Policy* 23 (1995): 395–401; Hadi Dowlatabadi, "Assessing the Health Impacts of Climate Change," *Climatic Change* 35 (1997): 137–44; Indur M. Goklany, "Relative Contributions of Global Warming to Various Climate-Sensitive Risks"; Richard S. J. Tol and Hadi Dowlatabadi, "Vector-Borne Diseases, Development, and Climate Change," *Integrated Assessment* 2 (2001): 173–81; Bjørn Lomborg, ed., *Global Crises, Global Solutions* (Cambridge, UK: Cambridge University Press, 2004).

120. Hanh H. Dang, Axel Michaelowa, and Dao D. Tuan, "Synergy of Adaptation and Mitigation Strategies."

121. Indur M. Goklany, "Strategies to Enhance Adaptability."

122. Indur M. Goklany, "Affluence, Technology and Well-being," *Case Western Reserve Law Review* 53 (2002): 369–90.

123. Office of Development Studies, "Global Public Goods 'A Highly Rewarding Investment,'" *Briefing Note 3*, UNDP, www.undp.org/globalpublicgoods/globalization/background.html (accessed June 24, 2004).

Chapter 11

1. United Nations Population Division, *World Population Prospects: The 2004 Revision, Population Database*, http://esa.un.org/unpp/ (accessed December 12, 2005).

2. United Nations Population Division, *Long-Range World Population Projections: Based on the 1998 Revision*, www.un.org/esa/population/publications/longrange/longrange.htm (accessed December 12, 2002).

3. See chapter 2.

4. Indur M. Goklany, "Saving Habitat and Conserving Biodiversity on a Crowded Planet," *BioScience* 48 (1998): 941–53; Indur M. Goklany, "The Future of Industrial Society" (paper presented at the International Conference on Industrial Ecology and Sustainability, University of Technology of Troyes, Troyes, France, September 22–25, 1999); Carroll Ann Hodges, "Mineral Resources, Environmental Issues, and Land Use," *Science* 268 (1995): 1305–12; Theodore Panayotou and Jeffrey R. Vincent, "Consumption: Challenge to Sustainable Development or Distraction," *Science* 276 (1997): 55–57; Mark Sagoff, "What's Wrong with Exotic Species?" *Report from the Institute for Philosophy and Public Policy* 19 (Fall 1999): 16–23.

5. See, for example, Jesse H. Ausubel and H. Dale Langford, eds., *Technological Trajectories and the Environment* (Washington, DC: National Academy Press, 1997); Jesse H. Ausubel, "Resources and Environment in the 21st Century: Seeing Past the Phantoms." *World Energy Council Journal* (July 1998): 8–16; Indur M. Goklany, "The Importance of Climate Change Compared to Other Global Changes," in *Proceedings of the Second International Specialty Conference on Global Climate Change: Science, Policy, and Mitigation/Adaptation Strategies*, Crystal City, VA, October 13–16, 1998 (Sewickley, PA: Air and Waste Management Association, 1998); Indur M. Goklany, "Meeting Global Food Needs: The Environmental Trade-Offs Between Increasing Land Conversion and Land Productivity," *Technology* 6 (1999): 107–30; Arnulf Grübler, *Technology and Global Change* (Cambridge, UK: Cambridge University Press, 1998); Nebojsa Nakicenovic, Arnulf Grübler, and Alan McDonald, eds., *Global Energy Perspectives* (Cambridge, UK: Cambridge University Press, 1998).

6. Sandra L. Postel, Gretchen C. Daily, and Paul R. Ehrlich, "Human Appropriation of Renewable Fresh Water," *Science* 271 (1996): 785–88; David J. Pimentel, James Houser, Erika Preiss, Omar White, et al., "Water Resources: Agriculture, the Environment, and Society," *BioScience* 47, no. 2 (1997): 97–106; Peter H. Gleick, *The World's Water: The Biennial Report on Freshwater Resources* (Washington, DC: Island Press, 1998).

7. World Health Organization (WHO), *World Health Report 2002* (Geneva: WHO, 2002), Annexes 2, 3, 11, 12, 14–16.

8. Food and Agriculture Organization (FAO), FAOSTAT database, 2006, www.apps.fao.org (accessed February 21, 2006).

9. Indur M. Goklany, "Strategies to Enhance Adaptability: Technological Change, Economic Growth, and Free Trade," *Climatic Change* 30 (1995): 427–49.

10. Estimated at around $250 billion annually by 2050; see Indur M. Goklany, "Saving Habitat and Conserving Biodiversity on a Crowded Planet."

11. See, for example, FAO, *The State of Food and Agriculture 1996* (Rome: FAO, 1996).

12. Intergovernmental Panel on Climate Change (IPCC), *Climate Change 1995: The Economic and Social Dimensions of Climate Change* (Cambridge, UK: Cambridge University Press, 1996).

13. Indur M. Goklany, "Richer Is More Resilient: Dealing with Climate Change and More Urgent Environmental Problems," in *Earth Report 2000, Revisiting the True State of the Planet,* ed. Ronald Bailey (New York: McGraw-Hill, 1999), pp. 155–87.

14. Indur M. Goklany and Merritt W. Sprague, *An Alternative Approach to Sustainable Development: Conserving Forests, Habitat, and Biological Diversity by Increasing the Efficiency and Productivity of Land Utilization* (Washington, DC: Office of Program Analysis, Department of the Interior, 1991); Indur M. Goklany, "Strategies to Enhance Adaptability: Technological Change, Economic Growth, and Free Trade"; Indur M. Goklany, "The Importance of Climate Change Compared to Other Global Changes."

15. FAO, *Global Forest Resources Assessment 2000* (Rome: FAO, 2000), chapter 49, p. 345.

16. Indur M. Goklany, "Saving Habitat and Conserving Biodiversity on a Crowded Planet" Indur M. Goklany, "Meeting Global Food Needs."

17. FAO, "The State of Food and Agriculture 1996"; Sandra L. Postel, Gretchen C. Daily, and Paul R. Erlich, "Human Appropriation of Renewable Fresh Water."

18. Terry L. Anderson, "Water, Water Everywhere But Not a Drop to Sell," in *The State of Humanity,* ed. Julian Simon, E. Calvin Beisner, and John Phelps (Cambridge, MA: Blackwell, 1995), pp. 425–33.

19. Allan R. Hoffman, "Water, Energy and Sustainable Development, United States Department of Energy," presentation to Water Policy in the Americas Roundtable, Organization of American States, June 15, 2000.

20. Texas Water Desalination Board, "Desalination—Frequently Asked Questions," www.twdb.state.tx.us/Desalination/Desal/Frequently%20asked%20questions.asp (accessed February 10, 2006).

21. David Corbus, "Desalination and Water Purification for Villages," National Renewable Energy Laboratory, December 1999, www.nrel.gov/villagepower/pdfs/briefs_2000/desalination.pdf (accessed February 8, 2003); Peter Weiss, "Oceans of Energy," *Science News* 159 (April 14, 2001), www.sciencenews.org/20010414/bob12.asp (accessed February 8, 2003); *Economist,* "Sunshine and Showers," October 21, 1995, p. 84; *Discover,* "Pump it Up," July 1995, pp. 18–20.

22. These estimates are based on 2003 data from FAOSTAT's Food Balance Sheet for the world. FAO, *FAOSTAT 2006,* http://faostat.fao.org (accessed December 10, 2006). It includes estimates for milk, butter, and eggs.

23. FAO, *The State of World Fisheries and Aquaculture (SOFIA) 2004*, www.fao.org/sof/sofia/index_en.htm (accessed February 10, 2006), henceforth SOFIA 2004.

24. Ismail Serageldin, *Toward Sustainable Management of Water Resources* (Washington, DC: World Bank, 1995).

25. Indur M. Goklany, "Meeting Global Food Needs."

26. Massimo Livi-Bacci, *A Concise History of World Population*, trans. Carl Ipsen (Cambridge, MA: Blackwell, 1992).

27. FAO, *SOFIA 2004*, table 1; FAO, *The State of World Fisheries and Agriculture (SOFIA) 1998*, www.fao.org/sof/sofia/index_en.htm (accessed February 10, 2006).

28. FAO, *SOFIA 2004*, table 1.

29. Ibid.

30. FAO, *SOFIA 2004*, table 4.

31. Donald R. Leal, *Homesteading the Oceans: The Case for Property Rights in United States Fisheries* (Bozeman, MT: Political Economy Research Center, 2000).

32. Rosamond L. Naylor, Rebecca J. Goldberg, Jurgenne H. Primavera, Nil Kautsky, et al., "Effect of Aquaculture on World Fish Supplies," *Nature* 405 (2000): 1017–24.

33. WRI, *World Resources 1998–99 Database* (Washington, DC: WRI, 1998); and FAO, FAOSTAT database, 1998, http://apps.fao.org.

34. Rosamond L. Naylor, Kjetil Hindar, Ian A. Fleming, Rebecca Goldberg, et al., "Fugitive Salmon: Assessing the Risks of Escaped Fish from Net-Pen Aquaculture," *BioSience* 55 (2005): 427–37.

35. James H. Tidwell and Geoff L. Allan, "Fish as Food: Aquaculture's Contribution," *EMBO Reports* 2 (2001): 958–63.

36. Kenneth H. Coale, Kenneth S. Johnson, Francisco P. Chavez, Ken O. Buessler, et al., " Southern Ocean Iron Enrichment Experiment: Carbon Cycling in High- and Low-Si Waters," *Science* 304 (2004): 408–14; Ken O. Buesseler, John E. Andrews, Steven M. Pike, and Matthew A. Charette, "The Effects of Iron Fertilization on Carbon Sequestration in the Southern Ocean," *Science* 304 (2004): 414–17; Edward R. Abraham, Cliff S. Law, Philip W. Boyd, Samantha J. Lavender, et al., "Importance of Stirring in the Development of an Iron-Fertilized Phytoplankton Bloom," *Nature* 407 (2000): 727–30; Philip W. Boyd, Andrew J. Watson, Cliff S. Law, Edward R. Abraham, et al., "A Mesoscale Phytoplankton Bloom in the Polar Southern Ocean Stimulated by Iron Fertilization," *Nature* 407 (2000): 695–702; Andrew J. Watson, D. C. E. Bakker, A. J. Ridgwell, P. W. Boyd, et al., "Effect of Iron Supply on Southern Ocean CO_2 Uptake and Implications for Glacial Atmospheric CO_2," *Nature* 407 (October 12, 2000): 730–33.

37. Kenneth H. Coale, et al., "Southern Ocean Iron Enrichment Experiment."

38. James K. B. Bishop, Todd J. Wood, Russ E. Davis, and Jeffrey T. Sherman, "Robotic Observations of Enhanced Carbon Biomass and Export at 55ES during SOFeX," *Science* 304 (2004): 417–20. See also Quirin Schiermeier, "Iron Seeding Creates Fleeting Carbon Sink in Southern Ocean," *Nature* 428 (2004): 788.

39. Rex Dalton, "Ocean Tests Raise Doubts over Use of Algae as Carbon Sink," *Nature* 420 (2002): 722.

40. Indur M. Goklany, "Meeting Global Food Needs."

41. See figure 4.1.

42. WHO, "Water, Sanitation and Hygiene Links to Health: Facts and Figures Updated November 2004," www.who.int/water_sanitation_health/publications/facts2004/en/index.html (accessed February 24, 2006).

43. WHO, "Indoor Air Pollution and Health, Fact Sheet 292," June 2005, www.who.int/mediacentre/factsheets/fs292/en/index.html (accessed February 24, 2006).

44. Indur M. Goklany, *Clearing the Air*.

45. Indur M. Goklany, "Strategies to Enhance Adaptability."

46. Indur M. Goklany, "Potential Consequences of Increasing Atmospheric CO_2 Concentration Compared to Other Environmental Problems," *Technology* 7S (2000): 189–213; Indur M. Goklany, "Integrating Strategies."

Chapter 12

1. Jared Diamond, *Collapse: How Societies Choose to Fail or Succeed* (New York: Viking, 2005), pp. 504–05.

2. United States Bureau of the Census (USBOC), *Historical Statistics of the United States, Colonial Times to 1970* (Washington, DC: Government Printing Office, 1975), p. 55, henceforth USBOC (1975).

3. Grecia Matos, Total United States Material Consumption, 1900–2000 (Reston, VA: U.S. Geological Survey, 2005); USBOC (1975); USBOC, *Statistical Abstract of the United States 2006* (Washington, DC: Government Printing Office, 2000); Energy Information Administration (EIA), *Annual Energy Review 2004* (Washington, DC: EIA/Department of Energy, 2004). Estimates of material consumption do not include materials embodied in exports or imports of goods. "Nonfuel organic chemicals" include primary nonfuel products from petroleum, natural gas, and coal.

4. Nonfuel organics (NFOs) include pesticides. However, by weight, the latter are a tiny part of the former. In 1997, the United States consumed 140 million metric tons of NFOs and less than half a million metric tons of pesticides (by weight of active ingredients). See Matos, *United States Consumption of Raw Materials*; Arnold J. Aspelin and Arthur H. Grube, *Pesticide Industry Sales and Usage: 1996 and 1997 Market Estimates* (Washington, DC: Office of Pesticide Programs, EPA, 1999), table 10. Trends for pesticides consumption show that they grew rapidly until 1979– growing 85 percent from 1964 (the first year for which data are available) to 1979, but then they declined so that by 1997 they were 58 percent above the 1964 level. By contrast, NFOs grew by 91 percent from 1964 to 1979, followed by a decline in the early 1980s because of high oil prices and a recession after which they resumed a more or less steady climb. By 1997, NFO consumption was 153 percent above 1964 levels.

5. Richard H. Steckel and Roderick Floud, eds., *Health and Welfare during Industrialization* (Chicago: University of Chicago Press, 1997).

6. Richard A. Easterlin, *Growth Triumphant: The Twenty-First Century in Historical Perspective* (Ann Arbor, MI: University of Michigan Press, 1996), pp. 161–62.

7. Richard H. Steckel and Rodericks Floud, eds., *Health and Welfare during Industrialization*.

8. Indur M. Goklany, "Strategies to Enhance Adaptability: Technological Change, Economic Growth, and Free Trade," *Climatic Change* 30 (1995): 427–49; Indur M. Goklany, "Factors Affecting Environmental Impacts: The Effects of Technology on Long-Term Trends in Cropland, Air Pollution, and Water-Related Diseases," *Ambio* 25 (1996): 497–503.

9. Easterlin, *Growth Triumphant*, pp. 161–62.

10. The Global Fund to Fight AIDS, Tuberculosis, and Malaria, Pledges and Contributions," www.theglobalfund.org/en/files/pledges&contributions.xls (accessed February 24, 2006).

11. Indur M. Goklany, "Richer Is More Resilient: Dealing with Climate Change and More Urgent Environmental Problems," in *Earth Report 2000: Revisiting the True State of the Planet*, ed. Ronald Bailey (New York: McGraw-Hill, 1999), pp. 155–87.

12. Associated Press, "Life Expectancy Plummets, North Korea Says," *New York Times*, May 16, 2000, p. A6.

13. Food and Agriculture Organization (FAO), *State of Food Insecurity in the World 2004* (Rome: FAO, 2004).

14. World Health Organization (WHO), *The World Health Report 2004* (Geneva: WHO, 2004); WHO, "Water, Sanitation, and Hygiene Links to Health: Facts and Figures, Updated November 2004," www.who.int/water_sanitation_health/publications/facts2004/en/index.html (accessed February 24, 2006); WHO "Indoor Air Pollution and Health," Fact Sheet 292, June 2005, www.who.int/mediacentre/factsheets/fs292/en/index.html (accessed February 24, 2006).

15. Based on the increase in population between 1950 and 2002 and cropland estimates for 2002, using data from FAO (2005).

16. Robert S. Chen and Robert W. Kates, "World Food Security: Prospects and Trends," *Food Policy* 19 (1994): 193–208.

17. Lord Palmer, in the United Kingdom Parliament, Lord Hansard, March 8, 2000, www.parliament.the-stationery-office.co.uk/pa/ld199900/ldhansrd/vo000308/text/00308-06.htm (accessed December 20, 2002).

18. Based on the change in $P \times A$ from 1950 to 2000 and emissions in 1950. See chapter 6.

19. Indur M. Goklany, "Factors Affecting Environmental Impacts: The Effects of Technology on Long-Term Trends in Cropland, Air Pollution, and Water-Related Diseases," *Ambio* 25 (1996): 497–503.

20. The figure for deaths due to water-related diseases is estimated by multiplying the 1900 death rate of 1860 per million (see chapter 6) by the current United States population, while that for emissions assumes that emissions per GDP would remain unchanged while GDP would continue to grow at its historical rate.

21. Nowadays population explosions are only associated with the developing world. In fact, the current population of the United States is more than 3.5-fold what it was in 1900. Similarly, despite wars and genocide, Europe's population increased by 86 percent during the latter half of the 20th century. FAO, *State of the World's Forests 2001* (Rome: FAO, 2001).

22. Goklany, "Strategies to Enhance Adaptability," 427–449.

23. See, for example, Wolfgang Lutz, ed., *IIASA Population Projection Results*, 1998, www.iiasa.ac.at/Research/POP/docs/Population_Projections_Results.html.

24. Indur M. Goklany, "Strategies to Enhance Adaptability."

25. Paul R. Ehrlich, Anne H. Ehrlich, and Gretchen C. Daily, "Food Security Population, and Environment," *Population and Development Review* 19 (1993): 1–32; Norman Myers, "Consumption: Challenge to Sustainable Development," *Science* 276 (1997): 53–55.

26. World Bank, *World Development Indicators 2005*.

27. United Nations Population Fund (UNFPA), *The State of World Population 1997* (New York: UNFPA, 1997); World Resources Institute, *World Resources 1996–97* (New York: Oxford University Press, 1996).

28. Joel E. Cohen, *How Many People Can the Earth Support?* (New York: W. W. Norton, 1995); Anne S. Moffat, "Ecologists Look at the Big Picture," *Science* 273 (1996): 1490.

29. World Bank, 1984; Massimo Livi-Bacci, *A Concise History of World Population*, trans. Carl Ipsen (Cambridge, MA: Blackwell, 1992); Bryant Robey, Shea O. Rutstein, and Leo Morris, "The Fertility Decline in Developing Countries," *Scientific American*

269, no. 6 (1993): 60–67; Wade Roush, "Population: The View from Cairo," *Science* 265 (1994): 1164–67.

30. Paul E. Ehrlich and Ann H. Ehrlich, *The Population Explosion* (New York: Simon and Schuster, 1990); Atiq Rahman, Nick Robins, and Annie Roncerel, eds., *Exploding the Population Myth: Consumption versus Population: Which Is the Climate Bomb?* (Brussels: Climate Network Europe, 1993); Paul R. Harrison, *The Third Revolution: Population. Environment and a Sustainable World* (London: Penguin Books, 1993); Vaclav Smil, *Energy in World History (Boulder, CO: Westview Press, 1994); Norman Myers, "Consumption: Challenge to Sustainable Development."*

31. Paul H. Reitan and Eric Reitan, "Our Unsustainable Present."

32. Jesse H. Ausubel and H. Dale Langford, eds., *Technological Trajectories and the Environment* (Washington, DC: National Academy Press, 1997); Jesse H. Ausubel, "Resources and Environment in the 21st Century: Seeing Past the Phantoms," *World Energy Council Journal* (July 1998): 8–16; Arnulf Grübler, *Technology and Global Change* (Cambridge, UK: Cambridge University Press, 1998).

33. Carolyn Raffensperger and Joel Tickner, eds., *Protecting Public Health and the Environment: Implementing the Precautionary Principle* (Washington, DC: Island Press, 1999); Indur M. Goklany, "Precaution without Perversity: A Comprehensive Application of the Precautionary Principle to Genetically Modified Crops," *Biotechnology Law Report* 20, no. 3 (2001).

34. See, for example, Christopher D. Stone, "Is There a Precautionary Principle?" *Environmental Law Reporter* 31 (2001): 10,789–10,799.

35. Friends of the Earth (FOE), "FoE Supports Tory GM Moratorium Call. What About the Precautionary Principle Mr. Blair," press release 1999, www.foe.co.uk/pubsinfo/infoteam/pressrel/1999/19990203170456.html.

36. See also Frank Cross, "Paradoxical Perils of the Precautionary Principle," *Washington and Lee Law Review* 53 (1996): 851–921; Jonathan Adler, "More Sorry Than Safe: Assessing the Precautionary Principle and the Proposed International Biosafety Protocol," *Texas International Law Journal* 35 (2000): 194–20; Gary Comstock, *Vexing Nature? On the Ethical Case Against Agricultural Biotechnology* (Boston: Kluwer Academic Publishers, 2000).

37. Indur M. Goklany, "From Precautionary Principle to Risk-Risk Analysis," *Nature Biotechnology* 20 (2002): 1075; Indur M. Goklany, "Applying the Precautionary Principle in a Broader Concept" in *Rethinking Risk and the Precautionary Principle*, ed. Julian Morris (Oxford, UK: Butterworth-Heinemann, 2000), pp. 189–228.

38. Indur M. Goklany, "Saving Habitat and Conserving Biodiversity on a Crowded Planet," *BioScience* 48 (1998): 941–53.

39. Indur M. Goklany, *Clearing the Air: The True Story of the War on Air Pollution* (Washington, DC: Cato Institute, 1999), p. 18.

40. See, for example, Linda G. Martin, "Population Aging Policies in East Asia and the United States," *Science* 251 (1991): 527–31; Indur M. Goklany, "Strategies to Enhance Adaptability"; Nicholas Eberstadt, "World Population Prospects for the Twenty-First Century: The Specter of 'Depopulation'," in *Earth Report 2000*, ed. Ronald Bailey (New York: McGraw-Hill, 2000), pp. 63–84; Anatoly Zoubanov, *Population Aging and Population Decline: Government Views and Policies*, UN/POP/PRA/2000/2, prepared for the Expert Group Meeting on Policy Responses to Population Aging and Population Decline (New York: UN Population Division, 2000).

41. Additional information on these issues can be obtained from the UN Population Division's website devoted to the Expert Group Meeting on Policy Responses to

Population Aging and Population Decline, www.un.org/esa/population/publications/popdecline/popdecline.htm (accessed February 9, 2003), henceforth UNPD Expert Group.

42. See UNPD Expert Group. In 1935, the year social security was enacted in the United States, 6.1 percent of its population was over 65; by 1998, this had risen to 12.7 percent; and by 2050, this could rise to 20.0 percent. USBOC (1975), p. 15; USBOC, *Statistical Abstract of the United States 1999* (Washington, DC: USBOC, 1999), pp. 15, 17.

43. Linda G. Martin, "Population Aging Policies in East Asia and the United States"; Nicholas Eberstadt, "World Population Prospects for the Twenty-First Century"; S. Rich, "Four in House Outline Social Security Cuts," *Washington Post*, September 28, 1994, p. A17; UNPD Expert Group.

44. UNPD Expert Group; R. Atkinson, "Worried Germany Grapples with Population Shrinkage," *Washington Post*, March 12, 1994, p. A14; World Bank, *World Development Indicators 2002, CD-ROM* (Washington, DC: World Bank, 2002).

45. Idur M. Goklany, "Strategies to Enhance Adaptability."

46. Ibid.

47. Jesse H. Ausubel, "Resources and Environment in the 21st Century: Seeing Past the Phantoms." *World Energy Council Journal* (July 1998); David S. Landes, *The Wealth and Poverty of Nations: Why Some Are So Rich and Some So Poor* (New York: W. W. Norton, 1998), David Tilman, Joseph Fargione, Brian Wolff, Carla D'Antonio, et al., "Forecasting Agriculturally Driven Global Environmental Change," *Science* 292 (2001): 281–84.

48. Paul H. Reitan and Eric Reitan, "Our Unsustainable Present: Why and What Can We Do About It?" *Electronic Green Journal* (December 1998), http://egj.lib.uidaho.edu/egj09/reitan2.html (accessed February 8, 2003).

49. Jesse H. Ausubel, "Resources and Environment in the 21st Century: Seeing Past the Phantoms"; Robert U. Ayres, "Economic Growth: Politically Necessary but Not Environmentally Friendly," *Ecological Economics* 15 (1995): 97–99; David A. Landes, *The Wealth and Poverty of Nations: Why Some Are So Rich and Some So Poor.*

50. Indur M. Goklany, "The Future of Industrial Society" (paper presented at the International Conference on Industrial Ecology and Sustainability, University of Technology of Troyes, Troyes, France, September 22–25, 1999).

51. Indur M. Goklany, "Strategies to Enhance Adaptability."

52. Paul R. Ehrlich, *The Machinery of Nature* (New York: Simon and Schuster, 1986).

53. Richard N. Cooper, "Trade," in *Encyclopedia Americana* (Danbury, CT: Grolier, 1987); Jesse H. Ausubel, "Does Climate Still Matter?" *Nature* 350 (1991): 649–52.

54. Jared Diamond, *Collapse*, pp. 193–97.

55. Indur M. Goklany, "Strategies to Enhance Adaptability."

56. Based on data from World Resources Institute, EarthTrends, http://earthtrends.wri.org/ (accessed January 18, 2003).

57. This rough estimate, based on data from World Resources Institute, Earth-Trends, www.wri.org (accessed July 12, 2005), assumes that each country's average cereal yields would be unaffected.

58. David L. Hawksworth and M. T. Kalin-Arroyo, "Magnitude and Distribution of Biodiversity," in *Global Biodiversity Assessment*, ed. Vernon H. Heywood, et al. (Cambridge, UK: Cambridge University Press, 1995), pp. 107–92.

59. Herman E. Daly, "The Perils of Free Trade," *Scientific American* 269, no. 5 (1993): 50–57; Herman E. Daly, *Beyond Growth: The Economics of Sustainable Development*

(Boston, MA: Beacon Press, 1996); Indur M. Goklany, "Strategies to Enhance Adaptability"; Indur M. Goklany, "The Importance of Climate Change Compared to Other Global Changes," in Proceedings of the Second International Specialty Conference on Global Climate Change: Science, Policy, and Mitigation/Adaptation Strategies, Crystal City, VA, October 13–16, 1998 (Sewickley, PA: Air and Waste Management Association, 1998), pp. 1024–41; Theodore Panayotou, and Jeffrey R. Vincent, "Consumption: Challenge to Sustainable Development or Distraction," *Science* 276 (1997): 55–57.

60. FAO, *State of the World's Forests 2001*, Annex 2, table 5, pp. 162–69.

61. FAO, *Global Forest Resources Assessment 2000* (Rome: FAO, 2000), table 46.2, table 49.1, pp. 311, 344.

62. Graciela Chichilnisky, "North-South Trade and the Global Environment," *American Economic Review* 84, no. 4 (1994): 851–74; Environmental Defense Fund (EDF), "25 Years After DDT Ban, Bald Eagles, Osprey Numbers Soar," press release, June 13, 1997, www.edf.org/pubs/NewsReleases/1997/Jun/e_ddt.html; FAO, *The State of the World's Forests 1997* (Rome: FAO, 1997).

63. FAO, *The State of the World's Forests 1997*; Michael Painter, "Introduction," in *The Social Causes of Environmental Destruction in Latin America*, ed. Michael Painter and William H. Durham (Ann Arbor: University of Michigan, 1995), pp. 1–21.

64. John Roper and Ralph W. Roberts, "Forestry Issues: Deforestation: Tropical Forests in Decline," Canadian International Development Agency, 1999, www.rcfa-cfan.org/english/issues.12-5.html (accessed December 17, 2002.)

65. Ibid.

66. FAO, *Global Forest Resources Assessment 2000*, Chapters 46 and 49.

67. See, for example, Caroline Taylor, "The Challenge of African Elephant Conservation," *Conservation Issues* 4, no. 2 (1997): 1, 3–11.

68. The race-to-the-bottom hypothesis has frequently been used to justify regulations at higher levels of aggregation. For instance, it has been cited as one of the justifications for the United States' Clean Air Act of 1970 which nationalized air pollution control for stationary sources in the United States. However, a detailed examination of the history of air pollution control in the United States shows that, consistent with the environmental transition hypothesis, communities and states were always striving to improve their well-being. In the initial part of the industrial era that meant apparently favoring economic development over environmental quality because with wealth it was possible to improve other aspects of well-being such as health, education, housing, and so forth. However, over time, as evidenced by air pollution trends shown in figures 6-5 through 6-8, greater emphasis began to be placed on environmental quality because of increased recognition that to improve human well-being, the environment had to be cleaned up (see chapter 5). Thus, at all times, the race, if any, was really to the top of welfare, which, at low levels of economic development, looks like a race to the bottom of environmental quality, but at higher levels it better resembles a race to the top of environmental standards. This examination also suggests that the reason motor vehicle controls were nationalized first was to prevent a race to the top by individual states. See Indur M. Goklany, *Clearing the Air*, pp. 1–7, 87–109.

69. Daniel L. Millimet and John A. List, "A Natural Experiment on the "Race to the Bottom" Hypothesis: Testing for Stochastic Dominance in Temporal Pollution Trends," *Oxford Bulletin of Economics and Statistics* 65 (2003): 395–420; Jeffrey A. Frankel, "The Environment and Globalization," National Bureau of Economic

Research Working Paper no. W10090, November 2003, http://ssrn.com/abstract=467558; Brian R. Copeland and M. Scott Taylor, "Trade and Transboundary Pollution," *American Economic Review* 85, no. 4 (1995): 716–37; Lyuba Zarsky, "Havens, Halos, and Spaghetti: Untangling the Evidence about the Relationship between Foreign Investment and the Environment," Conference on Foreign Direct Investment and the Environment, Organization for Economic Co-operation and Development (OECD), Environment Directorate, The Hague, The Netherlands, January 28–29, 1999, www.nautilus.org/papers/enviro/zarsky_oecdfdi.html (accessed December 15, 2002); Jeffrey A. Frankel and Andrew K. Rose, "Is Trade Good or Bad for the Environment? Sorting out the Causality," National Bureau of Economic Research Working Paper no. 9021, 2002, www.nber.org/papers/w9201 (accessed December 22, 2002); David Wheeler, *Racing to the Bottom? Foreign Investment and Air Pollution in Developing Countries* (Washington, DC: World Bank, 2001), http://netec.mcc.ac.uk/WoPEc/data/Papers/wopwobaed2524.html (accessed November 10, 2002).

70. Judith M. Dean, Mary E. Lovely, and Hua Wang, "Are Foreign Investors Attracted to Weak Environmental Regulations? Evaluating the Evidence from China," World Bank Policy Research Working Paper no. 3505, February 2005, available at Social Sciences Research Network (SSRN), http://ssrn.com/abstract=659122; Andreas Waldkirch and Munisamy Gopinath, "Pollution Haven or Hythe? New Evidence from Mexico," June 2004, http://ssrn.com/ abstract=592721; Matthew A. Cole, Robert J. R. Elliott, and Per G. Fredriksson, "Endogenous Pollution Havens: Does FDI Influence Environmental Regulations?" University of Nottingham Research Paper no. 2004/20, http://ssrn.com/abstract=764124; Arik M. Levinson and M. Scott Taylor, "Unmasking the Pollution Haven Effect," National Bureau of Economic Research Working Paper no. W10629, July 2004, http://ssrn.com/abstract=565828; Jeffrey Frankel and Andrew Rose, "Is Trade Good or Bad for the Environment?"; Lyuba Zarsky, "Havens, Halos, and Spaghetti"; David Wheeler, *Racing to the Bottom?*; B. Smarzynska Javorcik and Shang Jin Wei, "Pollution Havens and Foreign Direct Investment: Dirty Secret or Popular Myth?" World Bank Policy Research Working Paper no. 2673, September 2001, http://ssrn.com/abstract=328240; Gunnar A. Eskeland and Ann E. Harrison, "Moving to Greener Pastures? Multinationals and the Pollution-Haven Hypothesis," World Bank Policy Research Working Paper no. 1744, January 1997, http://ssrn.com/abstract=604985.

71. World Bank, *World Development Indicators 2005*, http://devdata.worldbank.org/dataonline (accessed August 24, 2005).

72. Indur M. Goklany, "Richer Is Cleaner: Long-Term Trends in Global Air Quality," in *The True State of the Planet*, ed. Ronald Bailey (New York: Free Press, 1995), pp. 339–77.

73. William Langewiesche, "The Shipbreakers," *The Atlantic*, August 2000, www.theatlantic.com/issues/2000/08/ langewiesche.htm.

74. Theodore Panayotou and Jeffrey R. Vincent, "Consumption: Challenge to Sustainable Development or Distraction."

75. FAO, "Irrigation Potential in Africa: A Basin Approach," *FAO Land and Water Bulletin* 4, no. 12 (July 1997).

76. Indur M. Goklany, "Strategies to Enhance Adaptability."

77. Ibid.

78. World Bank, *Global Development Finance 2005* (Washington, DC: World Bank, 2005).

79. OECD, *OECD in Figures–2005 edition*, available at StatLink at http://dx.doi.org/10.1787/028807378487 (accessed February 24, 2006).

80. World Bank, *Global Development Finance 2005*.

81. See, for example, Jean Drèze, "Famine Prevention in Africa, Some Experiences and Lessons," in *The Political Economy of Hunger, Volume II*, ed. Jean Drèze and Amartya Sen (Oxford, UK: Clarendon Press, Oxford University Press, 1990), pp. 123–72; B. G. Kumar, "Ethiopian Famines 1973–1985, A Case Study," in *The Political Economy of Hunger, Volume II*, ed. Jean Drèze and Amartya Sen (Oxford, UK: Clarendon Press and Oxford University Press, 1990), pp. 173–216.

82. Goklany, "Strategies to Enhance Adaptability," 427–49.

83. Lester R. Brown, *Who Will Feed China?* (New York: W. W. Norton, 1995).

84. FAO 2006, http://apps.fao.org (accessed March 3, 2006).

85. Ibid.

86. See, for example, Richard Bernstein and Ross H. Munro, *The Coming Conflict with China* (New York: Knopf, 1997).

87. Based on 2002 data from G. Marland, et al., *National CO_2 Emissions from Fossil-Fuel Burning, Cement Manufacture, and Gas Flaring: 1751–2002* (Oak Ridge, TN: Carbon Dioxide Information Analysis Center, Oak Ridge National Laboratory, 2005), http://cdiac.ornl.gov/ftp/trends/emissions/hai.dat (accessed March 4, 2006).

88. Indur M. Goklany, "Meeting Global Food Needs: The Environmental Trade-Offs between Increasing Land Conversion and Land Productivity," *Technology* 6 (1999): 107–30.

89. Richard Tren, "Africa Needs DDT," *New York Times*, December 28, 2002, p. A34.

90. Jared Diamond, *Collapse*, p. 274; Indur M. Goklany, "Strategies to Enhance Adaptability."

91. Jared Diamond, *Collapse*, pp. 230, 229–230, 239–240.

92. BBC, "Famine and the GM Debate," November 14, 2002, http://news.bbc.co.uk/2/hi/africa/2459903.stm (accessed March 4, 2006).

93. Jared Diamond, *Collapse*, p. 341.

94. Joel Tarr, "The Horse—The Polluter of the City," in *The Search for the Ultimate Sink: Urban Pollution in Historical Perspective* (Akron, OH: University of Akron Press, 1996).

95. John von Neumann, "Can We Survive Technology?" *Fortune* (June 1955): 106–08, 151–52, reprinted in *Collected Works, Version VI* (New York: Pergamon Press, 1963): pp. 504–19. Von Neumann was referring to atomic weapons, but his question is pertinent to the entire human enterprise.

Appendix A

1. World Bank, *World Development Indicators*, http://devdata.worldbank.org/dataonline (accessed July 12, 2005).

Appendix B

1. Dora L. Costa and Richard H. Steckel, "Long-Term Trends, Health, Welfare, and Economic Growth in the United States," in *Health and Welfare during Industrialization*, ed. Richard H. Steckel and Roderick Floud (Chicago: University of Chicago Press, 1997), p. 72; and Angus Maddison, "Poor Until 1820," *Wall Street Journal, The Millennium*, January 11, 1999, p. R54.

2. United Nations Development Program, *Human Development Report 2000* (New York: Oxford University Press, 2000).

Index

About the Author

Dr. Indur M. Goklany has worked with federal and state govenment, think tanks, and the private sector for more than 30 years, and he has written extensively on the interactions between globalization, economic development, environmental quality, technological change, and human and environmental well-being. He was a U.S. delegate to the Intergovernmental Panel on Climate Change and to the team negotiating the UN Framework Convention on Climate Change. In the 1980s, he managed EPA's fledgling emission trading program before trading became popular. Among his policy innovations, which are increasingly going mainstream, are (a) that increasing the productivity and efficiency of land and water use to meet critical human needs for food, fiber, and timber is the most effective method of conserving habitat and biodiversity and (b) that sustainable economic development, technological change, and trade will make developing countries less vulnerable to future climate change while helping solve present-day climate-related problems and generally increasing their resiliency to all forms of adversity. He is also the author of *The Precautionary Principle: A Critical Appraisal of Environmental Risk Assessment* and *Clearing the Air: The Real Story of the War on Air Pollution*, both published by the Cato Institute (in 2001 and 1999, respectively).

Cato Institute

Founded in 1977, the Cato Institute is a public policy research foundation dedicated to broadening the parameters of policy debate to allow consideration of more options that are consistent with the traditional American principles of limited government, individual liberty, and peace. To that end, the Institute strives to achieve greater involvement of the intelligent, concerned lay public in questions of policy and the proper role of government.

The Institute is named for *Cato's Letters*, libertarian pamphlets that were widely read in the American Colonies in the early 18th century and played a major role in laying the philosophical foundation for the American Revolution.

Despite the achievement of the nation's Founders, today virtually no aspect of life is free from government encroachment. A pervasive intolerance for individual rights is shown by government's arbitrary intrusions into private economic transactions and its disregard for civil liberties.

To counter that trend, the Cato Institute undertakes an extensive publications program that addresses the complete spectrum of policy issues. Books, monographs, and shorter studies are commissioned to examine the federal budget, Social Security, regulation, military spending, international trade, and myriad other issues. Major policy conferences are held throughout the year, from which papers are published thrice yearly in the *Cato Journal*. The Institute also publishes the quarterly magazine *Regulation*.

In order to maintain its independence, the Cato Institute accepts no government funding. Contributions are received from foundations, corporations, and individuals, and other revenue is generated from the sale of publications. The Institute is a nonprofit, tax-exempt, educational foundation under Section 501(c)3 of the Internal Revenue Code.

CATO INSTITUTE
1000 Massachusetts Ave., N.W.
Washington, D.C. 20001
www.cato.org